REVOLUTIONARY MOVEMENTS IN WORLD HISTORY

FROM 1750 TO THE PRESENT

REVOLUTIONARY MOVEMENTS IN WORLD HISTORY

FROM 1750 TO THE PRESENT

VOLUME 3: R–Z

JAMES V. DeFRONZO

EDITOR

A B C • C L I O

Santa Barbara, California • Denver, Colorado • Oxford, United Kingdom

Library of Congress Cataloging-in-Publication Data
Revolutionary movements in world history : from 1750 to present / James V. DeFronzo, editor.
    p.   cm.
    Includes bibliographical references and index.
    ISBN 1-85109-793-7 (alk. paper) — ISBN 1-85109-798-8 (ebook)   1. History, Modern.
2. Revolutions.   I. DeFronzo, James.

D295.R49 2006
303.6'4—dc22

                                                          2006009532

10   09   08   07   06   05 / 10   9   8   7   6   5   4   3   2   1

Media Editor: Ellen Rasmussen
Media Resources Manager: Caroline Price
Production Editor: Vicki Moran
Editorial Assistant: Alisha Martinez
Production Manager: Don Schmidt
Manufacturing Coordinator: George Smyser

This book is also available on the World Wide Web as an ebook.
Visit abc-clio.com for details.

ABC-CLIO, Inc.
130 Cremona Drive, P.O. Box 1911
Santa Barbara, California 93116–1911

This book is printed on acid-free paper ∞.
Manufactured in the United States of America

Contents

Entries

VOLUME 3: R–Z

Maps

Contributors

Advisor
Cyrus Ernesto Zirakzadeh
University of Connecticut
Storrs, CT

Contributors
Howard Adelman
Griffith University
Brisbane, Queensland
Australia

David E. Adleman
University of Idaho
Moscow, ID

Ali Abdullatif Ahmida
University of New England
Biddeford, ME

Ayad Al-Qazzaz
California State University
Sacramento, CA

Craig Baxter
Juniata College
Huntingdon, PA

Marc Becker
Truman State University
Kirksville, MO

Angie Beeman
University of Connecticut
Storrs, CT

Leigh Binford
Benemérita Universidad
   Autónoma de Puebla
Puebla
Mexico

P. Richard Bohr
College of Saint Benedict and Saint
   John's University
St. Joseph, MN

Hamit Bozarslan
Ecole des Hautes Etudes en
   Sciences Sociales
Paris
France

Roger Brown
Saitama University
Saitama City, Saitama Prefecture
Japan

Malcolm Byrne
National Security Archive
Washington, DC

Henry F. Carey
Georgia State University
Atlanta, GA

Clayborne Carson
Stanford University
Stanford, CA

Francesco Cavatorta
Dublin City University
Dublin
Ireland

David Chandler
Monash University
Melbourne
Australia

James G. Chastain
Ohio University
Athens, OH

Albert K. Cohen
University of Connecticut
Storrs, CT

James DeFronzo
University of Connecticut
Storrs, CT

Judith Ewell
College of William and Mary
Williamsburg, VA

John Foran
University of California, Santa
   Barbara
Santa Barbara, CA

Will Fowler
University of St. Andrews
St. Andrews
United Kingdom

Andrew S. Fullerton
University of Connecticut
Storrs, CT

Venelin I. Ganev
Miami University of Ohio
Oxford, OH

John D. Garrigus
University of Texas at Arlington
Arlington, TX

Gordon Gauchat
University of Connecticut
Storrs, CT

Paul A. Gilje
University of Oklahoma
Norman, OK

Jungyun Gill
University of Connecticut
Storrs, CT

Roger S. Gocking
Mercy College
Dobbs Ferry, NY

Anthony Gorman
University of London
London
United Kingdom

Alexander Groth
University of California, Davis
Davis, CA

Josef Gugler
University of Connecticut
Storrs, CT

Geoffrey C. Gunn
Nagasaki University
Nagasaki
Japan

Ahmed H. Ibrahim
Missouri State University
Springfield, MO

George Joffe
Cambridge University
Cambridge
United Kingdom

Sanjay Joshi
Northern Arizona University
Flagstaff, AZ

Colin H. Kahl
University of Minnesota
Minneapolis, MN

Stathis N. Kalyvas
Yale University
New Haven, CT

Eran Kaplan
University of Cincinnati
Cincinnati, OH

Mark N. Katz
George Mason University
Fairfax, VA

Damien Kingsbury
Deakin University
Geelong
Australia

Mikolaj Stanislaw Kunicki
Institute for Human Sciences
Vienna
Austria

George Lawson
University of London
London
United Kingdom

J. J. Lee
New York University
New York, NY

Namhee Lee
University of California, Los
    Angeles
Los Angeles, CA

Deanna Lee Levanti
Braintree, MA

Anatol Lieven
New America Foundation
Washington, DC

Richard A. Lobban, Jr.
Rhode Island College
Providence, RI

Jean-Michel Mabeko-Tali
Howard University
Washington, DC

Theresa M. Mackey
Virginia Community College
Annandale, VA

James I. Matray
California State University, Chico
Chico, CA

Brian C. Melton
Liberty University
Lynchburg, VA

Valentine M. Moghadam
UNESCO
Paris
France

Evan Braden Montgomery
University of Virginia
Charlottesville, VA

Michael Mulcahy
University of Connecticut
Stamford, CT

Carlo Nasi
Universidad de los Andes
Bogota
Colombia

Malyn Newitt
King's College London
London
United Kingdom

Michael R. Nusbaumer
Indiana University-Purdue
    University at Fort Wayne
Fort Wayne, IN

Borden Painter
Trinity College
Hartford, CT

Stacie Pettyjohn
University of Virginia
Charlottesville, VA

Roger Price
University of Wales
Aberystwyth
Wales

Jennie Purnell
Boston College
Chestnut Hill, MA

Nathan Gilbert Quimpo
University of Amsterdam
Amsterdam
Netherlands

Kumar Ramakrishna
Nanyang Technological University
Singapore

Mike Rapport
University of Stirling
Stirling
Scotland

James F. Rinehart
Troy University
Troy, AL

Paul A. Rodell
Georgia Southern University
Statesboro, GA

Donald Rothchild
University of California, Davis
Davis, CA

Steven C. Rubert
Oregon State University
Corvallis, OR

Peter Rutland
Wesleyan University
Middletown, CT

L. Sabaratnam
Davidson College
Davidson, NC

Roland Sarti
University of Massachusetts
Amherst, MA

Paul Khalil Saucier
Northeastern University
Boston, MA

Eric Selbin
Southwestern University
Georgetown, TX

Deric M. Shannon
University of Connecticut
Storrs, CT

Julie Shayne
Emory University
Atlanta, GA

Priscilla M. Shilaro
West Virginia University
Morgantown, WV

James Sidbury
University of Texas at Austin
Austin, TX

Paul E. Sigmund
Princeton University
Princeton, NJ

Richard Stahler-Sholk
Eastern Michigan University
Ypsilanti, MI

Lynn Stephen
University of Oregon
Eugene, OR

Jill Stephenson
University of Edinburgh
Edinburgh
Scotland

Stephen M. Streeter
McMaster University
Hamilton, Ontario
Canada

Martin Stuart-Fox
The University of Queensland
Brisbane
Australia

Gebru Tareke
Hobart and William Smith
    Colleges
Geneva, NY

Arlene B. Tickner
Universidad de los Andes and
    Universidad Nacional
Bogotá
Colombia

Thomas Turner
Formerly of the National
    University of Rwanda
Dubuque, IA

Frédéric Volpi
University of St. Andrews
St. Andrews
Scotland

Veljko Vujačić
Oberlin College
Oberlin, OH

Samuel Watson
United States Military Academy
West Point, NY

Kathleen Weekley
University of Wollongong
Wollongong
Australia

Timothy P. Wickham-Crowley
Georgetown University
Washington, DC

Teresa Wright
California State University, Long
    Beach
Long Beach, CA

Cyrus Ernesto Zirakzadeh
University of Connecticut
Storrs, CT

Preface

Revolutionary movements, conflicts, successful revolutions, the transformations they attempt to bring about, and the support or opposition they provoke are all fascinating topics for a wide range of academic fields, including anthropology, economics, history, political science, psychology, and sociology, as well as for people in general. My interest in revolutions stems from several experiences including the U.S. Civil Rights movements and the conflict over U.S. involvement in Vietnam. As undergraduates, Roger Gocking, author of the entry on the Ghana's Independence Revolution, and I founded the Youth Interracial Council at Fairfield University whose participants from several colleges, such as Manhattanville College, and highschools, such as Convent of the Sacred Heart in Noroton, CT, helped run community centers and tutoring programs, discussion panels, and fund raising musical performances in Connecticut and New York. Some of us also participated in in the university's Upward Bound Program for local highschool students (I taught an English grammar and literature course). Roger and I, along with approximately fifty other students, organized what was apparently the first anti-Vietnam War demonstration at the university and participated in the great 1967 New York City anti-war demonstration led by the Reverend Martin Luther King Junior. When we graduated, my younger brother Donald, later mayor of New Britain, CT, and currently state senator and sponsor in 2005 of the state's first public campaign financing election law, carried on in the Youth Interracial Council. Work in the Youth Interracial Council resulted in the award of the university's Saint Ignatius Loyal Medal. Roger headed to Stanford University and eventually became a college professor and expert on West African history. I enrolled at Indiana University. For three years I taught as a lecturer in Sociology at Indiana University's branch campus in Fort Wayne (Indiana University-Purdue University at Fort Wayne), participating in local social movement activity and writing for the city's activist newspaper, the *Fort Wayne Free*

Press. As a graduate student at Indiana University, a course on social conflict by Professor Austin T. Turk provided an opportunity for me to write a very long paper on revolution, guerilla warfare, and related topics, which was later published in a book, *Focus on Sociology* (Dubuque, IA: Kendall/Hunt), edited by professors Arnold O. Olson and Sushil K. Usman. Research for this paper and a short volunteer course on revolution which I taught one semester at IU in Fort Wayne, and later study, including work for the political crime section of my criminology course, resulted in the creation of the other large course, which with criminology, I taught every semester at the University of Connecticut for more than twenty years, Revolutionary Social Movements Around the World. This led to my writing a textbook for the course and similar courses, Revolutions and Revolutionary Movements (1991, 1996, 2007 forthcoming, Boulder CO: Westview). Most likely this book led to Mr. Simon Mason of ABC-CLIO asking me to prepare a proposal and to serve as general editor for this project, *Revolutionary Movemens in World History: From 1750 to the Present.* After more than a year of discussing the project with Simon and developing the proposal, the project began at the beginning of 2004. I have been tremendously impressed at the depth of knowledge of our contributors and working on this project was always extremely interesting and educative.

STRUCTURE OF THE ENCYCLOPEDIA

The encyclopedia includes two major types of entries, which appear in alphabetical order: revolution entries and theme or concept entries. The revolution entries—on revolutions and social movements—range in length from about 4,000 to 15,000 words and are divided into six main sections: Chronology; Background; Context and Process of Revolution; Impacts; People and Organizations; and References and

Further Readings. The theme or concept entries deal with topics related to revolution, such as colonialism and neo-colonialism, human rights and revolution, ideology and propaganda,, student movements and revolutions, war and revolution, women and revolution, terrorism, and theories of revolution. These entries generally range in length from about 3,000 to 4,500 words. Two longer theme entries deal respectively with documentaries on revolutions and revolution as the subjects of feature films.

ACKNOWLEDGMENTS

Above all, I am extremely grateful to our authors for the exceptional quality of the entries they wrote.

But many people in addition to the authors contributed directly or indirectly to the production of this encyclopedia. At ABC-CLIO I would particularly like to thank Simon Mason who invited me to develop the proposal for this project and who contributed valuable guidance, information, suggestions, and ideas for the project. Simon's colleagues at ABC-CLIO who also played important roles include, in alphabetical order, Ron Boehm, Valerie Boyajian, Craig Hunt, Alex Mikaberidze, Vicki Moran, Ellen Rasmussen, Wendy Roseth, Vicky Speck, Art Stickney, and Peter Westwick. Others at ABC-CLIO also contributed significantly and deserve appreciation. I would particularly like to thank Wendy, who was my direct contact and project editor for much of time.

Professor Cyrus E. Zirakzadeh of the University of Connecticut's Political Science Department, author of the entry on "The Spanish Revolution and Counter-Revolution," served as my advisor for this project and provided very important guidance and suggestions.

Jack Goldstone of George Mason University, who had edited the earlier *Encyclopedia of Political Revolutions* (Congressional Quarterly) and published a number of important works on revolution, and with whom I worked as an academic consultant on a documentary series on revolutions, provided valuable advice and suggestions from his own experience as an editor. Both Jack and Douglas Goldenberg-Hart of Congressional Quarterly also consented to allow several authors who had written for the earlier encyclopedia to write entries for this project.

My friend and former teaching assistant Jungyun Gill, author of the entry on "Student and Youth Movements, Activism and Revolution," provided valuable assistance, including important insights on Korean history and society, which helped me in the editing of the Korea entries. There are many UCONN students and faculty members to whom I would like to express thanks, in part for encouraging the creation of my revolutions' course, such as then Sociology De-partment Head Mark Abrahamson, and my book on revolutions that preceded this encyclopedia. In particular, my good friend Professor Al Cohen, the brilliant and well-known criminologist and author of the entry on "Terrorism" for this encyclopedia, provided much encouragement and many useful suggestions in the course of many conversations.

Many family members and other friends also provided important encouragement and assistance. I particularly would like to thank my brother and sister-in-law, Don and Diane DeFronzo, and their children, David and Karen, and my sister, Margaret Pastore, her friend David Timm, and her son, Michael. Thanks also to my parents, Armand and Mary Pavano DeFronzo, my uncle and aunt, Francis and Lenneye DiFronzo, my uncle and aunt, Alexander and Angie Pavano DiFronzo, my aunt Doris Pavano Pitts, and my cousin, Connie Manafort, and all my other cousins for their encouragement. Deanna Levanti (Americorps and graduate of UMASS), who researched and wrote the valuable entry on "Documentaries and Revolution," which lists hundreds of documentaries and the sources from which these may be obtained, provided much encouragement, as did her mother and stepfather, Sue and Tom Ryan, her brothers, Mathew and Evan, and her father, Charles Levanti.

Others who provided important encouragement were my wonderful and long-time friends Professor Jane Prochow, Massey University, New Zealand; and John McVarish of Hull, Massachusetts. John's daughter, Heather, was, to the best of my knowledge, first college student (James Madison University) to read one of the entries for the encyclopedia, the entry on the Iranian Revolution, which was used as a model for all revolution entries. Heather's reaction to it was very positive, enthusiastic, and encouraging. Professor Lance Hannon of Occidental College and Villanova University, another good friend, former teaching assistant, and coauthor on other projects, also provided valuable encouragement as well as suggestions for authors.

I would also like to thank my good friend, Professor Roger Gocking, Mercy College, author, as noted earlier, of the entry on "Ghana's Independence Revolution," for his valuable encouragement and assistance. Other good friends provided encouragement for this project. Thanks to Wendy Kimsey, my former teaching assistant, and her husband, David Fowler, their daughters, Zoe and Hannah, and Steve Merlino, also my former teaching assistant, and his wife, Kathy Mangiafico. Thanks also to Professor Walter Ellis and his wife Becky Ellis of Hillsboro College, Ted Rhodes and Joni Pascal and their children, Jesse and Rachel, and Sue Cook Ringle and Ken Ringle and their sons Dylan and Carter, and John Pearlman, and George Relue, a great friend and the co-founder, along with Ted Rhodes, and editor of the *Fort Wayne Free Press.*

I would also like to express gratitude to Professor William Doyle of the University of Bristol, Professor Josef Gugler of the University of Connecticut, author of the entry on "The Cinema of Revolution," Professor George Lawson of the London School of Economics, author of the entries on "Reform, Rebellion, Civil War, Coup D'état, and Revolution" and "Trends in Revolution," and Professor Roland Sarti of the University of Massachusetts, author of the entry on the "Italian Risorgimento," for their valuable suggestions of several authors.

Introduction

A *social movement* is a collective effort by a relatively large number of people to bring about, resist, or reverse social change. A *revolutionary movement* is a type of social movement whose leaders advocate structural change, the replacement of one or more major social institutions, such as a society's political system or its economic system. Social movements with goals not including structural change are generally called *reform movements* rather than revolutionary movements. *Revolution* is the term for a revolutionary movement that succeeds and accomplishes structural change.

Students of revolution disagree on whether other characteristics should be included in the definition. Some insist that a true revolution must involve participation by the large mass of a society's population. Others assert that only structural change brought about by violence qualifies as revolution. Still others argue that although violence is not a necessary element, only social transformations through illegal means should be labeled revolutions.

The editor of this encyclopedia does not agree with narrowing the conception of revolution by including any of these restrictions. The preference here is for a definition of revolutionary movement based solely on advocacy of institutional change and for revolution as the achievement of institutional change.

The revolutions and revolutionary movements covered in this project include many that were characterized by large-scale popular participation, illegal rebellion against existing governments, and violence, such as the Russian Revolution of 1917 and the Chinese and Vietnamese revolutions, and others that lacked one or more of these aspects. The political revolutions in Eastern Europe in 1989 and later in the Soviet Union, for example, were largely non-violent. And democratic elections brought leftist coalitions, supported in part by movements advocating structural economic change to power legally in Spain in 1936 and Chile in 1970. The resulting governments were crushed by right-wing counter-revo-

lutions spearheaded by the military and permitted or even aided by foreign powers. Efforts of people to structurally change their societies through legal democratic means merit the term *revolutionary*. In fact, it could be argued that the reason for the historic link between past revolutions and violence was precisely that democratic means to accomplish institutional change did not exist in many societies until recently.

WHAT MAKES REVOLUTION POSSIBLE?

Historically revolutionary movements were likely to occur and succeed when five factors were present simultaneously. One key element was the development of a high level of discontent with the existing political or economic systems among a large sector of a society's population. This popular or mass discontent has typically been the result of one of three processes: (1) A decline in living standards due to rapid population growth, economic problems or policies, war, or other factors; (2) a change in the moral acceptability of existing living standards in that people come to believe that their lives could and should be better (such a change in viewpoint can result from messages communicated by recognized moral authorities, such as religious leaders, or contact with people from other societies); (3) a period of general improvement in living standards followed by a significant decline (the period of improvement raises people's expectations for future improvements, which are frustrated by the later deterioration of economic conditions).

In order for the discontent to lead to a revolutionary movement, people must come to believe that their troubles are due not only to the current government leaders, but also to one or more of their society's social institutions. Directing blame in this way is often the result of the efforts of leaders of revolutionary movements and the ideologies they put forth. In the past, revolutionary leadership has often developed from a division within the so-called elite sector of a society. Elites are people with culturally defined characteristics qualifying them for leadership positions in society in general. In many societies these include at minimum high levels of intelligence, education, and talent. Elite members of society can become alienated from existing institutions for a number of reasons. Occasionally young people with elite traits become morally outraged at aspects of the social system or repressive government policies. Others may turn against the pre-revolutionary regime because they feel themselves to be the targets of discrimination or barred from opportunities due to the nature of the political, social, or economic systems.

Whatever the reason, the existence of a division within the elite sector, the second factor in successful revolutionary movements, simultaneous with mass discontent creates the possibility that dissident elite persons may provide leadership and organization for the members of the discontented mass of the population, along with an ideology to motivate, mobilize, and guide them. Such an ideology typically includes a systematic criticism of the existing regime and its policies, an explanation of the need for the revolutionary movement, a plan for overthrowing the governing group, and proposals for revolutionary changes to society. In order for a revolution to succeed, the revolutionary ideology should be characterized by a concept that provides a basis for unifying different groups and social classes in a revolutionary alliance to oust the existing regime.

The unifying motive constitutes a third important factor in successful revolutionary movements. A unifying theme may be hatred for a particular ruler, but nationalism in some form has usually served most effectively as a motive unifying different population groups against either colonial regimes or indigenous rulers or governments perceived as serving foreign interests.

A fourth essential element for the success of a revolutionary movement is the deterioration of the legitimacy and coercive capacity of the state. This may be due to devastating defeat in war blamed on the existing government, as was the case in the Russian Revolution of 1917, a state financial crisis such as that which contributed to the occurrence of the French Revolution in 1789, or loss of faith in a personalized dictatorship such as characterized the Cuban Revolution against the Batista regime in the 1950s. In such situations the pre-revolutionary government lacks the capacity to suppress revolutionary movements.

The fifth crucial factor is whether or not other nations intervene to help suppress a revolutionary movement. If the world is permissive toward a revolutionary movement in a particular society, in that other nations are unwilling or unable to assist an existing government in the repression of rev-

olutionaries, then the revolutionary movement has a chance of success.

Some students of revolution have stressed the importance of one of these factors, for example the breakdown of state authority, over the others. The orientation here is that a successful revolution almost always has involved the simultaneous presence of all five factors: mass discontent; a division among elites with some becoming revolutionary leaders; the development, propagation, and widespread acceptance of an ideology that in the process of defining the problems of the old regime and calling for its overthrow is able to unify different social groups and classes in support of the revolutionary effort; the deterioration of the coercive capacity of the state; and a world context at least temporarily permissive towards the revolutionary movement.

TRENDS IN REVOLUTION

Social conflict over political systems may be as old as civilization. The ancient Greeks experienced forms of democracy, oligarchy, and dictatorship. The Romans at one time abolished monarchy to create a republic. Senators opposed to the establishment of a dictatorship under Caesar killed him and lost a civil war and their own lives in an attempt to preserve the republic. At some point conflict among social elites for control of government came to resemble little more than a circulation of leadership personnel, and Europeans began referring to the revolving of competing elites in and out of control of government as "revolution." But gradually, with the coming of the philosophical concepts of the Enlightenment and the growing belief in the ability of humanity to control nature and alter society, revolution came to mean changing the system of government or other institutions, including the form of a society's economic system.

The American Revolution shifted the type of government in the former colonies from monarchy to republic and attempted to guarantee a wide range of freedoms and rights to citizens, although limited initially to white males. The French Revolution not only changed the form of government, at least temporarily, and abolished privileges of certain groups, such as the aristocracy and the clergy, it also involved proponents of sweeping economic transformations whose aspirations were largely frustrated, although their ideas and efforts inspired later generations of revolutionaries. The French Revolution's "rights of man and the citizen" concepts constituted a type of transnational revolutionary ideology threatening monarchal regimes throughout Europe. The monarchies reacted by forming a grand international counter-revolutionary military coalition to defeat Napoleon and crush the French Revolution. This international anti-revolutionary alliance functioned to some degree in the 1820s, 1830s, and

1840s to repress new multinational revolutionary efforts motivated both by ideals of the French Revolution and aspirations for national liberation.

Marx's historical materialist concept of socialism appealed to a wide range of intellectuals attracted by an ideology that not only supported the creation of what appeared to be a morally superior form of society, but also offered an apparently scientific analysis which seemed to demonstrate that socialism, and eventually communist utopia, were not only achievable but inevitable. The success of the Marxist Russian revolutionaries in seemingly bringing about the first social revolution in which workers and peasants actually seized state power and control of the economy, and destroyed the old ruling class, inspired revolutionaries in many other countries. But the Communists' establishment of one party rule sowed the seeds of Stalin's brutal dictatorship and, ultimately, contributed to discrediting their revolutionary model.

Lenin's theories of revolution and imperialism long held wide appeal for revolutionaries in many developing countries seeking to free themselves from colonial rule. Communist movements in China and Vietnam effectively became the vehicles of their people's national liberation, greatly contributing to their staying power long after the fall of Communist governments in Eastern Europe and the U.S.S.R. Although Marxism-Leninism became a major transnational revolutionary ideology for decades after the Russian Revolution, it eventually lost ground to non-Marxist nationalism, revolutionary democratic ideologies, and Islamic fundamentalism, especially after the 1991 disintegration of the Soviet Union.

FUTURE REVOLUTIONS?

Will the future be characterized by the number of revolutions that occurred in the past? Students of revolution disagree. Goodwin (2001, 273), refers to the period of 1945–1991 as an "age of revolutions" and offers arguments regarding why revolutions should become less frequent. He notes that some claim that growth in the power of multinational corporations and financial institutions has reduced the relative power of the state in many countries, making control of the state less valuable to potential revolutionaries seeking to bring about change. He also discusses what he considered the more plausible explanation, that without the example of the U.S.S.R. as a powerful industrialized alternative to a capitalist system, the attractiveness and feasibility of revolution decrease. However, Goodwin (273) believes that the spread of democracy, in part the result of certain revolutions of the Cold War period that "helped destroy European colonialism, toppled some of the century's most ruthless dictators and humbled the superpowers," is most responsible for the decline of revolution. He argues that democracies offer the opportunity for

voters to punish offensive government officials and to "win concessions from economic and political elites," thus reducing motives for revolution (277). But he qualifies his argument in a telling way by saying that the movements and revolutions least likely to occur are those that "would seriously challenge the capitalist world-system" (274). This assessment clearly points to an external element affecting the frequency of revolutions, not the internal attribute of whether a society's government is democratic or non-democratic.

Many of the "new" democracies of the recent wave of democratization from the late 1980s on, including Chile and Guatemala, had been democracies in the past, but military revolts overthrew the earlier democratic systems, often with great violence and loss of life. Those who had friends or family members killed, imprisoned or abused, or who were themselves the victims of torture, rape, or other mistreatment by members of the armed forces or police (who were virtually never punished) were profoundly affected. Victims of these types of crimes in any society generally avoid engaging in behaviors that they perceive will put them at risk of further victimization. Such is also the case for people who have survived such crimes and suffered repression and the loss of democracy because they favored a particular economic or political policy. If they know that the perpetrators of the crimes against them were not punished—and that these people or others like them are free to commit the same crimes again—they are not likely to even consider repeating the political choices that led to their plight. So in some cases, lack of visible revolutionary aspirations may not have been due to the new democracies, but rather to the lingering fear of state terrorism among their citizens.

Selbin (2001, 290) refers to the wave of democratization of the late twentieth century as "wider," but not necessarily "deeper." Focusing mainly on Latin America, he suggested that poverty and inequality have been increasing and so the motivation for revolutionary change should also be increasing. Selbin (286) stated that neo-liberal economic "globalization…appears strikingly similar to what was once called 'imperialism.'" He also noted (285–286) that "democratic institutions and free markets are not, in any broad historical perspective, natural allies" and as "neo-liberalism fails to deliver on its promise, revolution will become more likely."

In assessing the possible relationship between democracy and revolution, a question that must be asked is whether any revolutionary movement would seek to overthrow a genuinely democratic system, that is, one in which the military is committed to a democratic constitution and obedient to the elected government. If revolutionaries could win popular support, they would most likely not attempt to overthrow the democratic system, but rather use democracy and elections to take power and to carry out their plans for social change without resorting to the dangerous and costly option of violence.

Whether more revolutions will occur in the future cannot be forecast with certainty. The pace of the occurrence of revolutions may have at least temporarily slowed, perhaps not so much due to the wave of democratization as to the maintenance of a generally non-permissive international stance towards revolutionary economic change, particularly on the part of a number of U.S. administrations. The orientation of the United States towards implementing true democracy in other nations and respecting the electoral will of the people in those democracies is essentially the key to determining whether the pace of revolutionary change will accelerate or decline. A major implication is that elections in the United States may determine how permissive or non-permissive the world environment is towards revolutionary change. As has been widely noted, it was no accident that both the Iranian and Nicaraguan revolutions occurred during the human rights–focused U.S. administration of Jimmy Carter. After the reduction of what appeared to be previous near unconditional U.S. support for the pre-revolutionary right-wing regimes in both countries, opponents of these governments were apparently encouraged to mount or escalate major revolutionary efforts.

Real democracy is inherently revolutionary in societies where the majority of the population is impoverished and perceive themselves to be the victims of economic exploitation and/or imperialism. Non-permissive world contexts in the form of the actions of nations opposing radical change have blocked revolutionary movements on numerous occasions. In the twenty-first century, the answer to the question regarding whether revolutionary movements and change re-emerge as a prominent features of world history may be found within the world's wealthiest and most powerful nation.

> **See Also** American Revolution; Chilean Socialist Revolution, Counter-Revolution, and the Restoration of Democracy; Chinese Revolution; Democracy, Dictatorship and Fascism; East European Revolutions of 1989; Elites, intellectuals and Revolutionary Leadership; French Revolution; Iranian Revolution; Nicaraguan Revolution; Reform, Rebellion, Civil War, Coup D'état and Revolution; Russian Revolution of 1917; Russian Revolution of 1991 and the Dissolution of the U.S.S.R.; Spanish Revolution and Counter-Revolution; Student and Youth Movements, Activism and Revolution; Theories of Revolution; Transnational Revolutionary Movements; Trends in Revolution; Vietnamese Revolution

References and Further Readings

Brinton, Crane. 1965. *The Anatomy of Revolution.* New York: Vintage.

DeFronzo, James. 1996. (3rd edition forthcoming in 2007) *Revolutions and Revolutionary Movements.* Boulder, CO: Westview Press.

Foran, John. 2005. *Taking Power: On the Origins of Third World Revolutions.* Cambridge, UK: Cambridge University Press.

———. "Theories of Revolution." Pp. 868–872 in *Revolutionary Movements in World History: From 1750 to the Present* edited by James DeFronzo. Santa Barbara, CA: ABC-CLIO.

Goldfrank, Walter L. 1986. "The Mexican Revolution." Pp. 104–117 in *Revolutions: Theoretical, Comparative, and Historical Studies,* edited by Jack A. Goldstone. San Diego, CA: Harcourt Brace Jovanovich.

Goldstone, Jack A., ed. 1986, 1994. *Revolutions: Theoretical, Comparative, and Historical Studies.* Fort Worth, TX: Harcourt Brace College Publishers.

———. 1998. *The Encyclopedia of Political Revolutions.* Washington DC: Congressional Quarterly.

———. 2001. "An Analytical Framework." Pp. 9–29 in *Revolution: International Dimensions,* edited by Mark N. Katz. Washington DC: Congressional Quarterly Press.

———, Ted Robert Gurr, and Farrokh Moshiri, eds. 1991. *Revolutions of the Late Twentieth Century.* Boulder CO: Westview Press.

Goodwin, Jeff. 2001. "Is the Age of Revolution Over?" Pp. 272—283 in *Revolution: International Dimensions,* edited by Mark N. Katz. Washington DC: Congressional Quarterly Press.

Gurr, Ted Robert. 1970. *Why Men Rebel.* Princeton NJ: Princeton University Press.

Katz, Mark N. 1999. *Revolutions and Revolutionary Waves.* New York: Saint Martin's Press.

———, ed. 2001. *Revolution: International Dimensions.* Washington DC: Congressional Quarterly Press.

———. 2006. "Transnational Revolutionary Movements." Pp. 872–876 in *Revolutionary Movements in World History: From 1750 to the Present* edited by James DeFronzo.

McAdam, Doug, Sidney Tarrow and Charles Tilly. 2001 *Dynamics of Contention.* Cambridge, UK: Cambridge University Press.

Selbin, Eric. 2001. "Same as It Ever Was: The Future of Revolution at the End of the Century." Pp. 284-297 in *Revolution: International Dimensions,* edited by Mark N. Katz. Washington, DC: Congressional Quarterly Press.

Skocpol, Theda. 1979. *States and Revolutions.* Cambridge: Cambridge University Press.

REVOLUTIONARY MOVEMENTS IN WORLD HISTORY

FROM 1750 TO THE PRESENT

R

Reform, Rebellion, Civil War, Coup D'état, and Revolution

The relationship between the concepts of reform, rebellion, civil war, coup d'état, and revolution is one of the thorniest in the social sciences. Civil wars, for example, are often intimately bound up with revolutions. Each of the great revolutions of the modern era—France, Russia, and China—was preceded or followed by civil war, as were many other twentieth-century revolutions, including those in Cuba, Nicaragua, Afghanistan, and Angola. Rebellions (used here synonymously with revolts) too are difficult to pinpoint. The Mau-Mau uprising in Kenya during the 1950s ended in the overthrow of the British colonial regime, and thus became associated with revolutionary change. The 1381 Peasant Revolt in England nearly succeeded in overthrowing the British monarchy. Add to this complex picture the concepts of reform and coup d'état, and it is clear that these are categories that are difficult to disentangle.

CIVIL WAR

Civil wars are usually considered to be internal or domestic conflicts that involve both the government and a large body of non-state actors (including civilians), while featuring a considerable degree of violence. In this way, civil wars be-

come differentiated from inter-state wars that involve more than one state, and are distinct from fleeting moments of violence such as riots and strikes. The difficulty with this view is that civil wars often involve other states. For example, the contemporary conflict in the Democratic Republic of Congo, although ostensibly taking place within one state, also involves many others, including Zimbabwe, Angola, Namibia, and Uganda. The conflict also spread to many of its neighboring states, such as Rwanda and Burundi. The Russian Civil War that took place after the Bolshevik Revolution of 1917 involved armies from all over Europe, as did the Spanish Civil War of the 1930s. The Korean Civil War during the 1950s and the Vietnam conflict during the 1960s and 1970s were domestic struggles that assumed a global significance.

There are many types of civil war: some last decades (as in China), and others weeks (such as Finland, in 1918); some are secessionist movements confined to a particular region within a state (Chechnya in Russia, the Tamil majority provinces of Sri Lanka, East Timor in Indonesia), while others are struggles for control of an entire state (America, Guatemala, and Yemen). Some are rooted in ethnic rivalries (Yugoslavia and Rwanda) or religious belief (Sudan and Northern Ireland), while others have more to do with political ideology (China, Nepal, Georgia). Often, civil wars are a mixture of all of these elements. Evidently, civil wars come in many shapes and sizes. The concept itself goes back centuries, at least until the period of The Anarchy in England, during the early to mid twelfth century. It is a concept that has assumed a concrete reality in every corner of the globe.

Bombs fall on the presidential palace in Chile during the coup d'état of 1973. Soldiers supporting the coup led by General Augusto Pinochet take cover as bombs are dropped on the Presidential Palace of La Moneda on September 11, 1973. (AP/Wide World Photos)

COUP D'ÉTAT

The concept of coup d'état also goes back many centuries, perhaps being traceable to the role played by the Praetorian Guards in ancient Rome, who periodically intervened to determine who was to take stewardship of the Roman empire. Over the centuries the concept became confined to the takeover of a state by an alternative elite, often guaranteed or led by the armed forces. Coups, therefore, have assumed a much more narrow and contained meaning than civil wars, being more about a change in personnel than a violent conflict that induces a novel social and economic program. Coups became commonplace in Europe during the late Middle Ages and into the early modern period, then spread, over the past two hundred years or so, around the world. In recent times, coups have been most habitually observed in developing countries, particularly in Africa and Latin America, where they became frequent during the 1970s. Like civil wars, coups remain an endemic feature of world politics, as can be seen by the unsuccessful coup attempted by foreign-backed financiers and mercenaries in Equatorial Guinea in 2004, and the more successful ousting of rulers in Pakistan, Fiji, and Haiti over recent years.

Despite appearing to be a neater category than civil war, coups too are more complicated than they at first appear. First, like civil wars, coups are not simply domestic processes—hence the involvement of both the U.S. CIA and the Soviet KGB intelligence service in numerous coups, successful and unsuccessful, during the Cold War. Equally, coups have often sparked wars abroad, witnessed, for example, by the expansionist drive initiated by Japan after the 1936 attempted coup by members of the military corps. Nor are the effects of coups necessarily confined to rival elites scrambling and jockeying for position. After the coup by General Pinochet in Chile in 1973, the military junta set in place radical economic, political, and economic programs that significantly recast Chilean society over the fifteen years of the military dictatorship. Similar effects were produced by the Baathist coup in Iraq, the putsch against the monarchy led by Mu'ammar al-Qadhafi in Libya, and the Francoist coup (*golpe*) in Spain. Coups have often preceded more dramatic processes: the regime of Fulgencio Batista in Cuba was distracted by numerous attempted coups during the late 1950s, something that enabled the revolutionary army led by Fidel Castro to build up support in the eastern highlands of the country before advancing on Cuba's major cities.

Coups have many causes, some noble (such as the failed plot of July 20, 1944, to assassinate Adolf Hitler), while others are more mercenary: for example the UK- and U.S.-backed imposition of Shah Reza Pahlavi in Iran in 1953. Although the armed forces have been the leading actors in most coups, some coups have taken place despite them or even in opposition to them, seen most recently in the failed 2002 coup against Venezuelan president Hugo Chavez, a former paratrooper who enjoys the support of the vast majority of the armed forces. Coups, therefore, vary from being little more than a change of leadership, often prompted by the armed forces, to more significant political processes that can have dramatic consequences.

REBELLION

Like coups, rebellions have also tended to be seen as relatively limited processes. The Kett Rebellion of 1549 in Eastern England was not an attempt to overthrow the state, but more a reflection of the dissatisfaction felt in the region against the system of enclosures and private ownership sanctioned by the monarchy. The ongoing rebellion in the Chiapas area of Mexico is also predominantly a conflict contained within its regional stronghold. As well as being limited to local grievances, rebellions are sometimes associated with particular social groups, such as students (as in the May 1968 student rebellion in France) or indigenous groups (the Mapuche in Chile or the Quechua in Peru). Although these rebellions contain elements that threaten the security of incumbent regimes, they have failed to produce a lasting legacy that can genuinely challenge the authority of the central state. As such, rebellions can be understood as uprisings that are aimed at removing certain leaders or abolishing particular practices, without necessarily seeking to overhaul an entire social order. In that sense, they appear to be something short of a full-blown civil war or revolution.

However, upon closer inspection, rebellion too proves to be a rather elusive category. The Jacobite Rebellion in the eighteenth century, the Chinese Boxer Rebellion of 1900, and the 1916 Easter Rebellion (Rising) in Ireland are events that had a significant impact on both domestic and international history. Rebellions, like civil wars and coups, have a long and distinguished lineage, going back at least two thousand years to the Roman slave uprisings and the revolt by the people of Judea against their imperial masters. Disenfranchised groups, from slaves to peasants, have often been in a state of virtually continuous rebellion against their masters and seigneurs, processes that have induced revolutions in numerous states (Algeria, Mexico, and Nicaragua among them). Many groups in contemporary societies form alliances to rebel against state authority on issues ranging from the price of oil to freedom of religious belief. Rather than serving as a discrete unit of analysis, rebellions also appear to defy easy summation.

REFORM

Of all these categories, reform appears the easiest to capture. After all, the long path of parliamentary reform in Britain is considered the principal reason why revolution has not taken place in modern British history, despite at times conditions that have appeared ripe for it. Reform movements are generally seen as advocating social change short of the rapid, more fundamental institutional transformation associated with revolution. Reformism is co-determinous with gradualism and the resolving of particular problems through nonviolent means, such as the enactment of civil rights legislation in the United States as a result of protests by various disenfranchised groups.

However, once more, reality is somewhat removed from this standard interpretation. On numerous occasions, the attempt by governments to reduce the prospect of radical action by instituting reform programs has served only to hasten rather than prevent revolution. In France, for example, the program of limited reform instigated by the regime of Louis XVI only emboldened the provincial *parlements,* the newly empowered bourgeoisie (business, merchant, and professional classes), and peasants taking part in rural uprisings. As Alexis de Tocqueville pointed out, the weakness of the monarchy was revealed by its reforms, allowing the "middling" classes of burghers, merchants, and gentry to press for more radical steps. Defeat in the Seven Years War with England, the example of a successful bourgeois revolution in America, and the growth of new ideas like equality and nationalism all combined with elite fracture in turning reform into revolution.

REVOLUTION

Revolutions have been a common theme in world history, yet there have been many different types of revolutions. In ancient Greece, the idea of revolution was linked to a circular movement contained within Aristotle's trinity of democracy, oligarchy, and tyranny. In the European Middle Ages, the concept was used to denote a sense of return to a pre-existing order. Following the French Revolution, revolution came to mean a more pronounced, radical rupture from past arrangements. Revolutions became associated with glorious fights to the finish in which the old order would surrender to

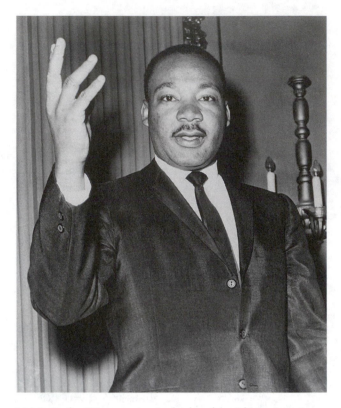

Martin Luther King was a major leader of the African American Freedom Struggle and Civil Rights Movement. The Civil Rights Movement was generally viewed as reformist since most of its leaders advocated nonviolent means and the opening of existing political and economic institutions to equal access and participation by all groups rather than the rapid replacement of exiting institutions with new ones, as is characteristic of revolution. King, though, unlike some other major civil rights leaders of his time, became a staunch opponent of U.S. military intervention in Vietnam and more critical of certain aspects of the U.S. economic system shortly before his assassination. (Library of Congress)

the might and right of revolutionary armies. During the nineteenth century, the liberal (or bourgeois) revolutions of America and France became considered as archetypal, reaching their apogee in the 1848 "Springtime of Nations" in Europe. Following the mid-century rise of Communism, primarily via the work of theorists like Marx and Engels and the practical example provided by the 1870 Paris Commune, revolution came to be associated with an inevitable, violent shift from one type of social system (such as capitalism) to another (Socialism). The ideas of Marx and Engels were extended by numerous twentieth-century revolutionaries—Lenin, Mao, and Castro among them—who variously added a role for revolutionary parties, peasants, and guerrillas in the formation of revolutionary processes. After the collapse of Communism, many people argued that revolution had taken

yet another turn, becoming variously "negotiated" or conjoined with reform processes to generate a new category of "refolution."

The rarest, but most thorough, type of revolution is usually described as a "social revolution." Social revolutions, such as those experienced in France, Russia, and China, can be seen as the rapid, mass, forceful, systemic transformation of the principal institutions and organizations in a society. They are systemic in that social revolutions are processes in which the major institutions and organizations in a society are transformed. Ways of doing business and competing politically must change, alongside shifts in values and attitudes, if an example of radical change is truly to warrant the label "social revolution." Social revolutions are not merely about the introduction of elections, instituting programs of land reform, or the opening up of news media outlets to allow mild critiques of the status quo; they are something much more fundamental and comprehensive. Social revolutions seek to overturn a society's social, economic, and political structures, and to recast its international relations, all within a relatively short time frame. This differentiates social revolutions from evolutionary change, which is comprehensive but takes place over the long term; reform programs, which take place in the short term but do not engender fundamental change; and political revolutions, which seek a modification of a society's political arrangements but leave its economic and social arrangements largely intact. Social revolutions are long-term processes in that the seeds of a revolutionary crisis emerge over decades rather than months, and yet they are also the result of short-term triggers that serve to ignite the revolutionary process.

To constitute a social revolution, systemic change must be the result of a significant contribution from social movements in civil society and must substantially involve the wider public. Although led by an elite, social revolutions are mass events in which the population is prepared to defy the old regime and overturn the existing order. This distinguishes social revolutions from processes of reform from above and coup d'état. Lenin and Castro may have seized power with only a handful of well-armed, committed revolutionaries, but their regimes were supported and sustained by popular legitimacy—at least in the short-to-medium term (although in both cases, the iron fist of dictatorship was never too far from the surface).

Social revolutions also have a *constitutive* effect on world politics. The French Revolution, for example, introduced into the public domain concepts such as "nationalism," "Left," and "Right," and what Eric Hobsbawm, the British historian, calls its "most lasting and universal consequence"—the metric system. Although the initial direction of the revolutionary program was subverted by Robespierre's "Terror" and Napoleonic dictatorship, its impact traveled far and wide: counter-revolutionary alliances were formed to crush the revolution; other uprisings were carried out in its name; and reform programs were initiated to prevent such events happening elsewhere. Social revolutions, both as concept and practice, appear to affect the very makeup of the international order.

Revolutions, therefore, may be social, bourgeois, Communist, peasant, negotiated, and more. The term has come to be used to describe all forms of dramatic change, as in the conservative "Thatcher revolution" that shook up British politics in the 1980s, the information revolution that heralded the move toward a service-oriented or knowledge-based economy, the Chinese Cultural Revolution initiated by Chairman Mao in 1966, and the more contemporary "Bolivarian revolution" undertaken by Venezuelan president Hugo Chavez. To go with this cornucopia are an equal number of theories and definitions, from the most simple to the most complex, explaining what revolutions are and how they come about. Several schools of revolutionary theory compete in a seemingly endless squabble about what constitutes a revolution, and how revolutions are like or unlike other types of radical change. As with the other categories outlined above, revolutions appear to vary in form across time and place, as well as according to the prejudices and politics of those who observe them.

CONCLUSION

Although the study of radical change does not appear to be well suited to universal schema, that does not stop scholars from trying. The problem, as indicated by this survey, is that it is difficult to subsume all categories of social change within a single, catch-all taxonomy. Civil wars, reforms, coups d'état, rebellions, and revolutions are intricately connected and overlapping, running into each other at numerous junctures. They may be roughly viewed as points along a continuum of social phenomena differentiated by unique levels of popular participation, organization, rapidity of change, violence, and overall impact (both domestic and international), as well as other factors. Revolutions can be distinguished from other types of social change by the fact that, during revolutions, the context of social action and the goals of opposition alliances are more far-reaching. Revolutionary social movements involve social groupings that seek to fundamentally recast the existing order within a relatively short space of time. In other words, revolutions can be differentiated from other processes of change by their scope, rapidity, and effect.

George Lawson

See Also Afghanistan: Conflict and Civil War; African American Freedom Struggle; Algerian Revolution; American Revolution; Anarchism, Communism, and Socialism; Angolan Revolution; Chechen Revolt against Russia; Chilean Socialist Revolution, Counter-Revolution, and the Restoration of Democracy; Chinese Revolution; Cinema of Revolution; Congo Revolution; ; Cuban Revolution; Documentaries of Revolution; East European Revolutions of 1989; European Revolutions of 1848; French Revolution; Guatemalan Democratic Revolution, Counterrevolution, and Restoration of Democracy; Iranian Revolution; Iraq Revolution; Italian Fascist Revolution; Japanese New Order Movement; Kenyan Mau Mau Rebellion; Korean Civil War; Libyan Revolution; Mexican Revolution; Nazi Revolution: Politics and Racial Hierarchy; Nicaraguan Revolution; Paris Commune of 1871; Polish Solidarity Movement; Russian Revolution of 1917; Russian Revolution of 1991 and the Dissolution of the U.S.S.R.; South African Revolution; Spanish Revolution and Counter-Revolution; Sri Lankan Conflict; Student and Youth Movements: Activism and Revolution; Theories of Revolutions; Transnational Revolutionary Movements; Trends in Revolution; U.S. Southern Secessionist Rebellion and Civil War; Venezuelan Bolivarian Revolution of Hugo Chávez; ; Vietnamese Revolution; War and Revolution; Women's Movement of the United States; Zapatista Movement; Zimbabwean Revolution

References and Further Readings

Garton Ash, Timothy. 1999. *History of the Present: Essays, Sketches and Dispatches from Europe in the 1990s.* London: Penguin.

Goldstone, Jack, ed. 1998. *The Encyclopedia of Political Revolutions.* London: FitzroyDearborn.

Halliday, Fred. 1999. *Revolution and World Politics: The Rise and Fall of the Sixth Great Power.* London: Macmillan.

Hobsbawm, E. J. 1990. *Echoes of the Marseillaise: Two Centuries Look Back on the French Revolution.* London: Verso.

Lawson, George. 2005. *Negotiated Revolutions: The Czech Republic, South Africa and Chile.* Aldershot, UK: Ashgate.

Skocpol, Theda. 1979. *States and Social Revolutions: A Comparative Analysis of France, Russia and China.* Cambridge: Cambridge University Press.

Tilly, Charles. 1978. *From Mobilization to Revolution.* New York: Random House.

Tocqueville, Alexis de. (1856) 1998. *The Old Regime and the Revolution, Volume I.* Chicago: University of Chicago Press.

Russian Revolution of 1917

CHRONOLOGY

1649	The creation of serfdom binds many peasants to particular estates.
1689–1725	Reign of Peter the Great.
1713	The capital is moved to St. Petersburg.
1762–1796	Reign of Catherine the Great.

1812   Napoléon's invasion of Russia, which ends in failure. The French Revolution is defeated, and the power of Europe's absolute monarchies is reinforced.

1825   Decembrist Uprising: Liberal Russian officers are influenced by the positive ideals of the French Revolution; they object to the continuation of an absolute monarchy in Russia, rebel, and are defeated.

1853–1856   Russia suffers defeat in the Crimean War at the hands of technologically more advanced nations, motivating Czar Alexander II to launch a program to modernize the country. This includes providing Western educations to thousands of young Russians.

1861   The serfs are emancipated, but many former serfs face economic hardship.

1863   Publication of Chernyshevsky's *What Is to Be Done?* This book is thought to have inspired Lenin's concept of a dedicated intellectual revolutionary elite (or vanguard) that would educate and lead the working class and peasant majority to support Socialist revolution.

1870   Vladimir Ilich Ulyanov (Lenin) is born.

1881   Assassination of Czar Alexander II by Narodnaia Volia (People's Will).

1898   Organization of the Russian Social Democratic Party.

1903   Russian Social Democratic Party begins to split into the Bolshevik faction ("majority"; in 1918 named the Communist Party) and Menshevik ("minority") faction.

1904–1905   Russo-Japanese War results in devastating defeat for Russia.

1905   Russian Revolution of 1905. To retain power, the czar permits the creation of a Russian parliament, the Duma.

1906–1917   Stolypin land reform program attempts to encourage peasants to leave the traditional peasant communes in which land was owned collectively and become individual, private landowning farmers. The peasant communes had been a source of support for the Revolution of 1905, and the czar's advisers hope that landowning independent farmers will become conservative politically and supporters of the czar's regime in the countryside.

1914   After a Serbian terrorist assassinates Archduke Franz Ferdinand, heir to the Austro-Hungarian throne, Austria invades Serbia. Russia comes to Serbia's defense, triggering a series of declarations of war among nations linked by pre-war alliances and beginning World War I.

1914–1917   Russia's relatively poorly equipped and poorly led army is repeatedly defeated. Millions of Russian peasant and worker soldiers die: in combat, from disease, or from freezing to death. Millions more are wounded. The flow of food from the countryside to the cities is disrupted as resources are diverted to the Russian army, as are the trains that were used to bring grain from farms to the urban centers. The Romanov dynasty rapidly loses most of its remaining legitimacy and popular support because of its incompetent war policies and the scandalous behavior of a charismatic but morally dissolute monk, Rasputin, upon whom the royal family becomes dependent; Rasputin has a seemingly miraculous ability to stop the bleeding of the czar's son, heir to the Russian throne, who suffers from hemophilia.

1916   In December, a member of the extended royal family and his associates attempt to save the reputation of the Romanov dynasty and Czar Nicholas II by ridding the monarchy of the seemingly evil influence of Rasputin by murdering him.

1917   On February 23 by the Julian calendar, which Russia follows at that time (March 8, modern calendar), thousands of women demonstrate for bread on International Women's Day and are joined by hundreds of thousands of industrial workers. Petrograd military units refuse to suppress the demonstration, and the czar is forced to abdicate. National power is officially handed over to a Provisional Government made up of leading figures in the czar's parliament, the Duma, who come largely from Russia's tiny professional and business upper-middle class. The vast majority of people in the Petrograd area, who are workers, peasants, soldiers, and sailors, elect committees (soviets) to whom they owe their direct allegiance, including the Petrograd Soviet. In this situation of dual power, the Provisional Government can survive only as long as it enjoys the support of the Petrograd Soviet.

In September, after the Provisional Government loses what limited legitimacy and popularity it originally enjoyed through disastrous and unpopular policies, including continuing the war against Germany and failing to carry out land reform, the Bolsheviks gain greater popular support and achieve majorities with both the Petrograd and Moscow city Soviets.

On October 25, (November 7 according to the modern calendar) military units loyal to the Petrograd Soviet seize major government buildings, disband the Provisional Government, and take national power. Mensheviks and the more conservative or Right Socialist Revolutionaries protest the Bolshevik-led Soviet seizure of power. The Bolsheviks form a temporary leftist coalition government with their allies the Left Socialist Revolutionaries.

In November, the multiparty election for a Constituent Assembly to organize a new political system is held. The Bolsheviks appear to win majorities in the large cities (where less than 20 percent of the population live), but only 24 percent of the total popular vote. In contrast, the Socialist Revolutionaries win in much of the countryside and obtain the largest percentage of the popular vote nationwide—about 41 percent.

1918   On January 5, the Constituent Assembly meets. Most elected delegates criticize Bolshevik (Communist Party) behavior and policies. After one day, this most democratically elected national assembly in Russia's history until the 1990s is forcibly disbanded by the Bolshevik-dominated Soviet government. Dissatisfaction with the Bolsheviks increases. Rebellions against the Soviet government break out in various parts of Russia and the former czarist empire. The Russian Civil War begins.

In March, the Communists establish Lenin's concept of the dictatorship of the proletariat: exclusive Communist Party control of the government.

1922   The Civil War largely comes to an end with the victory of the Communist-led Red Army under the command of Leon Trotsky. Stalin becomes the general secretary of the rapidly expanding Communist Party as hundreds of thousands of workers and peasants join. The Communist Party enacts a rule permitting the expulsion of dissident and supposedly disruptive party members by a two-thirds vote of the Central Committee of the Communist Party.

1924   Lenin dies and leaves behind a statement calling for Stalin to be removed from power. The majority of the Central Committee ignore Lenin's warning and vote to maintain Stalin in the position of general secretary of the Communist Party.

1927–1929   Stalin wins the struggle for leadership. Trotsky is expelled from the Communist Party and then forcibly exiled from the Soviet Union.

1929–1930s   Stalin and his supporters launch the collectivization of agriculture program and continue the far more successful industrialization drive. Repression, conflict, and disruption in parts of the countryside result in famine and the deaths or deportation to Siberia of millions of people. Hundreds of thousands are expelled from the party, the government, or the military for actual or suspected opposition to Stalin's policies. Many are imprisoned or executed.

1939   The Hitler-Stalin Non-Aggression Pact allows the Nazi Germans to attack Poland without fear of Soviet interference and permits the U.S.S.R. to seize much of Polish territory in the event of such a war. As a result, Nazi Germany will go to war first with Poland

and then western European countries, and only later with the Soviet Union. On September 1, Germany invades Poland, beginning World War II in Europe.

1940   Trotsky is assassinated in Mexico.

1941   On June 22, Nazi Germany invades the U.S.S.R. Twenty-six to 27 million Soviet soldiers and civilians perish during the war.

1943   The Soviet Army forces the surrender of the German Sixth Army at Stalingrad.

1945   World War II ends.

1947   The Cold War begins.

1953   Stalin dies.

1956   Khrushchev denounces Stalin's crimes.

INTRODUCTION

The Russian Revolution was the first revolution in world history won by revolutionists who aimed to create a "socialist" society. This new social system was to be characterized by social (collective) rather than individual (private) ownership of major resources and industries, and was to provide people with equality of opportunity as well as the basic necessities of life, such as food, shelter, medical services, and education. The concept of a socialist society gained popularity in reaction to the injustices of early industrial society, such as extreme inequality, crowded urban slums, unsafe working conditions, exploitive child labor, and rule by the rich rather than real democracy.

The revolution went through a number of phases. In February of 1917 (according to the Julian calendar, which Russia followed at the time), massive demonstrations in the capital city, Petrograd, forced the czar to abdicate, and Russia became a republic. National policy was controlled by a Provisional Government composed of leading members of the czar's parliament, the Duma, while local administration was often in the hands of popularly elected revolutionary committees or large assemblies called soviets. In October (according to the old calendar), the Bolshevik-dominated citywide soviet of the capital, the Petrograd Soviet, overthrew the weakened Provisional Government, seizing state power. In 1918 the Bolsheviks, adopting the name Communist Party, established a political system in which the Communist Party alone controlled the national government.

After a brutal civil war, the Communist Party, under the leadership of Lenin and his associates, emerged victorious. Following Lenin's death in 1924 and a bitter leadership struggle, Joseph Stalin, general secretary of the Communist Party, became the dominant leader in the late 1920s. Stalin and his supporters created an authoritarian bureaucratic state ruled by a Communist Party elite that crushed real and potential opposition. After Stalin's death in 1953 and the denunciation of his crimes by the new Communist leadership in 1956, the U.S.S.R. moved away from the repressive Stalinist system and eventually abandoned the one-party form of government in the spring of 1990 in favor of multiparty democracy. In late December 1991, the U.S.S.R. ceased to exist, disintegrating into fifteen separate nations.

BACKGROUND: CULTURE AND HISTORY

Prior to the revolutionary movements that began to develop in Russia in the late nineteenth century, the Russian empire, which incorporated many ethnic, language, and religious groups, was governed by an absolute monarchy. Approximately 85 percent of the people were peasants, the large majority of whom were very poor. Russia had experienced an enormous 1812 invasion by a multinational French-led army under the command of Napoléon. The defeat of that invasion resulted not only in the toppling of Napoléon but also in the suppression of the ideals of the French Revolution and the reestablishment of the near total domination of absolute monarchies over the entire continent.

Ironically, in Russia, many of the officers who had helped to defeat Napoléon felt betrayed when Russian nationalist fervor, which had surged in reaction to the invasion and motivated thousands of Russians to give their lives in defense of the motherland, was used to reinforce the czar's dictatorship rather than improve the lives of the mass of Russia's people or permit them any significant role in the political system. Defeating foreign aggression was one thing, but many Russian officers supported some of the reforms of the French Revolution and wanted them for Russia. In December 1825, shortly after the death of Alexander I and faced with the prospect of the rule of the unpopular Czar Nicholas I, many of these officers attempted to carry out a revolution. Officers involved in the conspiracy in the north of Russia aimed to create a constitutional monarchy system that would end the absolute power of the czar and give a major political role to at least educated Russians with significant property. In the south of Russia, in contrast, the officers involved in the "Decembrists' Revolt" apparently intended to end the monarchy and turn Russia into a republic. The rebellion in the north was immediately suppressed in St. Petersburg with the loss of many rebel lives. The southern revolt was defeated after a few months, and several of the leaders were executed. Although the Decembrist Revolt was crushed, it inspired many later Russian revolutionaries.

The prospect of revolution in Russia was enhanced significantly by Czar Alexander II's response to Russia's defeat by Britain and France in the 1853–1856 Crimean War. Concluding that the advanced military equipment of those smaller nations, the product of their much more developed technology and industrialization, had brought them victory over Russia despite its huge advantage in population, the czar decided to launch a series of policies and reforms to modernize Russia. These included far-reaching changes in the system of agriculture and in educational policy.

To begin a process of modernizing agriculture, the czar abolished serfdom in 1861. Serfdom had been established in 1649 as a means of binding peasants to the land and, in so doing, ensuring the landowners a reliable labor force. A little more than half of the peasants were serfs before 1861. Most serfs welcomed emancipation, but before long many were bitterly disappointed. First, former serfs were required to pay for the sections of land that their mirs (peasant communes) received in "redemption payments" to compensate the previous owners, payments often stretching out over many years. Second, to raise funds as part of the czar's modernization program, Russia had to expand the amount of its agricultural products sold on the international market through increased taxation. Peasants needing to feed their families and burdened with redemption payments and high taxes often concluded that their emancipation from slavery had been replaced with a financial enslavement in which many, in order to survive, under even relatively miserable conditions, fell deeper into debt. As the desperation of poor peasants grew, increasing numbers became receptive to the concepts of Russian populism, which called for a more democratic political system and for freeing the peasants from the repression and economic exploitation of the czar's government. This movement gave rise to both small groups of terrorists—such as Narodnaia Volia (People's Will), which assassinated Czar Alexander II in 1881—and to a mass political party with enormous peasant support, the Socialist Revolutionary Party.

The modernization plan also included an expansion of Western-style education for many upper- and middle-class young people. Although these classes made up only small percentages of Russian society, since the total population of the czar's empire was approximately 150 million, education to Western science and culture reached tens of thousands of young people. Many of them were struck by the government's demand that they learn modern Western technologies, sciences, and forms of economic organization but still submit to an anti-democratic absolute monarchy that permitted no effective political participation except to members of the royal family, and that supported an economic system in which so many Russians suffered from extreme poverty.

A significant number of the educated young organized or joined revolutionary movements. Some were attracted to Marxism or to the anarchistic ideas of Michail Bakunin and became involved in Marxist Socialist or anarchist-related movements, such as populism. A small number formed terrorist groups, such as People's Will, to violently attack the czar's regime and prepare the way for a freer, more socially just society by first destroying the existing repressive system. Lenin's older brother Alexander, a brilliant science student at St. Petersburg University, became involved with a group of radical students who plotted to assassinate Czar Alexander III. When Lenin was seventeen, his twenty-one-year-old brother was caught with a bomb built into a hollowed-out encyclopedia volume intended for the assassination; Alexander was tried and executed, along with several of his associates who also refused to ask for mercy.

Like his older brother, Lenin became committed to the concept of a group of dedicated revolutionary intellectuals playing an essential role in transforming Russia—but not through terrorist violence, such as assassination; rather, it was to be by organizing, educating, and leading the masses of people to revolution. Writings extolling the need for a highly committed revolutionary elite, such as *The Catechism of the Revolutionary* by anarchists Sergei Necheav and Mikhail Bakunin, had a significant impact on Lenin. He seemed especially impressed by Chernyshevsky's 1864 novel, *What Is to Be Done;* in 1904, he explained to a friend that "Chernyshevsky's great service was not only that he showed that every right-thinking and really decent thinking person must be a revolutionary, but something more important: what kind of revolutionary, what his principles ought to be, how he should aim for his goal, what means and methods he should employ to realize it" (Volkogonov 1994, 20).

From these works, the views of Karl Kautsky of the German Social Democratic Party, and his own analyses, Lenin concluded that workers on their own would likely develop concern only for improving wages and working conditions. It was up to revolutionary intellectuals to inspire the workers with the vision of a new social order that would eliminate the actual root causes of much of their economic misery. But Lenin proposed that this revolutionary elite should organize and lead the masses not only during the revolutionary struggle but also after the revolutionary victory, during the process of rapidly transforming society's economic and social systems. That notion became manifested in the concept of the vanguard party, the Communist Party, which would have exclusive control over the post-revolutionary government. This was Lenin's attempt to operationalize Marx's concept of the dictatorship of the proletariat, the political situation in which, for the first time in history, the working people of society would control the government. But whereas some Marxist revolutionaries argued that the rule of the proletariat could and should come about through free multiparty elections, Lenin held that the dictatorship of the working people should be exercised through giving exclusive control of the state to a party of dedicated revolutionaries that truly represented the interests of the workers and peasants.

The ultimately dominant revolutionary leadership emerged from the Marxist-inspired Russian Social Democratic Party, founded in 1898. A key dispute in 1903 was whether the party should be governed by totally democratic procedures, in which the votes of new members would be equal to those of long-time members. Lenin and his associates held that total democracy in the party would be suicidal, since undoubtedly the party would be infiltrated by czarist agents who, if given the right to participate equally in voting for leaders and in determining policy, could possibly exert significant influence on, or even gain control of, the party. Lenin advocated that major decisions in the party should be made only by long-term, highly trusted revolutionaries who could not possibly be czarist agents. He also argued that in order to mobilize the working classes effectively, the party had to maintain a high level of discipline and unity. On several votes taken at the 1903 meeting—such as the election of certain party officials and committees—candidates or policies favored by Lenin won. Thus Lenin's supporters began calling themselves the Bolshevik ("majority") faction of the Russian Social Democratic Party, while those generally in opposition to Lenin's policies became known as the Menshevik ("minority") faction. The split in the Russian Social Democratic Party became essentially permanent after 1912, with the two factions functioning as separate parties.

The major and most historically significant disagreements between the two factions centered on the issues of the characteristics of the post-monarchy government and economy. The Mensheviks believed that the monarchy should be replaced with a multiparty democratic political system and that capitalists should continue to industrialize Russia, thereby increasing the size of the urban industrial working class, the proletariat, which Marx argued would be the political basis for a transition to socialism. A Marxist political party could then potentially be voted into power. In contrast, Lenin and his Bolsheviks (who in 1918 would adopt the name Communist Party) concluded that once the monarchy was overthrown, Marxist revolutionaries should take advantage of the circumstances and seize sole control of the government and begin rapidly transforming society to benefit the large majority of Russia's people, who were peasants and workers. This would mean completing in-

dustrialization under a revolutionary-controlled government rather than through the process of private capitalist investment, as Marx had generally thought would be the case. (Late is his life, Marx did consider the possibility of "bypassing the capitalist stage of development" in Russia by building a modern, collectively owned economy "on the basis of the common ownership of land characteristic of the village mir" (McLelland 1983, 305). When, after the October Revolution of 1917, the Bolsheviks did establish a one-party government, that act had major consequences outside as well as within Russia. Marxist-inspired Socialist movements in various countries such as France and the United States began to split over support of, or opposition to, Lenin's one-party system. Those who favored the Menshevik, democratic approach generally adopted or retained the expression "Socialist Party" (as in French Socialist Party or American Socialist Party), while those who favored Lenin and the Bolsheviks followed the Bolshevik lead in adopting the title Communist Party (French Communist Party or American Communist Party).

CONTEXT AND PROCESS OF REVOLUTION

By the beginning of the twentieth century, Russia, with a population that was still at least 80 percent rural, was characterized by worker unrest, widespread peasant dissatisfaction, the existence of a number of revolutionary movements, and terrorist violence, including assassinations of government officials. As the turmoil began to seriously threaten the continuation of the Romanov dynasty, a conflict over territory in the Far East led to the outbreak of the 1904–1905 Russo-Japanese War. The czar and his ministers felt that war with Japan would rally nationalist support to the monarchy, overcoming, at least temporarily, class conflict and internal disorders, and that victory over Japan would enhance the legitimacy of the czar's government. But the Japanese navy annihilated much of the Russian fleet. Russia's defeat, coupled with previously existing circumstances, led to the outbreak of protests and rebellions among civilians and mutinies of some military units. A particularly brutal event was the violent suppression of a demonstration at the Winter Palace on Sunday, January 22, 1905, of thousands of workers, women, and children led by a priest, Father Georgii Gapon, appealing for the czar's assistance to alleviate their economic hardship. Unknown to the demonstrators the czar was away, but his security forces decided to open fire, killing more than a hundred people (Thompson 1990, 181). The massacre, which became known as "Bloody Sunday," spurred anti-Romanov insurrections. In Petrograd, a revolutionary council, or soviet, was established that eventually included Trotsky, then a Menshevik, among its leaders.

In order to save the monarchy and end the rebellions, the czar agreed to permit freedom of speech and assembly, and the creation of a national parliament, or Duma, to be elected by male voters. While the czar would remain the head of the government and the commander of the armed forces, the Duma was, in theory, to have veto and confirmatory power over laws proposed by the czar. The creation of the Duma and what appeared to be a constitutional monarchy satisfied the immediate demands of those upper- and upper-middle-class Russians who had demanded a participatory role in government. Since the majority of the armed forces had remained loyal to the czar, those workers and peasants still in rebellion, deprived of most of their former upper- and middle-class allies, were gradually suppressed, often violently. The Duma, in reality, became more of an inconvenience than a real check on the czar's absolute power, since the czar repeatedly dismissed it or altered the requirements of eligibility to vote in order to weaken or control it.

The czar's government launched a series of reforms— such as legalizing labor unions and providing accident and health insurance programs for certain types of workers—in order to decrease the likelihood of a new revolutionary upsurge. In particular, the so-called Stolypin land reform was intended to increase the percentage of Russian peasants who owned and farmed land privately, rather than as members of the traditional commune (mir) system. Peasant communes had been a major source of revolutionary activity in rural areas during the 1905 rebellion. Whether these measures would have been sufficient to prevent the outbreak of a new revolution will never be known.

Competition for control of the world's resources and European ethnic tensions combined to set the stage for the outbreak of World War I. The immediate flash point was the murder in Sarajevo of the heir to the throne of the Austro-Hungarian empire, Franz Ferdinand, by a Serbian assassin. Serbian nationalist extremists were attempting to force the Austro-Hungarian empire to permit Serbian-populated areas it controlled to unite with Serbia. When Austria invaded Serbia in response, Russia, Serbia's ally, declared war on Austria, triggering a series of declarations of war by nations bound by previous treaties—and beginning World War I. In the years before the war, a number of Socialist leaders had argued that the working people of Europe should never again allow themselves to be ordered to war by their ruling elites. But once war had broken out, most people, including many Socialist activists, became inflamed with nationalist fervor and supported their nation's mobilization for war, including in Russia the Mensheviks and Socialist Revolutionaries. But Lenin and other Bolsheviks opposed the war as an atrocity in which the ruling classes of Europe would send millions of their peasants and workers to be killed by the peasants and workers of other nations. Lenin's goal was ultimately to transform World War I, in which millions of peasants and workers had been uprooted from their homes and given guns, from a conflict between nations into a struggle in which the peasants and workers of all nations would turn against and overthrow the ruling classes that had sent them to war. At a minimum, Lenin anticipated a high probability that the results of the war would destroy the remaining legitimacy of the Romanov dynasty and create an opportunity for revolution in Russia.

Faced with superior German weaponry, leadership, and organization, the Russians suffered successive military disasters. Russia's railroad system, used to supply soldiers at the front, had difficulty simultaneously bringing food from the countryside to the cities. Food scarcities, coupled with repeated defeats, caused a rapid surge in urban discontent. The czarina was German, and she relied for an extended period of time on the religious advice and healing services of a charismatic but morally dissolute monk, Rasputin, for her ailing hemophiliac son, the heir to the throne; these facts further eroded public confidence in the monarchy.

On International Women's Day in the capital, Petrograd (February 23, according to the calendar Russia followed at the time), thousands of working-class women staged a demonstration demanding bread; they marched through industrial areas and called on workers to come out and join them. Soldiers refused orders to suppress the demonstrations and strikes. With the capital in turmoil, the military situation desperate, and the loyalty of many military units rapidly disintegrating, the czar was forced to abdicate, ending the Romanov dynasty and the monarchy and transforming Russia into a republic. Those events constituted the February Revolution.

The new government was characterized by a system of dual political power. On the one hand, the czar's parliament, the Duma, used its members to create a new national governing group, the Provisional Revolutionary Government. This was recognized by Russia's wartime allies, Britain and France, as the new and legitimate government. But in reality, the Provisional Government, initially led by an aristocrat, Prince George Lvov, and later by the moderate Socialist Alexander Kerensky, could govern only so long as it enjoyed the support of the Petrograd Soviet. The soviets were the councils elected by workers, peasants, soldiers, or sailors to run local organizations as the authorities linked to the monarchy were rejected. Factory soviets, village soviets, regimental army soviets, and sailor soviets in the Petrograd area in turn sent some of their members to the citywide Petrograd Soviet. Since the members of the soviets were more directly and popularly elected by the people, usually from their own numbers, most people owed their allegiance first to the

Petrograd Soviet and only secondarily to the Provisional Government—and then only as long as it was supported by the Petrograd Soviet.

Through the spring and summer, the Socialist Revolutionaries and the Mensheviks dominated the Petrograd Soviet, while the Bolsheviks were a growing minority. But most of the Socialist Revolutionaries and the Mensheviks supported the unpopular and politically disastrous decisions of the Provisional Government to continue the war against Germany and to postpone a proposed sweeping land redistribution program. The resulting continued military defeats—coupled with a growing suspicion that the Provisional Government, given its upper- and upper-middle-class composition, did not really intend to carry out a significant land reform at all—destroyed its legitimacy. As a result, by the beginning of the fall, Bolsheviks, who had continuously demanded an immediate peace treaty with the Germans and land reform, had achieved majorities in a number of big city soviets, including Petrograd and Moscow.

No longer enjoying either significant popular support or the loyalty of military forces in the capital, the Provisional Government was easily ousted by soldiers and sailors under the command of the Petrograd Soviet on October 25, 1917, known as the October Revolution. The new Bolshevik-dominated government quickly concluded a truce with the Germans and later a treaty very costly to Russia—but in anticipation that Germany would soon experience its own Socialist revolution, return the surrendered territories to Russia, and aid Russia in industrializing.

Within weeks of the seizure of power by the Petrograd Soviet, a previously planned election for a Constituent Assembly to write a new constitution for Russia took place. The Bolsheviks won in a number of big cities, including Petrograd and Moscow, and appeared to receive most of the urban vote. But in terms of the total nationwide popular vote, the Bolsheviks finished second, with about 24 percent. The Socialist Revolutionaries won in the countryside, where the vast majority of the Russian people lived, and finished first in the popular vote, with about 41 percent. Other parties finished far behind. The Constitutional Democrats (Cadets), who favored a constitutional monarchy and some economic reform, received 5 percent, and the Mensheviks 3 percent (Dmytryshyn 1984, 78). When the Constituent Assembly met in Petrograd in January 1918 and the Bolsheviks realized that they could not control it, soldiers loyal to the Bolsheviks disbanded it after about twenty-four hours. The Bolsheviks, under Lenin's leadership, in effect established a political system in which only the Communist Party (the title the Bolsheviks adopted in 1918) could control the government. Later this would often be referred to as a Leninist, or dictatorship of the proletariat, system of government. But many groups opposed a Communist seizure of power, resulting in civil war

from 1918 to 1922. Elements of the czar's army, with the support of Great Britain, launched a military campaign to oust the Bolsheviks. The Right Socialist Revolutionaries attempted to set up an alternative revolutionary government. Military forces from Great Britain, Japan, the United States, France, and Italy intervened in Russia in support of the anti-Communist White Armies. On March 5, 1918, the Soviet government, fearing a possible attack on Petrograd, moved the capital to Moscow. But ultimately the Communist-led Red Army, which would grow to 5 million under the command of Trotsky, defeated the White forces.

At the conclusion of the civil war, the top leaders of the Communist Party, which was growing rapidly in membership with the influx of tens of thousands of workers and peasants, decided to create the position of general secretary of the Communist Party, in order to oversee the expanding party and the development of an administrative party bureaucracy. While some major party leaders desired important government positions through which they could play a public role in transforming Russian society, Stalin, who had demonstrated considerable organizational skill in the past, accepted the position. This assignment would be a crucial element in Stalin's rise to power.

Stalin was able to place many of his associates in important positions in the party and in government ministries. Lenin became aware, however, of Stalin's tendency toward violence and disrespect for other party members, and also of the development of a growing government bureaucracy that was becoming insensitive to the needs of the people. During 1923, though extremely ill, he attempted to communicate his concerns to other party leaders. In particular, he left a statement that was read to the party Central Committee after his death in 1924, recommending that Stalin "should be removed from his position of General Secretary" (Fitzpatrick 1982, 99). Stalin, aware of the existence of the letter, convinced some key party figures to ignore it. Thus despite Lenin's warning, Stalin continued as general secretary.

Following Lenin's death, Stalin began to accumulate more power. He and his associates made use of a 1922 measure that allowed for the expulsion of party members thought guilty of forming organized groups in opposition to party policies; thus began a process of continually removing dissidents from the party. Trotsky, who too late realized what Stalin and his supporters were doing, attempted to resist the process but was at a disadvantage, for several reasons. Many Bolsheviks, fearing the establishment of a one-man dictatorship as an outcome of their revolution (as had occurred when a successful revolutionary general, Napoléon, seized control of the French Revolution), thought that Trotsky, former commander of the victorious Red Army, was the primary threat; they consequently allied with Stalin against him. Furthermore, Stalin, being from a lower-class background, as many

Armed Bolshevik revolutionaries gather in Petrograd in 1917. (Forbes, Edgar Allen, *Leslie's Photographic Review of the Great War*, 1919)

of the newer members of the Communist Party were, could often communicate with them and the larger population more effectively than could the highly educated Trotsky. And Stalin's position as general secretary of the Communist Party gave him a huge organizational advantage over Trotsky and his supporters.

Trotsky was expelled from the Communist Party and then from the Soviet Union in the late 1920s. After years of continually criticizing Stalin and the perversion of socialism that was developing in Russia—involving elitist rule by an authoritarian bureaucracy and reliance on eliminating or terrorizing critics—Trotsky was murdered at his home near Mexico City by a Stalinist supporter in 1940.

Stalin and his followers, in firm control from the late 1920s on, launched a series of radical policies. Collectivization of

agriculture took place in the late 1920s and the early 1930s. The motives included an attempt to create more efficient farming by pooling land, machinery, and farm animals, coupled with the introduction of improved agricultural practices, so that fewer people would be needed to grow the crops. The surplus labor no longer needed for agriculture would then be available for the country's intensified industrialization drive. Other goals were to improve the flow of agricultural products from the countryside to the cities and to foster a more cooperative (socialist) as opposed to competitive (capitalist) culture in the countryside. Since many peasants already farmed in cooperative-type settings, mirs, and since poor peasants often desired access to more land and the equipment that the collective farms would provide, some peasants favored collectivization. However, the kulaks, or rich peasants, often

Vladimir Lenin, leader of the Bolshevik Revolution and leader of Russia (1917–1924). (Library of Congress)

among the most productive and hardworking, generally opposed surrendering their land, farm animals, and machinery to the collectives. The collectivization process thus provoked widespread opposition, social turmoil, and near civil war conditions in parts of the countryside between those peasants, party officials, and militia enforcing collectivization and those peasants resisting it. The country lost millions of farm animals as many rich peasants sold them for slaughter or simply killed them rather than turn them over to the collective farms. The disruption of agriculture, the loss of farm animals, the deportation to Siberia of hundreds of thousands of resisting peasant families, coupled with poor weather conditions, contributed to famines in some areas, in which millions of people are estimated to have perished.

In contrast to the flawed collectivization of agriculture, the industrialization drive was vastly more successful. While these changes were under way, Stalin's regime implemented a totalitarian social system in which virtually all major social institutions were placed under the control of the Communist Party and the state. In addition, harsh repression of dissidents, real or suspected, resulted in the mid-1930s in the execution or imprisonment of millions of Russians, including the elimination of many high-ranking officers of the armed forces.

While Stalin and his associates were imprisoning and executing many of the original Bolshevik leaders who had helped to bring about the 1917 revolution and were creating an authoritarian totalitarian system in Russia, the German National Socialists, or Nazis, who preserved capitalism while asserting the superiority of Germanic peoples over what they termed inferior races, including Slavic Russians, were establishing their racist totalitarian society. Part of the popular appeal of the Nazis was the fear among many Germans—especially aristocrats, businessmen, and prosperous farmers—of the threat of Bolshevism and the Soviet Union.

In line with Hitler's publicly proclaimed goal of obtaining "living room" for the German people in fertile territories to the east, Germany invaded the Soviet Union in June of 1941. The German war of conquest, racial purification, colonization, and extermination of the Russian Communist Party (whose ideology, among other things, asserted the anti-Nazi concept of equality of the races) resulted in the deaths of an estimated 26 to 27 million soldiers and civilians of the Soviet Union (Volkogonov 1991, 505). The initial inability of the Soviet armed forces to resist the invasion has been blamed partly on Stalin's previous purges of skilled Russian military officers, as well as his failure to heed intelligence warnings and prepare effectively for the Nazi aggression. On the other hand, the Soviet Union's rapid pre-war industrialization had created a huge number of factories, many of whose machines were placed on railroad cars and shipped east to escape the Nazi onslaught. Many of these were used in the production of tens of thousands of tanks, airplanes, artillery pieces, and other weapons that helped the Soviet armed forces to win the epic battle of Stalingrad, drive the Germans and their allies out of the Soviet Union, and play a major role—many argue the major role—in crushing the Nazi regime.

Following the war Stalin's leadership was publicly praised, while his mistakes were publicly ignored. Soviet armies occupied much of eastern Europe and assisted in the installation of Communist Party governments there. In another crash program, the Soviet Union developed atomic weapons. In 1953, Stalin died. Shortly thereafter, the head of Stalin's secret police, Lavrenti Beria, was arrested by top generals of the Soviet armed forces, tried for numerous crimes, and executed. On February 25, 1956, the new leader of the Soviet Union, Nikita Khrushchev, denounced the atrocities committed under Stalin's rule before the 1,436 delegates to the Twentieth Party Congress (Volkogonov 1998, 207). That began a process of de-Stalinization eventually leading to the Eastern European revolutions of 1989, the abandonment of the Leninist, one-party system of government in the Soviet Union in 1990, and the dissolution of the Soviet Union at the end of 1991.

IMPACTS

The Russian Revolution of 1917 was humanity's first major experiment with Socialist revolution. Lenin and his Communist Party operationally defined Marx's general concept of the dictatorship of the proletariat for later generations as the exclusive rule by one party, the Communist Party. That decision drastically increased divisions within the world Socialist movement between the democratic (typically, Social Democrat parties) and the authoritarian branches (usually, Communist parties until the 1990s). The one-party political system was copied in China, North Korea, Vietnam, Cuba, and, after World War II, in a number of Eastern European states, but also, minus the Marxist ideology, in a number of non-Communist and even anti-Communist countries. The Communist Party of the U.S.S.R. trained and aided revolutionaries from many other countries, including China, Korea, and Vietnam. The Leninist style of government stigmatized Marxism as an anti-democratic ideology in the minds of hundreds of millions of people. While Lenin's one-party system may have greatly expanded worker and peasant social and economic opportunities and the rapid industrialization of the Soviet Union—and in so doing contributed significantly to the defeat of Nazi Germany in World War II—it had enormous negative consequences. Many who fought for a democratic revolution in Russia saw their hopes crushed and were themselves persecuted. The death of Lenin permitted Joseph Stalin eventually to emerge as the dominant Communist leader, and to transform Lenin's one-party dictatorship into, in effect, a brutal one-man dictatorship. Stalin's policies resulted in the deaths of millions of innocent people, including many of the old Bolshevik leaders who had worked with Lenin to bring about the revolution. Stalin and his supporters carried out a divisive collectivization of agriculture that resulted in the oppression and deaths of millions of people. He purged the Soviet military of capable but distrusted officers. That and Stalin's willingness to sign a non-aggression pact with Hitler's regime contributed to devastating Nazi victories against Poland, France, and other nations, as well as, after the surprise German attack on the Soviet Union in June of 1941, the deaths of 26 to 27 million citizens of the Soviet Union.

After World War II, the Stalin-led U.S.S.R. assisted local Communist parties in dominating political systems in Poland, Hungary, Romania, Bulgaria, Czechoslovakia, and East Germany. Even after Stalin's death, the Soviet Union crushed an anti-Communist nationalist rebellion in Hungary in 1956 and a liberal Communist reform movement in Czechoslovakia in 1968. While suppressing social movements it opposed, the Soviet Union provided crucial assistance to pro-Socialist and pro-Communist nationalist revolutionaries in defense of their revolutions in Vietnam and Cuba.

Inherent flaws in the Stalinist-shaped Soviet Union coupled with enormous economic and military pressure from the United States and its allies ultimately led to the destruction of the Soviet Union. This had other important consequences. Marxist-Leninist revolutionary ideology, in the view of many potential revolutionaries, lost much of its appeal. The world became, to a great extent at least, temporarily uni-polar economically and politically, dominated by the capitalist democracy of the United States. Leftist political parties such as the Chilean Socialist Party, formerly revolutionary political movements such as the African National Congress in South Africa, and even Communist Party–controlled governments in China, Cuba, and Vietnam were inclined to adapt to the capitalistic-dominated world economic environment by supporting or permitting a wide range of capitalistic economic activity, domestic and foreign, within their borders, in order to advance economic and social development.

The Russian Revolution of 1917, for a considerable time, inspired, aided, and encouraged many revolutionaries in poverty-stricken societies characterized by huge inequalities and social injustice. Its long—though temporary and greatly flawed—existence contributed to the victory of other Communist revolutions that have proved far more successful and durable. But for many millions around the world, the Russian Revolution has served as a prime example of how a revolution, led by often brilliant and dedicated people and promising a future utopia, can go drastically wrong.

PEOPLE AND ORGANIZATIONS

Anarchism

Anarchism is a political ideology that opposes the concept of a government with strong coercive powers. The Socialist (collectivist) version holds that resources and the means of production should be owned collectively by associations of workers whose efforts would be coordinated, when necessary, through federation, while maintaining a high degree of local independence and freedom of action. The capitalist (individualist) version advocates that resources and means of production be privately owned.

Bakunin, Michail (1814–1876)

Bakunin, son of a landowning Russian aristocrat, was the creator of the international Anarchist Movement. Bakunin's anarchist version of socialism differed from Marx's views in several important ways. First, while Marx believed that after the overthrow of the capitalist state, a new worker-controlled state would be created with strong coercive capabilities, and that it would exist until society had transformed to the point where different economic classes no longer exist, Bakunin argued that such a government would ultimately prove just as repressive as, or even more repressive than, a capitalist-controlled government. Instead, Bakunin advocated the immediate elimination of a strong central government and its replacement by a federation of relatively autonomous and self-governing local communities, in which major productive resources would be collectively owned. Second, Marx felt that the revolutionary struggle should be centrally organized and that a revolutionary political party should be formed to fight for the interests of working-class people, including through parliamentary participation. Bakunin, in contrast, opposed forming a workers' political party and felt that the revolutionary struggle should be carried out more through local initiative and groups, such as unions of workers. For Bakunin, a political party was inherently dictatorial; in creating one and competing for control of the state with other parties, revolutionaries would explicitly recognize the legitimacy of what he viewed as an illegitimate, repressive and exploitive central government.

Bolshevik (Majority) Party

This was the faction of the Russian Social Democratic Party led by Lenin that emerged in 1903 and effectively operated as an independent political party after 1912, adopting the title Communist Party in 1918. The Bolsheviks dominated the Petrograd Soviet in the fall of 1917, when it overthrew the then unpopular Provisional Government. Bolshevik leaders supported the creation of a political system in the Soviet Union in which only one party, the Communist Party, would control the government.

Communism

Communism is the stage of social development following the socialist phase, according to Marx's theory of historical materialism. During the socialist phase, the major resources of a society and the major means of production were to be socially (collectively) owned, while inequality was to be reduced, equality of opportunity established, and a system implemented for providing all people with the basic necessities, such as food, medical services, shelter, and education. Ultimately, as socialism produced economic abundance and a new cooperative culture and psychology, specialization of labor would decrease, differentiation of people into separate social classes would come to an end,

the need for government with strong powers of coercion would decline, and the state, as previously known, would cease to exist. Society would then achieve the highest form of development: communism. Whereas in the socialist stage of development, people would receive benefits in direct relation to their level of work and contribution to society, in the communist stage people's psychology would have shifted morally to the point that they would expect to receive benefits more directly in relation to their needs. No society ever claimed to reach the communist stage. Communist Party–led states claimed to be at the socialist stage of development. That is why the Soviet Union was titled the Union of Soviet Socialist (not Communist) Republics, and why Vietnam is titled the Socialist (not Communist) Republic of Vietnam. However, in general political discourse, as opposed to Marxian theory, the expression "Communism" has often been used to refer to a society in which the government is controlled exclusively by the country's Communist Party.

Czar Nicholas II (1868–1918)

Nicholas II was the last czar of Russia and the Romanov dynasty. He has been viewed historically as a somewhat indecisive ruler of questionable abilities. He suppressed the 1905 Revolution in part through the creation of a Russian parliament, or Duma, which he repeatedly attempted to ignore or undermine. He committed Russia to World War I, eventually taking direct command of the armies, but the result was a series of disastrous defeats, millions of casualties, and extreme hardship and suffering throughout the country. He abdicated in early 1917 and was murdered, along with his wife, children, and other associates, by Bolshevik soldiers of the Yekaterinburg Soviet as anti-Bolshevik forces approached the city of Yekaterinburg on July 17, 1918.

Duma

The Duma was the parliament created by the czar to satisfy the demands of at least part of Russia's population and in so doing help bring an end to the 1905 Revolution. The Duma was to have the power to confirm or block laws proposed by the czar. In practice, the czar periodically ignored or dismissed the Duma, or changed election laws to try to increase the percentage of conservative, pro-monarchy members. After the czar's abdication in early 1917, members of the Duma established the Provisional Government, which was overthrown later in 1917 by the Bolshevik-led Petrograd Soviet.

Kerensky, Alexander (1881–1970)

Alexander Kerensky, the son of a school headmaster, was a lawyer and a moderate Socialist of the Socialist Revolutionary Party.

After the abdication of the czar, Kerensky became first the minister of justice and then the minister of war in the Provisional Government headed by Prince George Lvov. When Prince Lvov became unpopular because of his policy of continuing the war against Germany, he was forced to resign; Kerensky became head of the Provisional Government on July 8. While an advocate of democracy, Kerensky quickly destroyed his earlier popularity by ignoring the will of most of the people and continuing the war, resulting in further defeats for Russian forces and mass desertions. When the Provisional Government was overthrown on October 25, 1917 (according to the calendar that Russia followed at the time), Kerensky fled to Finland and then to France, where he continually criticized the Communist Party government of the U.S.S.R. During World War II he went to the United States, where he died in 1970.

Lenin (Vladimir Ilich Ulyanov) (1870–1924)

Lenin, the brilliant son of a regional inspector of schools, was the leader of the Bolshevik faction (in 1918 renamed the Communist Party) of the Russian Social Democratic Party. When Lenin was seventeen his older brother, Alexander, a university science student, was executed for being involved in a plot to assassinate the czar. Lenin became a determined Marxist revolutionary. But he was also somewhat influenced by certain aspects of Russian anarchism, such as the emphasis that some prominent anarchists put on the creation of dedicated activists totally committed to revolution. Lenin has been credited with introducing several major innovations in Marxist revolutionary theory. First, he proposed that workers and peasants required the inspiration and leadership of revolutionary intellectuals organized into a "vanguard party," the Communist Party, in order to develop revolutionary consciousness and mobilize to transform society. Second, Lenin operationalized Marx's concept of the "dictatorship of the proletariat," the rule of the vast working majority of society, as exclusive Communist Party control of the government in a one-party political system. Third, Lenin attempted to explain the failure of Marx's prediction that the most advanced industrial societies would be the first to experience a revolution to socialism through his Theory of Imperialism. Lenin believed that the advanced capitalist countries through imperialist domination and exploitation of most of the lesser-developed countries of the world were able to, in effect, use much of the resources of those societies to improve the living conditions of the working classes of the advanced nations. This development removed the motivation for revolution, extreme economic hardship, which Marx thought would drive most of the workers in industrial societies to fight for socialism, and made all the classes of the advanced societies partners in the exploitation of the lesser-developed countries. But once revolutions in lesser-developed societies had cut off the favorable economic benefits flowing from those countries to the imperialist nations, economic conditions for most people in the imperialist nations would worsen leading to socialist revolutions. Thus in Lenin's view a key to world revolution was revolution in relatively underdeveloped and exploited nations such as China, and other countries of Asia, Africa, and Latin America. Lenin's Theory of Imperialism was an inspiration to many revolutionaries including China's Mao and Vietnam's Ho Chi Minh.

After the czar abdicated in the February Revolution of 1917, Lenin advocated a seizure of power in October by the Petrograd Soviet which was then dominated by the Bolsheviks. As the civil war came to an end in 1922, Lenin favored the economically productive pragmatic policy of permitting farming for profit and much private business activity in his New Economic Program while at the same time centralizing authority and tightening discipline in the Communist Party. By late 1922, however, Lenin became worried that a domineering, oppressive bureaucratic system was developing in Russia and that Stalin, who had become the general secretary of the Communist Party in 1922, was too violent, brutal, and rude to be trusted with such power. Severely restricted from political activity by illness during 1923 and until his death on January 21, 1924, he was unable to persuade other Communist leaders to reverse their repressive bureaucratic tendencies or to remove Stalin from power.

Marx, Karl (1818–1883), and Marxism

Karl Marx was a social scientist, political activist and is widely considered the most influential advocate of Socialist revolution. He was born in Trier, Germany, to an upper-middle-class Jewish family (his father was a lawyer) and had a number of rabbis in his family background. After attending the University of Berlin for four years, Marx began a career in journalism, becoming editor of the *Rhenische Zeitung*, but the liberal paper was shut down by the Prussian government. Marx moved to Paris, where he worked with both French and German revolutionaries and met Friedrich Engels, whose family was involved in the cotton-spinning business in Manchester, England; he would become Marx's life-long friend, financial supporter, and a major contributor to what would become known as "Marxism." After spending several years in Brussels studying, writing, and engaging in political activism with revolutionary groups of workers, Marx moved with his wife, Jenny Westphalia, to London, where he would live the rest of his life.

Marx and Engels over a number of years produced several major works involving a creative synthesis of concepts from Hegelean philosophy concerning the importance of antagonistic ideas and forces, English economic studies, and French revolutionary ideas and experience. At the center of their analyses was Marx's formulation of historical materialism, which asserts that the study of history reveals that the culture (values, norms, and shared knowledge) of societies, social class configuration, forms of government, social change, and even the psychology of individuals stem from the mode of production in the society (the ways in which life-sustaining resources and wealth are obtained from nature). The mode of production includes the forces of production—the productive technologies and labor force available at a particular stage of history—and the relations of production (or economic system): that is, the ways people are organized to make use of the forces of production. Ideally, the relations of production facilitate the efficient operation of the forces of production. But as the forces of production improve, the relations of production may not adapt and actually become a restraint on more effective production. According to the theory of historical materialism, major social change results when this incompatibility or contradiction between the forces of production and the relations of production becomes too great. Further progress in humanity's ability to improve the material conditions of life requires a change in the relations of production. This shift involves conflict between economic classes.

An economic class, according to Marx, is a category of people who occupy the same general position in the relations of production, carry out the same type of economic function, and share similar material interests. When a period of contradiction develops between the forces of production and the relations of production, the class that dominates and benefits from the maintenance of the existing relations of production, which are now impeding further economic development, will eventually come into conflict with and be defeated by an emergent "class which has the capacity and incentive to introduce" new relations of production "required to accommodate the advance of the productive forces" (Shaw 1983, 209). Thus, according to historical materialism, major social change has come about because of improvements in productive forces that in turn have led to class conflict, changes in the relations of production, and replacement of the old dominant class by a new dominant class. Such a transition is accompanied by changes in society's "superstructure" (culture and other social institutions) to support and facilitate the operation of the new relations of production.

Marx predicted that after the capitalist class had carried out the industrial revolution and brought the "proletariat"—the class of urban industrial workers who operated the new technologies—into existence, certain characteristics of the capitalist system, such as wasteful competition and lack of ability to cooperate effectively to advance the productive forces of society, would constitute a restraint on further economic development. As the economic system faltered, the capitalist class would place an increasing burden on the industrial working class by lowering wages and increasing working hours; intensifying hardships would provoke a rebellion by the proletariat that it would ultimately win. The victory of the proletariat would bring about a transition to the socialist stage of economic development in which the working majority of society would control government and during which all major resources and industries would be owned by the worker-controlled state. Further economic development would then proceed much more rapidly than under capitalism because the use of existing scientific knowledge and technology would be more coordinated and effectively utilized to bring about new advances in the forces of production. Eventually the socialist stage of development would generate enormous wealth, eliminate social classes, create a new culture and psychology of cooperation, and reduce the level of specialization of labor. The need for the state (government) as a coercive institution would fade away. These developments collectively would constitute the advent of the Communist stage of social development.

Marx not only worked as a writer and social theoretician; he also engaged in political activism, serving as an elected member of the General Council of the First International, the International Working Men's Association (1864–1876), an international federation of working-class organizations whose members were drawn largely from Western and Central Europe (Johnstone 1983, 233). Marx helped to organize its meetings and participated in its debates and the formulation of its policies.

The impact of Marx's work, much of which was published posthumously, increased after his death. Eventually the expression "Marxism" was used to refer to Marx's ideas. A number of additional concepts were added to Marxism by later writers and political activists. It is highly probable that Marx would not agree with all of what became known as Marxism by the twenty-first century. And many "Marxists" disagree among themselves.

In the 1890s, Georgii Plekanov introduced the expression "dialectical materialism" to describe Marxism. Lenin contributed the notions that Marxist concepts had to be communicated to the workers and peasants by revolutionary intellectuals, and that the post-revolution government should be controlled exclusively by the revolutionary vanguard party, the Communist Party. Mao is credited with adapting the Marxist perspective to China by emphasizing the revolutionary potential of the peasants. Stalin is blamed for transforming Soviet Marxism into a static doctrine that lacked the ability to adapt to changing conditions and was used to impose rigid and damaging conformity on citizens and social institutions. After the death of Stalin, more flexible and democratic versions of Marxism proliferated.

Marxism-Leninism

This widely used expression refers to a major revolutionary ideology. A prominent Marxist aspect of this set of ideas is the theory of historical materialism, which predicts that changes in productive technology would create the conditions for the working-class majority of modern society to overthrow the capitalist ownership class and establish its control over government. Lenin contributed his views on how to achieve the victory of the working class. He believed that this would be accomplished through creating a party of highly dedicated revolutionaries, initially primarily intellectuals, to mobilize, organize, and lead the working class. Once victory was achieved, the revolutionary party should, according to Lenin, establish exclusive control of the government in order to defend the revolution and rapidly transform society for the benefit of the large majority of its members. Lenin's Theory of Imperialism is also a crucial element of Marxism-Leninism that has had great appeal to revolutionaries in developing societies. This concept holds that the working classes of the advanced capitalist nations have been in a sense bribed into collaborating with their capitalist ruling classes by receiving benefits from the imperialist exploitation of the resources and the labor power of lesser-developed countries. But once revolutionaries in developing countries gained control of their own nations and ended the unfair exploitation of their societies' resources, the resulting working-class hardships in the imperialist nations would finally motivate the working classes there to overthrow capitalism. Thus the struggles and successes of revolutionaries in developing countries would be the key to bringing about world Socialist revolution.

Menshevik (Minority) Party

The faction of the Russian Social Democratic Party that opposed the Bolshevik faction, the Mensheviks held that a multiparty democratic system should be introduced in Russia after the end of the czar's absolute monarchy. They believed that a period of capitalist development would be necessary to industrialize Russian society, greatly enlarge the size of the industrial proletariat, and provide the requirements for socialism. Democratic elections would be the mechanism, in the Mensheviks' view, through which the proletariat would come to control society and transform the economy from capitalism to socialism.

People's Will (Narodnaia Volia)

People's Will was a terrorist group that emerged from the anarchist-influenced Populist Movement in nineteenth-century Russia. When the Populist movement failed to mobilize large numbers of peasants for revolution, some revolutionaries adopted tactics of extreme violence to strike at the ruling group and inspire the workers and peasants to overthrow the system. In 1881, People's Will succeeded in assassinating Czar Alexander II, after which a number of its key leaders, including Sophie Perovskaya, were executed.

Petrograd Soviet

At the grassroots level, the soviets were councils elected by workers, peasants, soldiers, and sailors to exercise authority once the governmental authority of the czar's regime—including that of his appointed officials and military officers—was rejected. Delegates from the local soviets made up the large city soviets, such as the Petrograd City Soviet and the Moscow City Soviet. The Petrograd City Soviet, characterized by a majority of Bolshevik (Communist Party) members in the fall of 1917, seized national power from the Provisional Government in the October Revolution of 1917.

Rasputin, Grigory (1872–1916)

Rasputin was a monk from an unusual sect within the Russian Orthodox Church which held that the path to salvation was through first sinning, in order then to be able to confess and be forgiven. He claimed to possess healing powers and was considered very charismatic by many who knew him. Brought to the attention of the royal family, he seemed to have a mysterious ability to control the bleeding to which the czar's son, who suffered from hemophilia, was prone. The czar and czarina became dependent on Rasputin for advice on certain state policies and the appointment of some governmental officials. He was accused of having sexual relations with many women, scandalizing the czar and czarina, interfering with the war effort, and contributing to the monarchy's loss of legitimacy. On December 30, 1916, Rasputin was murdered by Prince Felix Yusupov, a member of the Duma Vladimir Purishkevich, and Grand Duke Dmitri Pavlovitch, the czar's cousin, in what they considered an attempt to save the Romanov dynasty and Russia.

Red Army

The Communist-led armed forces that defended the Bolshevik Revolution and, under the leadership of Trotsky, defeated the White Armies in the Russian Civil War of 1918–1922.

Russian Social Democratic Party

The Russian Social Democratic Party was a Marxist-inspired Russian revolutionary organization founded in 1898 from the earlier Liberation of Labor group. By 1903, the party had begun to split into the Bolshevik faction, led by Lenin, which ultimately created a one-party political system in Russia, and the Menshevik faction, which favored replacing the Russian monarchy with a multiparty democratic political system.

Russian Socialist Revolutionary Party

This party was organized in 1902. In contrast to the Marxist Russian Social Democratic Party, the Socialist Revolutionary Party's ideology, while influenced by Marxism, incorporated important concepts from Russian anarchism and previous movements and organizations, such as Populism and People's Will. Among these were the belief that Russia could move directly from feudalism to socialism without having to undergo an extended phase of capitalist development, as Marx had theorized. The Socialist Revolutionaries (SRs) hoped that the traditional land-sharing communes, or mirs, to which many Russian peasants belonged, could serve as the basis for the development of an agrarian system in which all land was owned collectively by village cooperative farming communities. They emphasized the notion that in Russia the peasants would be the central revolutionary class, rather than urban workers as Marx had thought. Instead of a strong, coercive central state, the Socialist Revolutionaries envisaged a future federation of local collectives in which the local communities would maintain a high level of autonomy. In the view of the Socialist Revolutionaries, the role of revolutionary activists was to arouse the revolutionary consciousness of the peasants and workers, rather than to assume control over them. According to the ideology of the Socialist Revolutionaries, the revolution was to come from a mass insurrection of the lower classes, who would sweep away the old repressive institutions and then create a new system of federated Socialist communities. Many Socialist Revolutionaries, in contrast to the Marxist Social Democrats, believed that one useful way in which to inspire the masses to revolution was through the assassination of officials of the pre-revolutionary government. In 1917 a minority of the Socialist Revolutionaries, the Left SRs, allied with the Bolsheviks, while the Right SRs supported the Provisional Government and later opposed the Bolshevik regime.

Socialism

In Marx's theory of the stages of historical development, socialism is the phase immediately following the proletarian revolution to overthrow capitalism. Under socialism the major resources of a society and the major means of production were to be socially or collectively owned through the worker-controlled government. Inequality was to be greatly reduced, equality of opportunity established, and a system implemented for providing all people with the basic necessities of life, such as food, medical services, shelter, and education. Different social classes would continue to exist as well as, for many people, remnants of the pre-revolution capitalistic culture and psychology. Therefore material incentives would still be a primary motivation for many people to work, and a strong central state with powerful coercive capabilities (police and army) would be necessary to protect the revolution and economic development programs. Ultimately, as socialism, through its more efficient use of resources, labor, and technology in comparison to capitalism, produced economic abundance and a new cooperative culture and psychology, different social classes would cease to exist, specialization of labor would be greatly reduced, the need for government with strong powers of coercion would decline, and the state, as previously known, would cease to exist. Society would then achieve the highest form of development, communism. No society has ever claimed to reach the communist stage of development. Communist Party–led states claimed to be at the socialist stage of development. That is why, for example, the Soviet Union was titled the Union of Soviet Socialist (not Communist) Republics.

The concept of socialism as a moral and economic system had been promoted by a number of writers and activists before Marx, including Compte de Saint-Simon, Charles Fourier, Robert Owen, and Pierre-Joseph Proudhon. But Marx developed the theory of historical materialism which predicted that technological progress would eventually lead to the creation of the material conditions for the advent of socialism, and the political circumstances to bring socialism into existence as a pervasive phase of social development.

Soviets

At the grassroots level, the soviets were councils elected by workers, peasants, soldiers, and sailors to exercise authority once the governmental authority of the czar's regime, including that of his appointed officials and military officers, had been rejected. Delegates from the local soviets made up the large city soviets, such as the Petrograd City Soviet and the Moscow City Soviet.

Stalin, Joseph (Iosif Vissarionovich Dzhugashvili, 1879–1953)

Stalin was one of the major leaders of the Russian Communist Party who, after Lenin's death, eventually emerged to become the virtual dictator of the Soviet Union. He was born in Georgia, a small nation conquered by the czar's army and incorporated into the Russian empire. His father was a shoemaker who was a heavy drinker and often physically violent; his mother was a washerwoman. Stalin was one of the few top Bolshevik leaders who came from the lower classes. His mother obtained entrance for him into a Christian Orthodox seminary, virtually the only way a poor child could receive an education in pre-revolutionary Russia. Exposed to revolutionary ideas, Stalin abandoned his religious schooling and joined the Bolshevik faction of the Russian Social Democratic Party. He reportedly participated in bank robberies to help fund the movement, and helped recruit workers to the party. Eventually Stalin was arrested and sent to Siberian exile in 1913, but he was able to return to Petrograd after the czar was overthrown in 1917. He played significant roles in the October Revolution and the 1918–1922 Civil War. Having demonstrated considerable organizational skills, in 1922 he accepted the position of general secretary of the Communist Party, while other top Bolsheviks occupied government ministerial posts. But as membership in the Communist Party grew dramatically, Stalin's position as head of the party gave him an enormous advantage, since the staff members he supplied to government ministries often felt that they owed their positions to him. Although Lenin, in a statement read to top party leaders at the time of his death in early 1924, accused Stalin of being too brutal and rude to continue as head of the party, most of the members of the Central Committee chose not to remove Stalin. After Lenin's death, Stalin eventually emerged as the dominant leader for several reasons. Probably most important was Stalin's position as general secretary of the Communist Party. Another factor in Stalin's favor was that a number of top Communist leaders apparently underestimated his intelligence, ruthlessness, and paranoia. They chose to form alliances with him against Trotsky, whom they may have initially feared as emerging as a dictator, since Trotsky, like Napoléon after the French Revolution, had led a revolutionary army to victory against domestic foes of the revolution and against foreign military intervention. Trotsky's post

civil war partial withdrawal from politics while Stalin rapidly built his power base also played into Stalin's hands. Also, since Trotsky stressed the need for international revolution, some interpreted this as a lack of loyalty to the Soviet Union and a lack of commitment to making the Russian Revolution succeed. Trotsky's continual criticism of the new bureaucracy and its decisions was portrayed as self-centered obstructionism at a time when unity and dedication were needed to build weak Russia rapidly into an industrial power. Stalin's working-class origins and style of speaking led many of the hundreds of thousands of newer members of the Communist Party—who were themselves workers or peasants—to identify with him, rather than with the other top Bolshevik leaders who, like Trotsky, were from upper-middle-class backgrounds, highly educated, and often Jewish. The actual foreign capitalist hostility to the Soviet Union also motivated many Russians to accept limitations on freedom and an authoritarian government under Stalin for defensive reasons. As dictator from the late 1920s on, Stalin used his leadership position to determine the outcome of the Russian Revolution. His supporters forcefully launched a brutal collectivization of agriculture that in some areas caused much disruption and famine, leading to the deaths of millions of people. But his government also carried out a spectacularly successful and rapid industrialization program. Stalin's regime, apparently fearing a military-based internal rebellion against Stalin's leadership, removed and destroyed much of the armed forces leadership during the 1930s. Despite Stalin's persecutions and initial military blunders, the Soviet people, at enormous cost, repelled the German Nazi invasion. Possibly while planning still further persecutions, Stalin died in 1953.

Trotsky, Leon (Lev Davidovich Bronstein, 1879–1940)

Trotsky, son of a rich Ukrainian peasant of Jewish ancestry, was a major leader of the Russian Revolution and the commander of the victorious Red Army during the Russian Civil War of 1918–1922. He was also a prominent revolutionary theoretician viewed by many as second only to Lenin in his intellectual contributions to the revolution. He was less successful as a politician after the Civil War and lost in a power struggle to Joseph Stalin, who expelled him from the Communist Party and the Soviet Union in the late 1920s. Trotsky, who before 1917 had been associated with the Menshevik, or democratic Socialist, wing of the Russian Social Democratic Party, and who had once predicted that Lenin's concept of a highly disciplined organization of revolutionaries could one day lead to a dictatorship, criticized Stalin and his supporters for imposing authoritarian rule and domineering bureaucracy in the Soviet Union, as well as crushing dissent within the Communist Party. Trotsky also believed that Russia would be susceptible to the development of a repressive dictatorship if only Russia experienced a revolution to socialism in the immediate post–World War I era, since it would be militarily threatened by technologically superior capitalist societies and would be forced to impose harsh measures on the population in order to industrialize rapidly. Trotsky termed the perverted form of socialism that developed under Stalin's leadership "Stalinism." In exile, he attempted to organize an international Communist movement alternative to that led by the Soviet Union. Many of his supporters and even family members were imprisoned or killed by Stalin's regime. Trotsky himself was assassinated by a Stalinist supporter at his home near Mexico City in 1940.

White Armies

White Armies referred to the assortment of military forces that opposed the Communist-led Red Army during the Russian Civil War. Most of these were led by former czarist military officers, and some were aided by foreign countries, in particular Great Britain. Because their economic policies typically benefited the rich, and because they were aided by foreign powers, which made them vulnerable to being labeled instruments of foreign imperialism, the White Armies lacked sufficient popular support and were defeated.

James DeFronzo

See Also Anarchism, Communism, and Socialism; Armed Forces, Revolution, and Counter-Revolution; Chinese Revolution; Cinema of Revolution; Democracy, Dictatorship, and Fascism; Documentaries of Revolution; East European Revolutions of 1989; Elites, Intellectuals, and Revolutionary Leadership; Human Rights, Morality, Social Justice, and Revolution; Ideology, Propaganda, and Revolution; Inequality, Class, and Revolution; Literature and Modern Revolution; Music and Revolution; Nazi Revolution: Politics and Racial Hierarchy; Paris Commune of 1871; Population, Economic Development, and Revolution; Reform, Rebellion, Civil War, Coup D'état, and Revolution; Russian Revolution of 1991 and the Dissolution of the U.S.S.R.; Student and Youth Movements, Activism and Revolution; Terrorism; Transnational Revolutionary Movements; Vietnamese Revolution; War and Revolution

References and Further Readings

Bottomore, Tom, ed. 1983. *A Dictionary of Marxist Thought.* Cambridge, MA: Harvard University Press.

———. 1983. "Communism." Pp. 87–90 in *A Dictionary of Marxist Thought,* edited by Tom Bottomore. Cambridge, MA: Harvard University Press.

Daniels, Robert V. 1993. *A Documentary History of Communism in Russia.* Lebanon, NH: University Press of New England.

DeFronzo, James. 1996.(3rd edition forthcoming) *Revolutions and Revolutionary Movements.* Boulder, CO: Westview.

Dmytryshyn, Basil. 1984. *The U.S.S.R.: A Concise History.* New York: Scribner.

Dunn, John. 1972. *Modern Revolutions.* Cambridge: Cambridge University Press.

Fetscher, Irving. 1983. "Development of Marxism." Pp. 309–312 in *A Dictionary of Marxist Thought,* edited by Tom Bottomore. Cambridge, MA: Harvard University Press.

Fitzpatrick, Sheila. 1982. *The Russian Revolution: 1917–1932.* New York: Oxford University Press.

Getty, J. Arch, and Oleg Naumov. 1999. *The Road to Terror: Stalin and the Self-Destruction of the Bolsheviks, 1932–1939.* New Haven, CT: Yale University Press.

Goldstone, Jack, ed. 1998. *The Encyclopedia of Political Revolutions.* Washington, DC: Congressional Quarterly.

Greene, Thomas. 1990. *Comparative Revolutionary Movements.* Englewood Cliffs, NJ: Prentice-Hall.

Johnstone, Monty. 1983. "The Internationals." Pp. 233-238 in *A Dictionary of Marxist Thought,* edited by Tom Bottomore. Cambridge, MA: Harvard University Press.

Katov, George. 1967. *Russia 1917: The February Revolution.* New York: Harper and Row.

McLelland, David. 1983. "Karl Heinrich Marx." Pp. 302–305 in *A Dictionary of Marxist Thought,* edited by Tom Bottomore. Cambridge, MA: Harvard University Press.

Ostergaard, G. 1983. "Anarchism." Pp. 18–19 in *A Dictionary of Marxist Thought,* edited by Tom Bottomore. Cambridge, MA: Harvard University Press.

Palij, Michaeil. 1976. *The Anarchism of Hector Makhno, 1918–1921.* Seattle: University of Washington Press.

Rabinowitch, Alexander. 1976. *The Bolsheviks Come to Power.* New York: Norton.

Salisbury, Harrison. 1981. *Black Night, White Snow.* New York: Da Capo.

Shaw, William H. 1983. "Historical Materialism." Pp. 206–210 in *A Dictionary of Marxist Thought,* edited by Tom Bottomore. Cambridge, MA: Harvard University Press.

Sweezy, Paul. 1983. "Socialism." Pp. 444–446 in *A Dictionary of Marxist Thought,* edited by Tom Bottomore. Cambridge, MA: Harvard University Press.

Thompson, John M. 1990. *Russia and the Soviet Union: An Historical Introduction.* Boulder, CO: Westview.

Tucker, Robert, ed. 1975. *The Lenin Anthology.* New York: Norton.

Tumarkin, Nina. 1997. *Lenin Lives! The Lenin Cult in Soviet Russia.* Cambridge, MA: Harvard University Press.

Ulam, Adam Bruno. 1965. *The Bolsheviks: The Intellectual and Political History of the Triumph of Communism in Russia.* New York: Macmillan.

———. 1978. *A History of Soviet Russia.* Orlando, FL: Harcourt Brace Jovanovich.

Volkogonov, Dmitri. 1991. *Stalin: Triumph and Tragedy.* London: Weidenfeld and Nicolson.

———. 1994. *Lenin: A New Biography.* New York: Free Press.

———. 1996. *Trotsky: The Eternal Revolutionary.* New York: Free Press.

———. 1998. *Autopsy for an Empire: The Seven Leaders Who Built the Soviet Regime.* New York: Free Press.

Von Laue, Theodore H. 1971. *Why Lenin? Why Stalin?* New York: Lippincott.

Wilson, Edmund. 1972. *To The Finland Station.* New York: Macmillan.

Wolf, Eric. 1969. *Peasant Wars of the Twentieth Century.* New York: Harper and Row.

Russian Revolution of 1991 and the Dissolution of the U.S.S.R.

CHRONOLOGY

Soviet History

1917   Bolshevik Revolution leads to creation of the Union of Soviet Socialist Republics, formed of fifteen republics and ruled by the Communist Party.

1924   Founder Vladimir Lenin dies; is replaced by Joseph Stalin.

1929–1931   Stalin launches a crash industrialization drive and the forced collectivization of peasant farms.

1935–1937   Massive purges of potential opponents to Stalin's rule decimates Soviet society and especially Communist Party officials and Soviet army generals.

1941–1945   Nazi invasion causes 27 million Soviet deaths. Stalin emerges victorious and takes over eastern Europe, including East Germany. The Baltic states (Estonia, Latvia, and Lithuania) are incorporated into the Soviet Union. The Soviet takeover of eastern Europe launches the Cold War.

1949   The Soviet Union explodes an atomic bomb.

1953   Stalin dies; he is replaced by a collective leadership in the Politburo, the top organ of the Communist Party's Central Committee.

1956   Nikita Khrushchev, the new Communist Party leader, makes a "secret speech" to the 20th Party Congress denouncing Stalin's purges of innocent victims. Nevertheless, in November 1956, an anti-Soviet uprising in Hungary is ruthlessly repressed.

1957   The Soviet Union launches Sputnik, the world's first satellite, and puts the first man into space in 1961.

1961   The Soviet Union breaks with Communist China over ideological and strategic differences.

1964–1982   The Communist Party is headed by General Secretary Leonid Brezhnev, a cautious leader who avoids reform, cracks down on dissidents, and builds up the Soviet nuclear arsenal.

1968   Brezhnev invades Czechoslovakia to prevent the Communist government there from introducing reforms.

1979   Brezhnev invades neighboring Afghanistan to preserve a pro-Soviet government there.

1982–1984   Brezhnev dies and is replaced by Yuri Andropov, the former head of the KGB (Committee of State Security), who starts an anti-corruption drive. He is ill and soon dies.

The Start of Reforms

1985   In May, the Politburo appoints the youthful Mikhail Gorbachev as general secretary.

In November, Gorbachev meets U.S. president Ronald Reagan in Geneva.

In December, Gorbachev appoints the outspoken Boris Yeltsin, formerly a party boss in Sverdlovsk, to head the Moscow City Communist Party, to tackle corruption and inefficiency.

1986   Gorbachev starts campaigns against corruption and alcoholism.

In March, an explosion at the Chernobyl nuclear reactor in Ukraine, the worst nuclear accident in world history, contaminates extensive territory and causes great anxiety in the population. Gorbachev launches reforms of glasnost (press freedom), perestroika (cautious economic reform), and "new thinking" in foreign policy. He begins arms control talks with U.S. president Ronald Reagan.

1987   In January, Gorbachev calls for "democratization," by which he means multiple candidates in elections, while preserving the Communist Party monopoly. It will take him two years to persuade party conservatives to implement this reform.

In June, a new law on state enterprises weakens central controls over the economy.

In summer, the first mass demonstrations by nationalists occur in the Baltic countries (Estonia, Latvia, and Lithuania) and in Armenia, south of the Caucasus Mountains.

In November, Gorbachev fires Boris Yeltsin, head of the Moscow City Communist Party, for rudeness.

In December in Washington, Gorbachev signs a treaty under which the United States and the U.S.S.R. agree to remove all the medium-range nuclear weapons from Europe.

1988   In February, demonstrations in the Armenian enclave of Nagorno-Karabakh lead to attacks on Armenians living in Azerbaijan, and Azeris living in Armenia. By the end of the year, 300,000 Armenians and Azerbaijanis flee their homes, and the Soviet Army imposes martial law.

In May, President Ronald Reagan visits Moscow for the first time; stops talking about the "evil empire."

In October, Gorbachev has himself appointed president of the Soviet Union.

1989   In February, the last Soviet troops leave Afghanistan.

In March, elections for the new U.S.S.R. Congress of People's Deputies see humiliating defeats for Communist Party candidates and the victory of nationalists in the Baltic and Caucasus republics. Yeltsin wins election from the Moscow district. The proceedings of the congress are televised live.

In April, nationalist unrest spreads to Georgia, focusing on Georgian independence and the rights of the Abkhaz minority. On April 9, Soviet troops disperse Georgian protestors in

Tbilisi, killing twenty-one, an action condemned by democrats across the Soviet Union and by foreign leaders.

In spring,"Round Table" talks between Communist leaders and opposition groups in Poland and Hungary lead to the formation of non-Communist governments.

In June, the Hungarian government dismantles the border fences with Austria (the "Iron Curtain"). East German citizens try to get to Hungary, in order to flee to the West.

In July, a wave of strikes by Russian coal miners forces the government to increase wages and food supplies.

In November, the opening of the Berlin Wall means an end to travel restrictions for East Germans. Communist governments are toppled in East Germany, Czechoslovakia, Bulgaria, and Romania.

In December, the Lithuanian parliament renounces the country's 1940 incorporation into the Soviet Union.

1990   In March, elections to parliament in the fifteen republics that make up the Soviet Union and in regional councils. Pro-democracy deputies form a majority in some key cities, including Moscow. The new Lithuanian parliament declares independence. In response, Gorbachev declares an economic blockade on Lithuania. The U.S.S.R. Congress abolishes Article 6 of the Soviet Constitution, recognizing the "leading role" of the Communist Party. Gorbachev creates a new Federation Council composed of the leaders of the fifteen main republics and the twenty-one ethnic republics within the Russian Republic.

In May, the Russian Supreme Soviet (parliament) elects Yeltsin as president of the Russian Republic.

In June, the U.S.S.R. Congress rejects Gorbachev's plan to introduce a "regulated market economy," objecting to the lifting of price controls.

In July, the 28th Congress of the Communist Party is dominated by conservatives who reject Gorbachev's reforms. Key radical leaders such as Yeltsin leave the Communist Party. Yeltsin declares that the Russian Republic is prepared to adopt the radical "500 day plan" for conversion to a market economy.

In September, Gorbachev is granted new powers by the U.S.S.R. Congress to rule by presidential decree, bypassing the U.S.S.R. Congress, for eighteen months. He launches a conservative economic stabilization program.

In December, Gorbachev creates a new Security Council, with control over the KGB, police, and the army. Liberal foreign minister Eduard Shevardnadze resigns, protesting that "a harsh dictatorship is coming."

The End Game

1991   In January, the Soviet army attempts a crackdown in Lithuania, killing thirteen protestors and triggering protests in Moscow and abroad. Many enterprises switch their tax payments to the Russian Federal Republic government and refuse to send money to the Soviet government.

In March, a referendum is held on the preservation of the U.S.S.R. The vote is boycotted by Armenia, Moldova, Georgia, Estonia, Latvia, and Lithuania. In the other nine republics, 76 percent of voters approve the idea of preserving a common state.

In April, Gorbachev and the leaders of nine republics draft a new union treaty. The Soviet government introduces an economic anti-crisis program, with 60 percent price increases.

In June, Yeltsin wins election as president of the Russian Federal Republic, gaining 57 percent support in a free popular vote.

In July, leaders of the G7 countries, meeting in London, turn down a proposal for a massive aid package, a new Marshall Plan, for the Soviet Union.

On August 19, one day before five republic leaders have agreed to meet and sign the new union treaty, Gorbachev's own vice president, Gennady Yanaev, declares a state of emergency and has Gorbachev arrested in his vacation villa.

On August 20, Soviet troops refuse to storm the building of the Russian parliament in Moscow, where Boris Yeltsin has taken refuge. Yeltsin calls on all soldiers to obey him as president of the Russian Federation.

On August 21, the coup collapses in the face of widespread popular protests. The coup leaders are arrested, and Gorbachev is freed. Yeltsin refuses to accept the authority of the Soviet government.

December 7–8, Yeltsin meets in Minsk with the presidents of Ukraine and Belarus, Leonid Kravchuk and Stanislav Shushkevich. They agree to create a new Commonwealth of Independent States (CIS). Gorbachev is not present at the meeting.

On December 22, a meeting in Alma Ata sees eight more Soviet republics join the CIS. Estonia, Latvia, Lithuania, and Georgia refuse to take part, although Georgia joins in 1992.

On December 31, the Union of Soviet Socialist Republics ceases to exist.

INTRODUCTION

The collapse of the Soviet Union in 1991 was one of the defining events of the twentieth century. It signaled the end of the Cold War, a half-century-long conflict that threatened the world with nuclear destruction, and that caused a number of "hot" wars from Angola to Vietnam. It also signaled the end of communism as an alternative to capitalism and democracy.

Fifteen years after the Soviet collapse, we can only guess what history's final verdict will be when it comes to explaining why the second most powerful country in the world disintegrated in the space of a few years. Which leader will historians credit for bringing about such a momentous change? Mikhail Gorbachev, or Boris Yeltsin—or Ronald Reagan? Will we remember, or will we forget, the role of dissident intellectuals like Andrei Sakharov and Alexander Solzhenitsyn?

And what about the leaders of East European protest movements, such as Lech Walesa and Vaclav Havel?

If the jury is still out on the causes of the Soviet collapse, it is equally premature to try to evaluate the lasting consequences. Reportedly, when Chinese leader Zhou Enlai was asked by Henry Kissinger in 1972 what he thought was the legacy of the 1789 French Revolution, he replied that "it is too soon to tell."

Historians and political scientists have not yet forged a consensus on why and how the Soviet Union collapsed. Many argue that the collapse was inevitable, that it was bound to happen sooner or later. But that does not explain why it happened precisely *when* it did, or *how* it did.

Most observers agree that the Soviet Union was a failed experiment that had long ago lost its viability as an alternative model to Western capitalism. The Soviet economy was highly inefficient and unresponsive to consumer demand. The political system was based on coercion rather than consent. The state devoted massive resources to controlling information flows and eliminating dissent.

What is puzzling is that this system collapsed so quickly, within a few years. Was the system doomed to fail in 1991, or could it have staggered on for a few more years, or decades? If the system was fatally flawed, why didn't it expire in 1933, during the great famine; or in 1941, when Nazi armies reached the gates of Moscow; or in 1953, after the death of the all-powerful Joseph Stalin?

The Soviet system did have certain strengths. It survived for seventy-five years, emerged victorious from World War II, and managed to challenge the United States for global leadership during the Cold War. The regime created by Vladimir Lenin and Joseph Stalin produced a modern, educated, urban society, with a standard of living that was impressive to Third World countries, even as it lagged well behind that of the developed West. Although the political system denied basic freedoms to the population, it did ensure the country's independence from foreign domination—an important consideration that made the Soviet model attractive to many leaders of newly de-colonized states in the Third World in the 1950s and 1960s.

The Soviet Union was the first self-styled "workers' state" dedicated to the overthrow of capitalism. It claimed a global revolutionary role: its purpose was to replace the entire international system. Unique among states, the Union of Soviet Socialist Republics did not include any geographic or ethnic marker in its title. ("Soviet" is Russian for "council.") This means that the "revolution" that ended Soviet power was not just a product of domestic developments within that country. It must also be seen in an international context. Once Moscow lost faith in its ability to defeat the West, the state also lost its very reason for existence.

BACKGROUND: CULTURE AND HISTORY

What, then, were the deep structural flaws in the Soviet political model that laid the foundations for the Soviet collapse? They can be grouped into five categories: nationalism, military competition, political succession, economic stress, and social change.

Nationalism

Nationalism was the key single variable that brought about the Soviet collapse. It was both a deep structural flaw and a proximate cause.

At the beginning of the twentieth century, most of the peoples of the world were living under empires. They did not enjoy self-rule, but were controlled by distant rulers who belonged to a different nationality. By the century's end, *all* of those empires had collapsed: Ottoman, Habsburg, English, French, Dutch, Belgian, and Portuguese.

The Soviet Union was a multinational state—although its rulers denied that it was an empire, and tried to promote a new concept of citizenship, "the Soviet people," which transcended ethnic identity. But the Soviet Union disintegrated, like the other multinational empires. One cannot help concluding that if the Soviet Union had been as ethnically homogeneous as China, it would probably still be in existence.

Ethnic Russians made up just 52 percent of the Soviet population of 290 million. (In contrast, 85 percent of China's population are Han Chinese.) The remaining 140 million included representatives of 160 distinct ethnic groups. There were 50 million Slavs, such as Ukrainians and Belarussians; 40 million Muslims, mainly in Central Asia; and the numerically small but proud and ancient nations of the Caucasus. Fearful of Russian nationalism, Lenin created the Soviet Union as an ethnic federation, with fifteen major nations each given their own Soviet republic. The Russian Republic itself was a federation, with autonomous republics for twenty-one indigenous groups living on its territory (including the Muslim Tatars and Chechens). The Russian Republic was something of an anomaly, because it had less autonomy from the Soviet federal government than the other republics. This was because ethnic Russians dominated the central apparatus of the Soviet state, but it still left some Russians, paradoxically, feeling that their national interests were less well represented than those of other nations.

During the Soviet era, the Communist Party, aided by the KGB, kept a tight grip on political expression. Especially under Stalin, any signs of nationalist sympathy were vigorously repressed. But the federal structure did ensure that minority languages and cultures were fairly well preserved, at least for the thirty-six groups that had their own republic. Political and intellectual elites in each republic developed a strong sense of national identity, and they tried to defend the interests of their region, within the limits imposed by the central controls of the Communist Party and planning ministries.

When Gorbachev opened the door to free speech after 1985, with his policy of glasnost, or "openness," the first people to respond were nationalist activists in the Baltic states (Estonia, Latvia, and Lithuania); the Caucasus (Armenia, Georgia, and Azerbaijan); and western Ukraine. The Baltic republics and western Ukraine had been incorporated into the Soviet Union only in 1940, and most of their inhabitants never accepted the Soviet occupation. The Caucasus republics and Central Asia were occupied by the czars in the nineteenth century. There were some strong ethnic rivalries among the peoples of those regions. For example, Georgians wanted full control over ethnic minorities in Abkhazia and Ossetia, while ethnic Armenians living in Karabakh resented the fact that their province was included in Azerbaijan. These disputes, which had simmered for decades, triggered violent conflict between rival groups in 1988–1989.

These ethnic disputes were troublesome, but they were confined to about 10 percent of the Soviet population. There was little unrest in Central Asia, in part because the Communist leaders of the region kept a tight grip. Such conflicts could in principle have been managed—just as Communist China successfully represses secessionist movements in Tibet and Xinjiang. Apart from the Baltic states, Mark Beissinger (2002) has shown that most of the violent ethnic conflicts were "horizontal" (against local rival groups) rather than "vertical" (against Moscow).

Nationalism played a decisive role not so much in mobilizing the masses but in providing an exit strategy for disaffected regional Communist elites. The decisive nationalist movement was that of Russia itself. Unable to remove Gorbachev from power as president of the Soviet Union, Boris Yeltsin instead removed the Russian Federation from the U.S.S.R., leaving Gorbachev a president without a country. We do not usually think of Yeltsin as a nationalist, since he came to power through democratic elections and stood up in defense of human rights. But it was Yeltsin's drive for Russian sovereignty that brought an end to the Soviet Union in 1991.

Military Defeat

Historically, most empires have collapsed following a defeat in war, or the inability to win a war at a cost acceptable to the people. The Soviet Union was no exception. In the 1980s it lost two wars—the Afghan war and the Cold War.

In 1979, Leonid Brezhnev sent 120,000 troops into Afghanistan, on the southern border of the Soviet Union, to prop up a Marxist, pro-Soviet regime. Despite ruthless force, driving millions of Afghans into exile, Moscow was unable to crush the resistance. The United States helped the Afghan fighters based in Pakistan with money and weapons—including shoulder-fired Stinger missiles that could bring down Soviet helicopters. Although at least 15,000 Soviet soldiers died in Afghanistan according to official figures (Borovik 2001, 281), the main cost was political—it blackened Moscow in the eyes of the international community. Gorbachev tried to persuade the United States to stop supporting the resistance, in order to get peace with honor in Afghanistan. Soviet troops withdrew in 1989, but fighting continued and the pro-Moscow government was finally overthrown in 1992.

In response to the invasion of Afghanistan, the United States boosted its defense spending. In 1983, President Ronald Reagan announced a space-based defense system to protect the United States from nuclear attack. The so-called Star Wars program deeply alarmed the Soviet military. They did not believe that the system would work, but they were afraid that taking countermeasures would overburden the Soviet military budget. Also, they feared that the research program could produce a new generation of conventional weapons (such as precision-guided munitions) that would give the United States the edge in future wars.

Mikhail Gorbachev entered arms control talks with the United States in the hope that he could persuade Reagan to halt the Star Wars program. Gorbachev did not imagine that by negotiating an end to the Cold War he would trigger a chain of events that would lead to the collapse of the U.S.S.R.

The end of the Cold War meant that the Soviet military did not actively resist Gorbachev's moves to withdraw from Eastern Europe. The latter no longer had any strategic value, if the Soviet state was no longer preparing itself for all-out war with the United States.

Political Succession

A key factor in the Soviet breakdown was the problem of political succession and the passage of generations. A fundamental weakness of the Soviet system was the lack of a succession mechanism. General secretaries could not be criticized, and they could not be removed. They stayed in office until they died. The sole exception was the removal of Nikita Khrushchev in 1964: his flaws included disastrous farm reforms, defeat in the Cuban missile crisis, and an administrative shake-up that threatened the unity of the Communist Party.

The inability to remove leaders applied not just at the top, but at every level in the party hierarchy. Incompetent leaders stayed in office for decades. New ideas, and new leaders, were not tolerated. Stalin had not faced this problem, because he systematically purged the ranks of party leaders. After Stalin's death, party leaders agreed not to conduct mass purges. For twenty years, from 1965 to 1985, as the party leadership aged, urgently needed reforms were postponed.

The Brezhnev generation had been born around 1910, and their formative experience was World War II. In the 1980s, these men in their seventies still dominated the Politburo and Communist Party bureaucracy. Only in 1985, with the appointment of Mikhail Gorbachev, did the Politburo open the door to a new generation of political leaders—who had started their careers after the death of Stalin.

Economic Stress

The Soviet Union was the world's first Marxist state, in which private ownership of the means of production was outlawed and all the nation's farms, stores, and factories were taken into state ownership. Many Western economists believed that such a system could not function, but the Soviet Union survived for seventy-five years.

The inefficiencies of central planning are well known—the long lines for goods, the poor quality of consumer products, the black market for blue jeans. Many people conclude that economic inefficiency was responsible for the collapse of the Soviet system.

But that is only partly true. The official Soviet Gross Domestic Product (GDP) grew at impressive rates in the 1950s and 1960s, and the economy did produce a steady improvement in living standards for ordinary citizens. However, this economic growth was extensive rather than intensive, based on natural resources (land, minerals, manpower) and high rates of forced saving and investment. By the 1960s, the easily obtained resources were running out. The inefficiencies of the overly centralized economy meant that many resources were wasted. Soviet farms in particular were extremely inefficient. After 1962 the Soviet Union often had to import food to meet consumer needs. While the Soviet system was reasonably good at generating scientific innovations, such as the launch of Sputnik in 1957, it was hopeless at introducing them into mass production.

Soviet economists recognized the need for change. But Leonid Brezhnev, general secretary of the Communist Party from 1964 to 1982, feared that economic reform would lead to political liberalization. It was fear of such a development that led to the Soviet invasion of Czechoslovakia in 1968. In the 1960s the Western economies were forging ahead, while the Soviet economy was falling behind. But the Soviet Union was the second largest oil exporter in the world, and it benefited from the surge in oil prices after the Mideast crises of 1973 and 1979. That helped the country to import food, new technology, and scarce consumer goods.

Michael Ellman and Vladimir Kontorovich (1998) have shown that the Soviet GDP was not decreasing in the early 1980s (the slump began only in 1990), and that the economy could have stumbled on for many more years. Tighter discipline could have squeezed out more growth, while also crushing dissent. That was the approach favored by former KGB chief Yuri Andropov, who took power in 1982. But he was struck down by kidney disease just thirteen months later. Had he lived, the Soviet Union could still be here today.

Above all, it was the half-hearted economic reforms launched by Gorbachev after 1985 that disrupted the functioning of the planned economy. That, together with the dislocations caused by political liberalization, had produced goods shortages and rampant inflation by 1989, leading to more popular protests and systemic collapse.

The revolution of 1989–1991 also exemplifies the role of rising expectations. Since the death of Stalin, Soviet power had rested less on fear and more on the promise of material improvements. For decades official propaganda told the Soviet people that their lives were getting better, but actual living standards fell short of their expectations.

Social Movements and Social Values

Social mobilization was not a decisive factor in the Soviet collapse—outside the nationalist movements. There was no social revolution in Russia in 1991, on a par with the revolutions of 1789 and 1917, or Iran in 1979. Mass mobilization was limited largely to Moscow and other major cities and was of short duration. The "democratic movement" did not produce a lasting political organization (such as Poland's Solidarity trade union).

Despite much talk of a resurgent civil society, there was little evidence that grassroots organizations played a pivotal role in the events of 1985–1991. The strongest social movement was that of the environmentalists, which had spread rapidly in response to the 1986 Chernobyl nuclear disaster. They had some success in publicizing ecological problems, even closing down some polluting plants. But their leaders went on to win election to regional and national office in 1989–1990, and the Greens dissolved into the broader democratic movement.

The erosion of ideology played an important part in the Soviet collapse. Most ordinary people had little if any faith in the official Marxist-Leninist ideology. A gradual disillusionment with stagnant living standards and bureaucratic red tape contrasted with glimpses of a freer world: from smuggled news magazines, vacations in Bulgaria, or just listening to rock songs over the radio. The hollowing out of the official ideology during the political stagnation of the Brezhnev era meant that party conservatives were not able to mobilize supporters in opposition to Gorbachev's reforms—and they were outnumbered by followers of Boris Yeltsin, who was calling for even more radical change.

Even most of the ruling elite no longer believed in the ideology; their sons and daughters certainly did not. Gorbachev's decision to allow free speech in the mass media (glasnost) exposed the gap between official propaganda and people's real opinions. Nevertheless, voting patterns in free elections since 1991 suggest that about one-third of the Russian population were true believers, still committed to Soviet values.

The main impact of ideological decay was at the elite rather than the mass level. The lack of confidence in their own system fatally eroded the resolution of the Soviet elite. Even the hard-liners who tried to seize power in August 1991 were not confident in their own legitimacy, and they lacked the will to use force in defense of values they now saw as outdated.

In the past few years it has become quite common to argue that "globalization" doomed the Soviet state. The argument is that new information technologies made it impossible for the Soviet leadership to seal off the country from a true understanding of how far their country was falling behind the developed West.

This argument is only partly valid. The big breakthroughs in global communications technology—satellite TV and the Internet—only spread to Russia *after* 1991. Before that, the only means of communication into the Soviet Union were smuggling printed matter across the border and international radio broadcasting. Up to the bitter end the Soviet state was fairly effective at blocking these information sources: jamming international radio news, for example. Most East Europeans were freer to travel to the West and had a better idea than Soviet citizens about what life there was like. Even the East Germans, who could not travel, were often able to pick up West German television. But the international information revolution was not a decisive factor in the fall of Communism.

CONTEXT AND PROCESS OF REVOLUTION

The dissolution of the Soviet state played out very quickly, in a flurry of accelerating change that stood in stark contrast to the decades of stagnation that had preceded it. It was a revolution in which the key players were elites, and not the mobilized masses. It was a top-down rather than bottom-up process, although at several stages mass reactions were critical in enabling one elite faction to defeat another. It is impossible to explain the demise of the U.S.S.R. without granting decisive roles to Mikhail Gorbachev and Boris Yeltsin, two individuals whose caustic rivalry brought down the mighty structures of Soviet state power.

The end game consisted, essentially, of seven steps

1. Mikhail Gorbachev is appointed general secretary (1985).
2. Gorbachev decides to launch reform in domestic and foreign policy.
3. An explosion of nationalist discontent in the Soviet periphery throws Gorbachev on the defensive (1988).
4. Gorbachev's half-hearted economic reforms cause a breakdown of the central planning system.
5. Gorbachev introduces limited free elections when he finds that bureaucrats are blocking his reforms. Boris Yeltsin uses these elections to build a power base for himself in the Russian Republic.
6. Popular protests in Eastern Europe cause the regimes there to tumble, one after the other.
7. Soviet hard-liners stage an abortive coup in August 1991 that exposes the lack of support for Gorbachev and enables Yeltsin to dissolve the Soviet Union.

The Rise of Gorbachev

In April 1985 the Soviet Politburo decided to elect Mikhail Gorbachev as general secretary. His three predecessors had died, one after the other, over the preceding three years: each of them had been too sick to govern effectively. Gorbachev was healthy, and at fifty-four he was twenty-one years younger than the average Politburo member. Although the conservatives feared that he would stir things up, the moderates concluded that a new, more decisive leader was precisely what their country needed to meet the challenge posed by U.S. president Ronald Reagan, who had launched a political offensive against what he called the "evil empire." Other challenges included a stagnant economy, the unwinnable war in Afghanistan, and continuing unrest in Poland. The Solidarity trade union movement there had nearly toppled the Communist government in 1980, and only the imposition of martial law in December 1981 had saved the regime.

The second critical factor was the character of Mikhail Gorbachev. He was intelligent, decisive, and self-willed. Gorbachev's goal in reforming the Soviet state was to make it more competitive with the United States. The irony is that in trying to save the Soviet Union, he unwittingly brought about its destruction. He was, then, a reluctant or accidental revolutionary.

The main power base for Gorbachev was the Communist Party—the very institution that he was trying to reform. During his time in office Gorbachev tried to develop other sources of power. He drummed up political and financial support from Western leaders. He enlisted the Russian intelligentsia to promote his reforms. And he tried to mobilize public opinion behind his agenda. But Gorbachev was not popular among ordinary Russians. His speaking style was rather stiff, they resented his elegant wife, and they blamed him for the growing economic problems and ethnic conflict.

As general secretary, Gorbachev had to work with a state and party that was deeply hostile to change. The officials who ran the party and state apparatus were known as the *nomenklatura,* so called because their jobs were on lists (*nomenklatura*) that had to be filled with candidates approved by the relevant Communist Party committee. The nomenklatura were rewarded with privileges such as better apartments, limousines, access to special shops, limited foreign travel, and ensured entry for their children to elite educational institutions. Gorbachev's great disappointment was that few party officials responded positively to his call for change or *perestroika* (literally, "reconstruction"). Most of the nomenklatura resisted change until the bitter end, and in doing so they doomed the Soviet Union. Gorbachev was fully aware of the contradictions in being a reformist general secretary. He later described himself as "a product of that very nomenklatura and at the same time its anti-product, its 'gravedigger,' so to speak" (Brown 1996, 316). By stripping the Communist Party of its supervisory powers, he was undermining the key bureaucratic structure that held together the Soviet Union.

Perestroika

Gorbachev started out with moderate domestic initiatives: an anti-alcohol campaign (which was deeply unpopular), and a policy of openness, or *glasnost,* to promote more free discussion in the mass media. But he had achieved little in his first year in office. Things changed with the explosion of the Chernobyl nuclear reactor in April 1986, a disaster that nearly caused millions of casualties. The accident was caused by sloppy safety procedures and an unauthorized experiment by the plant director. It showed that Soviet bureaucracy was not only annoying but also positively dangerous. Across the country there were demonstrations outside dozens of nuclear facilities, demanding information about their operations. This upsurge of public activism was unprecedented in Soviet history. Popular fear of eco-catastrophe replaced fear of KGB persecution.

After Chernobyl, glasnost began to spread: at first in the theater, then in limited-run magazines, then in national newspapers, and finally on the television. With Gorbachev's encouragement, intellectuals, editors, and journalists steadily and cautiously pushed back the limits on press freedom. For a public starved of free speech for decades, it was exhilarating, but also a little frightening. Suddenly, all the problems that the inflexible Soviet bureaucracy had ignored for decades burst onto the nation's television screens: the housing shortage, the health crisis, Stalin's repressions.

Nationalist Unrest

Among the first to respond to the new freedom were nations that had nurtured their grievances for years—the Armenians in the province of Karabakh, which had been awarded to Azerbaijan in 1923, and the Balts, who had been forcibly incorporated into the Soviet Union in 1940. Gorbachev sent troops to quell demonstrations in the Caucasus and arrested the nationalist leaders in Armenia and Azerbaijan. Gorbachev had not foreseen the nationalist unrest, and he had no strategy for dealing with it. Because he wanted to preserve the Soviet Union, he was unwilling to grant the Balts independence. In Estonia and Latvia, Russian migrants made up 40 percent of the population, so Moscow used their presence as an excuse to deny independence. Lithuania was more assertive, because there Russians made up only 15 percent of the population.

Gorbachev's crackdown on nationalism caused many Russian democrats to switch their support to a new rising star in the Communist Party, Boris Yeltsin. Yeltsin was the party boss in Sverdlovsk, an industrial city in the Ural Mountains. Gorbachev appointed him to head the Moscow City Party and launch perestroika in the nation's capital. However, the personalities of these two strong-willed men clashed, and Gorbachev fired Yeltsin in 1987.

Economic Failure

Gorbachev tried to reform the central planning system by "democratizing" it. The idea was to use popular pressure from below to encourage officials to be less corrupt and more efficient. In 1987 managers were given more freedom to run their factories, but in return they had to put themselves up for election by the workers. The reform was a disaster. Managers used their new freedom to ignore plan targets, while placating their workers with wage increases, triggering an inflationary spiral. Gorbachev resisted the introduction of private property and real market reform. Despite a surge in the money supply, the government postponed raising official prices, meaning that store shelves emptied even faster. Limits on small-scale entrepreneurial activity were lifted, leading to a boom in street-corner trading and individual services. But the main state-owned farms and factories were left untouched. The longer reform was delayed, the worse was the economic situation and the more radical the corrective measures that were needed. It was left up to Gorbachev's successor, Boris Yeltsin, to bite the bullet of price liberalization and privatization in 1992.

Democratization

In the face of mounting pressure, Gorbachev decided to introduce semi-free elections. His goal was to outflank the party conservatives, whom he blamed for blocking the reforms. In the elections for a new U.S.S.R. Congress of People's Deputies in March 1989, the Communist Party was the only party allowed to compete, but across the country there were humiliating defeats for party candidates at the hands of independent candidates nominated by local trade unions and social organizations.

Yeltsin returned from political oblivion, winning election from the Moscow district. In the Baltic and Caucasus republics, the elections were won by nationalists. The 1989 election was for the federal U.S.S.R. parliament. In March 1990 there were elections to parliaments in the fifteen national republics and in regional councils. Pro-democracy deputies formed a majority in some key Russian cities, including Moscow. These elections undermined the legitimacy of the Communist Party and provided a platform for a new generation of political leaders. Gorbachev did not put himself up for election: he was appointed president by the unelected Supreme Soviet in 1988. Having freed the democracy "genie," Gorbachev would not be able to stuff it back into its bottle.

Revolution in Eastern Europe

Meanwhile, dramatic developments were taking place in the outer ring of the Soviet empire. People in Eastern Europe seized the opening provided by Gorbachev to push for an end to Communist rule. The Communist leaders in Hungary and Poland chose to lead in the dismantling of Communism in order to get on the right side of history—and maybe to save their own careers. Leaders in East Germany and Czechoslovakia resisted reform—and appealed to Gorbachev for permission to crack down. Then, in June 1989, Chinese leaders authorized the shooting of hundreds of protestors on Tiananmen Square. (The demonstrations actually coincided with a state visit to Beijing by Gorbachev.)

Gorbachev did not want to go down in history as a butcher, so he vetoed the use of force to stop the protests in East Germany. The 500,000 Soviet troops based in East Germany stayed in their barracks. Gorbachev's principled stance sealed the fate of the East German regime: by November, the Berlin Wall was opened. One after another, all the Communist governments of Eastern Europe abandoned their monopoly on power.

The collapse of the Soviet empire in Eastern Europe emboldened the Baltic nationalists and Russian democrats—and demoralized Soviet conservatives. If Gorbachev was unwilling to use force in East Germany, it was going to be very difficult for him to use force in Lithuania—or Moscow.

In 1990–1991, as political legitimacy shifted from the Soviet president to the elected Russian parliament, many provincial industrialists switched their tax payments from the Soviet (federal) budget to that of the Russian Republic, controlled by Yeltsin. By mid 1991, the Soviet government was bankrupt.

Gorbachev drew admiring crowds during his visits to Western capitals, but his international prestige did not help him at home. The arms control agreements he signed did not provide any visible improvements at home. He was, however, able to negotiate a withdrawal from Afghanistan in 1989, bringing an end to that unpopular war.

The most concrete assistance from the West was financial. Between 1985 and 1991, Gorbachev received about $50 billion in low-interest loans, including a $10 billion grant from Germany in return for Gorbachev's approval of German unification in 1990. These funds covered the importation of scarce food and consumer goods, and kept the battered economy running for a few more years.

Countdown to the August 1991 Coup

In 1990–1991, these diverse pressures mounted into a "perfect storm" for Gorbachev. Inflation and goods shortages triggered a wave of strikes by miners and steelworkers. The newly elected parliaments provided a public platform for Gorbachev's nationalist and democratic critics. The nation's news media brushed aside the censors and embraced full-scale press freedom.

Gorbachev began making contingency plans for a state of emergency, at the same time that he was trying to broker a deal that would preserve the Soviet Union as a loose confederation of states—although only eight of fifteen republics were willing to sign the treaty. These two trends came together in August 1991, when Gorbachev's own cabinet launched a coup d'état, just days before the new union

Russian president Boris Yeltsin (holding papers), atop a tank in Moscow in August 1991, urges the Russian people to resist a hard-line takeover of the central government. (AP/Wide World Photos)

treaty was due to be signed. Gorbachev and his wife were detained in their holiday villa, while his vice president, Gennady Yanaev, went on television to announce that power was in the hands of the State Committee for the State of Emergency.

The coup failed. The soldiers and KGB special forces sent to storm the Russian parliament and arrest Yeltsin refused to act when they saw that the building was ringed by unarmed demonstrators. The coup leaders themselves were hesitant: it was learned later that several of them were drunk. After a tense forty-eight hours the coup collapsed, and its leaders were arrested. Gorbachev was freed, but when he returned to Moscow he found that he no longer had a country to govern. Yeltsin signed decrees banning the Communist Party and taking control over the Soviet armed forces on the territory

of the Russian Republic. In December, Yeltsin met with the presidents of Ukraine and Belarus in Minsk and agreed to create a new Commonwealth of Independent States, which was later joined by nine other Soviet republics. The Soviet Union was officially dissolved and replaced by fifteen new independent states.

Evaluation

Scholars differ over whether Gorbachev or Yeltsin deserves more credit for the breakup of the Soviet Union. Gorbachev initiated the reforms and made the crucial decision not to use force to try to hold the country together. But his intention was to save the U.S.S.R. Yeltsin was more consistent: he embraced democracy and was willing to give up the Soviet Union if that was the only way to preserve democracy. Soviet Communists blame both men for destroying the Soviet Union in their selfish struggle for power. They also accuse the West of manipulating the two men to bring about the destruction of the U.S.S.R. Given the costs of post-Soviet transition, neither man is very popular among ordinary Russians today.

Other observers are reluctant to grant such a pivotal role to individual leaders. David Kotz and Fred Weir (1997) argue that the Soviet Union fell because the elites who ran it decided that they could have a better life if they ditched the Soviet system. As the economy disintegrated in the wake of Gorbachev's bungled reforms, many members of the party elite abandoned the sinking ship of state Socialism and launched the lifeboats of market capitalism. Indeed, most of the leaders of post-1991 Russia came out of the ranks of the old party-state elite—or at least they were the sons and daughters of the old elite. And they benefited handsomely from the transition to capitalism. (By 2005, Russia had thirty-seven dollar billionaires, the second highest number in the world after the United States.) However, just because individuals from the old elite benefited from the transition by seizing opportunities to make money does not mean that they caused those events to occur. The introduction of capitalism in Russia was essentially spontaneous and unexpected. It was the result of human action but not of human design.

IMPACTS

The fall of the Berlin Wall in 1989 is one of the turning points in world history, on a par with 1789 or 1917. Whether or not the events of 1989–1991 were a revolution in the traditional sense of the word, or merely a system collapse, they changed the structure of the international system that had been in place since 1945, and they caused a shift in domestic politics in states all around the world.

A New World Order?

In the spring of 1989, U.S. scholar Francis Fukuyama (1989) wrote an influential essay in which he argued that the breakdown of Communist regimes in Eastern Europe signaled the "end of history." By that he meant the end of a model of social development alternative to what U.S. president Bill Clinton called "market democracy." After the Soviet collapse the Chinese Communists still clung to one-party rule, but even they had embraced capitalist methods for running their economy since 1978. Fukuyama predicted that with the fall of Communism, the world would no longer be divided into two rival ideological camps.

The end of the Cold War left the United States as the undisputed world leader. It was now the dominant military power, and no longer had to fear imminent destruction in a Soviet surprise attack. That allowed the United States to cut military spending by a third (the "peace dividend"). The United States reduced its forces in Europe but did not dismantle the North Atlantic Treaty Organization. (The Soviet-led military alliance, the Warsaw Pact, dissolved in 1991.)

George H. W. Bush, U.S. president from 1989 to 1993, talked about the need for a "new world order" to replace the Cold War. But that vision presupposed a partnership with Gorbachev's Soviet Union, which no longer existed. The first—and last—sign of that partnership was Gorbachev's acquiescence in the U.S.-led invasion of Iraq in 1991, to reverse its occupation of Kuwait. U.S. president Bill Clinton, who took office in 1993, focused on domestic issues and the promotion of international free trade. Clinton continued to pursue good relations with Russia, though corruption, authoritarianism, and the war in Chechnya made Boris Yeltsin a less attractive partner as the decade wore on.

Several times in the 1990s the United States and her allies launched "humanitarian interventions" to try to prevent gross abuses of human rights. The new threats to U.S. security came now from "non-traditional sources"—the proliferation of nuclear materials from Soviet arsenals; the instability caused by "failed states"; and the spread of organized crime and international drug trafficking. However, Russia was a reluctant partner in those efforts, and the United States failed to articulate a clear vision for international cooperation to deal with them. U.S. policy drifted toward isolationism, until the September 11 attacks gave it a new mission—the global war on terror.

Nationalist Conflicts

The "end of history" did not mean an end to conflict. New motives for fighting surfaced to replace the ideological rivalry of the Cold War: nationalism and religious fervor. Harvard professor Samuel Huntington argues that a "clash of civilizations" would replace the clash of ideologies of the post-1945 era (Huntington 1993).

Three of the Communist states were ethnic federations: the Soviet Union, Yugoslavia, and Czechoslovakia. All three broke up after 1989: powerful evidence for the idea that nationalism filled the political vacuum created by the crumbling of ideology. The breakup was violent in Yugoslavia but peaceful in the case of Czechoslovakia, which split amicably into the Czech and Slovak republics in 1992.

Nationalism triggered open warfare within the former Soviet Union: in Moldova, Azerbaijan, and Georgia. The fighting ended in cease-fires in 1992, but there has been no progress toward a lasting peace. The secessionist regions (TransDniester, Karabakh, Abkhazia, and South Ossetia) prevented the sovereign states from establishing control over their territory, thanks to military assistance from Russia. But they have been unable to win international recognition, their economies have collapsed, and they are pockets of anarchy that serve as a base for organized crime. Meanwhile, 800,000 refugees in Azerbaijan and 300,000 in Georgia are still unable to return to their homes.

A Wave of Democratization

The end of the Soviet empire ignited what Michael McFaul (2002) has called the "fourth wave" of global democratization. The East European states enthusiastically embraced free elections, and most embraced economic "shock therapy" to make the transition from state planning to capitalism as rapidly as possible. Remarkably few of the countries tried to look for social democratic, welfare-state solutions that might avoid the extremes of central planning and liberal market capitalism. All of them suffered from a "transition recession" that saw living standards plummet by a third, but most started growing strongly after three to five years of adjustment. By 2004, eight of the former Socialist countries had become full members of the European Union: an event that would have been inconceivable in 1985.

Within the former Soviet Union itself, the record of post-Communist transition has been mixed, at best. Although the countries all pay lip service to democracy, fair elections are rare. There are more personal freedoms than in Soviet times, but there is also more crime and corruption. In most places, the Communist elite stayed on in power after the Soviet collapse, rejecting Communist ideology in favor of the rhetoric of markets, democracy, and national independence. Only in the Baltic countries, Armenia, and Georgia did new rulers emerge from the ranks of the nationalist movement. In all other places, the person who headed the republic when the U.S.S.R. collapsed in 1991 calmly took over as president of the new country. In Central Asia, leaders fixed elections and used police-state tactics to stay in power. In Belarus, Aleksandr Lukashenko won election on a populist platform in 1994, then went on to establish a personal dictatorship. In Ukraine, the first post-independence president lost an election in 1994 and stepped down. His successor, Leonid Kuchma, tried to hand-pick his successor, but popular protests (the "Orange revolution") in December 2004 thwarted his effort to rig the election.

In Russia, Boris Yeltsin stayed on as president, calling out the army in 1993 to disband the Congress, which objected to his radical economic reforms. Yeltsin oversaw the privatiza-

tion of most of the Russian economy, with choice oil fields and metals plants sold for a pittance to favored insiders. Russian politics came to be dominated by a small, incredibly wealthy group of billionaires, the "oligarchs." Yeltsin won a second term in 1996, in an election widely regarded as unfair because the television stations rallied behind the president, against his Communist challenger. In December 1999, Yeltsin passed on the presidency to his chosen successor, the former KGB veteran Vladimir Putin. Putin recentralized power by establishing control over the oligarchs, the television stations, and regional leaders. Putin's state bears some of the features of the old Soviet Union, including patriotic nostalgia and a strong police presence. But Putin has sought cooperation with the West, and has not tried to reverse Yeltsin's market reforms.

The Soviet collapse meant an abrupt end to diplomatic and financial support for Soviet allies around the world. From Albania to Benin, dictators who used Marxist rhetoric to justify authoritarian rule changed course after 1989, and started holding free or semi-free elections. Communist regimes in Cuba, Laos, North Korea, and Vietnam clung to power, although even they launched economic reforms in varying degrees.

Likewise, right-wing authoritarian leaders around the world also sensed that the United States would no longer be so tolerant of repressive methods in the name of battling Communism. The most striking example of this dynamic was the dissolution of apartheid in South Africa. Prime Minister Frederik de Klerk realized that with the Soviet Union gone, the United States would no longer support South Africa as a bulwark against Marxist regimes in Angola and Mozambique. So in February 1990, just three months after the fall of the Berlin Wall, de Klerk released Nelson Mandela from prison and went on to allow free elections, on the understanding that the civil and property rights of the white elite would be preserved. In 1994 a black majority government was elected. It is hard to imagine such a rapid and relatively peaceful end to apartheid if the Berlin Wall had not fallen.

PEOPLE AND ORGANIZATIONS

Andropov, Yuri (1914–1984)

Head of the Committee on State Security (KGB) from 1967 to 1982 and general secretary of the Communist Party from 1982 to 1984, Yuri Andropov brought Gorbachev to Moscow and chose him as his number two.

Brezhnev, Leonid (1906–1982)

General secretary of the Communist Party from 1964 to 1982. Brezhnev brought about steadily improving living standards, but no political or economic reform. Under his leadership, the Soviet Union sent troops into Czechoslovakia in 1968 and into Afghanistan in 1979.

Commonwealth of Independent States (CIS)

The CIS was the loose confederation formed in December 1991 to replace the Union of Soviet Socialist Republics. Eleven former Soviet republics joined the CIS, which was later joined by Georgia. The Baltic republics of Estonia, Latvia, and Lithuania refused to take part.

Communist Party of the Soviet Unioin (CPSU)

Formed by Vladimir Lenin, the CPSU was the only party allowed to operate between 1918 and 1990. It tightly controlled all political and economic activities in Soviet society, but was fatally weakened by the reforms launched by Gorbachev in 1985.

Gorbachev, Mikhail (Born 1931)

After graduating in law from Moscow State University, Gorbachev returned to his home province of Stavropol and worked his way up the Communist Party bureaucracy. Brought to Moscow as party secretary for agriculture in 1978, he joined the Politburo in 1979 and was made general secretary in 1985. He was appointed Soviet president in 1989; he left office in December 1991.

Khrushchev, Nikita (1894–1971)

Head of the Soviet Communist Party from 1953–1964 and soviet premier from 1958–1964, Khrushchev was the last leader prior to Gorbachev to try to implement structural reforms, which eventually led to his dismissal.

Nomenklatura

Nomenklatura was the informal name for the top 1–2 million Communist Party officials who ran the party and state bureaucracy.

Politburo

The Politburo was the committee, with ten to fifteen members, that headed the Communist Party of the Soviet Union.

Yanaev, Gennady (Born 1937)

A trade union leader whom Gorbachev appointed Soviet vice president, Yanaev headed the committee that declared a state of emergency in August 1991 and had Gorbachev arrested in his vacation villa.

Yeltsin, Boris (Born 1931)

Former construction chief and then party official in the Urals city of Sverdlovsk, Yeltsin was appointed head of the Moscow City Communist Party in December 1985 by Gorbachev, who fired him in 1987. Yeltsin won election to the U.S.S.R. Congress in 1989, and in 1990 he was elected president by the Russian Republic parliament. He won a direct election for the Russian presidency in June 1991.

Peter Rutland

See Also Afghanistan: Conflict and Civil War; Chechen Revolt against Russia; Democracy, Dictatorship, and Fascism; Documentaries of Revolution; East European Revolutions of 1989; Ethnic and Racial Conflict: From Bargaining to Violence; Human Rights, Morality, Social Justice, and Revolution; Hungarian Revolution of 1956; Nationalism and Revolution; Polish Solidarity Movement; Population, Economic Development, and Revolution; Reform, Rebellion, Civil War, Coup D'état, and Revolution; Russian Revolution of 1917; Yugoslavia: Dissolution.

References and Further Readings

Aron, Leon. 2000. *Yeltsin: A Revolutionary Life.* New York: St. Martin's.

Aslund, Anders. 1991. *Gorbachev's Struggle for Economic Reform.* Ithaca, NY: Cornell University Press.

Beissinger, Mark. 2002. *Nationalist Mobilization and the Collapse of the Soviet State.* New York: Cambridge University Press.

Borovik, Artem. 2001. *The Hidden War: A Russian Journalist's Account of the Soviet War in Afghanistan.* Oak Lawn, IL: Grove/Atlantic.

Breslauer, George. 2002. *Gorbachev and Yeltsin as Leaders.* New York: Cambridge University Press.

Brown, Archie. 1996. *The Gorbachev Factor.* New York: Oxford University Press.

Cox, Michael, ed. 1999. *Rethinking the Soviet Collapse: Sovietology, the Death of Communism and the New Russia.* London: Frances Pinter.

Dawson, Jane. 1996. *Eco-Nationalism: Anti-Nuclear Activity and National Identity in Russia, Lithuania, and Ukraine.* Durham, NC: Duke University Press.

Dunlop, John B. 1995. *The Rise of Russia and the Fall of the Soviet Empire.* Princeton, NJ: Princeton University Press.

Ellman, Michael, and Vladimir Kontorovich. 1998. *The Destruction of the Soviet Economic System.* Armonk, NY: M. E. Sharpe.

English, Robert. 2000. *Russia and the Idea of the West.* New York: Columbia University Press.

Fish, M. Steven. 1997. *Democracy from Scratch.* Princeton, NJ: Princeton University Press.

Fukuyama, Francis. 1989. "The End of History," *National Interest* 6: 3–18.

Goldman, Marshall I. 1992. *What Went Wrong with Perestroika?* New York: W. W. Norton.

Hosking, Geoffrey. 1993. *The First Socialist Society: A History of the Soviet Union from Within.* Cambridge, MA: Harvard University Press.

Huntington, Samuel P. 1993. "The Clash of Civilizations?" *Foreign Affairs* 72 (3) (summer): 22–49.

Kotkin, Stephen. 2003. *Armageddon Averted: The Soviet Collapse, 1970–2000.* New York: Oxford University Press.

Kotz, David, and Fred Weir. 1997. *Revolution from Above: The Demise of the Soviet System.* New York: Routledge.

Ligachev, Yegor. 1996. *Inside Gorbachev's Kremlin: The Memoirs of Yegor Ligachev.* Boulder, CO: Westview.

Malia, Martin. 1990. "To the Stalin Mausoleum," *Daedalus* 119 (spring): 295–344.

Matlock, Jack. 1995. *Autopsy on an Empire: The American Ambassador's Account of the Collapse of the Soviet Union.* New York: Random House.

McFaul, Michael. 2002. "The Fourth Wave of Democracy and Dictatorship," *World Politics* 54 (2): 212–244.

Remnick, David. 1993. *Lenin's Tomb: The Last Days of the Soviet Empire.* New York: Random House.

Rutland, Peter. 1993. "Sovietology: Notes for a Post-Mortem," *National Interest* 31: 109–122.

Strayer, Robert W. 1998. *Why Did the Soviet Union Collapse?: Understanding Historical Change.* Armonk, NY: M. E. Sharpe.

Suny, Ronald G. 1993. *The Revenge of the Past: Nationalism, Revolution and the Collapse of the Soviet Union.* Stanford, CA: Stanford University Press.

Yeltsin, Boris N. 1991. *Against the Grain: An Autobiography.* New York: Pan Macmillan.

Rwanda Civil Wars

CHRONOLOGY

1895–1896	In 1895 Germany begins to consolidate control over Rwanda. Continuing the Tutsi royal line, Yuhi Musinga becomes king, or *unwami* (1896–1931), after a year-long civil war with his brother over the succession to the throne following the death of their father, Rwabugiri (1860–1895).
1900–1914	In 1907, Germany appoints German "residents" for the different regions of Rwanda and constructs Kigali as the capital. In 1912, Ndungutze, the leader of the rebellion against both Germany and Musinga, is killed.
1910	A Brussels conference fixes the frontiers of Rwanda.
1916–1917	In 1916 the Belgian military replaces German rule and, in 1917, installs a colonial administration.
1923	The League of Nations designates Rwanda as a mandate territory under Belgian trusteeship.
1931	The Belgians replace Musinga with his son, Charles-Leon-Pierre Rudahigwa (Mutara III, 1913–1959). Catholicism becomes the quasi-official religion of Rwanda.
1933	After a census, Belgium issues identity cards designating citizens as Hutu (mainly agriculturalist, 85 percent), Tutsi (mainly cattle owners, 14 percent), or Twa (originally hunters and gatherers, 1 percent).
1957	The Bahutu Manifesto claims that the struggle within Rwanda is a conflict against both colonialists (*Bazungu*) and foreign Tutsi (Hamites).
1959	The king, Rudahigwa, dies following an antibiotic injection and is succeeded by King Kigeri V.
	Supported by Belgium, a Hutu revolt overthrows the Tutsi monarchy, kills 10,000 Tutsi, and forces tens of thousands of Tutsi to flee into exile.
1960	Rwanda's first local elections produce an overwhelming Parmehutu victory.
1960–1962	Tutsi refugee guerrilla bands, *Inyenzi* (cockroaches), attack Rwanda.
1961	A referendum abolishes the monarchy.
1962	Rwanda becomes independent. Grégoire Kayibanda, head of the anti-Tutsi Parmehutu Party, is installed as president.
1963	In December, following an *Inyenzi* attack from Burundi, the Hutu rulers kill 10,000 Tutsi in the fighting and execute 20,000 later as traitors; 150,000 Tutsi flee Rwanda and become refugees.
1973	In the Catholic seminaries and educational institutions, Tutsi are removed, following a

wave of "ethnic" violence. Major General Juvénal Habyarimana, a northerner from Gisenyi who later founds the National Revolutionary Movement for Development (MRND) in 1975, overthrows Kayibanda in a coup d'état.

1986   Habyarimana rejects the return of Tutsi refugees.

1987   Following a sharp drop in the price of coffee, Rwanda's chief export crop, the average GDP growth of 6.5 percent for the previous decade declines sharply.

1988   Habyarimana is "re-elected" with 99 percent support. A Washington Tutsi diaspora conference creates the Rwandan Patriotic Front (RPF), calling for refugee return.

1989   Poor weather and the total collapse of coffee prices results in a dramatic economic decline and a rise in unemployment.

1990   In July, Habyarimana commits himself to multiparty democratization. On October 1, the Rwandan Patriotic Front (RPF) invades Rwanda from Uganda; with the assistance of French and Zairian troops, the invasion is stopped and the two top military leaders are killed.

1991   On March 29, the cease-fire in Rwanda is made permanent by the N'Sele Agreement, providing for an immediate cessation of hostilities, withdrawal of foreign troops, the creation of a Neutral Military Observer Group (NMOG), an end to hate media messages, and the beginning of dialogue. Although the cease-fire breaks down in the summer, and the African observer group is removed from Rwanda to the Ugandan side of the border, the cease-fire is restored by the Gbadolite agreement in September.

1992   On March 7, following violence against Tutsi, fighting resumes, and the RPF advances. The number of displaced persons doubles to 180,000, and Habyarimana is forced to end fourteen years of one-party rule and form a new transitional coalition government, in-

cluding representation from all four parties. A major RPF attack in May on Byumba almost doubles the internally displaced population once again, to 350,000 (JEEAR 1996, Vol. 1, 77). In October the Arusha talks resume, and an agreement on presidential power and the transition to democracy is reached.

1993   In January, after signing peace protocols providing a new power-sharing agreement, opponents of the regime are arrested, and at least 300 Tutsi are slaughtered in what the International Commission of Investigation on Human Rights Violations in Rwanda initially dubs "genocide." After the RPF launches a new offensive in February, leading them to within 27 kilometers of Kigali, and 650,000 more Rwandans are displaced, new peace talks provide for the withdrawal of the RPF to their former positions. The Arusha agreement, signed on August 4, provides for power sharing, the repatriation of refugees, and a new integrated army and gendarmerie—just before Bacre W. Ndiaye, the UN special rapporteur on extrajudicial executions, in his report on his mission to Rwanda from April 8 to 17, implies that there has been genocide. Following the UNAMIR arrival in Rwanda, a coup in Burundi kills 100,000 to 150,000 Hutu and creates hundreds of thousands of refugees, most fleeing to Rwanda (ibid., 77–78).

1994   The inauguration of the new Broad-Based Transitional Government is continually delayed. Just after the Security Council extends UNAMIR's mandate for another six months, on April 6 a missile destroys the plane carrying the presidents of Rwanda and Burundi and the Rwandan chief of staff. A military coup follows; coup leaders murder a number of ministers, government officials, and the prime minister of Rwanda, Agatha Uwilingiyimana. The presidential guard capture ten Belgian peacekeepers who had been defending the prime minister and kill them. The war resumes, ending with a victory for the RPF three months later, but only after 800,000 Tutsi and moderate Hutu are killed in a systematic genocide; a million and a half refugees flee into Zaire and Tanzania (Prunier 1995, 265).

INTRODUCTION

Over the last century, the history of Rwanda has been punctuated by revolution: the double revolution from above in 1895–1896 that imposed both colonial rule and the most autocratic ruler in Rwandan history; the 1959 Hutu racist revolution from below that overthrew the Tutsi monarchy and then won independence from Belgium in 1962; the revolution from the inside in the 1973 coup d'état of Habyarimana; and the beginning of the revolution from the outside led by the RPF and the Tutsi refugees in exile in 1990 that co-opted the inside revolution of democratic forces. The RPF eventually won the war against the regime in July of 1994. Just before the final victory of the RPF, a combined coup d'état and racist revolution from above by the extremists took place on April 6, 1994. Before they were defeated, they killed 800,000 Tutsi and moderate Hutu in a ruthless genocide.

BACKGROUND: CULTURE AND HISTORY

Before the second millennium, hunters and gatherers (Twa, now 1 percent of the population) populated the region. By the 1400s both pastoralists (Tutsi cattle herders) and agriculturalists (Hutu) had moved into the region. The Rwandan kingdom was founded in the fifteenth century through an amalgamation of autonomous chiefs under the Abanyiginya royal clan. (Rudahigwa was the last king in that line.) In the seventeenth century, the Tutsi consolidated their economic and political power. In the eighteenth century, the Tutsi acquired military dominance with the centralization of power through a military and hierarchical organization of state and society. Hutu were incorporated into royal court rituals, as patron-client relationships developed, and as military, political, and administrative power structures were consolidated as the territory over which the monarchy held sway expanded. From 1860 to 1895, under the rule of *mwami* Kigeri Rwabugiri, the political and social position of the Hutu agriculturalists was even further diminished as the state and military capacity of the state grew, and as Hutu "statelets" in both eastern and western Rwanda were incorporated into the state. As new groups were consolidated into the expanding state, they were also defined as Hutu, even if they owned cattle. Hutu were increasingly defined by their inferior social status rather than their economic role.

European colonialists reinforced the superior political, military, economic, and social status of the Tutsis by type-

casting them as Europeans with black skins in the writings of the white fathers of the Catholic Church who arrived in Rwanda in 1900. The latter constructed one minority group, the Tutsi, as alien rather than indigenous, by creating a mythology of Tutsis as a separate group of quasi-Aryans (the Hamitic hypothesis) who invaded Rwanda from the north and gradually subjugated the indigenous Hutu population. When a Belgian "trusteeship" assumed control after the defeat of Germany in World War I, the process of racialization of the social divisions of Tutsi and Hutu accelerated. Reinforced by the church, and using state administration and educational "reforms," the Belgians consolidated the social and economic divisions into racial ones in the 1930s through the issuance of identity cards that characterized Rwandans as Tutsi, Hutu, or Twa *by race*, instead of by social status or economic role, even though all three groups had the same cultural practices and belonged to the Kinyarwanda-speaking peoples. That latter group was overwhelmingly dominant in Rwanda and Burundi but also in Uganda, the Democratic Republic of the Congo (Zaire), and Tanzania.

CONTEXT AND PROCESS OF REVOLUTION

Grégoire Kayibanda—leader of the Parmehutu (Parti du Movement de l'Emancipation Hutu) and one of the Committee of Nine who signed the Bahutu manifesto criticizing the Tutsi social, political, economic, and military domination in 1957—overthrew the Tutsi rulers of Rwanda in a violent uprising and inverted the power structure. Inspired by migrant Hutu laborers who had escaped the system of forced labor, local and regional power brokers united with a small, educated elite and a dependent, exploited, and resentful underclass. However, the new Hutu government kept the ideological underpinnings of the old government rooted in race and class. The idea of Hutu identified with subjugation was transformed into identification with power.

The 1959 revolt from below changed the internal power structure of Rwanda by reversing the historical pattern of discrimination against the Hutu. Hutus were given preferential treatment in the military, political, and educational spheres, and Tutsi leaders were driven into exile and discriminated against. Attempts to recover power by Tutsi exiles were rebuffed, and Hutu power was consolidated. In 1973, Major General Juvénal Habyarimana, a northerner from Gisenyi who later founds the National Revolutionary Movement for Development (MRND) in 1975, overthrew Grégoire Kayibanda, head of the anti-Tutsi MDR-Parmehutu Party, in an initially bloodless coup d'état and announced an

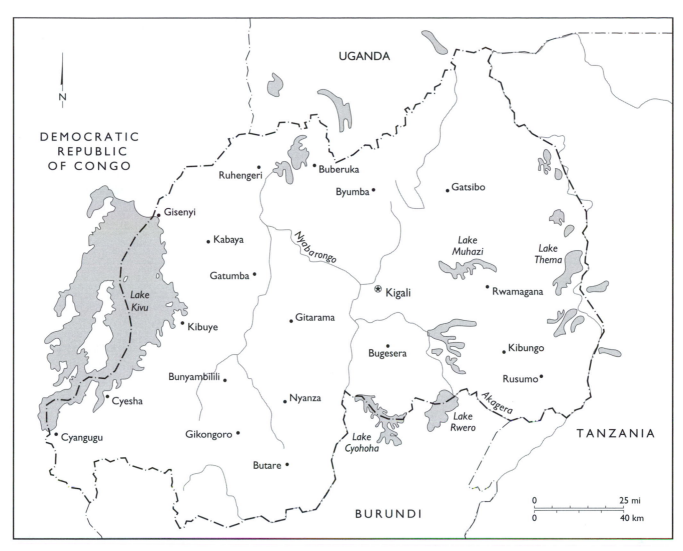

Republic of Rwanda: political conflict and ethnic strife led to the mass murder of hundreds of thousands of people beginning on April 6, 1994, before the victory of the rebel army, the Rwandese Patriotic Front (RPF), in July of that year.

end to ethnic politics; but Habyarimana favored Hutu northerners and restricted Tutsi participation in the professions and public life through quotas. This revolution from inside merely shifted Hutu domination over the Tutsi to northern versus southern Hutu supremacy.

The new rulers were supported by external overseas powers as the French replaced the Belgian patrons of the elite in Rwanda. By the 1980s, regional power brokers, such as Uganda and Zaire, played an increasingly important role, even as the revolution from the outside and inside began in 1990, with a two-pronged movement: the formation of the RPF in exile, with a determination to gain readmission for the refugees; and the domestic push from within for multiparty democracy and the protection of human rights. These movements were reinforced by the economic collapse caused by the crash in commodity prices and the push by the IMF and World Bank to initiate a structural adjustment program. The invasion of Rwanda by the Tutsi-dominated Rwandan Patriotic Front (RPF) from Uganda on October 1, 1990, and the rescue of the Habyarimana regime by French and Zairian military forces, which stopped the invasion in its tracks, began the three-and-a-half-year civil war that led to the eventual withdrawal of all foreign troops supporting Habyarimana.

After the 1990 RPF invasion, Yoweri Museveni, president of Uganda, who had secretly supported the RPF rebels, along with the prime minister of Belgium, Wilfried Martens, the president of Tanzania, Ali Hassan Mwinyi, and Habyarimana all agreed on a cease-fire based on the withdrawal of foreign troops and a commitment to resettle the Rwandese refugees. On October 26, a regional meeting of the leaders of Rwanda,

Burundi, Zaire, and Uganda at Gbadolite, Zaire, formally endorsed a cease-fire and called on the OAU (Organization of African Unity) to create a monitoring force to be based in Byumba, Rwanda. Zaire and Brussels withdrew their troops.

With each break in the cease-fire, the RPF consolidated power as it expanded its control over territory and produced more and more internally displaced people. Why was the RPF victorious with fewer troops and poorer military equipment? It was victorious because of excellent leadership, good discipline, high morale, and the sense of a just cause, in conflict with a divided, faction-ridden, and now somewhat corrupt polity with extremist ideologues increasingly taking over power and alienating potential allies. These defeats fostered the growth of extremism, led by the *Akazu,* a small extremist elite from the north who advocated an ideology of exclusion of the Tutsi and eventually extermination. They controlled the news media, particularly the press and Radio Mille Collines. They also trained and armed paramilitary militias. Nevertheless, a peace agreement was signed at Arusha on August 4, 1993, called the Arusha Accords, which provided for power sharing, integration of the armed forces, and refugee return. It did not result in peace. Following the missile destruction of the airplane carrying Rwanda's president and Rwanda's chief of staff on April 6, 1994, an extremist coup took over the government, killed the moderate political leadership, resumed the war against the RPF, and initiated a systematic genocide against the Tutsi domestic population until finally defeated by the RPF. More than a million and a half Hutu refugees (ibid., 312) fled into exile, as well as the defeated military and political *génocidaires* who had organized and participated in the massive slaughter.

The RPF took ten years to consolidate its power and attempt the most radical revolution in Rwandan history through an effort to alter Rwandan identity so that only Rwandan citizenship would be recognized in any formal operations of government. They defeated the Hutu extremist leaders in exile, restored peace to the country, oversaw the return of the vast bulk of the Hutu refugees, and tried to mete out justice through both a resurrected court system and, later, traditional, community-based *gacaca* "courts."

All, however, was far from rosy. Possibly with the guilt over inaction in the face of the genocide, the international community was either unable or unwilling to impose conditionality on its aid to Rwanda to ensure pluralism and true multiparty democracy in Rwanda. In 1995, Prime Minister Faustin Twagiramungu and Minister of Home Affairs Seth Sendashonga resigned to protest abuses by government troops; they subsequently fled into exile. The latter was murdered in Nairobi in 1998. In 2000, President Pasteur Bizimungu and the speaker of the national assembly, Joseph Kabuye Sebarenz, were forced out. Bizimungu was charged with corruption, and Sebarenz fled into exile.

In an effort to forge a new Rwandan identity in which each citizen would be first and foremost a Rwandan, a new flag and national anthem were introduced in 2001, and, in 2003, a new constitution was confirmed by a referendum that made "divisionism," "revisionism, negationism and trivialization of the genocide" illegal. In the presidential elections of August 2003, President Paul Kagame, who had led the RPF to victory in 1994, won 95 percent of the vote, while the former prime minister, Faustin Twagiramungu, who had returned from exile to run against Kagame, saw his party banned and all twelve provincial campaign managers arrested; Twagiramungu received 3.7 percent of the vote. Even though Paul Kagame, the leader of the RPF, was elected president with a very large majority, Rwanda still awaits a proper democratic revolution that will ensure the full protection of human rights and a pluralist polity.

IMPACTS

Even without full democracy, the domestic impacts were profound. Instead of an occupying power geared to nation-building, as in Kosovo and Iraq, a Tutsi-dominated government of exiles who were raised in English took power in an unprecedented effort to govern a state in which French had been the dominant foreign language and in which families of the victors had been the victims of the genocide. They threw out the idea of a state based on the domination of radically separate identities and one that did not allow refugees to return. They created a state in which membership, instead of being defined by class and ethnicity, was defined by *natio,* nativity; all members were formally equal in a state that retained responsibility for all its members—members who retained the right to return and the right to be protected by the state. The gradual separation of political and ritual/magical power that had begun in the fifteenth century was consolidated with the separation of church and state in the twentieth century, a separation that took place unfortunately only with the genocide and the termination of the close identity of many church leaders with the power elite and the *génocidaires.* A process of education that began with colonization became a matter of universal right, rather than a method of reproducing social and political distinctions between Tutsi and Hutu and a matter of privilege for the few. The state once again resumed its monopoly over coercive power (there were no longer militias associated with political factions); at the same time, the supremacy of civilian over military power became the accepted norm. Finally, the consolidation of society under a new myth of unitary citizenship, backed by a growing domestic coalition in favor of both inclusion and accommodation, rather than exclusion and confrontation, was the most important result of this long revolutionary process.

Rwandan Patriotic Front leader Paul Kagame (center right, unarmed) tours a rural area with his troops. (Joel Stettenheim/Corbis)

The revolutions and civil wars in Rwanda have had far-ranging impacts on the surrounding region, totally out of proportion to the small size of the country. Although the Tutsi refugees from 1959 to 1966 had an impact on their immediate neighbors—particularly the Tutsi who fought for Museveni in Uganda and helped bring him to power in 1986—the last series of counter-revolutions and revolutions in the 1990s, in which genocide was the most eventful and horrific by-product, had the greatest repercussions. As the United Nations failed to intervene in the Rwandan genocide in an effective manner, it also failed to intervene when the former FAR (Rwandese Armed Forces) and the interahamwe, which had fled with the refugees after their defeat by the RPF, took control and militarized the refugee camps in Zaire. They used them as bases first to launch attacks back into Rwanda and then, when their losses became unbearable, to continue the genocide by attacking Tutsi in the Congo. Eventually, Rwanda and Uganda backed a rebel army in Zaire that ended up overthrowing Mobutu, the ailing president, and installing Laurent Kabila as ruler. As the alliance fractured, civil war broke out anew and escalated into a pan-African war as neighboring countries fought for

their own security as well as for power and the exploitation of the natural resources of the Congo (primarily the mineral wealth of coltan [Columbite-tantalite], diamonds, copper, cobalt, and gold). In the second stage of that civil war, after the proxy of Rwanda and Uganda, Kabila, fell out with his sponsors, the international community stood by as at least another 2 million Congolese died. (In a written statement to the 58th session of the UN Commission on Human Rights, the International Federation of Human Rights on February 12, 2002, claimed that there had been 3 million deaths.)

The effects of the events in Rwanda on her sister country, Burundi, were profound. When the first democratically elected Hutu, Melchior Ndadaye, became prime minister of Burundi and was subsequently assassinated by Tutsi extremists in October 1993, an inter-ethnic killing spree took the lives of 50,000 to 100,000 and forced at least 300,000 refugees to flee, mostly into Rwanda (ibid.; Prunier 1995, 199 ; JEEAR 1996, 78). The hands of the Hutu extremists in Rwanda were strengthened in the face of this example of Tutsi behavior. So too, the genocide in turn reinforced the intransigence of the Tutsi extremists in Burundi, and, in the dragged-out civil war, many more innocent civilians died or were forced to flee.

There were also international repercussions, especially in Paris, Brussels, and Washington. France, instead of enlarging the space for the French culture and language (*francophonie*), saw that space shrink at the same time as the country was widely characterized as abetting genocide. Belgium went through a self-flagellating inquiry into the causes of the death of its ten peacekeepers. Guilt-ridden at its obstruction to supporting peacekeeping, the United States is now all too ready to label any incident of mass slaughter—for example, Darfur—as genocide. The Rwandan genocide has been the greatest embarrassment to the United Nations system since it was created. A low-tech genocide managed to kill people at a far faster rate than the industrialized murder machine of the Nazis *while UN troops were in the country,* and while the airport was accessible to land European and U.S. troops within several days' notice. Most studies concluded that the genocide could have been stopped or significantly mitigated with a relatively small but effective force.

UNAMIR II (UN Assistance Mission to Rwanda II) stood by in April of 1995 when as many as four thousand civilians were killed by Rwandan government troops in the effort to empty out the last internally displaced persons camp at Kibeho. When the United Nations proved impotent to reverse the military control that the *génocidaires* had established over the refugee camps in the Congo, and when those forces began to slaughter Tutsi in the Congo as well as to attempt to destabilize Rwanda, Rwanda itself took responsibility for clearing out the militants, in November 1996. To the surprise, and contrary to the predictions, of NGOs (non-governmental organizations) of mass starvation and disease among the refugees—and contrary to warnings of the fear among the refugees of returning to Rwanda—almost 650,000 refugees walked home to Rwanda. The international community subsequently gave implicit support to Tanzania when it "forced" the return of another half-million Rwandan refugees on its soil, contrary to the terms of the Geneva Convention, which insisted upon voluntary return only. The dramatic failure of the United Nations became all the more embarrassing when the Joint Evaluation of Emergency Assistance to Rwanda (JEEAR) Report of 1996 revealed that the force commander had sent UN headquarters information on the plans for the genocide well in advance, and that the human rights mechanism of the United Nations and NGO human rights organizations had also reported on the existence of a small, organized conspiracy by extremist Hutus to slaughter Tutsis. General Romeo Dallaire, the force commander of UNAMIR, was not even informed of the existence of these human rights reports as part of his briefing but discovered the conspiracy through other means. However, since the genocide in Rwanda, human rights officers are regularly incorporated in peacekeeping missions. Although states were burdened by guilt for their inaction in response to the genocide, governments have tended to remain passive or even overlook or excuse human rights abuses within Rwanda.

On the other hand, cables reporting violence or potential violence are no longer buried in a "black box" but spotlighted; there is a much greater awareness of the importance of early warning signs. Through the auspices of the Intergovernmental Authority on Development (IGAD), the countries of the Horn of Africa have set up a Conflict Early Warning and Response Network called CEWARN, with corresponding state institutions called Conflict Early Warning and Early Response Units (CEWERUs). There has also been a recognition that the way in which aid and financial assistance to developing countries are offered can exacerbate the conditions for violence.

Although widespread support for post-genocide international and state trials of the perpetrators has tried to make up for the culture of impunity that had become so pervasive internationally, there has been little impact from using international courts as a tool to isysdm.cpcleandefrsysdmnhibit such actions by making hate-mongers subject to the full force of international law before such hate crimes are committed. Other instruments in preventing revolutionary movements from turning into "terror" machines, such as monitoring and controlling the flow of arms, have begun to improve on the monitoring side, almost directly as a result of the Rwanda catastrophe, but it is hard to see any consistent impact on the control dimension. Certainly, the specter of the Rwanda genocide has haunted all discussions since that time, when cases of internal violence in Bosnia, Kosovo, East Timor, Sierra Leone, Liberia, Cote d'Ivoire, and Bunia have been thrust into the spotlight of world opinion; increasingly, coalitions of the willing have chosen to act rather than stand by and wait for a UN imprimatur. But, given the recent spate of killing and ethnic cleansing in Darfur, there has been no discernible impact on action, as distinct from words, in other countries, such as Sudan.

Report after report on Rwanda insisted "never again," and the Brahimi Report to the United Nations in 2000 insisted that peacekeeping forces be properly and adequately supplied and equipped for robust action, and also provided with broad rules of engagement based on realistic scenarios, not wishful thinking, that take into account potential and unforeseen obstacles. Troop deployments for peacekeeping have improved, especially if a Western state takes direct responsibility for the operation, but there is a long way to go if consistency and true effectiveness are to be criteria for the prevention and mitigation of the mass slaughter of civilians. On the other side of the ledger, NGOs and the ICRC (International Committee of the Red Cross) have lost the "neutral humanitarian space" that had been reserved for humanitarian aid, as humanitarian workers fell under increasing suspicion for supplying information on local violence, human rights abuses, and especially the exploitation of the mineral wealth of the Congo. For example, in April 2001, six ICRC staff members were murdered near Bunia in Ituri.

PEOPLE AND ORGANIZATIONS

Akazu

Akazu was the entourage of northern Rwandan extremists around President Habyarimana's wife.

Bagosora, Colonel Théoneste (Born 1941)

Bagosora was director of services in the Ministry of Defense under Théoneste Habyarimana; he was believed to be the coordinator of the April 6 coup and genocide, and was tried at Arusha.

BBTG

The Broad-Based Transitional Government was provided for in the Arusha Accords.

CDR

The Coalition for the Defense of the Republic (Coalition pour la défense de la république) was the most extreme Hutu party, formed in 1992 and adamantly opposed to the Arusha Accords.

DAMI

Detachment d'assistance militaire et d'instruction, the French military mission to Rwanda, was accused of helping to train FAR soldiers and interahamwe militia members.

FAR

Forces Armées Rwandaises, Rwandese Armed Forces, formed under the Habyarimana regime.

GOMN

The Groupement des Observatuers Militaires Neutres was the OAU Neutral Military Group set up in 1993 to observe the cease-fire signed between the RPF and the Rwandan government

Habyarimana, Juvénal (1937–1994)

An original member of the Committee of Nine who was made head of the Ministry of the National Guard and Police in 1965, Habyarimana became president of Rwanda through a coup on July 5, 1973, on the basis of a new constitution centralizing power in the presidency and legalizing only his own MRND party. He was elected president on December 24, 1978, beginning a succession of five-year terms that ended when his airplane was shot down on April 6, 1994.

ICTR

The International Court Tribunal for Rwanda was formed in Arusha, Tanzania, for trying the perpetrators of genocide in Rwanda.

Interahamwe

Interahamwe ("those who attack together") was the militia of the MRND Party.

Inyenzi

This term means "cockroaches," the derogatory name for the Tutsi refugees who took up arms against the Hutu government, first in the early 1960s; it was later used to depict the RPF fighters.

Kagame, Paul (Born 1957)

President of Rwanda, Kagame was a Tutsi refugee raised in Uganda who fought with Museveni's guerrillas, becoming head of military intelligence for the Uganda National Revolutionary Army (NRA) when Museveni became president of Uganda. Kagame enrolled in the U.S. General Staff College in Leavenworth, Kansas, at the time of the October 1990 invasion; he became head of the RPF when both Fred Rwigyema and Chris Bunyenyezi, RPF commanders, were killed in October 1990.

Kayibanda, Grégoire (1924–1976)

Founder of the Mouvement Social Mahutu, Kayibanda was editor in chief of the Catholic newspaper *Kinyameteka* that, in 1956, documented Tutsi abuses. He was an original member of the Committee of Nine, leader of Parmehutu, and Rwanda's first president until overthrown by Habyarimana in 1973. Kayibanda died in prison.

MDR

Mouvement démocratique républicain, the Democratic Republican Movement, was founded in 1991 as the successor to Grégoire Kayibanda's MDR-Parmehutu. Under Faustin Rucogoza, the MDR became the main opposition party to the Habyarimana regime.

MRND

The Mouvement Révolutionnaire National pour le Développement, National Revolutionary Movement for Development, President Habyarimana's party, was founded in 1975; it became the MRNDD in 1991.

MRNDD (formerly MRND)

Mouvement Révolutionnaire National pour le Développement et la Démocratie was the new name given the MRND in July 1991.

Ntaryamira, Cyprien (1965–1994)

Ntaryamira was the first Hutu elected president of Burundi. He was killed in an airplane crash with President Habyarimana on April 6, 1994.

Parmehutu

Parti du Mouvement de l'Emancipation de Bahutu, Parmehutu, was the party of Grégoire Kayibanda, the first president of independent Rwanda.

RPA

Rwandan Patriotic Army, the RPA, was the army of the RPF.

RPF

Rwandan Patriotic Front, the RPF, was the political arm of the RPA, and the dominant coalition partner after the RPF victory in 1994.

RTLM, or RTLMC

Radio-Télévision Libre des Mille Collines ("One Thousand Hills Free Radio") was the private radio station of the extremists, founded in mid 1993. It broadcast hate propaganda against the Arusha Accords and Tutsis.

Rudahigwa, Mutara III (1913–1959)

Rudahigwa, king of Rwanda, died mysteriously in Burundi in July of 1959. His death triggered the Tutsi attempt at independence and the Belgian-backed revolt of the Hutu in November against the Tutsi and the new Tutsi king: Kigeri V.

Rwigyema, Fred Gisa (1957–1990)

Rwigyema fought in Museveni's Ugandan rebel movement and was appointed deputy army commander and deputy minister of defense when Museveni took power. He became head of the RPF and leader of the October 1, 1990, RPF invasion; he was killed on October 2, 1990.

Sindikubwabo, Théodore (Born 1928)

Member of the MRND(D), coming unusually from Butare, speaker of the assembly in the previous coalition government, and acting president of the genocidal government of Rwanda from April 9 to July 19, 1994, Sindikubwabo personally instigated the genocide in Butare after replacing Jean-Baptiste Habyarimana as préfet with Sylvain Ndikumania on April 20, 1994.

UNAMIR

The United Nations Assistance Mission to Rwanda was a UN peacekeeping mission launched in October 1993 as part of the Arusha Accords.

Uwilingiyimana, Agatha (1953–1994)

Agatha Uwilingiyimana was a Hutu, a member of the MDR, minister of education in the first genuine coalition government, in April 1992, and vice president and prime minister of Rwanda in the July 17, 1993, cabinet, which was authorized to sign a peace agreement. Along with members of her family (excepting her five children, who were flown out on a French airplane), she was murdered on April 7, 1994.

Howard Adelman

See Also Colonialism, Anti-Colonialism and Neo-Colonialism; Congo Revolution; Documentaries of Revolution; Ethnic and

Racial Conflict: From Bargaining to Violence; Human Rights, Morality, Social Justice, and Revolution; Terrorism

References and Further Readings

Adelman, Howard, and Astri Suhrke, eds. 1999. *The Path of a Genocide: The Rwanda Crisis from Uganda to Zaire.* Rutgers, NJ: Transaction.

Barnett, Michael. 2002. *Eyewitness to a Genocide: The United Nations and Rwanda.* Ithaca, NY: Cornell University Press.

Carlsson, Ingvar, Han Sung-Joo, and Rufus M. Kupolati. 1999. *Report of the Independent Inquiry into the Actions of the UN during the 1994 Genocide in Rwanda* [December 15]. New York: United Nations.

Carnegie Commission on Preventing Deadly Conflict. 1997. *Preventing Deadly Conflict: Executive Summary of the Final Report.* New York: Carnegie Corporation of New York.

Dallaire, Roméo. 2003. *Shake Hands with the Devil.* Toronto: Random House Canada.

Des Forges, Alison. 1999. *Leave None to Tell the Story: Genocide in Rwanda.* New York: Human Rights Watch.

Joint Evaluation of Emergency Assistance to Rwanda (JEEAR). 1996. *The International Response to Conflict and Genocide: Lessons from the Rwanda Experience.* 5 vols. Copenhagen: DANIDA.

Jones, Bruce. 2001. *Peacemaking in Rwanda: The Dynamics of Failure.* Boulder, CO: Lynne Rienner.

Mamdani, Mahmood. 2001. *When Victims Become Killers: Colonialism, Nativism, and the Genocide in Rwanda.* Princeton, NJ: Princeton University Press.

Newbury, Catherine. 1988. *The Cohesion of Oppression: Clientship and Ethnicity in Rwanda, 1860–1960.* New York: Columbia University Press.

Otunnu, Ogenga. 1999. "An Historical Analysis of the Invasion by the Rwanda Patriotic Army (RPA)." Pp. 31–49 in *The Path of a Genocide: The Rwanda Crisis from Uganda to Zaire,* edited by Howard Adelman and Astri Suhrke. Rutgers, NJ: Transaction.

Prunier, Gérard. 1995. *The Rwandese Crisis (1959–1994): From Cultural Mythology to Genocide.* New York: Columbia University Press.

UN Commission on Human Rights. 1994. "Report on the Situation of Human Rights in Rwanda." R. Deqni-Séqui, Special Rapporteur of the Commission on Human Rights. May 25. New York: United Nations.

S

Salvadoran Revolution

CHRONOLOGY

1528   El Salvador is conquered by the Spanish.

1821   El Salvador attains independence from Spain.

1832   Failed peasant revolt led by Anastacio Aquino.

1881–1882   Laws are passed that privatize municipal land and land held by indigenous and ladino communities.

1931   Arturo Araujo wins democratic election in January; the military overthrows Araujo in December and replaces him with the vice president, General Maximiliano Hernández Martínez.

1932   A failed peasant rebellion is followed by the massacre of up to 30,000 people; Hernández captures and executes Agustín Farabundo Martí. Thus begins forty-six years of military rule.

1944   Hernández is ousted in a military coup, but the cycle of military rule continues.

1961   The Central American Common Market is created.

1969   El Salvador invades Honduras in what is widely (and erroneously) interpreted as a "Soccer War." Honduras expels more than 100,000 Salvadorans and closes its borders.

1970   The Popular Forces of Liberation, El Salvador's first armed guerrilla group, is formed.

1972   Colonel Arturo Molina becomes president following election fraud against José Napoleón Duarte of the National Opposition Union.

1975   The Salvadoran government spends $30 million to host the Miss Universe pageant. National Guard troops fire on a student protest in downtown San Salvador, killing thirty-seven people.

        Father Rutilio Grande is assassinated.

1976   President Molina decrees a moderate land reform in the departments of San Miguel and Usulután but pulls back in the wake of threats and a negative advertising campaign by the private sector.

1977–1979   The country is wracked by a spiral of protests, demonstrations, disappearances, death squad murders, and small-scale guerrilla actions.

1979   A group of young, progressive officers carries out a successful coup d'état known as the Young Officers' Coup against the government of General Humberto Romero.

1980   On March 24, Archbishop Oscar Arnulfo Romero is assassinated while saying Mass. Rebel political-military groups join forces to form the Farabundo Martí Front for National Liberation (FMLN) in October.

1981   On January 1, 1981, the FMLN carries out its first "Final Offensive," which, though unsuccessful, establishes it as a serious military force. Military and death squad repression in urban areas becomes so severe in the wake of the offensive that rebel groups redeploy to the countryside in northern Morazán, Chalatenango, and elsewhere.

In December the Salvadoran army's Atlacatl Battalion, trained by the United States, massacres more than 1,000 civilians in the vicinity of El Mozote in Morazán Province. More than 12,000 civilians are murdered during the year, mostly by government military and security forces.

1982   The United States sponsors the election of a Constituent Assembly in order to create the fiction of an elected government caught between the "extreme right" (death squads and oligarchs) and the "extreme left" (FMLN guerrillas and their supporters).

1982–1983   FMLN fighters clear their base areas of government military and security force detachments, establish training camps, and inflict important defeats on the poorly trained and poorly led Salvadoran army.

1984   In the midst of a civil war, Napoleón Duarte of the Christian Democratic Party is elected president of El Salvador in what some observers call "demonstration elections" (Herman and Broadhead 1984, 5). His election corresponds with a shift in government mili-

tary strategy toward the use of air power, rapid troop deployment, and civic action programs to "win the hearts and minds of the civilian population."

1985–1986   The guerrillas respond to the U.S.–imposed strategy by breaking up into small units and dispersing their troops to conduct small hit-and-run actions throughout the country.

1987   Five Central American presidents sign the Central American Peace Plan in San José, Costa Rica. The plan contributes to a political opening in urban areas and leads to the return of civilians linked to the FMLN and their participation in national elections in 1989.

1989   In March, Alfredo Cristiani of the Nationalist Republican Alliance (ARENA) wins the presidency.

On November 11, the Farabundo Martí Front for National Liberation carries out a "Final Offensive," invading the capital city of San Salvador and other cities. Air force bombing of working class neighborhoods eventually forces them to retreat, but not before FMLN combatants occupy the wealthy Escalón neighborhood and take over the Sheraton Hotel.

On November 16, during the height of the assault, the Salvadoran High Command sends a unit of the Atlacatl Battalion to the campus of the Central American University, where they murder Ignacio Ellacuría, Segundo Montes, and four other priests; they kill the priests' housekeeper and her daughter as well.

1992   On January 16, the Salvadoran government and representatives of the FMLN sign peace accords in Chapultepec Castle in Mexico City, bringing the civil war to an end. Under the auspices of the United Nations Observer Mission (ONUSAL), a phased demobilization of FMLN combatants ensues over the course of the year.

1993   On March 15, the United Nations' Truth Commission releases its report on wartime human rights violations, attributing 95 percent to the Salvadoran military and security forces (85 percent) or death squads linked to them (10 percent), and the remaining 5 percent to the FMLN. Three days later, President Alfredo Cristiani moves a blanket amnesty law through the ARENA-dominated legislature.

1994   In March, the first general elections, widely known as the "elections of the century" take place, with the FMLN supporting Rubén Zamora of the Democratic Convergence. Zamora loses in a run-off to Armando Calderón Sol of the ARENA Party, but the FMLN wins sixteen municipalities and seven seats in El Salvador's unicameral legislature.

1995   El Salvador's crime rate reaches a historic high. Statisticians register more homicide deaths except for the worst years of the civil war.

2006   In the election for national legislature's eighty-four seats, the FMLN wins approximately forty percent of the popular vote and thirty-two seats. The FMLN also wins the mayoral race in the capitol, San Salvador.

INTRODUCTION

The Salvadoran Revolution, which lasted roughly from 1980 to 1992, ended in peace accords following several years of negotiations between the Salvadoran government and the Farabundo Martí National Liberation Front (FMLN). The accords ended decades of military domination and established electoral democracy in El Salvador, though they had little effect on wealth or income distribution.

BACKGROUND: CULTURE AND HISTORY

In 1980 El Salvador was a small but densely populated country, packing 4.4 million people into an area about the size of Massachusetts. Over 550 persons per square mile and no remote, unpopulated hinterland made El Salvador an unlikely candidate for a guerrilla war. A brief examination of its history will help explain the conditions that led to civil war, as well as how the "people became the mountains" for rebels seeking to overthrow the government.

Prior to the Spanish conquest, El Salvador lay on the periphery of the great Mesoamerican civilizations. The Spanish arrived in 1524 and established a permanent settlement four years later. However, El Salvador lacked important deposits of precious minerals and attracted few Spanish settlers; for that reason, its economy became largely dependent on agriculture. Over the course of almost five centuries one export crop followed another, as boom gave way to bust, followed by the search for a profitable substitute. Cacao peaked in 1570 and was in full decline by 1610. Indigo, the source of a deep-blue dye popular in English and U.S. textile industries, proved profitable from 1700 to 1850, at which point Asian competition and then the development of aniline dyes sent it spiraling into decline.

Then came coffee, which proved particularly disruptive of land tenure and rural labor relations. Some analysts view the coffee economy, which grew rapidly between 1850 and 1920, as an antecedent cause of the civil war. El Salvador's coffee-growing areas are located above 750 meters on the flanks of the volcanoes, a few miles inland from the narrow coastal plain. In order to gain control of them, El Salvador's small, post-colonial elite—which controlled both economic and political affairs—created laws in the early 1880s to force the breakup and sale of community-held lands. Displaced peasants either relocated to unsettled areas or became integrated into a low-wage coffee-plantation labor force. The area planted in coffee grew from 42,000 hectares in 1901 to 97,000 hectares in 1932 (Lauria-Santiago 1999, 134); by the late 1920s, coffee accounted for more than 90 percent of Salvadoran exports (Montgomery 1982, 46).

The Great Depression of 1929–1932 exposed the weakness of this one-crop, export-oriented system. International demand collapsed, and coffee prices plummeted. In order to protect their investments, plantation owners dismissed workers and sliced the wages of those who remained. This economic crisis unfolded precisely at a moment of democratic opening that challenged the historic control of a few elite families. In 1931, the progressive Arturo Araujo was elected president in El Salvador's first democratic election.

The same period saw the development and radicalization of labor unions such as the Regional Federation of Salvadoran Workers, led by Agustín Farabundo Martí, a Marxist and founder of the Salvadoran Communist Party whom the government expelled on several occasions for his political activities. Araujo was deposed in a military coup in December of 1931 and replaced by the vice president, General Maximiliano Hernández Martínez. When the Hernández administration prevented likely Communist victories in January 1932 legislative and municipal elections, Martí planned an uprising. However, General Hernández arrested the leader, Martí, and quickly quashed the rebellion. He followed the military victory with a generalized massacre of between 10,000 and

30,000 indigenous and mestizo peasants, mainly in the western provinces of Sonsonate and Ahuachapán. El Salvador then devolved into a thoroughgoing police state that would be administered by the military for the next forty-six years. In what has been described as a "protection racket state" (Stanley 1996, 6–7), senior military officers occupying government positions benefited from corruption and kickback schemes, and employed the army and security forces to ensure the labor peace demanded by the oligarchy.

Hernández himself established a dictatorship that lasted until 1944, after which he was replaced by a series of generals until the formal restoration of civilian control in 1979. Social tensions in rural areas were kept in check by the National Guard and the Treasury Police as well as (from the 1960s) a broad network of civilian informants organized through the National Democratic Organization (ORDEN). The National Police patrolled the cities. All of these forces were led by officers trained at the General Gerardo Barrios Military School. After 1960, most officers also received courses in counterinsurgency at the Panama-based U.S. School of the Americas, where they internalized a simplistic anti-Communism that attributed every domestic social movement, protest, or demand for change as evidence of a Communist plot originating in Moscow and/or, after the 1959 Cuban Revolution, Havana.

Following the end of the Second World War, the agrarian economy diversified into sugarcane, cotton, and cattle, the last two stimulated by expanding international markets. However, the principal beneficiaries remained the same families that controlled coffee production, processing, and sale. Rather than improving the lot of the average rural dweller, agrarian diversification probably undermined it further by commercially developing South Coast areas of the Usulután and San Miguel departments that had previously served as a refuge for dispossessed peasants fleeing the coffee zones.

Many people also flocked to the cities, and some became incorporated into a small industrial sector, the growth of which benefited from the creation of the Central American Common Market in 1961. An even larger number of Salvadorans left the country in order to work in Honduran banana plantations. But that safety valve, too, disappeared with the outbreak of the four-day "Soccer War" in 1969. Although the war was publicly attributed to a dispute over the results of a World Cup soccer elimination series, it is better understood in terms of economic disequilibria between the two countries generated in part by El Salvador's advantageous trade position within the regional common market. El Salvador won the brief war, but Honduras closed its borders and expelled an estimated 100,000 Salvadorans, whose return aggravated economic pressures and social tensions. By 1975, some 40 percent of the rural population was landless, up from 11.8 percent in 1961 and 29.1 percent in 1971

(Montgomery 1982, 80). At that point, El Salvador exhibited one of the most unequal concentrations of land and income in Latin America.

The first armed leftist guerrilla group, called the Popular Forces of Liberation, formed in 1970, splitting off from the electorally minded Salvadoran Communist Party. After recovering from the failed 1932 rebellion, the small, clandestine Salvadoran Communist Party had adopted the Moscow "stage theory" of social and political evolution, which maintained that only a fully developed industrial capitalism could eliminate the "backward relationships" of agrarian semifeudalism and pave the way for Socialism. However, Castro's successful overthrow of the Batista dictatorship in Cuba in 1959 generated debate over the official party line. During the remainder of the 1970s, three additional revolutionary political-military organizations formed, all with historic links to the Salvadoran Communist Party: the Peoples Revolutionary Army (1972), the National Resistance (1975), and the Central American Workers Party (1976).

Small and relatively ineffective at first, the revolutionary Left benefited over the decade from combined economic, political, and ideological developments that inclined growing numbers of people toward armed rebellion. The possibility for a political resolution faded when José Napoleón Duarte, a reformer and popular Christian Democratic Party mayor of San Salvador, ran for and apparently won the 1972 presidential elections, only to have his victory stolen and his supporters' protest violently repressed by the army. Efforts to address growing landlessness in 1976 were snuffed out when the oligarchy mobilized against the government's effort to expropriate and redistribute underused cotton and ranch land in the South Coast region.

Finally, Vatican II (1962–1965) and the 1968 Latin American Bishop's Conference at Medellín, Colombia, moved a few bishops and many priests to take up a "Preferential Option for the Poor." Beginning in the late 1960s—and increasingly during the first half of the 1970s—many priests organized Christian base communities and trained lay catechists (peasants or workers) to interpret the Bible in the context of local realities. Although its founders envisioned Liberation Theology as a self-dignifying, self-help ideology, it was inevitable that its social and historical analysis of poverty—influenced in part by Marxist sociology—would incline many Catholics to join popular movements for change, particularly when self-help efforts proved insufficient to remedy the grave social and economic problems they confronted.

The march toward civil war and revolution might have been averted at various points during the 1970s but for (1) the vehement opposition of the small, closely related oligarchy to any suggestions of land or wealth redistribution and (2) the readiness of the anti-Communist military that ruled on the oligarchy's behalf to imprison, torture, and "disappear" individuals and groups speaking in favor of or attempting to bring about change. In addition, both oligarchy and military remained haunted by the memories of 1932, when machete-wielding indigenous peasants temporarily seized several towns in the Izalco region before being routed by army forces. Electoral fraud, resistance to land reform, and repression of the Catholic Church, student organizations, unions, and other groups convinced growing numbers of increasingly politically conscious Salvadorans of the need for structural change and the impossibility of bringing it about under the system set in place in 1932.

CONTEXT AND PROCESS OF REVOLUTION

The government began to lose control of the situation beginning in 1977, with the fraudulent election of General Humberto Romero. Military and security forces met mass protests, strikes, and demonstrations with open repression; death squads linked to the government security apparatus and often controlled by Major Roberto D'Aubuissón stalked unionists, teachers, students, and others. The progressive church, blamed by the Romero military government for having implanted Communist ideas through the teachings of Liberation Theology, was also targeted, beginning with the murder of Father Rutilio Grande in 1975. Small guerrilla units—the germs of the future FMLN army—carried out kidnappings, bank robberies, and assaults on police and security force targets in major cities and countryside. Unions, student organizations, peasant organizations, and other groups grew in size and political sophistication, and coalesced into a series of "popular blocs" linked to one of the five rebel political-military organizations. They demanded an end to the repression of the military government.

In October 1979, with the country on the brink of revolution, young, progressive, mostly junior-grade military officers seized control in an almost bloodless coup. They formed a five-person civilian-military junta as part of a transition government but were outmaneuvered by older, conservative, politically savvy superiors linked to the oligarchy. Despite promises of change, repression intensified. The junta underwent several metamorphoses, as civilians and progressive officers resigned or were forced out, eventually leaving conservative officers and a group of Christian Democrats, among them José Napoleón Duarte, who had returned from exile. On March 24, 1980, an assassin murdered Archbishop Oscar Arnulfo Romero—widely regarded as a spokesperson for the poor ("the voice of those who have no voice")—as he said Mass, and the possibility of compromise or a negotiated so-

In the spring of 1980 Archbishop Romero, leader of the Catholic Church in El Salvador, called on the government of the United States to stop sending weapons to the El Salvadoran army because of the army's human rights abuses, and he called on El Salvadoran soldiers to disobey orders to kill unarmed people. Shortly afterward he was assassinated, apparently by right-wing conservative extremists. (AFP/Getty Images)

lution became remote indeed. In October of that year, the anti-government political-military organizations joined together and formed the FMLN. A state-sponsored land reform carried out in the midst of repression, as well as the nationalization of banks and coffee exports, failed to halt either the drive toward unity or the growth and radicalization of the opposition movement.

In January of 1981 the FMLN carried out coordinated attacks in major cities with the aim of sparking a mass insurrection and toppling the government in order to present the incoming U.S. president, Ronald Reagan, with a fait accompli and to replicate the recent (1979) Sandinista victory in Nicaragua. The offensive established the FMLN's military capacity but stretched thin the resources of a small, inexperienced, and poorly armed and equipped guerrilla army. With urban repression mounting, the FMLN retreated to rural areas, weathered a series of army incursions (accompanied by numerous large-scale massacres of civilians), and recuperated its strength. The military's slaughter of civilians backfired when surviving family members flocked to join the FMLN. The rebels cleared northern Morazán, eastern Chalatenango, and other areas of small, preexisting National Guard and Treasury Police posts, established training bases, and rearmed with fresh weaponry smuggled into El Salvador from Nicaragua. By mid 1982, the guerrilla army was inflicting serious defeats on a demoralized Salvadoran military run by corrupt officers and staffed mainly with forced recruits.

Beginning in late 1983, the U.S. government successfully imposed a major military reorganization on its ally as a condition for further military assistance. The United States trained and advised the Salvadoran army in the tactics of "low intensity" warfare based on enhanced use of air power and lightening-quick air mobile strikes. The government cordoned off guerrilla "controlled zones" to wreak hardships on civilians remaining in them, and government troops made more selective use of repression and carried out propaganda campaigns to "win the hearts and minds" of the civilian population that provided FMLN forces with food, information, a recruitment base, and logistical assistance. U.S. military and economic assistance financed this project with up to $1 million daily in the mid 1980s, $6 billion during the course of the war (Schwartz 1991, 2–3). In 1984 the Reagan administration "sold" the policy to Congress by promoting democracy in the midst of war via elections (boycotted by the FMLN), won by José Napoleón Duarte of the Christian Democratic Party. However, all contending political parties represented either historical parties of the Right, the most conservative faction of the Christian Democrats, or the "new right" ARENA Party.

The FMLN countered the U.S. strategy by breaking up large units vulnerable to air attack and air mobile assault into small, self-contained ones, and expanded the war to previously peaceful provinces. They employed sharpshooters, hit-and-run operations, and ambushes, and they set mines and booby traps for invading forces. The FMLN also made the decision to raise the economic costs for the capitalist class by burning coffee crops, downing electric pylons, and extracting taxes from landowners where possible. A network of urban commandos harassed military and police forces in the cities. Periodically the rebels demonstrated their military capability by massing dispersed forces in order to attack, and occasionally overrun, military bases. Not only did these spectacular operations contradict Salvadoran and U.S. government claims that the military was winning the war, but they also demonstrated the depth of FMLN intelligence information about the Salvadoran army, without which such precision operations could not have succeeded.

The FMLN proved that it, too, could utilize what was widely viewed as the democratic façade designed and put in place by the United States. With rebel assistance and political advice, civilian supporters in rebel-controlled areas and elsewhere protested continuing human rights abuses. From 1986 on, displaced persons and refugees—many sympathetic to the FMLN—demanded the right to return to and live peacefully in their "places of origin," even when these were located in contested zones or those controlled on a day-to-day basis by the FMLN.

The last five years of the war (1987–1992) unfolded with few major changes, in what has often been referred to as a strategic stalemate. Despite having increased its numbers six-fold, to an estimated 60,000 troops; having modernized its equipment and improved its training, and raised the level of professionalization of the officers' corps—all under U.S. tutelage—the Salvadoran military was unable to defeat the FMLN. But neither could the FMLN, despite the successes it enjoyed, overthrow the Salvadoran government, which benefited from a seemingly endless stream of U.S. economic and military assistance. The last concerted effort on the part of the FMLN to do so failed, and yet, ironically, played a key role in the peace negotiations that ended the armed conflict.

On November 11, 1989, the FMLN put its troops, including reserves, on the line in a series of all-out surprise assaults on the major cities. The guerrillas occupied large areas of San Salvador for several days, placing the army on the defensive; they began to withdraw only when the Salvadoran High Command called on the air force to bomb the working class districts in which the rebels had entrenched themselves. Following this second "Final Offensive"—in which an estimated 500 FMLN were killed—many rebel troops became demoralized, abandoned the struggle, and returned home or left the country. However, the Salvadoran High Command erred by ordering the wanton murder of six Jesuit priests (as well as their housekeeper and daughter) working at the Jesuit Central American University in the midst of the offensive; among them was Ignacio Ellacuría, the university's rector and a world-renowned intellectual.

The murder of the Jesuits threatened further U.S. aid. Their assassination, along with the end of the Cold War, a decline in rebel military strength (which contributed to the FMLN leadership's embrace of the goal of a multiparty democracy), and the arrival in the White House of the more pragmatic George Bush combined to set peace negotiations on a track that eventually bore fruit on January 16, 1992, when representatives of the five FMLN groups and the government of Alfredo Cristiani signed Peace Accords at Chapultepec Castle in Mexico City.

The Salvadoran Revolution is often referred to as a "class-based" revolution because it set rich against poor with few crosscutting ethnic or religious ties to complicate matters, as occurred in Guatemala, Peru, and elsewhere. As in virtually all post-colonial Third World revolutions, though, the majority of the population remained neutral. The Salvadoran government, and particularly the military institution, systematically referred to the rebels as "terrorists" and "delinquents," and refused to entertain criticisms of the oligarchy or the government that ruled on its behalf. Early in the war the military and military-linked death squads suppressed newspapers and radio stations that did not follow the official line. Almost until the end they maintained a monopoly on the mass media. The guerrillas fought back through their own propaganda, graffiti, and broadcasts on two clandestine radio stations: Radio Venceremos (We will Win) and Radio Farabundo Martí. The guerrillas also solidified links with supporters in both Europe and the United States. They raised money for the guerrilla cause and attempted to counter the official U.S. anti-Communist justification for intervention by pointing to the long history of poverty, exclusion, and repression that underpinned military rule and the coffee economy, and emphasizing the home-ground nature of the Salvadoran Left. Musical groups in guerrilla-controlled areas and outside El Salvador, documentary films created by independent filmmakers as well as an FMLN collective, and a plethora of testimonial books were also used by FMLN spokespersons and their international supporters to counter the material advantages of domestic and international opponents.

IMPACTS

The civil war has had an enduring effect on all aspects of Salvadoran society. Most significantly, it reduced the power of the agrarian bourgeoisie and cleared the way for the ascendancy of the transnational businessmen within the Salvadoran capitalist class, supported by the United States and oriented toward finance and export markets. Arguably, this process began in the mid 1980s with the structural adjustment policies put into place during the Christian Democratic administration of José Napoleón Duarte, but it picked up steam with the ascent of the more conservative ARENA Party in 1989 and became consolidated in the post-conflict period during two successive ARENA administrations (1994–1999, 1999–2004). While neo-liberal transnational economic policy has gained dominance throughout Latin America, perhaps nowhere—with the possible exception of Chile—has it attained the breadth and depth it manifests in El Salvador, which offers one of Latin America's most "business friendly" environments. The FMLN did not intend this to happen, but it has undeniably been one of the consequences of the war.

The 1992 Peace Accords focused mainly on issues of public security, human rights, and electoral politics. Because the ARENA government refused to negotiate on tax policy or wealth distribution, the accords hardly touched the unequal economic relations that were a principal cause of the armed conflict. They did contemplate land distribution to former soldiers, FMLN guerrillas, and their supporters as a means of providing some demobilized combatants and politically organized civilians with a stake in the post-war system. Together, the 1980 land reform, designed by the United States to derail the revolutionary movement, and the post-war land distribution mandated in the Peace Accords to reintegrate former guerrillas and government soldiers back into civilian life redistributed 25.5 percent of all agricultural lands, affecting 23.6 percent of the rural population, roughly half the households engaged in agriculture (McReynolds 2002, 150). However, the market-oriented reforms promoted under the neo-liberal model deprived most land recipients of access to credit and technical assistance, and opened the gates to a flood of cheap food imports that drove down domestic food prices, in some cases below the cost of production.

The war generated a mass exodus of political and economic refugees to the United States and elsewhere, and wartime migrants served as beachheads for continuing migration in the post-war period. A significant proportion of native-born Salvadorans currently live and work in the United States. In 2001 they remitted about $1.92 billion to El Salvador, equal to 17 percent of gross national product (Lungo 2002, 874). Some researchers argue that international migration has become a constituent element of the dominant economic model. In the context of a chronic balance-of-payments deficit, the ability to import foreign goods depends on the continued "export" of Salvadoran workers, who then make possible the "import" of remittance dollars used to purchase machinery, food, and consumer goods on the international market.

War-induced migration has been a double-edged sword. Returning migrants—some expelled by the U.S. government—also "remitted" U.S.-style youth gangs and gang culture to El Salvador, and these have proliferated in both rural and urban areas. Gang youth and (more seriously) organized criminal mafias, the latter often composed of former soldiers and/or guerrillas, obtain easy access to military weaponry left over from the war. Poverty and alienation combined with guns and grenades resulted in more annual homicide deaths (upwards of 7,000) during the mid 1990s than occurred in all but the worst years of the armed conflict (Call 2003, 841). Youth gangs probably account for no more than a small percentage of the homicide deaths, but they offer citizens a concrete target on which to focus vague fears of post-war loss of social and economic control tied in part to the country's rapid globalization. The government, aided by the news media's inclination toward the spectacular and the macabre, reinforces public apprehension of youth crime as a means of tightening the law and increasing the public security budget—policies that may undermine some of the advances that followed the peace accords.

On a more positive note, the peace accords reduced the size of the army and removed it from internal policing functions, except in extraordinary circumstances. The accords abolished the repressive security forces, replacing them with a civilian-controlled National Civilian Police. FMLN guerrillas demobilized, turning their weapons over to the United Nations Observers Mission (ONUSAL), and formed a political party that has become the nation's number two political force. While the FMLN has failed to win either the presidency or outright control of the unicameral legislature, it made steady gains at the polls and in 2006 held thirty-two of eighty-four seats, as well as the mayoralties of San Salvador and most other large cities. In order to gain votes the FMLN has had to moderate its political line, one result of which has been an increase in internal conflicts and divisions.

The civil war also helped alter the religious contours of El Salvador, since many Catholics treated conversion to evangelical Protestantism as a "life insurance policy" against military and security force repression. Evangelical Protestantism continued to increase after the war in the context of social and economic displacements. Responding to Protestant gains, domestic political pressures, and changing Vatican policy, the post-war Catholic Church moved away from Liberation Theology.

Other war-related transformations include a tremendous increase in the number and importance of both national and international nongovernmental organizations (NGOs) in the society, as well as the rise of a vibrant women's movement. Many post-war women's organizations began as FMLN appendages controlled by male commanders but distanced themselves from the FMLN as former female fighters and activists used the post-war political space to criticize FMLN policies and practices pertaining to women.

Few people in El Salvador escaped unaffected from the twenty-year cycle of government repression and civil war. Thousands of survivors were scarred permanently as a result of their experiences, yet few resources have been made available to help the war wounded (amputees, blind people, etc.) or those mentally disabled by more than a dozen years of warfare and government repression (combat veterans, family members of the murdered and disappeared, etc.). Despite Cristiani's 1993 Amnesty Law and his admonition that Salvadorans put the past behind them in order to focus on the present and future, the struggle for historical memory continues in politics, within the Catholic Church, in homes, and on the street. In the absence of a clear victory by either side, and in the wake of a "negotiated revolution" that left most people economically worse off than before the conflict, Salvadorans will continue to debate the whys and wherefores of the civil war, the lessons to be drawn from it, and the responsibilities that should be assumed by the different participants.

PEOPLE AND ORGANIZATIONS

Atlacatl Battalion

The battalion was one of five rapid-response battalions trained by U.S. Special Forces at the beginning of the 1980s. Among Salvadoran military units, the Atlacatl became particularly well known for committing spectacular, large-scale human rights abuses. In December 1981, the Atlacatl massacred at least 1,000 people in the vicinity of El Mozote, Morazán, and on November 16, 1989, an Atlacatl unit killed six Jesuits and their housekeeper and daughter at the Central American University. The battalion was demobilized in 1992 as part of the Peace Accords.

Christian Democratic Party

The Christian Democratic Party was founded in 1960 as an alternative to both right (military) and left (Communist) organizations. The party won the presidency in 1984, but widespread accusations of corruption set the stage for its defeat at the hands of the conservative Nationalist Republican Alliance in 1989. The party was wracked by a series of internal divisions and splits after the war and has never recovered its former stature.

Cristiani Burkard, Alfredo Felix (Born 1943)

Alfredo Cristiani was born into a family of wealthy coffee growers. He obtained a business administration degree from Georgetown University and devoted himself to business until he entered politics in the 1980s. He rapidly ascended within the ARENA Party, which was attempting to project a more moderate public image and reduce its association with death-squad organizer and party founder Roberto D'Aubuissón. The quiet-spoken Cristiani won the presidency in 1989 and presided over the peace process and the first years of reconstruction. But he also promoted a neo-liberal economic model through privatization, a regressive tax policy, and open markets.

D'Aubuissón Arrierta, Roberto (1943–1992)

D'Aubuissón served as a major in the Salvadoran intelligence service until he was removed following accusations of involvement in planning a coup in 1979. He combined his intelligence capability with money and other forms of material assistance provided by wealthy, conservative Salvadorans to organize and direct death squads during the 1980s. In 1981 he founded the Nationalist Republican Alliance as a political vehicle for his conservative ideas. In 1982 he served as president of the Constituent Assembly and two years later ran for president, unsuccessfully, against the U.S.-backed José Napoleón Duarte. In the late 1980s ARENA attempted to moderate its image in order to broaden its following, and D'Aubuisson took a back seat to Alfredo Cristiani and others. He is widely believed to have planned the March 24, 1980, assassination of Archbishop Oscar Romero.

Duarte, José Napoleón (1925–1990)

Duarte was a civil engineer (B.S. Notre Dame, 1948) and one of the founders of the Christian Democratic Party. He served two very successful terms as elected mayor of San Salvador during the 1960s and ran for the presidency in 1972. However, the military denied his numerical victory, and Duarte was sent into exile. He returned in 1980 and served two years as interim president at the behest of the legislature, with the backing of the United States. In 1984 Duarte won the presidency in a runoff election against Roberto D'Aubuisson, but his implementation of austerity measures and his failure to end the war, along with widespread accusations of corruption among members of his administration, set the stage for the victory of the Nationalist Republican Alliance in 1989. He died of stomach cancer in 1990.

Ellacuría, Ignacio (1930–1989)

A Spanish Jesuit priest who arrived in El Salvador in 1949, Ellacuría became perhaps that nation's foremost intellectual, the author of numerous books and articles, and a key proponent of Liberation Theology and the "Preferential Option for the Poor." During the civil war Ellacuría served as rector of the Jesuit Central American University. He and other Jesuits remained steadfast in their quest for a peaceful solution to the conflict but were also staunch critics of the Salvadoran government. Ellacuría was murdered in the early morning hours of November 16, 1989, by members of the Salvadoran Atlacatl Battalion.

Farabundo Martí Front for National Liberation (FMLN)

The FMLN was formed in 1980 out of the Communist Party, Popular Liberation Forces, Peoples Revolutionary Army, National Resistance, and the Central American Workers Party, the last four having split from the Salvadoran Communist Party at some point during the 1970s. During the civil war,

the FMLN retained its unity despite internal frictions and differences of opinion among the component groups. Following the 1992 Peace Accords, the FMLN metamorphosed into a political party, but two years later the Peoples Revolutionary Army and the National Resistance withdrew to form the Democratic Party. During the ensuing years the FMLN has enjoyed substantial electoral success in the legislature and the major cities, despite internal conflicts between "orthodox" and "renewal" wings.

Hernández Martínez, Maximiliano (1882–1966)

Hernández was a general in the Salvadoran military and became vice president to President Arturo Araujo following the January 1931 election. When Araujo was overthrown in a coup d'état in December, Hernández took his place. He successfully put down a peasant uprising called by the Salvadoran Communist Party and ordered a massacre that led to between 10,000 and 30,000 deaths, mostly in largely indigenous areas of western El Salvador. Hernández then installed himself as dictator and ruled the country until he was ousted in 1944.

Martí, Agustín Farabundo (1893–1932)

Martí was a radical law student from a well-to-do landowning family. Jailed and exiled on several occasions, he traveled throughout Central America and Mexico. He participated in the founding of the Guatemalan Communist Party and served as Augusto Cesár Sandino's private secretary during the struggle against the U.S. occupation of Nicaragua. In 1930 Martí founded the Salvadoran Communist Party. In the wake of the 1932 municipal electoral fraud, which deprived various Communist Party candidates of probable victory, Martí plotted to overthrow the government of Maximiliano Hernández Martínez. Martí was arrested prior to the rebellion along with two co-conspirators, and was tried and shot on February 1, 1932.

National Conciliation Party

Formed in 1961, the National Conciliation Party, often known as the "party of the military," was the third (and last) in a line of state parties going back to 1932. It controlled the presidency and legislature until President General Humberto Romero was ousted in October 1979 during the Young Officers' Coup. The party lost power and influence with the rise of the Christian Democrats and the "new Right" ARENA Party, but in recent years has recovered some of its former strength.

Nationalist Republican Alliance (ARENA)

The Nationalist Republican Alliance or ARENA Party is a conservative, right-wing party of wealthy landowners founded by Roberto D'Aubuissón in 1981 to challenge the Christian Democratic Party, at that time supported by the United States government. ARENA won the 1982 Constituent Assembly elections but did not gain control of the government until 1989, with the presidential victory of Alfredo Cristiani. During the post-war period, ARENA has moderated its political perspective. ARENA candidates have won all three post-war presidential elections (1994, 1999, 2004), although the party lost the mayoralties of most of the country's large cities to the FMLN beginning in 2000.

Romero y Galdámez, Oscar Arnulfo (1917–1980)

Archbishop Oscar Arnulfo Romero, known to many Salvadorans as "the voice of those who have no voice," served as archbishop of El Salvador from 1977 until he was assassinated while saying Mass in church on March 24, 1980, by a professional "hit-man," probably sent by Roberto D'Aubuissón. Born in San Miguel in eastern El Salvador, Romero entered the priesthood in the 1940s and rose through the ranks to become bishop of the diocese of Santiago de María (1974–1977). Considered quiet and noncontroversial, Romero was the government and oligarchy's choice for taking over the office of archbishop following the retirement of Archbishop Luis Chávez y González. Once installed in San Salvador, however, Romero proved a champion of the poor and outspoken critic of government human rights violations. His masses were broadcast to all parts of the country on YSAX, the archdiocese's radio station. Romero's fate was probably sealed when, a day before his death, he urged government soldiers to refuse orders to fire on the civilian population.

Truth Commission

The 1992 Peace Accords that ended the civil war mandated the creation of a Truth Commission under United Nations supervision. The commission was composed of three prominent international jurists, one each from Colombia, Venezuela, and the United States. The commission released its report on March 15, 1993, following a nationwide, four-month investigation. It attributed 95 percent of the human rights violations to the military (85 percent) and death squads tied to the military (10 percent), and the remaining 5 percent to the FMLN. The commission named names in the cases of many egregious human rights violations and decreed that the perpetrators be excluded from holding public office for ten years.

United Nations Observer Mission to El Salvador (ONUSAL)

Better known as ONUSAL, the UN Observer's Mission presided over the cease-fire and FMLN demobilization following the 1992 Peace Accords. ONUSAL also monitored compliance with the accords and was charged with the establishment of a Truth Commission to investigate wartime human rights violations.

Leigh Binford

See Also Armed Forces, Revolution, and Counter-Revolution; Cinema of Revolution; Cuban Revolution; Democracy, Dictatorship, and Fascism; Documentaries of Revolution; Guatemalan Democratic Revolution, Counter-Revolution, and Restoration of Democracy; Guerrilla Warfare and Revolution; Human Rights, Morality, Social Justice, and Revolution; Inequality, Class, and Revolution; Music and Revolution; Nicaraguan Revolution; Population, Economic Development, and Revolution; Reform, Rebellion, Civil War, Coup D'état, and Revolution; Student and Youth Movements, Activism and Revolution; Terrorism;Trends in Revolution; Women and Revolution

References and Further Readings
Americas Watch. 1991. *El Salvador's Decade of Terror: Human Rights since the Assassination of Archbishop Romero.* New Haven, CT: Yale University Press.
Anderson, Thomas P. 1992 [1971]. *Matanza.* Willimantic, CT: Curbstone.
Argueta, Manlio. 1983. *One Day of Life.* New York: Aventura.
Baloyra, Enrique. 1982. *El Salvador in Transition.* Chapel Hill: University of North Carolina Press.
Binford, Leigh. 1996. *The El Mozote Massacre: Anthropology and Human Rights.* Tucson: University of Arizona Press.
Bonner, Raymond. 1984. *Weakness and Deceit: U.S. Policy and El Salvador.* New York: Times Books.
Browning, David. 1971. *El Salvador: Landscape and Society.* Oxford: Clarendon Press.
Call, Charles T. 2003. "Democratization, War and State-Building: Constructing the Rule of Law in El Salvador," *Journal of Latin American Studies* 35(4): 827–862.
Dunkerley, James. 1982. *The Long War: Dictatorship and Revolution in El Salvador.* London: Verso.
Hammond, Jack. 1998. *Fighting to Learn: Popular Education and Guerrilla War in El Salvador.* New Brunswick, NJ: Rutgers University Press.
Herman, Edward S., and Frank Broadhead. 1984. *Demonstration Elections: U.S.-Staged Elections in the Dominican Republic, Vietnam, and El Salvador.* Boston: South End.
Lauria-Santiago, Aldo. 1999. *An Agrarian Republic: Commercial Agriculture and the Politics of Peasant Communities in El Salvador, 1823–1914.* Pittsburgh, PA: University of Pittsburgh Press.

Lauria-Santiago, Aldo, and Leigh Binford, eds. 2004. *Landscapes of Struggle: Politics, Society and Community in El Salvador.* Pittsburgh, PA: University of Pittsburgh Press.

Lindo-Fuentes, Hector. 1990. *Weak Foundations: The Economy of El Salvador in the Nineteenth Century.* Berkeley: University of California Press.

Lungo, Mario. 2002. "La política migratoria del actual gobierno. Una revisión crítica," *Estudios Centroamericanos* 648: 873–878.

Macdonald, Mandy, and Mike Gatehouse. 1995. *In the Mountains of Morazan: Portrait of a Returned Refugee Community.* London: Latin America Bureau.

McClintock, Michael. 1986. *The American Connection.* Vol. 1, *State Terror and Popular Resistance in El Salvador.* London: Zed.

McReynolds, Samuel A. 2002. "Land Reform in El Salvador and the Chapultepec Peace Accord," *The Journal of Peasant Studies* 30 (1): 135–169.

Montgomery, Tommie Sue. 1982. *Revolution in El Salvador: Origins and Evolution.* Boulder, CO: Westview.

Pearce, Jenny. 1986. *Promised Land: Peasant Rebellion in Chalatenango El Salvador.* London: Latin America Bureau.

Robinson, William I. 2003. *Transnational Conflicts: Central America, Social Change, and Globalization.* London: Verso.

Schwartz, Benjamin. 1991. *American Counterinsurgency Doctrine and El Salvador: The Frustrations of Reform and the Illusions of Nation Building.* Rand Corporation.

Stanley, William. 1996. *The Protection Racket State: Elite Politics, Military Extortion, and Civil War in El Salvador.* Philadelphia: Temple University Press.

Stephen, Lynn, trans. and ed. 1994. *Hear My Testimony: María Teresa Tula, Human Rights Activist of El Salvador.* Boston: South End Press.

Whitfield, Teresa. 1995. *Paying the Price: Ignasio Ellacuría and the Murdered Jesuits of El Salvador.* Philadelphia: Temple University Press.

Williams, Robert G. 1986. *Export Agriculture and the Crisis in Central America.* Chapel Hill: University of North Carolina Press.

Wood, Elizabeth Jean. 2000. *Forging Democracy from Below: Insurgent Transitions in South Africa and El Salvador.* Cambridge: Cambridge University Press.

———. *Insurgent Collective Action and Civil War in El Salvador.* Cambridge: Cambridge University Press.

Slave Rebellions in the United States

CHRONOLOGY

1619	First Africans sold into British North America at Jamestown, Virginia.
1676	Bacon's Rebellion in Virginia.
1680–1710	Virginia becomes a slave society.
1695–1705	South Carolina becomes a slave society.
1712	Slave uprising in New York City.
1722	Slave uprising in Virginia.
1723	Slave uprising in Virginia.
1729	Slave uprising in western Virginia, including formation of short-lived maroon community.
1739	Stono Rebellion in South Carolina.
1741	"Great Negro Plot" in New York City.
1760	Tacky's Revolt, Jamaica.
1775	Thomas Jeremiah and "Preacher" George hanged for insurrectionary activity in South Carolina.
	Lord Dunmore's Proclamation offers freedom to Virginia slaves who will fight on the side of the British against American revolutionaries.
1775–1783	American Revolutionary War.
1776	Declaration of Independence signed.
1777	Vermont's constitution prohibits slavery.
1780	Pennsylvania passes the first post-nati emancipation law, which guarantees freedom to children born of enslaved mothers once they reach the age of 28.
1784	Rhode Island and Connecticut pass post-nati emancipation laws that promise gradual emancipation to children born of enslaved mothers.
1789	Constitution of the United States goes into effect.
1791–1804	Haitian Revolution.
1792	Cotton gin invented by Eli Whitney.
	"Black Loyalists" leave Nova Scotia to settle Sierra Leone.

1794	French Republic abolishes slavery in its colonies.
1795	Point Coupée Conspiracy, Louisiana.
1795–1796	Second Maroon War, Jamaica, in which a community of escaped slaves or "maroons" fights the colonial government, loses, and is deported, first to Nova Scotia and later to Sierra Leone.
1799	New York passes post-nati emancipation law.
1800	Gabriel's Conspiracy, Richmond, Virginia.
	Settler uprising in Freetown, Sierra Leone.
1802	France reinstitutes slavery in its colonies.
1803	Louisiana Purchase.
1804	New Jersey passes post-nati emancipation law.
1808	Great Britain and the United States independently outlaw the Atlantic slave trade.
1811	German Coast slave uprising, Louisiana.
1812–1815	War of 1812.
1814	The defeat of the Upper Creek Indians at the Battle of Horseshoe Bend opens the Deep South to plantation agriculture.
1816	Slave uprising, Barbados.
	American Colonization Society is organized for the purpose of transporting free black Americans from the United States to Africa and helping them settle there.
1820	Missouri Compromise allows Missouri to be admitted to the Union as a slave state but forbids slavery in any other part of the Louisiana Purchase territory north of 36°30′ N latitude.
1822	Denmark Vesey Conspiracy.
1823	Slave uprising, Demerara (present-day Guyana).

1827	New York abolishes slavery.
1829	David Walker publishes *An Appeal to the Coloured Citizens of the World*.
1831	January, William Lloyd Garrison begins publishing *The Liberator* in Boston.
	August, Nat Turner Rebellion, Southampton County, Virginia.
1831–1832	Baptist War slave uprising, Jamaica.
1833–1838	Great Britain abolishes slavery in its empire.
1835	Slave conspiracy, Adams County, Mississippi.
1839	*Amistad* found off the coast of Long Island.
1841	Slave uprising occurs on board the *Creole* as it transports Virginia slaves for sale at New Orleans.
1848	France and Denmark abolish slavery in their colonies.
1859	John Brown leads raid on Harper's Ferry, Virginia (now West Virginia).
1860	Christmas slave conspiracy, Dallas, Texas.
1861–1865	United States Civil War.
1862	Second Creek slave conspiracy, Mississippi.
1863	Abraham Lincoln issues the Emancipation Proclamation.
1865	Thirteenth Amendment to the Constitution is ratified, abolishing slavery in the United States.

INTRODUCTION

Slavery came to British North America early in the seventeenth century, and it survived in the United States until it was abolished as a result of the Civil War in 1865. Throughout the more than 200 years of its existence, the enslaved struggled against their bondage. The second half of the twentieth century witnessed an explosion of historical scholarship on slavery in the United States that has established the variety and complexity of American slavery and the resulting variety and complexity of enslaved Americans' struggles against their masters and their conditions. Slave rebellion—concerted, collective violent action through which the enslaved sought to escape from slavery or to overthrow it—constituted the most radical form of slave resistance. Slave rebellions were forbiddingly dangerous for the enslaved, but evidence of slave rebellions has survived from the seventeenth, eighteenth, and nineteenth centuries.

BACKGROUND: CULTURE AND HISTORY

Until roughly 1800 slavery was one of the most ubiquitous institutions in human history, and throughout history slaves have resisted their bondage. Nonetheless, the Haitian Revolution (1791–1804) is the only recorded example of slaves rising, overthrowing their masters, and establishing a government of their own in place of that of their former masters. Understanding the history of slave rebellion in any slave society must proceed from the daunting odds represented by this startling fact. Those odds are particularly germane to the history of slave rebellion in the United States where, despite local variations, free Europeans always significantly outnumbered enslaved Africans, immeasurably increasing the already overwhelming odds against successful rebellion. This simple demography militated against frequent slave rebellions in North America. But questions about the slave rebellions that did occur took on particular significance for understanding slavery in the American South.

The United States was founded through a violent revolution in which residents of Britain's colonies defended their rights against a metropolitan government that they considered oppressive, and in doing so, American revolutionary leaders explicitly claimed that "all men" were endowed with rights to "life, liberty and the pursuit of happiness." This lent a unique meaning to violent resistance to slavery in the United States: such resistance clearly violated statute law and thus constituted criminal activity, but when understood as an attempt to defend the natural right to human liberty upon which the nation had been founded, slave rebellion could also be understood as part of a struggle to force the nation to live up to its own explicit creed. This understanding informed some slave uprisings as well as anti-slavery activists' discussions of such uprisings, and it also shaped white southerners' responses to insurrections and insurrection scares.

Over the duration of slavery's existence in what became the United States, there were only a few cases of large-scale uprisings in which enslaved people collectively took up arms and attacked their oppressors in clear-cut slave rebellions.

Though scholars argue over the precise definition of a slave rebellion and thus about the number that occurred, only three—the 1739 Stono Rebellion in South Carolina, the 1811 German Coast Rebellion in Louisiana, and the 1831 Nat Turner Rebellion in Virginia—produced even a moderately significant surviving documentary record. All three were brutally repressed. Conspiracy scares—incidents in which slaves were reported to have planned to rebel against their masters but in which the plot was discovered before enslaved conspirators could put their plans into action—were much more frequent and were put down with similar violence. Because so much of the history of slave rebellion is a history of what oppressed people were reported to have said and planned secretively, and because such plans generally came to light in the context of viciously repressive efforts to uncover evidence that inquisitors were already convinced existed—efforts that routinely involved torturing witnesses reluctant to say what interrogators wanted to hear and rewarding those who testified to what prosecutors sought—the records upon which our understanding of these events is based are unusually unreliable, and our knowledge of slave rebellion is unusually uncertain.

CONTEXT AND PROCESS OF REBELLION

Colonial Period

Chattel slavery was legally recognized throughout colonial British North America. African peoples were enslaved in all of British America for most of the seventeenth and eighteenth centuries, but large-scale plantation slavery only emerged in the Chesapeake and the Carolina low country around the turn of the eighteenth century. Slavery became the central defining institution in the "slave societies" that developed around tobacco cultivation in Virginia and Maryland, and rice cultivation in Carolina and Georgia. Slaves fought against their condition in northern "slave-owning" societies as well as in southern slave societies, and the nature of slaves' resistance was influenced by the societies in which they lived.

In colonies north of Maryland, where slaves always comprised significantly less than 20 percent of the settler populations, collective resistance by the enslaved appears less frequently in the records and often involved allegations of relatively broad-scale cooperation with bound or impoverished European working people. Slaves in these northern societies often worked in artisan households or on the docks as part of multiracial workforces. The degree to which enslaved blacks worked with and lived beside free but often impoverished whites affected the rebellions and conspiracies that developed.

The two most famous examples of collective slave resistance in northern colonies both arose in New York City, one in 1712 and the other in 1741. The records of both incidents are shrouded in even greater uncertainty than those of most slave rebellions, but in both cases a cross-racial alliance was reported—enslaved Africans allegedly combining with Indians and whites in 1712 and with impoverished whites in 1741. In 1712 a group of slaves set fire to a building and then killed white men who came to extinguish the blaze. The rebels were reportedly allied with local Indians, and some contemporaries believed they were inspired by a local Huguenot school teacher. Thirty years later, in 1741, a series of fires at prominent city buildings were attributed to a group of slaves and white working people, all of whom were suffering economic hardship due to a harsh winter that had frozen the port and all of whom socialized together at a waterfront tavern. Authorities responded to both incidents with horrific brutality, burning, torturing, or hanging more than twenty alleged conspirators in 1712 and approximately thirty in 1741. In neither case does the surviving record permit more than marginally reliable distinctions to be drawn between elite fears and rebellious actions, but these scares underscore the degree to which northern slaves lived in a world of labor that encompassed the free and the enslaved as well as people of European, indigenous American, and African descent. Conspiracy scares that occurred in other northern colonies probably followed similar patterns, but only rumors of most of these incidents have survived in the records, so nothing precise can be said about them. In slave-owning societies, slaves' resistance often overlapped with the resistance of free people with whom slaves worked and socialized.

Reported rebellions and conspiracies were much more frequent in southern slave colonies, though in all but a few of these cases the surviving documentary record is too thin to say much about the goals, strategies, motivations, and often even the actions of the alleged participants. During the first decades of the eighteenth century, wealthy white Virginians imported large numbers of Africans, and during those very decades, Virginia experienced several significant uprisings by slaves. Not surprisingly, these African-born rebels often sought to escape not just from slavery but from the colony's European settler society and probably hoped to re-create the ways of life they had been forced to leave behind in the Old World.

At least once, rebellious slaves escaped into Virginia's Dismal Swamp; another time a group fled into the Blue Ridge Mountains. Each group sought to found a maroon society (a community of runaway slaves that remained outside the control of the plantation regime). White Virginians, conscious of the subversive and disruptive influence of maroons on Jamaica's plantation society, quickly mobilized the militia and Native American mercenaries to hunt down and destroy the escaped slaves' communities. Though other incidents are less fully documented—and there is hardly a surfeit of information about these maroons—it seems likely that groups of slaves who rose against their masters in 1722 and 1723 also hoped to escape and settle in independent maroon communities. By the middle of the eighteenth century, Creole slaves (American-born slaves) came to dominate Virginia's plantations, and the colony grew populous enough to diminish the possibility of rebellious slaves moving beyond the bounds of white settlement. Partially as a result of these changes, reported insurrections and conspiracies became less common, and patterns of slave resistance shifted away from collective uprisings.

South Carolina turned to slave labor at roughly the same time as the Chesapeake, but slavery became more dominant in the low country where rice, rather than tobacco, was the staple, and where the deadly disease environment of the rice swamps fueled South Carolina's steadier and more persistent engagement with the Atlantic slave trade. As a result, South Carolina continued to be dominated by African-born slaves throughout the colonial period, a fact that helped shape patterns of collective resistance. Another factor influencing slave resistance in South Carolina was the neighboring Spanish colony of St. Augustine along the Atlantic coast of Florida, for the Spanish welcomed and guaranteed freedom to slaves who escaped from South Carolina. Scant surviving evidence documents most early alleged conspiracies and uprisings by enslaved South Carolinians, but there were a number of reports of conspiracies and small uprisings among low-country slaves during the 1720s and 1730s, and a slow but seemingly steady flow of South Carolina runaways found their way to St. Augustine.

In 1739 South Carolina's largest slave uprising occurred, and it reflected the recent African origins of its participants as well as the lure of freedom in St. Augustine. In September of that year, a group of men who had recently been enslaved during civil wars in the kingdom of Kongo rose up on a plantation on the Stono River just southwest of Charleston. They killed the owner of the plantation and a number of other whites whom they encountered as they marched down the road toward St. Augustine where they are assumed to have been headed. Lt. Governor William Bull happened to be riding on that road and saw the Kongolese military procession of the rebels. He escaped on his horse and raised a militia force that dispersed the insurrectionaries and put down the uprising. Militia men killed an unknown number during the military encounter and then tortured and executed others after the battle, exhibiting the severed heads of rebel slaves on mile posts along the road to discourage future uprisings. The colonial legislature responded by codifying the province's brutal slave code into the Negro Act of 1740. Slave unrest continued in colonial South Carolina following the Stono Rebellion with periodic rumors of conspiracies to rebel, but never again would a planned, large-scale insurrection occur in the colony or the state.

When placed within the context of the constant and ongoing struggles between masters and slaves over the nature of work and the autonomy of slave communities, the numerous white reports of slave conspiracies and uprisings throughout the colonial period underscore the refusal of enslaved Africans to accept the condition in which they found themselves in British North America. The rejection of slavery most often took the form of collective violent rebellion in places where and at times when the majority of the settler population was enslaved and large majorities of the enslaved were Africans who had been born free and sold into the Americas. Such conditions rarely prevailed in North America. The Stono Rebellion suggests that collective resistance was even more likely in cases in which a large number of enslaved Africans living in a single community shared military training and traditions. In a fundamental sense, the traditions of resistance that characterized slave rebellions during the colonial period were often continuations of collective identities that reached directly back to ethnically specific Old World cultures in Africa. Though the evidence is too sketchy to be certain, several of the slave rebellions and conspiracies that occurred in Virginia before 1730 and in South Carolina before 1770 probably took their shapes as a result of the cultures and traditions of the African societies from which the rebels had been brought to America.

The Age of Revolution

Many slaves fought for their freedom in a variety of ways during the American Revolution. In 1775, John Murray, Fourth Earl of Dunmore, the royal governor of Virginia, issued a proclamation offering freedom to any slaves who escaped from rebel masters and joined the governor's "Ethiopian Regiment" to fight to reduce white Virginians to due submission to the Crown. Though Dunmore and the black soldiers were quickly expelled from Virginia, the proclamation opened the door for slaves to seek freedom by joining and fighting with the British against the American revolutionaries, and many chose to pass through that door. Reasonable estimates suggest that 25,000 "black loyalists" ran to British armies over the course of the war. Another 5,000 black soldiers fought on the "patriot" side during the revolution. Some of these black patriot soldiers were enslaved when they joined up, and many were granted freedom for fighting. In part because the war offered many alternative potential paths

to freedom while simultaneously ensuring that the free population was militarily mobilized, there were few insurrection scares and no slave rebellions during the war (1775–1783).

That conspiracy scares were rare is not, however, to say that they did not occur or that they were unimportant. In 1775, as white South Carolinians were hesitantly moving into open rebellion against George III, they reported two different incidents involving rebellious blacks. In one, an enslaved man called "Preacher George" by his prosecutors was purportedly inciting followers to rise, kill their masters, and join the British who, George allegedly said, had promised freedom to the slaves. In the other, Thomas Jeremiah, a free black boat pilot, allegedly planned to help lead British ships through the difficult passage into the city of Charleston so that they could bring liberty to his people. George and Thomas Jeremiah were both executed.

Black support for the British government could sometimes be difficult to distinguish in practice from a slave uprising. This is best illustrated by the exploits of Colonel Tye in New Jersey during the Revolutionary War. Colonel Tye had been enslaved but had escaped and was living as a fugitive prior to the war. When hostilities reached New Jersey, he signed on with the British and was made an officer of the militia unit that he organized, a unit of formerly enslaved people. They raided the countryside, exacting revenge on former masters while supporting the king's cause. On the one hand, it makes little sense to view Colonel Tye and his followers as slave rebels: they were fighting on the side of a legal government against those seeking to overthrow it. On the other hand, it makes even less sense to ignore the continuities between Tye's resistance to slavery before the revolution, when it was clearly illegal, and that during the revolution when he operated under the aegis of the Crown. The thousands of black soldiers who fought for Great Britain during the American Revolution were not slave rebels but, given their use of collective violence as a means to pursue liberty, neither are they irrelevant to the history of slave rebellion during the revolution.

Reported conspiratorial activity among slaves remained rare during the first eight years following the Peace of Paris (1783). During those years several northern states moved to abolish slavery either immediately or gradually, and antislavery movements gained momentum in a number of states like New York and New Jersey that continued to recognize the institution. Freeing slaves became easier and more common in Maryland and Virginia, though neither state came close to passing general emancipation. Most importantly for the history of slave rebellion in the United States, a stronger federal union was formed when the Constitution was ratified (1788), and this occurred at the same time that legislation and court decisions in northern states began to establish a distinction between free northern states and slave southern states. The

1790s saw new patterns of slave resistance in the United States.

The 1791 uprising of the enslaved on the northern plain of the French colony of Saint Domingue, an uprising that initiated what became the Haitian Revolution, coincided with a sharp increase in reported slave conspiracies in Virginia, substantial reports of conspiratorial activity in Spanish Louisiana, and significant scares in the Carolinas and Georgia. The exact relationship between events in Saint Domingue and North America is often difficult to discern and certainly varied by time and place. The port cities of Charleston, South Carolina, Norfolk, Virginia, and Baltimore, Maryland, received many white and black refugees from Saint Domingue during the revolution on that island as did New Orleans in its Spanish, French, and American periods. Whites in all of these towns grew uneasy, especially in response to the presence of black refugees, as well as to black sailors from ships trading with Hispaniola. They reported overhearing numerous discussions in which blacks spoke admiringly of the slave revolution then taking place and discussed the possibility of emulating Toussaint-Louverture and his formerly enslaved freedom fighters. Authorities frequently came to believe that such talk was part of an active effort to organize rebellion, and they were almost surely right in some cases. But the circumstances surrounding most of these events remain too murky to discern where evidence of black conspiratorial activity ends and the projection of white fear begins.

During the decade following the first uprising in Saint Domingue, enslaved North Americans organized several substantial and quite different conspiracies that nearly culminated in rebellions, although they were betrayed by informers at the last moment. The first occurred in Spanish Louisiana. Spain had acquired Louisiana in the wake of the Seven Years War (1756–1763), and white Louisianans imported large numbers of enslaved Africans during the last quarter of the century. As a result, the enslaved population of the region had grown increasingly African at the very time that British North American slave populations were growing increasingly Creole. A significant ethnically based Mina conspiracy was uncovered in Point Coupée Parish in 1791 on the eve of the first uprising in Saint Domingue. Just four years later, in 1795, a larger conspiracy was betrayed on the eve of its planned implementation.

The Point Coupée Conspiracy of 1795 was the only North American conspiracy that appears to have involved a complex combination of Creole slaves and slaves of various African ethnicities of the sort that characterized the Haitian Revolution, and white Louisianans were convinced that its leaders took direct inspiration from events in the Caribbean. The records produced in the repression of the conspiracy are as problematic as those from other conspiracies, but given Louisiana's proximity to Saint Domingue and the constant commerce between New Orleans and the islands, reports that some ties existed seem more likely true than not. The conspiracy was put down with characteristic brutality: twenty-three slaves convicted of having joined the plot were hanged and their severed heads were nailed to posts along the banks of the Mississippi River to terrorize any of their brethren inclined to pursue a similar plan.

Just five years later enslaved Virginians formed an extensive conspiracy to overthrow slavery in the largest and wealthiest state in the new United States. Throughout the summer of 1800, groups of Creole black Virginians in and around the state capital of Richmond congregated after church meetings, at slave-community barbecues, and in area slave quarters to discuss rising up and ending slavery in the state. Gabriel, a blacksmith who belonged to a planter named Thomas Henry Prosser, emerged as the leader of these Creole conspirators, and he and his lieutenants formed a plan to attack and seize the town and then to hold Governor James Monroe hostage until white Virginians abolished slavery in the state.

Blacks in Richmond had been overheard discussing the Haitian Revolution during the preceding eight years, so Gabriel and his followers knew of events in the Caribbean and probably found them inspiring. But records produced by white Virginians' repression of the conspiracy made scant mention of Saint Domingue. They suggest instead a conspiracy fueled by a volatile mix of a belief that the enslaved were God's chosen people with the language of liberty as it had been used by white Virginians during the American Revolution. Gabriel and his followers were betrayed on August 30, 1800, the day the rebellion was to begin, and many alleged conspirators were arrested. Authorities searched for and found some of the weapons that Gabriel and his blacksmith brother Solomon had made, though they seem to have found far fewer scythe-swords than trial testimony would have led one to expect. Approximately seventy men were tried for conspiring to rebel, twenty-six were hanged, and eight were convicted but had their sentences commuted to deportation. Gabriel and his followers, inspired by Atlantic revolutions and by their belief that slavery violated God's laws, failed in their attempt to seize the revolutionary mantle claimed by their masters.

The last major act of collective violent slave resistance of the revolutionary era resembled the uprisings of the colonial era more than those that occurred contemporaneously. In 1811 a group of slaves living in the German Coast region of the United States' recently acquired (1803) territory of Louisiana, rose and marched in the direction of New Orleans. This rebellion, which is only beginning to receive the scholarly attention it deserves, was probably the largest slave insurrection in the history of the United States, with reports of over 100 rebels. It occurred in a region whose slave population had grown rapidly during the years immediately preceding the 1808 closure of the Atlantic slave trade, and thus in a region that was home to many recently imported African-born slaves. Many of these "saltwater" slaves originated in the Kongo region, and the German Coast Rebellion, much like the earlier Stono Rebellion, appears to have reflected military traditions from that region. White Louisianans were convinced that it was led by a free mulatto refugee from the Haitian Revolution, suggesting the influence of Atlantic revolutionary ideas on the rebellion, though it is difficult to discern whether the Haitian connection existed in whites' minds, blacks' minds, or both.

Upon getting word that slaves on two German Coast plantations had attacked their masters and were marching on New Orleans, William C. C. Claiborne, Louisiana's territorial governor, called out both the local militia and a force of United States army troops under General Wade Hampton. The troops attacked and dispersed the rebels, killing more than sixty slaves in the military encounter. Eighteen more were captured, tried, and executed. Two whites are known to have been killed in the rebellion, and an unknown number of enslaved people were killed by whites in frenzied reaction to the uprising. Whites believed the slaves were marching on New Orleans with the intent to conquer the town, and Hampton argued that they had been inspired by the Spanish as part of an ongoing skirmish regarding the border separating the land the United States had purchased from France and Spanish Florida. Recent scholarship suggests that it is more accurately understood to be an uprising of Kongolese former soldiers, similar to the Stono Rebellion, and thus somewhat anomalous among North American rebellions during the Age of Revolution.

The era of the American Revolution was a momentous one in the history of slavery in the new nation. A transatlantic anti-slavery movement emerged with striking rapidity, leading states to the north of Maryland and Kentucky to take decisive steps—some quickly and immediately, others more gradually—to abolish slavery within their limits. Partially in response to the same movement, the national government closed the Atlantic slave trade. At the same time, Haiti offered a nearby example of a revolution that rejected racial limitations on those who could claim natural rights.

Events not directly related to revolutionary politics and ideology also shaped slavery and slaves' responses to their oppression. Despite a large influx of enslaved Africans between 1803 and 1808, the United States' rapidly growing slave population became an increasingly Creole population. At the same time, the white population of the new nation was growing even faster than that of bondspeople. This meant both that whites remained a majority not just in the nation, but in the southern states, and that white settlement became increasingly dense, rendering slaves' chances of forming successful maroon societies even less promising than they had been in early eighteenth-century North America. Much of the expansion of white settlement in the South and the corresponding spread of slavery into the old Southwest was fueled by the invention of the cotton gin, which opened the upcountry of South Carolina and Georgia and the vast territories of Alabama, Mississippi, Louisiana, and eastern Texas to cotton cultivation. All of these factors contributed to changing patterns of collective slave resistance, as Creole-led conspirators sought to demand equal rights within the land of their birth more often than to escape from the Euro-American societies into which their parents or grandparents had been sold.

The Antebellum Era

Conditions for collective violent slave resistance in the United States became even less promising after the American Revolution than they had been previously. The growing and well-armed white population of the South continued to hold overwhelming advantage over the enslaved in any calculation of potential military power. The white South also became increasingly defensive and aggressive toward the threat of rebellion in response to a growing sense of isolation in the world, as first the northern states (1780–1804), and then Great Britain in its Caribbean colonies (1833–1838), and then France and Holland in their sugar islands (1848) outlawed slavery. In 1776, slavery had existed throughout the Americas. By 1850, slavery had become a truly peculiar institution, thriving only in the American South, Brazil, and the Spanish colonies of Cuba and Puerto Rico.

The white South's great strength at home combined with its increasing fear that it was on the losing side of history to create a poisonous mix for the enslaved: a slave society in which successful rebellion was virtually impossible but in which masters were periodically acutely attuned to the danger of insurrection. Only one large-scale slave rebellion came to fruition in the antebellum South, but many more conspiracies to rebel were "uncovered." Authorities who believed a rebellion to be in the works used brutal techniques to interrogate suspected conspirators, corrupting virtually all of the evidence available to historians who seek to reconstruct these events. Such records obviously reveal a great deal about white fears, but scholars are increasingly divided regarding their reliability as evidence of blacks' planned resistance to slavery.

The Denmark Vesey Conspiracy has become the flashpoint for disagreements about the reliability of the evidence produced during the repression of slave conspiracies. From the time of the conspiracy until 2001, the account of the conspiracy that was published by magistrates involved in the trials of alleged participants was treated as a largely reliable account of the efforts of enslaved South Carolinians to win their freedom. According to this document, in 1822 a free black man named Denmark Vesey led a major conspiracy in Charleston, South Carolina. Vesey, a carpenter, had been sold into slavery in South Carolina, but he won a lottery and bought his freedom with the prize. Vesey's was seen as perhaps the most complex slave conspiracy in the history of the United States. He brought together Gullah-speaking slaves from the rice parishes outside Charleston and very assimilated slaves from the city itself; he melded religious traditions from the countryside with the gospel preached in Charleston's African Methodist Episcopal (A.M.E.) Church; he spoke of his experiences as a mariner in the black republic of Haiti and of congressional debates over the admission of Missouri into the union as a slave state. He organized a conspiracy that combined the secular radicalism of natural rights philosophy with millennialist faith that God would aid his enslaved chosen people.

The magistrates' account held that Vesey and his followers had planned to rise up and take the city, call on supporters from the rice parishes to flock to their banner, and then bring slavery to an end within the state. If they proved unable to hold the city, then the rebels planned to seize ships in Charleston's harbor and sail to freedom in Haiti. Vesey's conspiracy, like Gabriel's, was betrayed before the rebellion occurred. White South Carolinians tried more than 100 alleged conspirators, convicted forty-nine, and hanged thirty-seven. They also closed down Charleston's A.M.E. church and, in the wake of the conspiracy, became more convinced of the need to take drastic steps to protect slavery within the union.

In 2001, historian Michael Johnson published an essay that revealed the published "Official Report" of the court that tried the conspirators, the document that formed the basis of the standard interpretation, to have been a deliberately misleading account of the trials designed to justify the actions of the examining magistrates. After carefully reconstructing the trials as they probably occurred, rather than as they were presented, and after analyzing the roles of a few star prosecution witnesses, Johnson reached the conclusion that there was no slave conspiracy, and that the event that had long been considered one of the largest and most sophisticated conspiracies in the history of North American slavery was, instead, a conspiracy against Denmark Vesey that resulted in a mass judicial lynching. Not surprisingly, this effort to overturn a century and a half of historical certainty has proven controversial, and some scholars question Johnson's conclusions. What is less open to doubt is the degree to which he has shown the willingness of white officials, even in a highly publicized case, to induce people to give false testimony, alter the record, and produce a narrative of conspiracy with little reliable relation to the actions that may or may not have been pursued by accused slaves.

This discovery is particularly unsettling for scholars of antebellum slavery, because none of the numerous other reported slave conspiracies from the antebellum era produced the sort of rich documentary record that permitted Johnson to reveal the distortions in the "Official Report" of the Vesey Conspiracy. The existence of conspiracies in Mississippi in 1835 and 1862 or in Dallas, Texas, on the eve of the Civil War rests on the slimmest evidentiary foundation, and in each of these cases—among the three most significant alleged conspiracies prior to emancipation—there are good reasons to doubt that scholars will ever be able to reach a consensus on even the basic question of whether a slave conspiracy existed.

No such uncertainty exists regarding the most famous slave revolt in the history of the United States, that led by Nat Turner in Southampton County near the southeastern border of Virginia during the summer of 1831. Turner had long been known as a religious visionary or eccentric in the community, and in 1831 he began to receive messages from God calling him to lead his people in a battle to fight evil. He confided his plan to very few followers, counting either on divine assistance or the bitterness of the enslaved to win him followers once he joined battle against the unrighteous.

On August 21, Turner and five followers began attacking plantation houses, killing the white inhabitants and recruiting the slaves who had belonged to the now-dead masters. Perhaps as many as seventy slaves joined Turner's rebellion, and they killed at least fifty-seven white Virginians. Virginia militia units called out to meet Turner dispersed his forces, killed many, and arrested others. Many more enslaved Virginians were killed by area whites' savage vigilante response to the rebellion. In the official response, forty-five slaves were tried for participating in Turner's rebellion, and eighteen were hanged. Turner was among those eighteen, though he hid in the woods and escaped capture for about a month. After being tried and convicted and while awaiting execution, he dictated his *Confessions,* which immediately became a best seller and is still widely read. In the *Confessions* he revealed his conviction that God had ordained that the slaves should be free and his belief that he himself had been appointed to bring God's justice to earth and to vanquish God's enemies. In addition to the immediate reaction to Turner's rebellion, in which an unknown number of black Virginians and North Carolinians were killed, the rebellion excited tremendous anxiety throughout the white South, leading legislatures to pass harsher restrictions on slaves and masters to institute crackdowns on slaves' day-to-day autonomy.

A newspaper cartoon depicts the violent slave uprising led by Nat Turner that began on August 22, 1831, when Turner killed his master and his master's family. The revolt only lasted about a week but Turner eluded capture until October of that year. He was later tried and hanged for the crime. (Library of Congress)

If the conditions became increasingly unfavorable for slave rebellions on land throughout the antebellum period, ships transporting slaves remained one of the few locales in which the enslaved might reasonably hope to overwhelm their oppressors and seize freedom. About ten years after the Nat Turner Rebellion, two shipboard rebellions created major public issues in the United States, and in both cases the rebellious slaves won their freedom. The first case involved recently enslaved Africans who were sold into slavery in Spanish Cuba where the Atlantic slave trade, while technically illegal, continued unabated. While being transported from one part of the island to another aboard the ship *Amistad* in 1839, the slaves rose up, killed most of the crew, and ordered the captain to sail them back to their homes near Sierra Leone. The captain sailed east during the day when his captors could use the sun to determine the ship's direction, but then used the stars to backtrack and sail west and north each night, taking the ship to the United States where it was discovered off the coast of Long Island. The status of the *Amistad* rebels became a celebrated cause among abolitionists, and ultimately they won judicial recognition of their freedom in the Supreme Court, after which they returned to Africa.

The *Amistad* rebels were judged to be free precisely because they were not United States slaves. But two years later (1841), a group of enslaved Virginians who were being transported to be sold in New Orleans aboard the *Creole* rose up and took control of the ship when it was about 150 miles away from the British-owned Bahamas Islands. The *Creole* sailed to port in the Bahamas, and behind their leader, Madison Washington, the rebels appealed to British law—England had abolished slavery during the preceding decade—to establish their freedom. The United States government fought Britain's recognition of the *Creole* rebels' rights, but it lost, and the slaves gained freedom. Both of these shipboard rebellions became major diplomatic incidents while causing significant sectional strife within the United States. The success of the rebels in winning their freedom also underscores through contrast the harsh prospects faced by those who engaged in collective violent resistance to slavery on land in the United States. Slaves could achieve and exploit temporary military superiority on ships without facing immediate intervention by a large and well-armed militia.

The beginning of the Civil War radically changed the prospects for slaves inclined to use violence to contest their oppression, but it did so by offering an alternative path for them to pursue rather than by increasing the prospects for a successful rebellion. Even before Abraham Lincoln and Congress offered freedom to slaves who fled to Union armies, enslaved southerners began to escape from bondage and volunteer to fight against their masters. By the end of the war black soldiers—both escaped southern slaves and free black men from northern states—comprised about 10 percent of the soldiers fighting for the Union cause, and they joined up despite having to struggle to win pay equal to that of white soldiers.

IMPACTS

Recent scholarship has cast significant doubt on much that was once thought to be known about slave rebellion in the United States, but not on the persistent efforts of the enslaved to struggle against their bondage. Historians have documented a rich tradition of day-to-day resistance that ranged from work slowdowns to feigning illness to sabotaging agricultural implements to suicide. Southern slaves also engaged in many smaller scale acts of violent resistance that did not rise to the level of major rebellions. Such acts included individual slaves' decisions to fight back when whipped, secret attempts to poison masters, and individual violence against masters, overseers, or other white southerners, as well as single-plantation uprisings in which a slave community attacked a master or overseer. It is also clear from the many conspiracy scares reported in southern newspapers and official records that enslaved southerners regularly spoke of freedom and of the prospects for achieving it. Herbert Aptheker, who has made the only systematic attempt to count all such incidents, found approximately 250 scattered through the southern records, with many scares in each state that had large numbers of slaves. Determining whether such talk was just talk, was edging toward implementation, or was on the verge of culminating in rebellion may be impossible in most cases, given the nature of the illegitimate court proceedings used to repress many alleged conspiracies—illegitimate even according to the loose rules governing slave trials in the antebellum South. This does not mean that such conspiracies did not exist. It means

instead that we may never know which conspiracies existed and which did not.

The significance of slave rebellions for the study of slavery in the United States has also changed dramatically in the last fifty years. During the 1940s, when Herbert Aptheker published *American Negro Slave Revolts,* the reigning orthodoxy within the American academy held that slavery was a benign institution that was ideally suited to the racial character of African people. Aptheker's determination to recover a tradition of militant resistance to slavery spoke forcefully to the racism implicit in his contemporaries' scholarship. The second half of the twentieth century witnessed an explosion of scholarship on American slavery that has securely buried the image of the happy slave, and the earlier need to recover stories of heroic rebels has come to seem dated—at times even condescending.

In an era in which it would be difficult to find a single respectable historian who doubts that enslaved Americans consistently resisted bondage with the tools they had at their disposal, scholarship on slave rebellions has lost its central organizing focus. Conspiracies and rebellions that were once portrayed as part of a single tradition of militant slave resistance are now more likely to be viewed as discrete events best understood within their local and temporal contexts, as events that can more usefully shed light on the specific local worlds in which they occurred than on "the slave's" response to the peculiar institution.

Slaves' traditions of resistance only rarely led toward large-scale revolts in North America in the manifestly unfavorable conditions that existed in the South. The power of those traditions is, however, manifest in the fact that, over the course of the Civil War, about one-fifth of the black men of military age who lived in the United States joined the Union armies to fight against their masters and for freedom. The black soldiers who escaped from bondage to fight for the destruction of slavery illustrate the fundamental, if incomplete, way that the Civil War broadened American citizenship by permitting black Americans to fight for inclusion within the republic's claimed allegiance to natural rights without fighting against the republic.

PEOPLE AND ORGANIZATIONS

Brown, John (May 9, 1800–December 2, 1859)

John Brown was a white antislavery activist who attempted to stimulate a slave rebellion in Virginia in 1859 by taking over the federal arsenal in Harpers Ferry, Virginia (now West Virginia), and calling upon enslaved Virginians to join him. His small insurgent "army" was defeated, and he was arrested, tried, and executed.

Gabriel (ca. 1776–October 10, 1800)

Gabriel was an enslaved blacksmith who led a conspiracy among slaves in the Richmond, Virginia, area in the summer of 1800. The conspirators planned to seize the town, take Governor James Monroe hostage, and demand their freedom. They were betrayed on the day of the planned uprising, and Gabriel was eventually hanged.

Garrison, William Lloyd (December 10 or 12, 1805–May 24, 1879)

William Lloyd Garrison was an anti-slavery journalist and activist. In 1831 he founded *The Liberator*, which quickly gained influence as an important voice for the immediate abolition of slavery.

Jeremiah, Thomas (Died 1775)

Thomas Jeremiah was a free black boat pilot in Charleston, South Carolina, who was accused of conspiring to guide the British army into Charleston's harbor. He was arrested and hanged.

Maroon Societies

Maroon societies were communities of escaped slaves usually established in otherwise unsettled and remote areas where slave owners and their militias would have difficulty finding or surprising them. Their existence was viewed as a source of encouragement for other slaves to escape from or rebel against slave owners.

"Preacher" George (Died 1775)

"Preacher" George, as he was called in the surviving court records, was a South Carolina slave who claimed that God had set black South Carolinians free, and that the conflict between South Carolina and England (the American Revolution) was the result of Carolinians refusing to free their slaves. He was arrested and hanged.

Toussaint-Louverture (ca. 1743–April 7, 1803)

Toussaint-Louverture emerged as the most important leader of the Haitian Revolution (1791–1804), the only successful slave revolution in the history of the Americas.

Turner, Nat (October 2, 1800–November 11, 1831)

Nat Turner was a slave who lived in Southampton County, Virginia, and led one of the largest slave uprisings in North American history in the summer of 1831.

Vesey, Denmark (ca. 1767–July 2, 1822)

Denmark Vesey, a free man of color, lived in Charleston, South Carolina. In the summer of 1822 he was accused of leading a large and complex slave conspiracy. He was executed on July 2, 1822.

Walker, David (September 28, 1785–June 28, 1830)

David Walker, a free man of color, was born in Wilmington, North Carolina, and moved to Boston during the 1820s. There he became a small shopkeeper, an anti-slavery activist and journalist, and the author of the *Appeal to the Coloured Citizens of the World*. He died shortly after publishing the *Appeal*, probably of tuberculosis.

Whitney, Eli (December 8, 1765–January 8, 1825)

Eli Whitney was a white man from Connecticut. While visiting a plantation in Georgia in 1793, he invented the cotton gin, a machine that removed seeds from short staple cotton. The invention of the cotton gin effectively opened the Deep South to plantation agriculture.

Tye, Colonel (Died September 1780)

Colonel Tye was an escaped New Jersey slave who joined the British during the American Revolution and became the leader of a band of loyalist black militiamen. Tye and his men attacked patriot leaders until Tye was shot in a raid. The wound appeared minor at first, but it became infected, and he died from it.

James Sidbury

See Also African American Freedom Struggle; Documentaries of Revolution; Ethnic and Racial Conflict: From Bargaining to Violence; Haitian Independence Revolution; Human Rights, Morality, Social Justice, and Revolution; Music and Revolution; U.S. Southern Secessionist Rebellion and Civil War

References and Further Readings
Aptheker, Herbert. 1943. *American Negro Slave Revolts*. New York: Columbia University Press.

Craton, Michael. 1982. *Testing the Chains: Resistance to Slavery in the British West Indies.* Ithaca, NY: Cornell University Press.

DuBois, Laurent. 2004a. *Avengers of the New World: The Story of the Haitian Revolution.* Cambridge, MA: Harvard University Press.

———. 2004b. *A Colony of Citizens: Revolution and Slave Emancipation in the French Caribbean, 1787–1804.* Chapel Hill: University of North Carolina Press.

Egerton, Douglass. 1993. *Gabriel's Rebellion: The Virginia Slave Conspiracies of 1800 and 1802.* Chapel Hill: University of North Carolina Press.

———. 1999. *He Shall Go Out Free: The Lives of Denmark Vesey.* Madison, WI: Madison House.

Elkins, Stanley. 1976. *Slavery: A Problem in American Institutional and Intellectual Life.* 3rd edition. Chicago: University of Chicago Press.

Finkelman, Paul, ed. 1989. *Rebellions, Resistance and Runaways within the Slave South.* New York: Garland.

French, Scot. 2004. *The Rebellious Slave in American Memory.* Boston: Beacon Books.

Frey, Sylvia. 1991. *Water from the Rock: Black Resistance in a Revolutionary Age.* Princeton, NJ: Princeton University Press.

Genovese, Eugene D. 1974. *Roll, Jordan, Roll: The World the Slaves Made.* New York: Pantheon.

———. 1979. *From Rebellion to Revolution: Afro-American Slave Revolts in the Making of the Modern World.* Baton Rouge: Louisiana State University Press.

Hall, Gwendolyn Midlo. 1982. *Africans in Colonial Louisiana: The Development of Afro-Creole Culture in the Eighteenth Century.* Baton Rouge: Louisiana State University Press.

Harding, Vincent. 1981. *There Is a River: The Black Struggle for Freedom in America.* New York: Harcourt Brace Jovanovich.

Higginson, Thomas Wentworth. 1969. *Black Rebellion: A Selection from Travelers and Outlaws.* New York: Arno Reprint.

Johnson, Michael P., et al. 2002. "The Making of a Slave Conspiracy, Parts 1 and 2," *The William and Mary Quarterly,* 3rd ser., 58 (2001): 913–976; 59 (2002): 135–202.

Mullin, Gerald W. 1972. *Flight and Rebellion: Slave Resistance in Eighteenth Century Virginia.* New York: Oxford University Press.

Mullin, Michael. 1992. *Africa in America: Slave Acculturation and Resistance in the American South and the British Caribbean, 1736–1831.* Urbana: University of Illinois Press.

Roberts, Kevin David. 2003. "Slaves and Slavery in Louisiana: The Evolution of Atlantic World Identities, 1791–1831." PhD diss. Austin: University of Texas.

Sidbury, James. 1997. *Ploughshares into Swords: Race, Rebellion and Identity in Gabriel's Virginia, 1730–1810.* Cambridge: Cambridge University Press.

Stampp, Kenneth. 1956. *The Peculiar Institution: Slavery in the Ante-Bellum South.* New York: Knopf.

Thornton, John K. 1991. "African Dimensions of the Stono Rebellion," *American Historical Review* 96 (October 1991): 1101–1113.

———. 1999. *Africa and Africans in the Making of the Atlantic World, 1400–1680.* 2nd edition. Cambridge: Cambridge University Press.

Wood, Peter H. 1974. *Black Majority: Negroes in Colonial South Carolina from 1670 through the Stono Rebellion.* New York: Norton.

———. 1978. "'Taking Care of Business' in Revolutionary South Carolina: Republicanism and the Slave Society." Pp. 268–293 in *The Southern Experience in the American Revolution,* edited by Jeffrey J. Crow and Larry E. Tise. Chapel Hill: University of North Carolina Press.

———. 1986. "'The Dream Deferred': Black Freedom Struggles on the Eve of White Independence." Pp. 166–187 in *In Resistance: Studies in African, Caribbean, and Afro-American History,* edited by Gary Y. Okihiro. Amherst: University of Massachusetts Press.

South African Revolution

CHRONOLOGY

1652–1806   The Dutch East India Company establishes a settlement at the Cape of Good Hope for re-supplying ships traveling between Holland and its Asian Pacific colonies and trading interests. Dutch settlers come to southern Africa, later also German and French Huguenot settlers, in pursuit of land and new opportunities. Many indigenous Africans are dispossessed of their property and transformed into slave laborers. While the territory is under Dutch control, white colonists come to speak a form of the Dutch language called Afrikaans, which incorporates influences from some European and African languages. Those whites who speak Afrikaans are called Afrikaners.

1806   The British take the Cape settlement from Holland.

1820s   Thousands of English settlers arrive in South Africa.

1834   The British governor of the Cape Colony abolishes slavery.

1836–1856   Tens of thousands of Afrikaners move away from British rule in the Cape Colony, subdue and dispossess indigenous African peoples of the interior, and establish two independent Afrikaner republics based mainly on farming economies: the Orange Free State and the Transvaal Republic, also referred to as the Boer Republics.

1886   Gold is discovered in the Transvaal.

1899–1902   The Boer War takes place between the forces of the Boer Republics and the British, resulting in British victory and conquest of the Orange Free State and the Transvaal Republic.

1910   The Union of South Africa is established. The British choose to maintain the system of legal white racial dominance.

1912   The South African Natives' National Congress, later known as the African National Congress (ANC), is created by Africans to achieve racial equality and democracy.

1913   The white government enacts the Native Land Act, which limits the residence and land ownership of most indigenous Africans to so-called Bantustans (tribal homelands), which make up only about 13 percent of South Africa's territory.

1914   The National Party is created with the goals of uniting Afrikaner voters, a majority of the whites in South Africa, in support of the party and establishing Afrikaner control over South Africa through elections.

1921   Creation of the South African Communist Party (SACP). Eventually the SACP becomes one of the central allies of the ANC.

1928   The Afrikaner-dominated South African government creates the Iron and Steel Corporation of South Africa (ISCOR) and later other state-owned companies, in part to reduce British dominance of the economy, but also to provide job opportunities for poor Afrikaners.

1934   Many Afrikaners and white South Africans of British ancestry form the United Party in an attempt to provide strong leadership to help the country cope with the effects of the Great Depression.

1939–1945   The United Party and its allies bring South Africa into World War II on the side of Great Britain. Wartime industrialization brings many nonwhites into jobs and urban areas previously reserved for whites.

1948   The Afrikaner-dominated National Party wins control of the South African parliament by promising to roll back racial integration and reinforce racial separateness or "apartheid." The new government passes a series of laws over several years to accomplish its racial goals.

1949   The ANC adopts the Program of Action put forward by the ANC Youth League and advocated by Nelson Mandela, Walter Sisulu, and Oliver Tambo. The Program of Action transforms the ANC from an organization addressing mainly the concerns of elite indigenous Africans attempting to bring about change through occasional petitions to the white government into a more activist, militant movement focusing on the needs of the large majority of uneducated, exploited workers and employing mass actions such as labor strikes, boycotts of white businesses, and nonviolent civil disobedience.

1950   The South African government enacts the Suppression of Communism Act, which not only declares the South African Communist Party illegal, but also identifies working for racial equality as working for Communism.

1952   The ANC and other anti-apartheid groups launch the Defiance Campaign, a civil disobedience campaign to violate apartheid facilities segregation and other apartheid laws.

1955   The ANC and other anti-apartheid groups organize the Congress of the People, which proclaims the Freedom Charter calling for an end to apartheid and the creation of a nonracial democracy and a Socialist-type economic system.

1956   The white government arrests many anti-apartheid activists who participated in the Congress of the People and tries them for treason. In 1961 all defendants in the Treason Trial are found not guilty.

1959   The Pan-Africanist Congress (PAC) is created by anti-apartheid activists who defect from the ANC to pursue a black nationalist rather than multiracial approach and call for stronger actions to fight apartheid.

1960–1961	Most whites vote to reject the authority of the British monarchy and transform South Africa into a republic. South Africa withdraws from the British Commonwealth.
1960	In March, the Sharpeville massacre and related violence occurs; ANC and PAC are both declared illegal.
1961	Umkhonto we Sizwe, the ANC revolutionary army, begins sabotage attacks.
1962	Nelson Mandela is captured.
1964	Mandela is sentenced to life in prison at the Rivonia Trial.
1969–1977	Black Consciousness Movement (BCM). In August 1971, a number of previously organized activist groups sharing the black consciousness philosophy link up at the Black People's Convention at Bloemfontein under the leadership of Steve Biko, launching a nationwide movement.
1975	The Zulu-based Inkatha cultural organization is revived under the leadership of Mangosuthu Gatsha Buthelezi.
1976	Soweto Uprising against Afrikaans language requirements. Xhosa Transkei becomes the first supposedly "independent" African tribal homeland. By attempting to transform African tribal homelands into independent countries, the apartheid government intends to declare most African workers to be foreign laborers, not residents of South Africa.
1977	Steve Biko is killed while in police custody. Many BCM organizations are declared illegal.
1983	The white government institutes the Multi-Racial Constitution, widely viewed as a ploy to maintain apartheid. It bars indigenous South Africans, the large majority of the population, from voting or representation. The anti-apartheid United Democratic Front, later renamed the Mass Democratic Movement, is created to protest the Multi-Racial Constitution and fight for real nonracial democracy.

1985	A major anti-apartheid, pro-ANC federation of unionized workers is created and named the Congress of South African Trade Unions (COSATU).
1986	South African apartheid military forces are defeated at the battle of Cuito Cuanavale in Angola by a combination of Cuban, Popular Movement for the Liberation of Angola, and ANC forces.
1988	The ANC modifies its economic program by advocating a mixture of private and publicly owned enterprises subject to market forces, making the ANC more acceptable to South African business interests.
1989	F. W. de Klerk becomes president of South Africa and announces that he is forced to dismantle apartheid.
1990	Nelson Mandela is freed from prison; ANC, PAC, and SACP are re-legalized.
1990–1992	Intermittent negotiations take place on how to develop a new political system.
1992	The ANC adopts the tactic of mass action protests and labor strikes to achieve an agreement on creating a nonracial democracy.
1992–1994	Negotiations resume to end apartheid and create a new political and social system, accompanied by many protests and labor actions, and considerable violence, particularly between Inkatha and the ANC.
1994	The first post-apartheid election results in victory for the ANC under a temporary constitution.
1996	A permanent constitution is approved.
1999	ANC wins the second post-apartheid election by a larger majority, while voter participation declines significantly. Thabo Mbeki replaces Mandela as president of South Africa.
2004	ANC wins the third post-apartheid election by an even larger majority. Thabo Mbeki is re-elected president.

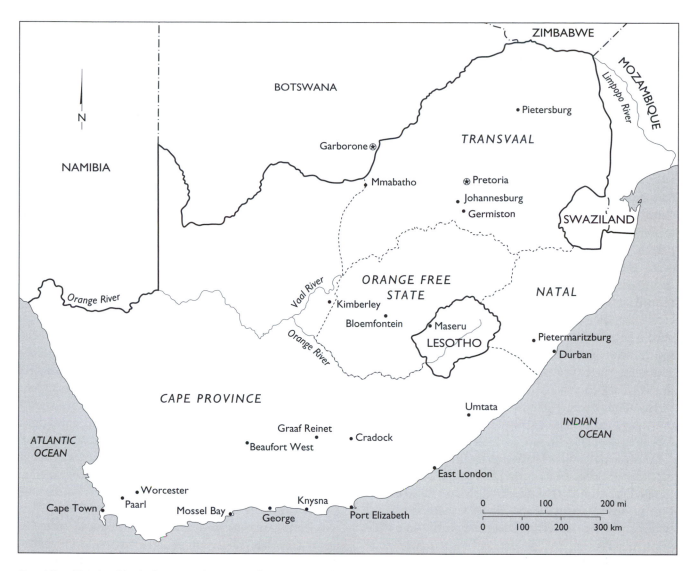

Republic of South Africa before 1994 showing its four provinces during the anti-apartheid revolutionary struggle. The post-apartheid constitution subdivided Cape Province and Transvaal resulting in the nine provinces of the new South Africa.

INTRODUCTION

In 1652 the Dutch East India Company established a settlement in southern Africa in order to refresh its ships traveling between Holland and Dutch colonial and trading interests in the Pacific. The indigenous African peoples were dispossessed of the land and its resources and transformed in many areas into propertyless laborers. After the British acquired the territory, enormous deposits of important and valuable minerals were discovered, including the world's largest known gold deposits. The white minority established a system of racial, political, and economic domination that was known, after 1948, as "apartheid"; it persisted until the 1990s. The leaders of the African National Congress and other groups fought for decades for racial equality. In 1994 a nonracial political democracy was established, and new opportunities were created for the majority of South Africa's people. But the country continued to be characterized by great inequalities and other enormous problems.

BACKGROUND: CULTURE AND HISTORY

In the late twentieth century, one major nation continued to assign political and economic rights on the basis of race: the Republic of South Africa. Persons of European ancestry, about 13 percent of the population, dominated the country, which included three other major racial categories: indigenous Africans, approximately 75 percent; Indians (Asian) about 3 percent; and Colored (mixed race), about 9 percent. The South African government also recognized the existence among indigenous Africans of ten major ethnic groupings with varying customs, languages, or dialects, the largest of which was the Zulu and the second largest the Xhosa.

European settlement of South Africa began in 1652, when the Dutch East India Company established a naval refreshment settlement at the Cape of Good Hope to provide fresh water, food, and other resources for its ships as they traveled the long distance between Holland and its colonies and trading interests in the east. Settlers arrived, often from Holland's poorer classes, seeking new opportunities, including the opportunity to own and operate large farms and ranches, often as big as 6,000 acres. The indigenous people were violently evicted when they attempted to resist, and many were transformed into slave laborers. Over time, the Dutch settlers, accompanied later by Germans and French Huguenots, developed a derivative of the Dutch language called Afrikaans, which incorporated influences from some European and African languages. The whites in southern Africa who spoke this language and shared the evolving African version of Dutch culture became known as Afrikaners. Afrikaners are estimated to make up about 60 percent of the people of European descent in South Africa.

After a series of wars between Great Britain and Holland, the British took possession of the Dutch Cape Colony in 1806. In 1843 the British also took the Afrikaner Port Natal (modern Durban) and bordering territory. By 1821, about 5,000 British settlers had arrived at the Cape. Eventually people of British descent would make up approximately 30 percent of South Africa's white population. Some Afrikaners began to fear that their language, culture, and religion—the Dutch Reformed Church—would gradually be replaced by those of the new ruling power. In 1834, many Afrikaners opposed the British governor's decision to abolish slavery. Thousands, especially young Afrikaners who wanted to establish large farms, which was becoming more difficult in the increasingly populated Cape Colony, began moving in heavily armed wagon trains into the interior and away from the British, first across the Orange River and then across the Vaal River. This outmigration of Afrikaners from about 1836 to 1856 became known as the Great Trek. The Trekkers defeated local indigenous African peoples who tried to resist the invasion. Eventually they established two new Afrikaner-controlled republics, the Orange Free State and the Transvaal (Across the Vaal River) Republic, also called the South African Republic. Most of the Afrikaners in these territories were farmers or *boers,* the Dutch word for farmers, so the Orange Free State and the Transvaal were often referred to by the British as the Boer Republics.

For a time the British seemed relatively unconcerned with the independent existence of the Boer Republics, perhaps de-

terred from intervening by the likely great cost of conquering them compared to their apparent limited value to the British empire. This view began to change rapidly when important minerals such as diamonds were found in southern Africa, especially with the 1886 discovery of vast gold deposits in the Transvaal. The gold ore, while plentiful, was often of moderate quality, and much of it deep underground. British mining companies were allowed to exploit the gold resource under terms set by the Transvaal government. The gold deposits, thought to be the largest known to exist in the world, increased British interest in politically controlling the Boer Republics and made such an effort economically feasible. One of the issues used as a justification to go to war was the British demand that British miners in the Transvaal be allowed to vote in the republic's elections.

The so-called Boer War broke out in 1899. The forces of the Boer Republics numbered as many as 40,000, often mounted fighters. The British were forced to commit approximately 250,000 soldiers to the war (DeFronzo 1996, 294). In order to deprive the Boer guerrillas of assistance from their families or other of their country folk, the British forcibly relocated tens of thousands of Boer families to concentration camps where an estimated 25,000 Boer women and children died (Omer-Cooper 1987, 146). The British burned many of the farms from which families had been removed to the camps. Through destroying the farms and imprisoning much of the population, the British made it more difficult for the Boers to continue the fight. In 1902 the Boer Republics were forced to surrender.

In 1910, the British government linked the defeated Orange Free State and the Transvaal to the Cape and Natal territories in a four-province federal system called the Union of South Africa. Each province was to have a legislature, and there would also be a parliament for the entire federation. Rather than establishing racial equality, the British decided that legal European racial supremacy would be maintained, apparently for several reasons. Undoubtedly some in Britain's government shared the racial prejudice of many Afrikaners against non-Europeans. But in addition, in the interest of convincing Afrikaners to cease armed resistance, the British decided to guarantee that white racial supremacy would be maintained despite the defeat of the Boer Republics. The policy also appeared to serve the economic interests of British mining companies and other industrial and business concerns by permitting them to pay non-Europeans less than workers of European descent, thereby keeping labor costs lower than they might otherwise have been.

The defeat of the Boer Republics had devastating consequences for many Afrikaners. As a result of the British destruction of Boer farms, the burden of taxation, and other economic trends, many Boers lost their land. To support themselves and their families, they had to move from the countryside to mining or industrial areas and seek jobs from British employers. This geographical relocation of much of the Afrikaner population following the Boer War became known as The Second Great Trek. Many of the impoverished Afrikaners were especially concerned with preserving white legal and political privileges to prevent effective economic competition from nonwhites. In addition, since they lacked significant property, clinging to an ideology of white racial superiority was psychologically gratifying to some poor Afrikaners.

Voting rights were restricted to persons of European descent except in the Cape Province, where some "economically prosperous" non-Europeans, "making up about one-seventh of all Cape voters," were temporarily allowed to vote (DeFronzo 1996, 294). Indigenous Africans were deprived of the vote in the Cape Province in 1936, and people of mixed race in 1956 (Radu 1987). Although the Boer Republics lost their independence, Afrikaner nationalists soon took advantage of elections to attempt to regain at least limited control of not only the Orange Free State and the Transvaal, but the entire Union of South Africa. The strategy involved convincing Afrikaners, who made up a majority of white voters, to unite behind the Afrikaner National Party, founded in 1914, which would then be able to take control of South Africa's provincial parliaments and the national government.

Afrikaner electoral unity was impeded by a number of factors. First, a serious division existed even before the inception of the Union of South Africa in 1910, since some Afrikaners, particularly in the Cape Province, either remained neutral during the Boer War or sided with the British. Just as the Afrikaner National Party was created, World War I broke out, causing a new division among Afrikaners. Some sided with the Germans, others with the British, and many wanted to remain neutral. Following the war and the renewed process of reconciliation, Afrikaner political power increased.

Afrikaner J. B. Herzog, a former official of the Orange Free State, was elected president of the Union of South Africa in 1924. The Herzog government launched a program to build Afrikaner economic power and improve economic prospects for poor Afrikaners. Control of the federal government provided the means for Afrikaners to begin to counter British domination of mining and industry by establishing state-owned corporations, such as the Iron and Steel Corporation of South Africa (ISCOR), founded in 1928. These economic organizations as well as other businesses were required to employ set quotas of white workers and reserve certain types of jobs for whites. Tariffs were instituted on the importation of manufactured goods to help spur the development of Afrikaner-owned businesses.

In response to the enormously damaging economic effects of the worldwide Great Depression, many of the members of Herzog's National Party and the party supported by many South Africans of British descent, the South Africa Party, led by a moderate Afrikaner Jan Smuts, decided to join together in 1934 to form a new political party for the good of the country, the United Party. Those Afrikaners who refused to join the United Party were members of the so-called Purified National Party (they eventually dropped the expression "Purified" to run for office under the title National Party). Some persons of British descent who opposed the United Party supported the Dominion Party.

The emergence of the Nazi regime in Germany followed by the outbreak of World War II in Europe further divided Afrikaners. Many Afrikaners agreed with aspects of the Nazi doctrine of Germanic racial superiority (since people of Dutch ancestry would be included in the superior racial category and since in their view South African society was based on the concept of racial supremacy). However, the United Party, with the assistance of the pro-British Dominion Party and the Labor Party, brought South Africa into the war on the side of Great Britain. Certain Afrikaners were accused of engaging in or planning sabotage to oppose the war effort and were incarcerated during the war, including some future government officials. Tens of thousands of South Africans participated in the war, although only white South Africans were allowed to serve as armed soldiers.

World War II had tremendous economic and social impacts on South Africa. Since British industry was converted to weapons production and German submarine warfare interfered with commerce, South Africa was forced to undergo a major development of industry. Many white men were away in the armed forces, so large numbers of nonwhite workers were recruited for jobs which in the past had been reserved for only whites and were drawn into urban areas. White farmers were often angry at the loss of nonwhite rural laborers who sought better-paying jobs in industry. When white soldiers returned from the war, many were outraged at the partial occupational and residential integration that had occurred during the conflict. The Afrikaner National Party promised to reverse racial integration and reinforce racial separateness (apartheid). In the momentous 1948 "Apartheid Election," the National Party defeated the United Party and proceeded to enact a series of laws to reverse the racial integration trends of the World War II period and reinforce separation, not only among the four major recognized racial categories, but also among the different ethnic (tribal) groups of the indigenous African majority.

D. F. Malan's National Party government enacted new laws that permitted the removal of thousands of indigenous Africans from urban areas to either tribal homelands or to townships outside major cities where workers whose labor was needed could reside. The Southwest Townships (Soweto) outside Johannesburg became home to hundreds of thousands of people who would be transported into the city in the morning to work and then back out again to Soweto when the work shift was over. Africans who were considered residents of tribal homeland areas (most of the indigenous African population) had the right to be outside their homeland territories only when contracted to work (according to the 1913 Native Land Act and the 1936 Native Trust and Land Act, the land area of all ten tribal groups together made up only about 13.5 percent of South Africa's territory). The new Pass Law required them, when outside their homelands, to at all times carry a personal pass book indicating current work contract, criminal record if any, and other important information. The Suppression of Communism Act of 1950 not only outlawed the multiracial South African Communist Party (SACP), but also allowed persons to be arrested and prosecuted for working to bring about racial equality.

Between 1948–1960, South Africa's National Party government established what has been referred to as a white-supremacist or master-race form of apartheid in which political policy appeared to be based on an assertion of white racial superiority. But changing international conditions began to motivate a shift in the legal form and public rationale for denying indigenous Africans the rights accorded to white South Africans. A central concern was the fact that European colonial control of Africa was coming to an end. Most African territories were declared independent states with new indigenous leadership. South Africa's leaders wanted to sell the country's industrial products to other African nations. Maintaining a stance of white racial superiority could interfere with this economic goal.

A possible solution was to begin a process of granting political independence to the tribal homelands or "Bantustans" within South Africa. If the tribal homelands, generally economically dependent on South Africa and controlled by leaders cooperative with and supported by white South Africa's government, were accepted by other nations as genuinely independent countries, racial discrimination in South Africa could be transformed into a type of discrimination employed by all nations. That is, most indigenous Africans would be denied the right to vote, equal education, residence, or other basic civil rights not on account of race, but on the basis of being foreign migrant laborers temporarily working in South Africa but legally citizens of other nations, the tribal homelands. The first homeland granted independence was Transkei (a Xhosa homeland) in 1976. But the United Nations overwhelmingly rejected the concept that Transkei was genuinely an independent country. Ultimately, five other tribal homelands were granted independence. Despite the fact that almost all other nations refused to recognize the homelands as independent states, the process of granting independence was apparently intended to serve other functions in preserving white domination such as intensifying divisions, rivalries, and cultural chauvinism among indigenous Africans, and

preventing them from uniting against the white government. Furthermore, educated indigenous Africans, instead of providing leadership for anti-apartheid movements, could be lured into jobs in the homelands' administrative bureaucracies and governments.

Eventually, a further significant modification was introduced into apartheid through implementation of the 1983 Multi-Racial Constitution. This was widely viewed internationally as another effort to maintain the essential aspects of apartheid in the face of growing world and domestic opposition. The government, however, publicized the 1983 constitution as a progressive reform. The constitution for the first time created separate national parliaments for some nonwhites in South Africa. In addition to a white parliament elected only by whites, there would be an Indian (Asian) parliament elected only by those South Africans of Asian descent and a Colored parliament elected only by mixed-race persons. Each parliament would theoretically deal separately with issues affecting only members of its own racial category and collectively with issues of concern to all three racial groups. However, the combined number of deputies in the Indian and Colored parliaments was significantly less than the number of deputies in the white parliament. This was important, since the president of the country was to be elected by representatives of the parliaments, and the white advantage in parliamentarians seemed to assure that a white president would always be selected. Furthermore, the president would have the authority to determine which issues were dealt with collectively by all three legislatures and which were to be dealt with by individual parliaments. Most indigenous Africans were outraged by this constitution, which omitted them from representation and continued to treat them as foreigners, citizens only of the tribal homelands. The new constitution seemed to be an effort to draw people of Indian and mixed racial ancestry into an alliance with whites against the indigenous African majority to ensure the continuation of white racial dominance.

CONTEXT AND PROCESS OF REVOLUTION

The British decision to maintain a system of white racial domination in the Union of South Africa motivated a small number of economically prosperous and relatively well-educated indigenous African farmers, professionals, and businessmen to create the South African Natives' National Congress in 1912, later renamed the African National Congress (ANC). The ANC adopted a nonviolent, generally legal, and nonconfrontational approach to working for a nonracial democratic system in South Africa. The members apparently hoped that moral arguments and international pressure would eventually convince white South Africans to establish racial equality. Membership in the ANC grew gradually, and by the outbreak of World War II in Europe, the ANC was considered influential enough among indigenous Africans to be asked by the United Party government to support South Africa's war effort against Nazi Germany. The ANC leaders decided to back the war.

After World War II, however, the ANC's support for the defeat of racist Nazi Germany did not result in increased racial equality in South Africa. Instead, whites elected the Afrikaner National Party, which launched its apartheid program to reinforce racial separateness and white domination. Younger members of the ANC in the ANC Youth League, such as Nelson Mandela, felt both betrayed by white voters and government officials and disillusioned with the legalistic, nonconfrontational methods of the older generation of ANC leaders. They decided to launch, in cooperation with the South African Indian Congress (SAIC), a large-scale civil disobedience effort, the Defiance Campaign of 1952, in which nonwhites attempted to use facilities legally reserved for whites only. The protest drew many new members into the ANC but was harshly suppressed by the government, which arrested thousands of participants.

The failure of the dramatic civil disobedience Defiance Campaign convinced younger members of the ANC, including Nelson Mandela, to develop new tactics. Some decided to form an alliance with the banned but still secretly operating South African Communist Party (SACP). Over several years the ANC, like the SACP (which had originally formed among white workers in 1921 but later worked for racial equality), formed a covert network through which the organization could continue to operate even if eventually declared illegal. Since the SACP included whites, some of its members, who concealed their party membership, could participate in government institutions and security forces and provide valuable information or other forms of assistance to the ANC. The ANC became a multiracial organization with some SACP members among its leadership.

The ANC and other anti-apartheid groups organized a Congress of the People, which met at Kliptown in June 1955 and involved several thousand people. There the participants proclaimed the Freedom Charter, a declaration that called for the end of apartheid and the creation of a nonracial democracy in South Africa, along with equality of opportunity and the provision of medical, educational, and other needed services for all. The charter also advocated ownership by the people of all the country's mineral wealth and its banks and much of its industry, along with government control of other economic activity and enterprises for the benefit of all South Africans. The government arrested scores of people who participated and tried them for trea-

son in 1956. The Treason Trial lasted four years, inflicting financial and other damage on the accused, all of whom were found not guilty in 1961.

Partly in response to the alliance between the ANC and the SACP, some ANC members decided to leave the organization and create a new anti-apartheid movement called the Pan-Africanist Congress (PAC) in 1959. The leaders of the PAC believed that indigenous Africans should lead the anti-apartheid struggle and rejected the multiracial ANC of the late 1950s. The PAC adopted a black nationalist approach "that the psychology of black South Africans, . . . crippled by decades of oppression and humiliation at the hands of whites, could only be rejuvenated by having the nation's blacks 'act alone in reclaiming South Africa from white domination' (Davis 1987, 11); the PAC's ideology gained popularity because it enhanced feelings of pride and importance among many young Africans and engendered a special sense of mission" (DeFronzo 1996, 307).

The PAC decided to launch a new civil disobedience protest in 1960 against the Pass Book Law. On March 21, many participants gathered in the town of Sharpeville without their pass books, expecting to be arrested. A number of police, possibly feeling threatened by the crowd, opened fire. Sixty-seven people died, most from wounds to the back as they tried to run away (Davis 1987, 12). Outraged by the shootings, thousands of people protested in the black townships outside white cities. The response of the white government was to outlaw both the PAC and the ANC on April 8, 1960.

After nonviolent efforts to end apartheid repeatedly failed, members of the ANC and its ally the SACP organized the ANC's armed guerrilla group, Umkhonto we Sizwe (The Spear of the Nation). The aim was to sabotage industrial and communication facilities in order to damage the economy directly and also indirectly by discouraging foreign investment. The South African government publicly portrayed Umkhonto we Sizwe (as well as the ANC as a whole) as a Communist terrorist organization out to destroy Christianity as well as individual tribal traditions. The date chosen to begin the Umkhonto sabotage campaign was December 16, 1961, the anniversary of the 1838 Afrikaner Blood River victory over the Zulu.

But in August 1962, Nelson Mandela was captured. He was charged with leaving the country illegally and later, along with other ANC leaders, of attempting to violently overthrow the government of South Africa. In 1964 Mandela and seven other captured ANC leaders were sentenced to life in prison and transported to the maximum security installation on Robin Island.

While the ANC attempted to recover from the loss of so many important leaders, another form of initially legal opposition to apartheid developed, the Black Consciousness Movement (BCM). Steve Biko and other young Africans in

Steve Biko. (Mark Peters/Getty Images)

able Africans became to the nation, the more self-confident they would be, and the more likely that the white minority would be persuaded to end apartheid. Like the ANC and the PAC, the BCM attempted to transcend ethnic divisions among indigenous Africans. Since the BCM stressed legality and nonviolence, and since its leaders, in barring white participation, seemed to be enforcing their own form of apartheid, the white government temporarily tolerated the movement, apparently hoping that the BCM would divert potential recruits from the ANC and the PAC. But in 1973 white authorities became alarmed by the movement's popularity and potential for contributing to future conflict and banned Steve Biko, restricting his activities and freedom of movement. The BCM activists and their message fostered an attitude of defiance and raised expectations of future progress. When instead of improvements the white regime instituted additional repressive, obstructionist, and humiliating policies toward the African majority, tens of thousands of people took to the streets in the 1976 Soweto Uprising.

Another major development helped set the stage for the Soweto protests. In 1974, after fighting Marxist-inspired anti-colonial revolutionaries for more than ten years, Portuguese troops, apparently influenced by the ideology of the revolutionary forces they tried to defeat, overthrew the authoritarian conservative government in Portugal that had sought to hold onto the profitable colonies of Angola, Mozambique, and Guinea-Bissau. The new leftist Portuguese government soon granted independence to the colonies. In Angola, separated geographically from South Africa by Namibia, which South Africa controlled, and in Mozambique, which borders South Africa, leftist regimes were established. Instead of friendly Portuguese colonial authorities, apartheid South Africa faced hostile governments opposed to its racially stratified system. The victory of African revolutionaries in Angola and Mozambique encouraged opponents of apartheid in South Africa.

The catalyst for the Soweto explosion of mass protest against apartheid was the decision of the white government to include compulsory Afrikaans language courses in the curriculum for African students and force them to accept it as the language for instruction in certain other courses, such as mathematics. Many people interpreted this as an attempt by Afrikaner whites to interfere with the education of African children by introducing the obstacle of Afrikaans, a language that had very little application outside of South Africa. School children in Soweto began a demonstration against the Afrikaans language requirement on June 16, 1976. Police used force to suppress it, killing many students. Demonstrations spread to other cities and towns. The protests, in some areas led by members of the BCM student organization SASM, went on for months, constituting the

1969 founded the South African Student's Organization, SASO, for black college students, apparently in part inspired by the U.S. Black Power Movement. Biko and his associates adopted the African nationalist approach. They believed that white domination had created a culture and psychology of subservience and feelings of inferiority among black South Africans that had to be replaced with pride in and an appreciation of African culture and heritage, and the psychological capacity to confront and defy white authority. A similar black consciousness organization for high school students, the South African Student Movement, SASM, was also established.

In August 1971, representatives of a number of activist groups sharing the black consciousness philosophy met at the Black People's Convention at Bloemfontein and launched the Black Consciousness Movement (BCM) nationwide, under the leadership of Steve Biko. Initially at least, the BCM was to use nonviolent, law-abiding tactics. Education and self-improvement were stressed, on the grounds that the more highly skilled and economically valu-

greatest and most continuous mass insurrection in South Africa during the twentieth century. An estimated 500 to 1,000 people were killed in confrontations with security forces (Lawson 2005, 125; www.anc.org.za/ancdocs/history/mk/mk-history.html). Anti-apartheid activists and suspected leaders of protests were arrested, and many died in police custody under suspicious circumstances often attributed by white officials to suicides or hunger strikes. Steve Biko was arrested in September 1977 and died in police custody. The repression crushed the BCM and its main student groups, SASO and SASM, and afterward thousands of young people flocked to join the ANC Umkhonto we Sizwe.

Along with Umkhonto sabotage efforts, the ANC pursued a multifront strategy against apartheid. In addition to armed struggle, ANC sympathizers repeatedly organized hundreds of community groups in South Africa to legally protest apartheid and stage demonstrations, labor strikes, and school and business boycotts in an effort to make South Africa internally ungovernable. Another facet of ANC strategy was to convince major nations to stop trade with and investment in South Africa to weaken the economy. This approach tended to force the government into one of two unsatisfactory alternatives: to try to covertly circumvent trade barriers, which often drastically increased the cost of trade, or to expand domestic industry to produce more products in South Africa, which made white industrialists more dependent on nonwhite labor and more vulnerable to strikes (Crawford 1998). Finally, the ANC sought to isolate South Africa diplomatically and culturally to increase whites' concern about being treated as international outcasts and undermine their moral self-perception.

As the government suppressed legal organizations because of anti-apartheid activism, new groups were repeatedly created, led by persons waiting for an appropriate opportunity to use their organizational network in a future anti-apartheid uprising. For example, after the BCM-influenced SASO and SASM were declared illegal, a new student organization, the Congress of South African Students (COSAS), many of whose leaders in reality supported the ANC, was established in 1979. The government's implementation of the 1983 Multi-Racial Constitution provoked a surge in organizing and sustained anti-apartheid protests that continued until the end of apartheid. In 1983, thousands of delegates from various parts of South Africa met in Cape Town to create a new, legal anti-apartheid federation. Called the United Democratic Front (UDF), it was made up of some seven hundred civic organizations including " . . . women's groups, labor unions, youth leagues, and religious councils" (Davis 1987, 87) and publicly disavowed violence. Although UDF leaders declared they were not controlled by the ANC, in reality many supported the revolutionary movement.

Later, after the UDF was banned in 1987, it re-emerged as the Mass Democratic Movement (MDM).

Probably the most important legal organization supporting the ANC was the Congress of South African Trade Unions (COSATU) founded in 1985. African labor unions were legalized in 1979 with the ultimately unenforceable restriction that they pursue purely economic and not political goals. In reality, most unions opposed apartheid, the large majority supporting the ANC and some the PAC. Legalization of African unions was in great part the result of the increasing reliance of the economy on African labor, including skilled African workers who could not easily be replaced in the event of strikes. Legalizing African Unions allowed employers to negotiate with an elected union leadership to reach agreements before costly strikes occurred or to more quickly end strikes. COSATU grew to an estimated 600,000 members within a few months and, even though the leaders originally indicated that their federation was independent of the ANC, they supported similar goals and "announced socialist aims and principles" (Davis 1987, 102).

Another large, significant, but non-ANC anti-apartheid organization was the Zulu-based Inkatha yeNkululeko yeSizwe (National Cultural Liberation Movement), founded in the mid 1970s in what is now KwaZulu-Natal. Chief Mangosuthu Gatsha Buthelezi led the organization into 2005. Based on an earlier Zulu cultural association founded during the 1920s, this organization became a political movement and was renamed the Inkatha Freedom Party (IFP) in 1990. While opposing apartheid, Inkatha for many years was also in conflict with the ANC. Buthelezi and other leaders of Inkatha criticized the ANC for resorting to violence, for calling for an international economic boycott of South Africa by other nations, which Buthelezi argued hurt indigenous Africans, and for advocating Socialism. For these reasons and because Inkatha leaders seemed for a time willing to consider a form of power sharing with whites short of a fully democratic system (a democratic system would put whites at a great electoral disadvantage), the white government praised Buthelezi and his Inkatha associates as responsible African leaders. Apartheid authorities were also more tolerant of Inkatha than other anti-apartheid groups because its promotion of Zulu culture was seen as serving to divide the African majority. The post-apartheid South African Truth and Reconciliation Commission found evidence that some Inkatha supporters, aided by special white security units, participated in the murder of hundreds of ANC supporters.

In addition to the 1983 Multi-Racial Constitution, the government instituted a series of reforms to quiet discontent while preserving white domination, including, in 1983, permitting African residents of townships to buy rather than only rent homes; in 1985, allowing persons of different races to marry; and in 1986, eliminating the Pass Law. But demands for the total end of apartheid increased. In 1988, after much internal debate, the ANC decided to publicly accept the concept of maintaining a mixed economy in South Africa, part privately owned and part state owned, subject to significant market forces rather than establishing a totally state-controlled economic system. This change made the ANC more acceptable to business interests. As the white leadership and public became increasingly convinced that the solution to the worsening economic crisis and continuing social turmoil within South Africa would require drastic political change, the government began to privatize major state-owned industries, including the Iron and Steel Corporation of South Africa in 1989. This shifted enormous economic resources into private white ownership rather than allowing them to be controlled by a future democratically elected ANC government.

White South African forces invaded several nearby African states that were providing support to the ANC. Although the South African army was defeated in 1986 at the Battle of Cuito Cuanavale in Angola by a combination of Cuban, Popular Movement for the Liberation of Angola, and ANC forces and withdrew from the country, most neighboring African nations stopped allowing the ANC to use their territory for armed actions against the apartheid regime. As Communist Party governments fell in Eastern Europe in 1989 and the Soviet Union suffered from economic crisis, Communist military assistance to the ANC declined. But the end of the Cold War also deprived white South Africa of its former support from Great Britain and the United States, who could no longer justify propping up or defending the apartheid regime in the absence of a viable international Communist threat. Searching for a way out of the crisis, white leaders decided there was no choice but to open negotiations with the leaders of anti-apartheid groups to structure a new political system.

This led to the release of Nelson Mandela and other ANC leaders from prison and the re-legalization of the ANC, PAC, and SACP in early 1990. Negotiations were conducted for more than three years while South Africa experienced repeated acts of violence, particularly by Inkatha supporters and special white security forces against ANC supporters, and large mass protests and labor strikes in support of the ANC. During negotiations, the National and Conservative parties, right-wing Afrikaner groups, Inkatha, and some homeland authorities formed a loose alliance against the ANC and its allies such as the SACP and COSATU. National Party leaders sought a system which, while allowing indigenous Africans a limited role in government, would effectively protect white control over the economy and the military and ultimately over the political system. In contrast, ANC leaders demanded the creation of a one person, one vote nonracial

democracy. With enormous popular support and the ability to shut down much of the economy through huge labor strikes, the ANC won general agreement for the establishment of a nonracial democratic system and for elections to be held in 1994 under a temporary constitution. South Africa was subdivided from four provinces into nine, permitting whites a sizeable proportion of the electorate for the legislature of the new Western Cape Province. All African homelands, including the six that the apartheid government had granted independence, were reincorporated into South Africa. An effort was made to assure all existing elites that their rights and property would be protected. To placate Inkatha, an agreement was reached to preserve the existence of the Zulu traditional monarchy. Seats in the 400-member parliament would be awarded to political parties in proportion to the share of the popular vote each party received.

When the 1994 election was held, the ANC received 62.7 percent of the popular vote compared to 20.4 percent for the National Party, 10.5 percent for Inkatha, 2.2 percent for the Afrikaner Freedom Front, and 1.3 percent for the PAC. Fifty-three of the 252 ANC members of the new parliament were also members of the SACP (Lawson 2005, 146). The parliament selected Nelson Mandela as the country's president and Thabo Mbeki, also of the ANC, as first deputy president. Since the National Party received over 20 percent of the vote, its leader, F. W. de Klerk, was designated as second deputy president. Soldiers of the South African Defense Force, the former homeland armies, the ANC Umkhonto we Sizwe, and the PAC's armed forces, the Azania People's Liberation Army, were combined to create the new South African military, the South African National Defense Force, under the command after 1998 of a former ANC Umkhonto leader. The country's nuclear weapons were reportedly dismantled earlier in 1991.

IMPACTS

The South African Revolution resulted in the end of the apartheid system and the establishment of a political democracy. After many years of peaceful and then armed resistance to white racial domination, the system was changed through a negotiation process accompanied by mass anti-apartheid protests; the impact of South Africa's unionized, militant labor movement; and international pressure. By negotiating an end to the conflict, rather than resolving it through civil war, many lives were saved, and the large majority of white South Africans remained in the country after the end of apartheid, preserving valuable capital and human resources. The peaceful settlement provided an encouraging model for nonviolently resolving conflicts in other countries. Another outcome was the cre-

Nelson Mandela, leader of the African National Congress and president of South Africa, 1994–1999. (Corel Corporation)

ation of a Bill of Rights that is one of the world's most comprehensive as part of South Africa's 1996 Permanent Constitution. It "not only guarantees freedom of speech, movement, and political activity and bans discrimination on the basis of race, gender, sexual orientation, age, pregnancy, or marital status, but also supports every citizen's right to adequate housing, food, water, education and health care" (DeFronzo 1996, 324).

The post-apartheid government generally increased social welfare benefits for poor South Africans and improved access to housing, electricity, clean water, and educational opportunities. While achieving steady, gradual economic growth since 1994, the ANC government tripled the number of people receiving social grants (child support, disability, or old age assistance) and created 700 new health clinics (Lawson 2005, 159–160). But in September 2005, the unemployment rate was still very high, estimated to be about 26.7 percent (http://www.statssa.gov.za/). The level of income inequality remained one of the highest in the world, and about half the population lived below the poverty line (Lawson 2005, 160). Widespread poverty may have contributed to the enormous AIDS problem, with approximately 11 percent of South Africa's population infected (Lawson 2005, 163). The disease, however, was not confined to the poor. By the end of 2005, sons of both Mandela and Buthelezi had died from AIDS.

Many South Africans were disillusioned that the ANC government did not do more to help them. In the 1999 election, the ANC's share of the popular vote increased to 66.4 percent, but since the total number of people voting declined significantly by about 3.5 million, the ANC actually received about 1.6 million fewer votes than it did in 1994 (http://electionresources.org/za/1999/99vs94/). In 1999, Thabo Mbeki succeeded Mandela as president and began a second term when the ANC won 69.7 percent of the vote in the 2004 elections.

Poverty and the millions of weapons available in South Africa have contributed to high levels of crime, including organized crime. In 2000 the homicide rate (number of homicides per 100,000 residents) was about eight times that in the United States (http://corporatism.tripod.com/homicide.htm), although according to the government, it declined by 31 percent from 1994 to 2004 (Lawson 2005, 152). Public opinion polls in South Africa indicate that people were most satisfied with the government in regard to areas where significant improvements had been made, such as basic services, education, and health care, and least satisfied with the government's performance regarding combating crime and creating jobs.

Africans best positioned to benefit from the end of apartheid were those with high levels of education or other pre-1994 advantages. Discontent arose among many regarding whether some of the revolutionary elite were co-opted by powerful white interests. In the view of most observers, the anti-apartheid struggle resulted in a drastic transformation and democratization of the political system, an enormous expansion of freedom, and the extension of welfare state policies to larger numbers of people, but little change in the basic economic system and level of inequality, except to enhance social mobility and economic opportunities for certain sectors of the population. The persistent high level of unemployment, attempts to further privatize government enterprises, failure to respond rapidly and effectively to the AIDS problem, and the extremely unequal socioeconomic system led to divisions in the ANC and criticisms of ANC moderates and their policies by some leaders of COSATU and the SACP.

Despite shortcomings, the success of the anti-apartheid movement and the courageous roles of revolutionary leaders such as Mandela, Sisulu, and Tambo continue to inspire people throughout the world.

PEOPLE AND ORGANIZATIONS

African National Congress (ANC)

The African National Congress, created in 1912 under the name South African Natives' National Congress, became the main anti-apartheid movement and, following years of struggle and repression, the governing party of South Africa after the 1994 post-apartheid election. The ANC began as an organization of relatively well-educated and economically prosperous indigenous Africans using moderate methods such as moral persuasion and petitioning the government for reforms. After the 1948 apartheid election, younger leaders began to employ more militant tactics including civil disobedience, and later, in combination with the South African Communist Party, sabotage carried out by the ANC's Umkhonto we Sizwe. The ANC's anti-apartheid strategy also involved widespread protest by many pro-ANC civic groups, international economic pressure, and cultural and diplomatic efforts to isolate white-ruled South Africa. In 2005, the ANC was a member of the Socialist International organization of political parties, which included the Labor Party of Great Britain and the Social Democratic Party of Germany. The ANC's Tripartite Alliance included COSATU and the SACP.

Biko, Steve (1946–1977)

Steve Biko was the main leader of what became known as the Black Consciousness Movement. It held that white domination had created a culture and psychology of subservience and a feeling of inferiority among many black South Africans that had to be replaced with pride in and appreciation of African culture and heritage and the psychological capacity to confront and defy white authority. Disillusioned with white liberals and the multiracial National Union of South African Students (NUSAS), which had discriminated against black college students, Biko withdrew from NUSAS and founded the South African Student's Organization, SASO, for black college students. A similar organization for high school students, the South African Student Movement (SASM), was also established. Despite the fact that the BCM's black nationalist approach fit in with apartheid policy of racial separateness and separate racial development, as opposed to the "Communist" multiracial approach of the ANC, white authorities eventually banned Biko in 1973, which restricted his organizational activities and freedom of movement. After the 1976 Soweto Uprising, in which SASM members played leadership roles, many BCM organizations, including SASM and SASO, were declared illegal. Steve Biko was arrested and died in police custody from what appeared to be maltreatment and lack of adequate medical attention.

Black Consciousness Movement (BCM)

The BCM was an initially legal anti-apartheid movement which, like the PAC, adopted an African nationalist approach. But unlike the PAC, the BCM was to use law-abiding tactics. BCM leaders claimed that white domination had led to a culture of subservience and a feeling of inferiority among many black South Africans that had to be replaced with a new self-confidence and pride in African culture and heritage. BCM leaders advocated education and self-improvement to build self-confidence and make blacks less dependent on whites, and because the more highly skilled and economically valuable Africans became to the nation, the more likely the white minority would be to end apartheid. One of the first black consciousness organizations was the South African Student's Organization (SASO), established by Steve Biko and his associates in the late 1960s among black college students. Activist groups sharing the black consciousness philosophy linked up at the Black People's Convention at Bloemfontein in August 1971, launching a nationwide movement under Steve Biko's leadership. Since the BCM stressed legality and nonviolence and seemed to be enforcing, through black nationalism, its own form of apartheid, the white government temporarily tolerated the movement, apparently hoping that the promise of gains through peaceful means would divert potential recruits from both the ANC and the PAC. But in inspiring self-confidence and hope in young Africans, BCM activists raised expectations of future progress. When the white regime engaged in further repressive policies toward the African majority, tens of thousands of people took to the streets in protest in the 1976 Soweto Uprising. South African security forces arrested many BCM leaders, including Steve Biko, who died in police custody, and banned BCM organizations.

Buthelezi, Mangosuthu Gatsha (Born 1928)

Buthelezi was the founder in 1975 and leader of the Zulu-based Inkatha organization, later called the Inkatha Freedom Party of South Africa, a rival of the ANC. A descendant of Shaka, originator of the Zulu nation, Buthelezi earned a history degree from the University of Natal in 1950 and was in the early 1950s an activist in the ANC Youth League. In 1953 he inherited the position of chief of the large Buthelezi tribe. In 1970 he was selected as the leader of the Kwa-Zulu homeland. He opposed apartheid and refused to participate in the apartheid government's plan to grant independence to the Zulu homeland. However, he and other Inkatha leaders also came to criticize the ANC for resorting to violence to oppose apartheid, for advocating Socialism, and for calling for an international economic boycott of South Africa to force an end to apartheid on the grounds that this would primarily injure indigenous South Africans. Because of his more moderate outlook, Buthelezi was referred to by apartheid officials as a responsible black leader, as opposed to what they called for years the ANC Marxist terrorists. After the first post-apartheid election in 1994, in which Inkatha received about 11 percent of the vote, Buthelezi became minister of home affairs in President Mandela's government, a post he also held during the first term of President Mbeki.

Congress of South African Trade Unions (COSATU)

COSATU is the federation of labor unions created in 1985 whose leadership sympathized with the ANC. With hundreds of thousands of members, COSATU became a powerful force against apartheid and in support of the ANC demand for a nonracial democratic political system. COSATU was a member of the ANC Tripartite Alliance, along with the SACP.

Congress of the People and the Freedom Charter

The Congress of the People, organized by the ANC and other anti-apartheid groups, convened at Kliptown in June 1955 and proclaimed the Freedom Charter. It called for the end of apartheid, the creation of a nonracial democracy in South Africa, equality of opportunity, and the provision of medical, educational, and other needed services. The charter also advocated ownership by the people of all the country's mineral wealth, its banks, and much of its industry, along with government control of other economic activity and enterprises for the benefit of all South Africans. The white government arrested scores of people who participated in the Congress of the People and tried them for treason in 1956. The Treason Trial lasted four years, inflicting financial and other damage on the accused, all of whom were found not guilty in 1961.

Conservative Party

This was the political party formed by whites who supported maintaining the earlier form of apartheid and objected to the 1983 Multi-Racial Constitution. In the 1989 election, the Conservative Party received about 31 percent of the white vote.

De Klerk, Frederik Willem (Born 1936)

F. W. de Klerk, a leader of the National Party, was the last apartheid-era president of South Africa. He was awarded the Nobel Peace Prize in 1993, along with Nelson Mandela. He responded to internal protests and external economic pressures and a deteriorating economic situation by announcing the necessity of ending apartheid and by freeing Nelson Mandela and re-legalizing the ANC, SACP, and PAC in 1990. After the 1994 post-apartheid election, de Klerk temporarily assumed the position of second deputy president.

Democratic Party

The Democratic Party was the white political party that officially opposed apartheid. In the 1989 election, the Democratic Party received about 20 percent of the white vote.

Fischer, Bram (1908–1975)

Bram (Abram Louis) Fischer was a brilliant Afrikaner lawyer and member of the South African Communist Party who successfully defended the accused 156 anti-apartheid activists in the 1956–1961 Treason Trial. In 1963–1964 he represented Nelson Mandela and his associates in the Rivonia Trial while secretly serving as the leader of the SACP. In 1965 he was arrested and held in prison until just before he died in 1975.

Hani, Chris (1942–1993)

ANC leader Chris Hani served as chief of staff of the ANC armed forces (Umkhonto we Sizwe) and chairperson of the South African Communist Party. In 1993, when he was assassinated by a white terrorist, he appeared to be the second most popular person in South Africa after Nelson Mandela and was seen as a threat both to conservative whites and to the more moderate leaders of the ANC.

Hani was born into a poor family in a rural town in the Xhosa Transkei homeland territory and for a while wanted to become a Catholic priest, a vocation that his father, an ANC member, reportedly opposed. When he was fourteen years old, he joined the ANC. In 1961, the year he graduated from Fort Hare University (run by the Department of Bantu Education), he joined the South African Communist Party, and in 1962 the ANC's Umkhonto we Sizwe. Hani fought in a unit assisting Zimbabwe revolutionary forces against the white-controlled Rhodesian army (Rhodesia was the pre-revolution name for Zimbabwe). In the 1970s and 1980s, he worked organizing Umkhonto units and new recruits, including many students who joined the ANC after the 1976 Soweto Uprising. Hani became chief of staff of Umkhonto in 1987. He returned to South Africa in 1990 after the ANC and the SACP were re-legalized. In 1991, he became the leader of the South African Communist Party. He was a charismatic speaker and campaigned vigorously for the SACP in townships throughout South Africa. On April 10, 1993, as he returned home in the racially integrated Dawn Park area of Johannesburg, he was shot and killed by an anti-Communist white linked to the Afrikaner Resistance Movement and the Conservative Party.

Inkatha Freedom Party (IFP)

This predominantly Zulu political party, based on an earlier Zulu cultural association, was founded in 1975 as Inkatha yeNkululeko yeSizwe (National Cultural Liberation Movement) in what is now KwaZulu-Natal. In 1990 its name was changed to the IFP. Chief Mangosuthu Gatsha Buthelezi led the organization into 2005. While opposing apartheid, Inkatha for many years was also in conflict with the ANC. Buthelezi and other leaders of Inkatha criticized the ANC for resorting to violence to oppose apartheid, for calling for an international economic boycott of South Africa to force an end to apartheid on the grounds that this would primarily injure indigenous South Africans, and for advocating Socialism. For these reasons—and because Inkatha leaders seemed for a time willing to consider a form of power sharing with whites short of a fully democratic system—the white government praised Buthelezi and his Inkatha associates as responsible African leaders. Apartheid authorities were also relatively tolerant of Inkatha, apparently because its promotion of Zulu culture was seen as serving to divide the African majority. The post-apartheid South African Truth and Reconciliation Commission found evidence that some Inkatha members, aided by special white security units, carried out the murders of hundreds of ANC supporters. Inkatha leaders refused to participate in much of the negotiation process leading to the first post apartheid election in 1994. ANC leaders, however, reached accommodation with Inkatha and selected its leader, Buthelezi, to be minister of home affairs from 1994 to 2004. In the 2004 elections, Inkatha received about 7 percent of the popular vote compared to 69.7 percent for the ANC.

Mandela, Nelson (Born 1918)

Nelson Mandela is considered the primary leader of the successful anti-apartheid struggle and was elected the first president of post-apartheid South Africa. He was awarded the Nobel Peace Prize in 1993, along with F. W. de Klerk.

Nelson Mandela was born into the Thembu people, part of the Xhosa ethnic group, as Rolihlahia Dalibhunga Mandela. A teacher reportedly gave him the English name Nelson. He joined the ANC in 1943, founded and led the ANC Youth League, and opened a law firm with his friend Oliver Tambo in 1952. He helped lead the 1952 anti-apartheid, civil disobedience Defiance Campaign. In 1956, after the Congress of the People and the proclamation of the Freedom Charter, he and many other activists were charged with treason. After a long trial, charges were dropped. When the ANC was banned in March 1960, Mandela went into hiding and helped organize the ANC revolutionary army, Umkhonto we Sizwe. Mandela was arrested in 1962, and in 1964 at the Rivonia Trial sentenced to life in prison for attempting to overthrow the government. In the late 1980s, as the apartheid system was deteriorating, government leaders began negotiating with Mandela about participating in the transition to a new form of government. In early 1990 he was released from prison to lead the ANC delegation in negotiations and steadfastly demanded the creation of a one person, one vote nonracial democracy. After the ANC won the majority of seats in the first post-apartheid election in 1994, Mandela became president from 1994 to 1999. Under his leadership South Africa maintained good relations not only with the United States and Western European countries, but also with countries that assisted the ANC during the anti-apartheid struggle, such as Cuba. Not hesitating to criticize international actions he considered wrong, he, along with other ANC leaders, strongly condemned the U.S.-British-led invasion of Iraq in 2003.

Mbeki, Thabo Mvuyelwa (Born 1942)

Thabo Mbeki became the second post-apartheid president of South Africa in 1999 and was re-elected in 2004. His father was a member of the ANC and the SACP. After illegally leaving South Africa, he earned a masters of economics degree at the University of Sussex. He returned to Africa in the early 1970s and worked in the ANC leadership in Zambia. When the ANC was re-legalized in 1990, he returned to South Africa. In 1994 Mbeki was elected first deputy president to Nelson Mandela. In 1999, he succeeded Mandela as president but has been criticized for being slow to react effectively to South Africa's AIDS crisis and for not doing enough to reduce inequality.

National Party

This Afrikaner National Party, which descended from the original National Party founded in 1914, won the 1948 elections and re-enforced racial separation by enacting a series of apartheid laws. It won all-white elections during

1948–1989 and received 20.4 percent of the popular vote in the first post-apartheid elections in 1994, finishing second to the ANC, which received 62.7 percent. Votes for the National Party declined in later elections and the party disbanded in 2005.

Pan-Africanist Congress (PAC)

The Pan-Africanist Congress was created by members of the ANC who objected to the ANC's multiracial approach to ending apartheid and preferred to create a new movement with exclusively indigenous African leadership. The PAC organized the anti–pass book protest in 1960 that was suppressed by the Sharpeville Massacre and other government violence. The PAC, like the ANC, was then declared illegal. The PAC created its own revolutionary army, the Azania People's Liberation Army. The PAC ultimately did not enjoy as much popular support as the ANC and won only 1.3 percent of the vote in the 1994 election compared to 62.7 percent for the ANC.

Sisulu, Walter Max Ulayate (1912–2003)

Walter Sisulu, with Nelson Mandela and Oliver Tambo, was one of the three major leaders who transformed the ANC from an elite group of liberal dissidents working totally within the legal framework of the white-controlled system to a revolutionary movement that succeeded in bringing about a nonracial democracy in South Africa.

Sisulu was born into a poor family in the Transkei region. He joined the ANC in 1940, and during the 1940s recruited both Nelson Mandela and Oliver Tambo into the organization. Sisulu worked with the multiracial South African Communist Party and the South African Indian Congress and helped promote the multiracial approach to combating apartheid. Accused with Mandela and others of organizing Umkhonto we Siwze, the ANC's revolutionary army, in 1964 he was sentenced to life in prison. He was released in the fall of 1989 and participated in the negotiation process to replace the apartheid system with a nonracial democracy.

Slovo, Joe (1926–1995)

Joe Slovo was a long-time leader of the South African Communist Party (SACP) and a cofounder of the ANC's revolutionary army, Umkhonto we Sizwe (MK). He was born in Lithuania, from which his parents emigrated to South Africa in part to escape anti-Semitism. As a teenager he worked as a clerk, joined the National Union of Distributive Workers, and then the SACP in 1942. He became a member of the SACP

central committee in 1953. During World War II he joined the South African army's Springbok Legion to fight the Nazis and served in North Africa and Italy. In the 1950s he and other members of the SACP worked with the ANC against apartheid, and he participated in drawing up the 1955 Freedom Charter. In 1961 he helped organize Umkhonto we Sizwe (MK). He left South Africa in 1963 and spent twenty-seven years in exile. At the ANC's Mozambique headquarters in 1982, his wife Ruth First was killed by a parcel bomb. In 1984, while serving as chief of staff of MK, Slovo was elected general secretary of the SACP. After the re-legalization of the ANC and the SACP in 1990, he returned to South Africa. Suffering from ill health, he declined to continue as general secretary of the SACP, and Chris Hani was elected to take his place. Slovo, a member of the ANC executive committee, played a major role in negotiations leading to the 1994 post-apartheid election in which he won a seat in parliament. The ANC government appointed him minister of housing before his death from leukemia on January 6, 1995.

South African Communist Party (SACP)

The SACP was founded in 1921 by white workers attempting to improve their wages, working conditions, and job security. Initially its leaders supported white racial dominance and discrimination against nonwhites as a means of protecting economic opportunities for white workers. Later some party members began to advocate working with and organizing nonwhite workers, and eventually the SACP became an ally of the ANC and a participant in the ANC multiracial anti-apartheid campaign. A number of SACP members became members of the ANC executive committee and leaders of the ANC revolutionary army, Umkhonto we Sizwe. Chris Hani, commander of Umkhonto in the late 1980s, later assumed the position of general secretary of the SACP before he was assassinated by white terrorists in 1993. Of the 252 ANC members elected to parliament in the post-apartheid election of 1994, fifty-three were also members of the SACP. Along with COSATU, the SACP was a member of the ANC Tripartite Alliance.

Tambo, Oliver Reginald (1917–1993)

Oliver Tambo was a college professor and ANC strategist who, with Nelson Mandela and Walter Sisulu, changed the ANC from an elite liberal group working within the legal framework of the white-dominated system to a revolutionary movement which ultimately transformed South Africa into a nonracial democracy. Tambo was born in Mpondoland in what is now the Eastern Cape Province. In 1941 he graduated with a bachelor of science from Fort Hare University and was recruited to teach science and mathematics at his old school, St. Peters College in Johannesburg. Many of his students went on to assume important positions in the ANC. In the early 1950s, Tambo left teaching to open a law practice with Nelson Mandela where they often represented poor defendants. In the early 1960s, Tambo was sent out of South Africa to establish ANC missions in other countries and mobilize foreign opinion against apartheid. With many other major ANC leaders in prison, Tambo assumed the position of president of the ANC after the previous president, Albert Luthuli, died in 1967. He continued to lead the ANC and effectively promote its cause around the world until the ANC was re-legalized in 1990. He returned to South Africa in 1991.

Truth and Reconciliation Commission

This commission was formed after the end of apartheid in the hope that revealing the truth about murders, disappearances, and bombings committed by defenders as well as opponents of apartheid would bring about reconciliation among South Africa's people. The new South African government offered immunity from criminal prosecution to many persons on all sides who committed acts of violence during the anti-apartheid conflict if they confessed their actions. Many people, including members of the white security forces, admitted to killings and other human rights abuses before the commission.

Tutu, Archbishop Desmond (Born 1931)

Bishop Tutu, who became head of the Anglican Church in South Africa, was a staunch opponent of apartheid. He continuously attempted to convince white leaders in South Africa that apartheid was against God's will. He was awarded the Nobel Peace Prize in 1985 for his efforts to end apartheid nonviolently. Once the ANC was elected to power in 1994, Bishop Tutu was appointed to preside over the Truth and Reconciliation Commission.

Umkhonto we Sizwe (MK)

MK or "Spear of the Nation" was the ANC's armed revolutionary force established in 1961. It engaged in economic sabotage and carried out many bombings, such as blowing up power transmission towers and part of the Sasol coal-to-oil conversion plant. In 1990, ANC leaders ordered the MK to cease military operations as negotiations got under way to end apartheid and create a new political system. After the end of apartheid, MK soldiers were integrated into the new South African armed forces.

United Democratic Movement (UDM)

The UDM was a federation of hundreds of anti-apartheid civic organizations that joined together in 1983 in reaction to the white regime's Multi-Racial Constitution. Most indigenous Africans, and many persons of mixed race or Asian ancestry, viewed the constitution as an attempt to preserve apartheid and began sustained, mass anti-apartheid protests. Many UDM leaders were sympathetic to the goals of the then illegal ANC.

United Party (UP)

The United Party was formed through a unification of many Afrikaners with many whites of British descent in 1934 in an effort to work together to bring South Africa out of the 1930s economic depression. The UP, with the support of some smaller white parties, brought South Africa into World War II on the side of Great Britain. Later many whites, especially Afrikaners, blamed the UP for the level of racial integration that occurred during the war. The UP was defeated by the Afrikaner-dominated National Party in the 1948 election.

James DeFronzo

See Also African American Freedom Struggle; Angolan Revolution; Cinema of Revolution; Colonialism, Anti-Colonialism, and Neo-Colonialism; Cuban Revolution; Documentaries of Revolution; Elites, Intellectuals, and Revolutionary Leadership; Ethnic and Racial Conflict: From Bargaining to Violence; Ghana's Independence Revolution: De-colonizing the Model Colony; Guerrilla Warfare and Revolution; Human Rights, Morality, Social Justice, and Revolution; Inequality, Class, and Revolution; Kenyan Mau Mau Rebellion; Mozambique Revolution; Nationalism and Revolution; Student and Youth Movements, Activism and Revolution; Trends in Revolution; Zimbabwean Revolution

References and Further Readings
Adam, Heribert. 1988. "Exile and Resistance: The African National Congress, the South African Communist Party, and the Pan African Congress." Pp. 95–124 in *A Future South Africa: Visions, Strategies and Realities,* edited by Peter L. Berger and Bobby Godsell. Boulder, CO: Westview.
Benson, Mary. 1986. *Nelson Mandela.* New York: Norton.
Berger, Peter L., and Bobby Godsell, eds. 1988. *A Future South Africa: Visions, Strategies and Realities.* Boulder, CO: Westview Press.
"CIA Tie Reported in Mandela Arrest." 1990. *New York Times,* June 10, p. A15.

Congress of the People 1955. 1987. "The Freedom Charter." Pp. 208–211 in *The Anti-Apartheid Reader: South Africa and the Struggle against White Racist Rule,* edited by David Mermelstein. New York: Grove Press.

Crawford, Neta. 1998. "South African Antiapartheid Revolts and Reform (1948–1994)." Pp. 446–450 in *The Encyclopedia of Political Revolutions,* edited by Jack Goldstone. Washington, DC: Congressional Quarterly.

Davis, Stephen M. 1987. *Apartheid's Rebels.* New Haven, CT: Yale University Press.

DeFronzo, James. 1991, 1996 (3rd edition forthcoming 2007). *Revolutions and Revolutionary Movements.* Boulder, CO: Westview.

Glaser, Daryl. 2001. *Politics and Society in South Africa.* Thousand Oaks, CA: Sage.

Gran, William. 1979. *Hot Shells: U.S. Arms for South Africa.* Boston: WGBH Transcripts.

Grundy, Kenneth W. 1993. "South Africa's Tortuous Transition," *Current History* May: 229–233.

"Inquest Finds South Africa Police Aided Zulus in Terror Campaign." 1994. *New York Times,* March 19, p. 1.

James, Frank. 1994. "The Black Middle Class," *Ebony,* August, 92–94, 96.

Karis, Thomas. 1986/1987. "South African Liberation: The Communist Factor," *Foreign Affairs, Volume 65* Winter: 267–287.

Kerson, Roger. 1987. "The Emergence of Powerful Black Unions." Pp. 276–282 in *The Anti-Apartheid Reader,* edited by David Mermelstein. New York: Grove Press.

Lawson, George. 2005. *Negotiated Revolutions: The Czech Republic, South Africa and Chile.* Burlington, VT: Ashgate Publishing.

Lazerson, Joshua. 1994. *Against the Tide: Whites in the Struggle against Apartheid.* Boulder, CO: Westview.

Le Roux, Peter. 1988. "The Economics of Conflict and Negotiation." Pp. 200–266 in *A Future South Africa: Visions,Strategies and Realities,* edited by Peter L. Berger and Bobby Godsell. Boulder, CO: Westview Press.

Lodge, Tom. 1983. *Black Politics in South Africa since 1945.* New York: Longman.

———. 2003. *Politics in South Africa: From Mandela to Mbeki.* Bloomington: Indiana University Press.

Magubane, Bernard. 1979. *The Political Economy of Race and Class in South Africa.* New York: Monthly Review Press.

Mandela, Nelson. 1994. *Long Walk to Freedom.* Boston: Little, Brown.

Marais, Hein. 2001. *South Africa: Limits to Change: The Political Economy of Transition.* London: Zed Books.

Mermelstein, David, ed. 1987. *The Anti-Apartheid Reader.* New York: Grove.

"A New Charter Wins Adoption in South Africa." 1996. *New York Times,* May 9, p. A1.

Norment, Lynn. 1994. "The Women of South Africa," *Ebony,* August, 98–100, 134.

Omeara, Dan. 1983. *Volkskapitalisme: Class, Capital, and Ideology of Afrikaner Nationalism, 1934–1948.* Cambridge: Cambridge University Press.

Omer-Cooper, J. D. 1987. *History of Southern Africa.* London: James Curry.

Price, Robert M., and Carl G. Rosberg, eds. 1980. *The Apartheid Regime.* Berkeley: University of California Press.

Radu, Michael. 1987. "The African National Congress: Cadres and Credo," *Problems of Communism* (July-August): 58–75.

Thompson, Leonard. 1985. *The Political Mythology of Apartheid.* New Haven, CT: Yale University Press.

———. 2001. *History of South Africa.* New Haven, CT: Yale University Press.

Warwick, Peter. 1983. *Black People and the South African War 1899–1902.* Cambridge: Cambridge University Press.

Wilson, Richard A., and Chris Arup. 2001. *The Politics of Truth and Reconciliation in South Africa: Legitimizing the Post-Apartheid State.* Cambridge: Cambridge University Press.

Wood, Elizabeth. 2000. *Forging Democracy from Below: Insurgent Transitions in South Africa and El Salvador.* Cambridge: Cambridge University Press.

Worden, Nigel. 2000. *Making of Modern South Africa: Conquest, Segregation, and Apartheid.* Oxford: Blackwell Publishing.

http://africanhistory.about.com/library/weekly/aa-BioChrisHani-a.htm accessed April 25, 2005.

http://www.anc.org.za accessed May 25, 2005.

http://www.anc.org.za/ancdocs/history/congress/began.html accessed May 4, 2005.

http://www.anc.org.za/ancdocs/history/mk/mk-history.html accessed May 24, 2005.

http://www.anc.org.za/people/slovo.html accessed May 31, 2005.

http://www.anctoday-admin@lists.anc.org.za accessed May 20, 2005.

http://corporatism.tripod.com/homicide.htm accessed November 7, 2004.

http://electionresources.org/za/1999/99vs94/ accessed May 30, 2005.

http://www.sacp.org.za/biographies/fbram.html accessed May 31, 2005.

http://www.statssa.gov.za accessed April 25, 2006.

South Korean Democracy Movement

CHRONOLOGY

1392–1910   Korea is called Choson ("Land of the Morning Calm") and has a centralized government with the Yi clan as a royal family. Buddhism and Confucianism are important in cultural and political life. Although the educated prefer Chinese for written language, commoners and women use Korean alphabet.

1910–1945   Japan colonizes Korea in 1910 and rules with complete control in the political, economic, cultural, and educational spheres until 1945. In the 1930s and 1940s, Koreans are forced to change their given names to Japanese names and forcibly mobilized for war. The collective memory of the colonial period remains by and large negative for most Koreans.

1919   After ten years of harsh colonial rule and inspired by Woodrow Wilson's idea of self-determination, close to two million Koreans rise to demand peaceful independence of Korea on March 1, 1919. Japanese suppress the protest with brutality, with deaths estimated as high as 7,500 (Cumings 1997, 155). The march gives rise to nationalist movements in and outside Korea, and becomes a historical symbol of Koreans' aspiration for independence.

1945–1948   Korea is liberated by the Allies in August 1945, when Japan is defeated in World War II. The United States divides Korea into North and South to expedite Japanese surrender and the Soviet Union agrees to the division. The United States Military Government occupies the southern zone until 1948, and the Republic of Korea is formed after a UN-sponsored election selects U.S.-educated Syngman Rhee as president. In Northern Korea, the Democratic People's Republic of Korea is established, and Soviet-backed Kim Il Sung is elected president.

1950–1953   The Korean War breaks out on June 25, 1950, as the North Korean army invades the South along the 38th parallel, following the guerrilla fighting and nine months of battles along the 38th parallel in 1949 that took hundreds of lives and involved thousands of troops (Cumings 1997, 247). The United Nations votes to intervene, and sixteen countries send arms and medical supplies. On July 27, 1953, North Korea and the United States sign an armistice agreement to end the war. The demilitarized zone (DMZ) is created, with Panmunjom remaining as the point of contact for future negotiations. The United States and the Republic of Korea sign a mutual defense treaty permitting U.S. troops to remain in South Korea indefinitely.

1960   High school and university students rise up to protest the massive voting fraud of the March presidential election in which Syngman Rhee is elected the president for the fourth time. He resigns in April and a parliamentary election in July inaugurates the Second Republic with Chang Myon as prime minister (1960–1961). Known as the April 19th Student Uprising, this event inspires future student protests in the 1970s and 1980s.

1961   On May 16, amid university students' demand to open a dialogue with North Korea and daily protests from various people due to rising living cost and unemployment, Major General Park Chung Hee leads a military coup overthrowing the Chang Myon government, promising to get rid of poverty and corruption. The Korean Central Intelligence Agency (KCIA), created to protect national security, is utilized mostly as a political weapon against the opposition. The junta also establishes an Economic Planning Board and directs an export-led economic growth strategy. In the 1963 presidential election, Park Chung Hee, having resigned from the military, runs as a civilian and wins the presidency.

1964   Negotiation for the Normalization Treaty with Japan begins. It is signed a year later, establishing diplomatic relations between Seoul and Tokyo, in exchange for Japanese economic assistance. The treaty is opposed by the majority of South Koreans, who feel that it exchanges Korea's national pride for economic aid. Massive protest against the treaty continues even after the treaty is signed in 1965.

1969   The ruling Democratic Republic Party (DRP) amends the constitution, under which the president could not run for another term, to allow Park Chung Hee a third presidential term in 1971. Popular opposition erupts, led by intellectuals and university students.

1970   Chon T'ae-il, a twenty-three year old garment worker, sets himself on fire in November 1970 protesting harsh working conditions and demanding the guarantee of three basic labor rights: an eight-hour workday, a minimum wage, and the right to unionize. His death triggers workers, slum dwellers, the unemployed, and students to protest against poor working conditions, the government's neglect of labor problems, and the lack of basic welfare programs for the urban poor, among other things.

1971   Park Chung Hee becomes president for the third time in what turns out to be the last direct presidential election until 1987 by defeating his opponent, Kim Dae Jung, with fraud and voter intimidation. In December, amid continuing protests against the election fraud and corruption of government officials, Park declares a national emergency, claiming that national security was threatened as the Nixon administration reduced the U.S. troops stationed in South Korea and as the United States began to negotiate with China for rapprochement.

1972   The historical Joint Communiqué is declared in July, with both North and South pledging to work to bring peaceful reunification of the peninsula. In October, Park declares martial law and a series of Yushin ("revitalizing") measures that include suspension of the national assembly, dissolution of all political parties, restrictions on civil liberties, and presidential rule-by-decree. The new constitution allows the president to be elected by an electoral college whose delegates are not themselves affiliated with a political party but elected by popular vote without political debate. Election of the president by the electoral college is also to be held without debate. Park Chung Hee is elected president by the electoral college in December 1972.

1973–1979   Dissidents and students continue to demand an end to the Yushin system and the establishment of liberal democracy by petitioning, issuing manifestos and statements, and organizing a national network of dissident groups, such as the National Coalition for Democracy (Minjujuui kungmin yonhap) in 1978 and the National Coalition for Democracy and Reunification (Minjujuui wa minjok t'ongilrul wihan kungmin yonhap) in 1979.

1979   Park Chung Hee is assassinated by the director of the Korean Central Intelligence Agency (KCIA) on October 26 amid nationwide protest against Park's authoritarian rule.

Martial law is declared in Seoul, and the prime minister is made acting president; the Army Security Command under Major General Chun Doo Hwan stages another military coup d'état in December and thwarts reform measures.

1980   On May 18, amid growing demands for political and social reforms by students, intellectuals, and workers after the death of Park Chung Hee, Chun Doo extends martial law to the whole of South Korea, bans all political activity, and arrests political leaders, including Kim Dae Jung. Citizens of Kwangju, the provincial capital of South Cholla Province, demand the lifting of Chun's measures, and the protest evolves into a citywide rebellion that comes to be known as the Kwangju People's Uprising. In August, Chun Doo Hwan is voted president of the Fifth Republic in the electoral college. Opposition leader Kim Dae Jung is convicted of anti-state activities and sentenced to death, but the sentence is later commuted.

1985   In May, a group of university students occupy the building of the United States Information Service (USIS), demanding an apology and admonishing the U.S. government for its role in the Kwangju massacre.

1987   In April, Chun Doo Hwan announces his decision to suspend discussion on constitutional revision, and citizens respond with nationwide demonstrations. Office workers and middle-class citizens join the students in weeks of street protest. On June 29, the ruling party's presidential candidate declares an eight-point "democratization reform" that includes an immediate constitutional amendment for popular election. In December, in the first popular presidential election in twenty-six years, the ruling party candidate, Roh Tae Woo, is elected by less than 37 percent of the votes, since the opposition is split among three candidates.

1997   With mounting foreign debts and rapid currency depreciation, the South Korean economy faces economic crisis, and the government accepts a large aid package from the International Monetary Fund (IMF). In December, Kim Dae Jung, a longtime opposition leader and pro-democracy advocate, is elected president.

2000   In a historic meeting between Kim Dae Jung and North Korean leader Kim Jong Il in June—the first face-to-face meeting between the leaders of North Korea and South Korea since the division of Korea in 1945—they agree to promote reconciliation and economic cooperation between the two countries. A handful of separated families meet, and both sides agree to start mail service and to reconnect road and rail links severed by the DMZ border.

INTRODUCTION

The South Korean pro-democracy movements of the 1970s and 1980s succeeded in bringing about a democratic government in 1987, after nineteen years of military dictatorship. Although it did not create an entirely new political system and changes were incremental and slow, the democratization brought new laws to protect the civil rights and liberties of South Koreans. The democratization in South Korea has made reconciliation between the two Koreas possible, which will have a significant impact on peace and stability of East Asia and the world.

BACKGROUND: CULTURE AND HISTORY

Korea was a unified nation for 1300 years before it was partitioned into North and South Korea in 1945. The Choson dynasty of Korea (1392–1910) was heavily influenced by Chinese culture but maintained a distinctive identity, as illustrated by the fact that Korea had its own unique alphabet, invented in 1446. Buddhism and Confucianism were introduced into Korea during the fourth century and have been important in the social, intellectual, and cultural life of Korea. Christianity was introduced in the eighteenth century and became one of the fastest growing religions in Korea.

Due to its location between China, Japan, and Russia, Korea had historically been subjected to frequent invasions by foreign powers, but it maintained its political independence until 1910, when Japan colonized it. Over the next thirty-six years, Japan had unlimited power over legislative, judicial, administrative, and military affairs in Korea through a powerful colonial state. The repressive measures and the general demand for national self-determination following World War I (1914–1918) led to what is now known as the March First Movement (1919), when roughly 2 million Koreans took to the streets in nonviolent demonstrations for independence. The movement was quickly suppressed. But even though it failed to gain independence, it provided a catalyst for the expansion of the nationalist movement, including the formation of a government in exile and armed Korean nationalist guerrilla activities abroad. As Japan invaded China and Southeast Asia in the 1930s and 1940s, it decreed measures to assimilate Koreans, outlawing the Korean language and Korean family names. More than 200,000 Koreans were also forcibly conscripted to military and factories, and more than 100,000 women, given the euphemism "comfort women," were forced to provide sexual service to the Japanese military (Cumings 1997, 179).

Although Koreans waged both diplomatic and armed struggle to regain Korea's independence throughout the colonial period, it was the Allied victory in World War II (1945) that ended colonial rule in Korea. The end of war also brought the Cold War, and the Korean Peninsula became a flash point between two superpowers. Korea was divided at the 38th parallel by the United States and the Soviet Union. Attempts to build a unified Korea failed, and both powers created separate governments along the 38th parallel. In August 1948, U.N.-sponsored elections led to the founding of the Republic of Korea (ROK) in the south. The United States Military Government, which ruled South Korea from 1945 to 1948, supported right-wing nationalists and suppressed leftist movements. Syngman Rhee, a nationalist who lived in exile in the United States for most of his adult life, emerged as a leader.

The North followed suit in September 1948 by establishing the Democratic People's Republic of Korea (DPRK) after the Soviet Union suppressed the moderate nationalists and gave its support to Kim Il Sung, a Communist who led anti-Japanese guerrillas in Manchuria. Both sides wanted to reunify the country. Political tension and armed skirmishes continued along the border, and the Korean War broke out in 1950, when North Korea launched an attack across the 38th parallel.

Although the war ended in 1953, a permanent peace settlement was not secured as a peace treaty was not signed. With close to 4 million military and civilian casualties, with half of Korea's industry and a third of all homes destroyed, the war had long-lasting impacts on both sides (Oberdorfer 1997, 9–10). The war left Koreans deeply scarred by atrocities committed by both sides, as many were accused of being supporters of the other side and then imprisoned or summarily executed. The existence of the Demilitarized Zone (DMZ), a mile-wide strip of no-man's-land, heavily fortified on both sides, became a symbol for the continuing political and military standoff between North and South Korea.

The Syngman Rhee government sustained itself mostly with economic and military aid from the United States. Rhee managed to win the 1952 presidential election by using the military to intimidate voters; he won again in 1956 and 1960 through massive voting fraud. The blatantly rigged election of 1960 led to a nationwide protest by high school and university students who, after 115 deaths and more than 1,000 injured, forced Syngman Rhee to resign in April 1960 (Cumings 1997, 344). This event is known as the April 19th Student Uprising and is remembered as a symbol of Koreans' aspiration for democracy.

CONTEXT AND PROCESS OF DEMOCRATIZATION

The moderate Chang Myon government (1960–1961), which came into power in the aftermath of the April 19th Student Uprising, made various efforts at political and liberal reforms. Unable to accommodate the demands by students and opposition parties for reconciliation with North Korea and more assertive diplomacy, however, the Chang government was besieged by daily protests, inefficient bureaucracy, and widespread corruption. The nine months of the Chang government's democratic experience was ended with a coup d'état on May 16, 1961, led by an army general, Park Chung Hee, who claimed he was determined to end corruption, fight Communism, and bring reunification. Korean citizens, disillusioned over the serious political disorganization and instability during the Chang Myon government, initially welcomed Park Chung Hee's call for a national economy to relieve the suffering of the people. During Park's tenure (1961–1979), Korea underwent rapid and dramatic industrialization and export growth that raised the living standard and made Korea the twelfth largest trading country in the world. Despite this achievement, Park's draconian political repression sparked decades-long opposition and gave rise to the pro-democratization movement that culminated in the 1987 Grand Uprising.

Opposition to the Park regime started in early 1964, when the government began a series of negotiations with Japan to normalize relations. But the Normalization Treaty was opposed by an overwhelming majority of Koreans, including some elements in the military. They saw the treaty as providing a way for Japan to rule over Korea once more and felt that by signing the treaty, they were exchanging Korea's national pride for economic aid. Normalization with Japan, they believed, should be preceded by Japan's sincere apology for its past colonial rule of Korea. Some Koreans also felt that cultural and economic cooperation between the North and South was more urgent than conducting talks with Japan.

Nevertheless, the Park government signed the treaty in 1965, despite a year-long protest involving tens of thousands of people. University students and intellectuals continued to oppose the Park government because the 1967 National Assembly was widely rigged and the ruling Democratic Republic Party (DRP) secretly passed a constitutional amendment in 1969 that permitted Park to run for a third term in 1971. (Under the previous constitution, the presidency was limited to two terms.) In April 1971, Park Chung Hee managed to win the presidential election, narrowly defeating his opponent Kim Dae Jung through fraud and voter intimidation. This would be the last direct presidential election in South Korea until 1987.

In the 1970s, as South Korea's industrialization policy created a massive urban migration, large slums began to grow around Seoul, the capital city, and there were increasing demands to satisfy the basic needs of the urban poor, such as jobs and housing. Workers also began to demand better working conditions, especially after a young garment worker, Chon T'ae-il, burned himself to death demanding the guarantee of three basic labor rights in 1970: an eight-hour workday, a minimum wage, and the right to unionize. In addition, the Nixon government in the United States reduced the number of American troops stationed in South Korea and began to negotiate with China. Park used all of these factors to justify his declaration of a national emergency on December 1971 that gave him the authority to ban public demonstrations, to control wages, rents, and prices, and, in essence, to rule by decree.

In October 1972, in a move that effectively and single-handedly wiped out any remnants of democracy in South Korea, Park declared martial law and the Yushin ("revitalizing") Constitution. This gave him the right to appoint a third of the National Assembly and dissolve it at will, and to appoint all judges and all members of the constitutional committee, which determined whether laws passed by the National Assembly were constitutional. More generally, the new constitution gave Park the authority to take whatever emergency measures might be needed whenever "the national security or the public safety and order is seriously threatened or anticipated to be threatened" (Hart-Landsberg 1993, 186). Utilizing the then-widespread fear of Communist victory induced by the fall of Saigon, South Vietnam, in 1975, Park issued more emergency measures restricting civil liberties and removing political opponents. The Korean Central Intelligence Agency (KCIA) was instrumental in repressing anyone challenging Park's political authority.

Throughout the Yushin era (1972–1979), students, workers, and intellectuals continuously and persistently opposed Yushin measures and sought to bring about democracy. Student activism has been a strong tradition in Korea, from the Choson period (1392–1910) and continuing into the colonial period. Along with students, dissident intellectuals, known in Korean as *chaeya insa*, actively engaged in various opposition movements, from organizing petition campaigns to issuing statements calling for democracy, to street demonstrations. Former politicians, Catholic and Protestant leaders, Buddhist priests, writers, journalists, lawyers, and leaders of women's organizations grouped themselves into various national organizations, such as the National Catholic Priests' Corps for the Realization of Justice, Council of Writers for Practicing Freedom, Association of Families of Political Prisoners, Association of Dismissed Professors, and National Congress for the Restoration of Democracy. Kim Dae Jung and Kim Young Sam, who were involved in these organizations and participated in the National Congress for the Restoration of Democracy, later became presidents of South Korea.

During the height of the political oppression under the Park regime, a group of theologians began to develop what is known as "*minjung* theology" (*minjung* means "common people") as a response to the political oppression and generally conservative stance of the church in Korea, the majority of which remained passive about the political situation. According to *minjung* theologians, the Bible showed that Jesus worked closely with the poor and oppressed; they saw that today's oppressed are *minjung* of South Korea, that Christians had to take action on behalf of their neighbors, and that there are long traditions of Christians participating in politics and social issues in Korea and elsewhere. Motivated by such a theology, a group of Christians became actively involved in the social movement for democracy and human rights during the 1970s and 1980s. Various Christian organizations such as the NCCK (National Council of Churches in Korea), YWCA (Young Women's Christian Association) and KSCF (Korean Student Christian Federation) also actively participated in the social movement, issuing statements and organizing prayer meetings, which were held weekly during the mid 1970s and attended by thousands.

But the pro-democracy movement in the 1970s was not led by a single ideology or group, but rather by a loose network of individuals who were united more by their opposition to the Park regime and their aspiration for liberal democratic ideals (such as individual liberty and revision of the constitution) than by any clearly articulated ideological doctrine or religious faith.

Starting from the mid 1970s, however, the notion of *minjung*, or "common people," came to identify and inform the struggle for democracy in South Korea, which gradually encompassed as its goals much more than liberal democratic political reform. The term *minjung* was never clearly defined and there was no consensus on its precise meaning, but it was popularly used to denote an alternative interpretive framework in which ordinary Koreans are thought to be the main

subjects of historical development, rather than just victims of oppression. Although workers and farmers were considered as true *minjung* in the *minjung* movement, in the late 1980s small business owners and "nationalistic elements" of the military were identified as a part of *minjung*. The *minjung* movement sought to bring democracy, justice, and reunification to Korea, as well as to rediscover and rejuvenate folk culture, which was perceived to have been undermined or lost during the process of South Korea's rapid industrialization and Westernization.

In March 1979, a pan-citizen group, "Citizens' Alliance for Democracy and National Reunification" (Kungmin Yonhap) was organized, composed of individuals from various groups mentioned above. The continuous anti-Yushin demonstrations culminated in general uprisings in the cities of Pusan and Masan in South Kyongsang Province, in which students and ordinary citizens took to the streets and attacked government buildings. Amid the increasing instability, Kim Jae Kyu, the director of the Korean Central Intelligence Agency (now known as the National Intelligence Service), assassinated Park on October 26, 1979, ending the much-hated Park regime.

Soon after Park's death, exuberant Korean citizens demanded political reform, and there were daily demonstrations by workers, students, and ordinary citizens. This brief period, called "Spring of Seoul," ended abruptly as General Chun Doo Hwan, then head of the military unit investigating Park's assassination, carried out another military coup on December 12, taking control of the army and subsequently thwarting efforts toward constitutional liberalization. On May 17, 1980, Chun Doo Hwan extended martial law to the entire country, dissolved the National Assembly, and arrested many politicians, including Kim Dae Jung. The citizens of Kwangju, capital city of South Cholla Province, rose up, demanded that martial law be lifted, Kim Dae Jung released, and Chun Doo Hwan step down. The brutal killing of protestors by the military's special forces angered the citizens of Kwangju, who took over the city for six days, forming an armed militia and governing themselves. The uprising was ended by the special forces storming the city on May 27 with tanks and armored personnel carriers, again brutally killing citizens. The exact number killed is unknown; the government figure is 164, but citizens' groups in Kwangju put the number as high as 2,000 (Clark 1988, 92).

The Kwangju massacre made the pro-democracy movement re-evaluate its previously held liberal democratic ideas and consider resisting not only the military dictatorship but also U.S. dominance in Korean affairs and the problems caused by the capitalist system. The post-Kwangju social movement activists also attributed the failure to achieve democratic reform partly to the lack of "scientific" analysis of Korean political economy and society. The pro-democracy groups became much more ideological, as some groups began to adopt Marxist ideas and some adopted the North Korean state ideology known as *Chuch'e sasang* ("ideology of self-reliance"). The previously mentioned notion of *minjung* also came to signify more radical ideas, as *minjung* was now defined as those who actively engaged in activities to bring about democracy and reunification.

One of the more pronounced features of the pro-democracy movement in the 1980s was its changed view toward the United States. Before the Kwangju massacre of 1980, the majority of Koreans saw the United States as an ally in their struggle for democracy. But the tacit (at a minimum) support by the United States of the military repression caused this view to change. The perceived role of the United States as an accomplice in the suppression of Kwangju transformed the struggle for democracy into a "nationalist struggle for independence from foreign intervention, and eventual unification" (Shin 1995, 514) rather than simply opposition to the military dictatorship.

Chun Doo Hwan became president of the Fifth Republic (1981–1988), and students, dissidents, workers, and slum dwellers continued their protests against his regime. The continuing demonstrations culminated in nationwide revolution in June 1987, spurred by a series of events earlier that year. In January, amid the continuing deals and negotiations among the political parties over the constitutional revision, a college student died during an interrogation in the headquarters of the National Security Planning Board (former KCIA). The death of Pak Chong-ch'ol galvanized the already widespread anti-government sentiment. Ordinary citizens from all walks of life attended Pak's commemoration services, held spontaneously in every major city, which quickly turned into protests against the Chun government.

Soon after Pak Chong-ch'ol's death, on April 13, 1987, Chun Doo Hwan announced his decision to suspend further discussion and consideration of constitutional revision until after the Olympics (held in 1988). Immediately after this announcement, there followed manifestos, prayer meetings, and hunger strikes denouncing Chun's decision by various individuals and groups including Buddhist monks, Protestant ministers and Catholic priests, and professors, lawyers, and medical doctors. The dissident groups and the main opposition party formed a pan-citizens' organization to oppose Chun's "4.13. decision" and to coordinate various protests, proposing a citizens' rally on June 10. On June 9, Yi Han-yol, a third-year student at Yonsei University, was hit by a tear-gas canister and fell into a fatal coma. The next day, 240,000 citizens—an unprecedented number—gathered in Seoul, and tens of thousands in twenty-two other cities to demand constitutional revision and the resignation of Chun Doo Hwan. Amid the daily street demonstrations, which gathered tens of thousands,

Chun's successor, Roh Tae Woo (one of his coconspirators in the 1979 coup), agreed to meet demands for political reforms with his eight-point proposal. This included the enactment of a new democratic constitution, direct popular election of the president, amnesty for Kim Dae Jung and other dissident leaders, and the creation of laws to protect the civil rights and liberties of the South Korean people. The events leading to the June 29 declaration are known as the Grand March of Democratization in South Korea. Since 1993, South Korea has seen two former pro-democracy advocates, Kim Young Sam and Kim Dae Jung, and a former human rights lawyer, Roh Moo Hyun, serve as president.

IMPACTS

Among the immediate impacts of the 1987 Grand March were a number of reforms in the political arena, including direct presidential elections. The 1987 presidential election was the first direct popular election in nineteen years. A new, democratic constitution took effect in February 1988. In March 1991 the first local elections in thirty years were held. Another notable development is the dramatic rise of the labor movement; since the 1987 Grand March, South Korean labor has undergone the most militant and successful labor activism of the four newly industrialized societies (South Korea, Taiwan, Singapore, and Hong Kong), pushing pay increases to double digits since 1987 and organizing 2,000 new unions in 1988 (Koo 2001, 153–217). Along with the rise in labor movement groups, various grassroots organizations of peasants and teachers that had been active in the anti-authoritarian movement in the 1980s have been reorganized into new national associations such as Korean Peasant Movement Coalition (Chonnong) and the Korean Teachers' and Educational Workers' Union (Chongyojo).

An equally notable development is the proliferation of various social groups known as "citizens' movement" groups. These focus on various issues, from environment to consumer protection to rights of the physically challenged to gender inequality (Kim 2000, 106–123). Many of these groups' participants are middle-class, white-collar professionals, religious leaders, and intellectuals. Another notable development since 1987 is that formerly more radical groups are working in coalition with newly organized and politically moderate citizens' movements to promote political reform and bring former political leaders to justice. Partly because of this effort and partly prompted by several months of public demonstrations by university professors, lawyers, and various individuals, two of the former presidents of Korea were prosecuted and imprisoned for the crimes they committed while in office, the first such cases in the history of Korea. Both Roh Tae Woo and Chun Doo Hwan

A student demonstrator stands to wave a banner over the crowd during a protest in Seoul, June 23, 1987. Students and other demonstrators who joined them all over South Korea protested the political and economic situation and eventually brought the regime of Chun Doo Hwan to an end. In October 1987, the National Assembly ratified a new constitution, which provided for direct presidential elections. (Patrick Robert/Sygma/Corbis)

were prosecuted and imprisoned in 1995 and 1996 on multiple charges of bribery, insurrection, and treason for their roles in the 1979 military coup that brought Chun to power and the May 1980 military crackdown in the Kwangju massacre (both were pardoned by Kim Dae Jung and released in December 1997).

Another significant impact of the democratic transition is South Korea's changed relation to North Korea. Although relations between North and South Korea continued to be troubled due to allegations about North Korea's possible nuclear weapons program, there was a significant movement toward peaceful coexistence starting with the Kim Dae Jung government. From 1998, the Kim government encouraged economic contact with North Korea in the hope of improving political relations. This approach, known as the "Sunshine" policy, eventually led to the historic meeting of the leaders of North and South Korea in Pyongyang, the North Korean capital, in June 2000. They agreed to promote reconciliation and economic cooperation between the two countries. Reconciliation between the two Koreas will help

to reduce tension and promote peace and stability in East Asia and in the world.

PEOPLE AND ORGANIZATIONS

Chon T'ae-il (1948–1970)

A garment worker in the garment district called Peace Market in Seoul, Chon set himself on fire in November 1970 after his numerous petitions to government agencies and newspapers about harsh working conditions failed to bring any changes. His death triggered workers' and students' protests over labor conditions in the 1970s.

Chun Doo Hwan (Born 1931)

President of the Fifth Republic of Korea, 1981–1988. Although South Korea achieved remarkable economic recovery while Chun was president, his lack of legitimacy (he came to power after suppressing the Kwangju People's Uprising), his suppression of political reform, and his and his relatives' illegal economic activities brought persistent protests from various sectors of society. In 1987 he picked Roh Tae Woo to be his party's presidential candidate and subsequently stepped down.

Headquarters of the National Movement for a Democratic Constitution (Kungmin Undong Ponbu)

As citizens' protests against Chun's announcement in April to postpone all discussion on the constitutional revision grew, the existing twenty-five pro-democracy movement groups established the Headquarters in May 1987 to coordinate all activities under a unified leadership. It held numerous public rallies and campaigns, culminating in the June 26 rally in which 1 million Koreans participated. The ruling government relented and agreed to meet the demands for reform on June 29.

Kim Dae Jung (Born 1925)

Eighth president of the Republic of Korea, 1998–2003. In the 1971 presidential election, Kim lost to Park Chung Hee by a narrow margin amid widespread obstructionist tactics by the ruling party. He was a vocal opponent of the Park regime and became a symbol of the pro-democracy movement throughout the 1970s and 1980s, as he endured several attempts on his life, imprisonments, house arrests, and exile. In December 1997, he was elected to the presidency, the first transition of power from the ruling party to an opposition party in Korea's history. In 2000 Kim received the Nobel Peace Prize for his work for democracy and human rights in South Korea and in East Asia, and for peace and reconciliation with North Korea.

Kim Young Sam (Born 1927)

President of South Korea from 1993 to 1998. Along with Kim Dae Jung, he was a longtime dissident leader during the presidencies of Park Chung Hee and Chun Doo Hwan, banned from politics from 1980 to 1985, and subjected to house arrests. Kim was an unsuccessful presidential candidate in 1987. In 1990 he merged his Reunification Democratic Party with the then-ruling conservative Democratic Justice Party to form the Democratic Liberal Party (DLP) in 1990, and in 1993 he became the first nonmilitary president in more than thirty years.

Korean Central Intelligence Agency (KCIA)

Soon after the 1961 military coup, Kim Jong-pil, a relative of Park Chung Hee and a fellow officer, established the KCIA to protect the state from foreign and domestic enemies. Over time, the KCIA was mainly used for political purposes by the Park regime to suppress dissidents and political opponents. The main legal apparatus used by the KCIA against the dissidents was the National Security Law (NSL), which mandated harsh felony punishments for activities considered to be "anti-state." Most of the pro-democracy activists who were arrested by the KCIA during the 1970s and 1980s were convicted of violating the NSL. The KCIA's name was changed in 1981 to the Agency for National Security Planning (ANSP) and again in 1999 to its current National Intelligence Service (NIS).

National Council of University Student Representatives (Chondaehyop)

A nationwide student organization created in 1987 in the aftermath of the electoral reform, this group developed a reunification movement and was responsible for carrying out protest against the Roh Tae Woo government. It was voted one of the ten most influential organizations in South Korea by a group of scholars and journalists in 1992.

National Democratic Youth and Student Federation (Minchu ch'ongnyon haksaeng yonhap)

This group of students at Seoul National University planned a nationwide student protest against the Park Chung Hee regime to be held on April 3, 1974. They had begun contacting individuals in universities nationwide when the plan was intercepted by the KCIA. Most of the individuals who were involved in this case became active in the democratization movement throughout the 1970s and 1980s as lawyers, publishers, opposition political party members, journalists, and scholars.

National Student Alliance (Chonhangnyon)

A nationwide university students' organization created in April 1985 which included sixty-two universities. It sought to link campus democratization with larger political reform issues. Under the slogan of "workers and students' alliance," many of its programs were centered on labor issues.

Park Chung Hee (1917–1979)

President of the Republic of Korea from 1963–1979, Park came to power in 1961, after carrying out a military coup against the Chang Myon government (1960–1961). In 1972 Park instituted the Yushin Constitution, under which he became the first indirectly elected president of South Korea, chosen by an electoral college. He ruled by decree through most of the 1970s. Although during his government South Korea achieved remarkable economic development (per capita income rose from less than $100 annually when Park took power in 1961 to more than $1,000 at the time of his death in 1979), his draconian Yushin rule spurred decade-long dissension (Oberdorfer 1997, 37). Park was assassinated by the Korean Central Intelligence Agency (KCIA) director Kim Chae Kyu on October 26, 1979.

Urban Industrial Mission (UIM)

Originating in the late 1950s as an interdenominational ministry to factory workers, it became instrumental, along with other Christian organizations such as Young Catholic Workers (JOC) Christian Academy, in educating workers about their rights and in some cases organizing workers to unionize in the 1970s.

Youth Coalition for Democracy Movement (Minch'ongnyon)

Established in September 1983 by former student activists, its publications on future directions, strategies, and tactics of the pro-democracy movement were critical in promoting the common goals of the movement and helped to connect university student activists to those active in various social movements.

Namhee Lee

See Also Armed Forces, Revolution, and Counter-Revolution; Cinema of Revolution; Democracy, Dictatorship, and Fascism; Documentaries of Revolution; Elites, Intellectuals, and Revolutionary Leadership; Korean Civil War; Student and Youth Movements, Activism and Revolution; War and Revolution

References and Further Readings
Clark, Donald N., ed. 1988. *The Kwangju Uprising.* Boulder, CO: Westview Press.
Cumings, Bruce. 1981. 1991. *The Origins of the Korean War.* 2 vols. Princeton, NJ: Princeton University Press.
———. 1997. *Korea's Place in the Sun: A Modern History.* New York: W.W. Norton.
Hart-Landsberg, Martin. 1993. *The Rush to Development: Economic Change and Political Struggle in South Korea.* New York: Monthly Review Press.
Kim, Sunhyuk. 2000. *The Politics of Democratization in Korea: The Role of Civil Society.* Pittsburgh, PA: University of Pittsburgh Press.
Koo, Hagen. 2001. *Korean Workers: The Culture and Politics of Class Formation.* Ithaca, NY: Cornell University Press.
Lee, Namhee. 2001. "Making Minjung Subjectivity: Crisis of Subjectivity and Rewriting History, 1960–1988." PhD diss. University of Chicago.
Oberdorfer, Don. 1997. *The Two Koreas: A Contemporary History.* New York: Basic Books.
Ogle, George E. 1990. *South Korea: Dissent within the Economic Miracle.* London: Zed Books.
Shin, Gi Wook. 1995. "Marxism, Anti-Americanism and Democracy in South Korea," *Positions: East Asia Cultures Critique* 3 (2): 508–533.
Sohn, Hak-Kyu. 1989. *Authoritarianism and Opposition in South Korea.* London: Routledge.
Wells, Kenneth M., ed. 1995. *South Korea's Minjung Movement: The Culture and Politics of Dissidence.* Honolulu: University of Hawaii Press.

Spanish American Revolutions of Independence

CHRONOLOGY

1759–1788	Charles III rules Spain and initiates period of Bourbon reforms.
1762	British occupy Havana.
1767	Jesuits are expelled from Spain and its colonies.
1775–1783	U.S. War of Independence.
1780–1781	Tupac Amaru II's Revolt in Peru.
1780	Comunero Revolt in Socorro (Colombia).
1781–1782	Tupac Katari's Revolt in Bolivia.
1788–1808	Charles IV becomes king of Spain.
1789	French Revolution.
1791	Haitian Revolution.
1797	British seize Trinidad, Tobago, and St Lucia.
1804	Haiti gains independence.
1806	British invade Buenos Aires.

1807   British invade Montevideo and Buenos Aires; Napoléon invades Portugal; Portuguese royal family and court transfer to Brazil.

1808   Mutiny of La Granja results in Ferdinand VII becoming king of Spain; French occupy Spain; Joseph Bonaparte becomes King Joseph I of Spain; Spanish War of Independence begins; Viceroy José de Iturrigaray is deposed in a palace coup led by the Spanish merchant guild in Mexico City (September).

1808–1813   Spanish War of Independence (Peninsular War).

1809   Creole revolts erupt in La Paz (July 16) and Quito (August 19).

1810   Creole revolts erupt in Caracas (April 19), Buenos Aires (May 18–19), Santiago de Chile (July 16), Bogotá (July 20), Dolores (Mexico, September 16). Spanish forces retaliate and Wars of Independence get under way.

1811   Hidalgo is executed (Mexico); revolt erupts in Banda Oriental (Uruguay); battles of Paraguarí and Taguarí (Paraguay); Paraguay gains independence; Venezuela declares independence.

1812   Constitution of Cadiz; royalists recapture Caracas and end First Venezuelan Republic.

1813   Constitution of Cadiz is implemented in Spanish America; Bolívar decrees *Guerra a Muerte* and briefly liberates Venezuela.

1814   Constitution of Apatzingán (Mexico); Battle of Rancagua (Chile); Ferdinand VII is restored to the Spanish throne and revokes the 1812 constitution; Montevideo is captured by insurgents.

1814–1815   Pumacahua's Revolt (Peru).

1815   Morelos is executed (Mexico); Artigas liberates Provincia Oriental (Uruguay); Spanish expedition succeeds in retaking Venezuela and Colombia. Bolivar goes into exile in Jamaica and Haiti.

1816   Dr. Francia becomes dictator of Paraguay (1816–1840); João VI becomes king of Portugal and Brazil.

1816–1820   Brazil invades Provincia Oriental (Uruguay).

1817   Mina's expedition to Mexico; San Martín's army crosses the Andes from Argentina into Chile; Battle of Chacabuco (Chile).

1818   Battles of Cancha Rayada and Maipú (Chile); Chile gains its independence; Bolívar liberates some regions of Venezuela.

1819   United States purchases Florida; Bolívar and Santander's army cross the Andes from Venezuela into Colombia; Battle of Boyacá (Colombia); Bolívar proclaims creation of Republic of Colombia (Gran Colombia), which includes Venezuela, New Granada (Colombia), and Ecuador.

1820   Riego Revolt in Spain leads to restoration of 1812 Constitution; San Martín leads seaborne liberating expedition from Chile to Peru.

1820–1823   The 1812 Constitution is restored in Spain.

1821   Mexico and Central America become independent; Battle of Carabobo (Venezuela); independence of Venezuela and Colombia.

1822   Agustín de Iturbide's Mexican empire is forged; battles of Bomboná (Colombia) and Pichincha (Ecuador); independence of Brazil; Ecuador is integrated into Gran Colombia; San Martín and Bolívar meet in Guayaquil.

1822–1844   Haitian occupation of Santo Domingo (Dominican Republic).

1823   Mexican empire ends; United Provinces of Central America comes into existence; Battle of Puerto Cabello (Venezuela); Bolívar arrives in Peru; slavery is abolished in Chile.

1824   Slavery is abolished in Central America; battles of Junín and Ayacucho (Peru); independence of Peru.

1825	Battle of Tumusla (Bolivia); independence of Bolivia; Spaniards abandon fortress of San Juan de Ulúa (Mexico).
1825–1828	Argentine-Brazilian War.
1826	Spaniards surrender Callao (Peru).
1828	Independence of Uruguay.

INTRODUCTION

By 1808 a conflagration of issues meant that Spanish America was on the verge of a revolutionary explosion. More than fifty years of Bourbon reforms had led to high Creole, mestizo, Indian, and slave discontent. Bourbon political, economic, military, and religious policies had succeeded in alienating the majority of the colonial population. The American War of Independence (1775–1783) had become a source of inspiration for many Creoles, and the French Revolution (1789) had been equally influential in spreading beliefs that exalted the need for equality, liberty, and fraternity. The Napoleonic occupation of Spain in 1808 resulted in a constitutional crisis that provoked the revolutions of independence. After ten to fifteen years of brutal civil war in most of Spain's colonies, the Spanish monarchy lost control of its entire empire in continental America, succeeding only in holding on to Cuba, Puerto Rico, and Santo Domingo.

BACKGROUND: CULTURE AND HISTORY

After 1760 there was an increasing sense among the population in Spanish America that Bourbon reformism was attacking the social bases and political values that had characterized the Spanish empire for over two and a half centuries. Under the Habsburgs, Spain's policy toward its colonies could almost be described as one of abandon. Centuries of inertia on the part of the monarchy had resulted in the colonies enjoying a high degree of autonomy. It was Charles III (1759–1788), a member of the Bourbon dynasty that had taken hold of Spain's destiny, replacing the Habsburgs in the wake of the Spanish War of Succession (1702–1713), who changed all of that. Determined to impose his own brand of enlightened despotism, Charles III energetically set about reforming his domains, determined to encourage social and agricultural improvement while tightening his administration's control over the empire. The changes he promoted have come to be known as the Bourbon reforms.

Under Charles III and Charles IV (1788–1808), the "second conquest of America" took place. This was a bureaucratic conquest. New viceroyalties were created. The previous district officers of the Spanish empire were replaced by intendants who set about closely supervising the American population. Government became far more centralized. While in 1750 the majority of existing administrators had been born and bred in the colonies, by 1780, over 72 percent were newcomers from Spain. The fact that the Creoles (white Spanish Americans of Spanish descent) were discriminated against and that most political posts went to Spaniards contributed to the heightening of tensions between Americans and Spaniards.

The majority of first-generation Creoles were aware that they could not rise in the colonial political hierarchy for the simple reason that they had been born in the Americas. This awareness of discrimination would become a determining factor in motivating them to rise up in arms against Spain. Nevertheless, the leap they needed to take to progress from criticizing the Spanish intendants to rebelling against them was not an easy one. They were bound to allegiance to the Spanish crown due to the ethnic fabric of the cultures in which they lived. They were terrified of the consequences of unleashing a revolution. The majority of the population, Indians, black slaves, and even mestizos (racially mixed Spanish Americans of Spanish-Indian descent), might inspire a race war in which they could very easily be wiped out, belonging, as they did, to a rather exclusive minority. At the end of the eighteenth century, out of an estimated total population of 17 million in Spanish America, only 3.2 million were whites, and of these, 150,000 were Spanish (Lynch 1973, 19). Most Creoles wanted a free hand in the running of their provinces and thus opposed the pressures that Bourbon Spanish domination represented. However, they would rather support the Spaniards than throw in their lot with revolutionaries, who were not prepared to protect them from the wrath of a discontented majority that hated them as much as they hated the Spaniards.

The Bourbon economic policies also created upheaval in the colonies. It was Spain's need for greater revenues that inspired the bureaucratic expansion in the first place. Spain's involvement in the Seven Years War (1756–1763), its war with Britain, renewed in 1779, its war with France in 1793, and its participation in the French Revolutionary and Napoleonic Wars, now serving the French (1796–1808), all meant that it became imperative for Spain to plunder the wealth of its colonies. Taxes were raised, monopolies were created, and trading laws were implemented to assist the Spanish economy while clearly damaging the interests of the local elites in the colonies. As a result of this new controlled economy, returns from America to Spain between 1778 and 1784 increased by 1528 percent (Lynch 1973, 12)! In addition to this, a mining boom at the end of the eighteenth century resulted in Spanish America yielding, in 1800, 90 percent of the total world production of silver, and the profits were spent on Spain's war efforts. By 1800 most Creoles were under the impression that their countries were being invaded by Spaniards, depriving them of all positions of political responsibility, and that their wealth was being plundered in order to subsidize foreign wars in which they had no interest.

Spain's ongoing wars with Britain, which entailed the loss of Trinidad, Tobago, and St. Lucia in 1797, resulted in a further grievance for the people of Spanish America: the creation of standing armies in the colonies. The British occupation of Havana in 1762 sent a very clear signal to Madrid that Spain needed to strengthen its defenses. In an attempt to protect its colonies, unprecedented numbers of Spanish officers and soldiers were sent out. However, given that most peninsular troops were needed to fight the different wars in Europe, it became necessary to form colonial military units, enlisting members from the local populations. The arrival of Spanish officers exacerbated the grievances of the Creoles by denying them the opportunity to attain the higher ranks in the army. The need to sustain the increased troops became another source of discontent, as it fell upon the local communities to feed, house, and pay for them. The means by which the soldiers were supported affected not only the Creoles, but also the majority of the population. In the long run, the formation of standing armies in the colonies not only created much discontent, it resulted in the creation of militias that would ultimately revolt against Madrid.

Church-state relations were to represent an equally important part of the Americans' rejection of Spain. One of the main ideas proposed by the Enlightenment was that the church's influence should be restricted. Religion and superstition must give way to the new scientific and philosophical ideas that dominated eighteenth-century France. Therefore the clergy were ousted from positions of political responsibility. A serious attempt was made to secularize education. Ecclesiastical immunities and privileges (*fueros*) by which the clergy were not expected to pay taxes were reduced. The need to raise revenue for the war efforts also meant that the church's wealth and properties ceased to be treated as inviolable. The Bourbon reforms met fierce opposition in Spanish America. This was due to the ethnic composition of the clergy, paired with the profound religious fervor that characterized the Indian and mestizo population of America. For although the church, as a whole, resented the assault the Bourbon reforms entailed, its hierarchy responded to the increased state pressure on its revenues by balancing its accounts to the detriment of its lower clergy. The higher clergy, all of whom were Spanish, ensured that their welfare was not affected while, in contrast, they allowed the lower clergy (Creoles and mestizos) to bear the brunt of the church's depleted funds. A disgruntled Creole and mestizo lower clergy discovered not only that their prospects of ascending in the ecclesiastical hierarchy were blocked by Spanish dominance of the church, but that their own personal and financial circumstances were profoundly affected by Bourbon fiscal demands.

On a deeper level, in a context whereby a new generation of Spanish bishops, appointed by the crown, arrived in the colonies advocating a new understanding of the church's role, the clash between traditional practices and those now espoused by certain members of the higher peninsular clergy became deeply unsettling. The bishops who arrived after 1760 attacked popular religious manifestations and cults, arguing that these were examples of superstition that needed to be eradicated in the name of a more enlightened church. In countries where Roman Catholicism had come to integrate a wide range of Indian practices, these views challenged the very essence of Spanish American devotion. Long-held indigenous festivities such as the Mexican Day of the Dead on All Saints Day, processions, pilgrimages, cults of "Indian" saints and, in particular, of the Virgin Mary in her many manifestations were suddenly considered to be fanatical by the higher peninsular clergy.

This generation-long Bourbon assault on the Church had serious repercussions in Spanish America. At one level the lower clergy were being pushed into adopting a confrontational stance by the way that they were being treated, both financially and morally. At another, it was precisely the parish priests who through daily contact with the suffering of their parishioners were in a position to realize the extent to which Bourbon Spain was responsible for the social deprivation of the early 1800s. Once the wars of independence began, a high proportion of leading revolutionaries were priests. It is significant that the revolts in which priests played a key role were characterized by their defense of a seemingly contradictory agenda whereby what was, at one level, a reactionary clerical backlash against the main secularizing tenets of the Enlightenment was, at another level, a radical movement against social injustice.

One specific decree that was to have major repercussions in the collective imagination of Spanish America was the expulsion of the Jesuits in 1767. Representative of Charles III's drive to restrict church influence was his order to expel the Jesuits, since they obeyed the pope and not the king. Over 2,500 Jesuits, most of them Creoles, were forced to abandon their homelands. This measure deprived Spanish America of its most outstanding educators, and the population regarded the Jesuits' life-long exile as an example of Bourbon despotism. In the first instance, the dismay of the populace was expressed in a number of riots and minor uprisings. Thereafter, a great resentment was borne by the communities the Jesuits left behind.

It was the exiled Jesuits who began the intellectual process of defining the particularity of the future nations they had been forced to leave. Ostracized in Europe, the Creole Jesuits took it upon themselves to refute the views generally accepted in Europe that the New World was an inferior continent. Offended by the writings of European philosophers and scientists, some of the exiled Jesuits wrote works of outstanding scholarship that defended their homelands' peoples, ecologies, and histories. Francisco Javier Clavigero, Juan Ignacio Molina, and Juan de Velasco, to name but a few, initiated a process of national reappraisal that soon caught the imagination of Europe as well as the Americas. Almost immediately after the exiled Jesuits' works started to be circulated in America, a wide range of Creole intellectuals went on to develop their rebuttal of European prejudices. Publications started to abound in the colonies celebrating the wealth and beauty of their regions, referring to them as their mother countries.

Coinciding with this proliferation of Creole writings, a leading Prussian scientist, Alexander von Humboldt, visited areas that are present-day Venezuela, Colombia, Peru, Cuba, and Mexico between 1799 and 1804. The books he wrote recounting his adventures, once he returned to Paris, were to become extremely influential. The fact that the writings of a European confirmed many of the views that had been defended by the Creole intellectuals served to validate what the Creoles already knew. It was Humboldt who predicted that with independence, the future prosperity of the different American nations would be extraordinary. Humboldt's writings, translated almost immediately into Spanish, led many Creoles to believe that all that was needed for them to enjoy the wealth of their regions was to become independent.

CONTEXT AND PROCESS OF REVOLUTION

Spanish America by 1808 was on the verge of revolution. Decades of Bourbon reforms had resulted in high levels of discontent among Creoles, mestizos, Indians, and slaves. The majority of the colonial population had become alienated by Bourbon political, economic, military, and religious policies. The American War of Independence (1775–1783) had inspired many Creoles. And the French Revolution (1789) had been just as influential in spreading beliefs that extolled the need for liberty, equality, and fraternity. However, while all of these issues meant that Spanish America was close to being consumed by revolutionary activity, a spark was needed to set the colonies on fire. This spark came from Spain.

In December 1807, Napoléon gave the order for the military occupation of the peninsula. On March 19, 1808, following the mutiny of La Granja, Charles IV abdicated in favor of his son, Ferdinand VII, who, in turn, left Madrid in April in the hands of the French to meet Napoléon at Bayonne. On May 5, only three days after the people of Madrid rose up in arms in a popular uprising against the invaders, Ferdinand relinquished his claim to the throne. Napoléon had his brother crowned King Joseph I of Spain, precipitating what is known in Spain as the War of Independence (1808–1813).

It was the French usurpation of the Spanish throne that unleashed the constitutional crisis that led to the outbreak of the revolutions of independence in Spanish America. With Ferdinand VII in France, once news of the seizure of Madrid reached the Americas, it became evident that the colonies had been left without a monarch they could obey. They could not take their orders from Joseph I, since he was a usurper. It was not clear whether they should obey the Spanish rebel juntas that were formed in the peninsula, since these had awarded themselves rights that had not been granted by the king. Throughout the summer of 1808, as news of the French occupation of Spain spread throughout the colonies, the different vice-regal and municipal authorities found themselves forced to decide who was responsible for the day-to-day running of their regional administrations. As long as Ferdinand VII was in France, it was clear that they would have to run the show themselves. Many Creoles realized that the time had come to seize the day. Most Spaniards posted in the colonies, aware that the next step from allowing the Creoles in would probably be independence, resisted the Creoles' attempts to become involved in the political administration of the colonies and sought guidance from the rebel juntas in Spain. Within two years of the French occupation of Spain, the political situation of most of Spanish America had descended into a state of brutal civil war. Between 1809 and 1810 Creole rebellions led to the capture of numerous cities and governments. The Spaniards retaliated, and all hell broke loose.

Between 1808 and 1825, most of Spanish America was ravaged by war. Control of the main cities changed hands as the development of the wars favored either the royalist or the patriot armies at different points in time. Developments in Spain further complicated matters, creating divisions both within the royalist and the patriot forces. In 1812, the rebel junta in Cadiz drafted one of the most progressive constitutions of the period. Responses in the colonies to the 1812 charter were fraught with contradictions. When the constitution began to be implemented in Spanish America in 1813, many liberal Creoles preferred to remain attached to Spain rather than support independence movements that, in some cases, appeared to be led by reactionary clerical traditionalists. For many Spanish administrators, in contrast, the implementation of the constitution was a blow to their attempts to crush the revolts, since it enabled the population at large, *castas* (racially mixed people) and Creoles alike, to elect their representatives in the *Cortes.* Once Ferdinand VII returned to power and revoked the constitution in 1814, the Spanish forces in the colonies became divided between those who were liberals and those who were absolutists. Their divisions became further exacerbated in 1820, when a liberal revolt in Spain succeeded in forcing the monarch to impose the 1812 charter all over again, only to overthrow it, once more, in 1823.

The revolutions of independence were a complex affair. It was not an easy case of Creoles fighting Spaniards. Creoles fought against Spaniards, against each other, against Indians, against *castas,* and against blacks. Divided between centralists and federalists, defenders of free-market economics and protectionist policies, abolitionists and slave-traders, republicans and monarchists, absolutists and constitutionalists, anti-clerical radicals and pro-clerical traditionalists, the Creole elites were only united by a fragile desire for independence. This desire remained, in many cases, hesitant, faced as they were with the threat of social dissolution and a race war in which they were numerically inferior. The Indians' response to the revolutions was equally difficult to categorize. In certain provinces where it became evident that the war was a power struggle between whites, their stance was one of notorious apathy. In other areas, Indians participated with vigor, sometimes fighting for the Spaniards, sometimes against. The *castas,* whether they were mestizos or *mulattos* (persons of mixed black and white ancestry), fought for both sides, depending on where they were from and what their particular context was. The black slaves, when they revolted, as was the case in Venezuela, took it upon themselves to attack all whites, regardless of whether they were patriots or royalists. In most cases local issues were key to motivating the colonial population to take one side or another. Ancient rivalries between and within local communities meant that different families and villages used the pretext of the revolutions to settle old grudges. They joined the patriots or the royalists in response to the side their local rivals adopted, regardless of whether they believed in grand and abstract terms such as *independence.* People fought for their regions, their districts, their village-based clans, for themselves. Notions such as Mexico and Colombia were not even commonly used by the high-ranking officers of the patriot-insurgent armies, let alone by the illiterate majority forced to fight for one cause or the other. The revolutions were characterized by murders, looting, pillage, rape. Banditry proliferated. It became common for people to change sides from patriot to royalist and back again, depending on circumstances, on who had the upper hand, on what favored their regional or personal interests. Regional rivalries also meant that as the emergent nations came into being, conflicts between them abounded. Buenos Aires' attempts to control Montevideo, Asunción, and La Paz meant that future Uruguayans, Paraguayans, and

Bolivians found themselves fighting the Argentineans with as much resolve as they fought the Spaniards.

The constitutional crisis of 1808 resulted in a mosaic of parallel yet not identical contexts in the colonies. The power vacuum that resulted from the French occupation of Spain provided the instability necessary for the discontent caused by fifty years of Bourbon reformism to erupt into violence. However, independence did not come easily. Between ten and fifteen years of war were fought before Spain's control of its colonies in continental America was brought to an end. The fact that the Spaniards were a minority no doubt meant that their winning the wars would prove almost impossible. Of the 40,000 Spanish troops dispatched between 1811 and 1818, the majority died of tropical diseases. However, due credit must be awarded to the military genius of those Creole generals who ensured that independence was achieved: Simón Bolívar (1783–1830), José de San Martín (1778–1850), Francisco de Paula Santander (1792–1840), and Antonio José de Sucre (1795–1830).

Mexico's Revolution of Independence

The Mexican Revolution of Independence (1810–1821) erupted on September 16, 1810, in the village of Dolores, when the Creole priest Miguel Hidalgo y Costilla summoned his parishioners to his church and inspired them to revolt against Spanish domination. The revolt was initially supported by Creoles who withdrew their support as Hidalgo's large and spontaneous army of 50,000 assaulted properties large and small, regardless of whether they belonged to Creoles or Spaniards, killing anybody who stood in their way. The colonial army, almost in its entirety, remained loyal to Spain, despite its predominantly Creole and *mestizo* makeup, and after December 1810, initiated a successful campaign of counterinsurgency. Hidalgo retreated to Guadalajara, where he became, as well as *generalísimo* (general of generals), *Su Alteza Serenísima* (His Serene Highness). Hidalgo was, however, captured and executed on June 30, 1811.

Nevertheless, the insurgency remained strong without Hidalgo. Another priest, José María Morelos, took over the leadership of the revolution while guerrilla armies, led by regional chieftains, surfaced throughout the colony. It was Morelos who gave the revolution a clearer ideological direction as well as a more disciplined approach to the military organization of the patriot forces. He supported the creation of a rebel congress, based in Chilpancingo, which went on to draft the 1814 Constitution of Apatzingán. However, Morelos was also captured and executed on December 22, 1815.

Following Morelos' death, the insurgency lost both its strength and its momentum. From a total of 80,000 members of insurgent militias, there remained, by 1816, no more than

8,000 poorly armed insurgents in the field, and these scattered over the vast territories of the country. Although Francisco Javier Mina, a Spanish liberal who joined the insurgents upon his arrival in Mexico, led the 1817 expedition that gave the revolution some respite, he was taken prisoner and was executed on November 11 that year. The years from 1810 to 1815 were the years of greatest revolutionary activity in Mexico. From 1816 to 1821 the Revolution of Independence was characterized by constant yet minor skirmishes that in no way resembled the large military campaigns of the previous years. Nonetheless, guerrilla warfare proved effective as it became clear to the high-ranking Creole officers in the royalist army that peace would not be restored until Mexico became independent. It was this realization, paired with the impact of events in Spain on the colonies in the wake of the restoration of the constitution, that led these Creole officers to finally turn their backs on Madrid and join forces with the insurgents.

On February 24, 1821, Colonel Agustín de Iturbide, one of the colonial government's more dedicated Creole officers, rebelled and proclaimed Mexico's independence with his Plan of Iguala. With the promise of Three Guarantees—that Mexico would be independent, that Roman Catholicism would be the official religion, and that all Spaniards could continue to live unharmed in Mexico—Iturbide succeeded in bringing old insurgents and old royalists together. Independence was formally attained on September 27, 1821, when the Army of the Three Guarantees marched into Mexico City. Iturbide had himself proclaimed Emperor Agustín I on May 18, 1822.

It was in response to the events in Mexico that Central America achieved independence from Spain in 1821. Prior to 1820, no unified independence movement had surfaced in Central America. It was only after news of the Plan of Iguala reached Central America that, on September 15, 1821, the authorities in Guatemala City issued their own declaration of independence. The other cities in the region followed suit and were integrated into Iturbide's Mexican empire (1821–1823). Once Iturbide abdicated (March 19, 1823), the five provinces of Guatemala, El Salvador, Honduras, Nicaragua, and Costa Rica (the elites of Chiapas opted to remain part of Mexico) established their separate independence in their joint declaration of July 1, 1823, whereby they became the United Provinces of Central America.

The Independence of the River Plate Provinces

The Vice-Royalty of the River Plate encompassed present-day Argentina, Uruguay, Paraguay, and Bolivia (after 1776), with its administrative capital in Buenos Aires. Its own wars of independence were different from the rest due to the im-

pact on the area of a British expeditionary force prior to the 1808 constitutional crisis. On June 27, 1806, as part of the war Britain was fighting against France and Spain, British troops took Buenos Aires. The Spanish viceroy, together with the majority of the Spanish elites, abandoned the port and took refuge in their country estates. It was left up to the Creoles and the lower classes of the port to confront the invaders. This they did with a vengeance, defeating the British on August 12, 1806, taking the British commander and 1,200 troops prisoner.

When a second British expeditionary force was defeated in Buenos Aires after it had succeeded in taking Montevideo in 1807, it became clear to the Argentinean Creoles that it was they and not the Spanish who had repulsed the invaders. When the Spaniards attempted to restore the old order they found that the Creoles in Buenos Aires, in military control of the provincial capital, were not prepared to let go of it. Therefore, when news arrived of the French occupation of Spain, Buenos Aires was already controlled by the Creole elites. However, it was not until May 18–19, 1810, that the Creoles in Buenos Aires, feeling that they needed to exert greater power over their province, staged the May Revolution that brought about the independence of Argentina. Thereafter, from 1810 to 1816, the conflicts that affected the region were mainly fought by Creoles against each other. The social dimensions that characterized the war in Mexico and the racial dimensions that characterized the wars in Peru, Ecuador, Colombia, and Venezuela were absent in the River Plate. The different economic interests of Buenos Aires and the interior led to clashes over the policies that were pursued: free market or protectionist respectively. Within Buenos Aires itself, Creole divisions resulted in the government changing hands on five occasions between 1810 and 1819. In 1820 the government changed hands on an average of once every two weeks, and it was only after Bernardino Rivadavia came to power in July 1821 that Argentina achieved some form of stability.

Montevideo, which remained deeply royalist in 1808, in part out of its own desire for emancipation from Buenos Aires, rejected the May 1810 Revolution from the outset. However, for the Uruguayan Creoles it became evident that supporting Spanish rule purely to avoid dependence on Buenos Aires was too damaging a policy to pursue. José Gervasio Artigas, a gaucho (Uruguayan cowboy) Creole renowned for his enlightened views, used the support of Buenos Aires to revolutionize his homeland. When the Spanish viceroy in Montevideo declared war on Buenos Aires in February 1811, the independence movement of the Banda Oriental was ignited. On February 26 a gaucho army was formed in the southwest corner of the province and pronounced the *grito de Asencio* (the Uruguayan call to arms). Artigas, with a small Argentinean force, moved into Uruguay, defeated the Spaniards at the battle of Las Piedras, and came close to taking Montevideo. Faced with the prospect of defeat, the viceroy allowed a Portuguese army to come to his rescue from Brazil. Fearing that the Portuguese might use their presence in Uruguay to annex the province for Brazil, the authorities in Buenos Aires signed a treaty with Montevideo (October 20, 1811) whereby Buenos Aires accepted Spanish control of the Banda Oriental as long as the Portuguese withdrew their forces.

Betrayed, Artigas led a heroic exodus of more than 16,000 Uruguayans out of the populated areas of the Banda Oriental into the wilderness, in the interior, announcing that the people from the Banda Oriental would never be subordinated to either Spain or Buenos Aires. Nonetheless, once the Portuguese evacuated the province, an uneasy alliance was formed between Artigas and the Buenos Aires junta that led to a joint siege of Montevideo in 1813. This alliance crumbled after Artigas demanded the independence of the United Provinces of the River Plate from Spain while awarding separate independent sovereignty to the Banda Oriental. The authorities in Buenos Aires declared him an outlaw and dispatched a new expeditionary army to Montevideo in 1814. After a further year of war, in February 1815, the Argentineans finally evacuated Montevideo, and Artigas became the ruler of the Provincia Oriental.

However, Uruguay did not achieve complete independence until August 27, 1828. Although Artigas ruled the Banda Oriental with noteworthy agrarian radicalism, his plans were thwarted in August 1816, when the Portuguese invaded. Between 1816 and 1820 Artigas led the war against the Portuguese, only to find himself defeated and seeking refuge in Paraguay, where he died thirty years later. Uruguay became, in July 1821, a province of Brazil, only achieving its own sovereign status after the Argentine-Brazilian War (1825–1828) came to an end.

Asunción also rejected Buenos Aires' authority. However, unlike Montevideo, its support for Spain did not last as long. The May 1810 Revolution in Buenos Aires served as the catalyst that provoked the independence movement of the region. The Paraguayan elites responded to the Buenos Aires junta by stating that they would remain loyal to Spain whilst maintaining fraternal relations with the port. When Buenos Aires sent General Manuel Belgrano to impose its control over the province, around 5,000 Paraguayans rose up in arms to defend their autonomy and defeated the Argentineans at the battles of Paraguarí (January 9, 1811) and Tacuarí (March 9, 1811). The Spanish authorities in Asunción played only a small part in the conflict, and after Belgrano retreated, the Creoles took over the provincial capital in the revolution of May 14, 1811. On May 17, Paraguay declared its independence from Spain and Buenos Aires. A Creole junta was formed and after two years of attempted liberal government allowed Dr. José Gaspar Rodríguez de Francia to become "Supreme Dictator of the Republic" in 1814. On June 1, 1816,

Dr. Francia was appointed "Perpetual Dictator" and went on to serve as *El Supremo* until he died in 1840.

Revolution in the Andes—from Buenos Aires to Lima

Although Buenos Aires was unsuccessful in its attempts to control Paraguay, Bolivia, and Uruguay, it was partly responsible for the liberation of Chile. José de San Martín, an Argentinean from Misiones who had fought in the Spanish War of Independence, returned to Buenos Aires in 1812 with the intention of joining the revolution and leading it from Argentina, over the Andes, to Chile, Peru, Bolivia, and Ecuador. For San Martín it became evident that as long as Peru was royalist, the independence of South America would be in jeopardy. Given that the three military expeditions Buenos Aires had dispatched to control La Paz had all ended in failure, San Martín came up with the idea of reaching Lima by heading first west to Chile and then north along the Pacific coast.

On January 9, 1817, with an army of 5,000, San Martín set his plan in motion. The timing of his expedition was crucial in determining its success. After seven years of conflict in Chile, whereby the Creole control of Santiago had come and gone, leading to the imposition of a particularly oppressive Spanish-dominated regime, most Chileans were ready to join a liberating army. The key leader of Chilean independence, Bernardo O'Higgins Riquelme, defeated at the battle of Rancagua (October 1–2, 1814) and forced into exile in Mendoza, joined forces with San Martín.

In what must have represented one of the most extraordinary feats of the revolutions of independence, San Martín's army crossed the Andes in two separate sections, managing to regroup at the other side at the appointed time. On the plains of Chacabuco, Argentinean and Chilean soldiers defeated the royalists (February 12, 1817) and went on to capture Santiago. On February 12, 1818, O'Higgins proclaimed the independence of Chile from Spain and Argentina. The royalists made one last bid to reconquer Santiago. Although San Martín was defeated at the battle of Cancha Rayada (March 19, 1818), he managed to reconcentrate his forces and strike a definitive blow against the Spanish forces in the battle of Maipú (April 5, 1818). Chile consolidated its independence. O'Higgins became the head of the Chilean government, and San Martín set about orchestrating the next stage of his plan: the liberation of Peru.

On August 25, 1820, San Martín's expedition, consisting of 4,500 Chilean troops and a large contingency of British mercenaries who had joined the Latin American revolutions following the end of the Napoleonic Wars in 1815, set sail from Valparaíso. They landed at Pisco and remained there for six

Chileans, led by General José de San Martín, fight for their independence from Spain in 1817. (Library of Congress)

weeks while San Martín waited for the Peruvians to rise up in arms and join his liberating army. This did not happen. The memory of Tupac Amaru's 1780–1781 revolt had played a key role in determining the Peruvian Creoles' patent ambiguity over the issue of independence. A second major Indian uprising (1814–1815), led this time by Mateo Pumacahua, meant that the Creoles had become even more reluctant to reject Spanish rule and protection than before. The end result was that between December 29, 1820, when the town hall of Trujillo launched its proclamation of independence, and January 1826, when the last Spanish stronghold in Callao capitulated, the government of Peru changed hands with alarming frequency. Lima was taken by San Martín and Spaniards alike; the Peruvian Creoles changed sides on a number of occasions; and in the end, it was left to Simón Bolívar, who arrived in Peru on September 1, 1823, to see independence consolidated after a further three years of violence. San Martín, in his despair, after meeting Bolívar in Guayaquil (present-day Ecuador) in 1822, decided to abandon Peru. He left the field clear for Bolívar and retired to Europe, where he died in 1850.

Revolution in the Andes—from Caracas to La Paz

Simón Bolívar was a highly educated aristocratic Creole from Caracas who had traveled extensively in Europe prior to the constitutional crisis of 1808. Well versed in enlightened philosophy thanks to the teachings of his mentor, Simón Rodríguez, and committed to the ideals of independence from an early age, his decision to join the revolution in Venezuela came naturally. Following the Creole revolt of April 19, 1810, in Caracas, Bolívar organized the return of Francisco de Miranda from his exile in London to lead the Venezuelan government. Miranda was a revolutionary who had fought against the British in the American War of Independence and ever since had been promoting the liberation of Spanish America in Paris and London. Together Bolívar and Miranda inspired the Creole elites to proclaim the independence of Venezuela on July 5, 1811. The First Venezuelan Republic came into being, and although it was initially led by a triumvirate, Miranda became its dictator in 1812, in the wake of the devastating earthquake of March 26, and in response to the Spanish counter-offensive initiated in Coro. Caracas fell to the Spaniards on July 25; Miranda was taken as a prisoner to Spain, where he died in 1816; and Bolívar escaped to New Granada (present-day Colombia).

From 1812 to 1823 Venezuela and New Granada were ravaged by war. The Spanish forces, enlarged after Ferdinand VII dispatched an expeditionary army of 10,000 men to the colony in 1815, were notoriously brutal in their effort to crush the rebels. Bolívar responded to their reign of terror with his June 15, 1813, proclamation of *Guerra a Muerte* (war to the death), whereby any royalist who refused to join the patriot forces would be punished by death before a firing squad. He led a Colombian expedition that succeeded in retaking Caracas on August 6, 1813, only to be forced into exile once more, in September 1814, after the royalists gained the upper hand again. In New Granada, Bolívar took Bogotá, on December 9, 1814, and from there he went to Jamaica, where he wrote his famous *Carta de Jamaica* (Jamaica Letter) (September 6, 1815) outlining his political beliefs. He visited Haiti, obtained weapons and men with the support of the Haitian president Alexandre Pétion (1807–1818) and led another expedition to Venezuela in May 1816 that was also repelled. Finally, in December 1816, Bolívar's long, yet ultimately successful, campaign to liberate Venezuela began with a second Haitian expedition that brought Bolívar to Guayana and from there to the Apure plains.

Supported by José Antonio Páez and Francisco de Paula Santander, the patriot forces started to force the retreat of the royalists between 1818 and 1819. With Bogotá once more under Spanish control after May 1816, Bolívar, following a similar strategy to San Martín, conceived of the idea of crossing the Andes to conquer Venezuela by reconquering New Granada first. On May 27, 1819, Bolívar and Santander crossed the mighty *cordillera*, reaching the village of Socha on July 5. From then on the Liberator's victories gathered momentum. He defeated the royalists at the crucial battle of Boyacá (August 7, 1819) and went on to take Bogotá. With Colombia liberated, he left Santander in charge of the new country and moved into Venezuela in September, leading a long campaign against the Spaniards that culminated in the final confrontation of Carabobo (June 1821). On June 29, 1821, Bolívar liberated Caracas, and the independence of Gran Colombia (incorporating Venezuela and Colombia, as had been decreed would happen, on December 17, 1819) was consolidated. Although 5,200 royalist forces held on to Puerto Cabello until they were finally defeated by Páez on November 10, 1823, Spanish supremacy in Venezuela was over.

With Venezuela and Colombia in patriot hands (Spanish resistance in Colombia was ultimately crushed in the battle of Bomboná [April 7, 1822]), Bolívar set about liberating Ecuador. This he did after his close friend and aide, Antonio José de Sucre, defeated the Spaniards at the battle of Pichincha (May 24, 1822). Sucre liberated Quito the following day, and on June 16, 1822, Bolívar entered the provincial capital, only to press on toward Guayaquil, which he formally incorporated into Gran Colombia on July 13, 1822. It was less than two weeks after this event that, on July 27, Bolívar met with San Martín in Guayaquil and agreed to proceed with his campaign in Peru.

On September 1, 1823, he arrived in Lima. Crippled by illness, he was forced to remain in Pativilca, a village north of the capital, while divisions among Creoles led to the

Simón Bolívar, late eighteenth–early nineteenth century South American revolutionary leader. (Library of Congress)

Spanish reoccupation of Lima (February 12, 1824). Once recovered, he established himself in Trujillo and, together with Sucre, set about organizing a new army. By April 1824, this army was 8,000 strong and ready for action. Benefiting from divisions in the royalist camp, Bolívar and Sucre led their army to victory at the battle of Junín (August 6, 1824). Thereafter, Bolívar left Sucre to harass the last major royalist army in the Andes while he set about taking Lima, which he did in December.

The final major and decisive battle of the revolutions of independence took place high up in the Andes, in Ayacucho, on December 8, 1824. Led by Sucre, the patriot forces routed the royalists, and on December 9 the Spanish high command offered its unconditional surrender. Although one Spanish stronghold held on, in Callao, until January 23, 1826, the independence of Peru was now consolidated. In the meantime, in Upper Peru, the brief monarchy that the Spaniard Pedro Antonio de Olañeta tried to impose collapsed after the battle of Tumusla (April 1, 1825). On August 6, 1825, under the supervision of Sucre, a newly formed assembly declared the independence of this new nation, stating that it would have as its name Bolívar (subsequently Bolivia), in honor of the great liberator.

IMPACTS

By 1825 Spain was no longer in control of its former colonies in continental America. However, while it was clear who had lost the Revolutions of Independence, it was less evident who had won. In most countries it was the Creoles who succeeded in rising to power. Nevertheless, since the Creoles were divided over a whole range of economic interests and political ideals, the onset of independence did not lead to a period of obvious emancipation. Ten to fifteen years of war had resulted in the almost complete destruction of those coveted industries that once had been so profitable for the Spanish monarchy. For many Indians, blacks, and *castas,* little had changed. One ruling class had replaced another. Notions such as liberty, fraternity, and equality were far from being achieved. Political independence was not the end, but the beginning of a tortuous series of cycles that continue to characterize the present. In the minds of many, full social and economic independence remains to this day incomplete and unfulfilled.

PEOPLE

Artigas, José Gervasio (1764–1850)

Artigas became the gaucho *caudillo* of the Banda Oriental (Uruguay) once the Revolutions of Independence got under way. Of Catalan parentage, Artigas grew up in the countryside, earning himself a reputation as a brave warrior and a gifted horseman fighting the Charrúa Indians in the late 1790s. Depicted as a bandit and a ruthless criminal by his enemies, his admirers saw him as an inspired and enlightened liberator. He was the leader of the first Uruguayan independence movement and fought against Spaniards, Argentineans, and Portuguese-Brazilians at different stages in order to achieve his dream of Uruguayan self-rule. His military victories included the battles of San José (February 26, 1811) and Las Piedras (May 18, 1811). However, he suffered the "heroic" defeat of the Paso del Catalán against the invading Portuguese forces on January 4, 1817, ultimately leading to the Brazilian annexation of Uruguay (Uruguay did not achieve independence until the 1825–1828 Argentine-Brazilian War came to an end). A nationalist, a radical federalist, and a populist, the liberal policies he tried to implement before he was defeated by the Portuguese invaders were noteworthy because of their progressive nature. Forced into exile in 1820, Artigas spent the rest of his life in Paraguay.

Bolívar, Simón (1783–1830)

Born in Caracas into a wealthy family, Bolívar benefited from an enlightened education and the opportunity to travel extensively. As well as a revolutionary, a military leader, and a politician, he was a man of ideas and a gifted writer. His ideology transcended class and national interests; he strove to achieve the liberation of all peoples (including slaves) and countries in Spanish America. More than anyone else, he was responsible for the liberation of Venezuela, Colombia, Ecuador, Peru, and Bolivia. However, although he succeeded in bringing about the independence of five countries, he failed to achieve his aim of establishing a federation of Spanish American nations. As time went by, his hopes, enthusiasm, and generous liberalism started to falter as the situation in the countries he had liberated degenerated into violence and anarchy. By 1830, not even five years after he had led the independence movements of northern South America, he had become an unpopular figure. His attempts to forge strong central governments were perceived as dictatorial and despotic. He died on his way into exile, afflicted with tuberculosis, despairing of Spanish America's ability to ever see progress and establish stability.

Charles III (1716–1788)

Charles III, king of Spain from 1759 to 1788, was a studious and erudite monarch. He played a key role in the conquest of Naples and Sicily before ascending to the throne and displayed great political skills during his time in Italy. Following his coronation, Charles III proved himself an energetic reformer and an eager student of the Enlightenment. More than any other eighteenth-century Spanish monarch, Charles III was responsible for the Bourbon reforms that dramatically changed Spain and its colonies' public administration. His reformism resulted in major shifts in Spain's fiscal policies, its public administration, church-state relations, education, and land tenure. Roads and bridges were built, communications were improved, and metropolitan control of the colonies was strengthened. Although he is remembered in Spain as one of the country's most gifted kings, his reforms generated major discontent in Spanish America, paving the way for the revolutions of the 1800s.

Charles IV (1748–1819)

Charles IV, the second son of Charles III, ruled from 1788 to 1808. But he was a weak and indecisive monarch who allowed much of his father's political and economic legacy to go to waste. Unlike his father, Charles IV was not interested in books or philosophy. He dedicated most of his time to hunting while his wife, María Luisa of Parma, and her lover, Manuel de Godoy (also known as "the Prince of Peace"), were seen as being the ones who decided what was best for the country. Charles III's Bourbon reforms were not reversed, but they were not monitored effectively. Much of the wealth they generated during Charles III's reign was squandered under Charles IV, although the European Wars were, in part, to blame. Ill-advised by Godoy, Charles IV allowed Napoléon to cross Spain to occupy Portugal in 1807. His ineptitude and reverence toward Godoy and Napoléon inspired his son, Ferdinand VII, to endorse the Mutiny of La Granja that forced his abdication in 1808. In exile, Charles IV moved to Rome in 1811, where he died eight years later.

Ferdinand VII (1784–1833)

Ferdinand VII, who ruled Spain 1808, 1814–1833, was Charles IV's son. Deeply resentful of Godoy's influence over his mother and father, Ferdinand had no qualms about supporting the 1808 Mutiny of La Granja that led to his father's (and Godoy's) removal from the political scene to make way for his rise to the throne. However, by the time he was crowned, the Napoleonic occupation of Spain was imminent. Ferdinand, who had given some thought to marrying into the Bonaparte family after his first wife died, went to meet up with Napoléon in Bayonne, in the hope that he could hang on to the Spanish crown within a Bonapartist Europe. But instead he was forced to renounce all claims to the throne. Thereafter, and while the Spanish War of Independence raged on, Ferdinand resided "captive" in Valencey and became known as *El Deseado* (the Desired One) by insurgents and royalists alike, who hoped he would favor their causes once he was restored to the throne. When he did in fact return to Madrid, in 1814, he proved himself a brutal despot, determined to reconquer Spanish America and crush the liberal movement. He garnered the hatred of Spain's liberals by revoking the 1812 constitution, but also disappointed the absolutists when he was forced to reintroduce the 1812 charter in 1820. In 1823, with the help of French troops, Ferdinand VII revoked the 1812 charter for a last time. He failed to reconquer Spanish America, despite an attempt to invade Mexico in 1829. He governed Spain despotically until he died in 1833.

Francia, José Gaspar Rodríguez de (1766–1840)

Brought up by Franciscan monks, Paraguayan Creole revolutionary and *Supremo* Gaspar Rodríguez de Francia studied theology in Asunción and Córdoba de Tucumán before becoming a lecturer at the prestigious Colegio Real de San Carlos (Asunción). It was only after he was expelled from the Colegio for professing unacceptable liberal ideas that Dr. Francia became a lawyer. As a lawyer he succeeded in rising in the provincial administration of Asunción, becoming one of the leading voices of its junta when the 1808 constitutional crisis was unleashed. Dr. Francia played a key role in leading Asunción's rejection of Argentine domination in 1810–1811. He went on to become one of Latin America's longest lasting rulers, governing Paraguay single-handed as its Supreme Dictator from 1816 until 1840. He succeeded in controlling Paraguay like no other *caudillo* of his day. Paternalistic with the Indians, brutal with the opposition, Dr. Francia established an original state-owned economy, was responsible for a novel agrarian reform, and ruled over Paraguay with an idiosyncratic style of despotism that entailed forcing Spaniards to marry Indians and preventing people from entering or leaving the country without his personal consent.

Hidalgo y Costilla, Miguel (1753–1811)

Miguel Hidalgo grew up in the Hacienda of Corralejo in Guanajuato (Mexico) and developed strong affinities with the land and its laborers. He studied theology in Valladolid (Morelia) and became a priest with radical tendencies. He cared about social injustice, agrarian discontent, the welfare of the Indians, and that of the more marginal sectors of colonial society. He was also a Catholic fundamentalist who was opposed to the Bourbon assault on the church. After Ferdinand VII was taken captive, he became involved in a number of Creole-led conspiracies aimed at forging a Mexican junta that could govern the colony in the king's absence. On September 16, 1810, on hearing that the Querétaro conspiracy had been discovered, Hidalgo started the Mexican Revolution of Independence in his parish of Dolores. He led his improvised revolutionary army to Celaya, Guanajuato, Valladolid (Morelia), and Monte de las Cruces, in the outskirts of Mexico City. The bloodbath he unleashed deterred most Creoles from supporting his revolutionary movement. Betrayed on his way to seek aid from the United States, he was taken prisoner, excommunicated, and executed in 1811. To this day Hidalgo is venerated as the founding father of Mexican independence.

Iturbide, Agustín de (1783–1824)

Iturbide was a typical affluent Creole, born in Mexico of Spanish father and Creole mother. He served in the colonial army as a landowning, high-ranking officer. Although he toyed with the idea of joining an 1809 conspiracy aimed at forging a Mexican junta that could govern the colony in the king's absence, he chose to remain loyal to the Spanish administration. Once the Revolution of Independence erupted in 1810, he fought for the royalists. However, in early 1821, following negotiations with insurgent leader Vicente Guerrero, Iturbide decided to change sides and authored the extremely successful Plan of Iguala (February 24, 1821), which paved the way for independence in September and succeeded in bringing together royalists and insurgents. Riding on his fame as the liberator of Mexico, he became Emperor Agustín I in 1822. His monarchical experiment was a failure, however, and he was forced to abdicate a year later. Iturbide was executed in 1824 after he returned from exile, unaware that during his absence he had been sentenced to death by the republican government.

Miranda, Francisco de (1750–1816)

Miranda was a dynamic, larger-than-life Venezuelan revolutionary and "precursor." Born and brought up in Caracas, he went on to travel the world and succeeded in participating in some of the most important events of his time and meeting some of the most outstanding people of his day. He fought against Britain in the U.S. War of Independence; traveled through Europe, North Africa, and Russia (becoming an intimate friend of Catherine the Great); joined the French Revolution; fought for Republican France against Prussia in the conquest of Belgium; and moved to Britain to avoid the guillotine. He dedicated all of his time to seeking international aid for his projected Venezuelan Revolution of Independence. A man of sophisticated ideas and inspiring writings, he led a failed expedition to liberate his homeland in 1806 but returned in 1810, invited by Bolívar, to become Venezuela's first president. Awarded dictatorial powers in April 1812, he was unable to defend Caracas from the Spaniards. Bolívar did not forgive him for this, and had him arrested and handed over to the enemy. Miranda was transferred to a prison in Spain. He died in his cell in Cadiz in 1816.

Morelos, José María (1765–1815)

Son of a carpenter, this Mexican mestizo priest and revolutionary of humble Afro-Mexican origins joined Hidalgo's insurgent movement in October 1810 and went on to become the revolution's main leader after Hidalgo was taken prisoner and executed. Between 1811 and 1815, Morelos led a successful campaign in the south of the country, controlling large areas of the present-day states of Michoacán, Mexico,

Guerrero, Morelos, Oaxaca, and Puebla. He gave the revolution a clearer ideological direction, bringing order and discipline to insurgent military organization and a strong constitutionalist impetus to his revolutionary government. Under Morelos a rebel congress was established in Chilpancingo which, inspired by his *Sentiments of the Nation,* drafted the progressive 1814 Constitution of Apatzingán. Morelos was captured on November 6, 1815. Like Hidalgo, Morelos was also excommunicated and executed.

O'Higgins Riquelme, Bernardo (1778–1842)

Bernardo O'Higgins was the estranged son of Ambrosio O'Higgins, an Irishman who served the Spanish crown, first as an administrator in Chile, and later as viceroy of Peru. He was sent to Europe at the age of fifteen and educated in England. In London O'Higgins became acquainted with Francisco de Miranda and his revolutionary clique. It was there that he developed his own revolutionary views. However, although he returned to Chile in 1802, he did not become involved in subversive activities until the 1808 constitutional crisis erupted. From 1810 to 1813 O'Higgins served the revolutionary cause and rose to become the commander in chief of the patriot army. Defeated by the royalists at the battle of Rancagua (1814), he was forced into exile in Argentina. There he joined forces with San Martín and participated in the extraordinary crossing of the Andes of 1817 that led to the eventual liberation of Chile. O'Higgins became the supreme director of the independent Chilean government and ruled as an enlightened despot. His radical liberal tendencies eventually undermined his popularity, and he was forced to abdicate in 1823. He went into exile and spent the remaining nineteen years of his life in Peru.

Páez, José Antonio (1790–1873)

Páez was a mestizo horseman of humble origins from the Venezuelan Apure plains (*llanos*). He proved himself a natural leader of the *llaneros* in the Revolution of Independence (1810–1822) and a particularly useful ally for Simón Bolívar to have in the region. Although their relationship was notoriously uneasy, they together inflicted a number of key defeats on the royalist forces. Following independence, Páez became the providential man who led the 1826 secessionist revolt of Valencia that eventually brought about the 1830 separation of Venezuela from Gran Colombia. Thereafter he was Venezuela's constitutionally elected president on three occasions (1830–1835, 1838–1843, and 1846–1847), establishing a dictatorship in 1861–1863. Starting with nothing, he became one of the wealthiest landowners of Venezuela. Despite the popularity he enjoyed in the 1830s and 1840s, he was exiled to the United States in 1863, where he died ten years later.

San Martín, José de (1778–1850)

Born in the remote Guaraní Indian territory of Yapeyú, San Martín was taken to Spain as a child and grew up in Madrid. He became a professional soldier. His military service led to his fighting Moorish and British troops, at different stages, in the 1790s and early 1800s, and being posted in different regions of Spain and North Africa. When the Spanish War of Independence exploded, San Martín proved himself a talented officer in the battles of Bailén (1808) and Albuera (1811). In 1812 he returned to Argentina and opted to join the revolution. San Martín crushed the last royalist forces in Argentina and was responsible for leading the expedition that, in 1817, crossed the Andes into Chile and liberated the region from Spanish control. In 1820 he led another ambitious expedition, this time from Chile to Peru. After two years of conflict, having failed to secure the independence of Peru, San Martín retired from the revolution after meeting Bolívar in Guayaquil. San Martín went back to Europe in 1822 and spent the rest of his life there, living in Brussels, Paris, and Boulogne-sur-Mer.

Santander, Francisco de Paula (1792–1840)

Francisco de Paula Santander was an affluent and well-educated Colombian Creole. A dedicated student, he succeeded in becoming a doctor at the age of seventeen in the prestigious Colegio del Rosario. When the Revolutions of Independence erupted in the region, Santander joined the patriot forces, met Bolívar in 1817, and became one of his aides. He fought in a number of important clashes and was part of Bolívar's notorious 1819 expedition across the Andes, from Venezuela into Colombia. Once New Granada (Colombia) became independent, Santander served as vice president (1821–1828), governing the country during Bolívar's long absences. He was a dedicated liberal and a radical federalist. His relations with Bolívar, however, became increasingly strained. As a result, he was forced into exile in 1828, spending the following four years in Europe. When he returned in 1832, he became president of Colombia (1832–1837) and enjoyed significant popularity, leading a moderate liberal government that promoted education and other enlightened reforms.

Sucre, Antonio José de (1795–1830)

Sucre was Simón Bolívar's most talented and loyal commander. A Venezuelan of modest origins, Sucre served in the Venezuelan Revolution under Bolívar. His military skills, his discipline, his courage, and his magnanimous nature endeared him to the Liberator who entrusted him with a number of important commands, placing him in charge of Guayana and the Orinoco basin in 1817. Promoted to general in 1818, Sucre was of key importance in the liberation of Quito, Peru, and Upper Peru (1822–1825). The battles of Pichincha (1822) and Ayacucho (1824) were won thanks to his military genius. A generous and compassionate liberal, he gave Bolivia a progressive government as the country's first president (1826–1828). Famed for his lack of personal ambition, he refused to serve as president for life, as was prescribed in the constitution, and chose to stand down after two years' service. He moved to Ecuador, then still a part of Colombia, and was elected deputy for the province in the national congress in Bogotá. He was killed by political enemies in highly treacherous circumstances as he made his way to Bogotá in 1830, ambushed in the mountains of Berruecos.

Will Fowler

See Also American Revolution; Elites, Intellectuals, and Revolutionary Leadership; Mexican Revolution; Nationalism and Revolution; Venezuelan Bolivarian Revolution of Hugo Chávez

References and Further Readings
Adams, Jerome. 1991. *Liberators and Patriots of Latin America: Biographies of 23 Leaders from Doña Marina (1505–1530) to Bishop Romero (1917–1980.)* Jefferson, NC: MacFarland.
Anna, Timothy E. 1978. *The Fall of the Royal Government in Mexico City.* Lincoln: University of Nebraska Press.
———. 1979. *The Fall of the Royal Government in Peru.* Lincoln: University of Nebraska Press.
Archer, Christon I., ed. 2000. *The Wars of Independence in Spanish America.* Wilmington: Scholarly Resources.
Bethell, Leslie, ed. 1987. *The Independence of Latin America.* Cambridge: Cambridge University Press.
Brading, D. A. 1991. *The First America: The Spanish Monarchy, Creole Patriots, and the Liberal State 1492–1867.* Cambridge: Cambridge University Press.
Bushnell, David. 1983. *Reform and Reaction in the Platine Provinces, 1810–1852.* Gainesville: University Press of Florida.
Collier, Simon. 1967. *Ideas and Politics of Chilean Independence 1808–1833.* Cambridge: Cambridge University Press.
Earle, Rebecca A. 2000. *Spain and the Independence of Colombia 1810–1825.* Exeter: University of Exeter Press.
Halperín Donghi, Tulio. 1975. *Politics, Economics, and Society in Argentina in the Revolutionary Period.* Cambridge: Cambridge University Press.
Hamnett, Brian R. 1986. *Roots of Insurgency: Mexican Regions, 1750–1824.* Cambridge: Cambridge University Press.
Kinsbruner, Jay. 1994. *Independence in Spanish America: Civil Wars, Revolutions, and Underdevelopment.* Albuquerque: University of New Mexico Press.

Liss, Peggy K. 1983. *Atlantic Empires: The Network of Trade and Revolution, 1713–1826*. Baltimore and London: Johns Hopkins University Press.

Lynch, John. 1973. *The Spanish American Revolutions 1808–1826*. London: Weidenfeld and Nicolson.

———. 1992. *Caudillos in Spanish America, 1800–1850*. Oxford: Clarendon Press.

———, ed. 1994. *Latin American Revolutions 1808–1826: Old and New World Origins*. Norman: University of Oklahoma Press.

Madariaga, Salvador. 1967. *The Fall of the Spanish Empire*. New York: Collier Books.

Maxwell, Kenneth R. 1973. *Conflicts and Conspiracies: Brazil and Portugal 1750–1808*. Cambridge: Cambridge University Press.

Rodríguez O., Jaime E. 1998. *The Independence of Spanish America*. New York: Cambridge University Press.

Van Young, Eric. 2001. *The Other Rebellion. Popular Violence, Ideology, and the Mexican Struggle for Independence, 1810–1821*. Stanford, CA: Stanford University Press.

Spanish Revolution and Counter-Revolution

CHRONOLOGY

1808   On May 2, a popular uprising against Napoléon's occupation of Spain takes place in Madrid, leading to six years of wars for national liberation, often with local militias of peasants and other non-aristocrats fighting French troops.

1814   King Fernando VII returns to Spain and re-establishes rule by aristocrats and the royal court.

1868–1869   Italian anarchist Giuseppe Fanelli visits Spain to organize Spanish sections of the First International and leaves copies of radical pamphlets and magazines, which contain some of Bakunin's writings and speeches.

1873   Spanish anarchists, inspired by the 1871 Paris Commune, launch local insurrections in various cities. Some of the communes survive for a couple months, until defeated by government troops.

1898   Spain loses several overseas possessions, including Cuba and the Philippines, in a war with the United States.

1921   King Alfonso XIII secretly orders a large contingent of Spanish soldiers to Morocco, where they are decimated by a smaller number of Moorish forces.

1923   On September 13, with the blessings of King Alfonso, the dictatorship of Miguel Primo de Rivera commences.

1931   On April 12, King Alfonso XIII holds municipal elections to placate opponents of the regime. Parties that favor abolishing the monarchy and establishing a parliamentary form of government emerge victorious in almost every major city.

On April 14, King Alfonso XIII leaves Spain, and a provisional Republican government begins to rule Spain.

On June 28, elections for the Spanish parliament (the Cortes) are held. The Spanish Socialist Workers' Party (PSOE) earns a plurality of seats in the Cortes, leading to a Republican-Socialist coalition government, with three ministries held by members of the PSOE.

1933   In January, anarchist uprisings take place in Barcelona, Madrid, and rural communities in Valencia and Andalusia. All are summarily defeated.

On November 19, parliamentary elections take place. Anarchist organizations, partly out of anger over the previously elected government's brutal repression of rural poor people's movements, boycott the elections. The socially conservative Spanish Confederation of Autonomous Rights Groups (CEDA) wins a plurality of seats in the Cortes. The conservatives' victory leads to a series of coalition governments in which the PSOE no longer holds any ministerial office but the CEDA does.

1934   In October, small-scale insurrections occur throughout Spain. Workers' communes appear in the province of Asturias and survive for approximately two weeks until they are defeated by aerial bombing and a large contingent of government forces, including troops from Morocco.

1936 On February 16, parliamentary elections are held. Anarchist organizations neither sponsor candidates nor call for a boycott. Socialists, Republicans, Communists, and other "Left" groups form an electoral alliance that wins a majority of seats in the Cortes. Republican parties then govern alone, without the Socialists participating in the cabinet.

In May and June, street fighting, general strikes, rural uprisings, and political assassinations escalate.

On July 17–20, a group of military commanders attempts a coup. Insurgent troops arrive from Morocco. The elected government, after attempting to wait out the crisis, distributes arms to various workers' militias.

On July 28–30, Italian and German aircraft and naval ships arrive to help the military rebels.

From July to October, transporting the Spanish Army of Africa from Spanish Morocco to Spain, Italian and German military forces rescue the geographically dispersed military insurgents from piecemeal defeat. Later, additional military aid from Fascist Italy and Nazi Germany will prove crucial in securing the rebels' victory.

On October 24, the elected government uses tanks from Russia in the conflict to fight Franco's forces.

1939 On April 1, the military insurgents triumph, officially ending the Spanish Civil War and its myriad anarchist experiments. The four-decade dictatorship of Generalissimo Franco commences.

INTRODUCTION

The set of events that we today call the "Spanish Revolution" was a clash of four distinguishable revolutionary projects. From 1931 until 1936, the leaders of the Spanish Workers' Socialist Party (PSOE) sought to remake the country through patient, electoral, and strictly legal means. At the same time,

many tens of thousands of workers participated in anarchist experiments with worker management of factories and libertarian Communism. In the midst of these working-class actions, roughly 5,000 young men (Payne 1961, 81, 278–279), inspired in part by the writings of José Antonio Primo de Rivera, joined the new quasi-Fascist Falange party and pursued a dream of an elite-created nationwide union of self-disciplined workers and industrious small business owners. Last but not least, the international Communist movement adopted a "popular front" strategy of inter-class reconciliation in the hope of forestalling further attacks by Western nations on the Soviet Union. In the end, none of the four revolutionary movements succeeded in achieving its goals. Instead, a three-year civil war broke out, culminating in a long-standing dictatorship that suspended elections, radically curtailed freedoms of speech and assembly, banned independent industrial and trade unions, and protected the privileges of the wealthy few.

Despite the emergence of a stable anti-Communist dictatorship, the revolutionary decade continues to evoke fond memories among radicals, largely because, in the words of anthropologist Jerome Mintz (1982, 2), "Spain is the only country in the world where anarchism developed into a major movement." Approximately 1 million Spaniards were members of the Anarchist union, the National Confederation of Labor (CNT)—a very impressive number given that the population of the country on the eve of the Spanish Civil War was roughly 24 million (Bookchin 1977, 1). Conversely, critics of revolutionary politics often cite Spain in the 1930s as an illustration of the dangers of confrontational behavior and utopian dreams.

BACKGROUND: CULTURE AND HISTORY

It is a commonplace to say that revolutions occur at moments of social and political crisis when the status quo no longer seems workable. The cliché fits the Spanish case, as the 1930s were preceded by three decades of constitutional upheaval, growing anti-church sentiment, and interclass violence.

The loss of key components of the Spanish empire—first at the hands of the United States in 1898 and then with the stunning 1921 military disaster in Morocco—preoccupied many members of the governing elite, who disagreed over the causes of their country's international decline and what to do with the handful of remaining colonies. High-ranking officers, whose social backgrounds were generally nonaristocratic, distrusted court politics (the Spanish king, Alfonso XIII, had secretly ordered the risky venture into Morocco) as well as the material greed and moral laxness of Spain's wealth-

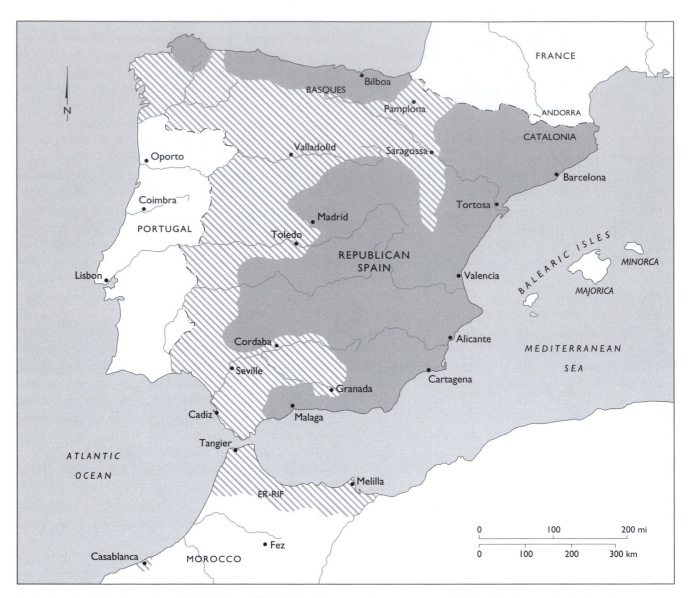

Spain, October 1936, during the 1936–1939 Spanish Civil War. The map shows areas controlled by the democratically elected government of the Spanish Republic (shaded) and areas controlled by the ultimately victorious forces, General Franco's military aided by his Italian Fascist and German Nazi allies (slanted lines).

iest residents. The contempt was mutual. King Alfonso was frustrated by the military leadership's refusal to comply with orders. Civilian politicians of almost every ideological stripe also believed that the military was incompetent and that far-reaching reform—in particular, updating the military's internal promotion policies—was badly needed.

Competing economic interests among property owners further divided the governing elite. Aristocratic families in the southern and central regions of Spain wanted high tariffs on food imports (to protect their domestic markets and incomes) but low tariffs on manufactured goods (to increase the landowners' purchasing power). Industrialists and manufacturers along Spain's northern border generally wanted

the opposite: an opportunity to import food at relatively low international prices (partly to help cap wage bills) and higher tariffs on manufactured goods to shield fledgling domestic industries from international competition. The dispute between these two property-owning classes was bitter. Some landowners encouraged anarchist rebellions in industrial cities and occasionally hired hit men to assassinate urban capitalists. Many members of the northern bourgeoisie, in turn, sponsored and joined regional "nationalist" parties, whose ambiguous goals varied from mild economic autonomy to outright secession.

At the turn of the century, discord and distrust also characterized relations between the wealthy and the poor. In cities and mines, wages rose and fell rapidly, in accordance to shifts in international demand for Spanish coal, steel, and manufactured goods. Proletarian radicalism grew in Catalonia, the country's primary manufacturing hub, and Vizcaya, its focal point for heavy industry. Anarchist, Socialist, and Communist groups competed for workers' loyalties, partly through militant rhetoric and dramatic individual and group actions, including general strikes and industrial sabotage. But as one moved downward within the unions' hierarchies, it became less clear what ideas distinguished one body from another. Occasionally the various workers' organizations cooperated—for instance, in planning and carrying out local strikes—and often workers would shift back and forth among organizations and sometimes simultaneously belonged to several ideologically distinct organizations. Three major general strikes took place during the first decade of the twentieth century. Capitalists, meanwhile, strove to secure their dominance through violence. For example, the Employers' Federation of Barcelona hired gunmen to shoot leaders of the anarchist, Socialist, and Communist movements. Armed workers' groups, such as the Anarchist Federation of Iberia (FAI)—responded in kind.

Interclass violence also was commonplace in the countryside—for example, in Extramadura and Andalusia, two immense agrarian regions that together constitute the southwest quadrant of Spain. In contrast to the rural poor in most other parts of Spain, many of whom labored on small plots to supplement low wages, the vast majority of poor people in Extramadura and Andalusia were landless and therefore were forced to migrate from estate to estate in search of seasonal employment. According to historian Edward Malefakis (1970, 346), "13 percent more children died in their first year of life in the Southwest than in the rest of nonindustrialized Spain on the average." Such abject conditions prompted regional banditry—a tradition that stretched back at least to the early eighteenth century—and periodic uprisings of as many as 10,000 landless people against a plantation. Local landowners, nervous about outbreaks of interclass strife, financed lynching parties and assassinations of suspected peasant militants. In addition, a special rural police force, the Guardia Civil, was created in the 1840s to rein in the brigands. By the end of the nineteenth century, systematic banditry against individuals had almost completely ended, to be replaced by larger uprisings against the state.

In the 1910s, landowners throughout Spain attempted to buy off class opponents in the countryside. The owners of estates helped neighboring farmers of modest means by establishing credit organizations and warehouses, by hiring out expensive machinery, and by sharing agronomic expertise. In the increasingly tense southwest, more progressive large landowners offered unused wasteland to selected members of the local proletariat whose behavior had been appropriately deferential. But most incidents of noblesse oblige were short-lived. Russia's 1917 revolution inspired small anarchist uprisings throughout rural Spain. In Andalusia, peasants scrawled "Viva Lenin" on walls, which understandably terrified property owners, large and small. The reaction was swift. Suspected agrarian radicals were imprisoned or deported, and almost the entire countryside found itself under martial law. With the poor forcibly silenced, landowners' interest in concessions dissipated. Upper-class privileges were exercised without pretext or gentlemanly facades. Poor people's traditional methods of securing their survival, such as watering of their farm animals and collecting firewood on large farms, now took place under armed guards, if at all.

Complicating patterns of economic disharmony within Spain was a heated dispute over the rights of the Catholic Church. The church had increasingly become a target for secular humanists, who believed that its monopoly of education was dampening the creativity and initiative of all Spaniards and was contributing to ignorance and simmering anger in the countryside. Conspiracy theories further fueled the debate over the possibly excessive political power of the Catholic Church. Historian Gerald Brenan (1950, 47–48) estimates that the Jesuits controlled "without exaggeration one-third of the capital wealth of Spain," including railways, mines, factories, banks, and shipping companies. Borkenau (1963, 9) reports that the church in the early twentieth century was not just "the largest landowner but the largest capitalist in Spain." The properties owned and managed by the Jesuits, in particular, prompted some of the church's more egalitarian believers to literally attack conservative churches on grounds that they housed corruption. Members of the conservative churches, in turn, launched counterattacks on liberal churches.

To revamp the military, to smother anti-church sentiment and interclass violence, and to prevent northern secessionist movements from spreading, King Alfonso in 1923 accepted what he hoped would prove to be a benevolent dictatorship. General Miguel Primo de Rivera, a member of Andalusia's petite aristocracy who was impatient with constitutions and political compromises, launched a successful coup in the name of nonpartisan national unity. He tried to reduce the sufferings of the poor by financing enormous public works and by consulting regularly with leaders of the Socialist-affliated trade union (the General Union of Workers, or UGT). Meanwhile, he attempted to reassure property owners by raising almost all tariffs, to calm civilian politicians by reforming the military, and to receive the church's blessings by outlawing verbal and physical attacks on its functions and resources. The dictator, wishing to be viewed and remembered as benevolent, consulted with those he considered moderates and jailed those he deemed extremists. He invited the Socialists to help administer the newly created labor-business arbitration committees and to sit on key planning committees. Primo de Rivera also permitted Socialist community centers to remain open but outlawed almost all centers and newspapers run by anarchists and Communists. He opened more than 6,000 primary schools and resettled roughly 4,000 peasants on land voluntarily sold to the state by the owners. Not given to profound ideological thinking, Primo de Rivera had no detailed thoughts about what a healthy Spanish society should look like. He was determined to remove current sources of conflict, however. In his opinion, once the military was reformed, the Bolshevik threat had passed, and the property owners' anger cooled, Spain would emerge a strong, vibrant, and unified nation.

But even best-laid plans can fail. Although the King Alfonso XIII and General Primo de Rivera got along famously, and although surprisingly diverse social groups—the military-officer caste, large landlords, urban capitalists, Socialist labor activists, and church leaders—initially embraced the dictatorship, each group, when asked to sacrifice its interests, began to itch for a different system of rule. The military repeatedly resisted efforts at reform, and groups of officers thrice attempted (unsuccessfully) to topple the dictatorship via coups. Rural magnates likewise opposed efforts at interclass reconciliation and refused to be generous to the havenots. Urban wages remained low and flat, despite rising prices for food, and the police shut down dozens of working-class meeting halls. When the world depression of the late 1920s finally rippled through Spain's countryside, large landowners cut already low wages. Meanwhile, mine owners tried to maintain profits by ignoring the judgments of arbitration committees, increasing working hours, and decreasing piecework rates. In response, miners rejected the UGT's pleas for patience and went on strike. Enormous public works projects, employing thousands of construction workers, exhausted the government's funds and ultimately had to be suspended. This exposed the PSOE and UGT to charges by rival labor groups that Socialist collaboration with the dictatorship had failed to generate jobs or raise wages. By the end of the 1920s, unauthorized strikes, business support for nationalist movements, and subversive activities by the military once again had become Spanish politics as normal. Miguel Primo de Rivera lost significant military support and was forced to step down as dictator in January 1930. He died of diabetes in March.

Unable to secure peace by censoring the press, dispatching security forces, or ruling solely by decree, King Alfonso XIII permitted municipal elections in 1930 and hoped that this concession would bolster the popularity of his regime. The constitutional gamble backfired. Openly anti-monarchical parties trumped their monarchical rivals in almost every major city. Numerous military units stationed in cities watched with approval as citizens celebrated in the streets. The king, supported by only a few die-hard monarchists, fled for England. The day that the king left, the victorious parties agreed to create a republican, liberal, and secular political order, directed by a democratically elected parliament. A constituent body crafted a new constitution that recognized freedoms of speech and assembly, and that prohibited further church involvement in education. The government cut all state financial support for the clergy and religious orders and limited the Catholic Church's right to wealth. Henceforth, no new titles of nobility would be recognized. All citizens were permitted to practice privately the religion of their choice (public acts of worship required prior government permission, however). The post-royal constitution also permitted divorce by consent, allowed women to vote, and made primary education compulsory and universal.

Although the founders of the new order were hopeful that they could rejuvenate their country, they feared the return of counter-revolutionary forces. They therefore passed laws intended to cripple anti-liberal and anti-democratic elements within the Catholic Church. Jesuits, in particular, were legally shorn of their property and were ordered to leave the country. A thorough purge of the church never occurred, however. Priests remained powerful in pockets of Spain, such as the mountains of the Basque-speaking provinces where clerics had developed ties with populist movements and organizations.

The new government's mixed signals to the church (partial persecution and partial acceptance) reflected its desire to build bridges with a wide range of interests rather than running roughshod over all opponents. In 1932, for example, the government passed a statute recognizing Catalonia's right to self-governance—an act that pleased a large number of Catalan businessmen. The government also gave two key cabinet posts to well-known conservatives in the hopes that the action would reassure large property owners that their rights would be respected.

The government, meanwhile, attempted to declaw the military by removing all judicial functions from the armed forces (for example, crimes of social disorder had been tried in military courts), offering generous retirement packages to older senior officers and requiring that all prospective cadets pass some university examinations. The closing of military courts, at a time when trade-union militias were sprouting and rural insurgency seemed to be persisting, troubled many senior officers. They feared that the new government was rendering Spain defenseless before international forces—not only rival states, but also Freemasonry and Marxism. The officer corps, partly because it was scarred by the failure of recent coup attempts, decided to accept the new regime, at least in the short run. In some officers' view, it probably would not last long.

CONTEXT AND PROCESS OF REVOLUTION

Evolutionary Socialism

Into this new kingless universe the Spanish Workers' Socialist Party stepped forward. Having watched social democratic parties grow in other parts of Europe, the Spanish Socialists were confident that they could peacefully create a Socialist order via the ballot box, if only all politically mobilized groups would respect the principles of free and fair elections and rule by elected officials.

In theory, land redistribution, legally protected unions, job protection, and other initiatives could have been achieved through Spain's parliament (called the Cortes), in which all groups could speak to each other and craft mutually beneficial policies. But patience was required. The success of a democratic-reformist strategy depended, for example, on workers cooperating with and not antagonizing capitalist groups whose initiatives and resources could generate further profit, wealth, and jobs. Bolshevik notions of violent class struggle and a dictatorship of the proletariat were utopian and counterproductive (or so the Socialists argued). Success also depended on business owners being willing to accept significant improvements in employees wages, benefits, and working conditions. Workers and business owners had to learn to trust each other and make compromises that would benefit all. Described from a slightly different viewpoint, long-standing class rivals had to learn to accept the legitimacy of parliamentary debate and compromise in deciding public policy, and this depended, in turn, on all political parties scrupulously adhering to parliamentary procedures.

Although among all parties the Socialists garnered the largest number of seats within the 1931 Cortes, the PSOE decided to keep a low profile and to rule alongside a group of urban, bourgeois, middle-class Republican parties that favored parliamentary rule, law and order, and individual rights (including property rules). The PSOE held only three ministries in the new coalition government, while members of a variety of republican parties held all other offices, including the prime ministry. But three offices should be enough (the Socialists reasoned) because the goal was neither to collectivize property nor to seize the goods of the wealthy, but to pass laws simultaneously advancing the interests of merchants, industrialists, urban workers, smaller farmers, and the rural poor against those of Spain's parasitic large landowners.

Urban business owners and large and small farmers remained uneasy with even partial Socialist rule, however. Although the Socialists always perceived themselves as acting moderately, the bourgeoisie disagreed. In their eyes, the new Socialist minister of labor, Francisco Largo Caballero, was a zealot, hostile to private property and blindly wedded to land redistribution. A believer in the effectiveness of arbitration committees—composed of an equal number of pro-labor and pro-business representatives with a government official acting as a potential tie-breaker—in promoting interclass peace, Largo Caballero quickly extended the jurisdiction of the committees to rural businesses. His admittedly modest laws transferring a few thousand acres of unused hacienda property to the landless were, according to bourgeois critics, the first steps to wholesale violations of the right of private property. Perhaps of equal concern, the Cortes passed legislation that curtailed landowners' historical prerogatives—for example, it prohibited landlords from recruiting laborers outside municipal boundaries so long as local residents remained unemployed, and from working farmhands more than eight hours a day without overtime.

Many landowners denounced the new agrarian laws, such as those protecting small tenants from arbitrary expulsion from the land that they labored on, as threats to the "economic interests of the entire nation" and as "the worst excesses of Bolshevism" (Preston 1984, 168). Unfamiliar with making concessions to workers, almost all large-property owners—urban and rural—insisted that the arbitration committees' judgments were not neutral and their decisions did not contribute to social peace. Having relied for decades on large pools of unemployed who would accept low pay and short-term jobs, owners of the latifundias, mines, and other large enterprises could not imagine increased wages and protected jobs as economically feasible.

During the first two years of the Republic, many business owners joined a new conservative electoral alliance that came to be called the Spanish Confederation of Autonomous Rights (CEDA). The CEDA, because of its insistence on the importance of respecting parliamentary rule of law (at least in the short run), sharply differed from the more militant monarchist groups that wished to scrap the new republican order altogether. Leaders of the anti-regime parties insisted that the new constitution gave all power to atheist Communists. One party's manifesto interpreted the new constitutional orders giving power to the "rabble that denies God and, therefore, the principles of Christian morality," that "proclaims instead of the sanctity of the family the inconstancy of free love," and that seeks the replacement of "individual property; the basis of individual well-being and collective wealth" with "a universal proletariat at the orders of the state." (Preston 1978, 33) In contrast, the titular head of CEDA, José Maria Gil Robles, believed that the constitutional rules of a political regime were transitory aspects of a country's history. What was crucial was the socioeconomic orientation of a government regardless of its constitutional shape, because ultimately (he believed) the existence of hierarchy, order, and merit determined the health of a country. These qualities, in turn, require the legal protection of religion, family, and property. A bourgeois party therefore should use existing political institutions and not fret about the constitutional rules—just use them to achieve the correct goals.

At the same time as disgruntled members of the bourgeoisie were coalescing into a single electoral force, the Socialists discovered that their presence in the cabinet did not guarantee implementation of legal initiatives. Local government officials, few of whom belonged to PSOE, frequently torpedoed the new economic reforms. Especially in the south, governors simply refused to enforce the laws and punish lawbreakers. Immune from serious threats, many large landowners who were found guilty of breaking labor laws paid neither fines nor back wages.

The PSOE's impotence stunned many of the rural poor. Frustrated and hungry, many poor folk participated in uprisings spearheaded by anarchist activists. Desperate day laborers broke machinery, invaded land, and destroyed deeds. The conservative press, pointing to the turmoil in the countryside, declared that the Socialists' sacrilegious approach to property rights had caused "collective kleptomania" to break out.

The Socialists faced working-class discontent in cities as well, because of the party's inability to alleviate the sufferings caused by the country's economic slump. Some key urban areas, such as Madrid, had experienced rapid population growth during the first two decades of the twentieth century. As buildings grew and new neighborhoods appeared, so did shortages of schools, roads, sanitation services (rubbish dumps and sewage ditches), and medical centers. The poor, arriving every day from the impoverished countryside, could accept these problems so long as jobs existed. But when the worldwide depression finally hit Spain around 1930, plans and contracts for new banks, factories, roads, and other enormous building projects disappeared. The ramifications of the sudden halt in large-scale construction were many. Ancillary businesses, such as metal and carpentry workshops, lost customers, as did restaurants and clothing stores. To survive, many business owners and contractors either released workers or cut wages. But not all businesses could protect themselves through such measures. Businesses using skilled and unionized workers were constrained by contracts, which were enforced via the government's institutional innovation, arbitration committees.

Political dissatisfaction came in two forms. Many urban small business owners, who initially did not mind the new regime, came to view it as an impediment to economic survival. During boom times, perhaps, they could afford to provide high wages and permanent jobs, but the depression had removed such favorable conditions. Meanwhile, low-skill laborers in construction, restaurants, and other so-called service sectors of the economy felt politically ignored (because they were either not unionized or not covered by the new labor legislation) and came to view the regime as a racket for the minority of well-paid workers in highly skilled crafts. By 1933, waiters and construction workers were challenging supervisors at work sites, rejecting arbitration-committee decisions, demanding more hours, and insisting on better wages. Fights sometimes broke out between unemployed workers and employed workers. Against directives from the Socialist party and its national union, construction and hotel workers launched citywide strikes, demanding job security, job sharing, and better pay. In response to workers' protests and unruly behavior, the trust of the middle class in rule by the Socialist-Republican coalition crumbled.

The urban economic crisis and social turmoil played into the hands of the anarchists, who distrusted the Republican government in general and viewed the PSOE as bourgeois Marxists. In 1933, the anarchists, and to a lesser degree the Communists, successfully called a series of industry-wide strikes, sometimes bringing production in enormous cities, such as Barcelona and Madrid, to a halt.

Working-class support for the Socialists, meanwhile, was rapidly disappearing in the countryside. By the early 1930s, international and domestic market conditions had prompted most landowners to cut production. In the agrarian south, 13 to 60 percent of the region's workers found themselves unemployed at any time, while between 40 and 60 percent of the cultivable land in Andalusia and Extramadura lay fallow (Preston 1978, 58; Preston 1984, 172–173). Both small and large landowners, trying to maintain revenue flows and to make ends meet, openly ignored laws governing overtime pay and workers' residency requirements. Workers did not respond kindly to such treatment. Crops, machines, and even buildings were burned. In some towns, armed insurrections took place. Many rank-and-file Socialists cooperated with the anarchists.

Trying to maintain the party's stature in workers' eyes, most Socialist leaders refused to denounce most acts of working-class violence and promised to immediately end the proletariat's sufferings. But in reality the party remained strictly legalistic in its conduct and the Socialist ministers drafted decrees banning strikes under certain circumstances. UGT officials tried to calm labor disputes, helped avert a major railway strike, and issued repeated statements about the absurdity of calling strikes at a time of high unemployment.

The Socialists' open expressions of sympathy for the poor played into opponents' hands, however. Leaders of CEDA insisted that members of PSOE were lukewarm in their respect for the rule of law and were, if anything, endorsing public disorder in the countryside and cities. Rural and urban property owners, who had backed Republican parties in 1931, voted for CEDA in the late 1933 elections. The CEDA then replaced the PSOE as the largest party within the Cortes, and a Republican-Conservative coalition was formed. The Socialists, once so confident of a legal and democratic road to social transformation, found themselves outside the government. Over the next two years, while CEDA politicians governed alongside leaders of various Republican parties, the leadership of the Socialist movement increasingly questioned the feasibility of its gradualist and scrupulously legalistic strategy. Hard times (combined with landowners' intransigence) made a mockery of their fairly mild economic reforms. Workers began deserting the UGT in droves, either withdrawing from trade unions altogether or joining the anarchist National Confederation of Labor (CNT). A leadership split quickly developed, pitting the true-blue Socialist evolutionists against militant unionists who feared the loss of rank-and-file members.

Rise of the Falange

While the Socialists were on the political sidelines, scratching their heads about what to do next, Fascists and anarchists tried to shape history. Their combined efforts would, among other things, further polarize class conflict within Spain, making the Socialists' evolutionary strategy more difficult than ever.

The largest Fascist party in Spain was the Falange, whose primary leader was José Antonio Primo de Rivera, the eldest son of Miguel Primo de Rivera, Spain's military dictator during the 1920s. A dutiful son, José Antonio believed that members of Spain's military and landowning classes had betrayed his father out of selfish interests. Spain needed unflinching rule by a selfless elite—people who would be tempted neither by material interests nor organizational loyalties but would seek only the glory and well-being of Spain. Democracy was not an option, he thought, because most people were too materialistic and shortsighted to pursue the nation's best interest. Peasants and small farmers were, for the most part, religiously devout and disciplined. Members of all other classes—regardless if rich or poor—were too morally corrupt to be trusted with power.

According to Primo de Rivera, a proper dictatorship would discipline both workers and capitalists, and would ban all working-class organizations and business organizations. The state would directly inform all citizens of their economic, military, and social duties. The self-centered freedom that Spanish liberals advocated would cease to exist. Instead, there would be liberty from worldly temptations thanks to the decisions of a creative minority, acting by intuition and not formulas. As he put it, "One achieves human dignity only when one serves" (Payne 1961, 32).

Primo de Rivera attracted interest and support from large property owners, because his denunciations of parliamentary politics struck a chord in their oftentimes pro-monarchic souls. But he also alienated many middle-class capitalists, perhaps because of his unrestrained denunciations of capitalist greed. He kept at arm's length from the CEDA. In his opinion, its rhetoric about defending "Christian civilization" was a ruse covering a corrupt machine that distributed favors to the rich while promoting the exploitation of the poor.

Primo de Rivera's passionate speeches outside the halls of government contained inflammatory images that encouraged armed action. The Falange's call for discipline encited many hundreds of middle-class thugs who enjoyed beating, shooting, and bombing members of working-class organizations.

During the first years of the Spanish Republic, Primo de Rivera's words and contemporary events involving Fascist parties in Germany and Italy worried the Socialist-Republican government. It banned the Falange's newspaper, *El Fascio,* and arrested hundreds of suspected Falange activists. Shortly before the 1933 parliamentary elections, complete freedom of speech was reinstituted. Primo de Rivera pooled resources with some other Fascist organizations, formed a single party, and ran candidates. The party's commitment to democratic rules of the game was qualified: "we desire that if on some occasion this [our program] must be achieved by violence, there be no shrinking from violence" (Payne 1961, 38). Hundreds of monarchists, retired soldiers, and, above all, passionate students joined the new organization, partly because they were fascinated with the activist yet selfless political style that Primo de Rivera was promoting ("Life is not worth the effort if it is not to be burnt up in the service of a great enterprise") (Payne 1961, 43).

In 1933, Primo de Rivera was elected to the Cortes and, despite his prior statements about parliamentary corruption and ineptitude, proved to be a conscientious lawmaker who carefully worded his presentations and was charming and generous in his interactions with ideological opponents. His friendship with Socialist leaders, in particular, confused followers, who began to wonder whether his commitment to self-sacrifice, violence, and national mission was a ruse. To preserve his leadership within the movement, Primo de Rivera spoke more frequently about the long-term need to resort to fists and guns while steadfastly opposing street violence as a short-term tactic. The temporal distinction was lost on many of his grassroots followers, who began to carry weapons inside hollowed-out schoolbooks.

In 1934, after three of its members became government ministers, the CEDA began to harass the rival on its right. Police periodically searched Falange centers. Primo de Rivera was called on impeachment charges for illegally carrying handguns. Colleagues within the parliament, including members of PSOE, secured a dismissal of charges. But outside the Cortes, the Falangist revolutionary movement was becoming uncontrollable. Receiving a constant flow of funds from monarchists and other wealthy benefactors who hoped to destabilize the parliamentary regime, local Falange units began street fights with anarchist, Communist, and Socialist youth groups. Killings mounted. By 1935, the Falange movement had attracted thousands of members, primarily white-collar professionals and service-sectors employees. Falange centers appeared in almost every major city.

The Falange's program, in the meantime, remained vague, calling for some sort of benign dictatorship, a "totalitarian state" that would discipline disorderly workers and at the same time eliminate artificial privileges enjoyed by the greedy rich. Banks would be nationalized and would provide easier credit for small businesses. The tiny plots of small farmers would be consolidated into larger, more efficient units of production, and redundant farmers would be resettled on unused lands or, perhaps, recruited for new industries financed by the state.

The outcome of the parliamentary elections of 1936, which returned the Socialists to power, temporarily silenced the Fascists. Election laws disproportionately rewarded broad coalitions that could attract large numbers of voters. No large conservative group wished to tie its fate to the Fascists, partly because Primo de Rivera constantly criticized capitalists' harsh treatment of laborers. In the opinions of some conservative politicians, the animating spirit of the Falange was unquestionably "Bolshevik." As a result of the Falange's isolation, not even one Fascist candidate was elected in 1936. Still, in the eyes of many politicians on the Left, the Falange—in its glorification of violence, its calls for self-discipline, and its cynical approach to elections and parliamentary politics—increasingly resembled the German Nazis. Although Primo de Rivera tried to appeal to anarchist and Socialist youth through his criticisms of corrupt capitalists, the grassroots cells of the Falange continued to attract middle-class males aching for a fight with the Socialist and Communist militias. As a result, paramilitary violence between quasi-political youth gangs rapidly escalated in the first half of 1936 and led to the Fascists being outlawed.

Anarchists' Response to Republican and Conservative Rule

At roughly the same time as the Falange formed and grew in numbers, the highly decentralized anarchist movement began to play a crucial role in the history of mainstream Spanish politics. The movement was not new, of course. Around the midnineteenth century, anarchist organizers from other countries visited small groups of artisans in Spain. In Barcelona and throughout the countryside, workers were in-

trigued by the anarchists' critique of idleness and inequality, found their visions of communal self-government exciting, and appreciated the services that local anarchist centers provided. Launching dozens of local revolutions, Spanish anarchists tried to imitate the 1871 Paris Commune and the 1917 Russian Revolution when democratically elected councils (soviets) of citizens, not the domination of the Communist Party, characterized the revolution. Unlike the Socialists, anarchists seemed to understand the desperation of the rural proletariat and small producers and seemed to gauge correctly the futility of trying to reform the government through elections and parliament. Also, unlike the Socialists, the anarchists' view of unions was radical. The anarchists' chief industrial union, the CNT, sought more than better wages, better work conditions, and job security. From the anarchists' perspective, the primary purpose of a union was to promote militant commitment to transforming society, not to sign binding agreements with business owners. Confrontation between employers and wage earners should be continual, and the forms of defiance should inspire and mobilize onlookers, not simply secure concessions. Hence, anarchist labor disputes often involved physical violence, from riots to bomb throwing to assassinations.

The anarchists' critique of the state seemed especially valid after CEDA's victory in the November 1933 parliamentary elections. Many impoverished Spaniards believed that the elections were neither free nor fair. In Andalusia and Extramadura, reported voting irregularities were widespread. The poor, needing to survive, often traded votes for promises of future employment, food, blankets, or other tangible goods. Known radicals were scared off from voting places, and the glass voting urns, which were monitored carefully by the thugs of local business owners, undermined voters' willingness to vote Socialist. The level of election fraud throughout Spain appeared so high that the minister of justice, Juan Botella Asensi, resigned in protest. The UGT's rank and file cried foul, but the Socialist leadership continued to believe that patience was wise and that the process, no matter how flawed, must be respected. After all, what could be accomplished by rejecting the outcome of imperfectly administered elections, other than giving further fuel to those who insisted that parliamentary rule was unworkable in Spain?

Members of the sprawling, disorganized anarchist movement were themselves divided in their attitudes toward the new political order. All dreamed of a future decentralized economic and political regime, in which local communities would rule themselves and laborers would manage their own collectivized factories and farms. But what should be done in the short run? Some anarchists counseled patience and favored cooperation with the government, respect for its laws, and participation in elections. Only after key reforms were in place, such as universal and secular education, could the jump to an anarchist order have a reasonable chance of success. More radical anarchists, such as those who belonged to the FAI, viewed the new parliamentary system as a silly pacifier, giving workers false hope and little material benefit. Sooner rather than later a revolution would be needed, and workers should be armed and ready for the upcoming event.

Even early in the republic (when the Socialists were partly in power), FAI-affiliated groups ignored unfavorable decisions by arbitration committees, launched wildcat strikes, marched menacingly on town halls, and hoisted black-and-red anarchist flags in public spaces. Anarchist uprisings appeared unexpectedly in remote, impoverished communities of Andalusia—for instance, Casas Viejas, where heavily armed rural police unceremoniously mowed down a few score of poorly armed villagers who had seized and collectivized local land.

But from the Socialists' point of view, laws must be respected. If the poor take matters in their own hands and reject constitutional processes, a bourgeois backlash surely will occur. Therefore for the country's own good, anarchist rebels must be repressed swiftly and thoroughly.

The government's efforts to reassure property owners by imprisoning and occasionally even killing anarchist rebels backfired more often than not. Both small and large capitalists, reading lurid stories about crazed anarchists defying political authorities and seizing land, became increasingly convinced that a peasant war was about to break out. Meanwhile, anarchist radicals pointed to police brutality as further evidence that the regime could not be trusted to protect workers' interests. FAI-led strike waves increased, frightening the bourgeoisie.

In hopes of containing the destabilizing force of the anarchists, the Socialist-Republican government outlawed a number of anarchist organizations in 1932. The repression was relatively half-hearted, however. anarchist groups continued to march and strike, even though their meeting places and periodicals were technically banned, and they added to their standard demands amnesty for political prisoners. Furious at the PSOE's protection of private property, its timid economic reforms, and its repression of peasants and the proletariat, anarchist leaders told their members to boycott the 1933 parliamentary elections. Most anarchists complied, which is one reason the CEDA triumphed.

Shortly after the elections, landowners in large numbers began to ignore existing social legislation. Clerics likewise ignored anti-church legislation, and parochial schools reopened. The government, meanwhile, started to dismantle the pro-labor laws that the Socialists had promulgated. The composition of the arbitration committees was altered to give property owners a bigger voice, and the rural jurisdiction of arbitration committees was curtailed. Rules outlawing the use of non-local labor were suspended. Accusations of police brutality against the poor increased.

Partly because of the lingering effects of the depression, the conditions of the poor rapidly worsened. About 619,000 wage earners, or roughly 12 percent of Spain's total workforce, lacked jobs at the time of the 1933 election. The number rose to 703,000 in less than half a year. By February 1936, more than 843,00 laborers (almost 17 percent of the workforce) were jobless (Preston 1978, 94, 178). This was startling by Spanish standards. Spanish industrial capitalism was relatively new, and agrarian capitalism was still based largely on domestic markets, so cyclical crises of underconsumption and overproduction were not well known. Perhaps more importantly, Spain lacked the range of social-welfare services to help the poor that existed in other countries.

Angry and hungry, local groups of workers, spearheaded by anarchists but including local chapters of militant Socialists and Trotskyites, launched general strikes. Usually these were brutally repressed. By 1935, innumerable local labor centers, whether anarchist or Socialist, were closed down. Newspapers critical of the government were banned. Tens of thousands were arrested. From the perspective of pro-labor parties, a "white terror" had been instituted.

Perhaps the most dramatic working-class action against the regime was the so-called Asturian revolution of 1934, in which northern coal miners had hoped to inspire a countrywide revolution. The region had suffered layoffs and wage cuts, and several major businesses were months behind in paying wages. During the revolution, several local communes were quickly established in the province of Asturias, some in accordance with anarchist principles. Everyday people organized their own transportation, managed hospital facilities, distributed food, and ran telephone services. In a few places, money was abolished and vouchers used.

The subsequent repression was savage. The government shipped mercenaries from Africa to Asturias. For more than two weeks, thousands of miners fought against better-armed opponents. More than 1,300 insurgents died during the short-lived insurrection (Atkinson 1967, 7). No questions about the government's actions were permitted in parliament, and press censorship was total (all Socialist newspapers were banned). Monarchists and anti-worker parties called for the reintroduction of the death penalty. When the government refused to execute convicted subversives, the monarchists accused the CEDA, now part of the government, of becoming "soft."

Following the defeat of the Asturian revolution, a large number of CEDA activists—especially the members of its youth wing, the Juventud de Acción Popular (Youth for Popular Action), known by the acronym JAP, began to dream of a putsch that would replace the republic with a military dictatorship in which unions would be closely regulated by the

Anarchist militia from the National Confederation of Labor wave their flags and rifles for the camera in Barcelona during the Spanish Civil War, ca. 1937. (Hulton-Deutsch Collection/Corbis)

government. A popular slogan among hierarchically oriented members of the JAP was "All power to the Jefe [Chief]." More than 270,000 gun licenses were issued to right-wing activists, facilitating armed attacks on prominent Socialist reformers (Preston 1978, 180).

Meanwhile, Gil Robles, the titular head of CEDA, assumed that he would be named the next prime minister of Spain. He believed that once in office, he would be able to reverse all the economic and religious reforms that the Socialist-Republican government had earlier enacted. Arbitration committees would be completely dismantled, the legislative powers of parliament would be significantly curtailed, and uncivilized parties and unions would be banned. A more hierarchical, non-rebellious, and spiritual Spain then would emerge.

Spain's president, however, was a die-hard Republican who feared that Gil Robles might transform Spain into an illiberal country, as had been done recently in Germany and Italy. Suspicious of Gil Robles's intentions, President Necito Alcalá Zamora called for new parliamentary elections. He hoped that the results would end the CEDA's plurality within the Cortes and thus enfeeble Gil Robles. The leaders of CEDA had very different expectations. Most Socialist and anarchist meeting places, after all, had been shut down. The CEDA thus was free to print tens of millions of flyers and posters with little opposition, to plant news stories that painted the PSOE and anarchists as gangsters and thieves, and to arrange for the delivery of groceries and clothes to the poor on election day.

To the conservatives' surprise, a very broad Socialist-Republican-Communist coalition, known as the Popular Front, won big at the polls. This time, unlike the elections of 1933, all major reformist and "Left" parties cooperated, and anarchist groups did not call for abstention. But the 1936 election coalition was fragile. The Socialist and Communist parties hoped to work after the election with the Republicans and other parties to pass mild social reforms, including partial nationalization of industry and redistribution of farmland. The Republicans, however, had other ideas. They believed that rural arbitration committees, laws strictly governing the length of a workday, and other economic policies during the first years of the republic had needlessly alienated Spain's bourgeoisie. What was needed was less, not more, economic reform.

The anarchists, the Socialists' trade union, and a quasi-Trotskyist party known as the POUM, meanwhile, were cautious about parliamentary politics. They agreed to join the election coalition in exchange for the release of political criminals and the defeat of CEDA. Otherwise, they were convinced that Spain was ripe for more radical social reform—and perhaps an immediate anti-capitalist revolution. Therefore, as soon as the election was over, labor parties should press for radical change and ignore the constitutional purists within the PSOE and the Republican parties. Past governmental actions—including repression in Asturias and at Casas Viejas—convinced many members of pro-labor organizations, with a combined membership of as many as 2 million workers, that working patiently through political institutions was futile.

Civil War and the Zenith of the Anarchist Revolt

A few leaders within CEDA responded to their electoral loss by conspiring with a sector of the military for an armed uprising. The military was divided over the legitimacy of the republic, but there were many officers, such as General Francisco Franco, who did not care what sort of regime was established so long as social order and respect for the existing distribution of wealth were restored. Franco's desire for peace was widely shared. Many officers were troubled by the clashes in the streets between youth gangs and by the growing unemployment throughout the country, exacerbated by months of heavy rains that destroyed grain harvests and limited large and small growers' willingness to hire workers and pay good wages. Still, it is worth remembering that the military was ideologically heterogeneous at this time. Some officers belonged to the conservative Spanish Military Union, some cultivated ties with the authoritarian Falange, some were staunchly pro-constitution and belonged to the anti-Fascist Republican Military Union, and a few belonged to the Communist Party.

By 1936, new waves of strikes crisscrossed the country. Both the rich and the poor expected the new Popular Front–dominated parliament to resuscitate the land reforms that the CEDA-Republican government had partially killed. Property owners, having watched their best electoral hope go down in flames, increasingly believed that only an armed revolution would save them; a few approached sympathetic generals, including Francisco Franco, and bankrolled the socially disruptive Falange youth groups.

Sensing that something was amiss, Socialist and Communist leaders urged grassroots activists to refrain from threatening verbiage and behavior. But the die was already cast. In July 1936 (only five months after the parliamentary election), a number of military units across Spain launched a coup against Spain's democratically elected government.

The government's response was slow. Leaders of the parliament hoped that domestic and international support for Spain's republican constitution would persuade the rebels to return to their barracks. Foreign powers refused to intervene, however, in part because Catholic organizations had for years promoted anti-republic sentiments in Western nations, convincing many citizens and governments that the Socialist-Republican regime was a threat to Christian civilization. Labor organizations across the country meanwhile clamored for arms with which to fight the military insurgents. The government refused to give workers access to armories because once armed, Socialist, anarchist, and Trotskyist units would (officials feared) terrify property owners and drive them into the arms of the rebellious military officers.

Once the Spanish Army of Africa, Moorish troops commanded by Spanish officers, arrived on Spanish soil, however, a war was inevitable. The military rebels, who were receiving artillery, airplanes, and other aid from Germany and Italy, felt strong enough to defeat the government's forces. To defend itself, the republic's government authorized workers' militias.

Amid the chaos of war, Spain's central government was weakened and forced to delegate authority to local bodies. Across Spain different political groups pursued their distinctive agendas. Anarchist experiments appeared in industrialized cities in northern Spain and in hundreds of rural communities. Radically democratic militias (in which rank-and-file soldiers voted every day for officers and even whether to follow orders from above) formed in many places, as did worker-run factories and small-scale collectivization of farmland. Author George Orwell, who had volunteered to fight in Spain against the military rebels, was amazed when he first visited Barcelona, a city in which anarchist groups and their allies, the POUM, were particularly well entrenched. Orwell observed workers' patrols keeping order; citizens from different backgrounds treating each other as equals; workers managing collectively run buses, cafes, barbershops, and telephone networks; and the absence of ostentatious dress in the downtown, retail section of the city. On the whole, he found the experience exhilarating: "There was much in it that I did not understand, in some ways I did not even like it, but I recognized it immediately as a state of affairs worth fighting for" (Orwell 1952, 5).

In some rural anarchist towns, money was technically abolished; in a few places, retail trade was outlawed; in several anarchist communities, coffee, alcohol, and prostitution

Militiamen load machine gun belts at a post behind lines at Toledo where they were fighting to stem the Fascist advance on Madrid, April 10, 1936. (AP Photo)

were forbidden. Coercion was still used, of course. Community police were typically armed, and businesses and farms above a certain size (the exact rules varied from place to place) were forcibly collectivized and their owners converted into wage-earners. Nonetheless, local bureaucracies were abolished. For the moment, those who physically toiled made their own decisions about social justice.

In the end, the numerous anarchist experiments failed. Some writers believe that the failure was due to the inappropriateness of anarchist principles in a modern society. Some insist that modern armies require hierarchy, as do factories, schools, hospitals, etc. Others, including Orwell, believed the opposite. Allegedly, armies in which members of a platoon are free to make their own decisions about missions and officers are more energetic, innovative, and efficient than machine-like troops who obey and do not question (Orwell 1952, 27–28).

Regardless of the long-term feasibility of anarchism, the anarchist communities were destroyed in part because of immediate international circumstances. The governments of advanced capitalist societies, such as the United States,

France, and Britain, frowned on Spain's Socialist and anarchist projects throughout the 1930s and looked favorably on the bourgeois leanings of the military rebels. In addition, U.S., British, and French businesses had investments in the territory controlled by the military insurgents, and Franco made certain the foreign properties were not harmed. The Western democracies therefore stayed out of the civil war, except for individual citizens who either sympathized with the Republic-Socialist government or ardently opposed the rise of Fascism in Europe. They volunteered to fight in Spain, sometimes forming their own battalions called the International Brigades and sometimes merging into Spanish platoons.

The Soviet Union, feeling threatened by the neighboring Nazi regime and recovering from years of struggle against counter-revolutionaries funded by Western powers, feared a social revolution in Spain because it might reignite Western governments' fears of noncapitalist regimes. The U.S.S.R. offered military and financial aid to the Spanish government but directed its contributions to groups other than the anarchists. As a result, anarchist and POUM units in combat areas often lacked basic equipment, while units away from the battlefields were often better armed. From the Soviet Union's point of view, the strategic reason for this arrangement was straightforward. By suffocating the more radical military units of the Republican-Socialist government, the Soviet Union ensured that the outcome of the civil war (if the military rebels were defeated) would not inflame Western governments and prompt them to resume their hostilities against the world's only Socialist country. Indeed, if the Western powers were not insecure, perhaps they would help the Soviet Union if it were attacked by Germany.

Lacking enough bullets and guns, the more revolutionary militia were slowly defeated. Those anarchist soldiers who survived combat discovered that when they returned from the front, they were ordered to lay down their guns and disband, as the Republican government, seeing itself on the verge of defeat, desperately sought to placate Western nations and receive additional aid.

In 1939, the civil war ended. Approximately 1 million lives had been lost (Jackson 1965, 526–40). The military rebels, now in power, outlawed all independent unions and radical parties. The Falange was an exception. In fact, it was the only party that the new regime permitted. It therefore enjoyed a tremendous influx of members. But this came at a cost. The Fascist party's revolutionary impulse was diluted, because many of the new members were careerists seeking government sinecures—hardly the creative, selfless minority Primo de Rivera dreamed of. In fact, many of the party's original idealists, including Primo de Rivera, had either been captured and executed by the elected government during the civil war or died in combat.

IMPACTS

The Spanish Civil War had enormous impacts on both the Spanish people and on other nations. Hundreds of thousands were killed in battle, and hundreds of thousands more were imprisoned or forced into exile. Tens of thousands were executed. Because the Western democracies failed to aid Republican Spain, the victorious Italian Fascist and Nazi German regimes were encouraged to launch new, aggressive ventures leading to World War II and the deaths of many millions of people, while the repressive right-wing dictatorship in Spain itself continued for decades after the destruction of its Fascist allies.

Could any of the four revolutionary projects that developed in Spain have succeeded? The apparent chances of success of these parties depend in part on one's views on the role of human choice in history. If one believes that particular individuals and (or) groups can set in motion different trains of events, then perhaps the unsuccessful Spanish revolutionary projects can lead to some warnings about what *not* to do. For example, some writers, such as historian Paul Preston (1978), believe that if the Socialists had not been so timid before the rich and so hostile toward the anarchists, the new democratic form of government could have cultivated more support among the poorer inhabitants of Spain and, consequently, the 1936 military rebellion could have been crushed in the bud. Reluctance to carry out needed reforms and avoidance of interclass conflict are luxuries that modern revolutionaries cannot always afford. A dramatic change in poor people's loyalties requires dramatic actions, not half-measures.

But other writers have drawn the opposite conclusion. They insist that the history of revolutionary politics in Spain teaches us about the dangers of unbridled combativeness and policy impatience in politics. Writers like Edward Malefakis (1970; 1971) contend that the civil war and triumph of an authoritarian regime could have been avoided if both the Left and Right had not been so intransigent and belligerent. The uncompromising rhetoric and violent behavior of the Falange and FAI, in particular, provoked their rivals into insurrections and coups. As Malefakis (1971, 37) puts it: "The short-sightedness of most radicals and rightists caused them to accumulate enemies by the wagon-load." Conciliatory politics could have led to a different outcome—or so writers such as Malefakis argue.

A goodly number of students of the Spanish revolution, however, doubt that any of the major revolutionary parties could have altered the outcome, because the objective conditions for the successful establishment of a revolutionary regime were simply absent. The structural obstacles were both domestic and international in scope, according to such writers as Juliá Santos (1984). Economic hard times made even minor economic reforms, such as limited workdays, prohibitively costly to private farmers and business owners. The world depression, combined with harsh weather, made the suffering of the poor worse than usual, prompting many to acts of violence. Then there was the hostility of the international community to radicalism in Iberia. Because of this conjuncture of circumstances, a peaceful path to Socialism could not occur, regardless of the tactical choices of the Socialists, the anarchists, the Falange, or the Communists. Both property owners and laborers lacked the material security and international support necessary for the time-consuming process of restructuring society.

Other authors, such as Shlomo Ben-Ami (1984), maintain that the objective challenges were hardly insurmountable. In fact, some conditions favored the measured social reforms desired by the PSOE and some moderates within the anarchist movement. During the Primo de Rivera dictatorship, economic modernization had been begun. Thanks to the government's expenditures on dams, roads, and schools, urban businesses were booming, urban workforces were mushrooming, literacy was increasing even in rural areas, and the old-fashioned patronage politics of the countryside had been undermined. (In addition, the heavy-handed policies of the Primo de Rivera regime cooled the military's interest in political intervention and convinced many anarchists that a democratic state was superior to authoritarian rule.) Social tensions existed, of course. But the spread of commerce, literacy, industry, and cities were greeted as boons by most sectors of society; property owners and the poor increasingly believed that cooperation under a democratic regime could work. All that was needed was further patience, goodwill, and wise policies.

It is doubtful that the debate between voluntarists, who emphasize the impact of parties' tactical choices, and structuralists, who emphasize the constraints posed by social conditions, can be easily resolved by appeals to the historical record, which includes incidents and events that support both positions. Moreover, both arguments, if taken to an extreme, result in the Spanish Revolution and counter-revolution appearing so unique in its personalities, groupings, and social and international conditions that it cannot be used for understanding other events.

Yet perhaps the history of Spanish revolutionary politics during the 1930s can be instructive in another way. The story of the Spanish Revolution and counter-revolution highlights the extent to which everyday people (and illiterate peasants in particular) can question the status quo and spontaneously create alternative social orders. As the scholar-activist Noam Chomsky (1969) has pointed out, the range of local experiments—from Casas Viejas, to Asturias, to Barcelona—can serve as a reminder that non-famous people who toil with their hands can also spontaneously create new rules about property, imagine unconventional norms about distributive justice, and adopt fresh methods of democratic policy making. It may be the revelation of the creative potential of various working classes, rather than any long-term regime restructuring, that makes the Spanish Revolution worthy of continued study.

PEOPLE AND ORGANIZATIONS

Communist Party of Spain (Partido Comunista de Espana—PCE)

Members of this Marxist party believed that conditions for a post-capitalist revolution did not exist in Spain during the 1930s and that therefore their primary task was to prevent the return of a dictatorial regime favoring large landowners. The party also wished to protect the Soviet Union from military harm and therefore tried to build a cross-class alliance against Fascism, which would weaken the threat of invasion by Germany while building bridges with Western democracies. Seeking to promote alliances with bourgeois parties and countries, the PCE opposed the revolutionary programs of Left groups, such as the anarchist CNT and the quasi-Trotskyist POUM.

Falange

The Falange was Spain's largest Fascist party. Its leader, José Antonio Primo de Rivera, espoused a theory of benign dictatorship in which a selfless, creative minority would discipline and direct both workers and property owners for the good of Spain. Members of its various youth organizations often engaged in street brawls with anarchists and Socialists.

Franco, Francisco (1892–1975)

General Franco was one of the organizers behind the military coup that mushroomed into the Spanish Civil War of 1936–1939. During the war, he declared himself *generalissimo* and the highest-ranking official not only within the military, but within the state. After the war, he headed a dictatorship for four decades.

General Union of Workers (Union General de Trabajadores—UGT)

The UGT was a large trade-union federation affiliated with the Spanish Socialist Workers' Party. It supported Socialist Party candidates, but its local branches periodically worked with anarchist groups—for example, during the Asturian insurrection of 1934. One of its most prestigious leaders, Francisco Largo Caballero, served between 1931 and 1933 as minister of labor in the Spanish government.

Guardia Civil

This national police force was created in the 1840s to end widespread peasant crime. Brutally efficient, the Guardia Civil helped shift the target of rural discontent from local landowners to the Spanish state, which may partly explain the appeal of anarchist ideas in the Spanish countryside.

Iberian Anarchist Federation (Federacion Anarquista Iberica—FAI)

A vanguard group within the National Confederation of Labor that at times engaged in armed action.

International Brigades

Thousands of volunteers, often Communist Party members, from many countries who came to Spain to defend the republic and fight against the Spanish military rebels and their Italian and German Fascist allies.

King Alfonso XIII (1886–1941)

King Alfonso was the last king to rule Spain before the republican constitution of the 1930s. Many Spaniards viewed him as politically incompetent, in part because he secretly ordered the ill-advised excursion into Morocco, which resulted in the deaths of thousands of soldiers. Opposed by almost all major political groups in Spain, King Alfonso left Spain in April 1931.

National Confederation of Labor (Confederacion Nacional del Trabajo—CNT)

This anarcho-syndicalist union advocated continual struggle (for example, it viewed contracts as not binding workers to workfloor passivity) and endorsed wildcat strikes and general strikes. It abstained from parliamentary politics and periodically urged members to boycott elections. It enjoyed large popular followings in the regions of Catalonia (especially the city of Barcelona), Aragon, the Levante, and Andalusia.

Popular Front

An electoral alliance of Socialists, Communists, Republicans, and other Left groups that formed before the 1936 parliamentary election and then disbanded. The alliance proved successful, winning a majority of seats in the Cortes.

Primo de Rivera, Miguel (1870–1930)

Miguel Primo de Rivera was a military officer who between 1923 and 1930 became dictator of Spain. He hoped to bring together Spain's warring factions and interests through public works that would produce jobs and profit businesses, arbitration committees that would help reconcile employers and employees, and the systematic repression of political parties.

Spanish Confederation of Autonomous Rights Groups (Confederacion Espanola de Derechas Autonomas—CEDA)

The largest political grouping of the non-insurrectionary Right, this confederation of conservative parties hoped to reverse the economic reforms and anti-church laws passed by the Spanish parliament between 1931 and 1933. A key leader of CEDA, Gil Robles, further believed that the specific form of a government should be irrelevant to property owners and Catholics, so long as the government (whether a monarchy, a dictatorship, or a democracy) is used to promote social order and rule by the meritorious.

Spanish Workers' Socialist Party (Partido Socialista Obrero Espanol—PSOE)

The PSOE, the largest workers' political party in Spain during the 1930s, sought to remake Spain patiently, through a strategy of electioneering and parliamentary coalition building. The party did well in the 1931 parliamentary elections and used its influence within the government to pass pro-labor legislation and to enact a modest redistribution of farmland.

Workers' Party of Marxist Unification (Partido Obrero de Unificacion Marxista—POUM)

This Marxist party, particularly strong in the region of Catalonia, was critical of Stalin's rule in the Soviet Union. In the 1936 parliamentary election, the POUM participated in the broad electoral coalition known as the Popular Front. During the Civil War, the POUM increasingly shared with the anarchists a belief in the benefits of labor militancy and participated in a range of revolutionary experiments. Unlike Spanish anarchists, the members of POUM believed that workers must not only control the workplace but seize governmental power.

Cyrus Ernesto Zirakzadeh

See Also Anarchism, Communism, and Socialism; Armed Forces, Revolution, and Counter-Revolution; Cinema of Revolution; Democracy, Dictatorship, and Fascism; Documentaries of Revolution; Inequality, Class, and Revolution; Italian Fascist Revolution; Literature and Modern Revolution; Nazi Revolution: Politics and Racial Hierarchy; Reform, Rebellion, Civil War, Coup D'état, and Revolution; Terrorism

References and Further Readings

Alpert, Micheal. 1984. "Soldiers, Politics and War." Pp. 202–224 in *Revolution and War in Spain 1931–1939*, edited by Paul Preston. New York: Methuen.

Atkinson, W. C. 1967. "The Domestic Crisis of the 1930's: Disillusion and Instability, 1898–1936." Pp. 1–8 in *The Spanish Civil War: Domestic Crisis or International Conspiracy?*, edited by Gabriel Jackson. Boston: D.C. Heath.

Ben-Ami, Shlomo. 1984. "The Republican 'Take-over': Prelude to Inevitable Catastrophe?" Pp. 14–34 in *Revolution and War in Spain 1931–1939*, edited by Paul Preston. New York: Methuen.

Bookchin, Murray. 1977. *The Spanish Anarchists: The Heroic Years, 1868–1936.* New York: Harper and Row.

Borkenau, Franz. 1963. *The Spanish Cockpit: An Eye-Witness Account of the Political and Social Conflicts of the Spanish Civil War.* Ann Arbor: University of Michigan Press.

Brenan, Gerald. 1950. *The Spanish Labyrinth: An Account of the Social and Political Background of the Civil War.* 2nd edition. Cambridge: Cambridge University Press.

Carr, Raymond. 1966. *Spain 1808–1939.* Oxford: Oxford University Press.

Chomsky, Noam. 1969. "Objectivity and Liberal Scholarship." Pp. 23–158 in *American Power and the New Mandarins: Historical and Political Essays*, edited by Noam Chomsky. New York: Random House.

Jackson, Gabriel. 1965. *The Spanish Republic and the Civil War, 1931–1939.* Princeton, NJ: Princeton University Press.

Macarro Vera, and José Manuel. 1989. "Social and Economic Policies of the Spanish Left in Theory and in Practice." Pp. 171–184 in *The French and Spanish Popular Fronts: Comparative Perspectives*, edited by Martin S. Alexander and Helen Graham. Cambridge: Cambridge University Press.

Malefakis, Edward E. 1970. *Agrarian Reform and Peasant Revolution in Spain: Origins of the Civil War.* New Haven, CT: Yale University Press.

———. 1971. "The Parties of the Left and the Second Republic." Pp. 16–45 in *The Republic and the Civil War in Spain*, edited by Raymond Carr. London: Macmillan.

Mintz, Jerome R. 1982. *The Anarchists of Casas Viejas.* Chicago: University of Chicago Press.

Orwell, George. 1952. *Homage to Catalonia.* New York: Harcourt, Brace and World.

Payne, Stanley G. 1961. *Falange: A History of Spanish Fascism.* Stanford, CA: Stanford University Press.

———1971. "The Army, the Republic and the Outbreak of the Civil War." Pp. 79–107 in *The Republic and the Civil War in Spain,* edited by Raymond Carr. London: Macmillan.

Preston, Paul. 1978. *The Coming of the Spanish Civil War: Reform, Reaction and Revolution in the Second Republic 1931–1936.* New York: Harper and Row.

———. 1984. "The Agrarian War in the South." Pp. 159–181 in *Revolution and War in Spain 1931–1939,* edited by Paul Preston. New York: Methuen.

Santos, Juliá. 1984. "Economic Crisis, Social Conflict and the Popular Front: Madrid 1931–6." Pp. 137–158 in *Revolution and War in Spain 1931–1939,* edited by Paul Preston. New York: Methuen.

———. 1989. "The Origins and Nature of the Spanish Popular Front." Pp. 24–37 in *The French and Spanish Popular Fronts: Comparative Perspectives,* edited by Martin S. Alexander and Helen Graham. Cambridge: Cambridge University Press.

Shubert, Adrian. 1984. "The Epic Failure: The Asturian Revolution of October 1934." Pp. 113–136 in *Revolution and War in Spain 1931–1939,* edited by Paul Preston. New York: Methuen.

Taylor, F. Jay. 1967. "American Catholic and Protestant Attitudes towards the Civil War." Pp. 90–100 in *The Spanish Civil War: Domestic Crisis or International Conspiracy,* edited by Gabriel Jackson. Boston: D.C. Heath.

Thomas, Hugh. 1971. "Anarchist Agrarian Collectives in the Spanish Civil War." Pp. 239–255 in *The Republic and the Civil War in Spain,* edited by Raymond Carr. London: Macmillan.

Whealey, Robert H. 1971. "Foreign Intervention in the Spanish Civil War." Pp. 213–238 in *The Republic and the Civil War in Spain,* edited by Raymond Carr. London: Macmillan.

Sri Lankan Conflict

CHRONOLOGY

The chronologies listed here are contested. Since neither academicians nor partisans of the two ethnic groups in the conflict have been able to agree on dates, two chronologies are listed here up to 1948.

A Sinhala Chronology

ca. 500 B.C.   Vijaya lands in Sri Lanka and marries Kuveni first, and then a princess from South India.

Gautama Siddhartha (known as the Buddha) preaches in North India.

ca. 270 B.C.   Devanampiya Tissa, king of Sri Lanka, converts to Buddhism.

ca. 205 B.C.   Elara (Tamil: Ellaalan) rules in central part of Sri Lanka.

Defeated in battle by Duttha Gamani about 161 B.C.

ca. 161 B.C.   Duttha Gamani rules the entire island.

Fifth century C.E.   Venerable Buddhaghosa visits and converts oral tradition and Sinhala Canon to written Pali. He depends primarily on the (Sinhala) *Maha Atthakatha* (Great Commentary) preserved at the Mahavihara in Anuradhapura. Sinhala scripts therefore become well-known around the Asian region.

997   Chola invasions from South India destroy Buddhist treasures such as the religious relics providing for legitimate authority of rulers.

1070   Vijayabaahu I defeats Cholas and reigns as king. Capital shifts to Polonnaruwa from Anuradhapura.

1158   Paraakramabaahu the Great [Sinhalese: Maha Paraakramabaahu] reigns as king.

1186   Nissanka Malla rules as king.

1505   Paraakramabaahu IX rules in Kotte in southwestern region.

1506   Portuguese arrive, and Portuguese control and eventual rule begins. Kandy remains unconquered.

1509   Vijayabaahu VI rules as king in Kotte. Negotiates with Portuguese.

Divides kingdom into three regions for his three sons.

1521   Bhuvenekabaahu VII rules in Kotte. Allows grandson Dharmapaala to be raised by Portuguese.

Vikramabaahu rules in Kandy. Portuguese intrigue to unseat king of Kandy.

Maayadunne rules in kingdom of Sitawaka.

1557   Bhuvenekabaahu is assassinated, and Don Joao Dharmapaala succeeds him.

1581	Raajasinghe succeeds Maayadunne in Sitawaka.
1592	Don Joao Dharmapaala dies and deeds the kingdom to the Portuguese.
1605	Senerath gains throne of Kandy.
1634	Raajasinghe, Senerath's son, succeeds to throne. He battles with the Portuguese, enabling the Dutch to control the island.
1657	Dutch rule begins in 1657. Kandy remains unconquered.
1686	Wimala Dharma Surya [Nayakkar descent].
1705	Narendrasinghe [Nayakkar descent].
1738	Wijaya Raajasinghe[Nayakkar descent].
1746	Keerthi Sri Raajasinghe[Nayakkar descent].
1779	Raajaadi Raajasinghe[Nayakkar descent].
1796–1798	Dual rule by British government and East India Company.
1797	Sri Wikrema Raajasinghe [Nayakkar descent; rule ends in 1815 when British capture the king of Kandy].
1798–1802	Sri Lanka now becomes a Crown colony.
1815–1948	Kandy is conquered by British. British rule the entire island.
1948	Sri Lanka becomes independent and parliamentary government begins.

Tamil Chronology of the Recent Past

1519	Sankili I succeeds to Tamil throne in Jaffna.
1591	Sankili II (Sankilikumaaran) is declared governor of Jaffna by the Portuguese on the condition that he has no contact with the Karaiyar generals.
1619	Sankili II allies with the Karaiyar general Migapulle from Mannar; he is defeated after prolonged fighting with the Portuguese.

1623	Sankili II is executed in Goa by the Portuguese, who destroy all big temples in Jaffna and Trincomalee.
1658	The Dutch take control of the seaboard provinces, which include Jaffna.
1796	British take the island from the Dutch. [Confirmed by the Treaty of Amiens in Europe 1823].
1948	Sri Lanka becomes independent from the British and parliamentary government begins.

Chronology From 1948

1948–1949	Acts of parliaments disenfranchise Indian Tamils.
1949	Tamil Federal Party formed.
1956	Sinhala made the official language.
1959	Prime Minister S.W.R.D. Bandaranaike assassinated.
1971	Janata Vimukti Peramuna (JVP) Sinhala nationalist revolution suppressed.
1972	Tamil Students' Movement divides into the Tamil New Tigers (TNT), Tamil Eelam Liberation Organization (TELO), and the Liberation Tigers of Eelam (LTTE).
1973	Pro-Sinhala affirmative action program affecting admission to institutions of higher learning created. Buddhism made the state religion.
1976	Tamil United Liberation Front established with the goal of pursuing secession of Tamil areas through parliamentary means.
1978	Tamil recognized as a national language, while Sinhala remains the official language.
1980s	Violent conflict between Tamil rebels and Sri Lankan army.
1987	Indian army units arrive to attempt to end the fighting.

1990   Indian military withdrawn from Sri Lanka.

1991   Rajiv Gandhi, former leader of India, assassinated.

2002   After some twenty years of fighting, peace efforts by Norway lead to the opening of peace negotiations in Thailand.

INTRODUCTION

Though Sri Lanka is a small island, it has been the location of at least two major revolutionary actions. Both these revolutionary movements—the Sinhala revolutionary movement and the Tamil revolutionary movement—can be termed nationalist, though they cloak themselves in neo-Marxist ideology.

In April 1971, the decidedly anti-Tamil group Janata Vimukti Peramuna (JVP), whose leaders aimed to overthrow the government and seize power, attacked a number of police stations, hoping to weaken the government. The attempt failed, and several adherents of the JVP were jailed. The leader, Rohana Wijeweera, was freed but later recaptured. (He was killed in 1990 while trying to escape.) He had recruited many followers through lectures during 1970–1971. Many members of the JVP movement came from among Sinhala university undergraduates, but there were also many others. This Sinhala nationalist revolution was suppressed.

The actions taken by the Sinhalese JVP may have provided an inspiration to many young Tamils, outraged by what they considered anti-Tamil government discrimination and impacted by the same political environment that motivated Sinhalese nationalist rebellion. Five years later, Tamils developed their own nationalist movements. In May 1976, the Federal Party, led by persons who advocated a federal structure to the Sri Lankan government, and the Tamil United Liberation Front, formed in 1976 on a secessionist basis, but espousing a parliamentary process for secession, met at Vaddukoddai in the Jaffna Peninsula. Their purpose was to embrace the aims of rebellious Tamil youth and declare Tamil separatism as a goal for Tamils who were candidates for Sri Lanka's parliament. This was in part an attempt to bring the radical Tamil youth movement under more moderate control. But it was too little too late. Tamil youth were already intoxicated by the goal of an independent Tamil state, which they intended to call Eelam.

Several Tamil movements emerged at this point. Among these, after a violent struggle, the Liberation Tigers of Tamil Eelam (abbreviated as Tigers) became dominant. Unlike the Sinhalese JVP, which sought only a change of government, the Tamil movement aimed at dividing Sri Lanka and creating a separate Tamil state. Since the struggle is ongoing, the number of deaths due to military violence is not yet ascertainable. In February 2003, the BBC reported that the International Commission of the Red Cross was still looking for 11,000 people who had disappeared during the civil war. The author's interviews with people in Sri Lanka indicated that more than 60,000 have died in the military clashes between the conflicting groups.

BACKGROUND: CULTURE AND HISTORY

The people of the island of Sri Lanka are divided among several languages and religions. The two major language groups are the Tamils (Tamil is often considered a Dravidian language) and Sinhalese (Sinhala is generally regarded as Indo-European). In the popular view, there are also two kinds of Tamils: those known as "Sri Lankan Tamils," who have lived on the island for centuries, predominantly in the coastal regions of the north and east, and have produced the current leaders who spearhead the separatist movement; and those known as "Indian Tamils" (also as "upcountry Tamils" and "estate Tamils") who were brought to the island by the British to work as laborers in the coffee and tea plantations in the central part of the island. Both speak the same language and are mostly Saivite Hindu (for whom the major god is Siva). There are also Christian and Muslim Tamils, but very few Buddhist Tamils.

The Sinhalese are predominantly Theravaada Buddhist and distinguish themselves from the Mahayaana Buddhists of Japan, ancient and medieval China, and Korea. Theravaada Buddhists are also known as Hinayaana Buddhists and tend to consider Buddhist monks as exemplars of devout believers. Buddhist monks are called *Theras,* and the word *Theravaada* may be roughly translated as the "way of the monks." The Buddhist believers in the island of Sri Lanka, particularly the ecclesiastical organization known as the Sangha, claim that the Buddha visited the island and cleansed it of unclean spiritual entities. The Hindu god Vishnu (not Siva of the Tamils) is an important part of the Sinhala pantheon, in which the Buddha takes a central place in power, prestige, and purity. Among the Sinhalese are small percentages of Muslims (alternatively known as Moors), Christians, and a group of original Sri Lankan hunters and gatherers known collectively as the Veddas.

The estimated mid-year ethnic composition of the island in 1989 was 74 percent Sinhalese, 18 percent Tamils (including both Sri Lankan and Indian Tamils), and about 6 percent Muslims (who often speak both languages) (http://www

.statistics.gov.lk/population/index.htm; see table 2.11). The 2003 Statistical Abstract for the country estimated the total literacy rate to be about 92 percent. In comparison, neighboring India had a rate of 61.3 percent in 2004 (World Bank 2004, Human Development Index 2004, 4). The relatively high level of literacy is partly related to the wide educational access the Sri Lanka welfare state has provided to its citizens.

CONTEXT AND PROCESS OF REVOLUTION

Several government actions since independence have alienated the large Tamil minority and resulted in major political repercussions. After gaining independence from the British in 1948, when the island was known as Ceylon, many Sinhala voters, quite unappreciative of Madison's warning in the American *Federalist Papers* about the tyranny of the majority endangering democracy, generally viewed the return of the island to its inhabitants as a return to the Sinhalese. They elected Sinhalese parliamentary representatives who enacted three policies that outraged the Tamils: they disenfranchised Indian Tamils, made Sinhalese the official language, and created a preferential university admissions policy known as "standardization."

Disenfranchisement

In 1948, and again in 1949, soon after the island was granted political independence, the Sri Lankan government disenfranchised Indian Tamils, who had been brought in by the British to work on plantations, as well as their descendants, even though born on the island. This was accomplished through two legislative actions. These were the Citizenship Act of 1948 and the Indian and Pakistani Residents Act of 1949.

In the nineteenth century, Indian laborers (India had not been partitioned into India and Pakistan at that time) had to march from island ports (such as Mannar in the northwest) to various locations where cash crops were being grown. These laborers helped the British denude the forests growing on steep hillsides and also provided labor for the export of coffee, then grown on the land that now was cleared of trees. Coffee production was disappointing, and the plantations switched to other crops. Eventually tea became the main source of foreign exchange earnings for the island's economy. Despite their productive work, these laborers were not allowed to freely select a candidate to represent them in parliament or to vote for whomever they wanted. Instead they were restricted to voting only for their single designated representative in parliament, who was often a ma-

jor plantation owner. The issue of denying citizenship to Tamils of Indian origin was related to the Sinhalese majority view that these laborers would vote contrary to Sinhalese interests and that some would support multiple trade union interests and even the formation of Socialist and Communist parties.

This legislation had several consequences. First, as a result of these acts of 1948 and 1949, many Indian Tamils became stateless; they did not belong either to India or to Sri Lanka. Second, the uneasy relationship between the central government in India and the government of Sri Lanka had to be resolved by pacts remedying the statelessness of the Tamil Indians. Agreements first made in 1964 between the late Mrs. Srimavo Bandaranaike, then prime minister of Sri Lanka, and Lal Bahadur Shastri, prime minister of India, and signed on June 28, 1974, by Mrs. Bandaranaike and Mrs. Indira Gandhi, stated that 375,000 Tamils were to become Sri Lankan citizens while 600,000 would change their citizenship to India (http://www.tamilcanadian.com/eelam/hrights/html/article/SU001021122313N205.html accessed October, 20, 2004). The website tamilcanadian.com adds that "out of a total of 600,000 apportioned to India, many did not apply for citizenship and many who were granted Indian papers did not leave the country at all. In 1984 for example, only 506,000 applied for Indian citizenship. Of these only 257,759 were granted citizenship and only 209,458 were repatriated." Natural growth through fertility increased these numbers somewhat, athough the fertility rate among these Tamils, also called Estate Tamils in more recent Sri Lankan reports, is very low. The Sri Lankan parliament later reconsidered the actions of 1948 and 1949 and tried to make amends with the Indian Tamils by introducing new legislation to change the citizenship status of this group and its children.

There is evidence of mutual exclusiveness between the Sri Lankan Tamils and the Indian Tamils. They share, however, a common language and religious heritage. Soon after the legislation preventing the Indian Tamils from voting was enacted, a group led by the lawyer S. J. V. Chelvanayakam broke away from the All Ceylon Tamil Congress (ACTC) and formed the Tamil Federal Party (FP) in 1949. The FP opposed the collaborationist position taken by the leader of the ACTC, who supported the legislation removing the general voting privileges of the Indian Tamils. The leaders of the Federal Party proposed transforming the centralized government of Sri Lanka into a more federalized system that would provide more local autonomy for the predominantly Tamil-populated regions. Since the 1980s, several Indian Tamil separatist leaders living in South India, along with South Indian political leaders influenced by the discrimination against the Indian Tamils, have supported the causes of the Sri Lankan Tamils.

Official Languages

The second law enacted against the Tamils was the official language law of 1956. In 1833, the Colebrooke-Cameron Commission advised the British governor to introduce English as the language of administration and courts. It also suggested that the English language be used in education. For years students were instructed in English. In 1951, the chairman of the Language Commission of the now independent Sri Lanka advised the government to switch to Sinhala only, since the Tamil seemed to enjoy the advantage of English, a language used in both South India and in Sri Lanka.

Following this recommendation, S. W. R. D. Bandaranaike campaigned in 1955 to make Sinhala the official language in 1956. Since Tamils in the northern province had an unfavorable natural agricultural ecology (rainfall is low and soil structure is not conducive to export cropping), they had actively sought to work in government administrative and professional positions under British rule. The position on language taken by Bandaranaike and his supporters in the Mahajana Eksath Peramuna [the MEP coalition formed in February 1956] seemed to destroy the career aspirations of many Tamils. Bandaranaike won the 1956 election, and despite a heated debate in the House of Representatives, engineered the successful passage of the Official Language Act (33) of 1956. The Language Act became effective in 1963. Even though in 1957 Bandaranaike and Chelvanayakam of the Tamil Federal Party came to an agreement about the use of the Tamil language as an official government language for the Northern and Eastern provinces and other things, this agreement was scuttled by Bandaranaike under pressure from Sinhalese Buddhist monks. In 1978, the government of J. R. Jayawardene provided for Tamil to be recognized as a national language while Sinhala remained the official language.

The legislation establishing Sinhala as the official language alienated the Tamils even further. If the first parliamentary action of removing the voting rights of Indian Tamil laborers in the Central, Sabaragamuwa, and Uva provinces had seemed too distant for many Sri Lankan Tamils, particularly those living in the northern and eastern provinces, the Official Language Act of 1956 was viewed as a direct attack on their rights and opportunities. Tamils in the northern and eastern provinces felt they had become victims of a tyrannical Sinhalese majority. Sinhalese anti-Tamil riots in 1956 and 1958 and the actions of several chauvinistic Sinhala-Buddhist organizations seemed to confirm this view.

Standardization

Bandaranaike was assassinated by a Buddhist monk in September 1959. His widow, Srimavo Bandaranaike (the first female prime minister in the world), succeeded him and acted to establish further Sinhala dominance over the Tamils. In 1973, she introduced a pro-Sinhala affirmative action program that promoted the entry of Sinhalese students to the island's universities at the expense of Tamil students. The new practice of "standardization" of university entrance scores by the government of Mrs. Bandaranaike gave preference to students who took the entry exams in Sinhala. Tamil students had previously done remarkably well in the university entrance examinations. Part of this success may have been due to parental pressure on Tamil youth and the increasing amount of competition among Sri Lankans in general, and among Tamils in particular. Most Tamils live in ecologically difficult circumstances, and university education seemed to them to be a way out, especially in professional fields such as engineering, medicine, and administration. As a result, Tamils appeared to have better academic performance at the university entrance level.

In 1973 the government of Srimavo Bandaranaike, however, implemented the preferential admissions system known euphemistically, and officially, as standardization. This resulted in strong drops in the admission of Tamils to the universities. While Sinhala admissions rose from 58.59 percent in 1945 to 78.10 percent in 1965, the admissions of Tamils dropped from 31.64 percent in 1945 to 19.1 percent during the same period (Sabaratnam 2001, 201). The government claimed that in order to redress the imbalances found before 1972, a new policy had to be both geographically based and language directed, so that rural takers of the admissions examinations were favored over urban takers (Tamil areas were often defined as more urbanized), and those answering in Sinhala had a better chance of entering the universities than those answering in Tamil. In 1973 Srimavo Bandaranaike also presided over a constituent assembly that made Buddhism the state religion.

The overall position of the Tamil community worsened in Sri Lanka after 1948. The belief among Tamils that this was due primarily to increasing discrimination by the Sinhalese against the Tamils has been an important cause of the current revolutionary conflict and has led some Tamil groups to take up arms in order to create a separate Tamil state primarily through violence. Tamil antagonism to government policies moved beyond the parliamentary opposition of the All Ceylon Tamil Congress and the Federal Party with the formation of a militant group called the Tamil Students' Movement. In 1972, this movement split into three groups called the Tamil New Tigers (TNT), Tamil Eelam Liberation Organization (TELO), and the Liberation Tigers of Eelam (LTTE). All three groups advocated violence against the Sinhala-dominated state. Eventually, the LTTE emerged as the only surviving group. V. Prabhakaran, who was active in the Tamil New Tigers, became leader of the LTTE, which claims

Tamil Tigers (Liberation Tigers of Tamil Eelam, LTTE), march on the road to Thopigila Camp in eastern Sri Lanka, March 4, 2004. (AP Photo/Julia Drapkin)

that it is carrying on the liberation struggle for Tamil Eelam and represents the Tamil population of Sri Lanka. However, this is disputed by more moderate Tamils and by the Sinhala-dominated state.

By the early 1980s, Tamil militants were engaged in violent resistance to the Sinhala-dominated Sri Lankan government. The Tamil offensive escalated in 1983, with increased attacks on government military units. Sri Lankan government counteroffensives in 1987 prompted India to air-drop food supplies to the Tamils. The Indian government led by Rajiv Gandhi pressured Sri Lanka to allow the deployment of Indian troops in parts of Sri Lanka to stop the fighting. While some Sinhalese political leaders viewed this as unacceptable Indian interference, the Tamil Tigers opposed Indian military actions because Gandhi advocated the creation of a federal political system in Sri Lanka that would provide more local self government for the Tamils rather than the creation of the independent Tamil state sought by the Tigers. The Tigers then began fighting Indian soldiers as well as Sri Lankan government troops, prompting the withdrawal of Indian forces in 1990. In 1991 Gandhi was assassinated, reportedly by pro-

LTTE Tamils (Sarin, 1998, Feb. 6, Indian Express) as the conflict in Sri Lanka continued.

IMPACTS

The Tamil Tigers

The Tigers seek a separate Tamil state called *Eelam*, a word derived from historical treatments of the island in Tamil literature. Some animosity against Sinhala Buddhists appears to come from devotional songs of the Tamil Hindu Saivites of the medieval period, songs that are currently used in Saivite temples. The history of ethnic conflict, the perceived anti-Tamil discriminatory parliamentary actions, and Sri Lankan government activity in areas claimed to be Tamil are the core ingredients of Tiger and Tamil grievances against the Sinhalese. The impact of the Tamil Tigers on Sinhala leadership has been significant. The Tigers (it is assumed) have assassinated several Sinhala politicians, such as President Premadasa, presidential candidates Gamini Dissanayake and Lalith Athuladmudali, as well as Rajiv Gandhi, a former prime minister of India who had sent the Indian military to Sri Lanka as a peacekeeping force (IPKF). Many moderate Sri Lankan Tamil politicians who have proposed more local autonomy for Tamils rather than complete independence have also been killed, including Amirthalingam, a Tamil leader of the parliamentary opposition and a major figure in a coalition of Tamil parliamentary groups, Sam Tambimuttu, and Neelan Tiruchelvam. Even the Tigers one-time deputy leader Mahendrarajah (also called Mahattaya) was killed.

While evidence regarding the perpetrators of these actions is sparse, there is a tendency to blame the Tigers because they have been ruthless toward their opponents, and popular opinion attributes these assassinations to the Tigers. More recently, the Tigers appealed to the Tamil populace not to follow a renegade (called Karuna) from their own Tiger ranks who participated in peace talks with the Sri Lankan government. Karuna (also called Muralitharan) endeavored to create another rebellious Tamil group located in the Eastern Province, which is supposed to be part of the Eelam state envisioned by the separatists.

The Sri Lankan Army

The Sri Lankan army, predominantly Sinhala, has also been blamed for excesses and has had a large number of desertions—50,000 by 2003 (BBC News, http://news.bbc.co.uk/1/hi/world/south_asia/2819603.stm, March 4, 2005). The government has in the past been severe in its punishment of such deserters and imprisoned some, and even punished relatives for protecting deserters. Many soldiers volunteer for the pay the army provides but find that the work is difficult and that they also risk their lives. Some have even maimed themselves so that they do not have to be in the government's military. Army deserters have often found that once they have achieved expertise with guns and ammunition through military training, monetary rewards in the criminal underworld and even in security work for private companies are higher than those of government military service. One important impact of the conflict between the Sinhalese and the Tamils is therefore its negative effect on the morale of the Sri Lankan government's military and also on relatives of soldiers.

The Civilian Population

Tens of thousands of people have died in the conflict and in ethnic riots, and several hundred thousand Tamil and Sinhala civilians have fled Sri Lanka for other countries. Their destinations have included Middle Eastern countries in search of professionals, such as teachers and nurses, and domestic servants, such as maids. They have also emigrated to Australia, New Zealand, Canada, other countries of the British Commonwealth, as well as India and the United States.

Peace Processes

There have been repeated international attempts to resolve the Sri Lankan conflict between the Sinhalese and the Tamils. The most recent was initiated by faraway Norway. Even before the division between the Karuna Eastern and Prabakharan Northern factions of the Tigers, the Norwegians in 1997, through Erik Solheim, a special adviser to the foreign minister of Norway and a former European Parliament member, offered to be intermediaries between the Sri Lankan (Sinhala-dominated) government and the Tamil Tigers. The Norwegian government indicated that it did not have interests in Sri Lankan resources and, therefore, in resolving the conflict for its own benefit. The Sri Lankan adversaries agreed to let the Norwegians mediate between opposing parties.

After some twenty years of fighting, the peace efforts by Norway led to the beginning of meetings on September 16–18, 2002, at Sattahip Naval Base in Thailand between representatives of the Sri Lankan government and the Tigers. In the first session, G. L. Pieris, speaking for the Sri Lankan government, stated that the present civil war in Sri Lanka was untenable. He said there should be compromise between the Sri Lankan government and the Tamil Tigers. Anton Balasingham, leading the Tamil Tigers at the negotiating table, argued that the Tamil Tigers were a legitimate representative of the Tamil people and would certainly play a crucial role in the development of Tamil regions. In the third session, the government of Sri Lanka and the Tamil Tigers agreed to explore the possibility of a federal structure within a united Sri Lanka that would provide Tamils with increased local autonomy.

In the meantime, surveys of the Sri Lankan population showed that people were uncertain whether the process initiated by Norway would truly bring about peace. The Center for Policy Alternatives in Colombo conducted a number of opinion polls of its own. Without regard to ethnic origin, most Sri Lankans wanted the two parties to the conflict to negotiate a settlement. Only about half agreed that a federal arrangement might improve the situation, though Tamils believed this to be a better solution than other ethnic groups in the country did. But opposition to the idea of federalism has been an important aspect of the Sinhalese political culture of Sri Lanka, since it has been viewed as a step toward dividing the country rather than uniting the different ethnic groups. In the Tamil areas there is a deep-seated fear of criticizing the

Tigers' original demand for independence by supporting federalism within Sri Lanka instead, since there is the perception that the Tigers will not tolerate dissent. The result is that the real level of Tamil support for a federal system is not known. In fact, poll takers have not been able to penetrate the Tamil regional borders. However, it is clear to the parties that failure at these negotiations will lead to a situation worse than before, where life could be difficult, brutish, and short. The negotiators dare not fail.

PEOPLE AND ORGANIZATIONS

Devananda, Douglas (Born 1955)

Devananda, a Tamil, was trained in Palestine and may also have received training in India. He was imprisoned in Welikade and Batticaloa in Sri Lanka as a Tamil separatist. But Devananda has also been a political bedfellow of the Sinhala parties. This collaborationist position is evident in the fact that he held a ministerial portfolio as minister of Hindu affairs in 2004 in the Sri Lankan government. He leads the EPDP (Eelam People's Democratic Party) which participates in the Sri Lankan parliament.

Eelam People's Liberation Revolutionary Front (EPRLF)

EPRLF began as a leftist group with a strong Trotskyite orientation. In 1982, its members formed a military wing and later engaged in several militant activities. The EPRLF has often supported the Tigers (LTTE) as a way of helping the cause of Tamil Eelam.

Eelam Revolutionary Organization of Students (EROS)

This is a youth organization that has often supported the Tigers.

Janata Vimukti Peramuna (JVP)

The JVP began as a Sinhala revolutionary party of the Left, mixing Marxist ideology with nationalist Sinhala sentiments. Its leader, Rohana Wijeweera, was captured and imprisoned, then released from prison by the leader of the UNP (J. R. Jayawardene). Under President Premadasa of the same party, he was shot while trying to escape from his government captors. The new JVP, changing its name slightly to Janata Vimuktasi Peramuna, became a parliamentary party and gained forty seats (up from sixteen) in the April 2004 election.

Liberation Tigers of Tamil Eelam (LTTE)

Led by V. Prabakharan (born 1954), the LTTE is commonly known as the "Tigers" and is one of the parties to the conflict and a participant in the peace talks with the government of Sri Lanka and the Norwegian government led by Erik Solheim. It claims to represent the Tamil people and has been the leader in the revolutionary struggle against the Sinhala state.

People's Liberation Organization of Tamil Eelam (PLOTE)

A Tamil organization advocating separatism. The political wing is led by D. Siddharthan. The more militant wing was led by Manikkathasan (1959–1999), who succeeded an assassinated PLOTE leader, Umamaheswaran, killed in July 1989. Manikkathasan was said to have gone to Lebanon and obtained experience with the Popular Front for the Liberation of Palestine (PFLP) led by George Habash. He returned to Sri Lanka in 1981, but the PLOTE became a minor force in comparison with the LTTE.

Sri Lanka Freedom Party (SLFP)

First formed in 1952 by the Oxford-educated leader S. W. R. D. Bandaranaike (1899–1959), the SLFP was initially defeated at the polls. In 1956, Bandaranaike, still leading the SLFP, came to power as prime minister in a coalition called the Mahajana Eksath Peramuna (MEP) ("People's United Front"). His government made Sinhala the official language. Unfortunately, Bandaranaike reneged on an agreement with the leader of the Tamil Federal Party for the use of the Tamil language as an official government language for the Northern and Eastern provinces after being pressured by Buddhist monks. He was assassinated by a Buddhist monk in 1959, because there had been a factional struggle within the cabinet and one of the factions had duped the assassin, a monk by the name of Somarama, into killing the prime minister with a revolver. After Bandaranaike's death, his widow Srimavo Bandaranaike (1916–2000), led the SLFP in the elections held in 1960, 1965, 1970, and 1977. In 1960, she became the first woman prime minister in the world. The SLFP in 2004 held about sixty of 225 seats in the unicameral House. Chandrika Kumaratunge (born 1945), the executive president of the country in 2004, is the daughter of both Bandaranaikes.

Tamil Eelam Liberation Organization (TELO)

India originally trained the members of TELO, founded in 1968, for guerilla activity in Sri Lanka. Two leaders, Kutti-mani and Thangathurai, were both killed in the maximum security prison in July 1983. Leadership was then assumed by Sri Sabaratnam, who was assassinated in 1986, probably by the Tamil Tigers led by Prabhakaran.

Tamil Nationalist Alliance (TNA)

This a parliamentary face of the Tigers. In the elections held in April 2004, it won twenty-two seats.

Tamil United Liberation Front (TULF)

This is a combination of several Tamil parliamentary groups seeking a separate Tamil state called Eelam. One of the component groups, mentioned above, is the All Ceylon Tamil Congress.

United National Party (UNP)

The UNP is the oldest political party in the country. It has been active in the political arena since the 1940s. The first prime minister of Sri Lanka, D. S. Senanayake, was from the UNP.

United People's Freedom Alliance (UPFA)

Composed of the SLFP and the JVP, this Sinhalese alliance is led by Chandrika Kumaratunge, who was born Chandrika Bandaranaike. In elections of 2004, the UPFA won 105 seats to the United National Front's (mainly the UNP) 82 seats. The JVP (now parliamentary and called the Janata Vimuktasi Peramuna and a member of the UPFA) gained 40 seats (it had formerly held 16 seats). Of the total of 225 seats in the parliament, the TNF (Tamil National Front) won 22 seats and other parties won 16 seats.

Lakshmanan Sabaratnam

See Also Documentaries of Revolution; Ethnic and Racial Conflict: From Bargaining to Violence; Human Rights, Morality, Social Justice, and Revolution; Terrorism

References and Further Readings
Amnesty for Sri Lankan Deserters, BBC NEWS, March 4, 2003. http://news.bbc.co.uk/1/hi/world/south_asia/2819603.stm accessed September 10, 2005.
Arasaratnam, Sinnappah. 1984. *Ceylon.* Englewood Cliffs, NJ: Prentice-Hall.
Columbia International Affairs On Line. www.ciaonet.org/olj/sa/sa_99rap01.html accessed October 25, 2004.
Department of Census and Statistics, Sri Lanka. http://www.statistics.gov.lk/population/index.htm accessed October 20, 2004.
De Silva, Chandra Richard. 1974. "Weightage in University Admissions: Standardization and District Quotas in Ceylon," *Modern Ceylon Studies* 5 (2): 152–178.
———. *Sri Lanka: A History.* 1987. New Delhi: Vikas Publishing.
Peace in Sri Lanka: The Official Website of the Sri Lankan Government's Secretariat for Coordinating the Peace Process (SCOPP). www.peaceinsrilanka.com/insidepages/PeaceTalks/PeacetalksMain.asp accessed May 20, 2004.
Rahula, Walpola. 1966. *History of Buddhism in Ceylon: The Anuradhapura Period, 3rd Century B.C.–10th Century A.D.* Colombo: M.D. Gunasena.
Rajeswari, P. R. 1999. "Ethnicity, Its Causes and Possible Solutions: The Case of Sri Lanka." *www.Ciaonet.org.* CIAO: Columbia International Affairs Online 23 (3) (June 13): 483–496.
Sabaratnam, Lakshmanan. 2001: *Ethnic Attachments in Sri Lanka.* New York: Palgrave.
Samarasinghe, S. W. R. de A. 1984. "Ethnic Representation in Central Government Employment and Sinhala-Tamil Relations in Sri Lanka 1948–1981." Pp. 173–184 in *From Independence to Statehood: Managing Ethnic Conflict in Five African and Asian States,* edited by R. B. Goldman and A. J. Wilson. London: Francis Pinter.
Sarin, Ritu. 1998. "Confessions of an accomplice." Indian Express, February 6. http://www.expressindia.com/ie/daily/19980206/03751004
Tamil Canadian Services. tamilcanadian.com/eelam/hrights/html/article/SU001021122313N205.html accessed October 20, 2004.
University Teachers for Human Rights (UTHR). 1990. *The Broken Palmyrah.* Jaffna Sri Lanka: UTHR.
Weerawardene, I. D. S. 1960. *Ceylon General Election 1956.* Colombo: Gunasena.
World Bank. 2004. *Human Development Report.* Washington, DC: World Bank.
Wriggins, W. Howard 1960. *Ceylon: Dilemmas of a New Nation.* Princeton, NJ: Princeton University Press.

Student and Youth Movements, Activism and Revolution

Many revolutionary movements have been preceded by student movements and periods of radical activism among young people. Social movements among students are important for the development and success of later revolutions primarily for two reasons. First, revolution by definition involves a criticism of one or more major social institutions and the aspects of culture that support them. Therefore, a new ideology is needed that explains the problems with existing institutions, why they should be changed, and with what they should be replaced. The point of origin for the new views about society has often been institutions of learning, where critical ideas were created or imported from other societies and communicated to students and from students to the larger population. Second, beyond the spread of new ideas, student movements have also been significant because they often produced an activist core or "elite" who played an important role in organizing people in revolutionary movements. Many revolutionary leaders, such as China's Mao Zedong, Cuba's Fidel Castro, and Nicaragua's Carlos Fonseca, became familiar with revolutionary concepts and developed organizational and leadership skills as student activists.

STUDENT MOVEMENTS

A student movement may be defined as a collective effort of students to achieve the goal of either bringing about or preventing social change. Although a particular student movement might focus primarily on either a political or a cultural goal, all student movements have both political and cultural aspects. (The meaning of "political" here refers to the capacity to affect social policies or social institutions.) Student movements can include student activities within universities as well as outside universities. Some revolutionaries have been involved in student movements that were not themselves revolutionary in nature before joining a revolutionary effort, while others were involved in student movements that were inherently revolutionary. A revolutionary student movement is a movement that calls for the replacement of one or more major social institutions, usually including the political system, and, if necessary, those elements of the cultural system that support the old institutions, and the creation of new cultural elements that support the new revolutionary society. Students have often tended to be leftist in their ideological orientation, but there has also been powerful rightist student activism, such as that which supported Fascist and Nazi movements during the 1920s and 1930s in Italy and Germany.

Student movements are diverse and range from protests against university administrations to movements that contribute to the downfall of governments. Some student movements focus primarily on bringing about cultural change such as destroying given identities, ways of thinking, norms, or values that are regarded by protesters as the means and products of past subordination and creating a new group identity that provides a sense of empowerment, pride, self-confidence, and equality. Students' involvement in the U.S.

Black Muslims (Nation of Islam) is viewed by many as an example of cultural radicalism. This group rejected much of the culture of African Americans as a product of slavery that functioned to create obedient servants and laborers convinced of their own inferiority. Instead, the Black Muslims created a new culture based on their version of the religion of Islam and adopted African names. This type of cultural radicalism is similar to that proposed by anti-colonial writers such as Franz Fanon, who argued that colonized peoples should rid themselves of elements of culture that serve the interests of their former colonial masters.

Other student movements have been revolutionary in advocating changing major social institutions without altering existing cultural values. For example, pro-democracy student movements in Eastern Europe in the 1980s called for abandoning the one-party government system and instead switching to a multiparty democratic political system. The Korean student movement in 1960 against a corrupt civilian dictatorship in favor of democracy and the Chinese student democracy movement of 1989 are further examples. These movements were based on the cultural value of democracy, which was already widely accepted in all these societies before the movements began.

The most change-oriented student movements are those that aim at replacing major social institutions, including the political system and often the economic system, and transforming much of the culture of a society. A major example of this type of student movement was the Chinese New Culture Movement during 1915–1919. The participants advocated a near total rejection of Confucianist values and norms, replacing Confucianism with Western culture. This included destroying the monarchy and replacing it with a democratic political system.

THE DEVELOPMENT AND ATTRACTION OF STUDENT MOVEMENTS

Student movements can offer participants a sense of power, moral superiority, and community through involvement. Social psychological perspectives on student movements have attempted, in part, to explain the motivation of student activists in terms of generational conflicts. The literature in regard to generational conflict seems to have two major explanatory themes: generational conflict as a consequence of the acceleration of social changes and generational conflict caused by an unconscious psychoanalytic factor, such as the Oedipal conflict. From the first perspective, rapid social changes result in the divergence between youth values and the dominant values, specifically those of the parents. For the second, generational conflicts are rooted in hatred toward the father that students experienced in their childhood. Later this hostility widens to larger objectives such as ousting political leaders or attacking whole social systems. In other words, existing institutions occupied by the older generation are the substitutes for students' fathers, and student protesters seek unconsciously to revolt against their fathers by challenging, for example, the government or university administrations (Feuer 1971).

But the generational conflict approach to explaining motivations of student activists does not account for why student movements exist at times in society when there is no rapid social change. Also generational conflict theories are inconsistent with findings from major social psychological studies. According to Flacks (1970), the primary constituency for the American student movement of the 1960s came from families in a new middle class composed of persons with critical attitudes toward the dominant culture. His findings imply that American student activists of the 1960s defended their parents' values rather than resisted them.

How does value continuity with parents lead to involvement in student movements and, for some students, to participation in revolutionary movements? One theory concerning this process was put forward by DeFronzo (1970). Noting that a number of observers of social movements have emphasized that many young people tend to be "idealistic" in believing in the desirability that society should correspond to the moral principles they learned in childhood, he attempted to explain the phenomenon of youthful idealism through applying Piaget's (1932) intellectual development research. In the final stage of intellectual development, which occurs at approximately the onset of adolescence (twelve–fifteen years), the child becomes capable of extended processes of inductive and deductive thought and turns his or her new deductive capability onto moral generalities internalized at an earlier period of life. If the child develops expectations from his or her moral generalities that turn out to be in conflict with aspects of social reality, he or she "experiences a type of moral dissonance or frustration which requires some form of adjustment." (DeFronzo 1970: 323). One type of response is to conclude that the social system is morally deficient and in need of change. Another form of adjustment is to accept some type of explanation for the apparent discrepancy and in so doing abandon idealism. Lipset (1967) and others argue that many young people tend to adopt the former response and attempt to bring society into greater conformity with their moral ideals, potentially bringing about social change.

In the initial stage of student activism the goals of student movement participants may be limited to altering a particular government policy or removing a particular political leader. If this is all students desire to change, their collective activity in pursuit of these goals is a reform student move-

ment. However, if their efforts fail, or if in succeeding to change a policy or remove a particular government leader, the objectionable social conditions remain unchanged, student movement participants may conclude that the cause of morally unacceptable social conditions is deeper than immediate policies or government personnel and may instead be due to social institutions, such as the nature of their society's political or economic systems. At that point discontented students may develop or be attracted to a revolutionary ideology that calls for sweeping structural change in society and possibly relevant aspects of culture.

THE IDEOLOGIES OF REVOLUTIONARY STUDENT MOVEMENTS

In modern times, several conceptually distinct types of revolutionary ideology have been influential. Revolutionary ideology popularly identified as Marxist or Marxist-Leninist includes the historical materialist notion that revolution associated with class conflict has been a major instrument of social progress. Traditionalist revolutionary efforts attempt to employ aspects of a society's existing or past culture to develop a revolutionary ideology. Democratic values and the desire for political democracy, like Marxism-Leninism, also became a transnational revolutionary phenomenon. And all three of these revolutionary perspectives have at times mixed with a fourth motivation for revolution: nationalism, the goal of freeing one's people from foreign domination and uniting them in a state capable of protecting their political and economic interests.

According to the Marxist view, old social institutions and the culture that supports them must give way to those that are new and more economically productive and beneficial. In particular, religion that explained human existence and the relation of humanity to God in ways that justified and supported the existing detrimental system should be viewed as the "opiate of the people," which culturally and psychologically drugged the exploited masses into accepting their fate. Therefore, revolutionary ideology for Marxists involved an effort to combat the perceived anti-revolutionary aspects of traditional culture, such as religion.

In contrast to the Marxist formulation, which attacks much of traditional culture as inhibiting needed revolutionary change, Ali Shariati, the famous Iranian sociologist whose writings helped inspire hundreds of thousands of students to participate in the Iranian Revolution of the 1970s, argued that the traditional cultures of many peoples who had suffered European colonization or domination included aspects that, if properly recognized and emphasized, could inspire revolution. He attempted to identify and spread awareness of these elements within Shia Islam, claiming that religion could be a revolutionary force to liberate the majority of people from exploitation. Although Shariati, who died shortly before the success of the Iranian Revolution, advocated a relatively democratic and equalitarian future society, other revolutionaries before and since Shariati's work have resurrected aspects of traditional culture and molded them into revolutionary ideologies that fostered authoritarianism and hierarchical nonequalitarian systems. These include the Italian Fascist leaders, who glorified the supposed virtues of Rome and attempted to restore Italy's past glory, and the German Nazis, who exalted not only traditional Germanic culture but also asserted Germanic racial superiority. Other revolutionary ideologies proclaiming the superiority of a particular people's cultural or religious traditions have sometimes attracted student support. Most recently, Islamic fundamentalism has emerged as a new transnational revolutionary ideology inspiring thousands of young people to struggle in behalf of traditionalist beliefs.

In many countries around the world in the late twentieth century, especially those whose people shared a sense of economic and military security, the appeal of more democratic political systems grew. This led to movements for democracy, often spearheaded by young people, in societies with diverse authoritarian regimes, including right-wing military oligarchies, monarchies, religiously dominated political systems, and one-party states.

Marxist-Leninist concepts, ideologies based on the exaltation of traditional culture, and democratic movements have all inspired the leaders of anti-imperialist nationalist revolutions seeking freedom from colonial rule or the overthrow of perceived neo-colonial regimes. Fidel Castro's revolutionaries attracted supporters and achieved widespread acceptance of the post-revolutionary regime not only through economic reform, but perhaps more importantly by demonstrating the capacity to free Cuba from and resist external domination. Ho Chi Minh was apparently drawn to Lenin's theory of the capitalist exploitation of less-developed parts of the world and his model for the construction of a revolutionary organization, not primarily because he was a Marxist but because he was a committed nationalist seeking the ideas and means with which to free Vietnam from foreign control.

The dominant revolutionary ideology among many young Iranians in the late 1970s was one or another form of Shiism. Ayatollah Khomeini was accepted by large numbers of Iranians as a revolutionary leader partly because he was firmly opposed to imperialism and repeatedly referred to the Shah's regime, which the revolution overthrew, as a tool of foreign interests. Although Khomeini and other fundamentalist leaders emphasized religious goals and Marxism-Leninism focused on class struggle, the popularity of both types of revolutionary ideologies was in part due to their role in gratifying nationalist aspirations by achieving anti-imperialist revolutions.

Similarly, democratic movements in certain societies assisted in the gratification of nationalist aspirations. When given the opportunity to freely express their political preferences, most people in Eastern European countries voted against leaders or parties thought in the past to have served foreign more than national interests. And in both the former Soviet Union and Yugoslavia, the advent of democratic political systems unleashed nationalist forces that contributed to the destruction of both federations.

STUDENT ACTIVISM AND REVOLUTIONARY MOVEMENTS: CHINA, SOUTH AFRICA, SOUTH KOREA, AND ISLAMIC FUNDAMENTALISM

As noted earlier, the student New Culture Movement (New Youth Movement) during 1915–1919 played a major role in bringing about the Chinese Revolution. This movement's leaders called for abandoning Confucianist culture and monarchal rule, and adopting Western values and a new democratic political system. The slogan of the movement was "Democracy and Science!" The students in the movement were appalled by the fact that much of their country was controlled by foreign powers and much of the rest by autocratic and corrupt warlords and landlords collaborating with other countries. Toward the end of World War I, many of China's student activists looked hopefully to the victorious allies to fulfill U.S. President Wilson's call for oppressed peoples to be allowed freedom and self-determination. But the students were shocked and disillusioned when instead of returning German-held Chinese territory to China, the Allies confirmed Japan's right to take possession. This brought about the May 4, 1919, student protest demonstration and the development of the so-called May 4 Movement. Many student activists became convinced that the reality they were experiencing was due to capitalist imperialism's intention to continue controlling and exploiting countries like China, as claimed in Lenin's writings on the subject. The Russian revolutionary leader believed that if revolutions occurred among exploited peoples like the Chinese, the eventual economic impact would bring about Socialist revolution in the advanced capitalist nations as well. Chinese students who had once protested in favor of emulating capitalist nations responded to perceived betrayal by adopting Marxism-Leninism as their ideology of national liberation and social revolution and established the Chinese Communist Party in 1921.

Student movements were also one of the key components of the anti-apartheid revolution in South Africa. Student ac-

South African students march in Soweto in July, 1976, demonstrating against the use of Afrikaans as a medium of instruction at their schools. Hundreds of students were killed or injured by the white government's forces attempting to suppress the protests. (Drum Social Histories/Baileys Archives/africanpictures.net)

tivism tended to have two parallel goals: (1) in the long run, to replace apartheid with nonracial democracy; and (2) to combat the apartheid educational system that was structured to indoctrinate African students to accept subordinate status to whites and to educate Africans only in those skills suitable to the limited number of occupations open to them. Since the number of Africans attending the few black colleges, such as Fort Hare University, was relatively low during much of the apartheid era, the mass of student activists were often high school or even middle school students. As the South African economy developed, white authorities, recognizing the need for an increasing number of skilled black workers, gradually expanded the number of African students. Although many African students joined the African National Congress, especially during the 1952 civil disobedience Defiance Campaign, a major surge in student activism occurred in the 1970s, in part due to the development of the Black Consciousness Movement (BCM) in 1971, which stressed black self-reliance and education to develop crucial technical skills as a legal strategy to undermine

apartheid. BCM activists organized the South African Student's Organization (SASO) at the university level and the South African Student Movement (SASM) for high school students. SASM in particular contributed a number of leaders for the 1976 Soweto student uprising in protest against the white government's attempt to impose an Afrikaans language requirement on African students. After months of continuing protests at various locations in South Africa, the white government in October 1977 banned SASM, SASO, and a number of other BCM organizations.

In 1979 a new group, the Congress of South African Students (COSAS), emerged to become the dominant student organization. Its leaders attempted to mobilize students at both the college and lower educational levels. COSAS was different from the BCM organizations in a number of ways. Like the ANC, with whom many of its leaders apparently sympathized, it advocated a multiracial struggle to end apartheid rather than the black nationalist approach of the BCM. It also favored working closely with labor unions and young people who were school dropouts, and staging protests and boycotts involving alliances of students, other young people, and workers. After the upsurge in protests against white South Africa's 1983 Multi-Racial Constitution, which omitted indigenous Africans from the vote and representation and appeared to be an attempt to lure mixed-race and Indian South Africans into supporting a modified version of apartheid, COSAS was declared illegal. But continuing student activism, in combination with labor strikes, ANC sabotage, international economic and diplomatic pressure, and the resulting economic crisis of the apartheid regime, played a significant role in bringing democracy to South Africa.

Few societies have experienced more student activism than South Korea. According to Kim (1989, 179), "Student activism is a time honored tradition in Korea. Students have taken part in and contributed to every major political and social event. The major causes of student movements have been national independence from colonialism, democracy in opposition to dictatorial and military regimes, economic independence, freedom to organize and national unification." Reflecting the Confucianist tradition, the people of South Korea have often looked to young scholars to take the lead in confronting problems. The hypocrisy, corruption, and repression of government throughout much of South Korea's history have often generated widespread support for student rebels. Major periods of student activism have included the April 19, 1960, high school and university student uprising against perceived fraudulent elections; the 1973–1979 student protests demanding abolition of the Yushin system, which had done away with the national assembly and political parties and allowed the president to rule by decree; the 1980 student participation in Kwangju City People's Uprising against military rule and arrests of leading dissidents, which was brutally suppressed by units of the South Korean army; and student leadership of the 1987 massive nationwide demonstrations, which finally brought about the restoration of democracy.

In the twenty-first century, one of the major transnational revolutionary ideologies has been Islamic fundamentalism. Islamic fundamentalist youth movements developed repeatedly in different countries and points in time, in great part due to the assertions of certain teachers that Islam and the larger society had become corrupted and needed to be purified. In the late twentieth and early twenty-first centuries, a major purveyor of Islamic fundamentalist tenets has been the Saudi Arabian Wahabist clergy through international educational efforts funded by Saudi oil money. The Saudi ruling monarchy, accused by Saudi exiles of corruption, self-enrichment, and serving foreign interests, may have permitted the funding of Wahabi international missionary activity as a way of maintaining the support or toleration of religious leaders and as a means of exporting fundamentalists who

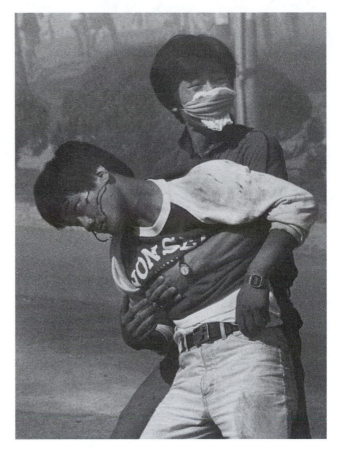

Mortally wounded pro-democracy student protestor Lee Han Yeol (Yi Han-Yol) in the arms of a comrade after being struck by a police tear gas canister during a demonstration June 9, 1987. This event sparked intensified popular protests for democracy in South Korea. (Reuters/Corbis)

might otherwise constitute a domestic threat to the royal family's domination. Wahabi clerics dispersed to other Islamic nations have established schools for millions of children who might otherwise remain illiterate and uneducated. Many of these students have been taught a very conservative form of Islam. This process has generated waves of young people for whom youthful idealism has centered on puritanical and extremely traditionalist interpretations of the Quran and Islamic law. Resulting youthful frustration with the lack of correspondence of social reality to religious ideals led many students to join fundamentalist revolutionary movements such as the Taliban ("religious students") in Afghanistan and parts of Pakistan, or one of the many other groups associated with the al-Qaeda network.

Historically motivated by youthful idealism to adopt diverse ideologies and manifest a wide variety of protest actions, student movements function as a major social and political force throughout the world.

Jungyun Gill

See Also Afghanistan: Conflict and Civil War; African American Freedom Struggle; Anarchism, Communism, and Socialism; Cambodian Revoluton; Chinese Revolution; Cinema of Revolution; Cuban Revolution; Documentaries of Revolution; East European Revolutions of 1989; Elites, Intellectuals, and Revolutionary Leadership; Guerrilla Warfare and Revolution; Human Rights, Morality, Social Justice, and Revolution; Ideology, Propaganda, and Revolution; Islamic Fundamentalist Revolutionary Movement; Iranian Revolution; Italian Fascist Revolution; Nazi Revolution: Politics and Racial Hierarchy; Nicaraguan Revolution; Salvadoran Revolution; South African Revolution; South Korean Democracy Movement; Theories of Revolutions; Transnational Revolutionary Movements; Vietnamese Revolution; Women and Revolution; Women's Movement in the United States

References and Further Readings

Abrahamian, Ervand. 1989. *The Iranian Mojahedin.* New Haven, CT: Yale University Press.

Atlback, Philip, Editor. 1989. *Student Political Activism: An International Reference Handbook.* New York: Greenwood Press.

Bundy, Collin. 1989. "South Africa." Pp. 21–36 in *Student Political Activism: An International Reference Handbook,* edited by Philip G. Atlbach. New York: Greenwood Press.

DeFronzo, James. 1970. "Revolution in the Twentieth Century." Pp. 317–338 in *Focus on Sociology,* edited by Arnold O. Olson and Sushil K. Usman. Dubuque, IA: Kendall/Hunt Publishing.

———. 1996. *Revolutions and Revolutionary Movements.* Boulder, CO: Westview Press.

Fanon, Franz. 1961. *Wretched of the Earth.* New York: Grove Press.

Feuer, Lewis S. 1971. "Patterns of Irrationality." Pp. 26–34 in *Student Activism,* edited by Paul D. Knott. Dubuque, IA: WCB.

Flacks, Richard. 1970. "Social and Cultural Meanings of Student Revolt: Some Informal Comparative Observations," *Social Problems* 17 (3): 340–357.

Gouldner, Alvin W. 1979. *The Future of Intellectuals and the Rise of the New Class.* New York: Continuum.

Kampwirth, Karen. 2002. *Women and Guerrilla Movements: Nicaragua, El Salvador, Chiapas, Cuba.* University Park: Pennsylvania State University Press.

Kim, Shinil. 1989. "South Korea." Pp. 173–182 in *Student Political Activism: An International Reference Handbook,* edited by Philip G. Atlbach. New York: Greenwood Press.

Lipset, Martin. 1967. *Student Politics.* New York: Basic Books.

Piaget, Jean. 1932. *The Moral Judgment of the Child.* London: Kegan Paul.

Rashid, Ahmed. 2000. *Taliban: Militant Islam, Oil, and Fundamentalism in Central Asia.* New Haven, CT: Yale University Press.

Wickham-Crowley, Timothy P., 1992. *Guerrillas and Revolution in Latin America: A Comparative Study of Insurgents and Regimes since 1956.* Princeton, NJ: Princeton University Press.

T

Taiping Revolution

CHRONOLOGY

1644   The Qing (1644–1911), China's last dynasty, is established by non-Chinese Manchus from beyond the Great Wall.

1814   Hong Xiuquan is born into a modest Hakka farm family in a village near Guangzhou, capital of Guangdong Province. He devotes his youth to studying the Confucian classics in preparation for the civil service examinations.

1828   Hong fails the prefectural exam in Guangzhou and therefore does not qualify for government appointment.

1830   Hong becomes a teacher in his village school.

1832   Liang Fa, China's first Protestant catechist, publishes *Good Words to Admonish the Age*, which insists that only conversion to Christianity (banned earlier by the Qing) can solve China's crises precipitated by domestic instability and Western encroachment.

1836   An American missionary secretly gives Hong a copy of Liang's book at the Guangzhou examination center, where Hong fails the test a second time.

1837   Distraught over his third failure, Hong reads *Good Words* and dreams he is Jesus' younger brother, commissioned by God to transform China into a "Heavenly Kingdom of Great Peace and Equality" (*Taiping Tianguo*).

1839   The First Opium War erupts when China is invaded by Britain for confiscating opium, which British merchants illegally sell in China to balance trade by regaining the cash that Britain has paid for Chinese tea, silk, and porcelain. The resulting Treaty of Nanjing (1842) opens China to international trade and Christian evangelism.

1843   After his fourth and final exam failure, Hong exhorts people to combat China's mounting problems by rejecting Chinese religion and fortifying Confucian ethics with Christianity's "stronger morality."

1844   Fired from teaching for his unorthodox ideas, Hong takes his religious message westward to neighboring Guangxi Province, where he and Feng Yunshan organize the God Worshipper Society to offer spiritual and material salvation amid the region's growing socioeconomic chaos.

1848	Yang Xiuqing and Xiao Chaogui mix indigenous folk religion and Christianity to convince the God Worshippers that the Heavenly Kingdom is about to descend. The Qing government interprets this millennialist faith as a threat to Chinese dynastic rule.
1850	Hong mobilizes 20,000 God Worshippers at Jintian village to prepare for an impending Manchu attack.
1851	On January 11, Hong establishes the Taiping Heavenly Kingdom with God as emperor and himself as God's vice-regent.
1852	At Yongan, Hong and his "brother kings" develop the Taipings' theocratic organization.
1853	One million Taipings capture Nanjing, where they initiate utopian institutions to dismantle Confucianism. Western diplomats visit Nanjing to evaluate whether or not to support the Taiping insurrection.
1856	Yang Xiuqing, the Taipings' administrative and military genius, attempts to depose Hong. By engineering Yang's assassination, Hong unleashes a fatal internecine bloodbath among the Taiping kings.
1859	Hong Rengan becomes Taiping prime minister but fails to gain approval to revive the faltering Heavenly Kingdom.
1860	The Ever-Victorious Army of European and American mercenaries bolsters Qing military forces in order to prevent a potential Taiping victory from canceling the West's opium trade in the name of universal equality under God.
1864	Hong Xiuquan dies on June 1, and his Heavenly Kingdom collapses on July 19.

INTRODUCTION

The momentous Taiping uprising (1851–1864) was China's first revolution and the world's bloodiest millenarian crusade. Interlinking domestic and foreign factors sparked this millenial insurrection through which the Taipings mortally wounded the Confucian old order and heralded China's twentieth-century revolutions.

BACKGROUND: CULTURE AND HISTORY

Taiping founder Hong Xiuquan grew up and taught school in a village near Guangzhou, capital of southernmost Guangdong Province. He belonged to south China's beleaguered Hakka (*kejia,* guest people) minority. This racially Chinese but linguistically and culturally distinct group had been pushed from its north China homeland by nomadic invaders centuries earlier and entered Guangdong around 1600. By then the most fertile land was already owned by the original settlers, called Bendi. Most Hakka became tenants and laborers of the Bendi, who treated them as uncivilized outcasts.

The Hong family had once been prominent in scholar-official circles and now owned a few farmland acres. Hong sought to revive his family's fortunes by seeking government office through success in the civil service examinations, which stressed obedience to emperor, hierarchy, patriarchy, and family. Once in government, he hoped to halt the Qing dynasty's decline and tackle the growing problems of economic hardship, social dislocation, ethnic strife, and opium smuggling in connection with China's First Opium War (1839–1842), through which the hitherto self-sufficient but now defeated Middle Kingdom was exposed to global economics and Western civilization.

In 1837, Hong's depression over failing the examination a third time coincided with his reading of *Good Words to Admonish the Age,* in which Liang Fa, China's first Protestant evangelist, claimed that God demanded China's immediate repentance of its recent moral breakdown if Chinese souls were to enter the Kingdom of Heaven. This notion prompted a series of messianic dreams, in which Hong saw himself transported to heaven, where a black-robed, blond-haired "Heavenly Father" rebuked Confucius and, identifying Hong as Jesus' younger brother, commissioned him to restore China's ancient commonwealth of "great peace and equality" (*taiping*), described in the pre-Confucian texts he had read. God recalled having ruled this utopia before China's devil-seduced emperors usurped his reign, imposed polytheistic Daoism and Buddhism, and polarized China by replacing God's "universal love" with Confucius' family-centered, "selfish" love. He told Hong that the vehicle for reconstituting theocratic government in China was the earthly implementation of the biblical Kingdom of Heaven (*Tianguo*), to be governed by God as emperor. As "heavenly king," God's vice-regent, Hong would dispense divine compassion equally to all Chinese regardless of their family connections.

After his fourth and final examination failure in 1843, Hong took up his mission. He smashed his school's Confucian tablet and his family's wooden idols while exhorting his relatives and neighbors to trigger the new order by being "born again" into Christianity, which the Qing emperors had

Greatest extent of Taiping control (as of early 1862). The coastal city of Shanghai was not itself controlled by Taiping forces. The solid line indicates the northward advance of Taiping troops in 1851–1853 to establish the Heavenly Capital (New Jerusalem) at Nanjing. The broken line represents the Taipings' unsuccessful northern campaign of 1853–1855.

banned in 1724 as anti-Confucian. Such heterodox preaching angered the village elders, who dismissed Hong from his teaching post. In early 1844, he took his message to relatives who had fled Bendi oppression in Guangdong for Thistle Mountain, a multiethnic frontier area in adjacent Guangxi Province, some 250 miles to the west.

The tripling of China's population and its catastrophic strain on land and crop resources during Qing rule created appalling suffering throughout Thistle Mountain. The recently arrived Hakka became wedged between two violent antagonists: wealthy, well-armed Bendi landlords eager to consolidate their landholdings on one side and Yao, Zhuang, and other tribal groups on the other. All of these communities fought each other over land and water rights. The coastal treaty-ports that the West imposed on China after the Opium War broke Guangzhou's monopoly on the country's foreign trade. As a result, 100,000 Hakka transport workers lost their jobs. So did thousands of Hakka miners when silver deposits dried up. Worse, demobilized Opium War volunteers, pirates fleeing British naval patrols, and secret society gangs flooded Guangxi to extort, rob, and kidnap; to run brothels, gambling dens, and protection rackets; and to smuggle opium to feed the growing addiction among dispirited peoples. The outflow of silver to purchase the drug devalued the local copper currency, thereby doubling land taxes and boosting commodity prices just as farm production began falling. Many struggling Hakka, now at the mercy of extortionate rents, usurious interest rates, and extralegal surtaxes, were driven from their rocky hillside plots into the downward spiral of poverty, lawlessness, and violence, which the corrupt Qing government refused to address.

Amid the doomsday omens of this apocalyptic world, Hong launched a campaign for social reform through individual Christian conversion. Merging Chinese and Protestant elements—the latter learned from the American Issachar Jacox Roberts and other missionaries in Guangzhou—he and his cousin, Feng Yunshan (also a failed examination candidate and former teacher), initiated 3,000 marginalized Hakka into a dozen God Worshipper Society congregations through baptism; united them as "brothers" and "sisters" in Bible reading, the Lord's Prayer, sermons delineating the coming Kingdom of peace and plenty, and Baptist hymns accompanied by firecrackers, drums, and gongs; and disciplined them by adhering to the Ten Commandments, which Hong reinterpreted to address such specific "sins" as "idolatry," interethnic feuding, "oppressing the weak," promiscuity, gambling, and abuse of opium, tobacco, and alcohol.

From 1848 to 1850, famine and typhus ballooned God Worshipper ranks. Hong dispensed disaster relief from the Hakka-inspired Sacred Treasury, while Yang Xiuqing, illiterate boss of Thistle Mountain's charcoalworkers, and Xiao Chaogui, a tenant farmer and Hong's brother-in-law, offered Hakka shamanistic faith healing in the name of the Christian Trinity. While performing Yao-inspired spirit possession and exorcism rituals, they spoke in trances for God and Jesus, making them a daily presence among the God Worshippers seeking deliverance. This charismatic appeal inspired a militant faith, sparked an orgy of idol smashing, and quickened expectations for the Heavenly Kingdom's imminent descent.

Bendi landlords, alarmed by the God Worshippers' loyalty to Christian God above Confucian emperor, ordered their militia to suppress Hong's congregations. In July 1850, Hong summoned 20,000 God Worshippers to Jintian village, where they donated their possessions to the Sacred Treasury, underwent military training, and cut their queue (symbol of Chinese subservience to the foreign Manchus) in preparation for Armageddon. The following winter, Qing troops attacked. Emboldened by divine injunctions spoken through Yang and Xiao to endure suffering, fight courageously, and respect noncombatants, the God Worshippers—including Hakka women under the command of Hong's sister—put up formidable resistance.

On January 11, 1851, Hong declared the inauguration of the Heavenly Kingdom of Great Peace and Equality (*Taiping Tianguo*). The God Worshippers' moral crusade was now a Taiping political uprising.

CONTEXT AND PROCESS OF REVOLUTION

In September 1851, 50,000 Taipings captured Yongan (the unemployed miners among them breaching the city wall), sixty miles northeast of Jintian. There, Hong developed his plan to extend theocratic control to the individual believer through a leadership pyramid integrating religious, military, and political authority directly from God through Hong, his chief of staff Yang Xiuqing, and four other subordinate kings (Feng Yunshan, Xiao Chaogui, Wei Changhui, and Shi Dakai under Yang Xiuqing as chief of staff). He modified the standard lunar calendar to emphasize the Sabbath and organized former government clerks, examination candidates, and pawnbrokers into an incipient bureaucracy. He segregated men and women—who were considered brothers and sisters under the same "Heavenly Father"—into separate military camps to enforce morality and facilitate mobile warfare. He then put the Taipings into Old Testament salvation history by issuing a patriotic call for all Chinese, including former enemies, to unite as God's "Chosen People" and march, Exodus-like, toward liberation from "devil" Manchu oppression into their Promised Land.

As the Taipings swept northward from China's southwestern periphery into the country's agrarian and commercial heartland, their promises of land distribution swelled recruitment. And the image of a judgmental warrior-God enforcing the Ten Commandments (now adapted to the rules of engagement) by rewarding bravery with Heaven and punishing cowardice with Hell inspired the fierce combat that enabled the Taipings to seize a string of prosperous river cities and thereby enrich their Sacred Treasury.

In March 1853, one million Taipings took Nanjing, China's former imperial capital, just west of Shanghai. They christened it "New Jerusalem." Hong governed on God's behalf and put the Taipings within the Bible itself by claiming to be the reincarnated Melchizedek, messianic priest-king who anticipated King David in the Old Testament and Jesus in the New. Hong unified his diverse followers through ceaseless prayer, Bible study, hymn singing, Sabbath services, baptisms, weddings, and funerals. Grace before meals enjoined the faithful to "Kill the [Manchu] demons!" Hong enforced discipline through floggings for dancing and tobacco and wine use, and summary beheading for opium smoking and failure to memorize the Ten Commandments.

In an unprecedented assault on Confucianism, Hong banned ancestor worship, simplified the Chinese language, and replaced the Confucian canon with the Taiping Bible (i.e., the first six Old Testament books, the complete New Testament, and a "Third Testament" recording the story of Hong's heavenly ascent and visions plus the divine pronouncements of God and Jesus in Thistle Mountain). He nationalized private property, made trade and commerce a government monopoly, and organized 25-person, occupation-specific units in separate men's, women's, and children's camps to produce around the clock for the Taiping state and army.

Hong's most radical reforms were on behalf of women. Although he gave harems to the kings, he compelled the rank and file to abandon the custom of polygamy. He also abolished other practices (some of which had already been rejected by the Hakka), such as footbinding, arranged marriage, wife purchase, widow suicide, and prostitution. And he decreed women's equal access to the military, education, examinations, and government.

Since the Taiping state must ensure that all Chinese share equally in God's Kingdom, Hong decreed that Taiping-occupied territory be placed under state ownership through a land system based on individual "congregations" of twenty-five families. There, a "sergeant" would lead daily church services, educate boys and girls using Bible texts, mediate disputes, recruit and train soldiers, supervise labor, and ensure that surplus grain was stored in the Sacred Treasury and that men and women were assigned equal amounts of similarly productive land.

Yang Xiuqing brilliantly coordinated the Taiping government and military. Although his campaign to capture Beijing had failed, the Taipings were riding high in 1856: they governed 30 million people in six provinces along a 300-mile stretch of the lower Yangzi River Valley. At this time, however, Qing statesmen like Zeng Guofan were already compensating for the ineffectual Qing army by assembling well-disciplined regional militias financed by landlord-gentry desperate to preserve the Confucian way of life even under Manchu rule.

That same year, Yang attempted to depose Hong by claiming to embody the Holy Ghost and thereby outrank Hong, who was merely God's second son. Hong ordered Wei Changhui to assassinate Yang, then commanded Shi Dakai to

kill Wei. This implosion of collective leadership was a mortal blow. Hong subsequently withdrew into mystical "heavenly matters." In the absence of God's voice uttered through Yang's "golden mouth," martial zeal waned. Meanwhile, Taiping commanders abandoned a coordinated, countrywide strategy and instead carved out their own regional power bases. By abandoning the land system in favor of preserving the landlord-tenant relationship and collecting traditional land taxes to support their armies, Taiping leaders reneged on their promise of free land that had initially attracted so many peasant followers to their movement.

In 1859, Hong Xiuquan sought to halt the Taipings' slide by appointing his cousin, Hong Rengan (an unsuccessful examination taker with close ties to Hong Kong and Shanghai missionaries), as "shield king." But the latter's proposals to adopt orthodox Christianity and create Western-style democratic, legal, economic, and social institutions were rejected by court rivals who had begun to revert to traditional Confucian court hierarchy and nepotism to preserve their power. Moreover, the Taipings squandered strategic advantage by refusing, for the sake of ideological purity, to cooperate with other rebels at the very moment Manchu forces were stretched thin fighting insurrections in every corner of the empire.

Although the Taipings prayed daily for their "foreign brothers and sisters," Christians in the West eventually condemned Hong's "abominable" doctrines. These included his insistence that God was revealed in China's ancient books as well as the Bible, his rewriting Scripture to rationalize Taiping teachings, and his preference for Old Testament vengeance over New Testament mercy. Meanwhile, Western governments, fearing that a victory for the equality-minded Taipings would end the foreigners' trading privileges (including the lucrative opium business), began reinforcing tattered Qing forces with American and European mercenaries and materiel by 1860.

The Manchus' siege of Nanjing early in 1864 choked off the Taipings' food supply. Hong ordered his starving faithful to eat weeds, which he dubbed "manna." On June 1, he died of malnutrition. The following month, New Jerusalem fell, and in November, Hong's teenage son, the "young lord," was executed. Mopping up operations stretched into 1866. By then, this civil war had taken between 20 and 40 million lives, destroyed 600 walled cities, and ravaged sixteen of China's eighteen provinces.

IMPACTS

Despite the time-honored efforts of China's emperors to control religion, messianic figures from society's margins often responded to catastrophe by prophesying apocalyptic de-

Dead bodies lie in the interior of Taku Fort after its capture by an Anglo-French force in August 1860 during the Taiping Rebellion. The rebellion was a major uprising in mid-nineteenth-century China, which came close to overthrowing the government of the Qing (Manchu) dynasty. (Hulton Archive/Getty Images)

struction of an orthodox order they condemned as evil and recruiting alienated followers into salvationist congregations, which often rose up when threatened with suppression. Yet their egalitarian notions did not extend beyond the sectarian elect or secret society cells. Their envisioned Daoist utopias and Buddhist millenniums lacked a blueprint and timetable for restructuring earthly society. Nor did they advocate alternatives to the restoration of virtuous Confucian rule in the next dynasty.

The Taipings were different. Their belief in a universal creator-God whose transcendence dwarfed the less powerful deities of other rebel groups and the Chinese monarch (a mere "Son of Heaven") shook Confucian China to its core. No other dissident movement had hitherto envisioned such revolutionary solutions to China's urgent problems as (1) social

and gender equality, (2) a Socialist alternative to private property, landlord-tenant ties, and labor management, and (3) the extension of totalitarian state control to individual grassroots congregations (the lowest level of government administration yet proposed in Chinese history).

The Taipings' theocratic kingdom was intended to reconcile China to the hostile modern world into which it had been thrust. But their revolutionary heirs utilized more secular approaches. Dr. Sun Yat-sen (1866–1925), a Hakka who called himself "Hong Xiuquan the second," looked to American-style republicanism. Ironically, regional fragmentation, created by the local militias formed to combat the Taiping menace, enabled Sun's revolutionary army to overthrow the Manchus in 1911 but prevented him from reunifying the country after the dynastic system had been discarded.

Mao Zedong (1893–1976) fashioned a millennial vision from another foreign ideology—Marxism-Leninism—and organized a revolution that included elements reminiscent of Taiping precedents: martial zeal, puritanical morality, and messianic struggle against demonized enemies (i.e., Chinese nationalists, foreign imperialists, and Japanese occupiers), a Long March toward the economic leveling of land reform and communes, a Marriage Law guaranteeing women legal equality with men, and an iconoclastic Cultural Revolution aimed at implementing the Communist utopia. In the end, though, Mao's utopian experiment has been no more permanent than Hong's. In recent years, the Chinese Communist Party has reinstituted traditional property rights and economic competition. These policies are reopening inequities that may spark yet another chapter in China's ongoing revolution.

PEOPLE AND ORGANIZATIONS

God Worshipper Society

A network of congregations organized by Hong Xiuquan and Feng Yunshan (1822–1852) throughout the Guangdong-Guangxi border region in 1844–1851 to rescue hard-pressed Hakka and other marginalized groups from moral breakdown, ethnic violence, social anarchy, and economic collapse wrought by China's intersecting internal and external crises. The God Worshippers synthesized Chinese folk religious and Christian Protestant initiation, purification, healing, and worship rituals; enforced the Ten Commandments to combat immorality, lawlessness, and opium use; and practiced gender equality and property sharing. The Qing government regarded their monotheism as a threat to imperial authority and began suppressing them late in 1850.

Hakka

For centuries, the Hakka (*kejia,* guest people) had fled repeated invasions of their north China homeland. Forced to become tenants of south China's Bendi (original settlers) majority, they worked as miners, stonecutters, charcoal- and dye-makers, and hired hands. Although many Hakka passed the civil service examinations and distinguished themselves in government, the Bendi dehumanized them because of their distinctive dialect and the poverty that necessitated their property sharing, monogamy, and rejection of female footbinding (which excluded women from manual labor and community self-defense). After 1800, tensions among the Hakka, Bendi, and tribal groups boiled over into inter-community violence. Pugnacious, self-reliant, and more recep-

tive to Christianity than other Chinese, the Hakka were the first converts to Hong Xiuquan's revolutionary movement, and their egalitarian traditions inspired the Taipings' most daring anti-Confucian reforms.

Hong Rengan (1822–1864)

Paternal cousin and early convert of Hong Xiuquan who, having been baptized and employed as an evangelist by Protestant missionaries in Hong Kong and Shanghai, was appointed prime minister in 1859 to revive Taiping fortunes. His proposals to transform Hong's pseudo-Christian faith into orthodox Protestantism, democratize Taiping rule, and westernize Taiping political, economic, social, educational, and philanthropic institutions were thwarted by rival kings. Nevertheless, his progressive ideas presaged those of a later generation of more successful Chinese reformers.

Hong Xiuquan (1814–1864)

Self-proclaimed younger brother of Jesus who launched a millenarian campaign to realize the pre-Confucian utopian goal of "great peace and equality" (*taiping*) through the biblical Kingdom of Heaven (*Tianguo)* come-to-earth. His identity as messiah, priest, and king was without Chinese precedent. Acknowledging that China was no longer the superior, stand-alone Middle Kingdom, Hong was the first Chinese intellectual to integrate Chinese and Western concepts into a post-Confucian national paradigm devoted to economic, social, and gender equality, universal education, and totalitarian governance of daily life. The Taiping kingdom was China's longest-surviving rebel utopia. Not since the assimilation of Buddhism centuries earlier had Confucian China faced so revolutionary an ideological threat.

Liang Fa (1789–1855)

A woodblock-printer-turned-Christian-propagandist, with a smattering of Confucian education, Liang was baptized and ordained as China's first Protestant evangelist by the missionary pioneers Robert Morrison (1782–1834) and William Milne (1789–1822). In 1832 he clandestinely published his *Good Words to Admonish the Age,* which Hong Xiuquan read several years later. The tract's apocalyptic denunciation of nineteenth-century China's moral decay, plea to reinforce a faltering Confucianism with Christian morals, and depiction of the monotheistic God and the theocratic Kingdom of Heaven precipitated Hong's messianic dream and informed much of his subsequent theological development.

Roberts, Issachar Jacox (1802–1871)

A Baptist missionary from Tennessee, Roberts broadened Hong's Christian knowledge beyond the contents of Liang's *Good Words* in the hope that, as a Chinese, Hong could Christianize China faster than the foreign missionaries could. During the spring of 1847, Roberts introduced Hong to church doctrine, liturgy, organization, and pastoral care as well as educational, publishing, medical, and other missionary good works in Guangzhou. Hong quickly integrated many of these elements into the God Worshipper Society and, in 1860, appointed Roberts the Taipings' director of foreign affairs. Initially a champion of the Taiping cause, Roberts, like many other Christians, grew increasingly disillusioned with Hong's theological "blasphemy" and ultimately advocated the Taipings' extermination.

Yang Xiuqing (Died 1856)

Illiterate Hakka labor boss in Thistle Mountain who, with Xiao Chaogui (died 1852), recruited famine and typhus sufferers into God Worshipper ranks by employing Hakka shamanism, aboriginal spirit possession, and folk ritual to offer Christian-style faith healing and to speak in trances for God and Jesus. The millenarian frenzy they unleashed provoked government attacks against the God Worshippers late in 1850 and accelerated Hong's timeline for inaugurating the Heavenly Kingdom. Yang became the Taipings' indispensable political and military organizer. But his assassination in September 1856, following his attempted coup against Hong, doomed the entire movement.

Zeng Guofan (1811–1872)

Born into a poor farming family in Hunan Province, north of Guangdong, Zeng achieved early examination success and quickly ascended the Qing bureaucratic ladder. Concerned, like the Taipings, about China's domestic and international woes, Zeng was convinced that China could be "restored" only by reaffirming traditional Confucian values and preserving the Manchu dynasty. As the primary defender of landlord-gentry interests against the Taipings, Zeng was the first of several Qing loyalists to organize regional militia aimed at reinforcing the disorganized Manchu army. After suppressing the Taipings in July 1864, Zeng initiated Sino-Western economic development projects, as Hong Rengan had earlier proposed, to bring "wealth and strength" to China.

Richard Bohr

See Also Chinese Revolution; Inequality, Class, and Revolution; Millenarianism, Religion, and Revolution; War and Revolution

References and Further Readings

Boardman, Eugene Powers. 1952. *Christian Influence upon the Ideology of the Taiping Rebellion, 1851–1864.* Madison: University of Wisconsin Press.

Bohr, P. Richard. 1998. "The Theologian as Revolutionary: Hung Hsiu-ch'üan [Hong Xiuquan]'s Religious Vision of the Taiping Heavenly Kingdom." Vol. 2, pp. 907–953 in *Tradition and Metamorphosis in Modern Chinese History. Essays in Honor of Professor Kwang-Ching Liu's Seventy-fifth Birthday,* edited by Yen-p'ing Hao and Hsiu-mei Wei. 2 vols. Taipei: Institute of Modern History, Academia Sinica.

————. 2003. "Jesus, Christianity, and Rebellion in China: The Evangelical Roots of the Taiping Heavenly Kingdom." Vol. 2, pp. 613–661 in *The Chinese Face of Jesus Christ,* edited by Roman Malek, S.V.D. 5 vols. Sankt Augustin, Germany: Institut Monumenta Serica and China-Zentrum.

————. 2004. "The Taipings in Chinese Sectarian Perspective." Pp. 393–430 in *Heterodoxy in Late Imperial China,* edited by Kwang-Ching Liu and Richard Shek. Honolulu: University of Hawaii Press.

Jen Yu-wen. 1973. *The Taiping Revolutionary Movement.* New Haven, CT: Yale University Press.

Kuhn, Philip A. 1978. "The Taiping Rebellion." Vol. 10, *Late Ch'ing [Qing],* pt. 1, pp. 264–317 in *The Cambridge History of China,* edited by John K. Fairbank. 15 vols. Cambridge: Cambridge University Press.

Michael, Franz, in collaboration with Chung-li Chang. 1966, 1971. *The Taiping Rebellion: History and Documents.* 3 vols. Seattle: University of Washington Press.

Reilly, Thomas H. 2004. *The Taiping Heavenly Kingdom: Rebellion and the Blasphemy of Empire.* Seattle: University of Washington Press.

Shih, Vincent Y. C. 1967. *The Taiping Ideology.* Seattle: University of Washington Press.

Spence, Jonathan D. 1996. *God's Chinese Son: The Taiping Heavenly Kingdom of Hong Xiuquan.* New York: Norton.

Wagner, Rufolf G. 1982. *Reenacting the Heavenly Vision: The Role of Religion in the Taiping Rebellion.* Berkeley: Institute of East Asian Studies, University of California.

Weller, Robert P. 1994. *Resistance, Chaos and Control in China: Taiping Rebels, Taiwanese Ghosts and Tianmen.* Seattle: University of Washington Press.

Terrorism

Most people believe that killing other human beings can only be justified in the context or war, and then only in accordance with the spirit and the letter of the laws of war, which are intended to minimize harm or injury to civilian populations and unnecessarily cruel or barbaric treatment of soldiers. Some of us believe that killing is also justified as punishment for homicide, provided that it is administered strictly in accordance with "due process of law," although the laws of most developed countries and of many of the American states do not allow capital punishment. In other words, we believe that human life is sacred; killing is, at best, a necessary evil. If people kill other people—especially innocent people—in large numbers, systematically, ruthlessly, brutally, we think of them as profoundly evil or crazy, possibly both.

In point of fact, humans have always slaughtered one another, frequently, in large numbers, and with little emotional or moral aversion, often accompanied by sacking, pillaging, and rape. The laws of war, as we know them, are a recent invention. The Crusades, dedicated to the sacred mission of recapturing the Holy Land from non-Christians, were a huge and prolonged exercise in wanton bloodshed.

> The First Crusade—the most idealistic, high spirited, and successful—set off on its two-thousand mile jaunt by massacring, plundering and slaughtering all the way from the Rhine to the Jordan. . . . Its conquest of the Holy City . . . was celebrated by the massacre of both Moslems and Jews. "In the temple and porch of Solomon," wrote the ecstatic cleric Raimundus de Agiles, "one rode in blood up to the knees and even to the horses' bridles, by the just and marvelous judgment of God." (Muller 1952, 239)

The appetite for inflicting death, suffering, and pain has also been manifest in the administration of criminal justice. The free use of the death penalty and the use of torture, not only to extract information but also to aggravate the pain of punishment, are part of relatively recent Western history. Such events were often held in public places so good citizens, cruising the square with their families, could be edified by these demonstrations of justice.

Recent history also provides us with examples of people not unlike us—humane, tolerant, schooled in civility and respect for human life—learning to live with, accept, and in various degrees, participate in the destruction of innocent human lives. What happened in Nazi Germany is the best example. The point is twofold: first, that Nazism was only yesterday, and second, that in the course of time millions of people, harmless people, more or less like you and me, became part of an enormous killing machine and most apparently lost no sleep over it. Even in recent years men have slaughtered each other by the thousands and the tens of thousands. Beginning on July 11, 1995, in the heart of Europe, Bosnian Serbs butchered their Muslim neighbors at Srebrenica—nearly 8,000 men and boys. Some Serbs have since been prosecuted for "the worst massacre of civilians since World War II" (*Hartford Courant,* July 10, 2005, p. A12).

This is not to say that the inclination to murder one's fellow man should be taken for granted, that an instinct to murder, rape, and plunder is always there just below the surface, or that the conduct we are concerned with here—terrorism—comes naturally to the human species and requires very little explaining. On the contrary, it remains one of the important ways human beings differ among themselves and, over time, from themselves; the differences must be explained; and the explanation is not obvious.

Studies of terrorism suggest, as does research on other forms of homicide and violence, that different individuals or groups may perpetrate terrorist acts for different reasons. Terrorism committed by individuals may in some cases be related to a serious psychological abnormality. Persons suffering from paranoid schizophrenia have sometimes distorted a political ideology or religious belief into a personal delusion that motivated the killing of a particular "guilty" person or category of persons. While only a tiny fraction of homicidal persons suffer from this type of psychosis, a much larger percentage, still a minority of all killers, are adept at homicide because, whether due to mistreatment during childhood or the result of neurological abnormalities, they feel little guilt for any aspects of their behavior. Such so-called psychopaths may be expected to excel as killers, not only in rebel groups but also in conventional armies.

But almost certainly much more significant are social and cultural causes. Economic deprivation or perception of threat have historically functioned to provoke terrorist violence, for example, on the part of governments facing foreign invasion or ruling classes fearing the revolt of lower classes. The members of the French revolutionary government in 1793, threatened by both counter-revolutionaries internally and foreign armies, and by their possible execution if defeated, instituted "The Terror," in which thousands were executed.

Ruling groups in many countries used extreme brutality and mass murder to repress political opposition. During the 1970s and 1980s, for example, right-wing military governments in Argentina and Chile were accused of causing thousands of people to simply disappear.

Combatants under intense stress or under orders have engaged in extreme forms of brutal violence against helpless civilians, including children, such as the Mi Lai massacre committed by U.S. troops in 1968 during the Vietnam conflict, or the slaughter of hundreds of people by El Salvadoran forces at El Mozote in 1981.

Another major explanation of terrorist violence entails the notion of cultures and subcultures—that is, systems of belief and practice that are shared by some community of people, encourage violence, and are transmitted and reinforced through social interaction. Subcultures that support and justify certain forms of violence have included extremist race- or religion-based ideologies. Such subcultures sometimes develop among oppressed and exploited people or are adopted by them from other groups or societies through the process of cultural diffusion.

Understanding and combating terrorism involves seeking answers to questions such as these: Why do we find such a culture *here, at this time?* Why is it located and distributed as it is within the larger social world? Why is it attractive to certain individuals or groups? Cultures that bear upon people-killing-people and the ways they are distributed in the social system change over time. For example, the culture that made possible the butchery (in the name of God and Christ and the Virgin Mary) that was part of the Crusades—that culture changed. How did Western culture, as it bore upon the conduct of war, transform over a relatively short time, and how do we explain the change? We may ask similar questions on a much smaller societal scale regarding the development or change over time in the subcultures of revolutionary groups.

Our understanding of terrorism may profit greatly from the application of cultural theory and research.

TERRORISM: DEFINITIONS, CHARACTERISTICS, AND DIMENSIONS

Bruce Hoffman (2002, 21), terrorism expert at the U.S. Rand Corporation, identified and analyzed 109 definitions of terrorism. He noted that the most common elements in the definitions, present in more than half of them, included violence, force, threat, fear, and a political aspect. James Poland, in his review of definitions, claimed that "Two common features are characteristic of . . . definitions of terror and terrorism. First, terrorism is a technique for inducing *fear*. . . . The second common denominator found in most definitions of terrorism is the achievement of some vague political objective (1988, 10)."

Certain definitions of terrorism limit the phenomenon not only to the political realm, but also specifically to acts by rebel or other dissident groups. Some terrorism writers, therefore, through their definitions, seem to avoid overtly recognizing the possibility of established governments engaging in terrorism. Eqbal Ahmad argued, in fact, that government officials like to describe modern terrorism as manifesting characteristics such as barbarism and constituting a threat to Western moral values, but typically do not put forward a specific definition of terrorism because this would commit them to "adherence to some norms of consistency (2002, 48)." The implication is that by providing a definition, government officials might at some point find themselves judged guilty of engaging in terrorism according to their own standards.

A number of students of terrorism have developed comprehensive typologies designed to identify a multitude of characteristics for analysis and to avoid the narrow constraints mentioned above. Terrorism can be categorized along several dimensions, including motive, agency, intended effects, types of targets, types of audiences addressed by acts or policies of terrorism, and the levels of effectiveness of terrorism. Motive typologies often have at least four categories, although a terrorist act may be the result of more than one motive: criminal (for example, terror is at times employed by organized crime); religious (to advance or defend religion according to the perpetrators' point of view); war (use of terrorism as a military tactic); political (such as the goal of changing government policy, or overthrowing a government, or crushing a dissident or rebel movement). Agency typologies refer to classification in terms of perpetrators, such as governments, anti-government groups, and private individuals, or persons employed as mercenaries in service to any of the former groups or individuals (such as the death squads financed by some pro-government persons in certain Latin American countries in the 1970s and 1980s).

An act of terrorism may be intended to force an adversary into negotiation or accomplish a structural goal, such as damaging the economic base of the adversary. Or it may be primarily symbolic-expressive, in which case the goal is psychological—to achieve a certain emotional state. The targets may include only those specifically blamed for certain policies or activities, or larger populations, even whole categories of people with a particular nationality or religion who are viewed as supportive of the adversary group and its policies. Audiences—those to whom the terrorist act is intended to communicate a message—include the members and immediate supporters of the terrorist group or government, populations whom the terrorists claim to represent, the members and supporters of the adversary group or government, and possibly other populations. The level of effectiveness of terrorism can be judged partly in relation to its impact on each type of audience. It may accomplish the intended effects with one or more audiences, but it may fail or be counterproductive with others.

Several aspects of the dimensions outlined above are elaborated or illustrated through examples in the following sections of this article. According to Cindy Combs (2003, 10) in the third edition of her popular book on terrorism, "Terrorism . . . involves an act of violence, an audience, the creation of a mood of fear, innocent victims, and political motives or goals." Terrorism, this definition suggests, is meant to inspire fear in the minds of some audience from whom the perpetrators want something. The primary object is not to punish the victims; they may be completely innocent. The object is to terrify some other audience and to motivate that audience to concede to the demands of the perpetrators.

When we think of terrorism, we often envision rebels making demands upon or seeking to destroy and replace an established government. However, governments themselves can employ terrorism in the sense of Combs' definition. Discontented crowds of people making demands upon the state but not yet prepared or equipped to engage in actual combat may provoke such a response. By violently suppressing such protests, a regime sends a message to other dissidents that they must cease further opposition. Events in the city of Andijon, Uzbekistan, in 2005 provided an example. There were accounts that government forces were involved in the shooting of a number of people engaged in a protest. Tom Casey, speaking for the U.S. Department of State, said that "There can be no excuse for this grave violation of the human rights of so many Uzbek citizens (New York Times, June 18, 2005, p. A6). Ironically, the United States had provided large amounts of equipment as well as training to Uzbek security forces to combat terrorism. The case is interesting because it suggests the complexity of the interrelationships that may be involved in episodes of terrorism and counter-terrorism.

The discussion of terrorism is often confounded by the fact that the word is both a descriptive term and an epithet. As a descriptive term, it specifies the characteristics by which we can recognize something when we see it. As an epithet it adds no information but conveys the moral judgment that what we are dealing with here is evil and immoral. When the Uzbek regime's forces fired into the crowd, in what many would view as a classic display of governmental terrorism, it described what it was doing as defending itself against the terrorism of the mob.

What the Combs' and other definitions seem to emphasize is that the goal of the act of terrorism is not primarily to punish the victims, it is to do business with a larger audience, to tell the audience in effect: *You know what we want from you. If you refuse, you can expect to get more of the same. You already know we are capable of it.*

It is consistent with many definitions of terrorism that the messages from the terrorists, be they government or rebels, can be directed to more than one audience. When Palestinian groups linked to Hamas or Islamic Jihad blew up buses or detonated bombs in a town square, they were indeed speaking to an Israeli audience. But they were also speaking to an Arab audience. To other Palestinians they were saying: *See what we do to the people who stole your land. With support from you—money, recruits to our cause, places to hide when the Israeli military comes looking for us—we will be even more effective. Some day we shall succeed in driving the Jews into the sea, and you can go back home.* To the extent that Islamic Jihad or other similar groups can claim that the Palestinian people respond positively to this message, they can in turn tell the Palestinian government: *The Palestinian people see us as their champions and will not tolerate efforts on your part to bring us under your command and control.* Such terrorist acts also speak loudly to other governments hostile to Israel that have provided important support to violent groups by way of money, training, and materiel.

Acts of terrorism by rebel groups in general can likewise send messages to various audiences beyond their prime adversaries. Through their actions, including violence, they speak to their own base: their active members, those they wish to recruit, and the populations from which they are drawn, whose interests they claim to represent, and from which they seek resources, help, and gratitude. Their attacks might also be intended to encourage other insurgent movements with similar ideologies to take up or continue the struggle against their own governments.

Governments fighting rebels may also have affinities to one another, growing out of a community of interests. If they perceive such a community of interests, one government may participate at a distance, so to speak, in counter-terror terrorism in another country by providing materiel, training, and intelligence, or even by sending its own counterinsurgency personnel. The United States, in its relationship to certain Latin American countries with repressive right-wing, pro-business governments, has provided forceful examples of this phenomenon. The El Salvadoran military unit accused of carrying out the slaughter of hundreds of children and unarmed civilian adults at El Mozote was U.S. trained. Rather than admitting the atrocity, the Reagan administration sought to certify that the El Salvadoran military had actually improved its human rights behavior in order to justify the continued flow of hundreds of millions of U.S. taxpayers' money to El Salvador's government and armed forces. At the same time, the U.S. government was accusing other nations of state-sponsored terrorism.

One must take pains not to incorporate into the definition of terrorism properties that are not essential to terrorism according to popular usage and understanding. A definition of terrorism that is consistent with usage would run something like this: *An act of violence or threat of violence by some individual, group, or organization intended to inspire terror in some audience.* Having defined terrorism in this fashion, students of the subject then face the task of identifying variations in the characteristics of those who commit acts of terrorism; of their victims or intended victims; of the audiences, both actual or intended; of their acts of violence; of the responses that terrorists seek to elicit from the various audiences; and so on. Finally, scientific analysis should also attempt to explain the variations along these dimensions and the interactions among these dimensions, such as the relationship between the choice of victims and the intended audiences, or the relationship between the sources from which the terrorists seek to obtain the resources they need and the demands that they make of the political entities they seek to terrorize.

Women farmers of El Mozote, El Salvador, carry the remains of their murdered family members in 2001. El Salvadoran government military forces murdered hundreds of people at El Mozote in 1981, including children. (Yuri Cortez/AFP/Getty Images)

Our object here is to illustrate, with the help of a few examples, that the world within which terrorism occurs, and which shapes the forms it takes and its successes and failures, is complex, often with a number of collective actors, audiences, and messages, and that analysis must often be correspondingly complex if it is to do justice to the phenomenon.

EXPRESSIVE TERRORISM

Most definitions of terrorism appear to stress an *instrumental* motive for terrorism: that is, the behavior is a means to an end, and that end is to persuade some entity to yield to the demands of the terrorists. Now consider another kind of killing that is a commonplace of criminology. Two men, usually in a public setting like a bar, start insulting each other. One of them is clearly getting the worst of it, being portrayed as stupid, cowardly, and unmanly. The identity that he cherishes is being mocked and belittled, and he can't think fast enough to do the same to the other guy. He is angry, bitter, helpless—and desperate. At some point he leaves, comes back with a gun, and "kills the son-of a bitch." As a result, the tension arising from a progressive accumulation of humiliation and hatred is dissipated. What he has done with the gun is itself a refutation of the other guy's claims. The killing is not instrumental in the sense that it is an effort to persuade

someone to make a deal. There may be an audience, but nothing is asked from the audience. The payoff lies not in what the terrorism persuades members of an adversarial audience to concede, but in the free—and lethal—expression of emotion. This behavior is not instrumental, but rather it is *expressive.*

If asked for an example of terrorism, most Americans would probably come up with the events of September 11, 2001. However, I suggest that the events of that day should be interpreted as largely expressive.

For many centuries the Near-Eastern world, largely Arab and overwhelmingly Muslim, was the center of civilization. Its great cities were alive with commerce and the literary and visual arts. Mathematics and the sciences flourished, and the world came there to learn. Their military forces were also powerful, inspiring fear, deference, respect, and admiration. In Europe they were turned back only at the gates of France.

But all that began to change as Europe emerged from the so-called Dark Ages. Gradually, fitfully, but without turning back, Europe began a millennium of growth, progress, commerce, and productivity; of science and technology; of supremacy of trade, exploration, and domination of the underdeveloped world. At the same time, whatever the reasons, the nations of the Near East stagnated. They tried to defend themselves against the armies and navies of the growing world powers of the West, but usually without success. They endured leaders who capitulated and became virtual puppets of Western imperialism. In their political and economic dealings with the West they learned to be deferential, respectful, and generally submissive. The people who once brought culture to the Western barbarians found themselves adusting to a world that was being molded by the Christian nations.

Many descendants of the followers and soldiers of Muhammad and Saladin found this state of affairs humiliating. They were resentful and bitter, and to some degree hostile to the West. But generally they did not articulate their hostility, because, given their relative lack of power, they could not afford to give offense to the Westerners with whom they did business.

And then there was 9–11. The whole world watched the destruction of the twin towers—the symbol of American power and American commercial ascendancy, the offices to which the whole world came hat in hand. People around the world watched the shock, the bewilderment, the confusion, the fear, the grief, and the incomprehension that seized the whole country. News agencies reported that people danced in the streets of Arab cities. The governments of Islamic nations gave the United States their solemn expressions of sympathy and the sympathy may have been in some degree genuine and even shared by wide sectors of their populations, but clearly it was not unalloyed. The joy of many was apparently immediate, spontaneous, visible, and public.

I suggest that the terrorists who participated in the events of that day were certainly playing to an American audience, but primarily to a Muslim audience, and that the primary object of the terrorism was not to obtain something from the United States. It was calculated terror, but they did not intend a deal. It was mainly a gift to the Muslim audience:

See the Twin Towers reduced to ashes. See the Americans running around wringing their hands, wondering, puzzled, terrified. Those who did this are our young men. They did it for us. The Americans have been cut down to size and we did it!

The United States was the audience, but nobody was asking anything of them. The Muslim world was also the audience, but nobody was asking anything of them either. They were, it can be said, the beneficiaries of 9–11. In what sense? The event was emotionally gratifying for those who identified with the perpetrators. Maybe even "therapeutic."

Since the events of 9–11 and largely in consequence of them, the United States became militarily engaged in Afghanistan and Iraq. In both countries it encountered much opposition, to a large extent encouraged and even directed by religious authorities. There is probably no more eloquent evidence for the expressive significance of 9–11 than the often repeated reference to the Americans as "infidels" and "Crusaders." This suggests that through the eyes of many in the Near East, what is happening now in Afghanistan and Iraq is part of a larger event that began long before 9–11 and is called the Crusades.

Explicating the events of 9–11 leads to an understanding of the complexity and the variety of circumstances and cultural meanings that interact to produce the events we call terrorism.

COUNTER-TERRORISM

Paul Pillar (2002) described at least four aspects of counter-terrorism: defend potential targets; weaken or destroy the capabilities of those who would commit terrorism; influence the intentions and plans of terrorists, in part by not giving in to their demands under the threat of terrorism; and deal with the root causes of terrorism which includes affecting antecedent conditions through means such as providing peoples with self-determination, alleviating political repression, bringing relief from depraved rulers, and economically supplying the means to escape from poverty and improve living standards.

Terrorist-hijacked United Airlines flight 175 flies into the South Tower of the World Trade Center in New York City during terrorist attacks on September 11, 2001. (Rob Howard/Corbis)

But a serious examination of the record uncovers inconsistencies, both past and contemporary, in U.S. foreign policy in dealing with root or underlying causes of terrorism. The U.S. government, in the view of much of the world, has not consistently opposed repressive and non-democratic regimes; instead, it has seemed to support such governments when this policy benefited its economic or political interests. For many years, extremely repressive regimes existed in parts of the Western Hemisphere, against which U.S. administrations took little effective action and with which U.S. corporations were free to do business. The right-wing military leaders who overthrew the elected leftist Chilean president Salvador Allende, whose government was strongly opposed by the Nixon administration, abandoned Chile's democratic constitution and established a dictatorship held responsible for the torture and death of thousands. They seized power, ironically, on September 11, 1973, creating a regime widely accused of state terrorism. In other parts of the world, U.S. administrations tolerated and continued to do business with monarchies and authoritarian governments while seeming to single out only those uncooperative with U.S. policy for severe criticism or harsher measures. These non-democratic societies were often characterized by extreme economic inequalities, leaving large sectors of their populations, including much of the Arab world, in poverty. In U.S.-occupied Iraq, an aspect of counter-terrorism policy seemed to exploit this situation by offering jobs and economic opportunity to those who would join the new U.S.-sponsored Iraqi military and police force. This seemingly selective, rather than universal, concern with fostering democracy and improving living standards may seriously hamper U.S. counter-terrorism efforts and undoubtedly provides effective recruiting arguments for terrorist groups. Unless and until inconsistencies and contradictions are eliminated, the war against terrorism will be difficult if not impossible to win.

Albert K. Cohen

See Also Algerian Revolution; Chilean Socialist Revolution, Counter-Revolution, and the Restoration of Democracy; Cinema of Revolution; Colonialism, Anti-Colonialism, and Neo-Colonialism; Documentaries of Revolution; Ethnic and Racial Conflict: From Bargaining to Violence; French Revolution; Guatemalan Democratic Revolution, Counter-Revolution, and Restoration of Democracy; Human Rights, Morality, Social Justice, and Revolution; Inequality, Class, and Revolution; Iranian Revolution; Irish Revolution; Islamic Fundamentalist Revolutionary Movement; Italian Fascist Revolution; Kenyan Mau Mau Rebellion; Libyan Revolution; Nazi Revolution: Politics and Racial Hierarchy; Palestinian Movement; Philippine Muslim Separatist Rebellions; Russian Revolution of 1917; Salvadoran Revolution; Spanish Revolution and Counter-Revolution; Sri Lankan Conflict; Vietnamese Revolution; Yugoslavia: Dissolution; Zionist Revolution and the State of Israel

References and Further Readings

Ahmad, Eqbal. 2002. "Terrorism: Theirs and Ours." Pp. 46–52 in *Terrorism and Counterterrorism: Understanding The New Security Environment*, edited by Russell D. Howard and Reid L. Sawyer. Guilford, CT: McGraw-Hill/Dushkin.

Binford, Leigh. 1996. *The El Mozzote Massacre: Anthropology and Human Rights.* Tucson, AZ: University of Arizona Press.

"Bosnia to Mark Massacre with Ceremony Memorial." *Hartford Courant,* July 10, 2005. p. A12.

Combs, Cindy C. 2003. *Terrorism in the Twenty-First Century.* 3rd edition. Upper Saddle River, NJ: Prentice Hall.

Danner, Mark. 1994. *The Massacre at El Mozote.* New York: Vintage Books.

Gareau, Frederick H. 2004. *State Terrorism and the United States: From Counterinsurgency to the War on Terrorism.* Atlanta, GA: Clarity Press.

Hoffman, Bruce. 2002. "Defining Terrorism." Pp. 3–23 in *Terrorism and Counterterrorism: Understanding the New Security Environment,* edited by Russell D. Howard and Reid L. Sawyer. Guilford, CT: McGraw-Hill/Dushkin.

Howard, Russell D., and Reid L. Sawyer, eds. 2002. *Terrorism and Counterterrorism: Understanding The New Security Environment.* Guilford, CT: McGraw-Hill/Dushkin.

Laqueur, Walter. 1998. *Origins of Terrorism: Psychologies, Ideologies, Theologies, States of Minds.* Baltimore, MD: Johns Hopkins University Press.

Muller, Herbert J. 1952. *The Uses of the Past: Profiles of Former Societies.* Oxford: Oxford University Press.

Pillar, Paul R. 2002. "The Dimensions of Terrorism and Counterterrorism." Pp. 24–45 in *Terrorism and Counterterrorism: Understanding The New Security Environment,* edited by Russell D. Howard and Reid L. Sawyer. Guilford, CT: McGraw-Hill/Dushkin.

Poland, James. M. 1988. *Understanding Terrorism: Groups, Strategies, and Responses.* Englewood Cliffs, NJ: Prentice Hall.

"Uzbek Ministries in Crackdown Received U.S. Aid." *New York Times,* June 18, 2005, p. A6.

Theories of Revolutions

Revolutions have powerfully shaped the world we live in and promise to do so well into the future. The revolutionary events in both Iran and Nicaragua in 1979 to China and Eastern Europe in 1989 and Chiapas today pose anew old puzzles for social theory even as they herald the changed situation of a post–Cold War, post–September 11 world. Alexis de Tocqueville's astute observation on the French Revolution rings just as true for any of these more contemporary upheavals: "never was any such event, stemming from factors far back in the past, so inevitable yet so completely unforeseen" (de Tocqueville 1955, 1). Virtually all modern revolutions took analysts by surprise and have led theorists into a variety of strategies to understand why these rare events have occurred.

The study of revolution is marked by fundamental theoretical and political controversy, beginning with the definition of the term itself. The best definition of social revolution has been provided by sociologist Theda Skocpol: "Social revolutions are rapid, basic transformations of a society's state and class structures; and they are accompanied and in part carried through by class-based revolts from below" (1979, 4). This definition, while not perfect or unambiguous, usefully underlines the salience of three factors—political change, economic and social transformation, and mass participation—as the hallmarks of revolution.

Explanations of what causes revolutions have centered on a cluster of factors, among them economic, political, demographic, ideological or cultural, and subjective factors. The history of such theorizing in the twentieth century can be usefully told in terms of "generations" of theories, with Jack Goldstone (1980) identifying three such generations up to the 1980s, and a fourth generation asserting itself since then.

THE FIRST TWO GENERATIONS

Social science models of the causes of revolutions date back to the 1920s and 1930s. Comparative historians such as L. P.

Edwards in *The Natural History of Revolution* (1927), Crane Brinton in *The Anatomy of Revolution* (1938), and G. S. Pettee in *The Process of Revolution* (1938) sought common patterns among such major revolutions as the French, American, English, and Russian. According to Jack Goldstone, this first-generation "Natural History of Revolution" school included:

- prior to revolutions, intellectuals cease to support the regime;
- prior to revolutions, the state undertakes reforms;
- outbreaks have more to do with a state crisis than active opposition;
- after the revolutionary coalition takes power, conflicts arise within it;
- the first group to seize power is moderate reformers;
- the revolution then radicalizes because moderates fail to go far enough;
- the radicals then bring about organizational and ideological changes, taking extreme measures to deal with problems and secure power;
- radicals impose coercive order ("The Terror") to implement their program in the midst of social dislocation;
- military leaders such as Cromwell, Washington, Napoleon, and Trotsky often emerge;
- "eventually things settle down and pragmatic moderates regain power" (Goldstone 1982, 189–192).

The critique commonly aimed at these pioneers of theory is that they merely *describe* the process of revolution rather than explain *why* revolutions occur. And yet, as description, this list is not at all bad, as the case of Iran, for example, bears out.

In the 1960s, a second generation of somewhat disparate American social scientists tried to explain why and when revolutions arise, using either social psychological or structural-functional approaches to collective behavior. Ted Robert Gurr (1970) and James Davies (1962) developed theories of political violence based on aggregate psychological states, notably relative deprivation. Davies proposed a "J-curve" in which economic growth leads to rising expectations but is followed instead by a downturn as a recipe for revolt. Within the then popular modernization paradigm, Neil Smelser and Chalmers Johnson looked for imbalances in the subsystems of a society that disoriented people and made them more prone to embrace radical ideologies. Smelser, in his *Theory of Collective Behavior* (1962) provides a comprehensive set of factors affecting the development of social movements, including structural conduciveness, strain, new beliefs, precipitants, mobilization, and social control.

The critique that is generally advanced of all of these approaches revolves around the difficulty of observing and measuring aggregate psychological states and societal disequilibrium, and the corresponding danger of sliding into a tautological argument that one can know such factors are present because a revolution has occurred—a danger for all who would theorize revolutions. They have also been dismissed as too "purposive" in seeking to explain revolutions in terms of the rise of oppositional actors in society. But this emphasis, along with the attendant concern for the values, beliefs, and ideologies of those involved, is a strength of these otherwise not-too-convincing theories, and in its way compares favorably with the more one-sidedly structural theories that would constitute the third generation.

THEDA SKOCPOL AND THE THIRD GENERATION

Beginning in the 1960s, and increasingly in the 1970s, a series of structural macrosociologies of revolution were elaborated, identifying actors and themes ranging from the state, dominant elites, and armies to international pressures, agrarian relations, and peasant mobilization as the keys to understanding social revolution. An obvious influential precursor was Karl Marx, who stressed the role played by class struggles as structured by the inequalities found in societies undergoing economic transition. Structural theories of revolution in contemporary social science were pioneered in 1966 by Barrington Moore, Jr.'s pathbreaking comparative study, *Social Origins of Dictatorship and Democracy*. Moore identified the vulnerable moment as that of the transition to capitalist agriculture and the changing relations among peasants, the state (usually a monarchy), landlords, and a nascent bourgeoisie in this period. He argued that successful commercialization of agriculture undercuts peasant revolution, that peasants must possess certain solidarity structures to rebel, and that they need allies to make a revolution. Eric Wolf's 1969 survey of six "peasant wars" found that as the commercialization of agriculture threatens peasants' access to land, middle peasants are best placed to rebel, allies must be found among the urban classes, and armed force is necessary to seize the state. Jeffery Paige's 1975 book on Third World peasant movements specifies that revolution occurs only where landed classes depend on the land itself (not capital, machinery, and technology) for their income and peasants are amenable to organization in their capacity as sharecroppers or migrant laborers.

Theda Skocpol's 1979 work, *States and Social Revolutions,* represents a landmark in the sociology of revolutions in arguing for a structural, as opposed to a "voluntarist" or "purposive" perspective. Her comparative study of France, Russia, and China yields a common pattern: political crises arose when old-regime states could not meet external challenges because of internal obstacles in agrarian and elite relations. In France, foreign wars led to fiscal crisis, which inefficient agriculture exacerbated. Efforts to tax nobles led to elite revolts; peasants took advantage of the crisis and were able to mobilize due to communal solidarity structures. In Russia, collapse in World War I led to state crisis; in China the Japanese invasion and World War II created an opportunity.

Various criticisms can be leveled at this model. It is unlikely that structures simply change *by themselves,* so change cannot be completely explained in structural terms. Further, while acknowledging some role for ideologies as "undoubtedly necessary ingredients in the great social revolutions," Skocpol insists that crises have not been made by actors, outcomes have been unintended, and ideologies have been shaped and confounded by structural situations and crises (Skocpol 1979, 170). These omissions detract from the overall power of what is otherwise *the* central study of revolutions written by a sociologist.

Charles Tilly is another eminent political sociologist who has made important contributions to the study of revolutions. His version of what came to be known as resource mobilization theory stresses the importance of studying the organizational and other resources available to contending groups (states, elites, challengers), and sees revolution as a condition of "multiple sovereignty," in which the population shifts its allegiance from the government to a contending group (1978). He also goes beyond Skocpol in his attention to ideological resources and the issue of state legitimacy, as well as the centrality of coalitions. More recently, this perspective has evolved into political process theory, with its attention to such factors as broad socioeconomic processes, expanded political opportunities, and actors' ability to frame their grievances in revolutionary terms.

A FOURTH GENERATION EMERGES

This leads us to a set of promising new directions in the sociological study of revolutions since the 1980s, suggesting the outlines of a new, fourth generation of theory. These include the interrelated issues of agency, political culture, and coalitions, and the dimensions of ethnicity (or "race"), class, and gender. The problem of agency is posed by its conceptual absence in the structural approaches of Skocpol and others. Social structure may illuminate both crises and outcomes, but past human actions, however much conditioned they may be, also help explain social structures. Neither individualism nor structuralism is the ultimate or only cause of social change.

Supplying a complex mediation between structure and action is the role of ideas, values, beliefs, ideologies. James

Scott's 1976 work on the moral economy of the peasantry refers to a norm of reciprocity in relation to the state and landlord that, if violated, can lead to rebellion. In some cases, revolutionaries tap long-standing cultural traditions (what Tilly calls the "cultural repertoire" of collective action); in others, they innovate these into rather new cultural orientations. This growing preoccupation with culture—now understood as "the cultural turn" in the social sciences—must be built into any serious theory of revolution today.

A final new direction in the sociology of revolutions leads back to the age-old question of who, precisely, makes them. Skocpol felt she was restoring the peasantry to center stage in the face of an urban bias in previous historiography on France and Russia. Critics of Skocpol and students of the revolutions in Iran, Nicaragua, and elsewhere then refocused attention on urban actors. The real challenge, however, is to study *coalitions* in revolutions, for multiclass alliances, often motivated by diffuse ideals such as nationalism, populism, or religion rather than particularistic ones such as Socialism, have made most of the revolutions in world history. In addition to class, it would be well to bear in mind (and until recently most scholars have not) the gender and ethnic composition of revolutionary coalitions so salient in the 1980s revolutions in Central America and in Chiapas today.

Signs of this emergent fourth generation can be discerned in a number of works of the last quarter of the twentieth century. In a study of the Mexican Revolution, Walter Goldfrank suggests a combination of necessary and sufficient conditions for Third World social revolutions: "(1) a tolerant or permissive world context; (2) a severe political crisis paralyzing the administrative and coercive capacities of the state; (3) widespread rural rebellion; and (4) dissident elite political movements" (1979, 148). John Walton's 1984 framework for the study of "national revolts" (nationwide violent conflicts that do not always lead to full-fledged social revolutions) also identifies several of these factors: uneven development, the role of the state, cultural nationalism, and an economic downturn. Farideh Farhi (1990) compares two important cases, Iran and Nicaragua, combining Skocpol's emphasis on the state and social structure with attention to the role of culture and ideology.

In a wide-ranging study of Eastern Europe, China, Vietnam, Cuba, Nicaragua, Iran, and South Africa, James DeFronzo identifies a loosely structured model of five factors, including (1) mass frustration, (2) dissident elites, (3) "unifying motivations," (4) a crisis of the state, "which may be caused by a catastrophic defeat in war, a natural disaster, an economic depression, or the withdrawal of critical economic or military support from other nations," and (5) "a permissive or tolerant world context," (1991, 10, citing Goldfrank). A more recent synthesis has been offered by Misagh Parsa (2000), who bids us focus attention on economic factors (particularly the degree of state intervention in the economy), the ideology of state challengers, and the political vulnerabilities of repressive regimes.

Other theorists—notably Jack Goldstone (1991), with a unique emphasis on the role of demography, and Jeff Goodwin (2001)—have extended Skocpol's state-centered approach into the early modern past and the contemporary Third World, respectively. These studies have produced compelling, but largely structuralist, explanations of why states break down; they are less useful as guides to how revolutionaries contribute to this process. At the opposite extreme is Eric Selbin (1999), whose study of Bolivia, Cuba, Nicaragua, and Grenada argues that the ability of revolutionaries to make effective ideological appeals to the population largely explains patterns of success or failure in these four cases. Finally, Timothy Wickham-Crowley's analysis of Latin American guerrilla movements (1992) is notable on at least two counts: while largely structuralist in inspiration, it begins to break with prior emphases on the state to consider aspects of social structure and the orientations of revolutionaries.

John Foran's work draws on many of the specific insights of this latest generation of scholars, trying to balance the poles of structure and agency, political economy and culture, state and social structure, internal and external factors. He argues that five interrelated causal factors must combine in a given conjuncture to produce a successful social revolution: (1) dependent development (a process of aggregate economic gains that leaves out much or most of the population, whose conditions of life actually worsen); (2) a repressive, exclusionary, personalist state; (3) the elaboration of effective and powerful political cultures of resistance, and a revolutionary crisis consisting of (4) an economic downturn, and (5) a world-systemic opening (a let-up of external international controls).

In *Taking Power* (2005), Foran examines over twenty cases to show that the combination of all five of these factors is required for a social revolution to succeed. Any other combination will result in a different outcome. If all of the above conditions are met, then, the model suggests, a revolutionary outbreak has optimal chances of occurring in which a multiclass, cross-racial, and all-gendered coalition of aggrieved social forces will emerge and coalesce to carry out a revolutionary project. Such broad coalitions will have the best chances for success in attaining state power.

These recent studies have all advocated multi-causal approaches to revolutions. They have gradually begun to explore the relationship of culture and agency to social and political structures. They have yet to settle definitively, however, the question of what particular combination of causes is most likely to explain revolutionary success and failure.

OUTCOMES

It is surprising that most scholarly theorizing about revolutions has focused on their causes rather than their outcomes. Two exceptions are the Natural History School discussed above, and Skocpol, who notes that the new states are more centralized and stronger vis-à-vis internal elites and lower classes and other states (Skocpol 1979, 162–163). Another is that of Foran and Goodwin (1993), who observe that once a measure of power is achieved, broad, heterogeneous coalitions tend to fragment, as their constituent elements begin to struggle among themselves over the shape of the new order. Scholars need to specify the coalitional dynamics and structural contradictions that have so often led to quite unintended (deviated, distorted, and disappointing) outcomes.

THE FUTURE OF REVOLUTIONS

Another frontier in the study of revolutions is posed by the rise of capitalist globalization after the end of the Cold War and its impact on the likelihood of revolutions in the future, or perhaps, new kinds of revolutions. The deepening inequalities of the current world economy would seem to suggest a definite future for revolutions, just as the inventiveness in tactics and orientation away from the direct seizing of state power of the Zapatista revolutionaries in Chiapas, Mexico, or the global justice movement's broad coalition of ecological, peace, labor, women's, indigenous, and many other movements point to the possibility of a worldwide, nonviolent transformation of the current system. Working against this is the foreign policy of the Bush administration and its indefinite war on terror. Only time and the actions of all sides will tell how to write this new chapter in the history and theory of revolutions. If revolutions have always surprised us, there is little reason to doubt they will continue to do so in the future, perhaps with more hopeful outcomes.

John Foran

See Also Armed Forces, Revolution, and Counter-Revolution; Chinese Revolution; Colonialism, Anti-Colonialism, and Neo-Colonialism; Cuban Revolution; Documentaries of Revolution; East European Revolutions of 1989; Elites, Intellectuals, and Revolutionary Leadership; European Revolutions of 1848; French Revolution; Inequality, Class, and Revolution; Introduction; Iranian Revolution, Reform, Rebellion, Civil War, Coup D'état, and Revolution; Millenarianism, Religion, and Revolution; Nationalism and Revolution; Population, Economic Development, and Revolution; Russian Revolution of 1917; South African Revolution; Student and Youth Movements, Activism and Revolution; Transnational Revolutionary Movements; Trends in Revolution; Vietnamese Revolution; War and Revolution

References and Further Readings

Brinton, Crane. 1952 [1938]. *The Anatomy of Revolution*. New York: Prentice-Hall.

Davies, James C. 1962. "Toward a Theory of Revolution," *American Sociological Review* 27 (1): 5–19.

DeFronzo, James. 1991.1996. (3rd edition forthcoming 2007) *Revolutions and Revolutionary Movements*. Boulder, CO: Westview Press.

Edwards, Lyford P. 1970 [1927]. *The Natural History of Revolution*. Chicago: University of Chicago Press.

Farhi, Farideh. 1990. *States and Urban-Based Revolutions: Iran and Nicaragua*. Urbana and Chicago: University of Illinois Press.

Foran, John. 2005. *Taking Power: On the Origins of Third World Revolutions*. Cambridge: Cambridge University Press.

Foran, John, and Jeff Goodwin. 1993. "Revolutionary Outcomes in Iran and Nicaragua. Coalition Fragmentation, War, and the Limits of Social Transformation," *Theory and Society* 22 (2): 209–247.

Goldfrank, Walter L. 1979. "Theories of Revolution and Revolution without Theory: The Case of Mexico," *Theory and Society* 7: 135–165.

Goldstone, Jack A. 1980. "Theories of Revolution: The Third Generation," *World Politics* 32 (3): 425–453.

———. 1982. "The Comparative and Historical Study of Revolutions," *Annual Review of Sociology* 8: 187–207.

———. 1991. *Revolution and Rebellion in the Early Modern World*. Berkeley: University of California Press.

Goodwin, Jeff. 2001. *No Other Way Out: States and Revolutionary Movements, 1945–1991*. Cambridge: Cambridge University Press.

Gurr, Ted Robert. 1970. *Why Men Rebel*. Princeton, NJ: Princeton University Press.

Moore, Jr., Barrington 1966. *Social Origins of Dictatorship and Democracy: Lord and Peasant in the Making of the Modern World*. Boston: Beacon Press.

Paige, Jeffery M. 1975. *Agrarian Revolution: Social Movements and Export Agriculture in the Underdeveloped World*. New York: Free Press.

Parsa, Misagh. 2000. *States, Ideologies, and Social Revolutions: A Comparative Analysis of Iran, Nicaragua and the Philippines*. Cambridge: Cambridge University Press.

Pettee, George Sawyer. 1938. *The Process of Revolution*. New York: Harper and Brothers.

Scott, James C. 1976. *The Moral Economy of the Peasant: Rebellion and Subsistence in Southeast Asia*. New Haven, CT: Yale University Press.

Selbin, Eric. 1999. *Modern Latin American Social Revolutions*. 2nd edition. Boulder, CO: Westview Press.

Skocpol, Theda. 1979. *States and Social Revolutions: A Comparative Analysis of France, Russia, and China*. Cambridge: Cambridge University Press.

Smelser, Neil. 1962. *Theory of Collective Behavior*. New York: Free Press.

Tilly, Charles. 1978. *From Mobilization to Revolution*. Reading, MA: Addison-Wesley.

Tocqueville, Alexis de. 1955 [1856]. *The Old Regime and the French Revolution*. Trans. Stuart Gilbert. Garden City, NY: Doubleday.

Walton, John. 1984. *Reluctant Rebels: Comparative Studies of Revolution and Underdevelopment*. New York: Columbia University Press.

Wickham-Crowley, Timothy P. 1992. *Guerrillas and Revolution in Latin America: A Comparative Study of Insurgents and Regimes since 1956*. Princeton, NJ: Princeton University Press.

Wolf, Eric R. 1969. *Peasant Wars of the Twentieth Century*. New York: Harper Colophon Books.

Transnational Revolutionary Movements

A transnational revolutionary movement seeks to foment a particular brand of revolution not just in one country, but in a group of countries or even the entire world. Three transnational revolutionary movements that have been particularly active in recent decades are Marxism-Leninism, Arab nationalism, and Islamic fundamentalism. The goal of Marxist-Leninists was to spread Communist revolution throughout the world. Arab nationalists sought to unite all the countries of the Arab world into a single state. Islamic fundamentalists seek to spread their brand of revolution throughout the Muslim world. In contrast to transnational revolutionary movements are nationalist ones, which seek to bring revolution just to one country.

In any given country, both transnational and national revolutionary movements may be motivated by the same basically nationalist concerns: the desire to rid their country of an unpopular authoritarian regime and/or an unwanted foreign presence, as well as the desire to change the existing pattern of uneven income distribution. The attraction of a transnationalist revolutionary movement, though, is that it can link these concerns across countries into an overarching narrative that points to a common cause for their grievances, proposes a common solution to them, and provides a common set of allies to achieve that solution. The internationalist (or pan-nationalist) narratives composed by Marxist-Leninists, Arab nationalists, and Islamic fundamentalists have had a strong appeal for many people in many countries.

These narratives, or revolutionary ideologies, appear to be a necessary ingredient for a transnational revolutionary movement to grow and spread. The existence of such a narrative alone, however, does not guarantee that it will do so. Marxist, Arab nationalist, and Islamic fundamentalist revolutionary ideologies were each developed long before they became politically powerful. To make them politically powerful it appears necessary that they give rise to a charismatic transnational revolutionary leader who not only achieves some extraordinary success (whether actual or illusory), but

Cuban economic minister Che Guevara during a speech at the Inter-American Economic and Social Conference in which he accuses the United States of plotting to assassinate Fidel Castro's brother and to provoke armed aggression. Guevara went on to participate in armed revolutionary struggles in Africa and Bolivia before he was captured and executed by Bolivian forces assisted by the U.S. CIA. (Bettman/Corbis)

who is able to project a sense of more success to come. For the Marxist-Leninists, this moment first came with the victory of the Russian Revolution led by Lenin and the formation of the Communist International (Comintern), which attempted vigorously to promote this brand of revolution in other countries. For the Arab nationalists, this moment came not so much when Nasser first came to power in Egypt in 1952 but through his ability to portray the 1956 Suez Crisis as a victory for Egypt (even though it was actually American pressure that led to the withdrawal of British, French, and Israeli troops). The success of the Iranian Revolution in 1979 galvanized Islamic fundamentalists elsewhere, even though Sunni fundamentalists did not accept the leadership of the Shiite Ayatollah Khomeini. Many Sunni fundamentalists were galvanized by the Soviet withdrawal from Afghanistan in 1989, since they believed that it was their struggle against Soviet occupation that caused this. The successful suicide attacks of September 11, 2001, which destroyed the World Trade Cen-

ter and damaged the Pentagon, appear to have had a similar effect.

Transnational revolutionary movements can have other important advantages over nationalist ones. The borders of many countries, usually drawn by European colonial powers, often lumped together different ethnic groups hostile to one another inside one country or divided an ethnic group between countries. The "nation" created by these boundaries has often seemed artificial to different groups inside it who have seen "nationalism" as an attempt by one group, often backed by foreign powers, to assert or maintain dominance. Transnational revolutionary movements, by contrast, offer people from disparate ethnic, religious, or other groups the opportunity to identify and unite with one another on a larger common basis. Marxism-Leninism was open to anyone, irrespective of their ethnic, religious, or even class background (indeed, this ideology that purported to speak on behalf of the poor often had great appeal to the children of the rich).

Arab nationalism was open both to Muslim and Christian Arabs throughout the Middle East. Islamic fundamentalism seeks to appeal to all Muslims: Arabs, Persians, Pakistanis, Central Asians, Indonesians, etc. In addition, as several cases since 9–11 have shown, there are non-Muslims who have been converted not just to Islam but to the Islamic fundamentalist revolutionary ideology as well.

Adherence to a transnational revolutionary movement also offers the prospect for receiving support from abroad. In a country where there may be several revolutionary (as well as nonrevolutionary reform) movements, the group receiving the most external support may have the advantage in the struggle for power that usually occurs after the old regime or foreign power is ousted. Support from the Soviet Union and other established Marxist-Leninist regimes helped Marxist-Leninist movements seize power in a number of Third World countries. The Islamic fundamentalist revolutionary movement has developed an elaborate support mechanism spanning many countries in both the Muslim and the non-Muslim worlds.

Transnational revolutionary movements also offer the prospect not just of transforming a nation internally, but of increasing its importance on the international stage through making it part of a large, powerful bloc. Alliance with the Soviet Union enabled the Marxist-Leninist leaders of even small Third World states, such as Fidel Castro of Cuba, to play a far more important international role than would have been possible otherwise. One important reason the Arab nationalists sought to unite all Arabs into a single state was the belief that a united Arab world could deal with the West more effectively than an Arab world divided into over twenty states. Many Islamic fundamentalists, including Osama bin Laden, want to re-establish the caliphate, not only to unite all Muslims under one government, but also to create an Islamic superpower.

Although the Marxist-Leninist and the Arab nationalist transnationalist revolutionary movements did not achieve their ultimate goal and the Islamic fundamentalist one appears far from doing so, all three have met with considerable success. In the decades after the Russian Revolution, several more Marxist-Leninist regimes came to power in eastern Europe, Asia, Africa, and Latin America. Most (though not all) of these were allied to the Soviet Union. After Nasser's rise to power, Arab nationalist regimes came to power in six other Arab states. After the Iranian Revolution of 1979, Islamic fundamentalist regimes came to power both in Sudan and in Afghanistan (though the Taliban regime there was ousted as a result of the U.S.-led intervention in 2001). Further, Islamic fundamentalist movements are not only active in many other Muslim states, but appear to have gained important influence within the regimes ruling some of them, including Pakistan and Saudi Arabia. And unlike the now moribund Marxist-Leninist and Arab nationalist movements, the Islamic fundamentalist transnational revolutionary movement is still growing and has the potential for further expansion.

The goals of transnational revolutionary movements are clearly much more ambitious than those of nationalist revolutionary movements. However, the obstacles faced by the former are also much greater than those faced by the latter. What status quo powers fear about revolution is not just the change it can bring about in one country, but the potential transnational revolutionary movements have for spreading to other nations and upsetting the existing balance of power. While one or more status quo powers may vigorously oppose nationalist revolution in an allied country, the new regime can often quickly integrate into the existing international system once the status quo powers realize that it is not seeking to export revolution. By contrast, vigorous attempts made by transnational revolutionary movements to foment revolution in several countries once they have seized power in one (or even beforehand) elicit a vigorous attempt by the status quo powers to prevent this. Sometimes this has led to intervention in order to reverse a revolution, such as the unsuccessful effort launched by several countries to oust Lenin and the Bolsheviks after they seized power in 1917, or the successful American-led intervention that ousted the Taliban regime in Afghanistan after it refused to surrender Osama bin Laden, the organizer of the September 11 attacks.

Short of direct military intervention to reverse a revolution (which often proves difficult anyway), status quo powers have often acted to prevent the spread of transnational revolution to other states. The onset of the Soviet-American Cold War in the late 1940s led to a decades-long American effort to contain the spread of Communism. In the latter stages of the Cold War, the U.S. government and its allies actively supported the internal opponents of several Third World Marxist-Leninist regimes that had come to power in the 1970s. In the wake of the Arab national revolutions in Syria and Iraq in 1958, the U.S. intervened in Lebanon and the U.K. intervened in Jordan in order to prevent the spread of further such revolution to those countries. The U.S. in particular acted to support Middle Eastern governments believed vulnerable to Khomeini's brand of Islamic fundamentalism in the 1980s and then to bin Laden's version of it in the 2000s.

Another problem that transnational revolutionary movements face is that their success in coming to power in one country may serve to inhibit the appeal of their ideology in a nearby country. The triumph of Marxism-Leninism in Vietnam, for example, was one factor that appears to have limited the appeal of this ideology in Thailand, Vietnam's traditional rival. The appeal of Arab nationalism in Saudi Arabia seems to have been limited by the fear that its triumph would have meant Egyptian dominance over that country. Khomeini's brand of Islamic fundamentalism had only limited appeal among Arabs who did not want to see the spread of Iranian influence to their countries.

Ironically, the coming to power of regimes espousing the same or similar transnational revolutionary ideologies in two or more countries does not necessarily mean that they will remain, or even become, allied to each other. Several fierce rivalries emerged between various Marxist-Leninist regimes, including those between the Soviet Union and China, the Soviet Union and Yugoslavia, Yugoslavia and Albania, China and Vietnam, and Vietnam and Khmer Rouge–ruled Cambodia. Rivalries also emerged among the three most prominent Arab nationalist regimes: Egypt, Syria, and Iraq. In addition, hostile relations emerged between two Islamic revolutionary regimes—Iran and Taliban-ruled Afghanistan. Adherence to a common transnational revolutionary movement has not enabled countries to overcome nationalist differences between them.

Furthermore, transnational revolutionary movements have sometimes not only failed to overcome nationalist or ethnic differences within nations, but have exacerbated them instead. During the Russian Revolution and the early years of the Soviet Union, Marxism-Leninism had a genuine appeal for many non-Russian minorities, since it offered them protections as well as opportunities for advancement that Russian nationalism did not. However, Stalin's ferocious treatment of the non-Russian minorities and their subordinate position vis-à-vis the Russians afterward served to encourage the emergence of non-Russian nationalisms and the breakup of the U.S.S.R. under Gorbachev. Arab nationalism encouraged counter-nationalisms among non-Arab minorities such as the Kurds of northern Iraq. Islamic fundamentalist rule in Iran has not eliminated tensions between Persians and non-Persians, while Taliban rule in Afghanistan exacerbated conflicts between Pushtuns (from whom the Taliban were largely drawn) and non-Pushtuns. Islamic fundamentalist rule in Sudan has also aggravated tensions between the Muslim north and the non-Muslim south.

Another problem faced by transnational revolutionary movements after they have come to power is that they have generally failed at fostering economic development. In general, these regimes have been riddled with corruption. Most have also been hostile to foreign investment, or have been unwilling to set up attractive investment policies even when they have sought it. Marxist-Leninist regimes promised higher living standards than those prevailing in the capitalist West, but only delivered inferior ones (Chinese living standards improved once the Marxist-Leninist regime there largely abandoned the Marxist-Leninist economic model). Arab nationalist governments did not deliver significant economic development—even in those countries such as Iraq, Libya, and Algeria that were rich in oil. Islamic fundamentalist regimes—including oil-rich Iran—have not yet built successful economies either. All these governments blamed their economic underperformance on Western (especially American) hostility. But the expenditure of these states' limited resources on attempts at spreading revolution as well as both the preservation and the comfort of the revolutionary elite has also contributed to their economic underperformance.

Finally, while transnational revolutionary movements have all promised, before coming to power, to establish regimes that truly reflect either "the will of the people" or "the will of God," what they largely succeeded in creating were authoritarian regimes that showed less reluctance to use force against their own citizens in order to remain in power than the pre-revolutionary regimes they replaced. This has often led to growing disillusionment with and cynicism about the transnational revolutionary ideology among the citizens living under the repressive regimes that espouse them. Ironically, a transnational revolutionary movement may be appealing to people who have not lived under it at the same time as people who have are disillusioned with it.

An important reason transnational revolutionary movements gain popular appeal has been their ability to persuade sufficient numbers of people that they can deliver a better life, unite different nations on the basis of a larger common identity, and defeat those whom they identify as their common opponents. By the same token, an important reason for the decline of such movements has been their inability to deliver the promised better life, failure to overcome national and other differences, and inability either to defeat the common opponent or to maintain the image of it as one.

The Marxist-Leninist revolutionary movement basically came to an end with the collapse of Communism in Eastern Europe in 1989 and the collapse of the Soviet Union in 1991. Marxist-Leninist regimes in the Third World were either overthrown or made peace with the West. Marxist-Leninist regimes do remain in power in China and Vietnam, but both are pursuing capitalist economic development as well as cooperation with the West. Cuba and North Korea are the only two countries where the regimes remain committed to the anti-capitalist and anti-imperialist Marxist-Leninist vision, but both of these countries are very poor. A few Marxist-Leninist revolutionary movements remain active in Latin America as well as in Nepal, but it appears highly unlikely Marxism-Leninism will ever regain potency as a transnational revolutionary movement.

Arab nationalism suffered a tremendous blow when Israel swiftly defeated Egyptian, Syrian, and Jordanian forces in the June 1967 war. There have been no additional Arab nationalist revolutions since 1969 (the two that year, in Sudan and Libya, were really coups). The most important Arab nationalist regime—Egypt—made peace not only with the U.S., but with Israel. The Arab nationalist regime in Sudan fell in 1985 and was replaced in 1989 by an Islamic fundamentalist one. The one in Iraq was overthrown in 2003 by a U.S.-led intervention. The others (Egypt, Syria, Libya, Algeria, and Yemen) remain in power, but all of them—along with the Arab nationalist wing of the Palestinians (the PLO)—face serious opposition from Islamic fundamentalists.

Will the Islamic fundamentalist transnational revolutionary movement suffer decline like the Marxist-Leninist and Arab nationalist ones? This is not something that appears likely to occur anytime soon, since the Islamic fundamentalist revolutionary movement now appears to be both active and growing. The Islamic fundamentalists, though, do not seem immune from the problems previously encountered by the Marxist-Leninists and Arab nationalists. The presence of enormous oil reserves in several Muslim states suggests that Islamic fundamentalist revolutionary movements managing to seize power in them might be able to keep the populace relatively satisfied economically. The experience of the Islamic Republic of Iran, though, suggests that Islamic fundamentalist revolutionary regimes will not necessarily use the proceeds from oil exports to develop their economies or improve living standards. The demonstrated willingness of Islamic fundamentalists to attack other Muslims also serves to limit the appeal of this transnational revolutionary movement.

Will other transnational revolutionary movements arise? This cannot be foretold. In order for this to occur, though, such movements will have to have an appeal capable of transcending narrow nationalism and holding out the prospect of uniting people and nations on a broader basis. Religion can serve as the basis for such an appeal, but there are not many other religions besides Islam with a wide transnational appeal. Christianity does have such an appeal, but republican democracy is so strongly entrenched in predominantly Christian countries that it is doubtful that a Christian fundamentalist revolutionary movement could gain much of a following in them. A Hindu fundamentalist movement has arisen, but this cannot form the basis of a transnational revolutionary movement since there are no predominantly Hindu countries to which it could spread beyond India except relatively small nearby ones such as Nepal and the Tamil parts of Sri Lanka. Other pan-nationalisms—such as pan-Turkism or pan-Africanism—could form the basis of a transnational revolutionary movement just as Arab nationalism (or pan-Arabism) did. These other pan-nationalisms, however, have so far proved weaker and less cohesive than Arab nationalism, and thus even less likely to form the basis

of a vigorous transnational revolutionary movement. The emergence of additional transnational revolutionary movements, though, cannot be ruled out. But even if one does not emerge, Islamic fundamentalism—the most active transnational revolutionary movement at present—will pose a serious challenge for many years to come.

Mark N. Katz

See Also Anarchism, Communism, and Socialism; Chinese Revolution; Cinema of Revolution; Documentaries of Revolution; Introduction; Iranian Revolution; Islamic Fundamentalist Revolutionary Movement; Russian Revolution of 1917; Student and Youth Movements, Activism and Revolution; Theories of Revolutions

References and Further Readings
Colburn, Forest D. 1994. *The Vogue of Revolution in Poor Countries.* Princeton, NJ: Princeton University Press.
DeFronzo, James. 1996. (3rd edition forthcoming 2007) *Revolution and Revolutionary Movements.* Boulder, CO: Westview.
Halliday, Fred. 1999. *Revolution and World Politics: The Rise and Fall of the Sixth Great Power.* Durham, NC: Duke University Press.
Katz, Mark N. 1997. *Revolutions and Revolutionary Waves.* New York: St. Martin's Press.
———. 2002. "Osama bin Laden as Transnational Revolutionary Leader," *Current History* 101 (February): 81–85.
Keddie, Nikki R. 1994. "The Revolt of Islam, 1700 to 1993: Comparative Considerations and Relations to Imperialism," *Comparative Studies in Society and History* 36 (July): 463–487.
Pillar, Paul R. 2003. *Terrorism and U.S. Foreign Policy.* Washington, DC: Brookings Institution.

Trends in Revolution

Revolution is a constant feature of world history, yet characteristics that are constant elements of all revolutions are difficult to identify. The term revolution has multiple lineages, among them the Greek concepts of *epanastasis* (revolt) and *neoterismos* (innovation), the Arabic terms *inqilab* (to rotate) and *thaura* (to revolt), the notions of *mered* (rebellion), *kom* (uprising), *marah* (revolt), and *kesher* (plot) in classical Hebrew, and the Chinese word *ge-ming* (change of life, fate, or destiny). Over the last 200 years, deriving in part from the work of Montesquieu, Voltaire, and Rousseau, the idea of revolution became more circumscribed. During this period, revolutions came to be seen as volcanic ruptures, quasi-astronomical realignments, and sharp breaks with the past from which societies could not turn back—ideas that were harnessed and exemplified by revolutionaries in

France and America. At the same time, the concept of revolution took on a kind of transcendental tilt that mythologized the revolutionary experience. The vision of a utopian future became profoundly linked to the concept of revolution, as did the notions of violence and inevitable, total change.

REVOLUTION AND VIOLENCE

The principal characteristic associated with revolutions has been violence. In the modern era, revolutions have been seen as festivals of violence, fights to the finish in which one side vanquishes the other. The 1789 revolution in France ushered in a decade of domestic strife, opening the way to Napoleonic dictatorship and continental war; the Bolshevik Revolution was followed by a four-year civil war in which foreign armies and their proxies fought fiercely with the Red Army; the two stages of the Chinese Revolution, first to establish a republic and then to build a Communist society, were separated by a battle for domestic dominance that lasted for three decades. Even after these revolutions, the new regimes struggled to impose their authority on their wider societies. Hence Robespierre's "Terror," Stalin's forced collectivization and purges, and Mao's Great Proletarian Cultural Revolution were all attempts to shore up revolutionary regimes against opposition at home and abroad, real or imagined.

Much of the theoretical connection between revolutions and violence stems from the work of Marxist scholars (and Karl Marx in particular), who saw revolutions as necessary for the transition from traditional to modern societies. Marx argued that the destruction of old forms of society in the industrial period would come about because of the contradictions and antagonisms between classes arising from the exploitation of the proletariat (working class) by the ruling class. Eventually workers would become aware of their importance and potential power and spontaneously rise to crush their exploiters. The resulting revolutions were certain to be violent, for ruling classes were unlikely to relinquish their position by choice.

Marx's initial conception of revolution was adopted by a number of his successors, most notable among them Vladimir Lenin, Leon Trotsky, Mao Zedong, Fidel Castro, and Che Guevara. Lenin extended Marx's initial formulation to include a vanguard role (leadership role) for a revolutionary party, while Trotsky focused on how revolutions were likely to take place in the developing world (or countries of the semi-periphery) rather than those at the center of capitalist development. Mao formally included the peasantry in the theory and practice of revolution; Guevara and Castro supplemented

Marxism through their concept of the revolutionary *foco*—a band of guerrillas who, through dedicated struggle, could create revolutions in seemingly unlikely settings.

The violence of the 1871 Paris Commune and the various revolutionary outbursts that followed during the early part of the twentieth century seemed to vindicate Marxist visions of sweeping, violent, and inevitable transformations. The storming of the Bastille, the raid on the Winter Palace, and the Long March undertaken by the remnants of Mao's army became part of revolutionary folklore, symbols of the might and right of the revolutionary struggle. If revolutions were to succeed, it seemed, they had to be violent. Marxism spread around the world, apparently able to explain gross inequalities and offering the way toward fairer, more just societies. For those who labored under the yoke of colonial rule or domestic tyranny, Marxism, with its attendant focus on the necessity of violence, appeared to provide the most compelling means of removing despots and eradicating social injustice.

Reflecting the violent struggles espoused by revolutionaries both in word and deed, revolutionary scholarship has tended to equate revolutions with heroic fights to the finish in which nothing less than death or victory would suffice. For certain scholars, the very essence of revolution lies in its violence. But this focus by both many scholars of revolution and revolutionaries themselves on the violent aspect of revolutions disguises a much more complex relationship between the two concepts than is commonly understood. If violence and revolution were codeterminous, then of the 1989 revolutions in Eastern Europe, only the Romanian uprising would qualify as a revolution. Yet given the partial nature of the Romanian transition since 1989, it is difficult to see how it warrants the label revolution. Social change, in the form of great scientific breakthroughs or wide-scale parliamentary reform programs have no necessary link with violence. In fact, as Johan Galtung (1996) and others point out, violence in its structural forms, such as repression, exploitation, marginalization, sexism, racism, and so forth, is used to *suppress* rather than instigate change. Violence is a means of maintaining order—the stifling of change—as much as a signifier of upheaval.

Often revolutions have been relatively peaceful seizures of power. Violence stemmed, for the most part, from battles *after* the initial takeover of state power, resulting from the need by revolutionary regimes to shore up their rule in the face of domestic and international attempts at counter-revolution, a cycle that can be observed, for example, in Iran by way of its war with Iraq and the brutal measures employed against the regime's "un-Islamic" foes after 1980. Hannah Arendt (1963), in a survey of the connection between violence and revolution, found that violence only became associated with revolutionary change through "The Terror" of the Jacobins during the French Revolution. The close link between revolution and violence is, therefore, a relatively modern connection. Violence has been neither a constant nor an indispensable aspect of revolutions.

REVOLUTIONS AND UTOPIAN IDEOLOGY

A second characteristic commonly associated with revolutions is the idea of "newness." Many theorists have demanded that, to be considered authentic, revolutions must be legitimized by a utopian vision promising nothing less than remaking the global order afresh. In this way, scholars came to see revolutions as characterized by ideological innovations that justified the degree of transformation undertaken and the excesses of the revolutionaries themselves. From the French call to arms of "liberty, equality, and fraternity" to Communist dreams of exporting class-based revolutions around the world, revolutionaries have been seen as ideologues espousing a vision that seeks to remold both domestic societies and the wider international order. On these grounds, many scholars argue that the events of 1989 in Eastern and Central Europe cannot be considered revolutionary because insurgents in Poland, the Czech Republic, Hungary, and elsewhere had no world vision to match the idealism of their predecessors in France and Russia.

But demanding that every revolution conjure a new world vision as an essential criterion for its definition would disqualify almost every case. Third World revolutionaries from Mao to Castro and Neto to Cabral have fused a basic grounding in Marxism with a dash of nationalism and an occasional sprinkling of messianic, populist fervor. All have looked to the past as much as to the present and future to legitimize their revolts. Even the leaders of the "great revolutions" in France, China, and Russia looked to the past as well as to a vision of a pristine future to justify their revolt. Mao's rhetoric, for example, was fundamentally rooted in Marxist thought, while also harking back to particularly Chinese conditions, history, and culture. To be revolutionary, therefore, ideas do not necessarily have to provide some new set of original precepts. Rather, revolutionary ideology coalesces around a fertile blend of the time-honored and the novel, inspirations to action in a given historical context. In this way, older ideals of freedom, justice, and equality are just as much part of revolutionary rhetoric as any claims of remaking the world anew. Revolutionaries in 1989 followed their predecessors by looking backward as well as forward, to the Springtime of Nations in 1848 as well as to the better-known revolutions of 1789, 1917, and 1949.

TOTAL VICTORY?

Revolutions, it is often claimed, change everything. And yet no revolutionary victory is as total as is often imagined. Evocations of starting afresh from a mythical year zero are mere bluster next to the reality of the constraints faced by revolutionary regimes. Even the paradigmatic revolution of the modern era in France changed less than is commonly thought. Much of the initial revolutionary project was overturned by the restoration of the Bourbons in 1815; many of the families who enjoyed positions of influence under the ancien regime retained their privileges during the first half of the nineteenth century (something that helps to explain the subsequent revolution of 1848). The institutions, norms, and customs of the old regime became reinvested in the new order in France, as in Russia, Mexico, China, Indochina, Iran, Nicaragua, Angola, and elsewhere. The reality is that revolutionary programs are often curtailed by institutions and structures inherited from the regime that revolutionaries depose, while many elements of their program are never initiated in the first place.

It is difficult, then, to find any single characteristic that runs constant through all instances of revolution over time and place. Revolutions have been conducted by nationalists, peasants, Communists, radical military groups, liberals, and religious fundamentalists. Underneath the generic category of revolution lies considerable variation in terms of the roles of violence and innovative ideology, and the overall outcomes of revolutions. Even the great revolutions of the modern era contained differing degrees of violence than is often considered to be the case, borrowed many of their ideas from others and from the past, and contained an unevenness of outcomes that would appear to invalidate them next to the general view of revolutions as necessarily violent, total transformations legitimized by a new utopian vision that aims to remake the world.

CONTEMPORARY REVOLUTIONS

Revolutions have evolved over time, from the traditional idea of a return to a previous order (for example the restoration of constitutional monarchy witnessed by the Glorious Revolution in England in 1688) to the liberal or bourgeois impulses toward (partial) democracy in the nineteenth century, to the more stirring goals of Marxists during the course of the twentieth century. The modern idea of revolutions as violent, total transformations sustained by radical new ideology appeared to be washed away by the relatively peaceful collapse of Communism in Eastern Europe in 1989. The relative ease with which Communist leaders abdicated their

Vaclav Havel (right), a dissident playwright and leading member of the Czechoslovak opposition Civic Forum, addresses Ladislav Adamec (left), the Communist prime minister, as the Czechoslovakian Communist party began negotiations with representatives of the opposition in Prague, November 1989. At the end of 1989, Havel was elected president of Czechoslovakia after the state-Communist system crumbled during the Velvet Revolution. (Joel Robine/AFP/Getty Images)

positions and allowed dissidents to establish regimes that threatened to eradicate the legacy of state Socialism caused a furor among scholars of revolution. If these changes were not violent, were they revolutionary? If insurgents did not promise anything more than signing up to the principles and statutes of a liberal world order, could they be seen as offering a truly revolutionary vision? If these transformations were negotiated between elites rather than fought out on the streets of Warsaw, Prague, and Budapest, were they really worth the label of revolution? Given the skepticism with which many commentators greeted the events of 1989, it is not surprising that over the decade or so that followed, revolutions disappeared from mainstream academic and political discourse. In an era seemingly best captured by Francis Fukuyama's (1992, 1) infamous phrase, "the end of history," the central revolutionary trend appeared to be a gradual, if stark, slide toward obscurity.

However, if there is no universal trait that characterizes a revolution, other than that of sweeping institutional (structural) change, there is no theoretical reason to suggest that revolution cannot take a contemporary form in keeping with contemporary conditions. In one sense, many elements of the transformations in Eastern and Central Europe, as well as others in southern Africa and elsewhere that accompanied the end of the Cold War, seem to conform to the traditional romanticism of revolutions: the fall of the Berlin Wall and the release of Nelson Mandela are some of the most dramatic moments in recent world history. Yet while many modern revolutions have been associated with armed rebellion, contemporary revolutions take on a somewhat different tilt—the power of the masses to be sure, but not that of the mob. Rather, the control of fervor and the dignity of protests rise above the social context defined by the old regime. Central to this success is that transformations are negotiated between rival groups rather than settled by firing squads or civil wars. In South Africa, apartheid-era combatants, many of whom had been involved in an armed struggle over a period of three decades, convened a series of conferences that ended with the advent of multiparty democracy. In the Czech Republic, three weeks of rapid dialogue between Communist leaders and opposition representatives ended with Vaclav Havel, a playwright, becoming the new president. Round tables replaced guillotines as the symbols of the newest means of revolutionary change.

Contemporary (or negotiated) revolutions are, therefore, not violent fights to the finish but relatively peaceful processes in which deals are struck between revolutionaries and their adversaries. Overt violence is contained; both sides seek a settlement of previously irreconcilable differences without recourse to coercive power. For many participants and observers alike, this lack of a revolutionary moment and the watering down of opposition demands and goals amounts to a betrayal of the revolution itself. But this misses a cardinal point. In South Africa, the Czech Republic, and elsewhere, negotiation offered a route out of impasse, an end to the tyranny of an authoritarian system, and containment of the excesses of oppressors and freedom fighters alike. In all of these cases, what had been peaceful opposition movements against dictatorial regimes had been forced into more violent methods of protest by the intransigence and tyranny of the old regimes. Negotiation provided both sides with a means to move on from a situation of armed equilibrium. The subsequent containment of violent struggles generated outcomes perhaps less melodramatic than past examples of revolutionary change—no tanks rolled down the streets of Pretoria displaying the crest of Mandela's African National Congress—but negotiation also delivered outcomes less damaging to the long-term social fabric of the countries themselves.

Along with the process of negotiation, perhaps the best illustration of the distinctiveness of negotiated revolutions is the role played by truth commissions. All revolutions require some mechanism for dealing with the injustices of the old order, a means of moving from old to new that establishes the authority and legitimacy of the incoming regime while also providing an outlet for people's sense of outrage and thirst for revenge. In the past, these needs were satiated through a mixture of firing squads, guillotines, show trials, gulags, and purges. But negotiated revolutions, founded on principles of restorative rather than punitive or retributive justice, institute truth commissions as an innovative way of dealing with these issues. Truth commissions are based on the need to generate a foundational narrative for a new social order out of which a collective rather than a disjointed history can emerge. They provide a moment when innocent as well as guilty people get the chance to tell stories that would otherwise go unheard. The truth commission is a weapon of the weak turned back against seemingly almighty oppressors. But at the same time, it performs this task in a novel fashion—by trading truth for punishment.

If the roles of violence and ideology are different in negotiated revolutions than in past examples of revolutions, so too is the level of change. One of the main critiques against labeling contemporary transformations like the one from apartheid to market-democracy in South Africa as revolutionary is that little has changed in the country since the first post-apartheid elections in 1994. Rather, it is argued, a cabal of big business and a newly enriched black bourgeoisie have carved up the spoils of an elite-contrived transition. Certainly it is true that things have changed less quickly in South Africa and other post-1989 states than some would have liked. The same charge, as noted earlier, could also be directed at many revolutionary states in the past. It is equally true that not all of the changes that have accompanied negotiated revolutions have been positive: in South Africa, as well as in the Czech Republic and other states like them, there has been an increase in inequality and corruption since the dissolution of authoritarian rule. All too often, societies undergoing negotiated revolutions have seen a commitment by international agencies to establishing free markets fail to be matched by a nurturing of the social and political institutions that are germane to the functioning of a consolidated democracy. Again, this mixed picture is hardly unique to these revolutions. All revolutions are unfinished; all are complex, messy affairs.

Yet, negotiated revolutions also induce sweeping changes from which there is no going back. In the Czech Republic, ideological uniformity has given way to an open society; the homogeneity of political life under Communism has been replaced by an often bewildering array of political parties and pressure groups; the tired, stagnant formula of central planning has made way for the uncertainty of market relations. South Africa has experienced a comparable shift from the restrictive system of apartheid to an open, competitive democracy; a protectionist economy dependent on state intervention has been liberalized and, to some extent, broadened and developed; a process of nation building, principally through the country's Truth and Reconciliation Commission, has helped to mold novel social institutions. While power-sharing agreements and commitments to honor the contracts of public servants ensure that there is a degree of continuity in these revolutions, this is hardly unusual set against the past experience of revolutions throughout world history.

CONCLUSION

Many of those scholars who deny the importance of revolution to the contemporary world do so because they mistakenly equate revolutions with certain inalienable, *essential* characteristics, seeing them as violent, utopian-driven, total transformations. Such a view is misguided, because it reduces revolutions to static objects rather than dynamic processes with features that change according to their historical and social contexts. Negotiated revolutions are the most recent example of the way in which revolution has been reinvented in a new historical environment. In the contemporary world, negotiated revolutions have become the principal means of generating transformations from authoritarian regimes to market-democracies. In the process, the utopian vision of past revolutions, which often resulted in extremism, is exchanged for a revolutionary ideology rooted in longer-term principles of freedom. A violent conflict between rival forces is replaced by the acceptance of mutual dependency and the undesirability of ongoing civil conflict. From a fight to the finish comes a process in which the old regime and revolutionaries together negotiate the destruction of the old order and the birth of a new nation. As such, negotiated revolutions represent a novel form of revolutionary change based around the idea of liberation rather than the dream of utopia.

George Lawson

See Also Anarchism, Communism, and Socialism; Chinese Revolution; Documentaries of Revolution; East European Revolutions of 1989; French Revolution; Iranian Revolution; Reform, Rebellion, Civil War, Coup D'état, and Revolution; Russian Revolution of 1917; South African Revolution; Theories of Revolutions; Transnational Revolutionary Movements

References and Further Readings
Arendt, Hannah. 1963. *On Revolution.* Harmondsworth, England: Penguin.
Dunn, John. 1989. *Modern Revolutions.* Cambridge: Cambridge University Press.
Foran, John, ed. 1997. *Theorizing Revolution.* London: Routledge.
Fukuyama, Francis. 1992. *The End of History and the Last Man.* London: Hamish Hamilton.
Galtung, Johan. 1996. *Peace by Peaceful Means.* London: Sage.
Garton Ash, Timothy. 1999. *History of the Present: Essays, Sketches and Dispatches from Europe in the 1990s.* London: Penguin.
Halliday, Fred. 1999. *Revolution and World Politics: The Rise and Fall of the Sixth Great Power.* London: Macmillan.
Kumar, Krishan. 2001. *1989: Revolutionary Ideas and Ideals.* Minneapolis: University of Minnesota Press.
Lawson, George. 2005. *Negotiated Revolutions: The Czech Republic, South Africa and Chile.* Aldershot, England: Ashgate.
Mandela, Nelson. 1994. *Long Walk to Freedom: The Autobiography of Nelson Mandela.* London: Little Brown.
Marx, Karl. 1948. *The Manifesto of the Communist Party.* London: Communist Party of Great Britain.
Wood, Elizabeth Jean. 2000. *Forging Democracy from Below: Insurgent Transitions in South Africa and El Salvador.* Cambridge: Cambridge University Press.

Turkish Revolutions of 1908 and 1919–1923

CHRONOLOGY

1299	Osman I establishes the Osmanli dynasty in western Anatolia with himself as the empire's first sultan. Europeans refer to the dynasty as the Ottomans. This is the origin of the Ottoman empire.
1389	Ottomans defeat the Serbian army at Kosovo.
1453	Ottoman army conquers Constantinople, later renamed Istanbul.
1520–1566	Ottoman empire reaches its greatest extent under Sultan Suleyman.
1571	Ottoman fleet is defeated and mostly destroyed or captured by a fleet of Venetian, Spanish, Papal, and other Italian ships at the Battle of Lepanto.
1683	Ottoman forces defeated at the Battle of Vienna.
1821–1832	Greek War of Independence from Ottoman rule.
1854–1856	Ottoman empire allies with Britain and France to defeat Russia in the Crimean War.
1876	Ottoman constitution is established.
1878	Constitution is abandoned by Sultan Abdullah Hamid II, who then rules as an absolute monarch. Serbia, Montenegro, and Romania gain independence from the Ottoman empire.
1908	The Committee of Union and Progress (CUP), also known as the Young Turks, forces the restoration of the 1876 Ottoman constitution.
1912–1913	First and Second Balkan Wars—Bulgaria, Greece, Serbia, and Montenegro form an al-

liance against the Ottoman empire, force the Ottomans out of most of their European territories, and then fight among themselves over division of the conquered regions.

1914–1918   Ottoman empire, under CUP leadership, participates in World War I as an ally of Germany against Russia, Britain, and France.

1915   Hundreds of thousands of Armenians, suspected of assisting or favoring Russia during the war, are forcibly relocated and many are murdered.

1919–1922   Mustafa Kemal (later given the surname Atatürk) leads Turkish forces to victory over foreign armies in Anatolia in the War of Independence.

1923   A national assembly abolishes the rule of the sultan and declares Turkey to be a republic.

1923–1938   Mustafa Kemal Atatürk leads Turkey in carrying out a major modernization program, including reforms involving separation of church and state, written script and language, education, technology, science, and gender roles.

INTRODUCTION

The Ottoman empire, originating at the end of the thirteenth century, developed into a multiethnic military power whose armies conquered many lands, including much of southeastern Europe. Its ruler, the sultan, eventually claimed to be caliph, spiritual ruler of all Muslims everywhere. In the nineteenth century, several European powers encouraged Greeks and other peoples to rebel against Ottoman rule. As the empire began to experience repeated military defeats, it became clear that its technology and armed forces had become markedly inferior to those of industrializing European nations. A secret rebel group of intellectuals, students, and younger military officers—the Committee of Union and Progress (CUP), also referred to as the "Young Turks"—staged a successful rebellion in 1908 to establish a constitutional monarchy system. But after the Ottoman defeat in World War I, much of the empire fell under the control of European powers, and Turkish-populated territory was penetrated by various foreign armies. A young Turkish general, Mustafa Kemal, rallied Turkish forces, and during 1919–1923, forced the withdrawal of foreign armies, ended Ottoman rule, and founded the Turkish republic. As

president he launched major modernizing reforms. The Turkish parliament recognized his leadership and achievements for his people by awarding him the surname Atatürk, "Father of the Turks."

BACKGROUND: CULTURE AND HISTORY

The Ottoman empire had its origin in western Anatolia at the end of the thirteenth century. Osman I founded what was initially one of a number of small Turkish states. He became the first sultan—a monarch combining the powers of both governmental and Islamic religious authority—of the Osmanli dynasty, which became known in Europe as the Ottomans. The Ottomans rapidly absorbed other Turkish states and began conquering non-Turkish peoples in Asia and Europe, including the 1453 capture of Constantinople. The empire reached its greatest extent during the reign of Sultan Suleyman (1520–1566). By then the Ottomans dominated some Christian populations such as the Serbs, the Greeks, and the Bulgarians. In the nineteenth century, the Ottoman sultan claimed the title of caliph, or religious leader of all Muslims anywhere in the world. But it had become apparent, after several military defeats, that the Ottomans had fallen significantly behind a number of major European nations in weapons technology. European powers encouraged separatist movements among European peoples under Ottoman rule. Many Greeks rebelled and fought a war of liberation from 1821 to 1832 with support from Russia, Britain, and France. An independent Greek nation was established although much of Greek territory remained temporarily under Ottoman control.

When Russia resumed military pressure on the Ottoman empire and destroyed a Turkish fleet in 1853, Britain and France began to fear the southward expansion of the Russian empire and its likely advance to Constantinople unless the Ottomans received major assistance. During 1854–1856, British and French forces allied with the Ottomans in the successful Crimean War against the Russians. Although on the winning side, Ottoman commanders were shocked by the far more advanced military technology of their British and French allies. This experience sparked renewed interest in modernizing the empire, especially its armed forces.

As part of the modernizing process, and also as a potential mechanism for holding the empire together in the face of rebellious movements among its multiethnic components, Sultan Abdullah Hamid II proclaimed a constitution and the establishment of a parliament in 1876. But in 1878 he decided to revert back to absolutist rule and suspended the constitution. At the time, popular opposition inside the empire was reportedly limited because many people had been taught to believe that the absolute power of the sultan was to their benefit, since the sultan was supposed to ensure justice and protect the weak from the corruption and exploitation of the upper and business classes, the very classes that dominated the parliament. But the suspension of the constitution and the subsequent political repression by the sultan's secret police, coupled with continued external military pressure and humiliating defeats by foreign armies, internal ethnically based rebellions, economic mismanagement of the government that led to much of the country's finances falling under the control of foreign powers, and distress at the slow pace of modernization, which was perceived to be partly due to conservative religious influence, contributed to the creation of a movement to reinstate the 1876 constitution and cope with the nation's problems.

The main activists were Turkish intellectuals and students residing in European countries such as France, who were exposed to both more democratic political systems and advancing industrial technologies, and young military officers serving disproportionately in Ottoman armies in the empire's European territories, particularly in Macedonia, where Western influences were relatively strong. These groups organized the Committee of Union and Progress (CUP), referred to as the Young Turks, with the goals of forcing the sultan to resurrect the 1876 constitution and allow an election for a new parliament, which would, they hoped, restrict the monarch's power and promote more successful and constructive government policies. Most CUP leaders apparently initially did not intend to destroy either the empire or the monarchy.

CONTEXT AND PROCESS OF REVOLUTION

The Revolution of 1908

Ottoman forces in Macedonia rose in revolt against absolutist rule in early July 1908. Other units sent to suppress the rebels refused to do so. As support for the movement spread, Sultan Abdullah Hamid II conceded defeat on July 24, restoring the constitution and a parliamentary system. CUP leaders and their political allies won control of the new parliament elected in the fall. But on April 13, 1909, more traditionalistic army officers, conservative politicians, and Islamic students concerned with restrictions on religious influence, encouraged by Sultan Abdullah Hamid II, staged a counter-revolution in Istanbul. This was soon suppressed by CUP-led military forces from Macedonia. In retaliation for the attempt at counter-revolution, the parliament removed Abdullah Hamid II from the sultanate and replaced him with his brother, Mehmad V. However, alleged electoral fraud by CUP supporters in the

next parliamentary election in 1912 forced the CUP government leaders to resign. The parliament was disbanded until a new election could be held, which ultimately did not take place until 1914 because of the outbreak of the First Balkan War in the fall of 1912.

But in January 1913, the CUP carried out a successful coup and reinstalled a CUP-led government. As a result of the First and Second Balkan Wars and a rebellion in Albania, the Ottomans lost the remainder of their European territories except for Istanbul and the neighboring area, while separately Italy acquired formerly Ottoman-controlled Libya.

Desperate to cope with surging nationalistic consciousness among the empire's remaining ethnic groups, such as the Arabs and the Kurds, most of whom were Muslim, some in the regime attempted to appeal to Islamic religious beliefs, including the claim of the Ottoman sultan to be the caliph of all Muslims, to hold the empire together and carry out government policies.

World War I

Prior to World War I, Britain and France viewed an alliance with Russia as far more beneficial than one with the Ottoman empire. Since Russia was a long-time military opponent of the Ottomans, CUP leaders brought the Ottoman empire into World War I as an ally of Germany. The CUP political party controlled the empire during the war, with Talat Pasha (1874–1921) as minister of the interior, Enver Pasha (1881–1922) as minister of war, and Cemal Pasha (1872–1922) as minister of the navy. Since many Armenians were sympathetic to Russia and lived in an area of strategic importance for the conflict, the Ottoman government in 1915 launched a policy of forcibly relocating much of the Armenian population, which degenerated into the mass murder of hundreds of thousands.

During the war, Ottoman military units under the leadership of Mustafa Kemal defeated British, French, Australian, and New Zealand forces at the Battle of Gallipoli. But the empire's armed forces were hard pressed to battle on multiple fronts, including against a major British-assisted rebellion in its Arab territories. With the defeat of its allies, the Ottoman government had no choice but to surrender in October 1918. The top CUP leaders, blamed for the persecution and atrocities against the Armenians, resigned and then fled. Later Armenian assassins killed Talat Pasha in Berlin in 1921 and Cemal Pasha in Tblisi, Georgia, in 1922, while Enver Pasha died in 1922 in combat against the Red Army in Turkistan (Tajikistan). The British occupied Istanbul and captured the sultan. Various nations of the victorious alliance seized parts of Anatolia in 1919, despite its largely Turkish population, with the Greeks occupying much of western Anatolia.

Mustafa Kemal, independent Turkey's first president (1923–1938). (Library of Congress)

The Revolution of 1919–1923

In May of 1919, Mustafa Kemal, the military hero who had little involvement in government up to this point, arrived at the port of Samsun on the Black Sea but then defied the sultan's orders and began to organize Turkish nationalists among the military and local militias to counter Greek and allied forces, and even Ottoman units still obedient to the sultan. In a series of victories during 1919–1922, referred to as the War of Independence, Mustafa's army forced the withdrawal of Greek and other foreign armed forces from Turkish territory. In April 1920, in further defiance of the Ottoman sultan, Mustafa's supporters, which included many from the CUP, established a Grand National Assembly to represent the Turkish nation, with Mustafa Kemal as its president. The assembly rejected the Ottoman government of Sultan Mehmed VI and the Treaty of Sèvres the sultan had agreed to, which had called for occupation of various parts of Anatolia by certain of the victorious World War I allied powers and the establishment of an independent Armenian state. Turkish military victories and popular support for Mustafa Kemal brought about the new 1923 Treaty of Lausanne, superseding the Treaty of Sèvres, in which the World War I victors recognized Turkish control of Anatolia. Later in the year, on October 29, the Turkish republic was proclaimed with its capital at Ankara and Mustafa Kemal as the country's president.

Mustafa's government launched policies intended to heighten the sense of Turkish nationalism and unity, some of which were accused of suppressing for decades aspects of other cultures within Turkey's boundaries such as that of its Kurdish minority, and carried out modernizing reforms. Separation of church and state was firmly established. People were encouraged to adopt Western-style clothing. Major efforts were made to expand literacy and education. A central aspect of this policy was to create a new Turkish alphabet based on Latin script rather than the Arabic script used by Turks for hundreds of years. This transformation of written language, launched in 1928, was credited with enabling illiterate adults and children to learn how to read and write faster. A process was begun that involved removing many Arabic, Persian, and other foreign elements from Ottoman Turkish to produce a more purified form of the Turkish language. One of the most revolutionary features of the modernization program was the big increase in the activity and roles of women outside the home.

In 1934, when the parliament passed the law requiring surnames for all Turkish citizens, it bestowed on Mustafa the name Atatürk (Father of the Turks).

IMPACTS

The Turkish Revolutions of 1908 and 1919–1923 had enormous impacts on the peoples of the Ottoman empire, the Middle East, and parts of Europe. In 1908, CUP military units defeated those loyal to the concept of absolute sultanic rule. The result was the establishment of a CUP-controlled parliament that greatly limited the power of the sultan. CUP leaders brought the Ottoman empire into World War I against Turkey's traditional enemy Russia and its allies Britain and France. This led to the deportation and massacre of much of Turkey's Armenian population thought to have been pro-Russian. The war resulted in the dismemberment of the empire and British and French occupation of certain Arab-populated areas, facilitating British access to the region's oil resources. The Ottoman government's accommodations to the victorious allies, who occupied the empire's capital, Istanbul, and the Greek and allied occupation of parts of Anatolia provoked the War of Independence by Turkish nationalists led by Mustafa Kemal. The success of Mustafa's military efforts forced the evacuation of foreign forces from Turkish-populated areas but also led to huge population relocations as hundreds of thousands of Greeks in Anatolia fled their homes when Greek forces were withdrawn, just as many

Turks and Muslims left Greece and certain territories that were separated from the former empire. The victory of the Turkish nationalist military effort and popular support for Mustafa Kemal's movement resulted in the destruction of the Ottoman government, the end of the Ottoman sultanate and caliphate, and the establishment of the Turkish republic. Mustafa Kemal's Turkish nationalist policies led to the removal of Arabic and Persian linguistic components from Ottoman Turkish and the creation of a more purely Turkish language. But the attempt to create a nation with a relatively culturally homogeneous population led to policies blamed for long repressing the language and certain cultural aspects of Turkey's Kurdish minority.

Mustafa accelerated modernizing policies begun earlier and initiated major new reforms aimed at separating church and state, greatly increasing literacy, education, and the study of science, and significantly expanding the role of women in society. Turkey's revolutions and Mustafa Kemal Atatürk's leadership provided inspiration for the attempts at political, economic, social, and educational modernization undertaken in later years by other nations, especially in the Middle East.

PEOPLE AND ORGANIZATIONS

Abdullah Hamid II (1842–1918)

Abdullah Hamid II was sultan of the Ottoman empire from 1876–1909. Sultan is a title for an Islamic monarch ruling with both religious and government authority according to Islamic religious law, the Sharia. The Turkish sultan in the nineteenth century also claimed the title of caliph or religious leader of all Muslims everywhere. In 1876 he allowed a constitution to be established but suspended it in 1878 to rule as an absolute monarch. Blamed for being repressive, failing to sufficiently modernize the country and the military, and being too accommodating to foreign powers, his rule was the target of the 1908 CUP-led revolution.

Atatürk, Mustafa Kemal (1881–1938)

Mustafa Kemal was a brilliant military officer who led the nationalist movement that founded the Turkish republic and conducted a program of rapid and radical modernizing reforms. He was born in Ottoman-controlled Salonika (in contemporary Greece), where his father was a lower-level government official. He attended a military academy, was influenced by the republican political systems of western Europe, and was impressed by their technological advances and economic development. He joined the CUP Young Turk

movement with similarly oriented officers, students, and intellectuals. During World War I, Mustafa played a major role leading Turkish armies to victory over Britain and its allies at the Battle of Gallipoli, and then later led Turkish nationalist forces against foreign armies and the Ottoman government in the War of Independence from 1919–1922, securing areas with Turkish-majority populations for a unified Turkish nation. In 1923 he led the national assembly that proclaimed the establishment of the Turkish republic and became its first president. Between 1923 and his death in 1938, he directed a sweeping modernization program separating church and state, greatly expanding literacy and education, adopting a Latin script for a Turkish alphabet in place of Arabic script, and widely expanding women's economic and political roles. Atatürk became a model for leaders attempting to modernize and economically develop their nations.

Cemal Pasha, Ahmed (1872–1922)

Cemal Pasha was one of the three central CUP leaders of the Ottoman empire during 1913–1918. He served as minister of the navy during World War I and was thought to have exercised important influence on internal and foreign policies. After the end of the war he left Turkey and eventually resided in Tbilisi. Blamed for playing a significant role in the persecution of Armenians, he was assassinated there on July 21, 1922.

Committee of Union and Progress (CUP)

The CUP was a secret organization of intellectuals, students, and young military officers who favored a constitutional political system in the Ottoman empire instead of the absolute authority of the sultan, anticipating that the new political system would lead to both economic progress and more effective policies for countering threats from foreign powers and safeguarding the empire. In 1908, pro-CUP military officers succeeded in gaining control of much of the army, leading to the creation of a type of constitutional monarchy and a parliament. The CUP led the country into and through World War I. While a number of CUP leaders fled the empire after the end of the war, many of its members supported Mustafa Kemal's 1919–1922 rebellion and War of Independence, and the establishment of the Turkish Republic in 1923.

Enver Pasha, Ismail (1881–1922)

Enver Pasha was a leader of the successful military revolt against Sultan Abdullah Hamid in 1908. In 1913 he became a major figure in the triumvirate that dominated the CUP-controlled Ottoman government from January 1913 through October 1918. He is thought to have played a major role in bringing the Ottoman empire into World War I on the side of Germany, and he served as minister of war. After the war he was killed while fighting with White forces against the Red Army on August 4, 1922, in territory that is now part of the Republic of Tajikistan.

Talat Pasha, Mehmed (1874–1921)

Talat Pasha was one of the three most important CUP leaders of the Ottoman empire, along with Cemal and Enver, during World War I. As minister of the interior he was accused of major responsibility for the expulsion of Armenians from the Ottoman empire's eastern provinces. At the end of the war, he left Turkey for Berlin, where he was assassinated on March 5, 1921.

Triumvirate Pashas

The expression *Triumvirate Pashas* referred to three major political leaders, Ahmed Cemal Pasha, Ismail Enver Pasha, and Mehmed Talat Pasha, who dominated the Ottoman empire's CUP-led government from January 1913 until the end of World War I.

Young Turks

Expression for members of the CUP.

James DeFronzo

See Also Arab Revolt of 1916–1918; Kurdish Movements

References and Further Readings

Ahmad, Feroz. 1969. *The Committee of Union and Progress in Turkish Politics, 1908–1918.* Oxford: Oxford University Press.

ataturk.com: "Ataturk, Mustafa Kemal: Founder and First President, Republic of Turkey." http://www.ataturk.com/index2.html accessed July 26, 2005.

BBC News. 2005. World | Europe | Country Profiles | Timeline: Turkey. http://news.bbc.co.uk/1/hi/world/europe/1023189.stm accessed July 28, 2005.

Hanioglu, Sükrü. 1995. *The Young Turks in Opposition.* New York: Oxford University Press.

Kansu, Aykut. 1997. *The Revolution of 1908 in Turkey.* Leiden: Brill.

Kayali, Hasan. 1997. *Arabs and Young Turks: Ottomanism, Arabism, and Islamism in the Ottoman Empire, 1908–1918.* Berkeley: University of California Press.

———. 1998. "Turkish Revolution." Pp. 484–486 in *The Encyclopedia of Political Revolutions,* edited by Jack A. Goldstone. Washington, DC: Congressional Quarterly.

Kinross, Lord. 1979. *Ottoman Centuries.* London: Harper Perennial.

Landua, Jacob M. 1984. *Atatürk and the Modernization of Turkey.* Boulder, CO: Westview Press.

Mango, Andrew. 2002. *Atatürk: The Biography of the Founder of Modern Turkey.* New York: Overlook.

Ramsaur, Ernest. 1957. *The Young Turks: Prelude to the Revolution of 1908.* Princeton, NJ: Princeton University Press.

Shaw, Stanford J., and Ezel Kural Shaw. *History of the Ottoman Empire and Modern Turkey.* Cambridge: Cambridge University Press.

Zürcher, Erik Jan. 1984. *The Unionist Factor: The Role of the Committee of Union and Progress in the Turkish National Movement.* Leiden: Brill.

U

U.S. Southern Secessionist Rebellion and Civil War

CHRONOLOGY

1619 The first African slaves arrive in Jamestown, Virginia, on a Dutch ship. These first slaves were likely treated as indentured servants.

1670s African chattel slavery becomes fully accepted in the British colonies.

1775–1783 The American revolutionary era leads a number of states and individuals to repudiate the practice of slavery. Slavery is abolished in Vermont, Massachusetts, and Pennsylvania. Virginia prohibits the external slave trade.

1783–1793 Due to declining soil quality brought on by years of poor farming techniques, many Southerners abandon growing tobacco in favor of other crops, such as wheat. In doing so, they lessen their dependence on slavery. Cotton is not yet grown on a widespread basis. The Constitution does nothing to emancipate slaves, but a number of individual slaveholders, including George Washington

and Patrick Henry, do so on their own. Many in the United States, in both the North and the South, at this time view slavery as a necessary evil but believe it will eventually die. They assume a process of gradual emancipation will take place.

1793 Connecticut native Eli Whitney, serving as a tutor to the children of a Georgia planter, invents the cotton gin to speed the processing of short-staple cotton. This provides the South with a labor-intensive crop to replace tobacco, making slavery appear to become profitable again.

1793–1820 A steady transformation of the Southern mind takes place as cotton production levels rise and profits increase. White Southerners move from thinking of slavery as a necessary evil to thinking of it as a benign influence and a right that should be guaranteed them.

1816–1828 In an attempt to protect the fledgling northern industries after the War of 1812, Congress passes very high tariffs on foreign goods. Southerners respond furiously, as the tariffs do little to help their region and in fact benefit the North at their expense.

1819–1820 Missouri petitions for statehood as a slave state. No slavery had existed in Missouri before it became a U.S. territory, and it would become the northernmost slave state. When a Northern congressman adds a provision to Missouri's admission providing for gradual emancipation, Southerners react harshly, claiming that the motion violates their civil rights. The Missouri Compromise allows Missouri's admission as a slave state, but prohibits slavery in the remainder of Louisiana Purchase north of latitude 36°30' N. This issue is very disturbing to many in the North, who had thought slavery was dying.

1820–1850   The Southern mind completes another stage in its transformation. During this time, Southerners begin to think of slavery not only as benign, but as positive. They assert that slavery is the natural state for blacks and that slavery as an institution should be praised and extended, not condemned and extinguished. They become increasingly insistent that any attempts to interfere with slavery, whatever the means, will be resisted. In the North, the continuing effects of the market revolution and other influences shift the region further toward an industrial economy, providing a sharp contrast to the South's wholesale dependence on agriculture. Northern industry depends greatly on textile production, which increases the call for Southern cotton.

1830s   The abolitionist movement begins in the North under the leadership of men like William Lloyd Garrison.

1832   Congress, deaf to the South's complaints, passes the second "Tariff of Abominations." John C. Calhoun of South Carolina promotes the doctrine of nullification and denies that the tariffs have any power in his state. President Andrew Jackson offers to lower the tariff and threatens force at the same time. South Carolina backs down after the other Southern states refuse to support it. Nullification is rightly regarded as a test run of a doctrine for the defense of slavery.

1836–1844   Southerners become more virulent in their defense of slavery, even pushing through a "gag rule" that bans slavery as a topic of dis-

cussion in Congress and prohibiting post offices from distributing abolitionist materials. This rule is eventually revoked by the determined efforts of John Quincy Adams.

1846–1848   Issues arising due to the Mexican War and the Wilmot Proviso divide Congress into three distinct camps: abolitionist, moderate, and virulently pro-slavery. None of the three is able to gain a majority. Congress virtually ceases to function.

1850   Some Southerners begin talking openly about secession. Henry Clay and Stephen Douglas manage to work out the "Compromise" of 1850, which holds the nation together for another ten years. Though billed as a compromise, in reality, each section votes only for the provisions that benefit it. It quiets the open debate on slavery for a short while.

1850s   A guerrilla war breaks out in Kansas as proponents of freedom and defenders of slavery fight for control of the new government. The publication of *Uncle Tom's Cabin* by Harriet Beecher Stowe and the visible enforcement of the fugitive slave law infuriate many in the North, swelling the ranks of abolitionists.

1856   A new party, the Republicans, run their first presidential candidate and come close to defeating the pro-slavery Democratic Party. The Republicans are a diverse group dedicated to one premise: there can be no further spread of slavery.

1859   John Brown, an unbalanced abolitionist crusader, attacks the arsenal at Harper's Ferry in what was then Virginia, hoping to start a massive slave revolt. His ploy fails but terrifies Southerners, whose greatest fear is an open, bloody slave rebellion like those in Haiti and the Dominican Republic. Virginia hangs Brown within six weeks of the crime. Abolitionists in the North treat Brown as a martyr, even engaging in public mourning for him. These public displays only further convince Southerners that the North is against them, and they take steps to increase their state militias.

1860   The South makes it clear that it will secede if Abraham Lincoln, the Republican candidate for president, wins the election that year. When Lincoln wins legally, though without a single Southern electoral vote, the South realizes that they are now a permanent minority and have lost control of the government. They apprehend that the North now has the power to vote to prevent slavery's expansion and even end it in states where it is already established. Though Lincoln promises to leave slavery untouched where it already exists, South Carolina secedes in December.

1861   In January, a number of Deep South states follow South Carolina's lead. Alabama, Mississippi, Georgia, Florida, and Louisiana secede. Texas joins them in February. Together, they form the Confederate States of America at Montgomery, Alabama. They devise a governing document that is a virtual copy of the United States Constitution, with a few notable exceptions (such as the explicit protection of the institution of slavery). One by one, federal institutions in the South surrender to the Confederates without a fight. After the garrison at Ft. Sumter in Charleston, South Carolina, refuses to evacuate, Confederate forces fire on the fort. Lincoln responds by calling for 75,000 volunteers to put down the rebellion, an act that prompts Virginia, Tennessee, North Carolina, and Arkansas to join the Confederacy. Lincoln begins the blockade of the Confederate coast. The inexperienced armies meet at the First Battle of Bull Run (Manassas) on July 21, resulting in a Confederate victory.

1862   Kentucky decides in favor of the Union after the Confederates violate its territory. Grant is nearly defeated at the Battle of Shiloh (April 6) but forces the Confederates into retreat. He begins operations toward Vicksburg. The Union navy also captures Jacksonville, Florida, and New Orleans, Louisiana. In the east, the Union advances on Richmond in the Peninsula Campaign, but Confederates under Robert E. Lee repel them during the Seven Days Battles (May 5 through July 2). Lee then turns and defeats a separate Union army at the Second Battle of Bull Run (Man-

assas, August 28–30), before marching north into Maryland. There, Lee suffers a strategic defeat and withdraws after the Battle of Antietam (Sharpsburg) on September 17. Lincoln takes this opportunity to announce the Emancipation Proclamation, freeing any slaves in areas still in rebellion against government authority as of January 1, 1863. Lee recovers from Antietam and defeats a much larger Union army at Fredericksburg, Virginia, on December 13.

1863   Grant moves against Vicksburg on the Mississippi River. After a number of failures, he manages to lay siege to the city. Lee defeats a vastly superior Union army at Chancellorsville (May 1–6) but then loses his campaign into the North at the Battle of Gettysburg (July 1–3) and retreats. Vicksburg surrenders on July 4, giving the Union virtually uncontested control of the Mississippi. Confederate forces in Tennessee under Braxton Bragg defeat Union forces at the Battle of Chickamauga (September 19). The Confederates then lay siege to Chattanooga, Tennessee, where the Union had withdrawn. Grant takes command of the entire western theater and breaks Bragg's chokehold on the city in a series of attacks in late November and early December. The Confederates retreat into Georgia. Lincoln begins recruiting black regiments.

1864   Lincoln places Grant in command of all Union armies. Grant and his subordinate, William T. Sherman, open a series of coordinated campaigns against the Confederates in Virginia and Georgia. Grant meets Lee's army in a series of bloody battles (The Wilderness, May 5–7; Spotsylvania Court House, May 8–21; Cold Harbor, June 1) that culminate in a siege of Lee's army at Petersburg, Virginia. Sherman presses steadily into Georgia. Confederate General John Bell Hood tries to defend Atlanta in three separate battles (Peachtree Creek, July 20; Atlanta, July 22; and Ezra Church, July 28) but fails. The city falls on September 2. Sherman then embarks on his infamous march through Georgia to the sea on November 15. Although he encounters no significant military opposition, Sherman destroys the infrastructure and morale of the state, denying its resources to Lee and leading to mass desertion among Georgia's troops in Virginia. He ends by establishing contact with the Union fleet at Savannah. After taking the city, Sherman offers it to President Lincoln as a "Christmas present" on December 24.

1865   Sherman leaves Savannah in January on a march through the Carolinas, planning to join Grant at Petersburg and overwhelm Lee. On April 2, Grant's forces finally breach Lee's defenses, and Lee orders the evacuation of Richmond. Lee tries to retreat west and join with other forces, but Grant pursues him and cuts him off. On April 9, Lee's forces surrender at Appomattox Courthouse, Virginia. Though other commanders would vie with each other for the title of the last to surrender, the rebellion practically ends with Lee. Only a few days later, on April 14, John Wilkes Boothe, a Southern sympathizer and professional actor, assassinates President Lincoln. The Thirteenth Amendment abolishes slavery in the United States. The Ku Klux Klan is founded in Tennessee. President Johnson champions Lincoln's plan for Reconstruction, and the Radical Republicans oppose him. Congress establishes the Freedmen's Bureau. Mississippi enacts the Black Code which is viewed in the North as an attempt to reintroduce slavery in disguise.

1866   The Fourteenth Amendment is approved by Congress. The powers of the Freedmen's Bureau are expanded.

1867   The Congress, controlled by Radical Republicans, pass their version of Reconstruction over Johnson's repeated vetoes.

1868   The Fourteenth Amendment is ratified.

1869   Ulysses S. Grant elected president. Though a Republican, Grant does not press forward with radical reconstruction as some in the North would like.

1870   The states ratify the Fifteenth Amendment. This amendment makes it illegal to discriminate against male voters based on race.

1876   Former Confederate General Wade Hampton is elected governor of South Carolina, demonstrating that the South has not changed significantly. A contested election between Republican Rutherford B. Hayes and Democrat Samuel Tilden drags on for months.

1877   In the Compromise of 1877, Southern Democrats agree to back Hayes in the contested election, if he will promise to remove Northern troops from the South.

1877–1879   The last federal troops leave the South. Without them, the local Republican governments collapse, making way for the return of white Democrats. This effectively ends the Reconstruction Era.

INTRODUCTION

The rebellion of the slave-holding states in the southern U.S. was the culmination of contradictions and pressures that had been active almost since the nation's founding. The central issue at stake, whether or not a nation dedicated to ideals of freedom could tolerate chattel slavery, was compounded by bickering over tariffs and states rights. The war settled many questions about the nature of the young republic permanently, but though it ended slavery, it did not settle deeper issues of racial equality.

BACKGROUND: CULTURE AND HISTORY

The United States has always been a nation of immigrants. As such, it has never existed as a nationalistic monolithic state. Significant distinctions between the moral, geographic, and economic situations of its people created powerful tensions between the northern and southern sections of the country. When it became apparent that the South could no longer legally oppose Northern attempts at abolitionism and tariff increases, the South rebelled, seeking to preserve the status quo antebellum by forming a new country. It is important to remember that early American history cannot be reduced to a mere preamble to Civil War, yet the war itself can never be understood without it.

While the majority of the early immigrants to what is now the United States shared the same skin color, it is wrong to assume that they all thought alike or pursued the same goals.

Even immigrants from the same country displayed very different visions and behavior, as evidenced in the settlements at Jamestown and Plymouth. As time passed and more European settlers arrived in North America, the situation only became more complicated as diverse colonies appeared, founded by various groups.

The colonists also found themselves divided by geography as much as ideology. New England, with its colder climate, stood far apart from the warm, steamy fields and swamps of southern Georgia. As the colonists began to spread westward, they passed other natural dividing lines; life on the coastal plain was much different from that of the piedmont, which was different from that of the mountains. Settlers who penetrated to the far side of the Appalachian Mountains into Alabama, Tennessee, Kentucky, and Ohio had very little in common with the more established people living on the coast.

If this were not enough, the steady trickle of African-born slaves into the English colonies provided yet another stark contrast. North America received only a tiny portion of all slaves transported from Africa (about 5 percent—the rest arrived in South America or the Caribbean), but their population grew substantially as the years passed (Tindall and Shi, 1996, 122). By 1790, they numbered nearly 700,000, the vast majority of them living in the South. In South Carolina, in fact, blacks soon outnumbered whites substantially (Boyer, et al. 1990, 352–353).

The First Great Awakening and other events leading up to the War for American Independence in 1776 gave the white settlers something in common and African slaves the hope that something could change. The colonies defended themselves against a British reassertion of imperial rights during the American Revolution, from 1775–1781, and emerged as one country, but not as indivisible as many assumed. There were at least two famous rebellions within the first twenty years of the country's existence, Shays' Rebellion and the Whiskey Rebellion, but neither amounted to anything significant.

More importantly, the very events and principles that had led to open rebellion against England began the processes that would eventually lead to disunion. The faith of the Awakening and all the talk of liberty and freedom, slavery and tyranny, had highlighted the evils of human bondage, leaving many of the founding generation with an abiding (if sometimes tragically ironic) hatred for the institution. In the North, entire states banned the practice. Even in the South, men like George Washington began to emancipate their slaves. But most Southerners could not bring themselves to follow suit in large numbers. Their economy remained tied to slavery, and so they preferred grand schemes of gradual emancipation, none of which ever translated into reality.

Still, it looked for a while like slavery in the United States might die on its own. During and after the Revolution, the North adopted a more diversified economy based on manufacturing. Poor farming techniques in the South had virtually destroyed the land for tobacco farming, so the South began to switch to other, less labor-intensive crops such as wheat. As the transition proceeded, the high cost of maintaining slaves made less and less financial sense. At the time, Southern cotton culture did not exist—very little cotton was grown in the South at all.

Everything changed in 1793 when a Connecticut man, Eli Whitney, invented the cotton gin, which easily removed the seeds from short-staple cotton. While Whitney had hoped his invention would benefit slaves by giving them more free time, it completely revitalized slavery in the South. Short-staple cotton could be grown virtually anywhere in the South and at tremendous profit. Also it required a great deal of labor, especially at picking time. White Southerners began to reverse themselves on the utility and morality of slavery.

Meanwhile, other sectional differences became more apparent. As the northern economy became more industrial, it sought protection from developed overseas competition in the form of very high tariffs. These protective tariffs did not benefit the South in any tangible way. Since the southern economy depended almost exclusively on agricultural exports and also relied heavily on manufactured imports, the tariffs forced Southerners to purchase inferior items at higher prices from Northern manufacturers instead of superior foreign-made ones. Also, when Britain could not export goods to the United States, the British began to shun Southern cotton. This, of course, struck at the very heart of the southern economy. In Congress, Southern representatives passionately fought the tariffs.

The first major crack in the foundations of the Union became apparent when Missouri applied for statehood in 1819 as a slave state. This caused controversy among Northern congressmen. First, Missouri would become the northernmost slave state, which worried the free states. Secondly, no slavery had existed in Missouri prior to U.S. acquisition. Many found the idea that slavery followed the United States flag disturbing. They also worried over the possibility of slave states outnumbering free states in the Senate.

In keeping with what many still thought to be the prevailing attitude toward slavery, a Northern senator introduced an addendum to the bill for Missouri statehood to slowly phase out slavery from Missouri after its admission. Southerners reacted with howls of anger. They insisted that slavery was a benign institution, an integral part of Southern life, and that in ending slavery in Missouri the federal government would be discriminating against white Southerners by excluding their property. They also knew that they must maintain a balance in the U.S. Senate to block anti-slavery bills that the more populated North might initiate in the House of Representatives.

Such a virulent defense caught many in the North off guard, and the Congress wrangled over it for the better part of a year before Henry Clay's Compromise of 1820 brought a temporary end to the bickering. The controversy endured, and Southerners, fearful of the destruction of their "peculiar institution," began retreating into a sort of bunker mentality.

From 1816 through 1828, Congress also angered the South by steadily increasing tariffs. Southerners fought the tariffs in 1816 and after, and each new tariff increased the discord between the sections. When the "Tariffs of Abominations," the highest tariffs in the history of the country to that point, passed into law in 1828, the South reacted angrily.

After the next Congress gave them no relief, John C. Calhoun of South Carolina proposed the doctrine of nullification, the idea that a state could call a convention and declare laws of Congress unconstitutional within its borders. South Carolina nullified the tariff and then threatened to secede if President Andrew Jackson took offensive action. Jackson responded by simultaneously offering to lower the tariff and passing the Force Bill, which authorized the use of armed force if South Carolina refused to back down. When the other Southern states refused to support such a radical position, South Carolina gave in, but not before nullifying the Force Bill. With that last face-saving measure, nullification ceased to be an issue.

While nullification dealt exclusively with the issue of tariffs, many scholars believe that Calhoun actually wanted to provide the South with a proven mechanism it could use in defense of slavery. Had nullification stood up to the test of the tariff, it could also have been used against any attempts to abolish slavery. After nullification, the South retreated even further into itself, becoming increasingly convinced that it must defend itself from a hostile Northern foe.

At this point, most Southerners considered further debate over the morality of slavery to be pointless, but the abolition movement had only just begun to grow powerful. The American Anti-Slavery Society, founded in 1833, inundated the South with abolitionist pamphlets and booklets. The southern states responded by making it a criminal offense to distribute abolitionist literature through the mail. Southern post offices destroyed any anti-slavery materials they found, and by 1860 some dedicated abolitionists actually lost their lives when caught traveling in the South with such literature. The American Anti-Slavery Society responded by sending numerous petitions to Congress calling for slavery's end. These pleas incorporated over two million individual signatures. In Congress, pro-slavery representatives managed to impose "gag rules" on Congress. From 1836 until 1844, any petitions or motions dealing with slavery faced immediate and indefinite postponement because of the rule, effectively preventing any debate. John Quincy Adams and Joshua R. Giddings succeeded in having the rules overturned in 1844.

Only two years later, in 1846, the issue of slavery took the national stage once again. Many in the North saw the war with Mexico that erupted that year as nothing more than an attempt to extend the power of slavery. In order to combat this, David Wilmot offered a proviso to a spending bill for the war that explicitly stated there could be no slavery in the lands acquired as a result of the war. The Northern-dominated House passed the bill, only to see it denied by the Senate, where slave states could force its defeat. Many Northern congressmen had grown tired of appeasing the South and so followed Wilmot's lead, attaching the Wilmot Proviso to many different pieces of legislation, all of which the Southerners vetoed in the Senate. Congress virtually ceased to function. By 1850, some Southerners began to talk openly of secession.

Only determined action in Congress prevented civil war in 1850. The "Compromise" of 1850 that saved the Union proved to be a compromise in name only. Originally proposed by Henry Clay and maneuvered past Congress by Stephen Douglas, it settled nothing permanently, as both sides voted only for the portions of the Compromise that benefited their section.

One of the Compromise's provisions, the stronger fugitive slave law, kept the issue of slavery alive and boiling during the 1850s. As Southerners enforced the law to capture escaped slaves in the North, some also abused it and kidnapped blacks who had never been slaves. (The court system set up by the law was inherently unfair to the accused.) This law, which compelled Northern compliance, brought the realities of slavery home to Northern people in real, visible ways. Harriet Beecher Stowe's *Uncle Tom's Cabin,* though melodramatic by modern standards, also made great strides toward making slavery real to Northerners.

In the middle part of the decade, a new party, the Republicans, formed. A loose coalition of a very diverse cross section of American society, they dedicated themselves to a single premise: there could be no further spread of slavery. The party encompassed radical abolitionists, gradual abolitionists, and outright racists who simply wanted slavery confined. In the election of 1856, the Republicans nearly took the presidency with their first candidate, John C. Fremont. Though the pro-slavery Democrats still controlled the White House, the Republicans knew they had a real chance to win with the election of 1860.

Republican gains in the North and west frightened the South, and events in 1859 did nothing to assuage their fears. That year, John Brown, an unbalanced abolitionist crusader made famous for his murderous exploits in Kansas, attempted to cause a massive slave uprising. With the backing of several wealthy Northerners, Brown and his men attacked the federal arsenal at Harpers Ferry, Virginia (now West Virginia), and then waited to arm the hundreds of slaves he expected would flock to him. He would then begin the bloody overthrow of the Southern state governments. No slaves came to Brown's aid. Instead, he and his men were taken by the Virginia militia and a company of Marines under the command of Colonel Robert E. Lee. Brown was quickly tried and hanged, but not before his grandstanding had made him a Christ-like martyr in the eyes of the abolitionist movement (many of whom did not know all of what Brown had done).

John Brown's raid touched a very raw nerve for most Southerners. For all their bluster about content slaves, slave rebellion frightened white Southerners more than anything else. They knew that it could mean widespread bloodshed and destruction, as was the case in Haiti and the Dominican Republic. To make matters worse, the radical abolitionists' near beatification of Brown sent a dire, if unintended, message to even average Southerners.

As the election of 1860 drew near, some states made it clear that they would secede if a "Black Republican" took the White House. Though many in the North thought this another bluffing tactic like the South had used in 1832 and 1850, the country had, in reality, come dangerously close to coming apart at the seams.

CONTEXT AND PROCESS OF REVOLUTION

The issue of slavery came to a head as the nation approached the election of 1860. The Republicans ran their second candidate for office on an explicit promise to limit the spread of slavery. Both sides realized that preventing the spread of slavery would kill it over time, and they had arrived at a place where they could no longer compromise: slavery would either continue to exist, or it would be destroyed, whatever the timetable. This realization pushed already paranoid Southerners into advocating secession. The North demonstrated equal determination in favor of union.

The election of 1860 would prove to be one of strangest in American history, as different groups tried to respond to the situation. The Democrats split down the middle along partisan lines after Southern delegates insisted that the party have an explicit pro-slavery plank in its platform. Southern Democrats nominated John C. Breckinridge and got just such a promise. Northern Democrats, tired of slavery interests dominating the party's plans, answered by nominating the more moderate Stephen A. Douglas. A third Southern party, the Constitutional Union Party, tried to avoid the issue of slavery altogether with their candidate, John Bell.

To the Republicans, this splintering of their opposition meant that if they remained united, their road to the White House would be all but assured. They chose a tall, lanky lawyer from Illinois named Abraham Lincoln. The Republicans did not want to look too radical, and Lincoln had not been on the national scene long enough to say much that could be used against him, at least when compared with the other frontrunner, William Seward. Ironically, Lincoln turned out to be more dedicated to ending slavery than many other Republicans.

The campaign turned into two, two-way races. In the North, Lincoln faced off with Douglas, and in the South, it was Breckinridge versus Bell. Lincoln did not even appear on the ticket in most Southern states, and Breckinridge had no hope of carrying any Northern ones. The Southern promise to secede if the "Black Republican" Lincoln won provided even more tension to an already electrified atmosphere. They realized what Lincoln's victory could mean for their "peculiar institution" and made it clear how high the stakes in the election were. Lincoln responded by trying to emphasize his promise not to harass slave owners in states where the evil was already established, but his promises fell on deaf ears.

When the results began to emerge in mid November, they fulfilled Southerners' worst fears. Lincoln took all of the Northern states plus California and Oregon. Bell took several Upper South states with the exception of Missouri, which gave its votes to Douglas, while Breckinridge carried all the Deep South slaveholding states. Lincoln had emerged the clear, legal winner in the electoral college, even though he had garnered only 40 percent of the popular vote. The South had lost control of the government and could not prevent a Northern assault on slavery or (and this was a secondary consideration) another rise in tariffs.

Lincoln and others made it clear that they did not believe that secession was a viable option, and that they intended to oppose it, peacefully, they hoped. They argued that the Constitution made clear that the Union was a perpetual one. That aside, the right of secession would invalidate federal power by making it clear that any state that wished could leave rather than have to conform to the government's will.

The opinion in the two sections split between Southern certainty and Northern doubt. The South perceived the North as one monolithic block of abolitionism, especially after John Brown's raid. Few doubted that the North would exercise its new-found strength and crush slavery. Many felt cornered and would even contemplate rebellion and secession to preserve the status quo. In the North, a sort of cynical disbelief predominated. The Southerners had threatened disunion on other occasions and had never followed through. Many did not expect this threat to be any different.

All doubting ended when South Carolina voted for secession in December of 1860. A string of Deep South states—Mississippi, Florida, Alabama, Georgia, Louisiana, and Texas—followed the Palmetto State's lead in January and

February of 1861. Representatives of these states met in Montgomery, Alabama, to form the Confederate States of America. They elected Jefferson Davis, a Mississippi senator and former secretary of war, their first president. The delegates also adopted a governing document that was a virtual copy of the United States Constitution, but it did include a few alterations. Some of the changes worked well—for example, the Confederate Constitution provided their president with a line-item veto over 100 years before U.S. presidents earned the privilege. Other changes, however, proved impractical or immoral. They limited the Confederate president, for instance, to one six-year term. This made Davis relatively ineffective from his first day in office, since he could never be re-elected.. More revealingly, they included a provision for the explicit protection of slavery.

The addition of a clause protecting slavery, when so much else remained unchanged, reveals a great deal about the causes and motivations surrounding the foundation of the Confederate States. The South had no interest in establishing anything substantially new, and so the attempt does not truly qualify as a "sweeping social revolution," at least in the sense of the rebels promoting radical change in society. The revolution, in fact, had been going on in the North, which had become an area based on industry and had grown more uniformly opposed to slavery (though many remained openly racist). Instead, the South fought to preserve on old order based on large-scale agriculture and slavery. The changes in the North and abolitionist activism made it impossible for the South to maintain itself as it had been, which prompted the rebellion.

One by one, federal institutions in the South, military and civilian, began to surrender to Southern state militias. Attempts at compromise failed. Also rabidly pro-Southern public speakers called fire-eaters, such as Edmund Ruffin of Virginia, spoke widely and loudly in favor of open war. Only two installations remained in Union hands by the time of Lincoln's inauguration, and Ft. Sumter, in the bay at Charleston, South Carolina, was the most important of these. The fledgling Confederate army surrounded the fort, intending to starve it into surrender. When Lincoln attempted to resupply the troops, the Confederates opened fire, marking the traditional beginning of hostilities.

In the immediate aftermath of Sumter, both sides had to marshal their forces. The United States army consisted of only 15,000 men at the beginning of the war, and many of the officers had resigned rather than fight against the South, while the Confederacy initially had no army at all, only a loose organization of state militias (McPherson 1982, 163). Lincoln called for 75,000 three-month volunteers to suppress the rebellion, and the slightly more far-sighted Davis asked for 100,000 one-year volunteers. Both sides would quickly ask their countries for more troops (McPherson, 1982, 164–168).

When Lincoln's call for volunteers made it clear that he intended to fight the South, a new string of secessions struck. Virginia, Arkansas, Tennessee, and North Carolina joined the Confederacy, and only quick action in the slave states of Missouri and Maryland kept them in the Union fold. These new states doubled the Confederacy's white population and also contained virtually all of the fledgling country's industry and railroads. Meanwhile, the state of Kentucky declared itself neutral, warning both sides to keep their troops clear of its borders. Lincoln was firmly convinced that if the Confederacy gained Kentucky's resources and huge white population, the war would become unwinnable and so he scrupulously observed this prohibition.

Both sides had their own advantages and disadvantages, and Union victory was not completely assured. The North had dramatic advantages in terms of population, industry, and railroads. The vast majority of the factories needed to manufacture cannons, guns, ammunition, and uniforms lay in the North, its railroad system allowed for easy transportation across a broad area, and it could field three troops for every Southern soldier. The South, on the other hand, embraced an immense territory. It would take millions of troops to conquer and hold all the rebellious states in terms of a traditional nineteenth-century war. The South did not have to conquer the North in order to win the war; it simply had to survive by outlasting Northern resolve. The South could also hope for intervention from foreign powers who depended heavily on Southern cotton exports. It was to Europe's advantage to see a further divided American continent.

The armies were still little more than chaotic mobs when they met in their first major battle at Bull Run (called Manassas in the South) in Virginia in the summer of 1861 (July 21). The Confederate Congress planned to meet in its new capital of Richmond, Virginia, that month, and Lincoln yielded to popular pressure to try to take the city before they could meet. Against the advice of his military advisers, he publicly ordered the army forward. Due to judicious use of railroads, Southern forces won the battle, and what began as a simple defeat became an embarrassing rout as the untried Union troops panicked during the retreat. During the rest of 1861, both sides continued to raise and organize their armies in the east and the west, but they now did so with more sober resolve.

The war embraced two major theaters of operation significant to the conflict's outcome. The eastern theater consisted of a small stretch of land in Virginia, Maryland, and Pennsylvania. Here, several major armies, most notably the Army of the Potomac and the Army of Northern Virginia, fought for control of a corridor of land from the Appalachian Mountains to the sea, and between the two capitals of Washington and Richmond. During 1862, the South managed to field a powerful combination of generals in the east, including Robert E. Lee and Thomas J. "Stonewall" Jackson, who repeatedly outmaneuvered their inept federal counterparts. Lee repelled two invasions of Virginia in 1862 and launched an invasion of Maryland that fall. For all his success, Lee lost the battle of Antietam in September. Managing to escape to Virginia, he humiliated the Union again at the Battle of Fredericksburg (December 11–15).

Easily as important as anything that happened on the battlefield, President Lincoln used the slim victory at Antietam to transform that nature of the war and take a stand on slavery in 1862. Up to this point, the North had insisted that it fought only to preserve the union, hoping to conciliate the South into ending the war early. Lincoln swept this away when he announced his preliminary Emancipation Proclamation. It declared all slaves in areas still in rebellion against the U.S. government as of January of 1863 forever free. In doing so, Lincoln raised the stakes significantly, and made it clear that full emancipation was not far off. He also provided for the recruiting of the first all-black military units in the army. Eventually, over 100,000 black soldiers would serve in the war, gallantly defying all critics. By the end of the conflict, they would make up a full 10 percent of all Union forces (McPherson, 1982, 350–355). This change in the nature of the war also ended any hope the Confederacy might have had of international intervention. Britain would not support a war to defend slavery, and France refused to act without British support.

The situation looked much different in the western theater in 1862. Geographically, the west was defined as the operational area stretching from the Appalachian Mountains in the east to the Mississippi River in the west. More practically, it encompassed every area where a western army saw service. By the end of the war, this also included the states of Alabama, Georgia, South Carolina, and North Carolina. This huge area of land proved to be impossible for the Confederacy to defend against the much larger and more numerous Union armies. Both governments looked at the west as a secondary effort, but in terms of command, the dynamics proved to be the exact opposite of the east. While western armies often became dumping grounds for failed Confederate leaders, they became proving grounds for the best Union generals of the war. Here, Ulysses S. Grant and William T. Sherman defeated Confederate armies with the same regularity that Lee and Jackson did U.S. forces in Virginia.

In 1862, Union forces gained important successes in the west. First, the Confederates violated Kentucky neutrality, pushing the state into Lincoln's waiting arms. Grant then took Fort Henry (February 6) and Fort Donelson (February 11–16) on the Tennessee and Cumberland rivers, north of Nashville. His success broke open the heart of the Confederate position in the west, forcing their armies to withdraw

down into Mississippi. Grant followed, but Confederates attacked him at Shiloh (April 6–7), nearly defeating him. Grant managed to hold on and even repulse them the next day. While Grant moved south, Confederate General Braxton Bragg invaded Kentucky, expecting the Blue Grass State to rally to the Confederate cause. In reality, his reception proved to be lukewarm at best. Bragg eventually made the controversial decision to retreat back into Tennessee after winning a confusing victory at Perryville (October 8). His opponent, now William S. Rosecrans, followed him. Bragg attacked at Stones River (December 31, 1862–January 2, 1863). Though he lost the battle, Bragg mauled the Union army so badly that Rosecrans refused to advance for another six months.

During 1862 the South, starved for manpower, started drafting soldiers into its armies. The North followed suit by the middle of 1863. In the South, wealthy planters and their families obtained exemption due to the need to oversee their slaves. In the North, individuals could buy their way out of service by paying a $1,000 bounty. This price naturally ensured that generally only rich Northerners could take advantage of it. Such blatant discrimination in favor of the wealthy led to grumbling on both sides, in and out of the armies.

The year 1863 saw both sides on the move. In the east, Lee won what has been called his greatest victory at the Battle of Chancellorsville (April 30–May 6), but also suffered a painful loss when Jackson died of pneumonia while recovering from wounds sustained in a friendly-fire incident. Lee took the opportunity afforded by his two resounding successes at Fredricksburg and Chancellorsville to launch a second invasion of the North. This effort met with defeat at the Battle of Gettysburg (July1–3). His army wrecked, Lee barely managed to retreat into friendly territory but would never again have the opportunity to invade the North.

Grant used this same time to set his sights on the stronghold of Vicksburg on the Mississippi River. But Vicksburg was inherently difficult to assault. Grant tried a number of times to attack the city successfully but failed, much to the amusement of some in the Northern press. Finally, Grant surrounded the city in May, after the battles of Champions Hill (May 16) and Big Black River Bridge (May 17), and began siege operations. As Lee's army sat silent and defeated on the fields of Gettysburg on July 4, the starved defenders of Vicksburg surrendered to Grant. With the fall of Port Hudson later in the war, the Union took full control of the Mississippi.

In Tennessee, Rosecrans finally moved against Bragg that summer and managed to maneuver the Confederates completely out of Tennessee, down into northwestern Georgia. There Bragg defeated Rosecrans at the Battle of Chickamauga (September 18–20), and the Confederates laid siege to the defeated Union army at Chattanooga, Tennessee. Meanwhile, Lincoln placed Grant in command of the entire

An attack by Confederate general James Longstreet's forces on a Union position during the Battle of Gettysburg on July 3, 1863. (Library of Congress)

western theater. With the help of reinforcements from the east, Grant broke the siege on Chattanooga (November 23–25), and the Confederate army retreated back into Georgia to wait out the winter.

Lincoln promoted Grant to lieutenant general and placed him in overall command of the Union armies on March 12, 1864, and the new campaign season opened with the first coordinated Union offensive of the war. Grant accompanied the Army of the Potomac against Lee in Virginia, while Sherman moved against Atlanta and the army now commanded by Joseph E. Johnston. Other forces operated against any smaller concentrations of Confederate troops in the South.

At this point, the best hope of the Confederacy lay in the upcoming U.S. presidential election. Even after the victories at Gettysburg and Vicksburg, portions of the Northern population remained impatient. The Democratic Party opposed Lincoln in 1864 on the grounds that the war was making no progress, and had degenerated into a bloody stalemate. Its candidate, none other than former Union military commander General McClellan, promised to end the war immediately, and many of his supporters expected a negotiated

peace. Lincoln's fate, and that of the war effort, therefore lay on how much progress his generals could make before the election.

In Virginia, Grant tried to outmaneuver Lee, but Lee refused to be taken in by a campaign of simple movement. Instead, the Overland Campaign (May–June) degenerated into a war of attrition when Grant took advantage of his numbers by dogmatically refusing to retreat. Eventually, Grant managed to pin Lee's army in the fortifications around Petersburg, Virginia, which covered an important rail link to Richmond that Lee could not afford to lose. Once there, Grant ground into Lee's army by extending the Union line whenever reinforcements arrived, and periodically testing Lee's lines. Desertion skyrocketed in Lee's army, but there was little he could do. His army as a whole would not move again until the very end of the war.

In Georgia, Sherman opened a campaign of maneuver against Johnston, who steadily retreated in the face of superior numbers. Aside from one major battle at Kennesaw Mountain (June 22) brought on by Sherman, Johnston retreated all the way into the defenses of Atlanta without putting up significant resistance. When it became apparent that Johnston would even give up Atlanta, Davis replaced him with the fiery Texan John Bell Hood. Hood launched three major attacks on Sherman's army—the battles of Peachtree Creek (July 20), Atlanta (July 22), and Ezra Church (July 28)—but lost each one badly. Afterward, Hood pulled back into the city's defenses. Sherman at first tried bombarding the city but eventually forced Hood to abandon it by cutting the railroads supplying the city. Sherman's troops occupied the city on September 1.

Sherman's victory, only about two months away from election day, ended McClellan's hope of becoming president. When the North went to the polls in November, Lincoln won re-election easily. With their political expectations dashed and all practical hope for a Southern military victory but a memory, the Southerners faced certain defeat. The war would not last another year.

Hood moved his army north into Tennessee, hoping to draw Sherman away from Georgia's fertile heartland, the best source of support Lee still enjoyed. Sherman dispatched enough troops to deal with Hood, and then marched his armies from Atlanta to Savannah, destroying crops, industry, and railroads throughout the region. Hood met with disastrous defeat at the battles of Franklin (November 30) and Nashville (December 16), losing virtually his entire army, while Sherman arrived safely at the sea, offering the city of Savannah to the recently re-elected President Lincoln as a Christmas present on December 24.

By 1865 it was obvious that the Confederacy had lost the war. In Virginia, Grant steadily wore down Lee, and Sherman began another march through the Carolinas to join him, patterned after his previous move through Georgia. The meager forces the Confederates pulled together to oppose Sherman had no hope of defeating him, as he proved in the battles of Averasboro (March 16) and Bentonville (March 19–21).

Lee's hard-pressed lines broke on April 2, before Sherman could reach the field, and Lee evacuated what he could of his army while the Confederate government scrambled to leave Richmond. Grant pursued Lee's retreat hard and fast, finally cutting off his escape at Appomattox Courthouse. Left with no other realistic options, Lee surrendered to Grant on April 9, 1865, ending the war for all practical purposes. Davis and his government either fled or were captured, some seeking asylum overseas. Other Confederate commanders vied for the honor of surrendering last, but by April 18 the final western armies had given up. The Confederacy ceased to exist except as a lingering hope for what could have been in the minds of ardent Southerners.

Southern partisans struck one final, serious blow against the North on the same day that the last of their field armies surrendered. A group of Southerners had infiltrated Washington, D.C., in order to kidnap Lincoln during the war. They

Confederate general Robert E. Lee, pictured here shortly after the surrender at Appomattox Courthouse in Virginia on April 9, 1865, was one of the most brilliant tacticians in American military history and the embodiment of Southern military prowess during the Civil War. (The Illustrated London News Picture Library)

had originally planned to hold him and other important members of his administration for ransom, but commuted the plot into one of revenge at war's end. John Wilkes Boothe, a member of the conspiracy, shot Lincoln in the presidential box of Ford's Theater in Washington as Lincoln and his wife watched a play. Surgeons carried Lincoln to a house across the street. The president lingered through the night but died the next morning. His assassination would have serious implications for the newly defeated South.

IMPACTS

The U.S. Civil War brought into fruition the seeds sown in the war for American independence; no longer would a nation that believed "all men are created equal" tolerate the abomination of slavery. Still, the painful surgery that had cut out the cancer of slavery had left deep and abiding scars on everyone involved, which the tumultuous period of Reconstruction did little to heal.

Reconstruction refers to the period between the end of the war and the final removal of all occupying forces from Southern capitals, during which time each state was readmitted to the Union. Needless to say, it had a very inauspicious beginning with Lincoln's assassination. In addition, the war had claimed the lives of over 600,000 Americans, more than any other war in the entire history of the United States. The first day of the Battle of Shiloh killed more men than all previous American wars combined. The massive loss of life affected the South more extensively than the North. Southern armies had lost nearly as many men as their counterparts, but this figure must be subtracted from a substantially smaller population. There was hardly a white Southern home or family who had not personally known someone killed in the war.

Before the war ended, Lincoln had fought with the increasingly powerful Radical Republican faction in Congress, trying to ensure a gentle return for the Southern states into the Union. The Radicals wanted to completely remake Southern society and demanded harsh terms, while Lincoln's preference leaned toward generous and forgiving ones. Unfortunately, the unrepentant Southern state governments assembled under Lincoln's plan strongly resembled their antebellum predecessors.

After Lincoln's assassination, Andrew Johnson tried to maintain Lincoln's plans. The Radical Republicans impeached Johnson, and though they failed to remove him from office, their plans carried the day. They quickly disfranchised most former Confederates, gave voting rights to most blacks without question, and in general set very rigid standards for the former states to meet before being readmitted to the Union. The Radical Republican approach fostered hatred and indignation in many white Southerners that still lingers in some places to the present day. The more immediate effect, though, was to remove many white Southerners from their positions of power and replace them with more compliant individuals.

The U.S. government quickly reduced the size of the army to but a shadow of its size at its wartime height. As the discharged men returned home, they expected to pick up the jobs they had left behind when they enlisted, but found many of them filled by other workers who had not enlisted. The government defused this potentially volatile situation by extending the Homestead Act, first passed in 1862, to the returning soldiers and displaced workers. This act allowed men to receive 162 acres of government-owned land for free, provided they live on the land and farm it for a period of five years. Thousands of families eventually took advantage of the Homestead Act, and it succeeded in preventing large-scale labor riots and unemployment. It also facilitated the post-war farming boom but presaged conflict with many American Indian cultures, as more and more whites pushed west.

Returning Confederates did not face a similar situation. Southern white manpower had been bled dry during the years of the war, and the majority of the region depended on large-scale agriculture. Union forces destroyed much of what little industry the region had before the war in an effort to starve the Confederate armies of supplies. The conflict had also decimated the cotton industry, and with its destruction even many of the wealthiest white Southerners found themselves destitute. During the war, the British and the French, the main buyers of antebellum cotton, had developed their own sources, and so what cotton Southerners did grow sold for pitifully low prices.

The most important and far-reaching change in the South was, of course, the destruction of chattel slavery. After the war, some four million black men, women, and children gained their freedom. Unfortunately, they had little else. Organizations such as the Freedman's Bureau took halting steps toward securing them land but with negligible or even negative results. What results they did gain hardly survived the Reconstruction period. With no money, no land, and no jobs, millions of blacks found themselves thrust back into dependence on white landowners. These men, who had generally been the largest slave owners before the war, loaned money to black families through the crop lien system or employed them as sharecroppers in exchange for a portion of crops produced. With prices falling and crops failing, these two systems predestined virtually every person caught in their grasp to a life of privation and ignorance.

The Thirteenth and Fourteenth amendments to the Constitution eliminated slavery and prevented the South from arbitrarily banning black men from the polls. While Reconstruction lasted and northern troops occupied Southern capitals, black men voted regularly and served in various positions in the state governments. But unrepentant white Southerners resorted to violence and threats to enforce their will. The most prominent of a number of such movements was the original incarnation of the Ku Klux Klan, led by former Confederate General Nathan Bedford Forrest of Mississippi. While this first version of the Ku Klux Klan would die off after Reconstruction, the pattern of beatings, rioting, and murder would remain consistent well into the twentieth century. The Klan, in particular, was re-created in 1905. At its peak in the 1920s it counted anywhere from three to eight million members, and was popular even in non-Southern states, such as Indiana (Tindall and Shi, 1996, 1094–1096).

The devastation of the war did force one transformation in the South, on at least a limited scale. With cotton agriculture devastated by the war, many younger Southerners began to turn to manufacturing, prompting a rapid industrialization of the region. Though significant, the depth of the change has been overstated by the proponents of the "New South," as the bulk of the economy remained tied to agriculture.

By the end of Ulysses S. Grant's second term as U.S. president, very little practical change for the better had been wrought in most Southern state governments. Political maneuvering in the contested election of 1877 brought an end to Reconstruction. In exchange for removing all Northern troops from Southern soil, several Southern Democrats agreed to support Rutherford B. Hayes in the election. When Hayes won and honored his end of the bargain, the Republican state governments collapsed one after another in the South. Each state then found ways to legally exclude blacks from voting or holding office. White Southerners trumpeted this as "redemption" and proclaimed the return of "home rule," which essentially meant white, Democratic government.

In the end, Reconstruction failed to heal the wounds inflicted by slavery and the war. Many Southern whites carried resentment toward the North for over one hundred years after the war ended. Though never serious enough to actually break out into open rebellion, it fostered the continuance of sectionalism and proved a boon to the Democratic Party in every presidential and congressional election until almost the 1980s. The South's racism led many to fight the civil rights movement viciously and remains a controversial problem to the present day as some abandon their hatreds and others cling tenaciously to them.

Black men and women had gained their freedom, but the failure of Reconstruction left them in a system that was little better, and in some ways worse, than what they had experienced as slaves. This continued discrimination and inequality doomed generations to poverty and ignorance. Though they would always fight for their rights and a better life, they would not begin to make much headway until the 1950s and 1960s.

PEOPLE AND ORGANIZATIONS

Barton, Clara (1821–1912)

Founder of the American Red Cross. Born in Massachusetts, Barton established a free public school in New Jersey before the war. After the First Battle of Bull Run, Barton advertised for medical supplies and established a relief organization that ministered to sick and wounded soldiers.

She later established a more permanent organization that followed the armies in the Virginia theater, helping with the sick and wounded. Her excellent efforts attracted national attention. She later began an effort to locate soldiers missing in action. Barton officially established the Red Cross in 1881.

Brown, John (1800–1859)

Abolitionist partisan executed for attempting to incite a slave insurrection. Brown, an unbalanced man who had failed at nearly everything he ever tried, found temporary fame as an abolitionist guerrilla fighter in Kansas, where he perpetrated the Pottowattamie Creek Massacre in 1856. With the financial backing of several prominent abolitionists, Brown attacked the arsenal at Harper's Ferry, Virginia, in 1859, hoping to start a massive slave revolt. Captured, Brown was quickly executed, but not before he had been lionized by the Northern abolitionist movement. Brown's raid and Northern response terrified Southerners, helping to further polarize the country prior to the election of 1860.

Bureau of Refugees, Freedmen, and Abandoned Lands

Government organization founded to help freed slaves through social work. The Freedman's Bureau suffered from a chronic lack of funds and a lack of cooperation in the South. Though well intentioned, most historians believe its impact was minimal.

Calhoun, John C. (1782–1850)

Pro-slavery, pro-Southern congressman. A U.S. senator from South Carolina, vice president, and secretary of war, Calhoun was a vocal proponent of Southern slavery and fought vigorously to defend it in the years leading up to the war. He tried to promote nullification as a defense against tariffs, and likely, as a defense against the abolition of slavery.

Confederate States of America

Government formed by the newly seceded states in 1861. It struggled with the war and inflation until its final demise in April of 1865.

Davis, Jefferson (1808–1889)

Mississippi senator and former secretary of war who served as the first and only president of the Confederate States.

Democratic Party

Before and during the war, a generally pro-Southern, pro-slavery political party. During the war it often argued against abolitionism and in favor of making peace with the Confederacy.

Douglass, Frederick (1817–1895)

Former slave and powerful abolitionist public speaker. Douglass escaped slavery and proved very effective in rallying Northerners against slavery before the war. Douglass's eloquence provided a living antithesis to Southern characterizations of blacks.

Fire-eaters

A group of rabidly pro-Southern public speakers who pushed the South toward secession. Including men like Edmund Ruffin and William Lowndes Yancey, the fire-eaters toured the South in the 1850s highlighting the South's perceived wrongs. Their inflammatory and popular speeches may have played an important role in many Southerners' decisions to vote for secession.

Garrison, William Lloyd (1805–1879)

Abolitionist newspaper editor. An early and outspoken leader of abolitionism, Garrison's anti-slavery paper, the *Liberator,* began publication in 1831 and established his reputation as the most radical of abolitionists. Garrison demanded the immediate abolition of slavery and promoted revolutionary measures to achieve it.

Grant, Ulysses S. (1822–1885)

Top Union general of the war. Born in 1822 in Ohio, Grant led a mediocre civilian life but excelled in the Mexican War. During the Civil War he established a reputation for dogged determination and sound strategy. Victorious in Tennessee and Mississippi, he caught Lincoln's attention, and the president placed Grant in command of the entire Union war effort in 1864. With the help of William T. Sherman, Grant used the Union's superior numbers to finally force Confederate surrender.

Jackson, Thomas J. (1824–1863)

Popular and talented Confederate general. "Stonewall" Jackson stood out as one of Robert E. Lee's chief lieutenants. His hard-driving nature and creative tactics regularly defeated federal armies. He died after the Battle of Chancellorsville in 1863.

Johnson, Andrew (1808–1875)

Vice president under Lincoln, first president of the Reconstruction era. After Lincoln's assassination, Johnson tried to promote Lincoln's conciliatory plan for Reconstruction, but the Radical Republicans in Congress nearly removed him from office through impeachment.

Lee, Robert E. (1807–1870)

Legendary Confederate general. Lee ranks as one of the most talented military leaders the United States has ever produced. After ascending to command of the Army of Northern Virginia in 1862, Lee conducted a series of brilliant campaigns with limited resources against powerful enemies. He went undefeated for nearly a year before losing the Battle of Gettysburg. When Grant took command in 1865, Lee proved a match for him, forcing Grant to resort to a strategy of attrition that eventually wore Lee down. After the war, Southerners enshrined Lee's memory, exalting him to near sainthood.

Lincoln, Abraham (1809–1865)

Lincoln's election served as the direct catalyst for Southern secession in 1860. Lincoln, a lawyer from Illinois, had run on a ticket of limiting the expansion of slavery, something the Southern states refused to countenance. In the first part of the war, Lincoln exercised a policy of conciliation toward Southerners and downplayed his abolitionism. When it became clear that conciliation was not possible, Lincoln turned the focus of the war to the elimination of slavery with his Emancipation Proclamation. He then prosecuted the war more seriously. Lincoln was shot on April 14, 1865 and died the next day.

Radical Republicans

Most ardent abolitionists of the Republican Party. This faction of Republicans called for an immediate, unconditional end to slavery and the elevation of black men and women to complete equality with whites. After the war, they tried to remake the South with their harsh reconstruction policies but failed, due to Southern intransigence and spotty enforcement.

Republican Party

Anti-slavery party. The Republican Party formed during the 1850s as a loose coalition of various groups all dedicated to one premise: no further spread of slavery. The election of the first Republican president in 1860 sparked the first wave of secession.

Sherman, William T. (1820–1891)

Union General. Born in Ohio, Sherman attended West Point but did not fight in the Mexican War. During the Civil War, he served as one of Grant's ablest lieutenants and is most famous for his controversial campaigns through Georgia and the Carolinas.

Brian C. Melton

See Also African American Freedom Struggle; American Revolution; Armed Forces, Revolution, and Counter-Revolution; Documentaries of Revolution; Human Rights, Morality, Social Justice, and Revolution; Music and Revolution; Slave Rebellions in the United States

References and Further Readings

Boyer, Paul S., et al. 1990. *The Enduring Vision: A History of the American People.* Lexington, MA: D.C. Heath and Company.

Castel, Albert D. 1992. *Decision in the West: The Atlanta Campaign of 1864.* Lawrence: University Press of Kansas.

Catton, Bruce. 1956. *This Hallowed Ground: The Story of the Union Side of the Civil War.* Garden City, NY: Doubleday.

Donald, David H. 1995. *Lincoln.* New York: Simon and Schuster.

Foner, Eric. 1988. *Reconstruction: America's Unfinished Revolution, 1863–1877.* New York: Harper and Row.

Foote, Shelby. 1958–1974. (3 volumes) *The Civil War: A Narrative.* New York: Random House.

Freeman, Douglas Southall. 1934–1935. *R. E. Lee: A Biography.* New York: C. Scribner's Sons.

Gallagher, Gary W. 1997. *The Confederate War.* Cambridge, MA: Harvard University Press.

Gerteis, Louis S. 1973. *From Contraband to Freedman: Federal Policy towards Southern Blacks, 1861–1865.* Westport, CT: Greenwood Press.

Grimsley, Mark. 1995. *The Hard Hand of War: Union Military Policy Toward Southern Civilians, 1861–1865.* New York: Cambridge University Press.

Hattaway, Herman. 1997. *Shades of Blue and Gray: An Introductory Military History of the Civil War.* Columbia: University of Missouri Press.

Jaffa, Harry V. 2000. *A New Birth of Freedom: Abraham Lincoln and the Coming of the Civil War.* Lanham, MD: Rowman and Littlefield.

Marszalek, John F. 1993. *Sherman: A Soldier's Passion for Order.* New York: Free Press.

McFeely, William S. 1968. *Yankee Stepfather: General O. O. Howard and the Freedmen.* New Haven, CT: Yale University Press.

McPherson, James M. 1982. *Ordeal by Fire: The Civil War and Reconstruction.* New York. Alfred A. Knopf.

———. 1990. *Battle Cry of Freedom: The Civil War Era.* New York: Oxford University Press.

———. 1997. *For Cause and Comrades: Why Men Fought in the Civil War.* New York: Oxford University Press.

Robertson, James I. 1997. *Stonewall Jackson: The Man, the Soldier, the Legend.* New York: Macmillan.

Simpson, Brooks D. 1991. *Let Us Have Peace: Ulysses S. Grant and the Politics of War and Reconstruction.* Chapel Hill: University of North Carolina Press.

———. 2000. *Ulysses S. Grant: Triumph over Adversity, 1822–1865.* Boston: Houghton Mifflin.

Tindall, George B., and David E. Shi. 1996. *America: A Narrative History.* 4th Edition. New York: W. W. Norton and Company.

U.S. War Department. 1881–1901. *The Official Records of the War of the Rebellion.* 127 vols. Washington, DC: Government Printing Office.

Warner, J. Ezra. 1959. *Generals in Gray: Lives of the Confederate Commanders.* Baton Rogue: Louisiana State University Press.

———. 1966. *Generals in Blue: Lives of the Union Commanders.* Baton Rogue: Louisiana State University Press.

Woodhead, Henry, ed., with the editors of Time-Life Books. 1998. *Echoes of Glory: Illustrated Atlas of the Civil War.* Alexandria, VA: Time-Life Books.

Woodworth, Steven E. 1995. *Davis and Lee at War.* Lawrence: University Press of Kansas.

———. 2001. *While God Is Marching On: The Religious World of Civil War Soldiers.* Lawrence: University Press of Kansas.

V

Venezuelan Bolivarian Revolution of Hugo Chávez

CHRONOLOGY

1811	Venezuelan independence war begins under Simón Bolívar's leadership.
1819	Colombia, Venezuela, and Ecuador are united under Bolívar's constitution.
1826	Pan American Congress in Panama represents Bolívar's vision of an American confederation without the participation of the United States.
1830	Venezuela becomes an independent republic. Bolívar dies.
1830–1858	Conservative and Liberal caudillos rule the country.
1859–1861	Civil wars. Ezequiel Zamora heads a movement against the oligarchs.
1870–1888	Dominance of modernizing liberal Antonio Guzmán Blanco.
1899–1945	Dictatorships by military men from the Andean state of Táchira.
1899–1908	President Cipriano Castro, a nationalist, harasses foreign companies and governments. The United States breaks diplomatic relations in 1908.
1908–1935	Juan Vicente Gómez allows no political opposition but treats foreign governments and oil companies with caution.
1914	Beginning of oil exploitation in Lake Maracaibo region. The subsidiaries of Standard Oil and Royal Dutch Shell dominate.
1928	Student revolt against Gómez, touted by many as the origin of the generation of democratic leaders.
1936–1945	Generals Eleazar López Contreras and Isaías Medina Angarita loosen political controls and pass (1943) the first law to restrict the actions of the foreign oil companies.
1941	Founding of Acción Democrática (AD), a social democratic party.
1945–1948	AD leader Rómulo Betancourt and young military men led by Marcos Pérez Jiménez overthrow Medina Angarita and usher in a democratic government. In November 1948, the military men push the civilians out and install a new military dictatorship.

1946	The Christian Democratic Party known as COPEI is founded.
1947	Democratic constitution is adopted.
1948–1958	Military junta, followed by dictatorship of Marcos Pérez Jiménez. In January 1958, civilians and military join to overthrow the dictatorship. Pact of Punto Fijo is signed by AD, COPEI, and other civilian and military leaders. The Communists are excluded.
1959–1964	Presidency of AD's Rómulo Betancourt. Marxists launch a guerrilla war.
1960	Venezuela joins Middle Eastern oil producers to form OPEC.
1961	Constitution establishes representative democracy.
1969–1974	COPEI president Rafael Caldera decrees amnesty, which brings most of the guerrillas back into legal political activity.
1971	A group of former guerrillas founds Movimiento Al Socialismo (MAS); others found the forerunner of La Causa R.
1974–1979	AD president Carlos Andrés Pérez presides over the bonanza years of oil revenues. He leads an expansive foreign policy and advocates South-South cooperation.
1976	Nationalization of petroleum and formation of national oil company, PDVSA.
1979–1989	Governments of Luis Herrera Campins (COPEI) and Jaime Lusinchi (AD). Beginning of Venezuela's crushing national debt. In February 1983, the currency is devalued. Both parties implement neo-liberal policies.
1982	Formation of Movimiento Bolivariano Revolucionario-200 (MBR-200) by Hugo Chávez and young military officers.
1989–1993	With promises to help the poor, President Carlos Andrés Pérez is re-elected, but his neo-liberal policies raise the prices of articles of prime necessity.
1989	February riots in Caracas, known as the *Caracazo*, protest Pérez's programs. Hundreds are killed when the military and National Guard restore order.
1992	Hugo Chávez leads a February revolt that fails but catapults him to national fame. A second military revolt in November also fails.
1993	President Pérez is impeached for corruption in May.
1994–1998	Rafael Caldera's second presidency, this time as an independent after renouncing his party. Continuation of neo-liberal policies.
1996	Chávez, released from jail, represents opposition to the entire Punto Fijo system.
1998	Chávez wins December elections with 56.2 percent of the vote. AD and COPEI effectively disintegrate.
1999	Popularly elected convention writes a new constitution, which is approved in popular referendum. Country is renamed Bolivarian Republic of Venezuela.
2000	Under the new constitution, Chávez is elected to a six-year presidential term by 59.76 percent of the vote. Chavistas also dominate Congress.
2001	Círculos Bolivarianos are launched to spur local political participation and community development.
2002	In April, military and civilian opposition removes Chávez from office, but popular reaction and the support of the pro-Chávez sector of the armed forces force his return two days later. The United States is embarrassed by its public failure to condemn a coup against a democratically elected leader.
2002–2003	In December–January a work stoppage takes place in the petroleum industry. The Chávez government dismisses over 11,000 white-collar PDVSA employees for participating in an illegal strike.

2003	Numerous "missions" are formed to bring health care, education, and services to the poor.
2004	Coordinadora Democrática, with U.S. support, forces a recall referendum in August. Chávez wins with 59 percent of the vote.
	In October, Chavistas sweep local and regional elections.
2006	Oil prices exceed $70 a barrel.

INTRODUCTION

Many of the heroic myths of Venezuela's historical past have become part of Hugo Chávez's revolution and appeal. His revolution is unique in that it is drawn from Venezuelan roots more than from any ideological theory or model. In his first five years in power (1999–2003), he established his legitimacy thorough national elections and a populist and nationalist program characterized by what he called participatory democracy. With the support of the masses and the army, he survived all attempts to unseat him by coup d'état, strikes, and a recall referendum. From 2004, high oil prices and a firmer grip on power allowed him to implement many of his social welfare measures.

BACKGROUND: CULTURE AND HISTORY

Under Simón Bolívar, Venezuela emerged as the leader of the continental drive for independence from Spain in 1811. The quixotic soldier envisioned a united Spanish America that could offset the power of Europe and the United States. Bolívar failed to achieve his dream, but the vision continued to inspire Venezuelans.

For most of the nineteenth century, *caudillos* (warlords) vied for power in Venezuela, although there was little to reward the winners. Poor infrastructure, conflict, and disease diminished the returns the small population received from cattle raising, cacao plantations, and Andean coffee. Venezuelans claim that the nineteenth century civil wars destroyed the elite and confirmed an egalitarian society free from racial prejudice. Even so, men of predominantly European descent have dominated the nation's politics and economics.

The late nineteenth century liberals brought order to the country but could not establish a stable representative democracy. Their failure opened the way for the military dictators who ruled between 1899 and 1945. Intellectuals justified their harsh rule by terming them "democratic caesars" and arguing that their rule was necessary until the "immature" Venezuelan population was ready for democracy.

Juan Vicente Gómez governed from 1908 to1935 and presided over the beginning of the petroleum industry. Gómez allowed the foreign companies, primarily the subsidiaries of Standard Oil of New Jersey and Royal Dutch Shell, to operate freely. By 1929, Venezuela was the world's leading exporter of oil. Relations with the United States were quite good, and Washington overlooked the harshness of Gómez's dictatorship.

A clandestine Communist Party formed in the 1920s, but the student demonstrations against Gómez in 1928 proved more significant in forming the generation that would establish the Punto Fijo representative democracy. Jailed and then exiled, many protesters like Rómulo Betancourt subsequently founded the social democratic party, Acción Democrática (AD). In the 1930s, Rafael Caldera led an anti-Communist, Christian student movement that later moved toward the center and became the Christian Democratic Party (COPEI). Some Venezuelans criticized the enrichment of the dictator and his cronies and advocated "sowing" the oil revenues more widely in the nation and among its citizens. The last two military dictators, Eleazar López Contreras (1935–1941) and Isaías Medina Angarita (1941–1945), tentatively moved toward social investment, curbs on the foreign oil companies, and mildly representative democratic institutions. Medina's openness and flexibility especially earned him affection as a reformist military officer.

Impatient for more rapid reform, Rómulo Betancourt's AD and young military officers overthrew Medina in 1945. Civilians and military leaders collaborated in drawing up a new constitution, holding elections, and establishing the bases for a populist nationalist government that punished corruption and promised social justice. But some became uncomfortable with the highly charged political climate and called on the armed forces to save the nation from chaos. In November 1948, the officers installed a new military dictatorship, highly attuned to the anti-Communism of the Cold War. They outlawed most political parties and labor unions, considered agents of divisiveness.

The 1940s democracy had put down deep roots, however, and in January 1958, a military-civilian alliance, including the Communists and the poor of the barrios, cast Marcos Pérez Jiménez from office. Admiral Wolfgang Larrazábal headed an interim junta that scheduled elections in December and decreed programs to help the urban poor. Many *caraqueños* (residents of Caracas) expressed their revulsion at the U.S.'s support of the dictatorship by physically attacking Vice President Richard Nixon's car during his 1958 visit. Determined to establish a stable democratic system, Caldera, Betancourt, other politicians, and business, military, and labor leaders met to sign the Pact of Punto Fijo. They vowed to uphold representative democracy and to turn their backs on the temptation of military coups. Significantly, Betancourt and Caldera excluded the Communists from the pact. Forced outside the political consensus, young leftists launched a guerrilla movement in the 1960s.

Thus began the Punto Fijo regimes that governed from 1959 to 1999, gaining a reputation for the hemisphere's most stable democracy. AD and COPEI alternated in power, and education, health care, industrialization, labor organization, and agrarian reform became the hallmarks of the new populism.

Labor and peasant organizations bloomed but depended heavily upon the parties for patronage and support. When oil prices were high and the government revenues abundant, political peace reigned. President Rafael Caldera in 1969 offered an amnesty that ended the guerrilla conflict. In 1971, former guerrillas formed the Movimiento Al Socialismo (MAS) and La Causa R (Radical). They became important political players, but lacked the discipline or patronage to achieve significant electoral victories. The armed forces remained aloof from electoral politics, taking pride in their role in saving the democratic system from the guerrillas.

Through the 1970s, the Punto Fijo governments were nationalistic without usually damaging relations with the United States. Although a founding member of the OPEC oil cartel, Venezuela continued to ship oil to the United States during the Arab oil embargo of the 1970s. The AD government of Carlos Andrés Pérez (1974–1979) nationalized the oil industry in 1976 and formed the state corporation PDVSA. The oil company became the most important in the increasing number of state-owned enterprises. Some of the oil largesse trickled down even to the poorest Venezuelans. Pérez aspired to Third World leadership by supporting the Nicaraguan Sandinistas and by offering loans and petroleum at reduced prices to poor countries in the region.

The good times ended abruptly when the 1983 currency devaluation, corruption, and mismanagement resulted in a crushing debt burden. Eager to please the International Monetary Fund (IMF), the presidents implemented austerity measures, eroding the new-found well-being of the poor. At the same time, friends of politicians found ways to profit even when banks, businesses, and government corporations collapsed. Congress charged Pérez with graft, but he evaded punishment. The two presidents who followed him did little either to end the debt crisis or to halt the corruption. Venezuelans became disenchanted with the two major parties. In 1982, some young military officers, including Hugo

Chávez, formed a secret organization, the Movimiento Bolivariano Revolucionario-200 (MBR-200), with a goal of restoring integrity and social justice to the country.

In 1988, Venezuelans re-elected Carlos Andrés Pérez. In January 1989, Pérez turned his back on populist politics when he issued several decrees that raised controlled prices on popular goods. The response was immediate and spontaneous: the *Caracazo* (exploding of Caracas). The poor in the shantytowns demonstrated, burned, and looted. The army and National Guard contained the riots, but with a cost of hundreds of deaths. Many of the officers and Venezuelans sympathized more strongly with the poor than with President Pérez.

In February 1992, Lieutenant Colonel Hugo Chávez led a military rebellion against the Pérez government, to the shock, if not the disapproval, of many. Chávez's movement failed, but a brief appearance on television to urge his colleagues to surrender made him a national hero. His charisma and his statement indicating that the revolution was only temporarily postponed made him the face of what seemed to be a viable opposition. A second military effort in November also failed, but congress removed Pérez from office for corruption in May 1993. An interim president served until the December 1993 elections could be held.

The old patriarch Rafael Caldera won the elections, but only by renouncing his party and running as an independent. Once in office, he too embraced the neo-liberal austerity program. In 1996, after his release from prison, Hugo Chávez argued that the Punto Fijo representative democracy had failed and had to be replaced. AD and COPEI disintegrated, offering no hope, no ideas, and no leaders. Many saw Chávez, like Simón Bolívar, or Medina Angarita, or even Wolfgang Larrazábal, as the honest military man who could implement reforms better than the civilians. The United States condemned Chávez as a *golpista* (leader of an attempted coup d'état), refused him a visa to enter the United States, and criticized his friendship with Fidel Castro. Even so, Chávez won the 1998 presidential election with 56 percent of the vote.

CONTEXT AND PROCESS OF REVOLUTION

Venezuela is a classic petroleum economy and the world's fifth largest exporter. Over half of government revenues and 73 percent of export earnings come from petroleum. Most Venezuelan oil goes to the United States, constituting 15 percent of U.S. imports. Chávez had to govern within the context set by the petroleum economy. Thus he did not reject capitalism, socialize the Venezuelan economy, or weaken or abolish the armed forces. Essentially, he sought to redistribute power and wealth within Venezuela's capitalist system; to empower the poor to take political action; to construct a nationalism that drew on Venezuela's past history; and internationally, to encourage the emergence of a multipolar world that would depend less on the United States.

Chávez's years in power (to mid 2005) fall into three stages. In his first two years (1999 to 2000), he established legitimacy and provided the outlines of his program. For the next two and a half years (2001 to mid 2003), he defended his legitimacy from an opposition that sought his ouster by any means. The more recent two years (mid 2003 to mid 2005), especially after the August 2004 referendum, allowed him to consolidate and deepen his revolution.

Chávez secured legitimacy through seven national elections held between 1998 and 2001, among which were two presidential contests (1998, 2000) and three relating to the Constitutional Assembly and constitution (1999). Chávez and his followers won each with well over 55 percent of the vote, although, as in the 1990s elections, the abstention rate was high: in the 1993 and 1998 presidential elections, 39.8 percent and 36.5 percent abstained respectively (Ellner and Hellinger 2003, 45).

The MVR (formerly MBR-200) and the coalition, Polo Patriótico, supported Chávez in the 1998 presidential election, but he chose not to organize a political party. Two leftist parties, La Causa R and MAS, proved his strongest allies, but both parties split over support of Chávez. Luis Miquilena and José Vicente Rangel became trusted advisors, but many on the Left viewed Chávez with suspicion. The traditional parties, AD and COPEI, continued to be impotent and disorganized. In the 2000 presidential elections, Chávez's old ally, Colonel Francisco Arias Cárdenas ran against him and came in second.

The constitution of 1999 retained civil liberties and the basic structure of the government. It provided for participatory democracy, indigenous rights, agrarian reform, a unicameral congress, increased presidential authority, a six-year presidential term, state intervention in the economy, a stronger social security system, and it renamed the country the Bolivarian Republic of Venezuela.

Chávez established contact with his base in speeches, television programs, and especially his call-in radio program *Aló Presidente.* His folksy style invoked nineteenth-century heroes like Simón Bolívar and the radical caudillo Ezequiel Zamora. The president denigrated Venezuelan oligarchs, "savage capitalism," the old parties, the business association Fedecámaras, PDVSA executives, the labor confederation CTV, the United States, and the private media, which maintained an unremitting hostility toward him. He called on *el soberano* (the sovereign), the people,

Venezuelan president Hugo Chávez waves to supporters on December 6, 1998, the date of presidential elections he won in a landslide. (AP/Wide World Photos)

to support him against these enemies. Many Venezuelans saw a man of color who looked and talked like them, and they resented the racialized epithets the opposition used to refer to Chávez. Chávez's rhetoric, and that of his enemies, provoked a class-based polarization that was relatively new to Venezuela and challenged the comfortable myth of egalitarianism.

Petroleum policy and foreign policy naturally intersected. Chávez worked to derive more revenues from petroleum and to bring PDVSA under government control. In 1998, petroleum sold at a low $12 a barrel. Acting autonomously, the oil executives were delivering only 20 percent of PDVSA's profits to the nation, had minimized cooperation with OPEC, and dealt independently with foreign companies. Many executives advocated the privatization of PDVSA. Portions of the company's profits went to fees to foreign companies, investments abroad, and high managerial salaries. PDVSA spokesmen resisted Chávez's initiatives and accused him of politicizing the global company. Chávez used personal diplomacy, including visits to Saddam Hussein and Mu'hammar al-Qadhafi, to strengthen the cartel, raise prices, and reassure OPEC leaders of Venezuela's commitment. Oil prices reached $30 a barrel by 2004, although as much from luck as from Chávez's efforts.

These initiatives angered Washington, as did Chávez's inter-American initiatives and friendship with Cuba's Fidel Castro. Chávez urged Latin American leaders to oppose the Free Trade Area of the Americas (FTAA) and to strengthen and expand Mercosur and other Latin American pacts. In bilateral issues, Chávez opposed U.S. military aid to Colombia, encouraged negotiations between the Colombian government and the guerrillas, and refused to allow United States planes to use Venezuelan airspace to intercept drug traffickers.

Chávez decreed a series of laws, including an agrarian reform law, in November 2001 that outraged the Venezuelan opposition. They charged that Chávez had acted dictatorially to attack private property without adequate debate, although it was unlikely that the elected Chavista-dominated National Assembly would have contested the laws. Rumors, accusations, and charges against Chávez filled the national and international press. U.S. officials frequently cautioned Chávez about his "misbehavior." In December 2001, business and oil leaders called a general strike to force Chávez's resignation. When that failed, dissident military leaders in cooperation with Fedecámaras removed Chávez from office on April 11, 2002. The interim president, businessman Pedro Carmona, made so many missteps that the rebellious military leaders acceded to the popular outcry and the sector of the military that supported Chávez and restored him to office two days later. Most American nations, except the United States, condemned the coup, and Washington was embarrassed at having, by its silence and criticism of Chávez, appeared to have endorsed a coup against an elected leader. In December 2002, the conflict spilled into the streets as military officers seized Caracas's Altamira Plaza, and oil executives and workers struck to close the industry down. After sixty days, the Ministry of Mines and Energy began to fire the strikers, and over 11,000 primarily managerial employees lost their jobs. By early 2003, both sides agreed grudgingly to work with the representatives from the Organization of American States (OAS), the Carter Center, and the United Nations to find a formula to end the crisis.

Thus began the third stage of Chávez's rule. He agreed to hold a recall referendum in August 2004 if sufficient petition signatures could be secured. After resolving a controversy over the legality of many signatures, Chávez prevailed in the referendum with 59 percent of the vote. The abstention rate dropped, suggesting that Chávez had energized the masses. The U.S. National Endowment for Democracy (NED) funded the opposition umbrella group, Coordinadora Democrática.

In spite of allegations of a fraudulent voting process, the Carter Center certified the election as fair.

After 2003, Chávez had the luxury of higher petroleum prices and no major disruptions, and he was able to deliver some of the benefits he had promised the poor. The government established missions to deliver health services, literacy programs, job training, and other services to the barrios. The most controversial was the Misión Barrio Adentro, which used Cuban doctors to deliver public health care in exchange for lower prices for petroleum purchased by Cuba. A few private estates were seized to expand the agrarian reform program. Chávez encouraged the growth and expansion of Círculos Bolivarianos to promote grassroots participation in the formation and discussion of public policy.

Although Chávez had triumphed in fair elections and had begun to provide real benefits to the poor, tensions within the country and between Venezuela and the United States remained high. Washington objected to Chávez's purchase of military equipment from Russia and held him responsible for several popular movements in the hemisphere, including the forced resignation of the Bolivian president in June 2005. Little firm evidence was offered in Venezuela or elsewhere for many of the accusations against him. Nonetheless, it was evident that he relished confrontation more than conciliation, and he did little to reassure his domestic or international enemies. Petroleum wealth afforded him that luxury.

IMPACTS

Hugo Chávez's rule differs more in style than in content from those of previous Venezuelan regimes. He wants to manage the petroleum economy for the good of the nation at large. In that goal, he resembles the Punto Fijo leaders of the 1960s and 1970s more than those of the last twenty years who embraced neo-liberal principles without applying them judiciously. Chávez's personal style and energy, the collapse of the traditional Venezuelan parties, the petroleum wealth, and the international debate on neo-liberalism have rendered him highly visible both nationally and internationally. Only the future can determine whether his "third way" between capitalism and Socialism will become a model or be reversed as an anachronism.

Chávez has had a major impact in five areas. First, he has introduced a radical and combative style and rhetoric in domestic politics and in diplomacy. His attacks on the Venezuelan elite and the United States have contributed to an unprecedented social cleavage in Venezuela and, to a lesser extent, to tensions abroad. Venezuelan political divisions today highly correlate with economic class, and the legacy of bitterness bodes poorly for an easy return to multiclass parties or politics. Internationally, his revival of OPEC's influence, his active personal diplomacy, and his fiery rhetoric have emboldened many in the Third World to challenge both globalization and United States dominance. At the same time, Chávez's multipolar world remains a dream, and poor countries often rationally choose to placate Washington rather than to ally with other weak nations.

Second, Chávez values the community over the individual and has modestly revived the role of the state in the Venezuelan economy. The constitution rejects privatization of oil, allows for an active land reform policy, posits the necessity for the state to control basic services and resources, and asserts the state's responsibility to care for and protect the poor. None of these principles is entirely new to Venezuela. Arguably, most Venezuelans share Chávez's belief that a petrostate has a special obligation to distribute the wealth that derives from that resource.

Third, Chávez has contributed to a reconstruction of Venezuelan heroes and nationalism in which rebels, rural folk, and people of color play a major role. The cult of Bolívar is nothing new to Venezuela, but seldom has his example been used so explicitly as a model for contemporary initiatives and to inspire hemispheric cooperation. Ezequiel Zamora, a *llanero* (a man from the plains, the cattle country of Venezuela), rebelled against the wealthy and the literate. Maisanta, another *llanero* and an ancestor of Chávez's, rebelled against Gómez's government and died in prison. These men previously had been considered primitive caudillos in contrast to people like Rómulo Betancourt and other middle-class urban students who formed the Generation of 1928. The new public history exalts Venezuela's uniqueness and revolutionary past, and it serves to give pride to many of the poor and persons of color.

Fourth, the commitment to participatory democracy has been enshrined in the constitution and the Círculos Bolivarianos. When the traditional parties dissolved, Chávez chose to go directly to the people rather than to form a new party. He has been much demonized for this, especially in the United States, but in the twenty-first century he has good company in his evading the constraints of representative democracy. A popular referendum removed a California governor from office, and popular demonstrations have forced the resignation of presidents in Ecuador and Bolivia. These events have been extraordinary, and the Venezuelan challenge will be to keep people educated and involved in public policies on a regular basis.

Finally, Chávez and his constitution have contributed to a stronger and more authoritarian presidency in Venezuela, with few checks on his actions. Military men hold many public and cabinet positions, giving them an enhanced political role. If Chávez completes his term in office and wins and completes a second term, he will have been in power for thir-teen years. Can this new "democratic caesar" spawn an authentically popular and participatory democracy? If Chávez can master that challenge, his impact will indeed be long-lasting, and he will have constructed a true revolution.

PEOPLE AND ORGANIZATIONS

Acción Democrática (AD)

Social Democratic Party founded in 1941 by Rómulo Betancourt. Alternated with COPEI in power between 1959 and 1999 under the aegis of the Punto Fijo agreement.

Arias Cárdenas, Francisco (Born 1950)

Military officer in MBR-200 with Chávez. Participated in 1992 coup. Later was elected governor of Zulia and then served in Caldera's administration. He ran against Chávez in the election of 2000 and came in second.

Caldera, Rafael (Born 1916)

Founder of COPEI in 1946 and signer of the Punto Fijo Pact of 1958. President from 1969 to 1973 and again from 1994 to 1998, although the second time as a political independent.

Caracazo

February 1989 Caracas riots protesting President Carlos Andrés Pérez's neo-liberal reforms. The National Guard and the military suppressed the outbreak, and hundreds of people were killed.

Carmona, Pedro (Born 1941)

Head of the business association Fedecámaras who was named president for two days after the April 2002 coup that briefly removed Chávez.

Carter Center

Founded by former U.S. president Jimmy Carter, the center was influential in mediating between Chávez and his opposition, and especially in certifying as legitimate the August 2004 recall referendum.

Chávez, Hugo (Born 1954)

Born on July 28, 1954, to two schoolteachers in the *llanos* state of Barinas, he entered the Caracas Military Academy in 1971. While involved in a counterinsurgency campaign, he became sympathetic with the guerrillas. He also admired military reformers like General Juan Velasco Alvarado of Peru and General Omar Torrijos of Panama. In 1982, he joined a group of officers, the MBR-200, to spearhead a radical reform movement. In February 1992, his group launched a failed military attack on the government. On television, Chávez urged his colleagues to surrender their arms since the rebellion had failed *por ahora* (for now). Released from prison in 1996, Chávez announced his candidacy for the presidency. He was elected in 1998 and again in 2000 (for a six-year term under the new 1999 constitution), and won a recall referendum in August 2004.

Círculos Bolivarianos (Bolivarian Circles)

Popular grassroots organizations that encourage participatory democracy.

Committee of Independent Electoral Political Organization (Comité de Organización Política Electoral Independiente—COPEI)

Christian Democratic Party founded by Rafael Caldera in 1946. Alternated in power with Acción Democrática between 1959 and 1999.

Confederation of Venezuelan Workers (Confederación de Trabajadores de Venezuela—CTV)

A labor confederation founded in 1936, representing somewhat less than one in five workers and almost entirely dominated by Acción Democrática. The CTV opposed Chávez and joined Fedecámaras, oil company executives, and the Coordinadora Democrática in strikes and protests to try to force Chávez out of office.

Constitution of 1999

Drawn up by the Chavista Constitutional Assembly in 1999 to replace the 1961 charter, it increased presidential authority, state control of the national oil company, and state intervention in the economy. It also introduced the concept of participatory democracy, provided for rights of indigenous peoples, and renamed the country the Bolivarian Republic of Venezuela.

Coordinadora Democrática

The umbrella organization that united the disparate groups supporting the coup of 2002 and the recall referendum of 2004.

Fedecámaras (Federation of Chambers of Commerce and Production—Federación de Cámaras de Comercio y Producción)

Federation of businesses and industries dating from the 1940s. Opposed Chávez.

La Causa R

Radical leftist party formed in the 1970s by former guerrillas. Gained control of the Guayana area through organization of steelworkers. The party subsequently divided between those who supported Chávez and those who opposed him.

Miquilena, Luis (Born 1919)

Union leader and founder in the 1940s of a non-Stalinist Communist Party. Considered one of Chávez's key ideological advisers since the 1980s, he had held several positions under Chávez, including minister of the interior and president of the Constitutional Assembly. He turned against Chávez at the time of the attempted coup in 2002.

Missions

Programs to deliver literacy, job training, and health care to the poor. Misión Barrio Adentro employed Cuban doctors to deliver health care to the poor.

Movimiento Al Socialismo (MAS)

Venezuelan Socialist Party founded in 1971 by former guerrillas. Journalist José Vicente Rangel became their presidential candidate several times. Many supporters of MAS, including Rangel, joined Chávez, but other prominent leftists opposed him.

Movimiento Bolivariano Revolucionario-200 (MBR-200)

Chávez's military lodge formed in 1982 with a plan to renew

the country. It was named for the 200th anniversary of Bolívar's birth in 1783 and carried out the 1992 coup attempt. Since Venezuelan law forbade the use of Bolívar's name in political parties, Chávez changed the name to Fifth Republic Movement (MVR) for the 1998 election.

National Constitutional Assembly (ANC)

Chavistas dominated the elected convention that wrote a new constitution in 1999. Neighborhood groups, environmental groups, indigenous groups, and similar organizations had considerable influence. A popular referendum in December 1999 approved the constitution.

National Endowment for Democracy (NED)

U.S. semipublic organization formed in 1983 to fund and encourage political opposition in countries judged to be authoritarian. NED has funded Chávez's opposition, and Chávez has accused those who received NED funds of treason.

Organization of Petroleum Exporting Countries (OPEC)

Formed in 1960 at AD's initiative with the goal of encouraging oil-producing developing nations to act together in setting production quotas and prices. Chávez has been a strong supporter of OPEC.

PDVSA (Petróleos de Venezuela, Sociedad Anónima)

Venezuelan national oil company formed in 1976, when the industry was nationalized. It is the largest company in Latin America, and some advocate its privatization. Chávez reaffirmed state ownership and brought the company more firmly under the control of the Ministry of Mines and Energy, but he had to fire thousands of executives in the process.

Pérez, Carlos Andrés (Born 1922)

AD president during the oil bonanza of the 1970s, which financed populist programs and an expansionist foreign policy. Pérez was re-elected in 1988, but his neo-liberal austerity measures set off the riots called the *Caracazo* in February 1989. The congress impeached and removed Pérez from office in May 1993.

Plan Bolívar

Launched in February 1999, the project assigned the armed forces to work on improvement of infrastructure and other public works designed especially to fight poverty.

Polo Patriótico (PP)

Political coalition that supported Chávez's candidacy in 1998.

Punto Fijo Pact

Political pact made by AD, COPEI, URD (Unión Republicana Democrática), labor, business, and the military in 1958 to pledge commitment to the rules of the democratic game. It launched the representative democratic system that lasted until 1999. The traditional parties' inability to cope with the economic crises of the 1980s and 1990s led to a popular rejection of all that *puntofijismo* represented.

Rangel, José Vicente (Born 1929)

Leftist journalist and politician who was a MAS presidential candidate several times. One of Chávez's primary advisers, he has held the positions of minister of foreign relations, minister of defense, and vice president.

Rodríguez Araque, Alí (Born 1938)

Former guerrilla and labor lawyer who joined the La Causa R party in Guayana state. Under Caldera, he headed the congressional committee on energy and mines. He broke with his party to become Chávez's main petroleum adviser. Served as minister of mines and energy, secretary general of OPEC, president of PDVSA, and foreign minister.

Rodríguez de Chávez, Marisabel (Born 1964)

Chávez's wife, a former newspaper columnist, who has been politically active. Elected to the Constitutional Assembly, she has been an advocate for children's rights, especially those of street children.

Súmate

Súmate means "join up." Under the leadership of María Corina Machado, this organization, part of the more general Coordinadora Democrática, helped spearhead the petition drive for the August 2004 recall referendum. Funded by the NED, Machado was accused of treason by Chávez's government. She became a cause celebre in Washington, and in June 2005 had an audience with President George W. Bush in the White House.

Judith Ewell

See Also Armed Forces, Revolution, and Counter-Revolution; Cuban Revolution; Documentaries of Revolution; Spanish American Revolutions of Independence

References and Further Readings

Blanco Muñoz, Agustín (interviewer). 1998. *Habla el comandante* (Hugo Chávez). Caracas: Universidad Central de Venezuela.

Buxton, Julia. 2001. *The Failure of Political Reform in Venezuela.* Aldershot, England: Ashgate.

Canache, Damarys. 2002. *Venezuela: Public Opinion and Protest in a Fragile Democracy.* Miami, FL: North and South Center Press/Lynne Rienner.

Coppage, Michael. 1994. *Strong Parties and Lame Ducks: Presidential Partyarchy and Factionalism in Venezuela.* Stanford, CA: Stanford University Press.

Coronil, Fernando. 1997. *The Magical State: Nature, Money, and Modernity in Venezuela.* Chicago: University of Chicago Press.

Ellner, Steve, and Daniel Hellinger, eds. 2003.*Venezuelan Politics in the Chávez Era: Class, Polarization, and Conflict.* Boulder, CO: Lynne Rienner.

Gott, Richard. 2000. *In the Shadow of the Liberator: Hugo Chávez and the Transformation of Venezuela.* London: Verso.

Hellinger, Daniel. 2003. "Political Overview: The Breakdown of *Puntofijismo* and the Rise of *Chavismo.*" Pp. 27–53 in *Venezuelan Politics in the Chávez Era: Class Polarization, and Conflict,* edited by Steve Ellner and Daniel Hellinger. Boulder, CO: Lynne Rienner.

Hillman, Richard S. 1994. *Democracy for the Privileged: Crisis and Transition in Venezuela.* Boulder, CO.: Lynne Rienner.

Karl, Terry Lynn. 1997. *The Paradox of Plenty: Oil Booms and Petro-States.* Berkeley: University of California Press.

Latin American Perspectives (2005) 141, vol. 32, no. 2 (March) and 142, vol. 32, no. 3 (May) (two entire issues devoted to Chávez).

Márquez, Patricia, and Ramón Piñango, eds. 2004. *Realidades y nuevos caminos en esta Venezuela.* Caracas: Ediciones del Instituto de Estudios Superiores de Administración.

McCauthan, Michael. 2004. *The Battle of Venezuela.* London: Latin America Bureau.

McCoy, Jennifer, and David Myers, eds. 2004. *The Unraveling of Representative Democracy in Venezuela.* Baltimore, MD: Johns Hopkins University Press.

United States Congress. Senate Committee on Foreign Relations. Subcommittee on Western Hemisphere, Peace Corps, and Narcotics Affairs. *The State of Democracy in Venezuela. Hearing.* 108th Congress, 2nd session, June 24, 2004.

Wilbert, Gregory, ed. 2003. *Coup against Chávez in Venezuela: The Best International Reports of What Really Happened in April 2002.* Caracas: Fundación Venezolano para la Justicia Global.

Wright, Winthrop R. 1990. *Café Con Leche: Race, Class, and National Image in Venezuela:* Austin: University of Texas Press.

Vietnamese Revolution

CHRONOLOGY

111 B.C.	China conquers the Vietnamese (the Viet people of the south). Most Vietnamese crave freedom from Chinese rule and repeatedly launch rebellions to regain independence. But over time, the Vietnamese adopt aspects of the Chinese Confucian cultural, political, and social systems.
40–43 A.D.	The Trung sisters organize and lead a rebellion against the Chinese, which forces the Chinese to temporarily withdraw. When the Chinese return and defeat the Vietnamese, the Trung sisters, rather than surrender, commit suicide. They are commemorated thereafter as heroes of the Vietnamese people and legendary examples of women leaders and soldiers.
939	The Vietnamese successfully rebel against the Chinese, resulting in an end to Chinese occupation.
1847–1883	In a series of violent conflicts, French forces defeat the Vietnamese in stages generally moving from south to north. The French rule Vietnam in three sections, along with the neighboring countries of Cambodia and Laos. They refer to all five territories collectively as their colony of French Indochina.
1911	Ho Chi Minh leaves Vietnam as a worker on a French ship that visits countries in Asia and Africa. He experiences colonial subjugation and exploitation on a global scale. Arriving in Boston, he later makes his way to New York, where he lives for months. There he is favorably impressed by how Asian immigrants are treated in the United States, where they are eventually granted citizenship and the right to vote. He views the United States as a nation created through a rebellion against an imperialist power, Great Britain. In September of 1945 he will declare Vietnam

an independent nation using words virtually identical to those of the U.S. Declaration of Independence.

1919   At the World War I peace conference in France, Ho Chi Minh is not allowed to present a proposal for Vietnamese local self-rule (autonomy) to the victorious Allied leaders. This leads Ho to conclude that Vietnam might have to be liberated through a violent struggle.

1920–1925   Ho Chi Minh, who had joined the French Socialist Party because its members advocated the most favorable policies toward France's colonial subject peoples, sides with those Socialists who, inspired by Lenin's revolution in Russia, split away to form the French Communist Party. Ho travels to Russia to learn about the Bolshevik Revolution. When the Soviet Union sends help to Sun Yat-Sen's republican revolutionary forces in south China, Ho Chi Minh joins the aid mission as a translator. But his main purpose is to organize Vietnamese patriotic exiles in south China into a revolutionary movement.

1925   Ho Chi Minh holds seminars on Vietnamese history, nationalism, and Marxist and Leninist ideas among young patriotic Vietnamese exiles in south China and with them creates the Revolutionary Youth League of Vietnam (Viet Nam Thanh Nien Cach Menh Dong Chi Hoi), an organization that will lead to the founding of the Vietnamese Communist Party in 1930.

1927   The Vietnamese Nationalist Party (Viet Nam Quoc Dan Dang, VNQDD), a non-Communist, pro-independence revolutionary organization inspired by Sun Yat-Sen's Chinese Guo Min Dang, is created. Its leaders plan violent attacks to drive the French out but generally fail to propose meaningful reforms to help Vietnam's poor peasants.

1930   Ho Chi Minh and other Vietnamese found the Vietnamese Communist Party (VCP—soon renamed the Indochinese Communist Party, ICP) in Hong Kong. From the VCP's inception, its leaders have two main goals:

anti-imperialism, freeing Vietnam from foreign control, and anti-feudalism, accomplishing a socioeconomic revolution by redistributing resources, including land, to the poor, in particular to Vietnam's large majority of people who are poor peasants.

The VNQDD (Vietnamese Nationalist Party) stages a mutiny of Vietnamese soldiers in the French-led Vietnamese colonial army at Yen Bay. Within a few days, the French crush the mutiny and arrest hundreds of members of the VNQDD, sentencing scores to death or life imprisonment. The significance and effectiveness of the VNQDD, a largely urban organization with limited support in rural areas, is greatly reduced by the French repression.

1940   France is defeated by Germany. Japanese forces occupy Vietnam to exploit its resources and use it for military purposes, but temporarily permit French authorities and armed forces in Vietnam to carry out their colonial functions.

1941   Ho Chi Minh, Vo Nguyen Giap, and other Vietnamese revolutionaries found the Communist-led nationalist movement, the Viet Minh (Viet Nam Doc Lap Dong Minh or League for the Independence of Vietnam).

1945   The Viet Minh and other allied pro-independence groups stage insurrections in over sixty Vietnamese cities in Vietnam's "August Revolution" (August 18–28), and on September 2 Ho Chi Minh proclaims Vietnam's Declaration of Independence at Hanoi.

1946–1954   The Franco-Vietnam or French Indochina War breaks out. The U.S. aids France while China aids the Viet Minh. Much of the French public turns against the war.

1954   In early May, thousands of elite French troops are surrounded by Viet Minh forces at the town of Dien Bien Phu and forced to surrender. The Geneva Peace Conference temporarily divides Vietnam into northern and southern sections with the understanding that in 1956 an election will be held through-out Vietnam for a new government for the entire unified country.

1954–1959   Ngo Dinh Diem, from a wealthy Catholic Vietnamese family, returns from the United States to Saigon to be the new anti-Communist leader of what the U.S. government calls South Vietnam. U.S. military advisers and CIA personnel help build an army for South Vietnam, the Army of the Republic of Vietnam or ARVN, initially from the ranks of the Vietnamese who served on the side of the French during the French Indochina War. Diem suppresses members of the Vietnamese Communist Party and supporters of the Viet Minh left behind in the south and refuses to allow the nationwide election called for in the Geneva Accords to select a government for a unified Vietnam.

1960   The National Liberation Front of South Vietnam (NLF) is formed as a successor, in effect, to the Viet Minh in the southern half of Vietnam. Similar to the Viet Minh, it is an alliance of nationalist groups under the leadership of the Vietnamese Communist Party. It is organized to fight the Diem-led, U.S.-backed Saigon regime in order to unify Vietnam. The Saigon and the U.S. governments refer to the NLF and its armed units, the People's Liberation Armed Forces, as the Viet Cong (Viet Communists).

1963   Diem is widely blamed for persecuting Buddhist monks opposed to his government; he is also accused of incompetent leadership viewed as leading to a probable victory for the Communist-led National Liberation Front of South Vietnam. On November 1, he is overthrown in a coup, approved by U.S. government authorities and led by officers in his own army. The next day he was murdered.

On November 22, President John F. Kennedy is assassinated in Dallas, Texas, and Lyndon Johnson replaces him as president of the United States.

1964   President Johnson accuses North Vietnamese naval forces of attacking U.S. ships in the Gulf of Tonkin in August. In response, the U.S.

Congress passes the Gulf of Tonkin Resolution, which gives the president authority to take actions necessary to protect U.S. personnel in Southeast Asia. This, in effect, gives President Johnson and later President Nixon the authority to conduct the Vietnam War.

1964–1973   Hundreds of thousands of U.S. troops arrive in Vietnam to combat Communist-led forces.

1968   In contrast to public statements by U.S. military leaders that the U.S. is winning the war, Communist-led forces simultaneously attack scores of South Vietnamese cities beginning on January 31, Tet, the Vietnamese New Year. The Tet offensive convinces many Americans that their leaders have been lying to them about the nature of the war or are incompetent, and that the war cannot be won and should not have been fought.

1973   The four parties to the conflict, the United States, the U.S.-backed Saigon regime of South Vietnam, North Vietnam, and its ally, the NLF of South Vietnam, conclude peace agreements intended to end the war and provide guidelines for a possible peaceful reunification of Vietnam.

1974   U.S. president Nixon is forced to resign or face impeachment and removal from office over the issue of obstruction of justice in the Watergate Affair.

1975   Communist-led forces launch an offensive in March, and Saigon surrenders on April 30, bringing an end to the war and resulting in the reunification of Vietnam under Communist leadership. Unified Vietnam is called the Socialist Republic of Vietnam (SRV) and Saigon is renamed Ho Chi Minh City.

1994–1995   The United States permits U.S. businesses to trade with and operate in Vietnam and establishes diplomatic relations with Vietnam.

INTRODUCTION

In 111 B.C., the Chinese conquered Vietnam and began an occupation that, despite desperate and heroic rebellions, such as that led by the Trung sisters in 40–43 A.D., would last until 939, when they were finally forced to withdraw. But Vietnam could not retain her hard-won independence. France, in 1847, began a series of wars against Vietnam that ended in 1883, when the last Viet territories fell. For decades young Vietnamese sought to create the means to liberate their nation from foreign control. The effort was difficult, dangerous, and sometimes led to deadly conflict among the Vietnamese themselves. In 1930 Ho Chi Minh and a small group of associates founded the Vietnamese Communist Party. This organization would, in 1941, create and lead a much larger nationalist movement, the Viet Minh, that through eight years of brutal conflict would finally force the French to withdraw. But only after a much more destructive conflict, the war with the United States, would the struggle over Vietnamese independence and unification come to an end.

BACKGROUND: CULTURE AND HISTORY

Vietnam is a long, narrow country of approximately 329,566 square km (127,246 square miles). China lies to the north and Laos and Cambodia to the west. The country's coastline borders the Gulf of Tonkin, the South China Sea, and the Gulf of Thailand. About 85 percent of the country's residents are ethnic Vietnamese. The other 15 percent include people of Cambodian or Chinese ancestry and members of tribal groups often located in the generally lightly populated highland areas. Most of the ethnic Vietnamese are concentrated in the relatively fertile lowland regions that make up about 20 percent of Vietnam's territory, including the river delta areas, especially the Red River Delta in the north and the Mekong Delta in the south (DeFronzo 1996, 119–120).

Before 111 B.C., Vietnam was a relatively loosely organized society that lacked a strong central government. But that year the Chinese began an occupation of Vietnam that lasted nearly continuously until 939 A.D., when the Vietnamese were able to force the Chinese out. During the more than one thousand years of Chinese occupation, the Vietnamese adopted aspects of the cultural, social, and political systems of the Chinese, including establishing an emperor similar to that in China as well as the Confucian examination procedures for selecting state administrators. The Vietnamese also adopted Chinese clothing styles. But most Vietnamese retained their own language and a fierce desire for independence from foreign control. The Vietnamese rebelled repeatedly against the Chinese, including the briefly successful 40 A.D. rebellion led by the legendary Trung sisters.

Modern European contact with the Vietnamese may have begun with a visit by Portuguese seamen to Vietnam in 1516. The Portuguese, too occupied with many far-flung colonial territories and trading interests in Asia, Africa, and South America to economically exploit and Christianize all of them, began taking French priests with them to Vietnam to help propagate Catholicism. The French priests periodically returned to France with stories of Vietnam and the resources and products available there. French merchants established trade with the Vietnamese. France's armed forces also developed an interest in Vietnam, in particular the French navy, attracted by the possibility of establishing one or more bases there in Vietnam's deepwater harbors to increase its operational effectiveness in the region. The activities of these three institutions led to France becoming the major European power involved with Vietnam. By 1847, the Vietnamese government became alarmed at the number of Vietnamese converting to Catholicism and took measures to limit missionary activity. This action precipitated a brief military conflict between France and Vietnam, which the French won.

France went to war against Vietnam repeatedly from 1858 to 1883. Progressively, starting with Vietnam's southern provinces, France gained control of all of Vietnam by 1884, as well as the neighboring countries of Laos and Cambodia. France divided Vietnam into three separate parts.

The southernmost area of Vietnam, which the French called Cochin China and which included Saigon and the Mekong Delta, was ruled directly by French administrators. Since France held this territory longer than it did any other part of Vietnam, French influence was strongest there. The other two sections of Vietnam were technically "protectorates," ruled indirectly by France through local Confucian officials whom, in reality, the French controlled. One of these parts, the long middle section of Vietnam that included the old imperial capital city of Hue, was called Annam by the French. Annam, meaning "the pacified south," was an expression used in previous times by the Chinese for Vietnam and suggested that the Vietnamese were a conquered, subject people. Many Vietnamese disliked being referred to as "Annamites" instead of Vietnamese. The French called the northernmost section of Vietnam, which included the cities of Hanoi and Haiphong and the Red River Delta, Tonkin. France designated Cochin China, Annam, Tonkin, Laos, and Cambodia the components of their French Indochina colony.

Many Frenchmen believed they were benefiting the people of Vietnam by bringing them Christianity, French culture, products and trade, economic development, and aspects of modern technology. The French presence not only politically transformed Vietnam from an independent nation into a French colony; it also changed Vietnam economically and culturally.

A number of the economic changes brought about by the French occurred or were accelerated under the administration of Paul Doumer, the French governor-general of Indochina from 1897–1902. His policies helped generate profits for France and French investors and colonists. Doumer

French Indochina showing the three colonial subdivisions of Vietnam (Cochinchina, Annam, and Tonkin), the Red River Delta in the north, and the Mekong Delta in the south, and several major Vietnamese cities including Hanoi, Haiphong, Hue (the old imperial capital), and Saigon (now Ho Chi Minh City), along with the countries of Cambodia and Laos and their respective capitals, Phnom Penh and Vientiane.

promoted the building of roads, bridges, and villages. His policies also expanded the lucrative sale of opium to the Vietnamese. A general French strategy was to transform the economy of Vietnam from one based on self-sufficient farming into to one that could generate a large number of materials and goods for the international market. The French developed iron, tin, and coal mines, typically in the Tonkin region, as well as some industry there to take advantage of the nearby mineral resources. Hundreds of rubber plantations operated in Cochin China and Cambodia, generating this valuable industrial substance for the world market. French hydraulic engineering projects brought water levels in much of the Mekong Delta, much larger than the Red River Delta, under control for rice cultivation, greatly expanding the amount of rice Vietnam exported for sale to other nations.

French policies tended to increase the concentration of land ownership, so that during the 1930s an estimated 70 percent of peasants either had no land or lacked sufficient land to grow the food needed to meet household needs (Karnow 1983, 117). Many of these people were forced to work in mines, on rubber plantations, or as laborers or sharecroppers on rice plantations. A minority of Vietnamese, usually favored by initial resources or fortunate opportunities, and a number of French settlers and investors became wealthy by selling Vietnam's resources and products internationally, while many more Vietnamese found that, instead of being able to grow their own food, their livelihood was based on the wages they could earn working for French enterprises or for other Vietnamese, and that these wages were in turn tied to the price for Vietnam's products on the world market. Both economic inequality and the hardships faced by a large number of peasants tended to increase.

The French established schools for thousands of Vietnamese, generally the children of the country's political, economic, or educated elites seeking for their children the knowledge and means to flourish within French-dominated Vietnam and in some cases motivated to learn the secrets of France's strength relative to Vietnam. France intended to generate a new Vietnamese elite that shared its language and culture, an admiration for the achievements of its civilization, and gratitude for the benefits it brought to Vietnam. If successful, Vietnam's upper class would become culturally and psychologically French and politically loyal to France (and possibly become citizens of France as well as Vietnam), and thus serve as the mechanism through which France could control the mass of Vietnam's people and protect access to its resources. By 1937, 2,555 Vietnamese had received French citizenship and 1,474 of these were residents of Cochin China, which then had less than a quarter of Vietnam's population (DeFronzo 1996, 127).

Politically, France not only controlled Vietnam through elements of the Vietnamese elite, but also through its military units and the Vietnamese colonial army it built. The French recruited thousands of Vietnamese to serve in a French-controlled colonial militia that functioned not only to keep order, but also to assist the French in subduing any rebellious Vietnamese. But France's policies also began to generate leaders for future movements of resistance to its rule. Vietnamese educated in French history of necessity learned about the French Revolution and its slogan of "liberty, equality, and fraternity" and that, from their point of view, the French were contradicting their own revolution's ideals in the way they treated the Vietnamese people.

CONTEXT AND PROCESS OF REVOLUTION

Vietnamese resistance movements to French rule developed in a series of phases. During the 1884–1900 period, some Confucian scholars, representing the pre-occupation political system, tried to stage protests or even revolts against French occupation. But these were usually local rebellions relatively easy for the French to suppress. Also, participation in these rebellions was limited by the fact that the old Confucianist system had proven unable to protect Vietnam from foreign conquest and was itself repressive. The character of opposition to foreign domination changed during 1900–1925 under the leadership of figures such as Phan Boi Chau (1867–1940) and Phan Chu Trinh (1872–1926). Though trained in the Confucian tradition, both of these scholars realized that new approaches were necessary to successfully throw off colonialism, and both advocated that young Vietnamese learn from France and other advanced nations the knowledge, technologies, and forms of organization and government that made these societies powerful. Then this new information could be used to strengthen the Vietnamese people so that they could free themselves. But whereas Phan Chu Trinh advocated nonviolent resistance to French domination and convincing the French to cooperate in eventually granting independence to Vietnam, Phan Boi Chau felt that violent methods were justified and might be necessary to free Vietnam from foreign control.

The work of these two scholars helped prepare young Vietnamese intellectuals to create modern pro-independence organizations during the 1925–1940 period.

The organizers of the new independence movements, often the children of Vietnam's elite families and Confucian scholars, had typically experienced Western education, either in schools operated by the French in Vietnam or in France or other countries. They tended to support the establishment of a republican form of government in Vietnam as opposed to a Confucianist monarchy and often blended aspects of foreign revolutionary ideologies with Vietnamese nationalism. The Vietnamese Nationalist Party (VNQDD) was established in 1927 and drew members primarily from among the 10 percent or so of Vietnamese living in urban areas, especially students and non-manual workers such as teachers, office clerks, and journalists. The party also secretly recruited Vietnamese soldiers who were employed in the French-controlled Vietnamese colonial army. The VNQDD's leaders patterned their organization, in part, after Chinese revolutionary Sun Yat-Sen's Guo Min Dang (National People's Party). However, the VNQDD leaders generally did not act as if they were really committed to a social revolution to benefit the vast majority of Vietnam's population who were poor peasants. As the VNQDD grew in membership, it remained mainly an urban nationalist movement that lacked a significant support network in the countryside. This meant that when the French moved to repress the VNQDD in towns and cities, its members had few places to find refuge inside Vietnam.

VNQDD leaders hoped that violent attacks, including assassinations, against French officials would inspire patriotic resistance and encourage the Vietnamese people to rise up, drive the occupiers out, and free the country. In February 1930, VNQDD supporters within units of the French-controlled Vietnamese colonial army staged an uprising at the town of Yen Bay. But other Vietnamese soldiers, with a few exceptions, did not or were not able to follow their example. The French quickly crushed the rebellion. More than 1,000 VNQDD party members were arrested, approximately eighty were sentenced to death, and one hundred to life in prison (DeFronzo 1996, 130). This repression effectively limited the future significance of the movement. Some VNQDD survivors joined Marxist-oriented groups and later the Communist-led independence movement. Others escaped to China or Japan. These countries sponsored resurrected versions of the VNQDD, which were viewed by many Vietnamese as manifestations of foreign interests.

In contrast to the limited effectiveness and fate of the VNQDD, the Vietnamese Communist Party (VCP) would prove far more successful. A major founder of the VCP and the main leader of the Vietnamese Revolution was Ho Chi Minh (1890–1969). Ho was born in rebellious Nghe An Province in north central Vietnam. His father was a prominent local scholar, and both his parents opposed French rule. At birth his parents named him Nguyen Sinh Cung. When he was eleven and entering adolescence, his father, following a Vietnamese custom, renamed him Nguyen Tat Thanh. But throughout his life, Ho used dozens of aliases. From 1919 to 1940, he was often known as Nguyen Ai Quoc (Nguyen Who Loves His Country, also translated as Nguyen the Patriot). But from 1941 on, the world knew him as Ho Chi Minh (He Who Enlightens) (Duiker 2000, 248–249). Ho's mother died in 1901, shortly after giving birth to her fourth child, and his father was eventually dismissed from his government posi-

Ho Chi Minh, founder of the Indochina Communist Party in 1930 and president of the Democratic Republic of Vietnam from 1945 to 1969. (Library of Congress)

tion for harshly punishing an influential person. Ho himself was expelled from school just before his eighteenth birthday for acting as a translator conveying the concerns of protesting peasants to French authorities.

In 1911, at the age of twenty-one, Ho left Vietnam as a worker on a French ship, not to return to his country for thirty years. He traveled to other places in Asia and to Africa and witnessed European colonialism, exploitation, and abuse of indigenous peoples. These experiences later drew him to the Russian revolutionary Lenin's analysis of capitalist imperialism. According to Lenin, imperialism involved not only using the wealth and labor power of less developed peoples to enrich the societies and ruling classes of Europe, but also making the working classes of these societies beneficiaries and participants in the exploitation of colonized people around the world. In Lenin's view, Socialist revolutions to empower poor people would tend to first take place in exploited, less-developed societies such as Vietnam, not in the advanced capitalist nations as Marx had originally predicted. In 1912, Ho visited the United States for several months, where he worked at various jobs, apparently briefly in Boston and then in New York City. He admired the fact that Asian immigrants to America could enjoy rights, eventually even citizenship and the ability to vote, which the Vietnamese could not exercise in their own country.

Ho studied American society and was captivated by the U.S. Declaration of Independence, which he viewed as a revolutionary and anti-imperialist proclamation directed against the oppression of a great power, Britain. Later, on September 2, 1945, Ho would use the words of the American Declaration of Independence to proclaim the independence of Vietnam from France and look to the United States for support.

Ho then traveled to Great Britain, where he apparently lived from 1913 to 1917, working for a time as an assistant pastry chef at the Carlton Hotel. Most likely in December 1917, Ho arrived in France, where, during World War I, tens of thousands of Vietnamese worked in French industries. Supporting himself through several jobs, he joined the Socialist Party, which at the time was the French political party advocating the most rights for France's colonial subject peoples. When in 1920 the French Socialist Party split over whether to support Lenin's Bolshevik policies in Russia, Ho, an admirer of Lenin's concern for the plight of exploited colonized peoples and his analysis of imperialism, sided with the Socialists who created the new French Communist Party.

In 1924, Ho journeyed to Moscow to learn the methods of the successful Bolshevik revolutionaries. There he participated in the Communist International (COMINTERN), a multinational organization established in the Soviet Union in 1919 to foster Communist-led revolutions in other countries. Soon Ho joined the Soviet aid mission to help Sun Yat-Sen's Republic of China in south China. There in 1925, with other patriotic Vietnamese exiles, he organized the Revolutionary Youth League of Vietnam, a forerunner of the Vietnamese Communist Party. In Hong Kong in February of 1930, Ho and other Vietnamese revolutionaries established the Vietnamese Communist Party. In October 1930, the Party was renamed the Indochinese Communist Party (ICP) to comply with the COMINTERN's policy, at the time, of adopting party titles that matched the names of colonies. Much later in November 1945, in a likely attempt to lessen hostility from the French, party members announced that they were dissolving the ICP, although in reality it apparently continued to operate in secret. In 1951, it publicly resurfaced as the Vietnamese Workers' Party (VWP). And in 1976, after the end of the war, it once again adopted the name Vietnamese Communist Party. In this article, for the sake of simplicity, we will use the expression Vietnamese Communist Party and assume the continuous existence of the VCP from 1930 on.

From its creation, the Communist Party advocated two major goals: *anti-imperialism,* freeing Vietnam from foreign control, and *anti-feudalism,* bringing about a socioeconomic revolution to redistribute resources toward Vietnam's poor majority. At times, the party's leaders emphasized the goal of freeing Vietnam first before carrying out a social revolution. At other times, priority was given to rallying support for social revolution. Ho reportedly always advocated placing priority on nationalism, the goal of making Vietnam once again a truly independent nation. He apparently had at least two major reasons for this strategy. First, Ho felt that giving priority to freeing Vietnam from foreign control would unite many patriotic Vietnamese of all social classes in the revolutionary effort. Second, since the affluent Vietnamese classes, including the big landowners, relied on foreign military assistance to maintain their privileges and suppress the large majority of Vietnam's people who were poor, independence would facilitate a social revolution. Without foreign support, Vietnam's wealthy minority would not be able to withstand the majority's demand for a redistribution of resources, including land.

Ho was arrested by British authorities in Hong Kong in 1931 and hospitalized, suffering, reportedly, from tuberculosis. Later he managed to leave British custody. For the next several years Ho is thought to have visited a number of countries, including China, Thailand, and Russia, often traveling on foot, in his efforts to organize Vietnamese exiles to support the revolutionary movement to liberate Vietnam. When the Chinese civil war between Mao Zedong's Communist-led forces and General Chiang Kai Shek's armies temporarily came to a halt as the two sides formed an alliance to fight the Japanese in 1937, Ho and other Vietnamese Communists believed, not always accurately, that they could more openly pursue their revolutionary goals in south China near the border with Vietnam.

France's defeat by Germany in the summer of 1940 led to the creation of the Vichy French government, which technically controlled France's overseas colonies and often appeared willing to collaborate with Nazi Germany and its allies. The Vichy government consented to Germany's request to allow Japanese troops to occupy French Indochina. Japan wanted to deploy troops there in order to cut off a possible southern supply route to Chinese forces, to use the region as a staging area for further military operations in nearby countries, and to exploit Vietnam's rice crop and other agricultural products, as well as its considerable mineral resources. For several years, the Japanese permitted the French armed forces in Vietnam to retain their weapons and carry out their colonial functions, which included suppressing the Communist-led independence movement.

In 1941 Ho Chi Minh crossed from China into Vietnam. In May, at Pac Bo with a number of associates, including Vo Nguyen Giap, he founded the Viet Minh or League for Vietnamese Independence, which was committed to freeing Vietnam from Japanese, French, or any foreign control. The Viet Minh was a large alliance of nationalist groups and individuals who accepted the leadership of the Vietnamese Communist Party and agreed to work in a common effort to liberate Vietnam. As thousands of persons joined the movement, both the United States and General Chiang Kai Shek's government in China recognized the Viet Minh as the only nationwide Vietnamese organization resisting Japanese occupation and provided assistance. The United States sent weapons to the Viet Minh's armed units and parachuted fifty agents of its Office of Strategic Services (OSS, the predecessor to the CIA, which was to be founded in 1947) to train Ho Chi Minh's soldiers.

As the Viet Minh grew in strength throughout most of Vietnam, the Japanese were losing the war in the Pacific and began to expect that U.S. and possibly British forces would invade Indochina. In fear that the French soldiers in Vietnam would join in a U.S.-led attack, the Japanese decided to disarm and arrest them in March 1945. In effect, the Japanese eliminated the repressive French colonial military apparatus without replacing it. This situation permitted a significant level of freedom, particularly in the countryside, for the Communist Party and the Viet Minh to organize and recruit new members with little interference. Then, after two Japanese cities were destroyed by U.S. atomic bombs, Japan agreed to end World War II by surrendering. Since the French colonial soldiers were in Japanese custody and the Japanese forces were demoralized due to their country's surrender, a tremendous opportunity presented itself to the Vietnamese nationalist movement. The imprisoned French were unable to suppress the Viet Minh, and the Japanese, who would soon leave Vietnam, were generally unwilling to use violence against the Vietnamese attempt to establish independence before a European imperialist power, France, returned to seize control.

The Viet Minh quickly moved to take advantage of the unique political and military situation by staging pro-independence insurrections throughout most of Vietnam. These uprisings, largely unopposed by the Japanese, are referred to as Vietnam's August Revolution of 1945. For ten days beginning on August 18, the Viet Minh and allied groups took effective control of sixty-four major Vietnamese cities, including Hanoi, Hue, and Saigon. On August 30 the largely figurehead Vietnamese emperor, Bao Dai, announced his support for the Viet Minh provisional government. Then on September 2, Ho Chi Minh addressed a crowd of several hundred thousand people in Hanoi, including U.S. OSS advisers, and proclaimed Vietnam's Declaration of Independence in wording nearly identical to that of the American Declaration of Independence.

But none of the victorious World War II Allied nations wanted to antagonize their ally, France, by publicly accepting Vietnam, which France claimed as a colony, as an independent country. Therefore, no major government recognized the Vietnamese Declaration of independence. Instead British and Indian troops under British command (India was then still a British colony) occupied the southern half of Vietnam below the sixteenth parallel to disarm and repatriate the Japanese troops there, and General Chiang Kai Shek's Chinese forces occupied the northern half of the country. The British released and rearmed the French soldiers that the Japanese had imprisoned, and more French troops arrived in Vietnam. The Viet Minh had no choice but to attempt to negotiate a compromise with France that would eventually lead to Vietnamese independence. Ho traveled to France in 1946 to try to work out a nonviolent resolution and avoid war.

A possible negotiated settlement involved the Viet Minh agreeing to allow French forces to reoccupy Vietnam in return for France granting Vietnam local self-government and then independence in five years. Vietnam would join the French Union of former French colonies. British, Indian, and Chinese forces withdrew as French forces continued to land in Vietnam. But not all issues were satisfactorily resolved. One problem was the future status of Cochin China, the region of Vietnam the French had occupied the longest. French colonial authorities and many French settlers there did not want to be part of a future independent Vietnam. As a compromise, the Viet Minh proposed that the people of Cochin China be allowed to vote on whether to unite with the other two parts of colonial Vietnam, Annam and Tonkin, in a single Vietnamese state. French colonial authorities in Cochin China feared that most people would vote for unification and opposed such a referendum. A further disagreement over whether the Viet Minh or the French had the right to collect fees from ships using the northern port of Haiphong led to fighting and a French naval bombardment of Haiphong in late November 1946. This was the beginning of the Franco-Vietnam or French Indochina War, which would last eight years and result in hundreds of thousands of casualties.

At first several French military leaders believed the war presented them with the opportunity to eliminate the Viet Minh within a matter of months. The Viet Minh, however, enjoying considerable support in the countryside and under the command of able military leaders such as General Vo Nguyen Giap, engaged in mobile warfare, fleeing from superior French forces and attacking vulnerable units, often simultaneously in several locations. The war in Southeast Asia became a concern of Cold War adversaries, with the United States eventually paying for nearly 80 percent of the French war effort and the new Communist-led government in China

Viet Minh soldiers take positions on a bridge during their takeover of Haiphong in 1954. Ho Chi Minh's forces took control of Haiphong after the U.S. navy evacuation of French forces from the area, shortly after the battle of Dien Bien Phu. (Corbis)

after 1949 providing assistance to the Viet Minh. Inside France many people became opposed to the war, and a large anti-war movement developed, as would later happen in the United States. As the morale of its troops declined, the French government concluded that it was necessary to negotiate an end to the war. But some French leaders apparently felt that if they could enter the negotiations immediately after winning a great victory, they could get more favorable terms from the Viet Minh, perhaps even retaining control of some portion of southern Vietnam, such as Cochin China.

In an attempt to achieve this victory, approximately 16,000 French combat troops were sent to occupy the town of Dien Bien Phu in northern Vietnam near the Laotian border deep within Viet Minh–controlled territory (Duiker 2000, 453–454). The French hoped to lure the Viet Minh into trying to take the town and then use French aircraft and artillery to destroy them as they tried to advance on French positions. The French, however, had fallen into a trap. Viet Minh soldiers dragged artillery pieces and shells up the mountains surrounding the town and dug tunnels for quickly concealing their cannons once they had fired a few shells. In this way, Viet Minh artillery destroyed the town's airfield and the French artillery bases without the French aircraft or artillery being able to knock out the Viet Minh guns.

The French at Dien Bien Phu were forced to surrender to the Viet Minh just as the negotiations to end the war opened in Geneva, Switzerland, on May 7, 1954. Despite their great achievement, the first time the rebellious forces of a colony had defeated the army of a colonial occupier in a battle of this type since the American revolutionary victory at Yorktown (although pro-independence rebels under Haitian General Jean-Jacques Dessalines did succeed in forcing the French to leave the island and in proclaiming independence in 1804), the Viet Minh leaders were extremely disappointed when the Soviet Union and China pressured them into accepting far less favorable terms than they had hoped. The Geneva Conference, attended by representatives not only of the Viet Minh and France, but also from many other nations, including Great Britain, the Soviet Union, and China, led to several major agreements. First, Vietnam would be temporarily divided at the seventeenth parallel latitude so that the fighting could be ended by having French troops and the Vietnamese allied with them, the "Vietnamese National Army," withdraw to the south of the seventeenth parallel while the Viet Minh moved north of the line. No new foreign troops were to be introduced into Vietnam. And in 1956 an election for a new government of a reunified Vietnam was to be held throughout all parts of the country. Fulfillment of the terms of the Geneva Accords was to be overseen by representatives from Canada, India, and Poland.

The United States government, however, did not agree to the Geneva Accords and decided to attempt to maintain Vietnam south of the seventeenth parallel latitude as a separate nation called the Republic of Vietnam, more commonly referred to as South Vietnam. A key aspect of this plan was to recruit a prominent Vietnamese who was recognized as a Vietnamese patriot but was also a strong anti-Communist to become the leader of South Vietnam. The person selected for this ultimately lethal assignment was Ngo Dinh Diem, who had been born into a wealthy Catholic Vietnamese family and had refused to join Ho Chi Minh's movement because it was Communist led. He had left Vietnam during the French Indochina War to eventually reside in a Catholic seminary in Lakewood, New Jersey, U.S.A. A government official in Vietnam before World War II, Diem had quit his position as interior minister since he objected to French interference in his work. This act had earned him a reputation as a Vietnamese nationalist. Among Diem's limitations, however, were that he was a Catholic, a religion shared by only about 10 percent of Vietnam's population (whom Diem would be accused of favoring), and that he tended to rule in a dictatorial style like that of the old Vietnamese emperors.

In July 1954 Diem was appointed prime minister of South Vietnam by the technical head of the South Vietnamese government, Emperor Bao Dai, whom the French had recruited to work with them during the French Indochina War. The next year, through a referendum widely viewed as "rigged," the position of emperor was eliminated, leaving Diem in control.

The United States sent thousands of weapons and military advisers to arm and train Diem's new army, the Army of the Republic of Vietnam (ARVN), many of whose members had previously served with the French. Relying on support from Vietnam's wealthier citizens, including the landlord class, Diem reversed the land reforms carried out by the Viet Minh in parts of South Vietnam and forced poor peasants to return land to the landlords or to pay for it. Diem's armed forces began arresting members of the Vietnam Communist Party and other prominent members or supporters of the Viet Minh. These people were relatively defenseless, since as part of the Geneva Accords many of the southern Viet Minh soldiers had been forced to move north of the seventeenth parallel.

It was widely believed in Vietnam and around the world that if the 1956 nationwide election called for in the 1954 Geneva Accords was held, Ho Chi Minh and the Viet Minh would receive a large majority of the popular vote. This would have meant that a united Vietnam would have a Communist-led government. Diem announced that the election would not be held, because, he indicated, it would not be fairly conducted north of the seventeenth parallel. Viet Minh supporters in the south were outraged by Diem's behavior and his refusal to comply with the Geneva Accords. They wanted to begin armed resistance to his regime and armed forces. The Communist-led government north of the seventeenth parallel, the Democratic Republic of Vietnam or North Vietnam, pressured its southern comrades to wait while more peaceful measures were attempted, such as relying on international pressure to force the Diem government and its primary supporter, the United States, to allow the election. Furthermore, the Vietnamese had recently suffered hundreds of thousands of casualties fighting the French; they were very fearful that armed resistance to Diem's regime would lead to war with the United States and result in even greater loss of life and devastation. In addition, there was uncertainty regarding whether or how much aid might be provided to the Communist-led Vietnamese forces from either the Soviet Union or China.

Finally in 1960 the southern Vietnamese Communists, supporters of the Viet Minh and other groups favoring reunification of Vietnam established a new Communist-led nationalist alliance in the south to resist and take up arms against the Diem government, the National Liberation Front of South Vietnam (NLF). Diem's regime quickly began calling the NLF the Viet Cong (Viet Communists). Once the NLF engaged in armed resistance, membership and morale in the NLF and the Communist Party in the south surged. Within a few years, the insurgency posed a serious threat to the Diem regime. Despite the presence of approximately 16,000 U.S. military advisers and the flow of U.S. weapons, by 1963 some observers concluded that the NLF was winning the war.

Diem, fearing a possible military coup by some of his own officers, periodically moved them from one region to another before they could organize plots against him. But this also impaired the war effort against the NLF, since constant rotation of ARVN commanders led to disorganization and lack of familiarity with local circumstances. Furthermore, as some Buddhist groups and monks began to protest his policies, he responded with repression by his special forces under the command of his brother. Both a number of his top ARVN generals and officials in the U.S. government concluded that Diem, once viewed as essential for preserving South Vietnam as an independent, non-Communist nation, had to be removed from power. With the consent of U.S. authorities, a military coup by South Vietnamese generals overthrew Diem's government on November 1, 1963. The next day, Ngo Dinh Diem and his brother were executed. The murder of Diem reportedly shocked U.S. President Kennedy, who apparently believed Diem would be exiled, not murdered. But he did not have long to react to events in Vietnam. Less than three weeks later, on November 22, while visiting Dallas, Texas, Kennedy himself was assassinated. This murder elevated the vice president, former Texas senator Lyndon Johnson, to the presidency. In South Vietnam, a group of ARVN generals took power. Eventually in 1967, one of these, General Nguyen Van Thieu, assumed the presidency of South Vietnam until virtually the end of the war in April 1975.

President Johnson was informed by his advisers that without large-scale U.S. military intervention in Vietnam, the NLF would likely win and Vietnam would be unified under a Communist-led government. But both moral justification and legal authority from the U.S. Congress were viewed as necessary before a major U.S. deployment of military forces to Vietnam could take place. The so-called Gulf of Tonkin Incident and Gulf of Tonkin Resolution would provide these. According to naval reports, on August 2, 1964, a U.S. destroyer, the *Maddox,* was attacked by North Vietnamese torpedo boats but suffered no damage or casualties. The navy also reported another possible attack two days later on a different destroyer. Later investigations suggested that if there had been an attack on the *Maddox,* it probably was provoked by either the presence of the *Maddox* in Vietnamese territorial waters or by other U.S. or South Vietnamese military action. But the event was presented to the American people and the U.S. Congress as an unprovoked act of Communist aggression against a U.S. vessel and its crew in international waters. The U.S. House of Representatives voted unanimously for the Gulf of Tonkin Resolution, and all but two members of the U.S. Senate also voted for it. The Gulf of Tonkin Resolution, which gave the president the authority to take actions necessary to protect U.S. personnel in Southeast Asia, in effect, provided the legal basis for waging the Vietnam War.

Just as French generals predicted a quick victory at the beginning of their war in Vietnam, American military leaders underestimated their opposition in Vietnam. As more U.S. troops landed in Vietnam, North Vietnamese soldiers entered the conflict, often by moving along a series of roads and paths called the Ho Chi Minh Trail. By the end of 1967, there were approximately 500,000 U.S. troops in South Vietnam, and U.S. military leaders indicated that America was well on its way to victory. Then beginning on January 31, Tet (the Vietnamese New Year) 1968, the National Liberation Front (Viet Cong) and the People's Army of Vietnam (North Vietnamese Army) simultaneously attacked nearly one hundred South Vietnamese towns and cities, taking several provi-

sional capitals and the old imperial capital of Hue. Fighting erupted in sections of Saigon itself, and the grounds of the U.S. embassy there were temporarily taken by a Viet Cong unit before it was wiped out. In weeks of fighting, the towns and cities seized by the Viet Cong or the North Vietnamese were retaken by U.S. and Saigon forces, but much of the surrounding countryside was no longer considered to be under U.S. control.

In the United States, the Tet offensive came as a tremendous shock to most Americans and resulted in a huge loss of popular support for the war. Many people believed that the U.S. political and military leaders, who had claimed the United States was winning and that the enemy was not capable of any serious attack on an urban area, had lied or been incompetent or simply did not understand the nature of the war. President Johnson, fearing defeat, decided not to run for re-election, even though he had won the previous election by one of the greatest popular vote margins in history.

Johnson's vice president, Hubert Humphrey, and antiwar peace candidates Senator Eugene McCarthy (MN) and Senator Robert Kennedy (NY) competed for the Democratic presidential nomination. After winning the California primary, Senator Kennedy appeared likely to get the nomination, but instead he was assassinated shortly after giving his primary victory speech. Humphrey won the nomination but lost the presidential election to Republican Richard Nixon.

President Nixon pledged to negotiate an "honorable" end to the conflict, but during his presidency the war continued for four more years and resulted in the deaths of some 26,000 more Americans and several times that number of Vietnamese. The Nixon plan for bringing U.S. involvement in the war to an end included "Vietnamization of the war." This meant delivering enormous quantities of military equipment to the South Vietnamese armed forces while simultaneously reducing the number of U.S. troops in Vietnam. The anticipated result was that the South Vietnamese military would become so powerful that on its own it could prevent a victory by the National Liberation Front and the North Vietnamese Army.

Finally in 1973, a peace settlement was negotiated among the four parties to the conflict: the United States and its ally the Saigon government of South Vietnam and the Hanoi government of North Vietnam and its ally the National Liberation Front (Viet Cong) of South Vietnam. Under the terms of the agreement, U.S. troops would leave Vietnam and the United States would get back its hundreds of prisoners of war. All Vietnamese troops would cease fire and could remain where they were. This included North Vietnamese troops who were in South Vietnam. The National Liberation Front of South Vietnam was to enter into negotiations with the Saigon government in an attempt to form a unified government in the south that would then attempt to negotiate a reunification of South Vietnam with North Vietnam. However, the peace agreement among the Vietnamese failed. While Saigon government forces were accused of breaking the truce by trying to seize territory controlled by the NLF, the North Vietnamese and the NLF prepared to resume the war.

Since President Nixon was forced to resign the presidency in August of 1974 over his involvement in alleged obstruction of justice regarding the Watergate Affair, and since the U.S. Congress was opposed to further major U.S. military involvement in Vietnam, when major fighting resumed in March 1975, the South Vietnamese forces were on their own. Despite their huge assortment of U.S. weapons and planes and the significant but temporary resistance of several units, the South Vietnamese army was defeated in a few weeks. Saigon surrendered on April 30, 1975. Following the end of the conflict, Vietnam was reunited into one nation, the Socialist Republic of Vietnam (SRV), under a government controlled by the Vietnamese Communist Party, and Saigon was renamed Ho Chi Minh City. The U.S.-Vietnamese War was estimated to have taken the lives of over 55,000 Americans and more than one million Vietnamese in the country as a whole, north and south (Duiker 2000, 554). Those missing in action (MIAs) were estimated at about 2,000 U.S. and 300,000 Vietnamese.

IMPACTS

The Vietnamese Revolution had enormous impacts on the Vietnamese people and much of the world, including France and later the United States. On September 2, 1945, Vietnam became one of the first nations colonized by European states to declare its independence, serving as an inspiration to many other people's struggling to free themselves from foreign domination and exploitation. The refusal of the French to peacefully accept an independent Vietnam and the failure of the major nations of the world to recognize and support Vietnamese independence led to thirty years of tragic warfare, brutality, war crimes, and the the deaths or physical or psychological maiming of millions of Vietnamese, Laotians, Cambodians, Frenchmen, and Americans. The wars also resulted in the expenditure or loss of many billions of dollars in destruction, postponement of economic and social development, and the need to care for thousands of orphaned children and seriously wounded soldiers and civilians. Years after the end of the conflict in 1975, many thousands of Vietnamese and Americans suffered from the harmful effects of the chemical defoliant Agent Orange, which was spread over much of Vietnam in an effort to remove forest cover protecting the Vietnamese fighting U.S. forces and make them easier targets. Many areas of Vietnam were unsafe due to the continued existence of thousands of buried landmines. Beyond the destruction in Southeast Asia, the Vietnam conflict may have prolonged the divisive and wasteful Cold War.

After the end of the war, 200,000 or more South Vietnamese government administrators and other officials and members of the South Vietnamese army were transported to special camps for a "re-education" process that lasted, depending on the individual, anywhere from months to years. Following release, many of these men and their families, along with others—more than one million people—left Vietnam to live elsewhere, including the United States (De-Fronzo 1996, 154).

Until 1986, unified Vietnam's leaders attempted to develop the country through centralized planning and maintaining state ownership of industrial enterprises. But by the mid 1980s, poor economic performance led to the adoption of the *doi moi* ("renovation") reforms. The new policies gave farmers greater control over what crops they grew and permitted direct foreign investment. After the reforms, the economy often grew at an annual rate of 8 percent while agricultural production doubled, and Vietnam became the world's second-ranking exporter of rice. By 2001, state-owned enterprises accounted for approximately 50 percent of industrial output, while foreign investment produced 30 percent, and privately owned companies about 20 percent (Manyin 2003, 12–13).

The Vietnamese Revolution contributed to the development of revolutionary movements in the neighboring countries of Laos and Cambodia. U.S. intervention in Cambodia to destroy NLF bases there, including bombing attacks that killed civilians, helped promote the ascendancy of an extreme anti-foreign branch in the Cambodian Communist movement that achieved control of much of the country in 1975 and proceeded to implement drastically repressive policies blamed for the deaths of more than a million Cambodians. The new Khmer Rouge government even entered into border conflicts with Vietnam, precipitating a Vietnamese invasion and occupation of much of Cambodia in late 1978 that ousted the brutal government there. Ironically, at the time both the United States and China opposed the Vietnamese occupation of Cambodia, and China even briefly invaded the northernmost part of Vietnam over the issue in early 1979, before quickly withdrawing after meeting heavy resistance.

Around the world, the peoples of many nations opposed first the French and later the U.S. attempts to suppress or limit the Vietnamese Revolution. Eventually many citizens of France and the United States turned against their nations' involvement in Vietnam. In the case of the United States, millions of young people accused their leaders of lying about the nature of the Vietnam conflict and criminally betraying the patriotism of thousands of Americans by sending them to fight in an unjust and unwise war. An anti-establishment counter-culture developed in the United States, accompanied by an increase in the use of illegal drugs by many members of anti-war protest movements as well as many war veterans who, under the pressure of war and the stress of separation from loved ones, often had easy access to opium and marijuana in Vietnam. The Vietnam War became perhaps the most divisive conflict among Americans since the U.S. Civil War. Some war veterans even formed an organization that opposed the war, Vietnam Veterans Against the War, one of whose leaders was a wounded war hero and future U.S. senator from Massachusetts, John Kerry.

After American involvement in Vietnam, the U.S. public's opposition to similar proposed actions in other parts of the world inhibited direct U.S. military interventions in the affairs of other nations for many years. Cubans, for example, felt that they may have been saved from a U.S. invasion both by the U.S. preoccupation with Vietnam and by later U.S. public sentiment against such military actions. Instead, U.S. intelligence agencies sometimes used covert techniques or relied on the military forces of allied nations to influence events in Africa, the Middle East, or Latin America.

The U.S. government and military learned valuable lessons from the Vietnam conflict. The drafting of young Americans into the armed forces contributed to the war's unpopularity. In response, the U.S. ended the draft and switched to a "volunteer army," drawing many recruits from those with resources too limited to get a college education or a good job without the training and financial aid that military service could provide. To reduce the level of U.S. casualties in later wars and ensure a necessary level of voluntary enlistment in the armed forces, more sophisticated "stand-off weapons," such as precisely guided missiles and bombs and remotely piloted armed aircraft, were developed so that enemy forces could often be destroyed from a safe distance. Since some American leaders blamed press reports of the Vietnam War for undermining public support, at least one further modification in conducting war, effective control of U.S. press coverage of military actions, seems to have been another outcome of the Vietnam conflict.

One aspect of the U.S. involvement in Vietnam appears to have been replicated in preparation for the U.S. invasion of Iraq in 2003, although whether this was intentional has been the subject of debate. Just as the story of a Vietnamese attack on naval ships in international waters was used in 1964 to stampede the U.S. Congress, through the Gulf of Tonkin Resolution, into support for a war in Vietnam, allegations by top U.S. leaders of what turned out to be nonexistent stores of weapons of mass destruction in Iraq were used to similarly motivate most members of Congress to vote to give the president the authority to take military action against that nation.

PEOPLE AND ORGANIZATIONS

Annam

The long central part of French colonial Vietnam between Cochin China and Tonkin. Annam included Hue, Vietnam's old imperial capital, and was ruled as a "protectorate" by France through local Vietnamese officials willing to cooperate with the French.

Army of the Republic of Vietnam (ARVN)

The army of the South Vietnamese Saigon regime, the Republic of Vietnam, backed by the United States, which existed from 1956 until the end of the war in 1975. A number of its members had served in the French-sponsored Vietnamese National Army, which was allied with France against the Viet Minh during the 1946–1954 French Indochina War.

Associated State of Vietnam (ASV)

This was the partially autonomous but French-dominated Vietnamese government set up in 1949 by the French and the Vietnamese allied with them during the French Indochina War. The Emperor Bao Dai, viewed by many as a puppet of the French, was technically its head of state. The ASV was replaced after the 1954 Geneva Conference by the U.S.-sponsored South Vietnamese government, the Republic of Vietnam, based in Saigon.

Bao Dai (1913–1997)

Bao Dai was the last emperor of Vietnam. Accused of cooperating with the Japanese during World War II, he abdicated in 1945 in favor of Ho Chi Minh's Viet Minh. He was restored temporarily to power in 1949 by the French as the supposed "head of state" of the French-supported Associated State of Vietnam. Later he appointed the U.S.-backed Ngo Dinh Diem as his prime minister of South Vietnam in 1954 but was ousted by Diem in a reportedly rigged referendum in 1955.

Cao Dai

An eclectic religion founded in the Cochin China region of French-controlled Vietnam in 1926. It combined aspects of Buddhism, Confucianism, and Taoism and included among its "saints" Buddha, Jesus, and Sun Yat-Sen. Like Hoa Hao, another relatively new religion, Cao Dai gained hundreds of thousands of adherents among economically displaced peasants in Cochin China seeking a sense of community, self-worth, and meaning in their lives. Also like the Hoa Hao, it organized its own armed militias and generally tended to ally with whatever political group seemed to best preserve its local autonomy and power.

Cochin China

The southernmost part of French-ruled colonial Vietnam, which included Saigon and the Mekong Delta. This was the part of Vietnam that the French controlled longest and was administered directly by French officials.

Communist International (COMINTERN)

An organization that included revolutionaries and representatives of revolutionary organizations from many nations, the COMINTERN was established in the Soviet Union in 1919 with the purpose of fostering Communist-led revolutions in other countries. Under Russian influence, it was often accused of pressuring foreign revolutionaries to carry out policies that were oriented to benefiting the interests of the Soviet Union.

Constitutionalist Party

A political party established in the Cochin China part of Vietnam during the 1920s, it was supported by pro-French Vietnamese large landowners and French settlers. Its leaders called for local self-government, but for Cochin China to remain associated with France. The Communist-led Viet Minh tended to view the Constitutionalist Party as an organization controlled by wealthy persons who were French sympathizers rather than true Vietnamese patriots.

Democratic Republic of Vietnam (DRV)

The government established by Ho Chi Minh and the Viet Minh in Vietnam in 1945. After the 1954 Geneva Conference, this was the name for the government in the northern half of Vietnam, also known as North Vietnam. In 1976, following the reunification of Vietnam, all of Vietnam was renamed the Socialist Republic of Vietnam (SRV).

Diem, Ngo Dinh (1901–1963)

Diem was the anti-Communist Vietnamese recruited by the U.S. Eisenhower administration to lead South Vietnam (the Republic of Vietnam) from 1954 until his murder by members of his own U.S.-backed South Vietnamese (ARVN) forces in November of 1963.

He was born into a wealthy Catholic Vietnamese family at Hue in 1901 and attended the French School of Administration in Hanoi, where he was a top student. He served under the French-supported emperor Bao Dai as interior minister until he resigned because of French interference in his duties. This earned him a reputation as a Vietnamese patriot. After World War II, he refused to ally with the Viet Minh and left for the U.S. When the United States sought to preserve the southern half of Vietnam as a separate non-Communist nation after the 1954 Geneva Conference, Diem returned from the United States to Saigon to lead South Vietnam. He used U.S. weapons, advisers, and other aid to build up South Vietnamese army and police forces, initially from the Vietnamese soldiers who had previously served the French, and used them to suppress the relatively defenseless Vietnamese Communists and their associates in South Vietnam.

He refused to hold the 1956 nationwide election called for in the 1954 Geneva Conference to select a government for a reunified Vietnam, apparently fearing that in a free election he would lose to Ho Chi Minh and the Viet Minh. In response, the Communists organized the National Liberation Front of South Vietnam to fight his regime and reunify Vietnam. His dictatorial ways, perceived favoritism of Vietnam's 10 percent Catholic minority, repression of certain Buddhist groups, and incompetence in conducting the war against the Communist-led NLF (Viet Cong) convinced U.S. representatives to consent to a military takeover by generals in the South Vietnamese army. During the military coup, Diem and his brother were quickly murdered November 2, 1963, just three weeks before the assassination of the U.S. president, John Kennedy.

Doumer, Paul (1857–1932)

Frenchman who became governor of France's Indochina colony in 1897 and in about five years made it a source of significant profit through economic changes and policies including the sale of opium to the Vietnamese. He was elected president of France in 1931 but assassinated the next year.

French Expeditionary Forces (FEF)

French military forces in Vietnam that fought the Viet Minh during the French Indochina War of 1946–1954.

Giap, Vo Nguyen (Born 1912)

General Giap was the most famous commander of Vietnam's Communist-led revolutionary armed forces. He was born in central Vietnam in 1912 to a family active in opposing French rule and experienced the death of his wife, daughter, and father at the hands of the French. He studied law and taught history and joined the Communist-led revolutionary movement. In 1941 with Ho Chi Minh, whose writings had inspired him in his youth, he helped found the Viet Minh. He organized and led the Viet Minh armed forces which fought the Japanese during World War II and then battled the French during the French Indochina War, achieving a major victory at the battle of Dien Bien Phu in May 1954. Later he was a major military leader in the war against the United States and the U.S.-backed South Vietnamese army.

Ho Chi Minh (1890–1969)

Ho was the legendary leader of the Vietnamese Revolution. He was born Nguyen Sinh Cung to parents strongly opposed to French rule in rebellious Nghe An Province in the northern Annam section of colonial Vietnam. At eleven, as he entered adolescence, his father, following a Vietnamese custom, renamed him Nguyen Tat Thanh. In 1911, after attending an elite French-run school in Vietnam from which he was expelled for involvement in protest activities, he got a job as a worker on a French ship and left Vietnam for the next thirty years. His travels took him to many parts of the world where he learned about European control of lands and peoples in Asia and Africa. This and his own experiences in Vietnam would later draw him to Lenin's analysis of capitalist imperialism and to the Communist movement as a vehicle for liberating Vietnam from foreign control. For a while he lived in Boston and New York, where he was amazed that Asian immigrants to the United States enjoyed greater political rights than the Vietnamese did in their own country. He viewed the American Declaration of Independence as an anti-imperialist proclamation (against Great Britain) and patterned the 1945 Vietnamese Declaration of Independence after it almost word for word.

In France Ho joined the Socialist Party and then in 1920 the new French Communist Party. In 1919, adopting the name Nguyen Ai Quoc (Nguyen The Patriot), he tried unsuccessfully to present the victorious World War I leaders with a proposal for local self-rule for the Vietnamese. In 1924, he journeyed to Moscow to learn about the revolutionary methods of the Soviet Communists and then joined the Soviet mission to aid Sun Yat-Sen's Chinese republican revolutionary movement in south China. There he organized a nationalist- and Marxist-oriented group among young patriotic Vietnamese exiles, the Revolutionary Youth League of Vietnam, and later helped found the Vietnamese Communist Party in Hong Kong in 1930. Sought by the French secret police, he reportedly returned to Russia with the help of friends and associates such as Mrs. Sun Yat-Sen (Duiker 2000, 210). In 1941 Ho re-entered Vietnam during World War II, when it was occupied by both Japanese and colonial French forces, to help found the Viet Minh with Vo Nguyen Giap and others. Around then he also adopted his most famous name, Ho Chi Minh (He Who Enlightens) (Karnow 1983, 690). On September 2, 1945, Ho proclaimed Vietnam's independence in a statement modeled after the American Declaration of Independence. But lacking sufficient international support, Ho and his Viet Minh fought the French for eight years in a war culminating in a great victory over the French at Dien Bien Phu in May 1954. Ho served as president of the Democratic Republic of Vietnam (North Vietnam) until his death in 1969 as Communist-led forces engaged in combat with the U.S. over the future of Vietnam.

Hoa Hao

Hoa Hao is a Buddhist reformist sect that takes its name from the Mekong town where it was founded in 1939. It attracted hundreds of thousands of adherents among economically displaced peasants in Cochin China, in part because of its simplicity and rejection of expensive rituals. Like the Cao Dai, it organized its own armed militias in an attempt to maintain local autonomy.

Indochinese Communist Party (ICP—Dang Cong San Dong Duong)

The Vietnamese Communist Party founded by Ho Chi Minh and his associates in 1930. From its outset, the party advocated the goal of ridding Vietnam of foreign occupation and achieving independence as well as the goal of radically redistributing resources and opportunity to benefit Vietnam's large majority, who were very poor. The Vietnamese Communist Party adopted the name Indochinese Communist Party from October 1930 until November 1945.

International Control Commission (ICC)

Observers from Canada, India, and Poland whom the Geneva Conference sent to Vietnam to oversee the 1954 Indochinese War cease-fire and the implementation of the Geneva Agreements.

Khmer Communist Party

Radical Communist party established by Pol Pot and others in Cambodia in the mid 1960s. It took the place of Cambodia's previous more moderate revolutionary party, originally set up in 1951.

Khmer Rouge

The name generally used for Pol Pot's extremist Cambodian Communist Party and its armed forces.

National Front for the Liberation of South Vietnam (NLF—Mat Tran Dan Toc Giai Phong Mien Nam)

The National Liberation Front of South Vietnam was the successor to the Viet Minh in South Vietnam. The NLF, formed under the leadership of the Vietnamese Communist Party, was an alliance of nationalist groups that opposed the U.S.-supported Saigon government and advocated the reunification of Vietnam. The Saigon regime and the U.S. military often referred to the NLF and its military units, the People's Liberation Armed Forces, as the Viet Cong, meaning Viet Communists.

Pathet Lao

The name for the Communist-led revolutionary armed forces of Laos. The Pathet Lao often cooperated with the Communist-led forces of North Vietnam and South Vietnam.

People's Liberation Armed Forces (PLAF—Nhan Dan Giai Phong Quan)

The People's Liberation Armed Forces was the name for the Communist-led military units of the NLF of South Vietnam and was often referred to by the U.S. military and by the U.S.-backed Saigon regime as the Viet Cong (Viet Communists).

Phan Boi Chau (1867–1940)

Phan Boi Chau was a Confucian scholar and nationalist who opposed French colonialism but concluded that efforts to free Vietnam must adopt more modern approaches since traditional Confucianist concepts had proved inadequate. He praised the determination, intelligence, and resourcefulness of the Vietnamese people and encouraged them to learn from the more advanced nations the knowledge that could free Vietnam. He tended to believe that violent methods were justified in pursuit of Vietnamese independence.

Phan Chu Trinh (1872–1926)

Phan Chu Trinh was a Confucian scholar and nationalist who opposed French colonialism but felt that traditional Confucianist learning had failed the Vietnamese people. He encouraged young Vietnamese to learn from the French and the people of other advanced nations the knowledge which could make Vietnam strong and free of foreign control. However, he advocated nonviolent methods to achieve independence and argued that the Vietnamese must modernize their technologies, culture, and political and economic systems, even if this process required a temporary continuation of Vietnam's colonial status.

Republic of Vietnam (RVN—Viet Nam Cong Hoa)

The formal title of the non-Communist government established in Saigon, South Vietnam, after the 1954 Geneva Conference with the assistance of the U.S.

Revolutionary Youth League of Vietnam (Viet Nam Thanh Nien Cach Menh Dong Chi)

Ho Chi Minh organized this revolutionary group among Vietnamese exiles in South China in 1925. Its members advocated freeing Vietnam from foreign control and accomplishing a socioeconomic revolution to benefit the country's poor majority. It was replaced by the Vietnamese Communist Party in 1930.

Socialist Republic of Vietnam (SRV—Cong Hoa Xa Hoi Viet Nam)

Title of the united Vietnamese nation after the end of the Vietnam War in 1975.

Thieu, Nguyen Van (1924–2001)

Thieu was president of South Vietnam (Republic of Vietnam) from 1967 to 1975. Previously he had served as a general in the South Vietnamese army (ARVN), and before that he had served in the French-sponsored Vietnamese National Army.

Tonkin

The northernmost section of French colonial Vietnam, which included the cities of Hanoi and Haiphong and the Red River Delta. Tonkin was ruled by France as a "protectorate" through Vietnamese officials willing to cooperate with the French.

Viet Cong (VC—Viet Communists)

The expression often used by the U.S. military and the U.S.-supported South Vietnamese regime in Saigon for the Communist-led NLF and its military units, the PLAF, of South Vietnam.

Viet Minh (Viet Nam Doc Lap Dong Minh— League for the Independence of Vietnam)

The Viet Minh was the anti-imperialist nationalist alliance created in 1941 under the leadership of Vietnam's Communist Party. The Viet Minh fought both the Japanese and French occupiers of Vietnam and finally forced the French to withdraw from Vietnam after the Franco-Vietnamese or French Indochina War.

Vietnamese Communist Party (VCP—Dang Cong San Dong Duong)

The original name for the Communist Party founded by Ho Chi Minh and his associates in 1930. From its outset, the party advocated both the goal of ridding Vietnam of foreign occupation and achieving independence, and the goal of rad-

ically redistributing resources and opportunity to benefit Vietnam's large majority, who were poor. After October 1930, it was often referred to as the Indochinese Communist Party (ICP) until November 1945, when it was supposedly dissolved. In 1951 it resurfaced and was called the Vietnamese Workers' Party (VWP) until the expression Vietnamese Communist Party was again adopted in 1976.

Vietnamese Liberation Army (VLA—Viet Nam Giai Phong Quan)

Official name for the armed forces of the Viet Minh from 1944 until the end of the war against the French in 1954. After the Geneva Conference it was replaced by the People's Army of Vietnam or PAVN, also referred to as the North Vietnamese Army by the U.S. government and military and the U.S.-sponsored South Vietnamese regime in Saigon.

Vietnamese National Army (VNA)

The armed forces of the French-supported Associated State of Vietnam during the Franco-Vietnamese or French Indochina War. After the 1954 Geneva Conference it was replaced by the U.S.-armed and -trained Army of the Republic of Vietnam or ARVN, also referred to as the South Vietnamese Army.

Vietnamese Nationalist Party (VNQDD—Viet Nam Quoc Dan Dang)

The VNQDD was the non-Communist nationalist resistance movement founded in Vietnam in 1927. This organization used violence in an attempt to drive the French out but was thought to lack a serious commitment to redistribute opportunity and resources to benefit Vietnam's large majority of rural poor. After the repression of its 1930 Yen Bay mutiny against the French, and without sufficient support in the countryside, the VNQDD's significance as an effective independence movement was greatly reduced, and leadership of the independence struggle was assumed by Vietnam's Communist Party.

Vietnamese Workers' Party (VWP—Dang Lao Dong Viet Nam)

The VWP was the name for the Vietnamese Communist Party from 1951 until 1976.

James DeFronzo

See Also Anarchism, Communism, and Socialism; Cambodian Revolution; Chinese Revolution; Cinema of Revolution; Colonialism, Anti-Colonialism, and Neo-Colonialism; Documentaries of Revolution; Elites, Intellectuals, and Revolutionary Leadership; Guerrilla Warfare and Revolution; Inequality, Class, and Revolution; Lao Communist Revolution; Literature and Modern Revolution; Nationalism and Revolution; Terrorism; War and Revolution

References and Further Readings

Adam, Nina S., and Alfred W. McCoy. 1970. *Laos: War and Revolution.* New York: Harper and Row.

Bain, Chester. 1967. *Vietnam: The Roots of Conflict.* Englewood Cliffs, NJ: Prentice-Hall.

Bergerud, Eric M. 1991. *The Dynamics of Defeat.* Boulder, CO: Westview.

Chandler, David P. 1983. *A History of Cambodia.* Boulder, CO: Westview.

DeFronzo, James. 1996. (3rd edition forthcoming 2007) *Revolutions and Revolutionary Movements.* Boulder, CO: Westview.

Duiker, William J. 1976. *The Rise of Nationalism in Vietnam, 1900–1941.* Ithaca, NY: Cornell University Press.

———. 1983. *Vietnam: Nation in Transition.* Boulder, CO: Westview.

———. 1995. *Vietnam: Revolution in Transition.* Boulder, CO: Westview.

———. 2000. *Ho Chi Minh.* New York: Hyperion.

Dunn, John D. 1972. *Modern Revolutions.* Cambridge: Cambridge University Press.

Duong, Pham Cao. 1985. *Vietnamese Peasants under French Domination.* Berkeley: University of California Press.

Etcheson, Craig. 1984. *The Rise and Demise of Democratic Kampuchea.* Boulder, CO: Westview.

Giap, Vo Nguyen. 1962. *People's War, People's Army.* New York: Praeger.

Karnow, Stanley. 1983. *Vietnam: A History.* New York: Viking.

———. 1990. "Hanoi's Legendary Giap Remembers." *New York Times Magazine* (June 24): 22–23, 36, 39, 57, 59–60, 62.

Khanh, Huynh Kim. 1982. *Vietnamese Communism.* Ithaca, NY: Cornell University Press.

Kolko, Gabriel. 1985. *Anatomy of a War.* New York: Pantheon.

Lacouture, Jean. 1968. *Ho Chi Minh: A Political Biography.* New York: Random House.

Manyin, Mark E. 2003. *CRS Issue Brief for Congress: The Vietnam-U.S. Normalization Process.* Washington, DC: Congressional Research Service.

Marr, David G. 1971. *Vietnamese Anticolonialism: 1885–1925.* Boulder, CO: Westview.

McAlister, John T., Jr. 1969. *Vietnam: Origins of Revolution.* New York: Knopf.

McNamara, Robert S. 1995. *In Retrospect: The Tragedy and Lessons of Vietnam.* New York: Random House.

Moise, Edwin E. 1983. *Land Reform in China and Vietnam.* Chapel Hill: University of North Carolina Press.

Race, Jeffrey. 1972. *War Comes to Long An.* Berkeley: University of California Press.

Stuart-Fox, Martin. 1997. *A History of Laos.* Cambridge: Cambridge University Press.

———. 2002. *Buddhist Kingdom, Marxist State: The Making of Modern Laos.* Bangkok: White Lotus.

Tai, Hue-Tam Ho. 1983. *Millenarianism and Peasant Politics in Vietnam.* Cambridge, MA: Harvard University Press.

Turley, William S. 1986. *The Second Indochina War.* Boulder, CO: Westview.

Turner, Robert F. 1975. *Vietnamese Communism.* Stanford, CA: Hoover Institution Press.

Werner, Jayne Susan. 1981. *Peasant Politics.* New Haven, CT: Yale University Press.

Wolf, Eric. 1969. *Peasant Wars of the Twentieth Century.* New York: Harper and Row.

Woodside, Alexander B. 1976. *Community and Revolution in Modern Vietnam.* Boston: Houghton Mifflin.

Zasloff, Joseph J. 1973. *The Pathet Lao Leadership and Organization.* Lexington, MA: Lexington Books.

War and Revolution

War and revolution are as old as history itself. Revolutions are internal revolts aimed at overthrowing the current state (government) and the elites who hold power, while wars are conflicts between states. History demonstrates that war and revolution can occur independently, but they are often interrelated. The large number of factors that may influence the interplay between war and revolution make a complete understanding of the relationship difficult, despite a rich history.

War and revolution share certain commonalities. Both involve an attempt to alter political control and/or the political structure of society. Frequently the intent is to also significantly alter the social structure, although the ability to actually achieve social transformation often falls short of original goals. In either case, the role of the state is central.

Revolutions always place the state in a defensive position in its effort to maintain control, while in wars the state may assume either a defensive or offensive position. A particular state may either fight defensive wars against external aggression or offensive wars to enhance its power and/or access to resources by seeking to control other states. The military establishment of each state plays a crucial role as the primary mechanism of defense, offense, and control.

The outcomes of both war and revolution are often affected by the prevailing nature and structure of the larger system of international relations among states, as is the success of any newly established regime that may result from war or revolution.

Scholars have referred to the often reciprocal relationship between war and revolution: war can be a cause of revolution and revolution can be a cause of war. Furthermore, one can occur in the midst of the other. Even in cases in which one was not a cause of the other, each may significantly impact the course and outcome of the other. In addition, wars between states may indirectly weaken a third state that is not involved in the war, for example by depriving it of resources normally obtained from one of the warring states, thereby making it more vulnerable to revolution. Similarly, a revolution in a noninvolved state may present a threat to other states currently at war and actually influence the war's outcome. War, however, is neither necessary nor sufficient for revolution, nor revolution for war. Indeed, most revolutionary movements have failed, regardless of the presence or potential of war. The interrelationship between war and revolution, nonetheless, has often been not only real, but of great historical significance.

WAR AS A CAUSE OF REVOLUTION

To fight any war requires the state to extract additional resources from the population. The longer the war, the greater the demand for resources, which results in greater strain on the citizenry. War-related resources take two forms: material and human. War requires a variety of material resources, ranging from foodstuffs to minerals to manufacturing capabilities. If these resources are unavailable internally, the state must purchase these from external sources. The redirection of material resources to the war effort can weaken the state's authority, because fewer resources are available to the population. Deprivation may lead to discontent, a fertile basis for revolution. This discontent may be further exacerbated if the war is unpopular, costly in the lost lives of citizens, or if there is little chance of victory.

Just as important is the need for human resources to staff the armed forces. Wars typically require increasing the size of the military, usually by arming and training a larger portion of the citizenry. To do so, however, can weaken the state's control over violence and increase citizens' demands for greater participation in the political process. In most cases, state authority is predicated upon controlling the military, particularly with regard to thwarting revolution. Increases in the size of a nation's armed forces can enhance the power position of the military relative to that of the country's government. Inability to ensure the loyalty of the armed forces may lead to its failure to defend the state or to outright military attempts to overthrow the existing government.

Any war has the potential to end in defeat. Such an outcome greatly enhances the likelihood of revolutionary efforts. Losing a war usually diminishes the status and capabilities of the state both externally and internally. Externally, the state experiences a loss of international power and influence. Often the victorious nation requires some sacrifice of resources from the defeated state, either through reparation payments or through the loss of land and population. Internally, defeat typically results in a continued burden on the population in the form of increased taxes, reduced wages, added working hours, or loss of property or freedom and may diminish loyalty to the current regime not only among civilians, but also in the military. Economic distress that leads to attempts to decrease spending on the military may carry risks for the state. Losing a war and reducing the size of the armed forces not only makes the state more vulnerable to foreign aggression, it simultaneously places skilled warriors outside the direct control of the government, thus making them more available for revolutionary recruitment. This possibility is more likely if the war was unpopular among the citizenry.

REVOLUTION AS A CAUSE OF WAR

Revolution can not only alter the power structure within a particular state, it can also alter power relations internationally. Those nations wielding the most power have a vested interest in maintaining current international relations. Because revolution within a particular state alters that state's political leadership, often resulting in the replacement of the previous ruling elite with a new one characterized by a radically different ideological outlook, revolution can be disrup-

tive and threatening to previous international power relations. The revolutionary regime's new leaders rarely support the old regime's international policies. Minimally, revolutions create a climate of international uncertainty.

Advocates of revolutionary ideologies rarely seek change only within the borders of one state. Instead, most ideologies are designed for application to all people, or at least to a group or class of people in numerous states. Successful revolutions are consequently often seen as increasing the potential for the spread of revolution to other countries, especially those in similar situations bordering the new revolutionary regime. As a result, others nations may strengthen their military as a means of increasing security against the revolutionary threat or even decide to destroy a new revolutionary government before it can inspire or aid revolutionaries in other countries. For example, the desire to prevent the spread of Islamic fundamentalist revolution to its own people was almost certainly a major reason for Iraq's 1980 invasion of the clerically dominated government of the Islamic Republic of Iran.

The likelihood of war is also increased because new revolutionary regimes are often seen as somewhat weak and disorganized, and therefore vulnerable to a military assault. Such beliefs are not necessarily well founded though, because revolutionary movements, when successful, are frequently swept into power on a widespread wave of citizen support and revolutionary fervor that can easily be mobilized against an external threat, as occurred when the armies of anti-revolutionary governments attempted to suppress the French Revolution or later the Russian Revolution of 1917.

Likewise, new regimes established through successful revolutions typically remain suspicious of other states. Just as some governments might attempt to combat a revolutionary threat by destroying a revolutionary state, the leaders of such a state may believe that their best chance of protecting and building their new society lies in attacking and defeating the armies of counter-revolutionary nations, as attempted, at first successfully, in defense of the French Revolution.

Revolutionary leaders may be overconfident in their ability to defend their revolution, spread their revolutionary ideals, and win further armed conflicts. Most analysts suggest that timing is a key factor in this regard. Newly established revolutionary regimes are generally seen as being more vulnerable in war in the short term but better able to amass citizen support and defend themselves in the long term. Revolutionary governments are often successful in improving their society's capacity to wage war. For example, before its revolution China was repeatedly defeated by Western armies, but post-revolution China was able to fight major Western powers to a stalemate in the Korean War. And after its revolution, Cuba was able to deploy thousands of its soldiers to Africa and repeatedly win battles on behalf of its revolutionary allies, including helping to defeat the white South African forces that invaded Angola in the 1970s.

CASE STUDIES OF THE RELATIONSHIPS BETWEEN WAR AND REVOLUTION

A number of major revolutions of the twentieth century involved interdependencies between war and revolution, including the Russian Revolution of 1917, the Chinese Revolution, the Vietnamese Revolution, and the Iranian Revolution of 1978–1979.

The Russian Revolution of 1917

The Bolshevik Revolution of 1917 was the first major revolution of the last century, and more importantly, it was the first successful Socialist revolution. This revolution was made possible in great part because continued participation in costly and unsuccessful wars destroyed the legitimacy of the czarist regime.

The revolution was rooted in a population made up overwhelmingly of peasants, with a small but significant minority of industrial workers. In 1904, in an effort to counter economic discontent and rally popular support for the regime, the czar entered into a war against Japan, which was portrayed to the people as easily winnable. Successive Japanese victories, however, forced Russia to seek peace terms through the diplomatic intervention of the United States. Disheartened by Russia's military defeat and faced with increased economic hardships, industrial workers and peasants attempted peaceful protests in 1905. The czar's troops fired on protestors at the Winter Palace in the capital, Petrograd, on January 22, killing scores of people in what became known as "Bloody Sunday." This event led to increased strikes and peasant uprisings. Several military units rebelled. But most of the armed forces remained loyal. After the czar agreed to allow the creation of a Russian parliament, or Duma, whose elected members would theoretically provide some level of political participation for the people and limit the czar's previous virtually absolute power, the rebellion lost momentum and the remaining insurgents were crushed.

But nine years later, the czarist regime led Russia into World War I. The army suffered repeated enormous defeats at the hands of the better-equipped and better-led Germans. Millions of Russian soldiers, the vast majority of whom were peasants and workers, were killed or wounded. The war caused huge shortages in the labor force needed to support the war effort and also to grow food and transport it to cities and towns. As hardships intensified, particularly in urban areas, demonstrations and workers' strikes occurred in Petrograd. In early 1917 troops sent to quell the disorders refused to fire on protestors, and many soldiers actually began to join them.

Faced with both popular rebellion and massive military mutinies, the czar was forced to abdicate. The leadership of the Duma transformed into a Provisional National Government, which temporarily ran the country as long as it had the approval of what many Russians perceived to be the more representative and popularly supported Petrograd Soviet of workers, peasants, soldiers, and sailors.

The provisional government's decision to continue the devastating war with Germany led to more catastrophic defeats, widespread desertions from the army, and the growth in popularity of the anti-war Bolsheviks who, through the Petrograd Soviet, seized power in October. Thus while participation in World War I resulted in the destruction of the monarchy, continued participation during 1917 helped turn the revolution in a more radical direction. The new Bolshevik-led Soviet government quickly withdrew from the war effort. Because of the Socialist ideology of the revolutionaries, the major international powers (Britain, the United States, France, Italy, and Japan) saw the revolution as a threat and sent troops to aid the anti-revolutionary forces during the Russian Civil War of 1918–1922. This foreign military intervention promoted the development of a siege mentality within the Soviet Communist Party. Fear of future foreign attack was used to justify authoritarian repression and contributed to the rise of Stalin's brutal regime.

The Chinese Revolution

By far the most populous country to experience revolution in the twentieth century was China. While China's pre-revolution political state structure and ideology had endured for hundreds of years, significant change began to occur early in the first half of the nineteenth century, due in part to the effects of the British victory over China in the 1839–1842 Opium War. The war was caused by China's refusal to agree to an expansion of the British opium trade. After defeat, China was forced to allow the British to market opium and other commodities in China, permit freedom for Christian missionary work, agree to British possession of Hong Kong and certain other Chinese territories, and pay war reparations to Britain. Later in the century China suffered other defeats.

The victories of foreign imperialist nations had major consequences for China and helped bring about later revolution-

Soldiers in Russia's Red Army parade before Leon Trotsky during the Russian Civil War, ca. 1918. (Library of Congress)

ary movements. China's economy suffered from the unfavorable trade relations structured by the victorious powers and the payments of war reparations. To meet its foreign obligations, the Chinese government raised taxes. To pay their taxes, the members of the landlord class tended to raise land rents and interest rates on loans to poor peasants. Those actions increased rural hardships and unrest, and led to huge peasant rebellions, including the Nian, 1853–1868, and the gigantic Taiping Rebellion, 1851–1864. Psychologically, defeat and exploitation by other nations instilled intense feelings of humiliation and hatred of foreigners among millions of Chinese, laying a popular basis for revolutionary nationalist movements. The inability of the Chinese Confucian monarchy, and specifically the ruling Manchu dynasty, to protect China's people from foreign defeat and exploitation undermined the legitimacy of the pre-revolutionary state. The main leader of China's Republican Revolutionary Movement, Dr. Sun Yat-Sen, viewed the destruction of the Manchu dynasty and the establishment of a republic form of government as essential to the freedom and welfare of the Chinese people.

The form that revolution was to take was influenced both by World War I and the Russian Revolution. Instead of returning Germany's colonial interests in China to the Chinese people, the leaders of the victorious WWI nations presented them to Japan. This action seemed to confirm Lenin's view that the capitalist nations were interested in continuing the economic exploitation of China and recruiting potentially troublesome Japan as a partner. Outraged young Chinese intellectuals, including Mao Zedong, formed the Chinese Communist Party in Shanghai in 1921. Sun Yat-Sen in 1924 accepted the Communists into his revolutionary nationalist movement and party, the Guo Min Dang (GMD), patterned the organizational structure of the GMD after that of the Russian Communist Party, and depended on military assistance from the Soviet Union to build his Republican Revolutionary Army in south China. After Sun's premature death in 1925, this army marched north to subdue or intimidate local warlord rulers and unite the country. In the midst of this conflict, General Chiang Kai Shek, who had emerged after Sun's death as the leader of the Republican Army, turned on his Communist allies in Shanghai in 1927, precipitating a new civil war. World War II later played a major role by causing a temporary truce in the civil war so that all Chinese could cooperate in fighting the Japanese invaders. Communist military achievements and social reform efforts in the conflict against the Japanese appeared to increase popular support for the Communist-led forces, facilitating their relatively rapid victory in the resumed civil war during 1947–1949.

The Vietnamese Revolution

From 1883 to 1954, France considered all of Vietnam to be under its authority. Despite rebellions and revolutionary movements for independence, the French maintained relatively tight control until the beginning of World War II. After France fell to Germany, the new French Vichy government allowed the Japanese to occupy Vietnam and exploit its resources. In response, Vietnamese revolutionaries under the leadership of Ho Chi Minh, Vo Nguyen Giap, and other Vietnamese Communists created a revolutionary nationalist alliance, the Viet Minh (League for Vietnamese Independence) to oppose both the Japanese and the French. Both the United States and China assisted the Viet Minh forces in their struggle against the occupying Japanese, facilitating the growth of the revolutionary movement. After developing popular support throughout most of the country, the Viet Minh declared Vietnam an independent nation on September 2, 1945, just after the Japanese, who had disarmed the French colonial forces in March, surrendered to the victorious Allies. But the French, whose own country had just been freed from the right-wing Vichy regime accused of collaborating with the Nazis, supported relatively rightist leaders for Vietnam rather than the Communist-led Viet Minh alliance. This led to the 1946–1954 French Indochina War.

This war resulted in the establishment of a revolutionary government in the northern half of Vietnam. Fearing the spread of Communist-led revolutions, U.S. leaders viewed the possible reunification of Vietnam under Communist leadership as a threat and attempted to keep the country divided through military force. The American war in Vietnam from 1964–1973 resulted in the deaths and injuries of millions of people. U.S. military interventions in neighboring Cambodia in pursuit of Vietnamese forces and weapons contributed not only to the growth of the Cambodian rebel army but to the victory in that country of an extremely anti-foreign branch of the Cambodian Communist movement. Thus the U.S. war in Vietnam indirectly helped create a brutal Cambodian regime blamed for the deaths of more than one million Cambodians. But the eventual success of the Vietnamese Revolution inhibited for some time direct U.S. military intervention in other nations.

Iranian Revolution of 1978–1979

As much or more than any modern revolution, the Iranian Revolution illustrates the potential interplay of revolution and war. In 1953, in the context of the Cold War, the United States helped install Iranian Shah Mohammad Pahlavi as, in effect, a pro-U.S. dictator complete with his own notorious secret police, the SAVAK. Deprived of the capacity for effective democratic opposition, anti-Shah revolutionary movements of both the Left and the Right (Shia fundamentalists) developed among Iranians.

The revolution ultimately succeeded, in 1979, in ousting the monarchy. Among the components of the anti-Shah revolutionary alliance, the Shia fundamentalist clergy, which included the charismatic and admired leader Ayatollah Ruhollah Khomeini, enjoyed the greatest popular support. As the dominant revolutionary force, Shia fundamentalists were able to create a fundamentalist-controlled government. The leaders of the Islamic Republic of Iran encouraged Islamic fundamentalist revolutionaries in other countries. Threatened by such a revolution, the Iraqi regime invaded Iran in September of 1980. This devastating conflict not only cost hundreds of thousands of lives, it also severely injured the economies of both nations, leaving Iraq tens of billions of dollars in debt to several nations, including Kuwait. Canceling this debt was apparently one of the motives for Iraq's invasion of Kuwait in 1990. Iraq's defeat in the 1991 Gulf War by the U.S.-led coalition weakened its secular government and encouraged rebellions by the Kurdish minority in the north and a large part of Iraq's Shia population in the south. These events were eventually followed by the U.S.-led military occupation of Iraq in 2003.

Another impact of the Shia Islamic fundamentalist victory in Iran's Revolution against a U.S.-backed and -armed regime (viewed by many as a victory over the United States itself) was to encourage Islamic resistance to the Soviet forces that occupied Afghanistan in the 1980s. This conflict led to the expansion of more radical forms of Sunni Islamic fundamentalism and to the formation of al-Qaeda from among many foreign volunteers who had fought against the Soviets. Further, the Soviet defeat in the Afghan War contributed to the de-legitimization of the U.S.S.R.'s Communist government, which helped bring about the Second Russian Revolution of the twentieth century, leading to the disintegration of the Soviet Union itself by the end of 1991.

CONCLUSION

As these case studies indicate, revolution can cause war (such as the U.S. war in Vietnam) or influence the course of a war (for example, revolutionary Russia's decision withdraw from

World War I). Furthermore, they show that war can cause revolution (the disastrous defeats of Russia's army during World War I undermined the authority of the czar's regime and motivated many soldiers and sailors to join the Bolsheviks) or can affect the course of revolution (foreign invasions provided an opportunity for revolutionaries in China and Vietnam to lead anti-imperialist alliances that won enormous popular support for the revolutionary forces and their leaders).

But these case studies also illustrate that the form of the interplay between revolution and war can vary widely. Local history and circumstances typically contribute unique characteristics that can determine or condition the war-revolution relationship. Consequently, our ability to generalize or to predict what relationships will develop is limited.

Michael Nusbaumer

See Also Afghanistan: Conflict and Civil War; Arab Revolt 1916-1918; Armed Forces, Revolution, and Counter-Revolution; Bangladesh Revolution; Cambodian Revolution; Chinese Revolution; Cinema of Revolution; Colonialism, Anti-Colonialism, and Neo-Colonialism; Documentaries of Revolution; Ethiopian Revolution; French Revolution; Guerrilla Warfare and Revolution; Iranian Revolution; Iraq Revolution; Irish Revolution; Italian Fascist Revolution; Korean Civil War; Kurdish Movements; Lao Communist Revolution; Nazi Revolution: Politics and Racial Hierarchy; Palestinian Movement; Philippine Independence Revolution and Wars; Russian Revolution of 1917; Russian Revolution of 1991 and the Dissolution of the U.S.S.R.; Terrorism; Theories of Revolution; Vietnamese Revolution; Yugoslav Communist Revolution; Zionist Revolution and the State of Israel

References and Further Readings

Adelman, Jonathan. 1985. *Revolutions, Armies and War: A Political History.* Boulder, CO: Lynne Rienner.

DeFronzo, James. 1996. *Revolutions and Revolutionary Movements,* 2nd edition. Boulder, CO: Westview Press.

Hagopian, Mark N. 1974. *The Phenomenon of Revolution.* New York: Harper and Row.

Motyl, Alexander J. 1999. *Revolutions, Nations and Empires: Conceptual Limits and Theoretical Possibilities.* New York: Columbia University Press.

Skocpol, Theda. 1988. "Social Revolutions and Mass Military Mobilization," *World Politics* 40: 147–168.

Walt, Stephen M. 1996. *Revolution and War.* Ithaca, NY: Cornell University Press.

Women and Revolution

This discussion of women and revolutionary movements in the late twentieth century addresses a number of themes: what is meant by revolution, the causes of the increased participation of women in revolutionary movements, the ways that women participate in revolutionary struggles, and the results for women in the aftermath of revolutions. Though the examples will be drawn largely from Latin American cases, the themes and patterns noted hold similarities with revolutionary movements throughout the world.

A question of particular interest to scholars of gender and revolution is what constitutes a revolutionary movement. Theda Skocpol defines revolutions in the traditional sociological sense: "Social revolutions are rapid, basic transformations of a society's state and class structures; and they are accompanied and in part carried through by class-based revolts from below" (1979, 4). Her definition, formerly widely accepted, has consistently come under criticism by what have come to be known as the fourth generation of scholars of revolutions (Goldstone 2001). In his review essay of the evolution of literature about revolution, Goldstone articulates the four generations of scholarship. He explains the various global shifts and empirical examples that account for the reconceptualization of the making and types of revolutions. He argues that the fourth trend in the scholarship on revolution—in contrast to the third approach, which focused on structural vulnerabilities of regimes as the cause of revolution—has emphasized the importance of also considering the roles of leadership, ideology, and processes of identification with a revolutionary movement in attempts to explain the success or failure of revolutions. These concepts have been emphasized in the literature on "contentious politics," the broader field of confrontational social movements. Expanding the study of revolution by incorporating the literature and theory on contentious politics—that is, oppositional social movements—helps in better understanding the roles of women in revolutionary movements. When a revolutionary movement is understood as an amalgam of organizations seeking to challenge the status quo in order to bring about long-term social transformation, the notion of what is a revolutionary movement expands, along with the idea of who is a revolutionary. With that expansion comes the space to analyze the roles of women (Shayne 2004).

Until fairly recently, revolutionary organizations, particularly those structured around violent tactics, tended to be a domain restricted to men. But there have always been exceptions. For example, in 40 A.D. the Chinese were temporarily driven out of Vietnam by a rebel army of 80,000 soldiers said to have been organized by two sisters, Trung Trac and Trung Nhi—the Trung sisters. The sisters are said to have trained thirty-six women, including their own mother, to be generals in their army. After the triumph, the Vietnamese people declared Trung Trac, the elder sister, their leader. However this victory was short-lived. According to folklore, after three years of battling the Chinese, the inevitable defeat of the Vietnamese people prompted the Trung sisters to maintain their honor by committing suicide. Their stories have been kept alive in Vietnam through everything from commemorative postage stamps to monuments (Women in World History, 2004).

More recent history has also included women revolutionaries. In the 1950s, for example, the three Mirabal sisters were leaders in the movement against the dictatorship of Rafael Trujillo Molina in the Dominican Republic. Beginning in the 1970s, Nobel Peace Prize winner Rigoberta Menchú Tum has been a leader for the rights of Guatemalan indigenous peoples. A handful of women revolutionaries have indeed received the recognition that their efforts and risks have warranted. However, these few cases, which have often reached mythological proportions, leave much of the history of women revolutionaries untold. According to several studies, the numbers of women revolutionaries have been increasing, and not just with a few exceptional leaders here and there.

What accounts for the increased participation of women in revolutionary movements? When considering guerrilla warfare, as opposed to contentious politics more generally, several social, political, and economic shifts have contributed to the increasing involvement of women. Karen Kampwirth, in her book *Women in Guerrilla Movements: Nicaragua, El Salvador, Chiapas, Cuba* (2002), offers a comparative analysis of women's participation in these four guerrilla struggles. Significant numbers of women participated in the three more recent cases, but far fewer in Cuba. She argues that four factors have contributed to the rise in numbers of women in guerrilla struggles. First are what she calls structural changes. She argues that socioeconomic shifts have impacted women's involvement in armed combat. Changes in the economies in Latin America led to increased participation of women in the so-called public sphere as income generators. As a result, women have grown more accustomed to living their lives outside the physical confines of the home and in many cases independent from men. Such shifts proved decisive to transformations in acceptable behavior for women, a process that has translated into increased political participation of women, including in guerrilla combat.

Second, she identifies what she calls ideological and organizational changes. These changes include the proliferation of the Marxist-Catholic doctrine of Liberation Theology in the region. Liberation Theology started to take hold in the 1960s. A typical manifestation of Liberation Theology was the creation of Christian Base Communities (CBCs) structured as consciousness-raising groups designed to implement social justice agendas while working within a Catholic framework. CBCs were decidedly progressive and were particularly appealing to women because of their religious roots. As such, they often served as the first site of leftist political education for many women who would later become guerrilla militants. Another organizational factor has been a shift in the type of guerrilla struggle waged. In Cuba, guerrillas—about 5 per-

A female guerrilla of the Zapatista National Liberation Army (EZLN), Chiapas, Mexico, 1994. (Keith Dannemiller/Corbis)

cent of whom were women (Kampwirth 2002, 118)—waged what is called a *foco* strategy of guerrilla warfare. It relied on a relatively small army or *foco* of guerrillas to wage the armed struggle. (In the case of Cuba this strategy succeeded.) This approach contrasted that taken in Chiapas, Nicaragua, and El Salvador, where revolutionary leaders had to mobilize much larger numbers of people to join the guerrilla armies. They waged what is called a *prolonged war,* a series of relentless and ongoing attacks designed to continuously weaken the enemy. Mass mobilization meant significantly more combatants and, thus, an increase in the participation of women to approximately 30 percent of guerrilla fighters in these three cases (Kampwirth 2002, 2–4, 84).

A third series of factors Kampwirth identifies are those she calls "political factors." Political factors include increased state repression coupled with the inability of the state to address the basic needs of women. And finally, she notes "personal factors" that have increased the number of women participants in guerrilla struggles, including family traditions of resistance, one's year of birth (which affects whether as a teenager or young adult a person was exposed to the development of a major social movement), and participation in preexisting social networks, particularly nonviolent yet radical social organizations such as militant student groups.

But other scholars have suggested that the real numbers of women involved in revolutionary activities have not necessarily gone up, but that due both to the expansion of the definition of revolution characteristic of the contentious politics approach and to the research of feminist scholars, more women who previously had fallen out of the purview of studies of revolution are now being acknowledged for their efforts. In her book *The Revolution Question: Feminisms in El Salvador, Chile, and Cuba* (2004), Julie Shayne argues that women participate in revolutionary movements in a variety of ways: as mothers, in support positions, as guerrillas, in leadership roles, as union and human rights activists, as politicians, and as alliance builders. She explains that the roles that women played tended to be the result of the same patriarchal, gendered division of labor present in civilian or nonrevolutionary life. However, despite the often sexist reasons for the positioning of women, their contributions were no less important to revolutionary movements than those of their male comrades.

With respect to guerrilla warfare, women have filled a variety of roles, including frontline and rearguard combat, mid- to high-level leadership, and what are typically referred to as logistical functions. Combat on both the rear and front lines of guerrilla warfare refers to women in face-to-face battle where weapons may be guns, hand grenades, or things like handmade bombs. Women have also played leadership roles, albeit in significantly fewer numbers than men (Luciak 2001). Such positions have been held by women at middle levels, where they are responsible for commanding an individual platoon or brigade. In some cases women have been responsible for strategizing decisions at the national level. For example, in El Salvador, one of the top members of the guerrilla leadership was a woman, Maria Marta Valladares (real name) aka Nidia Diaz (war name), who sat at the negotiating table and was responsible for working out a peace accord acceptable to the revolutionary movement she was representing.

Tasks considered to be logistical within a guerrilla movement include: working as medics and tending to wounded, delivering messages, transporting weapons, sewing uniforms, preparing food, accompanying male guerrillas from place to place, raising money, and operating rebel radio stations. In many cases women were more easily able to accomplish some of these tasks because assumptions about their passivity led to less suspicion than that elicited by male revolutionaries. For example, this was the case for women delivering messages from one guerrilla camp to another or accompanying a male guerrilla in order to help him pass as a part of a young couple rather than draw attention as a lone

male. In other cases, women were able to accomplish logistical tasks because expectations of behavior and attire connected to traditional ideas of femininity provided a certain degree of camouflage. For example, women were able to transport weapons by hiding them in their skirts, purses, and fabricated pregnant bellies. Similarly, in some cases women were even able to flirt their way out of dangerous situations.

In the noncombat aspects of revolutionary struggle and contentious politics women have also participated in a variety of local social movements, sometimes directly connected to larger national struggles while at other times more autonomous and outside the bounds of a larger revolutionary movement. Perhaps the most oft-cited example of women's participation in noncombat revolutionary movements is the mothers of the disappeared in Latin America (Arditti 1999; Fisher 1993). During the bloodier parts of Latin America's histories, the practice of "disappearing" suspected leftists and their sympathizers was a very common tactic used by military and paramilitary organizations. A "disappeared" individual is one who has been kidnapped, often in the middle of the night, and is never seen or heard from again. Families are never provided a body or any information regarding the victim's whereabouts or fate. The prevalence of this human rights violation prompted women to come together as mothers, grandmothers, sisters, and wives and pressure the military governments to provide information about their loved ones, cease the practice, and be held accountable for their actions. Their protests drew international attention to the systematic abuse of human rights. In many cases women activists in these organizations were the first to publicly denounce military regimes such as those in Argentina and Chile in the 1970s and 1980s. Additionally, women have been active in labor unions and other social organizations focused on economic betterment of their communities. In these cases the actions of women revolutionaries were not violent and were often seen as apolitical, but in many cases they were quite explicit in the revolutionary agendas that they advanced.

Another question that scholars of women and revolution have addressed is how revolutions are structured from an ideological and discursive point of view with respect to women. Valentine Moghadam (1997) has addressed this question through several cases, including Algeria, Iran, East Central Europe, Turkey, South Yemen, Afghanistan, and Nicaragua. Moghadam suggests that revolutionary movements are organized in one of two different ways: what she calls the women-in-the-family model or the women's emancipation model. According to Moghadam, the women-in-the-family model of revolution articulates that the roles of women revolutionaries reside in the realm of procreation; that is, birthing and rearing future revolutionaries. She uses the cases of Algeria, Iran, and East Central Europe to demonstrate her point. On the other hand, the women's emancipation model includes, at least rhetorically, concern for the lives of women in the revolutionary discourse. A revolutionary movement structured around such a paradigm might suggest that the eradication of sexism and emancipation of women is an integral part of the revolutionary agenda. In Moghadam's estimation, revolutionary movements in Turkey, South Yemen, Afghanistan, and Nicaragua organized themselves around this structure.

Implicit in Moghadam's argument is that such models are determined by male leadership as opposed to the women revolutionaries themselves. As a result of this top-down organizational style, women are often left disenchanted in the aftermath of revolutionary movements for which they risked their own and their families' lives. Similarly, when the rhetoric of egalitarianism that characterizes the women's emancipation model proves inconsistent with the treatment of women, both during and in the aftermath of revolutionary movements, the gendered sociopolitical landscape is often permanently transformed.

This leads to the next question: how have women fared in the wake of revolutionary movements? Some scholars have argued that one unintentional byproduct of revolutionary mobilization is feminism (for example, Kampwirth 2004; Randall 1992; Shayne 2004). There are several reasons for this. First, and related to Moghadam's women's emancipation model, women revolutionaries are often left with a deep sense of betrayal after revolutionary movements if their specific needs remain unaddressed and/or they feel they were subjected to sexism within the revolutionary movement. Additionally, the process of participating in a revolutionary movement often provides political and ideological training for women who later feel inspired to become involved in a feminist movement. Furthermore, participation in revolutionary movements serves, among other things, to transform women's self-perception into that of empowered political actors, which better positions them to feel confident about participating in and even leading a radical social movement like feminism.

Other scholars have argued that women's participation in formal democratic politics is increased in the aftermath of revolutionary movements. For example, in Ilja Luciak's (2001) analysis of El Salvador, Nicaragua, and Guatemala, he has concluded that despite the fact that in many cases women were held back both during revolutionary movements and in the political consolidation in the aftermath, women have seen a decided increase in their political opportunities. In contrast, however, some scholars have suggested that women's political positions and opportunities have actually diminished in the wake of some revolutionary movements, particularly in the context of transitions to democracy (Craske 1999; Goldstone 2001). It has been suggested that under an agenda focused upon the reconstruction of society, women have been pushed back into the domestic sphere by male revolutionary leaders in an attempt to create a new status quo based on the pre-revolutionary models of patriarchal governing. Other women may "voluntarily" withdraw from formal politics as a result of feelings of exasperation in confronting such sexist attitudes from their former comrades. Still others welcome the end of wars and political instability and appreciate the opportunity to spend time with their families from whom they were often separated. Another interpretation suggests that women's political organizing has not necessarily decreased in post-revolutionary periods, but rather has been redirected to other political activities, like the rest of civilian society, particularly those organized around neo-liberal economies (Franceschet 2003).

In conclusion, the participation of women in revolutionary struggles has been increasing as have the numbers of scholars committed to archiving their often untold histories. Women's participation has varied from low-level support tasks such as sewing uniforms to high-level tasks such as acting as guerrilla representatives and strategists. Similarly, women's revolutionary contributions extend beyond traditional notions of guerrilla warfare, as in the case, for example, of the mothers of the disappeared, and other similar organizations in which women were or are the leaders. The results for women in the aftermath of revolutions have been mixed— in some cases they have made significant gains in both formal and informal politics, while in others their revolutionary contributions have been unacknowledged and all but forgotten, contributing to the sense of resentment that was fundamental to the birth of feminism in the wake of revolution.

Julie D. Shayne

See Also Afghanistan: Conflict and Civil War; Chilean Socialist Revolution, Counter-Revolution, and the Restoration of Democracy; Chinese 1989 Democracy Movement; Cinema of Revolution; Cuban Revolution; Documentaries of Revolution; Guatemalan Democratic Revolution, Counterrevolution, and Restoration of Democracy; Nicaraguan Revolution; Salvadoran Revolution; Student and Youth Movements, Activism, and Revolution; Theories of Revolution; Vietnamese Revolution; Women's Movement of the United States; Zapatista Movement

References and Further Readings

Arditti, Rita. 1999. *Searching for Life: The Grandmothers of the Plaza de Mayo and the Disappeared Children of Argentina.* Berkeley: University of California Press.

Craske, Nikki. 1999. *Women and Politics in Latin America.* New Brunswick, NJ: Rutgers University Press.

Fisher, Jo. 1993. *Out of the Shadows: Women, Resistance and Politics in South America.* London: Latin American Bureau.

Franceschet, Susan. 2003. "'State Feminism' and Women's Movements: The Impact of Chile's Servicio Nacional de la Mujer on Women's Activism," *Latin American Research Review* 38 (1): 9–40.

Goldstone, Jack A. 2001. "Toward a Fourth Generation of Revolutionary Theory," *Annual Review of Political Science* 4: 139–187.

Kampwirth, Karen. 2002. *Women and Guerrilla Movements: Nicaragua, El Salvador, Chiapas, Cuba.* University Park: Pennsylvania State University Press.

———. 2004. *Feminism and the Legacy of Revolution: Nicaragua, El Salvador, Chiapas.* Athens: Ohio University Press.

Luciak, Ilja. 2001. *After the Revolution: Gender and Democracy in El Salvador, Nicaragua, and Guatemala.* Baltimore, MD: Johns Hopkins University Press.

Moghadam, Valentine. 1997. "Gender and Revolutions." Pp. 137–167 in *Theorizing Revolutions,* edited by John Foran. New York: Routledge.

Randall, Margaret. 1992. *Gathering Rage: The Failure of 20th Century Revolutions to Develop a Feminist Agenda.* New York: Monthly Review Press.

Shayne, Julie. 2004. *The Revolution Question: Feminisms in El Salvador, Chile, and Cuba.* New Brunswick, NJ: Rutgers University Press.

Skocpol, Theda. 1979. *States and Social Revolutions.* Cambridge: Cambridge University Press.

Wickham-Crowley, Timothy P. 1992. *Guerillas and Revolution in Latin America.* Princeton, NJ: Princeton University Press.

Women in World History. "The Trung Sisters." http://www.womeninworldhistory.com/heroine10.html accessed July 27, 2004.

Women's Movement of the United States

CHRONOLOGY

1848   The official birth of the woman suffrage movement is marked by the New York Seneca Falls meeting in July.

1850   The first National Women's Rights convention takes place in Worcester, Massachusetts.

The Fugitive Slave Act is passed, stifling black woman suffrage activities.

1857   The New York Married Women's Property Act is passed, noted as the most comprehensive piece of women's rights legislation in the United States.

1859   Black women make the first call for universal suffrage after the New England Convention of Colored Citizens.

1860   By now, fourteen states have passed legislation concerning women's property rights.

1865   Vassar opens its doors to middle-class white women.

1866   Elizabeth Cady Stanton and Susan B. Anthony organize a petition for woman suffrage, the first to be presented to Congress.

By the spring, the Fourteenth Amendment, intended to protect the legal rights of former slaves, is finalized. White women are very dissatisfied with the Fourteenth Amendment because it does not offer political rights to women. Abolitionists are also unhappy with the amendment because it largely offers only civil and not political rights to freedmen (Dubois 1978).

The American Equal Rights Association (AERA) is founded and includes both black and white suffragists. In conjunction with this association, African American women formed the interracial Philadelphia Suffrage Association.

1867   The American Equal Rights Association is defeated in New York and Kansas in its state-by-state campaign to gain the vote for women. When Republicans refuse to endorse woman suffrage, suffragists turn to Democratic presidential candidate George Francis Train, who agrees to fund the suffragist publication, "The Revolution." Most abolitionists and African Americans become alienated from those white suffragists who refuse to support the vote for black men while women continue to be denied the vote. During this time, many white women become increasingly racist in their approach, completely abandoning the call for universal suffrage.

1868   The suffragist paper "The Revolution" is published.

To the dismay of many feminists, pro-Republican suffragists support the Fifteenth Amendment, which gives the vote to black men while all women remain barred from voting. Pro-Republican suffragists support the amendment with the hope that a focus on woman suffrage will follow.

White middle-class suffragists begin seeking alliances with working women, forming the Working Women's Association in 1868. In September, the Women's Typographical Union is formed and is able to establish a local within the National Typographical Union.

1869   The National Woman's Suffrage Association (NWSA) is founded, led by Susan B. Anthony and Elizabeth Cady Stanton. This organization, which opposes the Fifteenth Amendment that grants rights to black men but not women, will pursue the expansion of women's rights at the national level.

The American Woman Suffrage Association (AWSA) is founded by Lucy Stone and others who support the Fifteenth Amendment, hoping its ratification will assist the achievement of the vote for women. The AWSA works for women's rights at the local level and attempts to achieve the vote for women through a state-by-state campaign.

Due to class conflict and the effective exclusion of working women, the Working Women's Association falls.

Women activists propose a Sixteenth Amendment for woman suffrage.

1870   The Fifteenth Amendment is ratified.

1871   In line with a suffragist strategy called the "new departure," Mary Ann Shadd Cary leads sixty-three women to vote in Washington, D.C. Though their votes are not counted, they are able to get elected officials to sign affidavits that verify their attempts.

1872   Sojourner Truth attempts to cast a vote in Michigan.

1873   Concerned with family problems brought on by the use of alcohol, a group of women form the Women's Christian Temperance Union. These women march into saloons, demanding that they be closed.

1881   The first volume of Stanton and Anthony's *History of Woman Suffrage* appears. The edi-

tors of the volume make no mention of black women suffragists in their coverage of the women's movement.

1890   After a bitter history of competition and ideological conflict, the NWSA and the AWSA reunite to form the National American Woman Suffrage Association (NAWSA). Some white women activists argue for "educated suffrage"—that the vote should be given to literate, educated women who, it is argued, will vote responsibly.

1892   Victoria Matthews and Marichita Lyons form the Women's Loyal Union, the first black women's club resulting from the black women's national club movement.

1912   Alice Paul and Lucy Burns introduce protest tactics that they have gleaned from their time in Europe. Using these methods, they revitalize the movement for a woman suffrage constitutional amendment.

1914   Suffragists Alice Paul and Lucy Burns establish the National Women's Party (NWP), formerly known as the Congressional Union.

1916   The National Association of Colored Women (NACW) prepares a "Declaration of Principles" at its Baltimore convention, offering support for a universal suffrage amendment to the U.S. Constitution.

1920   The Nineteenth Amendment, also known as the "Susan B. Anthony" Amendment, is ratified in August 1920, granting women the right to vote.

1920–1950   Feminism is said to have entered "the doldrums" after women obtained the right to vote, a period characterized by little to no activism. This lull in activism is attributed in part to women's expectations for greater inclusion in political life. But the existence of this lull is contested. Evidence indicates that women's activism, particularly among African Americans, continues throughout these years.

1963   Women's activism is said to be revitalized with Betty Friedan's book, *The Feminine*

Mystique. This publication appeals to white, middle-class housewives who feel a sense of emptiness in their lives.

1966   The National Organization for Women (NOW) is formed by college-educated and professional women after an attempt by a southern legislator to defeat the Civil Rights Act of 1964 by incorporating the word *sex* into the legislation.

1968   Members breaking from NOW's legislative focus form the Women's Equity Action League (WEAL). The Boston Women's Health Book Collective (BWHBC) is formed after a women's liberation conference in Boston.

1970   The BWHBC publishes the book *Women and Their Bodies,* later renamed, *Our Bodies, Ourselves,* now known as the bible of women's health.

1973   *Our Bodies, Ourselves* is translated into Spanish and gains wide use in medical schools. By this time, 350,000 copies have been sold.

1983   In June, a conference on black women's health organized by Byllye Avery of the National Women's Health Network (NWHN) leads to the creation of the National Black Women's Health Project (NBWHP) as part of the NWHN project on Black women's health.

1984   In an attempt to be more inclusive, the BWHBC includes a statement on race, class, ethnicity, and sexual preference in *Our Bodies, Ourselves.* The NBWHP becomes an independent organization.

1991   Julia Scott of the NBWHP attempts to develop interracial coalitions but is discouraged by what she sees as a lack of understanding from white women.

1992–Present   The women's movement is said to have become "professionalized." Women's rights activists continue to organize conferences and rallies, but also continue to face divisions along the lines of race, class, and sexuality.

INTRODUCTION

The U.S. women's movement was successful in securing basic civil, economic, and political rights through struggles carried out from the nineteenth to twenty-first centuries. However, the story of the women's rights movement is marked by deep divisions rather than harmonious unification. The path to women's rights varied for different segments of the population. Working-class white women and women of color utilized different methods from those of upper- and middle-class white women for obtaining the right to vote, given their differential access to education and employment. Strong divisions among African American women, white women, and men persisted throughout the suffrage movement. White women fought on the grounds of sexism, while black women necessarily fought both racism and sexism simultaneously. There were periods of interracial cooperation, but these coalitions were sporadic and short-lived. Race and class divisions that developed within the early phases of the women's movement persist at different levels in contemporary times, as women continue their struggle for equality.

BACKGROUND: CULTURE AND HISTORY

During the nineteenth century, women were seen as the property of their husbands and were relegated to domestic life in the social space that came to be known as "women's sphere." Women were not legally entitled to own property in their own names if they were married. They could not hold political office or even vote. Educational opportunities for women were extremely limited, and respectable job opportunities in urban settings were virtually nonexistent. The concept of a woman deciding of her own free will not to marry, apart from a religious vocation, was considered extremely abnormal. Black women faced other concerns, since they were barred from marriage during slavery, and after slavery they struggled to rebuild the families that had been sold away from them. Among free persons, men had dominant custodial rights of children, and the children of slave women were considered the properties of the slave master. Those who violated traditional norms, such as Sarah and Angelina Grimké, white South Carolinians who crossed into the political realm by attacking slavery and comparing the status of most American women to that of slaves, were quickly condemned by the clergy, who ordered them to return to their traditional womanly duties. In response to these demands, Sarah Grimké stated: "The Lord Jesus defines the duties of his followers in his Sermon on the mount . . . without any reference to sex or condition. . . . Men and women are CREATED EQUAL! They are both moral and accountable beings and whatever is right for men to do is right for women" (Grimké 1837, 16).

The industrial revolution over time began to offer some urban white women legitimate job opportunities outside the home, though often low-skill and poorly paid. The issues facing African American women were different, however, since they had *always* worked outside the home and did not have the luxury of separating the private and pubic spheres. After slavery, obtaining independence from men was a less significant issue for them than rebuilding families. However, black women and men faced enormous obstacles to reconstructing their families, not only due to the difficulty of finding lost family members, but also due to the unstable employment of black men and the underpaid employment of black women. The need for a better-educated citizenry opened the door slightly for some women to be trained as teachers and achieve an independent economic existence like that of men. Some of these women, such as Susan B. Anthony, educated to be a teacher, took advantage of their relative independence to play important leadership roles in the creation of the women's movement.

CONTEXT AND PROCESS OF THE WOMEN'S MOVEMENT

Women gained some admittance into colleges by 1834, but their coursework was restricted and they were not fully integrated into college life. It was not until 1865, when Vassar opened its doors to middle-class white women, that colleges began the process of fully integrating by gender. As women gained access to education, they found new avenues through which to work for social change. Women also began to fight for legal reform that would allow them to control their earnings and gain property rights (Burke 1980). By 1860, fourteen states had passed women's property rights legislation, including the 1857 New York Married Women's Property Act, hailed as the most comprehensive women's rights legislation in the United States at the time (Dubois 1978). But these advances did not give them access to political power, namely the right to vote.

Due to the political context of the nineteenth century, arguments for woman suffrage received much less support than those for education and property rights. During this period, women were denied autonomy and lacked even sexual rights within marriage. Therefore, granting political rights to women was attacked as a radical idea. Earlier struggles regarding property rights were more easily won, largely because they were viewed as within women's traditional domestic sphere. Demands for suffrage, on the other hand, implied more directly that women were equal to men.

Despite barriers to suffrage, women's rights activists found a home in the abolitionist movement. Many abolitionists espoused William Lloyd Garrison's ideology of egalitarianism, making the anti-slavery movement a logical place for suffragists to engage their struggle for the vote. Garrison believed that institutions were the source of sin rather than individuals. Armed with Garrison's analysis, women's rights activists began challenging clerical authority, which attempted to justify traditional gender roles. Suffragist Elizabeth Cady Stanton appealed to Garrisonian ideology in her speech at the Anti-Slavery Society:

> In the darkness and gloom of a false theology, I was slowly sawing off the chains of my spiritual bondage, when, for the first time, I met Garrison in London. A few bold strokes from the hammer of his truth, I was free! Only those who have lived all their lives under the dark clouds of vague, undefined fears can appreciate the joy of a doubting soul suddenly born into the kingdom of reason and free thought. Is the bondage of the priest-ridden less galling than that of the slave, because we do not see the chains, the indelible scars, the festering wounds, the deep degradation of all the power of the God-like mind? (As quoted in Dubois 1978, 34)

Even though the Garrisonian abolitionist movement offered activists such as Stanton a feeling of liberation, some historians contend that it also limited women's advancement, because it did not challenge the roots of sexism or offer a critique of the division of labor within the home. Garrisonian thought offered a starting place for suffragists, but once they began to espouse their own liberation, women soon found themselves excluded from the largely male-led and-organized anti-slavery movement. Out of this rejection emerged the 1848 New York Seneca Falls Women's Rights Convention, commonly seen as the birth of the women's movement. Some historians argue that this convention was organized after Elizabeth Cady Stanton and Lucretia Mott were excluded from the gallery of the 1840 World Anti-Slavery Convention in London. Stanton and Mott first met at this convention and forged a friendship, out of which emerged many years of activism starting with Seneca Falls (Burke 1980).

After the Seneca Falls convention, the suffrage movement expanded rapidly. Participation in the women's rights struggle grew primarily through local leadership, inspired by conventions and by suffragists who traveled from town to town educating women about the movement. This style of recruitment, depending largely on informal networks, also presented problems. Because there were no national or state organizations, membership was largely unstable. Also, continuing ties to the American Anti-Slavery Society temporarily inhibited the formation of a totally independent women's movement (Dubois 1978). Women's rights activists depended heavily on abolitionist support and even scheduled their conventions in conjunction with the Anti-Slavery Society's meetings. What's more, given this tight relationship with abolitionism, women's activism was forced to a halt during the Civil War, when its constituency was absorbed in the fight against slavery.

After the Civil War, the Anti-Slavery Society gained political influence and resources. Given their long-time relationship with abolitionists, women's rights activists expected to benefit from these resources. However, the next move for abolitionists was securing the vote for African Americans (namely African American men), while white suffragists were interested in gaining the vote for white women. This is not to say that all abolitionists supported the struggle for the black vote. Garrison himself, the leader of the Anti-Slavery Society, argued that abolition should be the end goal. Still, the bulk of abolitionists followed Wendell Phillips, Garrison's successor, who asserted that African Americans needed the vote to protect themselves from a racist society in which they were now at greater risk of violence.

Phillips encouraged women's rights activists to first work toward black suffrage, putting aside woman suffrage for the time being. He stated, "I hope in time to be as bold . . . and add to the last clause 'sex'! But this hour belongs to the negro" (Dubois 1978, 59). Stanton quickly responded, "My question is this: Do you believe the African race is composed entirely of males?" (Dubois 1978, 60). Though Stanton revealed an interesting contradiction in abolitionists' support of the black vote, she was herself guilty of pursuing rights mainly for white but not African American women. Many white suffragists employed arguments of moral superiority to prevent black women from achieving the vote before white women.

Much of the conflict over black male versus white female suffrage involved debates about the Fifteenth Amendment, which developed after women were excluded from the Fourteenth Amendment, intended to protect the legal rights of former slaves. In 1865, Stanton learned that the Fourteenth Amendment would specify men as the only citizens who could be granted political representation. In response, Stanton and Anthony organized a petition for woman suffrage, gaining ten thousand signatures by 1866. At this point, an attempt was made to unite white women and African Americans in a fight for universal adult suffrage.

Susan B. Anthony and Lucy Stone proposed universal suffrage to the Anti-Slavery meeting in January 1866. However Wendell Phillips, presiding officer, opposed a vote on the proposal. Hence, in May of 1866, suffragists organized their first women's rights campaign since the Civil War and created the American Equal Rights Association (AERA), pursuing their goals at the state level. The AERA activists launched two campaigns in 1867, one in Kansas and the other in New York, aimed at removing the words "white" and "male" from state constitutions and establishing universal suffrage in both states. After canvassing New York, women's rights activists obtained 28,000 signatures for their petitions. They sought the support of those with dual loyalties: that is, those who advocated both black male and woman suffrage. Therefore, white female suffragists called attention to the disenfranchisement of African American females—a strategy meant to secure support and resources from those still undecided. However, Ellen Dubois maintains that "the attention paid to black women was more rhetorical than real" (1978, 69). As Dubois points out, black women and men constituted only a minute percentage of women's rights and abolitionist organizations. Prominent black women, Frances Watkins Harper and Sojourner Truth, were active in the American Equal Rights Association but usually occupied the least powerful positions.

Unlike white women, black women consistently sided with abolitionists throughout the 1850s, evidence of their need to fight both sexism and racism. Also unlike their white counterparts, African Americans faced the frequent danger of lynching and had little protection against this violence. The threats and insecurity that African American women experienced often interfered with their struggle for equality. The passage of the Fugitive Slave Act in 1850 was one example of the impediments confronting African American women. The act allowed slave owners to recapture slaves who had fled, prompting those with the means to leave the United States. During these times, the intersection of race and gender was painfully disadvantageous for black women.

Black suffragists also differed from white suffragists in their early calls for universal suffrage. African Americans first advocated universal suffrage following the New England Convention of Colored Citizens in 1859. The call for universal suffrage did not come from white women activists until a decade later. Suffragists such as Lucy Stone, Lucretia Mott, and Susan B. Anthony at times worked alongside African Americans. But Elizabeth Cady Stanton was often alienated from black women by placing the cause of elite white women ahead of all other oppressions. Stanton also often compared the position of wealthy white women to the plight of the slave, which did not win her favor with black abolitionists or suffragists. However, though predominantly white, AERA did argue for both black and woman suffrage referenda in 1867. AERA's victory in securing authorization for these referenda in Kansas and New York spurred a countercampaign from the Republican Party, which separated abolitionists and feminists within the AERA. Republicans formed the "Anti-Female Suffrage Committee," and as a result, many abolitionists affiliated with the Republican Party left the feminist movement, while those supportive of both black and women's rights decided to endorse woman suffrage. The support feminists received, however, came too late to be of much assistance (Dubois 1978).

Injured by the defeat of the Kansas campaign and the attacks by Republicans, some white suffragists turned to the Democratic Party, a move that alienated what support they had left from African Americans and abolitionists. These white suffragists endorsed presidential candidate George Francis Train in 1867, who, while supportive of white women's rights, was also known for his extreme racism. Train appealed to white women's rights as a means of preventing African Americans from rising up against whites. He implored his audiences to choose "Beauty, Virtue, and Intelligence" over "Muscle, Color and Ignorance" (Dubois 1978, 95). Both Stanton and Susan B. Anthony supported Train's campaign, drawing on arguments of white moral superiority.

In contrast, at the close of the 1867 AERA convention, officers signed memoranda for the enfranchisement of both women and black men, yet these memoranda still excluded black women. Though this compromise offered some promise, conflict soon worsened as Stanton used AERA funds to support Train's campaign. Both Anthony and Stone protested Stanton's actions. Train's candidacy was short-lived, and he was defeated. What's more, growing conflict over black male versus white female suffrage led to the deterioration of the AERA. White women accused male abolitionists of abandoning woman suffrage completely, while black women criticized most white women activists as racists and elitists.

Alienated from previous supporters, white suffragists began searching for new allies and found them in the national labor movement. Now middle-class, white suffragists began attempting to align themselves with their working-class counterparts. In July 1868, "The Revolution" was calling for a new party that supported labor reform. Stanton was able to become a delegate to the National Labor Congress in September 1868, and Susan B. Anthony formed the Working Women's Association in that same year. Stanton encouraged working women facing exclusion from trade unions to create their own organizations. With Stanton's prodding, working women formed the Women's Typographical Union in 1868. By the second meeting of the Working Women's Association, Local 6 of the National Typographical Union (an all-male organization) had promised the Women's Typographical Union financial assistance and encouraged these women to apply to become a local unit within the national union.

Though suffragists had eagerly allied themselves with working women, the leadership positions of the Working Women's Association remained largely in middle-class hands. Class conflict resulting from the direct and indirect exclusion of some working women from the organization was a significant source of tension within the Working Women's Association and undoubtedly contributed to its demise. Overt exclusion of working women included an incident in which Elizabeth Brown, treasurer of the association, was removed from her position. Working women were excluded in covert ways as well. Association meetings were moved to middle-class homes and dues were increased to more than twice their usual rate (Dubois 1978). However, another factor played a role in the breakup of the organization. Female typesetters began aligning themselves with their male counterparts in Local 6, and this alliance weakened their coalition with middle-class white suffragists. In January of 1869, the women typesetters sided with Local 6 in its strike for union wages, but suffragists found themselves on the side of the employers. Susan B. Anthony argued for a training program for working women, inadvertently allowing employers to use women trainees as strikebreakers. Using women as strikebreakers had been a common tactic implemented by employers to alienate working-class women from working-class men. Anthony was heavily criticized by the labor movement, further dividing middle-class suffragists from working women. Finally in 1869, Anthony was removed from the National Labor Congress, bringing the coalition between working women and middle-class suffragists to an end, along with the Working Women's Association. Anthony and Stanton, left with their middle-class constituents, formed the National Labor Suffrage Association.

The demise of the Working Women's Association in 1869 was followed by debates concerning the Fifteenth Amendment. This Republican-sponsored amendment was intended to ensure that African American *men* had the right to the vote. Stanton and Susan Anthony took the anti-Republican position that white women suffragists should not support an amendment granting the right to vote only to black *men* while not also granting white women the right to vote. In contrast, Lucy Stone, along with her husband Henry Blackwell and others, felt that challenging the Republicans would offend a large group of woman suffrage supporters and former abolitionists, most of whom were pro-Republican. The debate over whether or not to support Republicans and the Fifteenth Amendment led to the creation of two separate organizations that represented this ideological divide among suffragists—Stanton and Anthony's National Woman Suffrage Association (NWSA) and Stone's American Woman Suffrage Association (AWSA).

The NWSA formed after a convention in May 1869 that Susan Anthony called together to promote a Sixteenth Amendment for woman suffrage. Hoping to inspire a united movement toward suffrage, Anthony and Stanton invited suffragists from whom they had been estranged, including Antoinette Brown Blackwell, Lucy Stone's sister-in-law. The convention did not go as Anthony had planned. After a keynote speech calling for a Sixteenth Amendment, Stephen Foster and Frederick Douglass accused Stanton of racism for opposing the Fifteenth Amendment and argued that the vote for African Americans carried with it an urgency of life and death that it did not carry for middle-class white women. However, Lucy Stone urged Douglass and others at the convention to unite with women in a struggle to end all oppression. Still, Stone's position was that women should work with Republicans to secure the vote for African American men before working on a Sixteenth Amendment. Most participants at the convention agreed with Stone's position. In response, those supporting Stanton's anti–Fifteenth Amendment position created the National Woman Suffrage Association (NWSA) two days later. Those agreeing with Stone's support for the Fifteenth Amendment joined the new American Woman Suffrage Association (AWSA) organized by Stone and Blackwell to fight for woman suffrage, while also supporting the Fifteenth Amendment. The NWSA and the AWSA also differed in that the NWSA generally employed tactics intended to bring change at the national level, while the AWSA usually worked for women's rights at the local level, hoping to achieve change state by state. African American women more often allied themselves with the AWSA, but also developed their own movement that focused more specifically on their unique experiences, needs, and goals.

During 1869–1874, when the white suffragist movement was divided between the NWSA and AWSA, black female suffragists developed a new approach that reinterpreted the Fourteenth Amendment. Pioneers of this strategy, known as the "new departure," worked to enfranchise women using the Constitution's definition of citizenship. In line with this new plan, both black and white suffragists set up voting tables across New Jersey in 1868, casting mock ballots alongside men. In 1871, Mary Ann Shadd Cary, a black woman activist, led sixty-three women to vote in Washington, D.C. She and her group were successful in pressing elected officials to sign affidavits verifying their attempts. Cary also asserted in front of the House Judiciary Committee that black men and women be afforded the right to vote and that the word "male" be struck from the Constitution. Cary argued that as a taxpayer, she should be afforded the same rights as men. Her activism inspired other prominent suffragists, such as Sojourner Truth, who in 1872 attempted to cast a ballot in Battle Creek, Michigan (Terborg-Penn 1998).

Because a larger constituency of black women affiliated themselves with AWSA in support of black male suffrage, conflict with white women in NWSA was inevitable. Members of the NWSA accused black male suffragists of being en-

Sojourner Truth, an escaped former slave, campaigned for the abolition of slavery and was the first known African American female suffragist. (Library of Congress)

tirely against votes for women, but historians cite evidence that these men actually advocated votes both for women and black men. Charles Langston, for example, publicly supported woman suffrage and persuaded a convention of African Americans in Kansas to advocate for impartial suffrage without regard to race or sex (Terborg-Penn 1998). Yet Olympia Brown, who had accused Langston of sexism, argued vehemently against "placing the dirty, immoral, degraded Negro before a white woman" (Stanton, Anthony, and Gage 1969, 23).

What's more, while most white women totally ignored African American women in the struggle for the vote, prominent African American men stood by them. W. E. B. Du Bois is most noted as consistently supporting political power for women. In his journal, the *Crisis,* Du Bois implored the African American community to support black women, and he also invited black suffragists to publish their work. Black men in South Carolina who had achieved the vote before the Fifteenth Amendment was ratified joined coalitions with black women to work for female suffrage. This is not to say that all black men supported black woman suffrage. Some held to traditional views of women's role in society, which complicated the struggle black women faced against both sexism and racism.

The Fifteenth Amendment was finally ratified in March 1870, but the leaders of AWSA did not receive the support for woman suffrage that they had expected as a result of helping to win the vote for black men. Also, potential black male political support for woman suffrage was severely weakened by the passage of legislation in southern states that effectively disenfranchised many black men. Eventually, the NWSA and AWSA would reunite, but not until 1890, and this reunification would continue to exclude African American as well as working-class women. White women suffragists, often lacking other political resources, would seek the support of black men from time to time, but they very rarely pursued political coalitions with African American women (Terborg-Penn 1998).

The 1880s marked the end of the first generation of black women suffragists. More militant and better educated by the end of the nineteenth century, the second generation of African American female suffragists continued arguments first promoted by Frances Harper and Mary Shadd Cary in the 1800s—that black women needed the vote to better their communities. During a time when violence against African Americans was worsening, black women continued to inspire their communities.

In the 1890s, when NWSA and AWSA reunited to form the National American Woman Suffrage Association (NAWSA), "educated suffrage" (the concept that the vote should be given to literate, educated women who would vote responsibly) gained wide support from both Southern and Northern white women. These suffragists viewed the exclusion of black women as a measure of expediency toward white female suffrage. Even Henry Blackwell, who had supported the Fifteenth Amendment, now argued for educated suffrage. At the 1895 NAWSA Convention, Stanton argued against universal suffrage for fear that politicians could easily manipulate illiterate voters (Terborg-Penn 1998).

Woman suffrage efforts, both black and white, flourished in separate club movements as well. As part of their work in the club movement, white middle- and upper-class women saw their purpose as upholding the moral and spiritual fabric of society. In 1866, middle- and upper-class women had established the YWCA (Young Women's Christian Association) to protect the morals of young women seeking work in the cities, and in 1873 they created the Women's Christian Temperance Union to fight for woman suffrage as well as to combat taverns and alcohol use, which were blamed for both spousal and child abuse.

Black women's clubs included the Women's Loyal Union, led by Victoria Earle Matthews in 1892, the Colored Women's Progressive Franchise Association, established by Mary Shadd Cary in 1895, and the National Baptist Convention of 1895. The development of these clubs increased the political power of black women by the twentieth century. The goal of the club movement was to achieve a Universal Suffrage Amendment that would allow women to vote in *any* election.

By the 1900s, suffragists were making substantial gains toward suffrage. In 1912, Alice Paul and Lucy Burns helped revitalize the movement toward a constitutional amendment. Drawing on tactics common to movements in Britain, Paul and Burns introduced marches, civil disobedience, and demonstrations to the organizations. In 1920 ratification of the Nineteenth Amendment to the U.S. Constitution, giving women the right to vote, was achieved. In response to the victory, the movement of white middle-class women declined. Some groups, such as the National Women's Party remained, but other organizations faded away for a variety of reasons, including the expectation that with suffrage would come institutional access and political power (Burke 1980). This began a period during which the women's movement was said to have entered the "doldrums." Yet this lull in activism did not characterize black women's organizations, and some social scientists also argue that white women did not completely halt their activism either (See Rupp and Taylor 1987). African American women of all classes actively engaged in women's rights campaigns in the mid 1900s. Among their organizations were the Women's Political Council (WPC), founded in 1946 before the Montgomery bus boycotts, and the Club From Nowhere (CFN), founded in 1956 during the boycotts (McNair Barnett 1995).

The Women's Movement, 1960–1990

While black women's organizing continued throughout the so-called doldrums, the activism of white middle-class women was said to have been reawakened in the 1960s, fueled by Betty Friedan's *The Feminine Mystique*. In this work, Friedan documented feelings of emptiness and discontent among college-educated, suburban, white housewives. With Friedan's publication, many of these women began questioning their homemaking roles and seeking meaningful alternatives. For some, this meant joining the Civil Rights and student protest movements.

Women active in the 1960s Civil Rights and student movements were often placed in less visible, non-leadership positions. Unsatisfied with their treatment in these movement organizations, women began forming their own independent groups and employed a tactic of "consciousness-raising" to stimulate people to analyze and question women's subordinate roles in society. This helped to create a sense of empowerment and spurred the growth of the movement (Morgen 2002). In 1966, the National Organization for Women (NOW) was formed by college-educated and professional white women. The organization was created after Virginia Representative Howard Smith attempted to sabotage the 1964 Civil Rights Act by adding the word *sex*. Comprehending Smith's real intention, women rallied in an effort to maintain the language including sex discrimination in the bill (Burke 1980).

NOW focused primarily on legislative actions, namely working for the Equal Rights Amendment and a pro-choice abortion rights agenda. But not all members of NOW were content with just working for these goals. In 1968, a group of members split off from NOW forming the Women's Equity Action League (WEAL), concerned mainly with economic issues. Though NOW continued to grow in membership, many radical women viewed the organization as elitist and conservative (Burke 1980).

The women's health movement faced similar criticisms. Like NOW, women's health organizations emerged from the activism of the 1960s. One of the best-known groups of this movement was the Boston Women's Health Book Collective (BWHBC). The BWHBC was established in 1968 after a women's liberation conference in Boston. The purpose of the group was to gather and convey knowledge on women's health that women were not receiving from the medical establishment. The women of the BWHBC spent months researching such topics as women's anatomy, menopause, pregnancy, sexually transmitted diseases, and nutrition. After dozens of meetings, they had produced an impressive set of papers that would later be published by the New England Free Press. By December 1970, the book *Women and Their Bodies,* compiled by the BWHBC, had sold 15,000 copies. By 1973, the book had a new title—*Our Bodies, Ourselves*—and had sold 350,000 copies, gaining wide use in medical schools. To this day *Our Bodies, Ourselves* is known as the bible of women's health.

By 1984, even though the BWHBC was largely white and middle class, its members had come to recognize the diversities of women's experiences and included in their book a statement about race, class, ethnicity, and sexual preference. Still some would criticize the BWHBC for "add and stir" approaches toward diversity. White feminists also continued to act as if women were a homogeneous group, focusing on reproductive rights as the key issue for women. White middle-class women defined reproductive rights as access to birth control and "choice," or the right to abortions. Reproductive rights for African American, Puerto Rican, and poor women, however, also meant safety from medical abuse. Historically African American and Puerto Rican men and women had been used as guinea pigs for medical experiments, and this history affected their trust of women's health organizations (Roberts 1999).

Out of this situation in which the needs of women of color were not being addressed, organizations such as the National Black Women's Health Project (NBWHP) arose. This project was born out of a conference on black women's health led by Byllye Avery. Avery had been working on the board of the National Women's Health Network since the 1970s. The first day of the conference in June 1983 was a very empowering and life-altering event for the women involved. One woman stated, "My heart was literally in my throat. To arrive on that campus (Spellman College) and see black women of every hue, blue eyes, fair skin, dark hair, no hair, dreadlocks, straight hair, and permed . . . I'd never been any place that was for black women only, I'd never been any place that was for women only" (Morgen 2002, 46). The conference reached a national audience, and this led to the immediate formation of the National Black Women's Health Project that summer. By March 1984, the NBWHP was an independent organization. Its mission statement emphasized a commitment to "defining, promoting, and maintaining the physical, mental, and emotional well-being of black women" (Morgen 2002, 46).

One of the goals of this organization, led by Julia Scott, was to develop coalitions with white women. Scott characterized the key difference between white feminist and black feminist organizing as having to do with single versus multiple issues:

> A group of people such as African American women and Hispanic women and Native American women who have been subjected to sterilization abuse, you know, the guinea pig kind of thing, and with the birth control pill and the excessive use of hysterectomies in our communities. We very seldom have the luxury of coming together and organizing on just one simple piece, that being the right to abortion, but we see that within the broader women's reproductive health agenda. (Morgen 2002, 48)

However, forging coalitions with white women did not always turn out to be successful. In 1991, Scott pinpointed one of the problems as a lack of empathetic understanding on the part of white women:

> You know at some point you've got to have white women understanding the issues . . . I think the divisions between the races are such that it is always going to be like an effort to put yourself in somebody else's place. . . . I think if white women look at their poor white sisters and the lives they have to live, they'll get the connection across racial lines. (Morgen 2002, 53)

Scott was pointing again to one of the major problems faced in interracial organizing—that is a failure to recognize that women of color experience unique situations that differ from white women's experiences. Hence, as with the suffrage movement, an ideology of sisterhood that emphasized gender over race and class was not beneficial to all women.

The Women's Movement of the Twenty-First Century

The racism and classism of which Julia Scott spoke continue to thrive within the twenty-first century women's movement. Morgen (2002) documents the exclusion of lower-class women and women of color from the women's health movement throughout the 1960s to 1990s. As was the case with the 1868 Working Women's Association, meetings of women's health organizations were held in the homes of white middle-class women, excluding the working class and women of color.

Friedman (1995) argues that the women's movement has reached a dead end in terms of its inclusiveness in that most attempts to include women of color and lower-class women resulted in tokenism, where marginalized women were fetishized. However, twenty-first century feminism has also moved toward theories of intersectionality, which propose the inclusion not just of women of color but also marginalized men. Feminists of color, in particular, have critiqued contemporary feminism as excluding not only women of color, but also lower-class white men and men of color in their analyses of oppression. Patricia Hill Collins (2000) and Yen Le Espiritu (1997), for instance, argue that feminists must embrace an intersectional approach to equality, one that recognizes the ways in which race, class, and gender intersect in the lives of both men and women.

Contemporary feminists continue to address the problem of representation and inclusiveness, but are also faced with a new issue—that of professionalization. Various segments of the contemporary women's health movement, for example, rely heavily on corporate sponsorship, whereas grassroots organizations steer clear of such ties (Ruzek and Becker, 1999). Gaining corporate sponsorship has assisted women's movement organizations financially, but this has also limited the range of tactics and issues they can choose. Professionalized organizations must remain loyal to their sponsors if they are to continue to receive financial support, and this has presented an additional dilemma for feminists of the twenty-first century.

IMPACTS

The U.S. women's movement has had enormous impacts domestically and internationally. In contrast to pre-1848 America, the old legal codes subordinating women to men have been largely eradicated. Women became able to independently own and inherit property and initiate divorce proceedings. Unlike millions of women condemned to illiteracy and relative ignorance in the past, women won equal rights to public education and came to constitute about half of the student bodies of U.S. colleges and universities. This revolution in educational opportunity not only culturally enriched the lives of women, it also provided them with the skills necessary to access a wide range of male-dominated occupations. Women not only achieved the right to vote but went on to become mayors, governors, congresspersons, senators, and cabinet members.

However, the gains cited above have largely benefited middle-class women, and many activists argue that poor women, especially poor women of color, face Third World conditions within the United States. Infant mortality rates for all racial groups have decreased, but the gap between whites and people of color has persisted. African Americans, for example, face more than twice the rate of infant mortality of white Americans (Center for Disease Control 2005). In fact, this ratio has not changed significantly since slavery (Roberts 1999). In general, women of color tend to have a shorter life expectancy and poorer quality of life than white women (National Institute of Health 2002). Black women face higher mortality rates for diseases such as breast cancer than white women, attributed in part to later detection and to inferior insurance coverage (The National Women's Health Information Center 2003). Some scholars and state health officials have also begun to draw connections between poor health outcomes and quality of life for middle-class people of color and everyday experiences with overt and covert racism (Feagin and McKinney 2003; New Jersey Department of Health and Senior Services 1996).

Women in general gained greater access to education, but they have higher poverty rates and earn less than men at each level of education. In 2003, men with four years or more of college earned $55,751 (median income) and women with the same level of education earned $35,125 (63 percent of men's income) (United States Census Bureau, 2005a). This gender gap in income had narrowed slightly since 1963. Adjusting for inflation, men with four years or more of college earned $40,679 (in 2003 dollars) in 1963, and women at the same level of education earned $20,546 (51 percent of men's income) (United States Census Bureau 2005b). Women with four years or more of college also had a higher poverty rate than men with the same level of education, 4.4 percent to 4.1 percent (United States Census Bureau 2004). African American women with four years or more of college had a poverty rate of 6 percent (United States Census Bureau 2004). What's more, consistent with the above discussion on quality of life, scholars continue to document everyday experiences with discrimination, particularly for women of color in academia

(Essed 2000; Collins 2000). So, while women have made marked improvements since the start of the women's movement, there is still much to be accomplished. Surviving for more than 150 years, the women's movement continues to fight on many fronts to secure greater economic, legal, and political rights.

PEOPLE AND ORGANIZATIONS

American Equal Rights Association (AERA)

Amid a deteriorating relationship with the American Anti-Slavery Society, women suffragists organized the first women's rights campaign since the Civil War in May 1866. At that point the women's movement became known as the American Equal Rights Association. AERA launched two campaigns in Kansas and New York, securing authorization for referenda on both black and female suffrage in 1867. Eventually conflict over black male versus white female suffrage would lead to the demise of AERA, contributing to the formation of two separate organizations—AWSA and NWSA.

American Woman Suffrage Association (AWSA)

The founders of the AWSA included Lucy Stone and her sister-in-law, Antoinette Brown Blackwell. The AWSA tended to work at the local level for women's rights, hoping to accomplish progressive changes state by state. Formed in 1869, this organization was in direct opposition to the NWSA, which opposed the Fifteenth Amendment. Suffragists of the AWSA hoped that after black men won the vote through the Fifteenth Amendment, abolitionists and black male voters would join them in the fight for white female suffrage. When this expectation was not met, Stone and other members of the AWSA joined forces with their rival organization, the NWSA, in 1890 to form the National American Woman Suffrage Association (NAWSA).

Anthony, Susan B. (1820–1906)

Born to a well-to-do Massachusetts Quaker family, Anthony and her long-time friend Elizabeth Cady Stanton are among the most noted suffragists of all time, likely due to the numerous organizations and activities that they organized together. Stanton and Anthony created the Women's National Loyal League in 1863, the American Equal Rights Association in 1866, and the National Woman Suffrage Association in 1869. Anthony's legacy as a women's rights activist was com-

memorated in 1920 when the Nineteenth Amendment granting women the right to vote was dubbed the Susan B. Anthony Amendment.

Boston Women's Health Book Collective (BWHBC)

The BWHBC grew out of a Boston women's liberation conference in 1968. The organization was established out of women's frustration with the male-dominated medical establishment that often ignored women's health concerns. After months of rigorous research and dozens of meetings, the BWHBC published a book called *Women and Their Bodies* in 1970. This book would later be named *Our Bodies, Ourselves* and would gain wide use within medical schools.

Burns, Lucy (1879–1966)

Burns studied in England at Oxford University, where she joined the Women's Social and Political Union. Along with her friend Alice Paul, Lucy Burns formed the Congressional Union for Woman Suffrage in 1913. After learning protest tactics in Europe, Burns and Paul introduced the tactic of large demonstrations into U.S. women's activism. Among her many accomplishments, Burns also edited the well-known feminist publication, *The Suffragist.*

Cary, Mary Ann Shadd (1823–1893)

Cary was the first African American woman to develop a suffrage association for black women. She was also the first woman to study at Howard University Law School in 1869. Though Cary began her studies at the age of forty-six, she could not graduate until she was sixty after Howard University Law School began admitting women. An advocate of the "new departure," Cary also worked for Frederick Douglass at his paper, *The New National Era.* Cary was also the first to propose the twentieth-century suffragist strategy of convincing the population (both black and white) that gaining the vote for African American women would allow them to uplift their communities and gain economic opportunities (Terborg-Penn 1998).

Colored Women's Progressive Franchise Association

The Colored Women's Progressive Franchise Association was established in 1895 by Mary Shadd Cary and was a product of the nineteenth-century women's club movement. The goal of this organization, along with other black women's clubs at the time, was to achieve a universal suffrage amendment that would grant all women the right to vote in any election.

Cooper, Anna Julia (1858–1964)

Cooper was born into slavery, the daughter of Hannah Stanley, a female slave, and George Washington Haywood, a white slave master. Often referred to as the female W. E. B. Du Bois, Anna Julia Cooper was a great intellectual of her time. She was admitted into a teacher training program and earned a M.A. degree at Oberlin College in 1884. Cooper wrote her first book, *A Voice from the South by a Black Woman of the South,* in 1892. Anna J. Cooper lived a long life, dying at the age of 105, just as the modern Civil Rights movement began.

Friedan, Betty (1921–2006)

Friedan was one of the world's most noted speakers on women's rights. Her 1963 book, *The Feminine Mystique,* was said to have sparked a second wave of feminism across the United States. Among her other publications are *It Changed My Life,* published in 1976; *The Second Stage,* 1981; and *The Fountain of Age,* 1993. Friedan had a long history of feminist activism. In addition to co-founding the National Organization for Women, the National Women's Political Caucus, and the National Abortion Rights Action League, Friedan led the movement to ratify the Equal Rights Amendment.

Grimké, Angelina (1805–1879) and Sarah (1792–1873)

Angelina and Sarah Grimké were among the first women's activists to speak publicly for abolition. Throughout their lives as women's activists, they refused to give primacy to either race or sex, choosing instead to fight on both fronts. Sarah and Angelina were also pioneers in challenging the confinement of women to the traditional sphere.

Harper, Frances Ellen Watkins (1825–1911)

Harper was a black woman who was born free. She was educated at her uncle's academy and worked extensively on women's rights and abolition. Harper bravely criticized those who would not recognize the significance of race in the bat-

tle for woman suffrage. Despite her privileged background, Harper worked as a domestic servant. She joined the abolitionist lecture circuit, speaking at the National Women's Rights Convention in May 1866, and was a founding member of the AWSA.

Mott, Lucretia (1793–1880)

Mott served as a Quaker minister in Massachusetts, her place of birth. Consistent with her Quaker upbringing, Mott was firmly opposed to slavery and traveled the world speaking on behalf of abolition. In 1840, Mott was elected as a delegate to the World Anti-Slavery Convention in London. It was here that Mott met Elizabeth Cady Stanton in the segregated women's section of the meeting. Forging a strong friendship, the two quickly organized the 1848 Seneca Falls Convention. Mott was also the first president of the AERA.

National American Woman Suffrage Association (NAWSA)

Unable to secure any significant gains in their separate efforts, the NWSA and AWSA joined forces in 1890 to form NAWSA. Many, but not all, members of this organization supported educated suffrage that barred African Americans from the vote. Also popular among many members of NAWSA were arguments of expediency, which stated that supporting the vote for African American women would delay the success of white women. NAWSA would help secure the right to vote for women in 1920.

National Black Women's Health Project (NBWHP)

The NBWHP was formed in March 1984 after a conference on black women's health led by Byllye Avery in 1983. The NBWHP's mission was to promote and maintain the physical, mental, and emotional well-being of black women. Though this organization attempted to forge coalitions with white women, the tendency of the latter to emphasize gender over race presented barriers to cooperation.

National Organizaton for Women (NOW)

NOW formed in 1966, a product of "consciousness raising" groups prevalent during the Civil Rights movement. The organization was created after an attempt was made to include barring sex discrimination as part of the 1964 Civil Rights

Act. Though this attempt was actually a joke by a Virginia legislator meant to discredit the act, the women who would later form NOW rallied around the inclusion of sex discrimination. In 1968, a group of members split from NOW, forming the Women's Equity Action League. Though NOW has been accused of elitism, conservatism, and racism, its membership continues to grow in the twenty-first century.

National Woman Suffrage Association (NWSA)

Elizabeth Cady Stanton and Susan B. Anthony were among the founders of this organization in 1869 and through it attempted to change laws and policies at the national level to advance women's rights. The leaders of the NWSA opposed ratification of the Fifteenth Amendment granting the vote to black men because it bestowed a constitutional right specifically on one sex, males. This caused a division in the women's movement, because other women's rights activists supported the Fifteenth Amendment and founded the rival American Woman Suffrage Association (AWSA). The NWSA spearheaded an effort to ratify a Sixteenth Amendment in support of woman suffrage. In 1890, after the passage of the Fifteenth Amendment, the NWSA united with the AWSA, creating the National American Woman Suffrage Association (NAWSA).

Paul, Alice (1885–1977)

Paul became the congressional committee chair of NAWSA in 1912. With the help of Lucy Burns, Paul also founded the Congressional Union for Woman Suffrage in 1913, which would later merge with the Women's Party to form the National Women's Party in 1917. By 1923, Paul drafted the first proposed Equal Rights Amendment to the Constitution.

Ruffin, Josephine St. Pierre (1842–1924)

The first African American woman to graduate Harvard Law School, Ruffin was an abolitionist and journalist who edited *Woman's Era* for seven years. She joined the Massachusetts Woman Suffrage Association in 1857 and helped to establish the National Association for the Advancement of Colored People in 1910.

Stanton, Elizabeth Cady (1815–1902)

Stanton is likely the most remembered feminist activist of all time. Stanton was one of the founders of the National Woman Suffrage Association and the co-founder of the 1848 Seneca Falls Convention. As a writer, Stanton was associated with the reform journal *Lily* in 1850, and she composed the now famous volumes of *History of Woman Suffrage, 1881–1902*. Stanton's methods for achieving suffrage were questioned by her colleagues, as she often espoused racist ideology, opposed the Fifteenth Amendment, and directly blocked African American women from her organizations.

Stone, Lucy (1818–1893)

Educated at Oberlin College, Stone was a lecturer for the Anti-Slavery Society and organized the first National Women's Rights Convention, which took place in 1850. She also assisted the development of the American Woman Suffrage Association. As members of the Equal Rights Association, Lucy Stone and her husband, Henry Blackwell, led the Kansas campaign of 1867.

Terrell, Mary Church (1863–1954)

Terrell was the first African American woman appointed to the Washington, D.C. School Board, a leader of the black women's club movement, and a member of NAWSA. Terrell came from an affluent family in Memphis. She earned a masters degree at Oberlin College and was president of the National Association of Colored Women. In her 1904 address to NAWSA, Terrell countered white women's accusations against black men who sold their votes, stating, "They never sold their votes 'til they found that it made no difference how they cast them" (Stanton, Anthony, and Gage 1969, 105–106). She also challenged white women to defend those of the oppressed race and not just the oppressed sex.

Truth, Sojourner (1797–1883)

Sojourner Truth was an abolitionist preacher originally from New York and the first known African American female suffragist. She was born into slavery with the name Isabella Baumfree (Painter 1996). She escaped from a slave owner in 1827. The next year New York state abolished slavery. Truth was able to afford attending movement conventions through her earnings from domestic labor and by money earned from performing songs and speaking. Though she was illiterate, Truth was well known for her articulate and impassioned lectures, including her well-known speech, "Ain't I a Woman." Her biographer, Nell Painter, states, "Whenever she spoke in the public, she also sang. No one ever forgot the power and pathos of Sojourner Truth's singing" (1996, 3).

Wells-Barnett, Ida B. (1862–1931)

Wells was born into slavery and faced a life of hardships. In 1892, she was forced out of her home by whites due to her protests of lynching. Prevented from publishing articles under her own name, Wells continued her writing under a pen name, Iola. She also pursued her work against lynching, both in the United States and in Western Europe. After marrying Ferdinand Barnett, she moved to Chicago and became involved with the Illinois Woman Suffrage Association.

Women's Equity Action League (WEAL)

WEAL was established in 1968 by a group of former NOW members who were unsatisfied with the latter organization's narrow focus on legislative concerns. WEAL's members wanted to also address economic issues affecting many women.

Women's Typographical Union (WTU)

The WTU was formed by working-class women in 1868. After their second meeting, the women of this union were able to achieve financial assistance from an all-male union organization known as Local 6. The WTU fought fervently and consistently against sexual discrimination in national unions, and against the use of women as strikebreakers. In 1869, only a year after its formation, the WTU was admitted into the National Typographical Union as the first all-female local.

Working Women's Association

Susan B. Anthony formed the Working Women's Association in September 1868 in order to develop alliances with working-class women. Though this organization assisted the formation of the WTU, it remained largely middle class in membership and excluded unskilled working women. Class conflict eventually led to the demise of the organization in 1869.

Angie Beeman

See Also African American Freedom Struggle; American Revolution; Documentaries of Revolution; Elites, Intellectuals, and Revolutionary Leadership; Human Rights, Morality, Social Justice, and Revolution; U.S. Southern Secessionist Rebellion and Civil War

References and Further Readings

Barry, Kathleen. 1988. *Susan B. Anthony: A Biography of a Singular Feminist.* New York: New York University Press.

Burke, Mary P. 1980. *Reaching for Justice: The Women's Movement.* Washington, DC: Center of Concern.

Collins, Patricia Hill. 2000. *Black Feminist Thought: Knowledge, Consciousness, and the Politics of Empowerment.* New York: Routledge.

Dubois, Ellen Carol. 1978. *Feminism and Suffrage: The Emergence of an Independent Women's Movement in America 1848–1869.* Ithaca, NY: Cornell University Press.

Duster, Alfreda M. 1970. *Crusade for Justice: The Autobiography of Ida B. Wells.* Chicago: University of Chicago Press.

Espiritu, Yen Le. 1997. *Asian American Women and Men: Labor, Laws and Love.* Thousand Oaks, CA: Sage.

Essed, Philomea. 2000. "Dilemmas in Leadership: Women of Colour in the Academy," *Ethnic and Racial Studies* 23 (5): 888–904.

Feagin, Joe R., Karyn D. McKinney. 2003. *The Many Costs of Racism.* New York: Rowman and Littlefield.

Friedan, Betty. 1963. *The Feminine Mystique.* New York: Norton.

———. 1976. *It Changed My Life: Writings on the Women's Movement.* New York: Random House.

———. 1991. *The Second Stage.* New York: Dell.

———. 1993. *The Fountain of Age.* New York: Simon and Schuster.

Friedman, Susan. 1995. "Beyond White and Other: Relationality and Narratives of Race in Feminist Discourse," *Signs,* 21 (1): 1–50.

Grimké, Sarah. 1837. *Letters on the Equality of the Sexes and the Condition of Woman: Addressed to Mary S. Parker.* Boston: Isaac Knapp.

McNair Barnett, Bernice. 1995. "Black Women's Collectivist Movement Organizations: Their Struggle During the Doldrums." Pp.199–222 in *Feminist Organizations Harvest of the New Women's Movement,* edited by Myra Marx Ferree and Patricia Yancey Martin. Philadelphia, PA: Temple University Press.

Morgen, Sandra. 2002. *Into Our Own Hands: The Women's Health Movement in the United States, 1969–1990.* New Brunswick, NJ: Rutgers University Press.

Painter, Nell Irvin. 1996. *Sojourner Truth: A Life, A Symbol.* New York: W. W. Norton.

Roberts, Dorothy. 1999. *Killing the Black Body: Race, Reproduction, and the Meaning of Liberty.* New York: Vintage.

Rupp, Leila J., and Verta Taylor. 1987. *Survival in the Doldrums.* New York: Oxford University Press.

Ruzek, Sheryl Burt, and Julie Becker. 1999. "The Women's Health Movement in the United States: From Grass-Roots Activism to Professional Agendas," *Journal of the American Medical Women's Association* 54 (1): 4–8.

Stanton, Elizabeth Cady, Susan B. Anthony, and Matilda J. Gage. 1969. *History of Woman Suffrage.* New York: Arno Press.

Streitmatter, Rodger. 1994. *Raising Her Voice: African American Women Journalists Who Changed History.* Lexington: University Press of Kentucky.

Terborg-Penn, Rosalyn. 1998. *African American Women in the Struggle for the Vote, 1850–1920.* Bloomington: Indiana University Press.

Centers for Disease Control. 2005. http://www.cdc.gov/omh/AMH/AMH.htm accessed on March 1, 2005.

National Institutes of Health. 2002. http://www4.od.nih.gov/orwh/wocEnglish2002.pdf accessed March 1, 2005.

National Women's Health Information Center. 2003. http://www.4woman.gov/minority/index.htm accessed March 1, 2005.

New Jersey Department of Health and Senior Services Blue Ribbon Panel Report. 1996. http://www.state.nj.us/health/fhs/bim.htm#preface accessed March 1, 2005.

United States Census Bureau. 2004. "Current Population Survey, 2004 Annual Social and Economic Supplement, Table POV29." http://pubdb3.census.gov/macro/032004/pov/new29_100_01 .htm accessed March 1, 2005.

United States Census Bureau. 2005a. "Current Population Survey, Annual Social and Economic Supplements, Table P-16." http://www.census.gov/hhes/income/histinc/p16.html accessed on March 21, 2005.

United States Census Bureau. 2005b. "Current Population Survey, Annual Social and Economic Supplements, Table P-17." http://www.census.gov/hhes/income/histinc/p17.html accessed on March 21, 2005.

Y

Yugoslav Communist Revolution

CHRONOLOGY

1918   Formation of the Kingdom of the Serbs, Croats, and Slovenes on December 1 through the merger of former Habsburg territories (Slovenia, Croatia, Bosnia-Herzegovina, and Vojvodina) with the independent kingdoms of Serbia and Montenegro. Serbia's King Aleksandar Karadjordjević becomes constitutional monarch.

1920   First general elections for Constituent Assembly are held on the basis of universal manhood suffrage. The newly formed Communist Party of Yugoslavia comes in fourth, with especially strong showing in the poorest regions of the country (Montenegro, Macedonia).

1921   Centralist Constitution, adopted on June 28, is boycotted by deputies of Croat Peasant Party. Communist Party of Yugoslavia banned.

1921–1928   Period of parliamentary rule characterized by politically unstable coalitions, high cabinet turnover, and strong influence of the king.

1928   Leader of Croat Peasant Party, Stjepan Radić, is shot in parliament by a Montenegrin deputy.

1929   King Aleksandar suspends constitution on January 6 and initiates, with the help of the army, a period of centralist authoritarian rule. The king reorganizes state administration into nine provinces that do not overlap with traditional regions in an attempt to foster Yugoslav state and national unity. The country's name is changed to Kingdom of Yugoslavia.

1934   During an official visit to France, King Aleksandar is assassinated by Croat and Macedonian nationalists. A three-man regency under Pavle Karadjordjević takes over, pending successor Peter II coming of age.

1937   Josip Broz Tito, future leader of Yugoslavia, is appointed head of the Communist Party of Yugoslavia.

1939   An agreement between government and leader of Croat Peasant Party (also known as the Cvetković-Maček Agreement or Sporazum) grants extensive autonomy to Croatia.

1941   On March 27, the regency and government are overthrown in a military coup after signing the Tripartite Pact with Hitler. On April 6, a combined attack (German, Italian, Hungarian, Bulgarian) on Yugoslavia begins with the severe bombing of Belgrade (the capital city). The Yugoslav Royal Army surrenders in mid April. Independent State of Croatia (incorporating all of Bosnia-Herzegovina) is proclaimed, with capital in Zagreb. It is headed by the leader of the pro-Fascist Croat Ustashe movement, Ante Pavelić. In Serbia, resistance is organized by remnants of the Yugoslav Royal Army under Colonel Dragoljub Mihailović, whose followers come to be known as Chetniks; Communist Partisans under Tito organize their own resistance movement. A three-cornered civil war ensues, pitting Pavelić's Ustashe against Mihailović's Chetniks and Tito's Partisans. Chetniks and Partisans become bitter opponents after a brief period of anti-Axis cooperation.

1943   On November 29, the Anti-Fascist Council for the National Liberation of Yugoslavia (AVNOJ) meets in Jajce (Bosnia), laying the foundation for the transformation of Yugoslavia into a federal Socialist state.

1944   On October 20, Belgrade is liberated in joint Soviet Red Army and Yugoslav Partisan operation. Partisans emerge as the dominant military force.

1945   On May 15, German units in Yugoslavia surrender; on November 29, the Federal Republic of Yugoslavia is formed, with Belgrade as the capital.

1946   First Communist constitution is adopted, officially recognizing five constituent peoples of the state (Serbs, Croats, Slovenes, Montenegrins, and Macedonians) and dividing the country into six federal units or "Socialist republics" (Serbia, Croatia, Slovenia, Bosnia and Herzegovina, Montenegro, and Macedonia), one autonomous province (Vojvodina), and one autonomous region (Kosovo). Vojvodina and Kosovo are both in Serbia.

1948   On June 28 the Communist Party of Yugoslavia is expelled from the COMINFORM.

The Tito-Stalin break has important consequences, as Yugoslavia becomes the first country in the international Communist movement to challenge the Soviet Union's undisputed leadership.

1950   First law on worker's self-management passed. In theory, state ownership of the means of production is abolished and workers become collective owners of "social property," running factories through elected working class councils together with managers. In reality, the party-state retains decisive control, although enterprises gradually gain more autonomy in economic decision making.

1952   Communist Party of Yugoslavia changes its name to League of Communists of Yugoslavia (LCY) in an attempt to demonstrate the inclusive character of Yugoslav Socialism. The party's role is no longer "vanguard of the working class" but rather "a guiding force" that rules in cooperation with broader social forces.

1953   The Socialist Alliance of the Working People of Yugoslavia is formed. In theory, the Socialist Alliance is the foundation of all state and "social self-governing" bodies, underscoring the theoretical separation of party and state.

1961   Conference of non-aligned states is held in Belgrade, adding to Tito's prestige as one of the founders of the Non-Aligned Movement, composed of newly independent countries from the developing world.

1963   Second Communist constitution is adopted. The country changes its name to Socialist Federal Republic of Yugoslavia (SFRY).

1965–1971   Period of political and economic reform, decentralization, and the rise of nationalist movements (especially in Croatia).

1974   Third Communist constitution is adopted, ceding far greater power to the republics and autonomous provinces. Tito is elected president for life.

| 1978 | Eleventh Party Congress implements collective leadership, whereby the representatives of the republics and autonomous provinces rotate as federal party and government presidents. |
| 1980 | Tito dies on May 4, at the age of 88. Yugoslavia enters a period of crisis. |

INTRODUCTION

In contrast to its East European counterparts, the Yugoslav Communist Revolution was an indigenous revolution organized by Yugoslav Partisans during the period of Axis occupation (1941–1945). The second distinctive feature of the Yugoslav Revolution was that it occurred in the context of a violent civil war that pitted various political forces and segments of Yugoslavia's ethnic groups against each other. The creation of a multiethnic army that put an end to civil war and liberated the country from foreign occupation created the precondition for Yugoslavia's independence from the Soviet bloc and the development of an alternative model of Socialism: these were the most important achievements of the Yugoslav Revolution. Internationally, the most significant aspect of the Yugoslav Revolution was that it legitimated the idea of separate roads to Socialism, influencing the emergence of "national Communism" throughout post-war Eastern Europe. In addition, Yugoslavia's self-management model of economic development provided an early example of limited market reforms in a Socialist economy.

BACKGROUND: CULTURE AND HISTORY

Yugoslavia (the land of the South Slavs) emerged as a unified state in the immediate aftermath of World War I (1918). As its first official name—Kingdom of the Serbs, Croats, and Slovenes—suggested, Yugoslavia was formed as a union of three constitutive peoples. Officially, Serbs, Croats, and Slovenes were considered "three tribes of the one-named Yugoslav nation." This doctrine, which came to be known as "unitarism," reflected the belief of a part of Yugoslavia's founding elites that a unified Yugoslav nation would emerge once all the South Slavs—historically divided between the Habsburg and Ottoman empires—were united in a common state. In practice, the divisions among Yugoslavia's constituent peoples proved stronger than the forces that bound them together.

The integration problems faced by the Yugoslav state were not surprising. The various Yugoslav peoples, although united by a common ethnic (South Slav) and widely shared linguistic background, were divided by centuries of distinct historical experience. The whole southeastern part of the future state (Serbia, Montenegro, Macedonia, Kosovo, Bosnia, and Herzegovina) fell to the Ottomans by the sixteenth century. By contrast, the northwestern regions (Slovenia, Croatia, and Vojvodina) came under Habsburg rule (Bosnia and Herzegovina became a Habsburg protectorate in the 1878–1914 period). Consequently, various Yugoslav regions and peoples were subjected to different types of imperial rule, administrative organization, economic systems, and cultural influences.

The Yugoslav peoples were also divided by religion. Serbs, Montenegrins, and Macedonians are Orthodox Christians; Slovenes and Croats are Catholics; and a considerable number of South Slavs in Bosnia and Herzegovina converted to Islam under Ottoman rule. Among the non-Slav minorities, the predominantly Muslim Albanians formed a territorially concentrated pocket in Yugoslavia's poorest region, Kosovo (bordering Albania). According to the best estimate of the ethnic composition of the new Yugoslav state (Banac 1984, 58), the distribution was as follows (1921 census): out of a total of some 12 million citizens, Serbs (with the ethnically close Montenegrins included) made up some 39 percent of the population (4,666,000), Croats 24 percent (2,857,000), Slovenes 9 percent (1,024,000), Bosnian Muslims 7 percent (728,000), Macedonians 5 percent (586,000), with large ethnic minorities completing the count (Germans, Hungarians, and Albanians were each between 400,000 and a little more than 500,000). The largest group of people, the Serbs, thus were only a relative majority, although they were also territorially the most dispersed ethnic group, forming a relative majority in Bosnia and Herzegovina, and a sizeable minority in Croatia.

The linguistic situation was somewhat less complex. Serbs, Montenegrins, Croats, and Bosnian Muslims were united by different dialects of a common language, in effect accounting for about 70 percent of the population (although the Catholic Croats wrote in Latin script, while the Orthodox Serbs preferred Cyrillic). Slovenes spoke a distinct language that was not easily understandable to Serbo-Croat speakers; Macedonian was more than a dialect (closer to Bulgarian than to Serbo-Croatian) but neither an officially recognized nor codified language until well after World War II; finally, Albanians spoke an altogether non-Slavic language. Bosnian Muslims and Macedonians were not considered distinct ethnic groups, but whereas the Bosnian Muslims were allowed to organize as a religious community, the Macedonians were labeled "southern Serbs," incorporated into the Serbian Orthodox Church, and subjected to assimilation policies.

The Yugoslav unification movement had a prehistory going back to the mid nineteenth century. In Croatia, romantic nationalist intellectuals advanced the "Illyrian" thesis, according to which all South Slavs were heirs of the ancient Illyrians (that is, of common ethnic stock). More importantly, the Illyrianists chose the Croat dialect that was closest to Serbian as the basis for the Croat language, thus paving the way for the future linguistic unification of Serbian and Croatian. But while the idea of Yugoslav unification was born in Croatia, Serbia became its self-proclaimed political center. A wave of successive insurrections against the Ottomans (1804, 1815) had resulted in the creation of an autonomous Serbian principality (1832). Well before its international recognition as an independent state (1878), Serbia had developed its own political, bureaucratic, and military institutions, as well as a program of the unification of all Serbs—whether under Ottoman or Habsburg rule—into a common nation-state. Moreover, under the impact of European liberalism, Serbia's liberals and populists ensured the adoption of a liberal constitution (1888) that effectively put an end to absolutist monarchical rule. A string of military victories in the two Balkan wars (1912–1913) brought Kosovo and Macedonia under Serbian sovereignty and augmented Serbia's political prestige. Serbia's transformation into a constitutional monarchy (1903–1914), with a modern parliament, vibrant political parties, and a free press, rendered it attractive as a potential center of the future state, despite its relative economic backwardness vis-à-vis the northwestern Habsburg territories (Slovenia, Croatia, and Vojvodina).

Developments in the Habsburg monarchy also favored the movement for South Slav unification. The long period of Hungarian misrule in Croatia pushed a segment of the Croat intelligentsia toward cooperation with the Serbs, formalized in the creation of a Croat-Serb coalition (1905). The formal annexation of Bosnia and Herzegovina by Austro-Hungary (1908) radicalized the pro-Serb and pro-Yugoslav movement in Bosnia, particularly among the young intelligentsia. On June 28, 1914, one of its members, Gavrilo Princip, assassinated Archduke Franz Ferdinand in Sarajevo, triggering a chain of international events that culminated in World War I. Austro-Hungary's punitive attack on Serbia (July 1914) unexpectedly led to a remarkable set of military victories for the Serbian army, which was defeated only after the combined German-Bulgarian offensive (1915). Even so, by 1918 the reorganized Serbian army reclaimed most of the territory of the future Yugoslav state, albeit at tremendous human cost. This collective sacrifice, combined with their pretension to make Serbia the center of Yugoslav unification, led Serbian elites to claim preponderance in the new state, despite the significant role of the Yugoslav Committee (formed by Slovene, Croat, and Serb intellectuals from the Habsburg lands) in the struggle for Yugoslavia's international recognition.

CONTEXT AND PROCESS OF REVOLUTION

The Communist Revolution in Yugoslavia (1941–1945) must be understood in the context of the national, social, political, and international problems faced by the inter-war state (1918–1941). The most difficult national problem was the Croat question. Although Croatia formally lost its independent medieval state in the twelfth century, when the king of Hungary was recognized by the Croat nobility as their ruler, the idea of Croat autonomy was preserved by the noble elite and subsequently incorporated into modern Croat national ideology. The long Croat struggle for autonomy in the Habsburg empire had left in the Croat elite a lasting suspicion of the central state, a political and cultural attitude that was transposed onto Yugoslavia. The political domination of Serbian elites, reflected in the passing of a centralist constitution (1921), alienated many Croats not only from the state, but increasingly from the Yugoslav idea as well.

The Serbian political experience was altogether different. After a century-long struggle for national unification, Serbian elites had developed a veritable cult of the central state. As a result, the political struggle between "Serbian centralism" and "Croat federalism" took center stage throughout the inter-war period, even as it was superimposed upon a whole set of other conflicts (economic, social, party-political, ideological). In the process, state-oriented Serbian elites sought to isolate Croat nationalists by courting Slovene and Bosnian Muslim politicians, while Croat elites supported all forces that favored state decentralization.

The social problem concerned the condition of the peasantry. Inter-war Yugoslavia was a predominantly peasant country (70 percent of the population), but the condition of peasantry varied greatly, from the small freeholders of Serbia to Ottoman era sharecroppers in semi-feudal Bosnia and Herzegovina, Kosovo, and Macedonia; the livestock producers and agricultural proletariat on the large estates of Vojvodina and upper Croatia (Slavonia); the peasants working cooperative farms in Slovenia; and those occupied with animal husbandry in the poor mountain regions (Montenegro, the Adriatic sea hinterland). In view of the tremendous diversity of social conditions, the ambitious land reform undertaken by the central government produced mixed economic results. Politically, however, the reform was a success, enabling a half million peasant families to acquire land and giving them a stake in the political order (Tomasevich 1955, 368). Even so, problems of agricultural overpopulation, the disparity between agricultural and industrial prices, lack of credit, and shrinking foreign markets (especially after the Great Depression) meant that the peasant question was not fully resolved. In the former Ottoman provinces (Bosnia, Macedonia, Kosovo), land reform disproportionately rewarded Serbian war veterans at the expense of the partially indemnified Muslim landlords, exacerbating ethnic resentment. The superimposition of social and national questions, however, was most evident in Croatia, where the Croat Peasant Party stood for both peasant populism and Croat nationalism.

Politically, inter-war Yugoslavia mirrored the problems of other East European countries: parliamentary life was unstable and contentious; parties were coteries of elites that courted rather than represented the electorate; the king was tempted to impose personal rule. Moreover, since the most powerful government-forming parties and the army were predominantly Serbian, the problem of non-Serb political representation was acute. Even so, the extent of opposition to King Aleksandar's dictatorship (1929–1934) was considerable among the Serbs as well, demonstrating that liberalism remained a significant force.

Yugoslavia's international position was precarious. Yugoslavia's neighbors—Italy, Hungary, and Bulgaria—had significant claims on Yugoslav territory, appealing to their co-nationals in Yugoslavia (in the case of Bulgaria to the Macedonians) and seeking territorial revisions of the Versailles treaty. Albania was militarily weak but served as a potential magnet for Kosovo Albanians. Hitler's takeover of Austria (1938) turned Nazi Germany into a threatening neighbor with preponderant economic influence in Yugoslavia. As a result, Yugoslav foreign policy after 1935 shifted from its traditional reliance on France to accommodation with Italy and Germany.

The Communist Party of Yugoslavia (formed in 1919 but officially named CPY in 1920) was a conglomerate of social-democratic parties from different parts of the country. The CPY's considerable success in elections for the constituent assembly (1920) turned it into the country's fourth largest party (12.4 percent of the vote) and the only party that could muster a following among all ethnic groups. The regime responded by adopting a law restricting Communist agitation (1920) and formally banned the party after the assassination of the interior minister by a Communist (1921). Henceforth, the CPY entered a period of internal turmoil that lasted into the late 1930s.

Like all other forces in Yugoslavia, the Communists had to take a stance on the national question. The first CPY leaders (predominantly Serbian Marxists) took the orthodox position that the national question was secondary to class struggle, and recognized the legitimacy of the Yugoslav state. In 1924–1925, however, this faction of the CPY suffered the severe criticism of COMINTERN officials (including Stalin), who took the position that the "national and peasant questions" were intimately related: hence Yugoslav Communists had to support "national-liberation" peasant movements throughout the country (e.g., the Croat Peasant Party), with

the goal of putting an end to the hegemony of the "greater Serbian bourgeoisie" and transforming Yugoslavia into a federation of Socialist republics on the Soviet model. For some ten years (1925–1935), the CPY followed this line, hoping to co-opt peripheral nationalism for the revolutionary cause. The COMINTERN's shift toward a broad anti-Fascist front policy (1936–1939) compelled the CPY to support Yugoslavia's state integrity, a policy that once more was reversed after the Stalin-Hitler pact (1939–1941). Thus, on the eve of World War II, the CPY seemed poorly poised to emerge as Yugoslavia's leading patriotic force.

The rapid collapse of the Royal Army and the partition of the country by Nazi Germany, Fascist Italy, Hungary, and Bulgaria (April 1941) suddenly opened new opportunities for mobilization. With the old order discredited, the royal government in exile, and the country partitioned among the occupiers, the Communists had a seemingly open field. Yet the constraints were serious: the former minorities (Italians, Germans, Hungarians, Albanians, and some Macedonians) welcomed the collapse of the state and the prospect of unification with their old/new homelands; a newly created Independent State of Croatia (incorporating all of Bosnia and Herzegovina) seemingly realized the Croat dream of independent statehood. Initially, only Serbia and Montenegro seemed like potential strongholds of mass resistance, but here the first resistance movement was organized by Colonel Mihailović of the Yugoslav Royal Army (the Communists waited until the Nazi attack on the Soviet Union on June 22, 1941). The Communists, however, had some distinct advantages: a small but disciplined organization with party cells throughout Yugoslavia (about 8,000 in 1941); a unified party elite of the Leninist type under Josip Broz Tito; a record of supporting minorities in the inter-war period, and an ideology that appealed to all those disappointed with the old order.

Nevertheless, the first two years of the war almost ended in Communist failure. In Serbia, Communist resistance provoked terrible Nazi reprisals, pushing the Serbian peasantry into Mihailović's camp, while zealous attempts to impose "Socialism" led to a similar result in Montenegro. It was the fanatical anti-Serbian policies of the Croat Ustashe that gave the Communists their first mass base among the Serb peasants of Croatia and Bosnia: as late as the end of 1943, when the Communists boasted about the multinational character of their army, fifteen out of twenty-seven Partisan divisions were still composed almost exclusively of Serbs, most of them peasant refugees who had fled Ustashe massacres (Burks 1961, 122).

The shortcomings of Mihailović's parochial and decentralized Chetnik movement were the second factor of Communist success. As select Chetnik commanders engaged in "revenge" campaigns against Croat and Bosnian Muslim civilians for massacres that had been perpetrated against the

Josip Broz Tito, president of Yugoslavia (1945–1981). One of the most accomplished guerrilla leaders of all time, Josip Broz Tito led Yugoslavia out of World War II and was responsible for reorganizing the country. (Library of Congress)

Serbs of Croatia and Bosnia, Mihailović's movement became identified with a narrowly understood Serbian cause. Consequently, Mihailović failed to attract non-Serbs, while his fear of Nazi reprisals condemned Chetniks in Serbia to passivity. The result was that (after 1943) the British began supporting Tito's Partisans at Mihailović's expense.

The Communists' appeal to various Yugoslav nationalities was the third critical factor in their success. During the first two years of the war, Communist propaganda cleverly avoided references to Yugoslavism, calling on individual Yugoslav nations to liberate themselves (i.e., Croats to liberate Croatia, Serbs Serbia, etc.). The promise of self-determination was made official at the second conference of AVNOJ (Anti-Fascist Council for the National Liberation of Yugoslavia) in November 1943, which laid the foundation for the future transformation of Yugoslavia into a federation of Socialist republics. More impressive still was the Communists' success in forging ethnically mixed units in which members of different nationalities fought side by side in the name of "brotherhood and unity." The recruitment of Croats was of paramount importance, as the Croat question had been the bane of inter-war Yugoslavia (Irvine 1993).

The fourth ingredient of Communist success was geopolitical. Although Yugoslav Partisans had taken control of much territory, the Soviet Red Army was critical to the liberation of Belgrade and the northwestern parts of the country. As a result, Soviet influence on Yugoslavia's post-war political development increased at the expense of Britain. The unexpected break with the Soviet Union (1948) radically altered the outcome of the Yugoslav Revolution, with important consequences for the Communist world.

IMPACTS

It was the indigenous character of the Yugoslav Revolution that led to the Tito-Stalin break. Armed with a large army and the aura of a national-liberation movement, Yugoslav Communists began rapidly nationalizing private property, collectivizing agriculture, and extending military support to Communist insurgents in the Greek civil war—all at a time when Stalin desperately wanted to avoid confrontation with a nuclear West and consolidate his gains in Eastern Europe. Tito's influence as the leader of a large resistance movement threatened to spill over into neighboring Balkan countries (Albania, Bulgaria), further undermining Soviet influence. The expulsion of Yugoslavia from the COMINFORM (1948) was meant to put an end to Yugoslavia's independence by removing Tito, with the help of Stalinists in the Yugoslav party. Instead, Tito became the first Communist leader to defy Stalin, paving the way for the emergence of "national Communism" in Eastern Europe.

The conflict with Stalin had enormous influence on the outcome of the Yugoslav Revolution. Expelled from the Soviet Bloc, Yugoslav Communists had to find their own road to Socialism, while seeking accommodation with the West. Their response was ingenious: by (theoretically) ceding the ownership and management of factories to working-class councils, transforming the party into a "guiding" (as opposed to commanding) force in society, allowing more scope for economic initiative, and assuming a leadership role in the "non-aligned movement," Yugoslav Communists succeeded in giving a new political identity to their revolution. Yugoslavia's pragmatic accommodation with the West was no ideological surrender either: the Non-Aligned Movement represented an international alliance of former colonies against Western imperialism.

Despite these changes, until the mid 1960s the Yugoslav regime retained all the main characteristics of Soviet-type political systems: the party-state "ruled" rather than "governed" society; the secret police enjoyed wide discretionary powers; all economic decisions were in the hands of party-appointed managers. After 1966, however, the Yugoslav regime gradually evolved from a classic totalitarian into a distinctly Communist authoritarian regime: the discretionary powers of the secret police were curtailed; the party experimented with multi-candidate elections and other forms of indirect representation; Yugoslav citizens acquired the right to travel abroad; economic reforms led to the emergence of a small-scale private service sector and resulted in inflation, unemployment, and the large-scale emigration of Yugoslav workers to Western countries—economic phenomena unique to Yugoslav Socialism; self-management became more of a reality, with working-class councils acquiring greater power in enterprises; significant Western aid helped raise consumption, while Western mass culture made inroads into everyday life. As a result, by the late 1960s, the Yugoslav Revolution appeared to be a relative success. Yugoslav Communists had industrialized the country without large-scale collectivization and mass terror, opened Yugoslavia to the West, introduced limited market reforms, and raised standards of living—accomplishments that provoked the envy of Soviet-Bloc populations and created a precedent for reforms elsewhere (e.g., Hungary). By the 1970s and early 1980s, however, the country entered a period of terminal crisis, as political decentralization, economic decline, Tito's death (1980), and Yugoslavia's reduced international significance as a buffer between NATO and the Soviet Bloc left the federal state weakened and divided. Ironically, the national question that the Communists boasted to have solved through "self-determination," federalism, and "brotherhood and unity" among Yugoslavia's peoples proved as intractable for them as for their inter-war predecessors. Worse still, in an attempt to place their shaken power on new foundations of legitimacy, local Communist elites became champions of their nations at the expense of Yugoslav unity.

Nevertheless, the Yugoslav Revolution had a lasting international impact. By openly defying Stalin's hitherto undisputed leadership, Yugoslav Communists asserted the right to pursue their own road to Socialism in consonance with the national interest. This precedent opened the way for the emergence of national Communism in Eastern Europe (Poland, Hungary). At a later date, China, Albania, and Romania followed independent paths from a more orthodox Communist position, while some Euro-Communist parties (Italian, Spanish) broke free from Soviet influence in the name of reformist ideas that were closer to the Yugoslav model of self-management Socialism. Yugoslavia's leadership role in the Non-Aligned Movement was no accident either: largely composed of former Western colonies that did not wish to become new Soviet dependencies (e.g., Egypt, India, etc.), their common ideological ground with Yugoslavia lay in nationalism rather than in their Socialist-style economic experiments.

PEOPLE AND ORGANIZATIONS

Aleksandar Karadjordjević (1888–1934)

First King of Yugoslavia, Aleksandar was successor to Peter I of Serbia from the Karadjordjević dynasty. As prince regent, Aleksandar led Serbian troops in the Balkan wars (1912–1913) and World War I (1914–1918). On December 1, 1918, King Aleksandar became the constitutional monarch of the Kingdom of the Serbs, Croats, and Slovenes. In January 1929, King Aleksandar suspended the parliamentary system, initiating a period of personal dictatorship with the help of the army. In order to foster state unity, the king reorganized the country into nine administrative units that cut across historic provinces (e.g., Croatia, Bosnia, Serbia) and renamed the country the Kingdom of Yugoslavia. King Aleksandar was assassinated by Croat and Macedonian nationalists during a state visit to France in 1934 (together with France's foreign minister Louis Barthou).

Anti-Fascist Council of National Liberation of Yugoslavia (AVNOJ)

AVNOJ was formed on November 26–27, 1942, in Bihać, Bosnia. A year later (November 29, 1943), the second session of AVNOJ (Jajce, Bosnia), laid the foundation for the federal reorganization of post-war Yugoslavia on the basis of the self-determination of its constituent peoples. After World War II, November 29 was taken as the founding date of Communist Yugoslavia, becoming a national holiday.

Chetniks

The Chetniks, from the word *četa* ("platoon"), originated as a Serb guerrilla movement in the Balkan wars (1912–1913). In the inter-war period, Chetnik veteran organizations played a conservative role, standing for Serbian traditions and Yugoslav state integrity against Croat "secessionists" and other minority movements. Although the resistance movement of General Mihailović in World War II was known informally as the Chetnik movement, there were Chetnik formations (led by Kosta Pecanac) that did not recognize Mihailović and collaborated with the German authorities in occupied Serbia. Other Chetnik commanders, although formally subordinate to

Mihailović, pursued independent policies in Croatia and Bosnia, where they were associated with the persecution of Croats and Bosnian Muslims.

COMINFORM

Communist Information Bureau or COMINFORM was created in 1947 (Warsaw) as an association of nine Communist parties (seven from Eastern Europe, plus those of Italy and France). The COMINFORM was designed to replace the defunct COMINTERN (Communist International, disbanded in 1943) as a new organization of Communist parties that would consult and exchange information without necessarily pursuing a unified pro-Soviet policy. In reality, the organization was dominated by the Soviet party. Yugoslavia's expulsion from the COMINFORM (June 1948) marked the beginning of the Tito-Stalin break.

Mihailović, Dragoljub-Draža (1893–1945)

Serbian and Yugoslav army officer (colonel in 1941) who organized the first resistance group in occupied Yugoslavia. Informally known as Chetniks, Mihailović's followers created a decentralized guerrilla movement with an overwhelmingly ethnic Serb following. In 1942, Mihailović was promoted to the rank of general and named official commander of the Yugoslav Army of the Homeland by the Yugoslav government in exile. Mihailović's movement was recognized as an important resistance force by the Allies, but its reluctance to openly engage German forces, its selective collaboration with Italian troops, and its war against the Communist Partisans gradually led to the withdrawal of Allied support. In 1945 Mihailović was captured, tried, and executed by the Communist regime.

Partisans

The informal name of the Communist-led resistance movement during World War II. The Partisans began as a small guerrilla-style force in 1941 and eventually grew into a large resistance movement with some 320,000 fighters by the end of 1943. The Partisans constituted themselves in two interrelated organizations—the People's Liberation Army and the more loosely organized Partisan Detachments of Yugoslavia. In territories under their control, the Partisans organized incipient civilian governments (People's Committees). By the end of the war, the Partisan army was organized into eight large army corps with more than 600,000 fighters recruited from all Yugoslav nationalities.

Pavelić, Ante (1898–1959)

Leader of the Croat Ustashe movement that he formed in 1929. As official head of the collaborationist Independent State of Croatia, Pavelić and his movement became associated with extreme racism and the brutal persecution of Serbs, Jews, Gypsies, and Croat resisters. In 1945, Pavelić escaped, finding refuge in Peron's Argentina and Franco's Spain, where he died (Madrid, 1959).

Tito, Josip Broz (1892–1980)

Leader of the Communist Party of Yugoslavia, Tito (his revolutionary name) was born Josip Broz in the Croatian town of Kumrovec on May 7, 1892, to a Croat father and a Slovene mother. Recruited into the Austro-Hungarian army to fight on the Russian front in World War I, Tito was captured. He was subsequently converted to the Communist cause during the Russian Revolution. A locksmith by profession, Tito returned to Yugoslavia in 1920, becoming a trade union and Communist organizer. During King Aleksandar's dictatorship (1929–1934), Tito was imprisoned, subsequently found his way to the Soviet Union, and was appointed to lead the CPY (1937). In World War II, Tito headed Yugoslavia's Partisan resistance movement, one of the largest in occupied Europe. Head of Communist Yugoslavia from 1945 until his death in 1980, Tito was one of the most prominent leaders in international Communism, celebrated for his record of anti-Nazi resistance, and respected for his defiance of Stalin as well as for his leadership role in the Non-Aligned Movement. In Yugoslavia, however, Tito's wartime charisma was institutionalized into an official state cult that reached great proportions, enabling him to assume dictatorial powers and turning him into an indispensable factor in the legitimacy and stability of the Communist state.

Ustashe

The Ustashe (literally, "rebels") was an extreme right-wing Croat nationalist movement that fought for the secession of Croatia from Yugoslavia by violent means. In 1941, the Ustashe came to power with Hitler's and Mussolini's support. The Ustashe's Independent State of Croatia incorporated Bosnia and Herzegovina, and had a significant Serb population. The Ustashe purported to deal with the "Serb question" by exterminating, expelling, or forcibly converting the Serbs to Catholicism. Realized with merciless brutality, the policy of the extermination of Serbs, Jews, and Gypsies soon provoked mass Serb resistance, alienated a considerable number of Croats, and filled up the ranks of the Communist Partisan movement in Croatia and Bosnia.

Workers' Self-management

The Yugoslav Communists' attempt to end the Soviet-style state-planned economy by granting ownership of factories to working-class councils. Although working-class councils were given considerable authority over investment and finance, enterprise managers retained veto power over decisions, acting as agents of the party-state. Nevertheless, Yugoslav self-management represented an important innovation, encouraging greater participation in decision making on the enterprise level.

Veljko Vujačić

See Also Documentaries of Revolution; Greek Civil War; Guerrilla Warfare and Revolution; War and Revolution; Yugoslavia: Dissolution

References and Further Readings

Avakumović, Ivan. 1964. *History of the Communist Party of Yugoslavia.* Aberdeen, Scotland: Aberdeen University Press.

Banac, Ivo. 1984. *The National Question in Yugoslavia.* Ithaca, NY: Cornell University Press.

———. 1988. *With Stalin against Tito: Cominformist Splits in Yugoslav Communism.* Ithaca, NY: Cornell University Press.

Bokovoy, Melissa. 1998. *Peasants and Communists: Politics and Ideology in the Yigoslav Countryside, 1940–1953.* Pittsburgh, PA: Pittsburgh University Press.

Burks, R. V. 1961. *The Dynamics of Communism in Eastern Europe.* Princeton, NJ: Princeton University Press.

Djilas, Aleksa. 1991. *The Contested Country: Yugoslav Unity and Communist Revolution 1919–1953* Cambridge, MA: Harvard University Press.

Djilas, Milovan. 1977. *Wartime.* New York: Hartcourt Brace.

Djokić, Dejan, ed. 2003. *Yugoslavism: Histories of a Failed Idea, 1918–1992.* Madison: University of Wisconsin Press.

Goldstein, Ivo. 1999. *Croatia: A History.* Montreal: McGill-Queen's University Press.

Irvine, Jill. 1993. *The Croat Question: Partisan Politics and the Formation of the Yugoslav Socialist State.* Boulder, CO: Westview Press.

Lampe, John. 2000. *Yugoslavia. Twice There Was a Country.* Cambridge: Cambridge University Press.

Pavlowitch, Stevan K. 1992. *Tito: Yugoslavia's Great Dictator.* Columbus: Ohio State University Press.

———. 2002. *Serbia: The History of an Idea.* New York: New York University Press.

Roberts, Walter R. 1973. *Tito, Mikhailovich, and the Allies, 1941–1945.* New Brunswick, NJ: Rutgers University Press.

Rubinstein, Alvin Z. 1970. *Yugoslavia and the Non-Aligned Movement.* Princeton, NJ: Princeton University Press.

Rusinow, Dennison. 1977. *The Yugoslav Experiment, 1948–1974.* Berkeley and Los Angeles: University of California Press.

Shoup, Paul. 1968. *Communism and the Yugoslav National Question.* New York: Columbia University Press.

Singleton, Fred. 1985. *A Short History of Yugoslav Peoples.* Cambridge: Cambridge University Press.

Tomasevich, Jozo 1955. *Peasants, Politics, and Economic Change in Yugoslavia.* Stanford, CA: Stanford University Press.

———. 1975. *The Chetniks.* Stanford, CA: Stanford University Press.

———. 2001. *War and Revolution in Yugoslavia: Occupation and Collaboration.* Stanford, CA: Stanford University Press.

Ulam, Adam. 1952. *Titoism and the Cominform.* Westport, CT: Greenwood.

Vucinich, Wayne S. 1982. *At the Brink of War and Peace: The Tito-Stalin Split in Historical Perspective.* Boulder, CO, and New York: Columbia University Press.

———, ed. 1969. *Contemporary Yugoslavia: Twenty Years of Socialist Experiment.* Berkeley and Los Angeles: University of California Press.

Zimmerman, William. 1987. *Open Borders, Non-Alignment, and the Political Evolution of Yugoslavia.* Princeton, NJ: Princeton University Press.

Yugoslavia: Dissolution

CHRONOLOGY

1980   On May 4, Marshall Tito, leader of post-war Yugoslavia, dies. Collective presidency takes over: each year, a president of the presidency is chosen from one of the republics or autonomous provinces on a rotating basis.

1981   Riots in Kosovo, an autonomous province within Serbia. The federal government imposes a state of emergency in the name of combating Albanian "irredentism."

1986   Serbian Academy of Sciences and Arts drafts "The Memorandum," a document widely seen as a manifesto of Serbian nationalism. "The Memorandum" complains that decentralization has undermined Yugoslav unity, crippled economic reform, and separated the Serbs in Kosovo, Bosnia, and Croatia from Serbia.

1987   Slovenian intellectuals publish a national program that calls for the transformation of Yugoslavia into a confederation of independent states. In April, new head of the Serbian party, Slobodan Milošević, visits Kosovo, promising to stop the emigration of Serbs from the province. In September, Milošević takes control of Serbia's party organization.

1988   In June, Yugoslav army authorities arrest three Slovenian journalists and an army officer for revealing military secrets, provoking national mobilization in Slovenia. In July and August, mass rallies in Serbia demand that Vojvodina and Kosovo be brought under Serbia's control. In October, the Vojvodina party elite resigns.

1989   In January, a mass rally forces the resignation of Montenegro's party elite. In February, Albanian miners in Kosovo go on strike, protesting purges of Kosovo party leadership. A state of emergency is imposed in the province. At the end of March, Serbia passes constitutional amendments formally bringing Kosovo and Vojvodina under its control. In September, Slovenia passes constitutional amendments in a first step toward national sovereignty.

1990   Federal government implements macro economic reforms. League of Communists of Yugoslavia breaks up when Slovenian and Croatian delegations leave the Fourteenth Congress in protest over Milošević's attempt to dominate the federal party. In April, Communists lose parliamentary elections in Slovenia and Croatia. Franjo Tudjman, a Croat nationalist, is elected president of Croatia. In July, Slovenian parliament passes a declaration of national sovereignty. In August, Serbs in Krajina region of Croatia erect barricades and demand local autonomy. In November, elections in Macedonia and Bosnia result in victory for nationalist parties. In Serbia and Montenegro the ruling Communists win elections; Milošević becomes president of Serbia. Referendum in Slovenia shows high support for national independence.

1991   In February, Slovenia and Croatia suspend federal laws in their republics; Serbs in Krajina declare their intention to split from Croatia and remain in Yugoslavia.

In late March, a secret meeting between Milošević and Tudjman takes place, raising suspicions that Serbia and Croatia are plotting to divide Bosnia. Presidents of all Yugoslav republics meet six times to resolve state crisis: Slovenia and Croatia want confederation or full independence; Serbia and Montenegro are for a strong federal state; Bosnia and Macedonia draft a compromise proposal.

On June 25, Slovenia and Croatia declare independence from Yugoslavia. After a ten-day conflict, the Yugoslav army withdraws from Slovenia; war breaks out in Croatia. In October, the European Union organizes a conference on Yugoslavia in The Hague and offers a plan for the transformation of Yugoslavia into an association of independent states; Serbia rejects the plan.

In December, Germany recognizes Slovenia and Croatia.

1992   In January, the European Union and the United States recognize Slovenia and Croatia. In March, Serb, Croat, and Bosnian Muslim leaders agree to establish ethnic cantons for each group in Bosnia and Herzegovina, but the Bosnian Muslim leader, Izetbegović, soon withdraws his agreement.

On April 6, the European Union recognizes Bosnia and Herzegovina after a referendum boycotted by the Bosnian Serbs. Serbian army and paramilitary forces begin an "ethnic cleansing" campaign against Bosnian Muslims and besiege the capital, Sarajevo. Serbia and Montenegro proclaim a new state—the Federal Republic of Yugoslavia.

In May, the UN Security Council imposes sanctions on Serbia and Montenegro.

In August, a London conference on the former Yugoslavia reaches an agreement to dismantle detention camps, lift sieges of major cities, and allow UN supervision of heavy weapons and delivery of humanitarian aid in Bosnia.

In October, international mediators Cyrus Vance and David Owen propose a plan for the creation of ethnic cantons in Bosnia (Vance-Owen plan).

1993   In January, Bosnian Croats and Muslims are in conflict in western and central Bosnia. In April, NATO enforces a no-fly zone in Bosnia.

In May, Bosnian Serb assembly rejects Vance-Owen plan, defying Serbia's president, Milošević. UN Security Council Resolution 827 establishes the International War Crimes Tribunal for the former Yugoslavia, with its seat in The Hague in the Netherlands.

In September, Milošević, Tudjman, and Izetbegović accept a new plan (Owen-Stoltenberg) to divide Bosnia into three ethnic entities (with 49 percent of territory going to Serbs; 33 percent to Muslims; 17.5 percent to Croats) with a figurehead central government; in October, Bosnian Serb and Bosnian Croat assemblies vote to revoke territorial concessions made to Bosnian Muslims.

1994   In February, an explosion at a Sarajevo marketplace attributed to Serbian forces propels NATO to enforce an exclusion zone for heavy weapons around the city. In Washington, talks begin on the formation of a Croat-Muslim federation.

In April, the Bosnian Serb army threatens to overrun the UN-protected safe zone of Goražde in eastern Bosnia; NATO responds with air strikes. Britain, France, Russia, and the United States set up a Contact Group to work together toward a cease-fire in Bosnia.

In June–July, the Contact Group presents new peace plan for Bosnia, according 51percent of the territory to the Croat-Muslim federation and 49 percent to the Bosnian Serbs. Bosnian Serbs reject the proposal.

In August, Serbia's president, Milošević, (who supports the Contact Group plan), imposes a political and economic blockade on the Bosnian Serbs. In response, Serbs from Bosnia and the Croatian Krajina declare their intention to form a common state. In September, Croats and Bosnian Muslims reach agreement on joint military command.

1995   In January, the Contact Group presents a plan for the reintegration of Serb-held Krajina into Croatia and promises full autonomy to Serbs (Z-4 plan).

In May, the Croatian army attacks across UN lines, reclaiming Serb-held territory in Slavonia (north-eastern Croatia); in response Krajina Serbs fire rockets into downtown Zagreb. Bosnian Serbs resume shelling of Sarajevo. NATO responds by air strikes against Bosnian Serbs, who, in turn, take 372 UN peacekeepers hostage.

On July 7–11, Bosnian Serb troops overrun the UN safe enclave of Srebrenica, expelling old men, women, and children, and executing some 7,000 Bosnian Muslim men.

On August 4–9, the Croatian army wages Operation Storm, retaking all of Krajina and parts of western Bosnia; 170,000 Serb refugees escape to Serbia.

In late August, NATO launches air strikes against Bosnian Serb forces for the shelling of the Markale marketplace in Sarajevo that killed thirty-seven and wounded eighty-five civilians.

In November, the presidents of Serbia, Bosnia, and Croatia negotiate in Dayton, Ohio, agreeing to bring an end to the war in Bosnia.

1997   The newly formed Kosovo Liberation Army (KLA) begins an armed struggle for Kosovo's independence from Serbia.

1998   Serbian police and army try to eradicate the KLA. By summer, some 200,000 Albanians are forced to leave their homes.

In October, NATO threatens bombing of Serbia. Milošević withdraws large army units from Kosovo. Two thousand European observers are placed in charge of monitoring the situation.

1999   In January, the bodies of forty-five Albanian civilians are found in the village of Račak (Kosovo); the massacre is attributed to Serbian police.

In February, the Contact Group organizes a conference in Rambouillet (France) with the aim of bringing peace to Kosovo. After two rounds of negotiations, the Albanian side signs a peace plan that falls short of guaranteeing Kosovo's national independence but promises NATO protection, autonomy, and a referendum at a future date. The Serbian side rejects the plan because of provisions that give NATO control over Kosovo and freedom of troop movement throughout Serbia.

On March 24, 1999, NATO begins bombing of Serbia and Montenegro. In response, Serbian army and paramilitary forces begin large-scale operations in Kosovo, killing about 10,000 Albanians and forcing 860,000 others to seek refuge in Macedonia and Albania. NATO bombing kills close to 1,000 Serb and Albanian civilians; 1,500 Serbian soldiers are killed in combat or by air strikes.

On May 27, the International War Crimes Tribunal indicts Milošević and other high-ranked Serbian civilian and military leaders for crimes against humanity.

In June, Milošević agrees (under pressure from NATO and Russia) to withdraw Serbian forces from Kosovo. Under UN Resolution 1244, Kosovo remains part of Serbia, but as a UN-administered entity protected by the NATO-led Kosovo Protection Force (KFOR).

In June–July, Albanian refugees return to Kosovo; more than 230,000 Serbs and Roma flee Kosovo; only about 10,000 have returned to Kosovo since 1999.

2001	The former president of Yugoslavia, Slobodan Milošević, is sent to the Netherlands to be tried as a war criminal.
2002	Milošević is put on trial for war crimes at the International Court of Justice in The Hague, Netherlands.
2006	Milošević dies before the end of the trial.

INTRODUCTION

The dissolution of Yugoslavia represents the most dramatic instance of state disintegration in post–World War II Europe. In contrast to the relatively peaceful breakup of the Soviet Union and Czechoslovakia's "velvet divorce," Yugoslavia's disintegration was marked by political violence, "ethnic cleansing," and other war crimes. Depending on the intellectual and political perspective of the observer, Yugoslavia's violent disintegration has been characterized as an instance of ethnic conflict, a civil war, or a case of foreign aggression against internationally recognized states (Serbia's and Croatia's aggression against Bosnia). Yugoslavia's violent dissolution had significant international consequences: the creation of five new independent states on the territory of the former Yugoslavia; the unprecedented engagement of international organizations in a domestic conflict, from the United Nations to the European Union and the NATO Alliance; the formation of the Contact Group for Bosnia composed of four great powers (United States, Britain, France, and Russia) and the NATO Alliance; and the establishment of the International War Crimes Tribunal for the former Yugoslavia in The Hague, Netherlands. The unresolved status of Kosovo (formally within Serbia but under a UN protectorate) and the uncertain status of the federation between Serbia and Montenegro mean that Yugoslavia's dissolution may not yet be complete.

BACKGROUND: CULTURE AND HISTORY

The dissolution of Yugoslavia must be understood against the background of three long-term factors that had an important impact on the crisis of the state: the troubled history of Yugoslavia's late unification in the context of considerable ethnic and religious diversity, the traumatic collective memories of ethnic conflict in the Yugoslav Civil War (1941–1945), and the unintended institutional consequences of ethnic federalism as the Yugoslav Communists' purported solution to the national question.

Yugoslavia ("the land of the South Slavs") was formed as a unified state after World War I (1918) through the union of the independent kingdoms of Serbia and Montenegro with South Slav provinces of Austro-Hungary (Slovenia, Croatia, Bosnia and Herzegovina, and Vojvodina). During the inter-war period (1918–1941), Yugoslavia was a constitutional monarchy with a king from the Serbian Karadjordjević dynasty. After World War II, Yugoslavia was reconstituted as a Communist federation of six republics (Slovenia, Croatia, Bosnia and Herzegovina, Serbia, Montenegro, and Macedonia) and two autonomous provinces within Serbia (Vojvodina and Kosovo).

From the time of its formation until its dissolution (1991), Yugoslavia was religiously and ethnically the most diverse state in Eastern Europe. In religious terms, the various Yugoslav peoples can be divided into three groups: Orthodox Christians (Serbs, Montenegrins, Macedonians); Catholics (Slovenes, Croats); and Muslims (Slavic Muslims in Bosnia

Yugoslavia from 1945 to its dissolution in 1991 showing, according to the 1974 Constitution, its six republics (Bosnia-Herzegovina, Croatia, Macedonia, Montenegro, Serbia, and Slovenia) and two autonomous regions within the Serbian Republic (Kosovo and Vojvodina), along with major cities.

and Albanian Muslims in Kosovo). The ethnic diversity of former Yugoslavia can be grasped from estimates of the last Yugoslav census (1991): out of some 23.5 million people, Serbs accounted for approximately 8.53 million (36. 2 percent of the total), Croats for 4.64 million (19.7 percent), Bosnian Muslims for 2.35 million (10 percent), Albanians for 2.18 million (9.3 percent), Slovenes for 1.76 million (7.5 percent), Macedonians for 1.37 million (5.8 percent), Montenegrins for 539,000 (2.3 percent), self-declared Yugoslavs for 705,000 (3 percent; the category "Yugoslav" was chosen by those who for personal or political reasons did not identify with any particular ethnic group), and other minorities (e.g., Hungarians, Roma, Italians, Slovaks) for the remaining 1.46 million (6.2 percent; Rusinow 1995, 353).

Yugoslavia's religious and ethnic diversity was tempered by relative linguistic unity. Although Serbian, Croatian, and Bosnian are now treated as separate languages, in the former Yugoslavia they were considered variants of a common language officially known as Serbo-Croatian or Croato-Serbian (spoken by Serbs, Croats, Bosnian Muslims, and Montenegrins, or about 70 percent of the total population, and writ-

ten in both the Latin and Cyrillic scripts). In addition, many Slovenes and Macedonians who speak distinct South Slavic languages also spoke Serbo-Croatian. This leaves Albanian as the only non-Slavic language spoken by a significant part of the population.

Yugoslavia's considerable religious and ethnic diversity was not always recognized as politically salient. At the time of the formation of the Kingdom of the Serbs, Croats, and Slovenes (the official name of the country until 1929, when it became the Kingdom of Yugoslavia), an influential segment of Yugoslavia's elite espoused the doctrine of "unitarism," i.e., the idea that the three constituent peoples of state—Serbs, Croats, and Slovenes—were "three tribes of one (South Slav) nation" (at that time Montenegrins, Macedonians, and Bosnian Muslims were not thought of as separate ethnic groups). This belief reflected the hope that a unified Yugoslav nation would emerge once all the South Slavs—historically divided between the Ottoman and Austro-Hungarian empires—were united in a common state. In practice, the divisions among the different Yugoslav peoples proved stronger than the forces that bound them together.

The central national problem of the inter-war period concerned the Croat question. Unlike Yugoslavia's smaller ethnic groups (with the partial exception of Slovenes), the Croats had a well-defined national ideology and a shared belief in the historical continuity of Croatia's autonomy in the Habsburg empire. Moreover, as the historical creators of the idea of Yugoslav unification, Croats considered themselves equal to the Serbs and sought guarantees against the Serbs' preponderance in federalism. The Serbian historical experience was altogether different. After a whole century of struggle for national independence against the Ottoman and Habsburg empires, Serbian elites had developed a veritable cult of the central state. As a result, the political struggle between "Serbian centralism" and "Croat federalism" took center stage throughout the inter-war period, even as it was superimposed upon a whole set of other conflicts (economic, social, party-political, ideological). The continued political domination of Serbian elites alienated many Croats from the Yugoslav idea, a situation only partly remedied by the constitutional recognition of Croatia's autonomy in 1939.

The Yugoslav national question had an international dimension as well. Yugoslavia's neighbors—Italy, Hungary, Albania, and Bulgaria—had designs on Yugoslav territory and were ready to mobilize their respective minorities (in the case of Bulgaria, controversially, the Macedonians) for the "irredentist" cause. The Nazi invasion (April 1941) enabled them to dismember Yugoslavia and helped unleash a civil war with lasting consequences. Three major forces emerged in Yugoslavia's civil war: the Croat Ustashe, an extreme nationalist movement that the Nazi and Italian occupiers placed at the helm of the greatly expanded Independent State of Croatia (that included Bosnia and Herzegovina); the Chetniks, a guerrilla resistance movement that claimed continuity with the Yugoslav Royal Army but remained overwhelmingly Serbian in composition and ideology; the Communist-led Partisans, who aspired to become a multiethnic and all-Yugoslav resistance force.

From the standpoint of long-term consequences, the most critical developments took place in the Independent State of Croatia, in which the Ustashe's brutal policy of the extermination, expulsion, and conversion (from Orthodoxy to Catholicism) of Serbs unleashed a bitter civil war among Serbs and Croats, with the Bosnian Muslims caught in between. The Serbian Chetniks' "revenge" raids on Croat and Muslim villages (some Bosnian Muslims had taken part in the massacres of Serbs) further poisoned Serb-Croat and Serb-Muslim relations. It was the Communist-led Partisans who reconstituted the Yugoslav state by mobilizing Serbs, Croats, and Bosnian Muslims into joint military units on the internationalist platform of "brotherhood and unity." Nevertheless, the war left an indelible mark on the collective memory of all three ethnic groups. For many Serbs, Croat nationalism became inseparable from the wartime Ustashe state; anti-Communist Croats saw the multiethnic Partisan army as a Serb-dominated force (Serbs from Croatia and Bosnia were overrepresented in Partisan ranks) that forcibly restored a centralist Yugoslav state and collectively punished the Croats for Ustashe crimes; and finally, some Bosnian Muslims carried bitter memories of Chetnik massacres while others resented the Ustashe's attempt to co-opt them for Croatian nationalism. Although such collective memories and sentiments were not equally influential throughout the three ethnic groups, they had deeper roots in the ethnically mixed parts of Croatia and Bosnia (the Krajina regions of Croatia and western Bosnia, Herzegovina, and eastern Bosnia), that is, some of the same regions in which war broke out in the 1990s.

The third long-term factor in Yugoslavia's dissolution concerns the institutional effects of ethnic federalism. Following the Soviet prototype, Yugoslav Communists organized ethnic groups in territorially based Socialist republics and autonomous provinces with their own political and cultural institutions, from Communist Party organizations to universities, academies of science, and unions of writers—de facto creating pseudo-states of and for the titular nations (Serbia for the Serbs; Croatia for the Croats, etc.). Since republics were also treated as units of administration and economic planning, conflicts over the distribution of federal resources inevitably acquired political and cultural (national) dimensions. The policy of transfer payments from the more developed republics (Slovenia, Croatia, and Serbia without Kosovo) to the less developed republics and provinces (Bosnia and Herzegovina, Montenegro, Macedonia, and Kosovo) exacerbated such conflicts.

A further contradiction of Communist federalism concerned the discrepancy between the territorial boundaries of republics and the geographical distribution of ethnic groups. Although republics were named after titular nations, all except Slovenia contained significant minorities. Since the Yugoslav constitution left unresolved the question of whether "nations" (peoples) or republics (territories) were the main units of self-determination, the territorially most dispersed ethnic group (the Serbs) had a vested interest in the "ethnic" interpretation, while territorially concentrated groups (e.g., Slovenes, Macedonians, and somewhat less, Albanians) espoused a "territorial" (republic or province-wide) interpretation of self-determination (the Croats mostly adopted the territorial interpretation, but Croats in Bosnia and Herzegovina opted for the "ethnic" one). In addition, the centrally located republic of Bosnia and Herzegovina had no clear titular nationality, since no group formed a clear majority (in 1991, Bosnian Muslims comprised 43.7 percent of the population, Serbs 31.4 percent, Croats 17.3 percent, self-declared Yugoslavs 5.5 percent [Rusinow 1995, 352]). Yugoslav

Communists hoped to overcome these potential problems through ideological campaigns designed to foster "brotherhood and unity" among Yugoslav peoples, and by imposing strict political limits on nationalist sentiment. However, by relying on Socialist ideology to keep the country together, they tied the preservation of the Yugoslav state to the survival of Socialism. As a result, the most important *contextual* factor in Yugoslavia's dissolution—the crisis of Yugoslav Socialism in the 1980s—inevitably led to the crisis of the multinational state.

CONTEXT AND PROCESS OF REVOLUTION

The crisis of Yugoslav Socialism had five interrelated aspects: generational, institutional, ideological, economic, and international. The deaths of Yugoslavia's chief ideologue Edvard Kardelj (1978) and leader Josip Broz Tito (1980) marked the end of the wartime Partisan generation in Yugoslav politics, leaving a legitimacy vacuum at the center. Institutionally, the 1974 constitution devolved most power to the republics and autonomous provinces, leaving the federal center weak and incoherent. Like other East European states, Yugoslavia accumulated significant external debt in the 1970s ($22 billion), making the problem of economic reform urgent. Such reform required a modicum of fiscal, political, and constitutional centralization that most republican elites (except in Serbia) deemed politically unacceptable. As a result, the economic question assumed the form of an institutionally irresolvable conflict between "federalists" (mostly from Serbia and the army leadership, but including liberal economists and Yugoslav-oriented reformists) and "confederalists" (led by Slovenia, but with varying support from elites in most republics and autonomous provinces [see Woodward, 1995, 63–73]). On the international level, Mikhail Gorbachev's reconciliation with the West diminished Yugoslavia's strategic importance as a "non-aligned" buffer between NATO and the Warsaw Pact. In addition, the collapse of Communism in Eastern Europe (1989) made other countries (Poland, Czechoslovakia, Hungary) a priority for Western leaders. Finally, the prospect of joining the European Union lured the most developed republics (Slovenia and Croatia) away from Yugoslavia, increasingly seen as a political and economic burden by their elites.

The political crisis of the Yugoslav state began with the Albanian riots in Kosovo (1981). Although an autonomous province within Serbia, after 1974 Kosovo was de facto a self-governing province whose higher educational institutions turned out a mass of Albanian-speaking graduates with few employment prospects. Moreover, despite large federal aid,

Kosovo remained Yugoslavia's poorest region, with very high birthrates. Informally, ethnic Albanians were associated with menial occupations and ranked lowest on Yugoslavia's scale of ethnic prestige. Finally, Kosovo's local elite (Albanian and Serb) was notoriously corrupt and ineffective. The combination of economic, social, and national grievances gave rise to the 1981 riots, in which one of the key demands of the demonstrators—the elevation of Kosovo's status to that of a Socialist republic—was interpreted by the Yugoslav party leadership as a first step to the Albanians' secession from Yugoslavia.

The imposition of martial law did little to solve Kosovo's problems. Even as Albanian dissent was suppressed by force, the Serb minority in Kosovo (by 1981 only 13.2 percent of Kosovo's population, down from 23.6 percent in 1961) felt under greater threat from Albanian "irredentism." This sense of threat was exacerbated by the fact that Serbia had only formal sovereignty over its autonomous provinces. In addition, in the Serbian national mythology Kosovo occupies a special status, both as the center of Serbia's medieval state and as the site of the Kosovo battle (1389), the main symbolic marker of the Serbs' subjugation to the Ottoman empire. Consequently, the problem of Kosovo's status assumed critical importance in Serbian politics. However, since the constitutional reintegration of Kosovo into Serbia required the consensus of the elites of republics and autonomous provinces with veto power in federal bodies, it could not be accomplished within the existing institutional framework.

The result of federal deadlock was the emergence of two diametrically opposed national programs—Serbian and Slovenian. The Serbian program envisaged federal recentralization, limited market reforms, and the constitutional integration of the autonomous provinces into Serbia, or—if Yugoslavia were to disintegrate—the creation of an enlarged Serbian state that would include Serbs from Croatia and Bosnia on the basis of self-determination. By contrast, the Slovenian program envisaged either the transformation of Yugoslavia into a confederation or full-fledged national independence. By 1988, these programs, first formulated by intellectuals, were co-opted by Serbia's and Slovenia's political elites.

Slobodan Milošević, the head of Serbia's Communist Party, capitalized on the grievances of Kosovo's Serbs, assuming leadership of a populist nationalist movement whose goal was to bring the autonomous provinces under Serbia's control. The mass rallies that toppled the elites of Vojvodina (October 1988) and Montenegro (January 1989) enabled Serbia to reassert control over Kosovo and changed the balance of votes in federal bodies in Serbia's favor (Serbia, Vojvodina, Kosovo, and Montenegro accounted for four out of eight votes in the collective presidency). The fear of Serbia's control over the federation provoked resistance in Slovenia and

Slobodan Milošević, president of Serbia (1989–1997) and of Yugoslavia (1997–2000). After Yugoslavia began to disintegrate in the late 1980s, Slobodan Milošević manipulated simmering nationalist sympathies which destroyed the multinational Yugoslavia, emerging as the most powerful man in the restructured Serbian-dominated nation. (AP/Wide World Photos)

Croatia, first within the party (Slovenia's and Croatia's delegations left the last Yugoslav Communist Party congress in January 1990), and then in the first multiparty elections (April 1990) that resulted in a victory for independence-minded parties (although Slovenia's president, Milan Kučan, was a reform Communist). The election of nationalist president Franjo Tudjman in Croatia was especially contentious, as it resurrected memories of wartime persecution among Serbs in Croatia and antagonized the army leadership in which Serbs from Croatia and Bosnia were overrepresented. The triumph of nationalist parties (Serb, Croat, and Bosnian Muslim) in Bosnia and Herzegovina, and the election of Milošević as president of Serbia (December 1990) effectively ended the hope that the popular federal prime minister Ante Marković would succeed in holding the country together through market reforms.

By spring 1991, clashes between Croatian police and Serb paramilitaries raised the specter of civil war in Croatia. The Yugoslav army, ostensibly stepping in to divide the two sides, effectively sided with the Serbs. When Slovenia and Croatia declared independence (June 1991), the Yugoslav army quickly withdrew from Slovenia, concentrating on "protecting" Serbs in Croatia and Bosnia, de facto establishing the boundaries of a greatly enlarged Serbian state. The aggressive character of army intervention (shelling of Dubrovnik, leveling of Vukovar) turned international opinion against Serbia. An important attempt to end the war was made at The Hague Conference on the Former Yugoslavia (October 1991), chaired by Lord Peter Carrington. Carrington envisaged the transformation of Yugoslavia into a loose association of states with limited common institutions that would guarantee minority rights in each of the constituent republics. When Serbia rejected the plan, Germany unilaterally recognized Slovenia and Croatia, a move soon followed by the other European Union countries and the United States. Simultaneously, a negotiated UN-monitored cease-fire temporarily stopped the war in Croatia. In April 1992, however, the conflict spilled over into Bosnia. The EU recognition of Bosnia—after a divisive referendum that was boycotted by the Bosnian Serbs—served as a pretext for Serbian military action.

Some of the worst "ethnic cleansing" campaigns, designed to murder and expel the Bosnian Muslims from areas claimed by the Bosnian Serbs, took place during the first few months of the war, which also witnessed the siege of Sarajevo by Bosnian Serb forces. In response, the international community imposed sanctions on Serbia, while the international press gave unprecedented publicity to war crimes (the murder of civilians, mass rapes) and the atrocious conditions in prisoner-of-war detention camps (mostly, though not exclusively, run by the Bosnian Serbs). Although the Bosnian Serb forces were guilty of the majority of war crimes, Bosnian Croat and Bosnian Muslim formations contributed their share. Moreover, by January 1993, Bosnian Croats and Muslims were engaged in a bitter conflict against each other in western and central Bosnia.

The next two years witnessed several attempts by the international community to stop the war through a combination of diplomacy, sanctions, and military intervention. Ultimately, U.S.-led Western strategy was to end the military preponderance of the Bosnian Serbs through the imposition of "no-fly zones," bombing, sanctions on Serbia, and the forging of a military alliance between the Bosnian Croats and Muslims. Simultaneously, Bosnian Serbs were promised autonomy on 49 percent of the territory of Bosnia and Herzegovina. The brutal execution of some 7,000 Bosnian Muslims by Bosnian Serb forces in the UN-protected "safe haven" of Srebrenica (July 1995) represented a turning point, paving the way for Western military involvement and the combined Croat-Muslim offensive (August 1995). The cumulative effect of military defeat, the expulsion of most of Croatia's Serbs, the loss of territory in western Bosnia, and air strikes by NATO forced the Bosnian Serbs to the negotiating table. In November 1995, the presidents of Serbia, Croatia, and Bosnia signed a peace agreement in Dayton, Ohio. The Dayton Agreements established Bosnia and Herzegovina as a federal state composed of two entities: the Federation of Bosnia-Herzegovina (predominantly Croat-Bosnian Muslim, 51 percent of territory), and Serb Republic (49 percent of territory).

Although the Dayton Agreements ended the war in most of former Yugoslavia, in 1998 armed conflict flared up in the southern Serbian province of Kosovo, where the newly formed KLA (Kosovo Liberation Army) sought to mobilize Kosovo Albanians for the cause of independence from the Federal Republic of Yugoslavia (later Serbia and Montenegro). The heavy-handed response of Serbia's police and army to KLA attacks supplied the Albanian guerrillas with thousands of recruits. By late 1998, the situation in Kosovo assumed critical proportions, with some 200,000 displaced Albanian civilians seeking shelter from the conflict. This humanitarian crisis prompted renewed U.S.-led diplomatic and military effort. When the Serbian delegation walked out of the peace talks in Rambouillet (France), refusing to accept the U.S.-drafted peace plan, NATO intervened by bombing Serbia (March 24, 1999). In response, Serbian army and paramilitary forces intensified the war in Kosovo, killing thousands of Albanians and forcing some 860,000 Albanian civilians to seek refuge in Macedonia and Albania. After eighty-eight days of NATO bombing and pressure from Russia, Serbia's President Milošević accepted to withdraw the Serbian army from Kosovo. Under UN Resolution 1244, Kosovo formally remained part of Serbia but de facto became a self-governing province under UN and NATO protection.

IMPACTS

The dissolution of Yugoslavia presented the most important challenge to the post–Cold War order in Europe. At a time when the European Union was breaking national barriers and other East European nations were developing democratic institutions and creating market economies, the war in the former Yugoslavia offered a powerful reminder of the destructive potential of nationalism. The conflicting territorial aspirations of Serbian and Croatian nationalism as articulated by their leaders—Milošević and Tudjman—proved particularly destructive, as they could be accomplished only by the "ethnic cleansing" of "unwanted minorities" and the dismemberment of Yugoslavia's ethnically most diverse republic—Bosnia and Herzegovina. The fact that the greatest number of war crimes was committed by the better-armed Bosnian Serbs (followed by the Bosnian Croats and Bosnian Muslims) indicates the relatively greater responsibility of Serbian nationalists for the violence in Bosnia and Herzegovina. Nevertheless, Yugoslavia's descent into war cannot be fully understood without taking into account the role of other nationalists (Croatian, Slovenian, Bosnian Muslim, and Kosovo Albanian) in the state's dissolution.

The peoples of the former Yugoslavia suffered the direst consequences: it is estimated that the wars in Croatia and Bosnia resulted in more than 200,000 deaths, and tens of thousands more were wounded. In addition, about 1.3 million people became refugees, and thousands of women (the figures remain contested; the women were predominantly Bosnian Muslim, but also Croat and Serb) became victims of mass rape (Alcock, Milivojević, and Horton 1998, 37–38, 233–234, 238–240). The character of the violence was more appalling than mere numbers can convey: villages were torched, women raped, children killed in front of their parents, bodies mutilated, prisoners of war tortured, civilians searching for food and shelter killed by snipers. The destruction of cultural monuments, especially churches and mosques, but also historic bridges (Mostar) and libraries (Sarajevo), were integral parts of the strategy of "ethnic cleansing" designed to eliminate the cultural foundations of an ethnic group's existence in a contested territory. The case of Srebrenica (July 1995), where 7,000 captured Bosnian Muslim men were executed by Bosnian Serb forces, evoked memories of the worst atrocities of World War II.

The dissolution of Yugoslavia led to the formation of five new states on its territory: Slovenia, Croatia, Bosnia-Herzegovina, Federal Republic of Yugoslavia (later Serbia and Montenegro), and Macedonia. Tragically, even after so much violence, several questions remain unresolved: the status of the federation between Serbia and Montenegro, the status of Kosovo as a prospective independent state, the future of Bosnia-Herzegovina as a state divided into two entities.

Yugoslavia's dissolution had very important international consequences. The unilateral recognition of Slovenia and Croatia by Germany (1991) raised important questions about the legitimate conditions of self-determination, secession, and external interference in the affairs of a sovereign state. The formation of the International War Crimes Tribunal for the former Yugoslavia (and Rwanda) created a precedent for the establishment of a permanent international war crimes court. The scale of diplomatic and military intervention by the Western powers (plus Russia) was unprecedented. The relative effectiveness of international sanctions versus military intervention against "rogue states," and the many unintended consequences of both strategies, were tested amply on Serbia. The bombing of Serbia (1999) was the first war fought by NATO in its history, setting a precedent for "humanitarian interventions" elsewhere (East Timor). The controversial character of armed intervention against a sovereign state without authorization of the UN Security Council and in seeming violation of existing international law raised questions about the limits of state sovereignty and created a precedent for subsequent unilateral U.S. military actions (Afghanistan; Iraq). The ultimate political consequences of these developments are still unknown. What can be safely said is that Yugoslavia's dissolution provided a testing ground for the development of new international norms and practices.

PEOPLE AND ORGANIZATIONS

Bleiburg Massacres

In May 1945, Yugoslav Partisans executed some 30,000 (perhaps more—the figures are contested) soldiers and civilians near the village of Bleiburg on the Austrian-Slovene border. Most of the victims were Croats fleeing from the defeated In-

dependent State of Croatia (there were a lot of Slovenes and a few Serbs as well). Although the Partisans were a multinational force, Croat nationalists see the Bleiburg massacres as an instance of Croat victimization by "Serb-Communist" forces (Serbs from Croatia and Bosnia were overrepresented among the Partisans).

Dayton Agreement

In November 1995, presidents Izetbegović (Bosnia), Tudjman (Croatia), and Milošević (Federal Republic of Yugoslavia) met in the Wright-Paterson Air Force Base in Dayton, Ohio. Under considerable U.S. pressure, the parties agreed to sign a peace agreement with the following main provisions: the federal organization of Bosnia-Herzegovina as a state composed of two entities—Federation of Bosnia-Herzegovina (mostly Croat-Muslim, 51 percent of territory) and Serb Republic (49 percent of territory); the separation of the armed forces of the two entities; the creation of a joint legislature; the return of refugees to their original place of residence; the implementation of peace by a NATO-led Stabilization Force (SFOR); the creation of the office of a U.N. High Commissioner with plenipotentiary powers.

Izetbegović, Alija (1925–2003)

The first president of independent Bosnia and Herzegovina, born in Bosanski Šamac (Bosnia). In 1970, Izetbegović published *The Islamic Declaration,* a programmatic document that asserted the superiority of Islam over secularism. In 1983, Izetbegović was put on trial for "hostile propaganda" against the Communist state and sentenced to twelve years in prison. Pardoned in 1988, Izetbegović emerged as the leader of the Bosnian Muslim Party of Democratic Action (1990). After his party won 44 percent of the vote in Bosnia's first free election (1990), Izetbegović was appointed president of Bosnia. In 1991–1992, Izetbegović sought a middle ground between Croat and Serb nationalists but ultimately sided with the Slovene-Croat proposal for a Yugoslav confederation, thus alienating the Bosnian Serbs. Izetbegović's decision to pursue Bosnia's independence in defiance of the Serb community (31.4 percent of Bosnia's population) proved controversial, serving as a pretext (not necessarily the cause) for Serbian military action in Bosnia.

Jasenovac

The largest concentration camp run by the Croat Ustashe in World War II, Jasenovac remains a symbol of the extermination of Serbs, Jews, and Gypsies in the Independent State of Croatia. In the 1980s, Serbian and Croatian historians contested the number of Jasenovac victims, with the former citing a figure of 700,000 and the latter bringing it down to as low as 30,000. Official post-war Communist figures of 500,000 victims have proven inflated; realistic sources speak of 100,000 to 200,000 victims. The Belgrade Museum of the Holocaust has gathered the names of 80,000 known victims; however, many more may be unknown. At least 13,000 (perhaps as many as 25,000) Jews were killed in Jasenovac, along with an unknown number of Gypsies and a small number of anti-Ustashe Croats. Whatever the exact numbers, it is indisputable that Jasenovac occupies an important place in the history of the Holocaust and genocide in World War II.

Karadžić, Radovan (Born 1945)

President of the Bosnian Serb Republic (1992–1996), Karadžić was born in Petnjica (Montenegro). A psychiatrist by profession, Karadžić emerged as the leader of the Serbian Democratic Party (SDS) in 1990. In November 1991, the SDS organized a referendum that showed widespread support among Bosnian Serbs for unification with Yugoslavia and/or Serbia. After Bosnia's international recognition (April 1992), Karadžić and the SDS set up an independent Serb Republic. An extreme nationalist, Karadžić lived up to his rhetoric: almost 90 percent of Croats and Muslims were killed or expelled from the Serb Republic in the 1992–1995 period. In 1996, the International War Crimes Tribunal indicted Karadžić for genocide and crimes against humanity. Since then, Karadžić has avoided all attempts to capture him.

Milošević, Slobodan (1941–2006)

President of Serbia and Federal Republic of Yugoslavia (later Serbia and Montenegro) from 1990 to 2000, Milošević was born in Požarevac (eastern Serbia). In 1987, Milošević emerged as a populist leader who capitalized on the grievances of the Kosovo Serbs to take control of Vojvodina, Montenegro, and Kosovo. With four votes in Yugoslavia's federal institutions, Milošević made an unsuccessful bid to dominate the Yugoslav party-state. In 1990, Milošević made clear that Serbia would seek to unite with Serbs from Croatia and Bosnia in case of Yugoslavia's breakup; in effect, this became a program for the creation of a "greater Serbia," even though Milošević—unlike some other extreme Serbian nationalists—never openly endorsed it. Despite considerable internal opposition, Milošević won the Serbian presidency in the first relatively free elections (December 1990) and proceeded to realize his program with the help of the Yu-

goslav army and Serbian paramilitaries. Milošević is commonly seen as the leader most to blame for the violence in the former Yugoslavia. Milošević's role in prodding, arming, and financing Serbs in Croatia and Bosnia and in fostering nationalist propaganda in Serbia is indisputable. Faced with considerable international and internal opposition, by 1993 Milošević distanced himself from the Croatian and Bosnian Serbs and refashioned himself as a peacemaker at the Dayton negotiations (November 1995). The crisis in Kosovo (1998–1999) proved to be Milošević's undoing. NATO's bombing of Serbia, his indictment by the International War Crimes Tribunal, and the growing strength of Serbia's internal opposition forced Milošević out of power after his defeat in the presidential elections of October 2000. In June 2001 Serbia's democratic government extradited Milošević to The Hague, where he died in 2006 while on trial.

Mladić, Ratko (Born 1942)

Colonel of the Yugoslav People's Army and subsequent head of the Army of the Serb Republic in Bosnia, Mladić was born in Kalinovik, Bosnia. In 1991, he was chief of staff of the Yugoslav army corps in Knin, the seat of the first Serb rebellion in Croatia. In May 1992, Mladić was promoted to general and appointed head of the Bosnian Serb Army (VRS). In the 1992–1995 period, Mladić became notorious for organizing the siege of Sarajevo and for his defiance of Western powers. Mladić committed his worst war crime in July 1995, when he ordered the execution of 7,000 Bosnian Muslim men in Srebrenica (eastern Bosnia). In June 1996, Mladić was charged with genocide and crimes against humanity. So far, he has avoided all attempts to capture him.

Tudjman, Franjo (1922–1999)

First freely elected president of Croatia, Tudjman was born in Veliko Trgovišće (northern Croatia). In World War II, Tudjman joined the Partisan movement, becoming one of Yugoslavia's youngest Communist generals. A military historian, in the late 1960s Tudjman turned away from Communism, espousing Croat nationalist ideas. In particular, Tudjman questioned the official figures of Serb victims in the Ustashe-run Jasenovac concentration camp as too high and attacked Yugoslav "unitarism" as a mask for continued Serbian hegemony. In 1971 Tudjman was sentenced to two years in prison for his role in the Croat nationalist movement. In 1989, Tudjman re-emerged as the leader of the Croatian Democratic Union (HDZ), a right-wing nationalist party. In April 1990, Tudjman was elected president of Croatia, a position he retained until his death. Although many

Croats perceive Tudjman as a hero who created an independent Croatia, he remains a controversial figure. Tudjman's discriminatory policies towards Croatia's Serbs and openly stated plans to partition Bosnia raise the question of his responsibility for the wars in Croatia and Bosnia.

Veljko Vujačić

See Also Documentaries of Revolution; East European Revolutions of 1989; Ethnic and Racial Conflict: From Bargaining to Violence; Human Rights, Morality, Social Justice, and Revolution; Nationalism and Revolution; Russian Revolution of 1991 and the Dissolution of the U.S.S.R.; Yugoslav Communist Revolution

References and Further Readings

Ali, Rabia, and Lawrence Lifshultz, eds. 1993. *Why Bosnia? Writings on the Balkan Wars.* Stony Creek, CT: Pamphleteer's Press.

Allcock, John B. 2000. *Explaining Yugoslavia.* New York: Columbia University Press.

Allcock, John B., Marko Milivojević, and John J. Horton, eds. 1998. *Conflict in the Former Yugoslavia: An Encyclopedia.* Santa Barbara, CA: ABC-CLIO.

Burg, Steven. 1983. *Conflict and Cohesion in Socialist Yugoslavia.* Princeton, NJ: Princeton University Press.

Burg, Steven, and Paul Shoup. 1999. *The War in Bosnia and Herzegovina: Ethnic Conflict and International Intervention.* Armonk, NY: M. E. Sharpe.

Cohen, Lenard. 1995. *Broken Bonds: Yugoslavia's Disintegration and Balkan Politics in Transition.* Boulder, CO: Westview Press.

———. 2001. *Serpent in Bosom: The Rise and Fall of Slobodan Milošević.* Boulder, CO: Westview Press.

Dragović-Soso, Jasna. 2002. *'Saviors of the Nation': Serbia's Intellectual Opposition and the Revival of Nationalism.* London: Hurst.

Glenny, Misha. 1996. *The Fall of Yugoslavia: The Third Balkan War.* New York: Penguin.

Hayden, Robert M. 1999. *Blueprints for a House Divided: The Constitutional Logic of Yugoslav Conflicts.* Ann Arbor: University of Michigan Press.

Judah, Tim. 2000. *Kosovo: War and Revenge.* New Haven, CT and London: Yale University Press.

Lampe, John. 2000. *Yugoslavia as History. Twice There Was a Country.* Cambridge: Cambridge University Press.

Magaš, Branka. 1993. *The Destruction of Yugoslavia.* London and New York: Verso.

Malcolm, Noel. 1995. *Bosnia: A Short History.* New York: New York University Press.

———. 1998. *Kosovo: A Short History.* New York: New York University Press.

Ramet, Sabrina P. 1992. *Nationalism and Federalism in Yugoslavia, 1962–1991.* Bloomington and Indianapolis: Indiana University Press.

———. 2002. *Balkan Babel: The Disintegration of Yugoslavia from the Death of Tito to the Fall of Milošević.* Boulder, CO: Westview Press.

Rusinow, Dennison. 1995. "The Yugoslav Peoples." Pp. 305–413 in *Eastern European Nationalism in the Twentieth Century,* edited by Peter F. Sugar. Washington, DC: American University Press.

Silber, Laura, and Allan Little. 1995. *Yugoslavia: Death of a Nation.* New York: Penguin.

Sudetic, Chuck. 1999. *Blood and Vengeance: One Family's Story of the War in Bosnia.* New York: Penguin.

Udovički, Jasminka, and James Ridgeway, eds. 1997. *Burn This House: The Making andUnmaking of Yugoslavia.* Durham, NC, and London: Duke University Press.

Vickers, Miranda. 1998. *Between Serb and Albanian: A History of Kosovo.* London: Hurst.

Wachtel, Andrew. 1998. *Making a Nation, Breaking a Nation: Literature and Cultural Politics in Yugoslavia.* Stanford, CA: Stanford University Press.

Woodward, Susan. 1995. *Balkan Tragedy: Chaos and Dissolution after the Cold War.* Washington, DC: Brookings Institution.

Z

Zapatista Movement

CHRONOLOGY

2000 B.C.– 250 A.D.	Pre-classic period of the Maya, now believed to be when the Mayan origin myth originated. A period of fully developed civilization spread out over what is now Guatemala, Chiapas, and the Yucatan Peninsula.
250–900	Classic period of the Maya, so-called by archaeologists because it was believed that Mayan civilization was at its zenith during this period, which included the development of writing, math, and astronomy.
900–1500	Post-classic period of the Maya marks the abandonment of large cities and the dispersal of the population.
1523	Luis Marín, one of Hernán Cortez's officers, arrives in Chiapas.
	Marín encounters fierce resistance from the highland Tzotzil and others. Diego de Mazariegos is sent to finish the conquest but is not able to do so until 1528, when he establishes Ciudad Real, now called San Cristóbal de las Casas.
1712–1715	Tzeltales, Tzotziles, and other highland peoples revolt against Spanish *repartimiento de mercancías,* a system of forced sales by which indigenous communities have to trade foodstuff, raw cotton, tobacco, and cacao beans for expensive finished goods.
1810	Mexico becomes independent, but Chiapas remains as a part of the Captaincy of Guatemala.
1823–1824	Chiapas first is a part of the independent United Provinces of Central America and then joins independent Mexico as a distinct province in1824.
1856	The Ley Lerdo privatizes church lands and private ranches and plantations grow.
1867–1869	The Custcat Rebellion occurs in highland Chiapas by Chamulas, who organize a regional religious shrine and attempt to defend access to land and markets and to religious and indigenous cultural practices.
1880–1930s	This period of debt servitude is tied to a plantation agricultural model of the late-nineteenth century that results in the selling off of approximately one-third of the surface area of Chiapas to foreign buyers under the

Porfiriato (1890–1910) and leaves approximately 80,000 out of 100,000 indigenous men moving around the state as migrant laborers.

1910–1920   Mexican Revolution in Chiapas is experienced through minimal land redistribution and the 1914 workers' law attempting to outlaw debt servitude.

1930–1980s   Agrarian reform and restitution of some ancestral lands to indigenous peoples as *ejidos* (commonly owned land).

1970s–1980s   Mexican student movement moves out of urban areas after 1968 Tlatelolco massacres and into rural areas, including Chiapas.

1974   First Indigenous Congress, "Fray Bartolomé de las Casas," brings together 1,230 Tzeltal, Tzotzil, Tojolabal, and Ch'ol delegates from 327 indigenous communities in Chiapas in a multilingual assembly that articulates shared demands.

1980   Founding of the Union of Unions, regional peasant organization with widespread political influence in the jungle region.

1983   First EZLN (Zapatista Army of National Liberation) organizers begin to work quietly in Chiapas.

1988   Mexican president Salinas de Gortari is elected in what is widely believed to be a fraudulent election.

1991   Emiliano Zapata Independent Peasant Alliance (ACIEZ) is founded in Puebla. In 1992 ACIEZ becomes national (ANCIEZ) and is the organization where significant parts of the clandestine leadership of the EZLN are participating—until it goes underground in October of 1992.

1992   Changes are made to Article 27 of the Mexican Constitution permitting privatization of communal land and ending the possibility for future land redistribution.

1994   On January 1, the North American Free Trade Agreement begins. The Zapatista Army of National Liberation (EZLN) occupies several cities in Chiapas. International protest stops a short war, and the Mexican government declares a unilateral cease-fire. A first round of peace negotiations with the EZLN fails. Two major political figures are assassinated in Mexico.

1995   Army occupies Zapatista territory in a major offensive. Major military occupation of Zapatista regions begins.

1996   EZLN and the Mexican government sign the San Andrés Accords on Indigenous Rights and Culture. Mexican government questions the peace accords it has signed and refuses to implement them.

1997   Paramilitaries emerge full force in Zapatista regions. Acteal massacre occurs, in which forty-six women, children, and male refugees are executed while worshipping.

2000   Institutional Revolutionary Party (PRI), which has been in power for seventy years, is defeated and Vicente Fox Quesada of the National Action Party (PAN) is elected, promising to end the Chiapas conflict in "15 minutes."

2001   Zapatistas make a historic march from Chiapas to Mexico City following the route of Emiliano Zapata. They campaign vigorously for the legislation of the San Andrés Accords on Indigenous Rights and Culture. In April, the Mexican Congress passes legislation on "Indigenous Rights and Culture" that is soundly rejected by the EZLN, a majority of indigenous organizations and communities, and twelve state governors.

2003   Zapatistas announce the creation of five *caracoles* (literally "shells," but meaning houses) that are the seats for five Juntas of Good Government that administer independent justice, education, government, and health systems in Zapatista autonomous Municipalities in Rebellion.

INTRODUCTION

The Zapatista Rebellion was publicly launched on January 1, 1994, in Chiapas, Mexico, by indigenous combatants and thousands more involved in a base movement of support. While Mexico's indigenous populations were often relegated to a romantic past history, the Zapatista Rebellion provided a political opening for indigenous peoples throughout Mexico and brought issues of indigenous rights to the fore, including land and resources rights, the right to self-determination in local systems of government and adjudication, cultural and language rights, health, education, employment, and housing. The Zapatista movement has also proven to be an inspiration for the global anti neo-liberalism movement through a model of self-development and government that draws on local experience and knowledge while incorporating international resources and connections.

BACKGROUND: CULTURE AND HISTORY

The Mayan peoples of Chiapas have a rich, ongoing, and living history that goes back at least three thousand years. Archaeologists are now busy reclassifying how they characterize Mayan societies before the arrival of the Spanish in 1523. While the period between 250 A.D. and 900 A.D. was referred to in the past as the classic period of the "zenith of Mayan culture," new discoveries suggest that Mayan civilization is much older than previously thought (see Estrada Belli et al. 1993). In addition, historians and social scientists have begun to validate Mayan native versions of their own history through the analysis of historical Mayan texts, through written self-history projects, and through narratives kept by community historians of events extending from 120 to 150 years in the past (see Benjamin 2000). Such a view of history reads the Zapatista Rebellion as part of a continuous historical thread of indigenous creativity and struggle.

Immediately following the conquest in Chiapas (1523–1528), indigenous peoples were wracked by decades of disease, slavery, and tribute. Within fifty years of the conquest, "pandemics of pneumonia, smallpox, and bubonic plague reduced the total indigenous population by two-thirds" (Benjamin 2000, 9).The encomienda system gave Spanish conquerors and their offspring grants of an Indian town or towns with rights to Indian labor and tribute. This condition placed indigenous peoples into positions often akin to slavery. After the encomienda system was outlawed, the elite families of San Cristóbal de Las Casas and elsewhere resorted to other ways of extracting wealth from the surrounding indigenous populations. In order to supposedly promote trade, repartimiento de mercancías was implemented—a system of forced trade by which indigenous communities were compelled to trade food, cotton, tobacco, and other products for expensive finished goods (Benjamin 2000, 8). By 1712, this sparked the Tzeltal rebellion, joined by Tzotziles and Choles (see Gosner 1992).

In 1824, Chiapas joined independent Mexico after briefly being a part of the United Provinces of Central America formed in 1823. Successive Chiapan governments between 1826 and 1844 progressively simplified the process by which private citizens could claim so-called terrenos baldios or vacant lands. By 1850, virtually all of the state's Indian communities had been stripped of lands that were not immediately adjacent to their communities and were labeled as "excess" (Rus 1983, 131–132). Elite ladino (mixed descent, similar to mestizo) families were able to transform more than a quarter of Chiapas's indigenous peoples into peons and laborers through obtaining land. The national Ley Lerdo of 1856, which privatized church lands and encouraged the privatization of all communal lands, resulted in the continued loss of land for indigenous peoples, first and most intensely in lowland regions nearer Spanish settlements, such as among the Tojolabales of Comitán (see Stephen 2002, 92–93; Mattiace 2003a).

During the Porfiriato period (1876–1910) in Mexico, highland indigenous peoples of Chiapas suffered extremely high levels of expropriation of communal lands, leaving them nothing or very small plots that resulted in the dependence of highland Tzeltals and Tzotziles on seasonal migratory labor in Chiapas' lowlands to feed themselves until the 1970s, and in some cases longer (see Rus and Collier 2003, 36–37). In other areas, such as in Tojolabal region, workers came to live on or near ranches and plantations, with no land of their own.

The Mexican Revolution (1910–1917) was felt indirectly and somewhat late by the indigenous peoples of Chiapas. While Carrancista soldiers arrived in 1914, and people were encouraged to petition the state to claim ancestral lands stolen from them, only six ejido grants (grants transferring land to collective indigenous ownership) were approved between 1915 and 1920 (Benjamin 1996, 130). Representatives of the Lázaro Cárdenas government (1934–1940) finally brought some of the gains of the revolution to the state. Communities were able to more successfully petition for land, debt servitude was finally ended, and state intervention in highland communities took off. Through the Chiapas Department of Indian Protection, a new system of governance in highland communities was implemented in which a group of bilingual (Spanish plus a Mayan language) indigenous scribes (official recorders and spokespersons, often known as secretarios) represented the communities in a wide range of dealings with the state government, including as labor union officers, heads of municipal agrarian committees, and leaders of the official party (what became the PRI) and the official peasant organization (CNC) (see Rus 1994).

In the lowlands, power dynamics continued to be concentrated in *haciendas,* but what was to become a large-scale migration and the foundation of new communities began through the establishment of hundreds of new *ejidos* in the Lacandon region. For those who founded *ejidos* in the jungle from the 1930s until the 1980s, receiving land grants was a transforming movement, from a period of "slavery" to "freedom." As most had been disconnected from their communities of origin for quite some time, the structure of the *ejido* became an important cultural and social part of daily life. The fact that some *ejidos* established in the Lacandon region involved multiethnic populations of Tzeltal, Tzotzil, and Ch'ol peoples as well as people from other parts of Mexico also resulted in a different kind of cultural and ethnic identification, which was important in the development of the Zapatista movement.

CONTEXT AND PROCESS OF REVOLUTION

The 1960s, 1970s, and 1980s in Chiapas were marked by several distinct processes and events that are critical for understanding the emergence of the Zapatista movement. Samuel Ruiz took over as bishop of the Catholic diocese of San Cristóbal de las Casas in 1960. In collaboration with Marist priests and nuns, he opened up catechist schools. By the early 1970s, thousands of young male and female indigenous catechists, whose role it was to assist the clergy in conveying religious teaching and services to the community, had been trained in the ideas of liberation theology, which called for the church to take an activist role in improving the lives of the poor and alleviating oppression. For the indigenous peoples of Chiapas, the themes of exodus from slavery, liberation, and an organizational and educational style that validated people's own sense of knowledge and history resonated well. In 1974, the statewide Indian Congress organized by Bishop Ruiz, with the help of Marist priests, nuns, schoolteachers, catechists, and advisers from the Maoist People's Union (UP), provided the first-ever forum in which 1,230 Tzeltal, Tzotzil, Tojolabal, and Ch'ol delegates from 327 communities came together to discuss issues of land, commerce, education, and health in their own languages (see Stephen 2002, 115–119). Never before had Chiapas's different indigenous peoples spoken with one another like this publicly, heard about common problems, or viewed themselves as one people.

Following the congress, a wide range of new organizations emerged, often under the banner of "peasant" rights and concerns. Outside grassroots organizers from various strands of the Left came to encourage the formation of unions of *ejidos.* In 1976, the United in Our Strength Ejido Union was formed in Ocosingo. The Land Liberty Ejido Union and Peasant Struggle Ejido Union formed in the Las Margaritas area that same year (Harvey 1998, 81–82). As these kinds of organizations grew, so did the population in the lowland jungle area, making it necessary for many communities to petition for extensions to their ejido land grants as new generations came of age (Stephen 2002, 120–124).

Concerned with a general crisis in the Mexican countryside represented by indigenous protests in Chiapas and elsewhere, the national government attempted to deal with discontent by creating the Supreme Indigenous Councils, regional organizations that were supposed to channel indigenous activism toward government-controlled programs. Some of these Supreme Indigenous Councils, such as the Tojolabal Council in Las Margaritas, became sites for independent organizations and for models of indigenous autonomous regional government that separated from their original government affiliations (Mattiace 2003b, 116; 2003a). In other areas of the state, the Independent Confederation of Agricultural Workers and Peasants (CIOAC) centered its demands on land reform and redistribution. *Ejido* unions focused on issues of production, such as access to credit, achieving high prices, and access to markets and transportation. The Emiliano Zapata Peasant Organization (OCEZ) formed in 1982 and fought a long, hard battle to recuperate land from local ranchers (see Harvey 1998). From 1982 to 1988 there were an average of two politically motivated killings of peasant activists per month (Harvey 1998, 160), providing clear evidence to many that it was impossible to accomplish change within existing structures.

In 1980, the Union of Ejidal Unions and United Peasants of Chiapas was formed, also known as UU or the Union of Unions. Bringing together 12,000 families from more than 180 communities, the UU represented a new level of organization for indigenous peoples of Chiapas. Because the demands of the UU appeared to be in line with the productivist strategy of the state (focused on the marketing of coffee, for example), the federal government did not see the organization as a threat. The Chiapan government did, however, working steadily to undermine leaders, harass them, and encourage them to defect to the government-sponsored peasant organization. In 1983, the UU split, and a new organization was formed, the Union of Ejidos of the Jungle, which came to represent more than 800 families. In 1988, this organization joined with others to form the ARIC-Union of Unions (ARIC-UU). It became the de facto subterranean government of a large region of the Lacandon jungle. (ARIC stands for Asociación de Interés Colectivo, Association of Collective Interest.)

Anthropologist Xothítl Leyva Solano has argued (2003) that the ARIC-UU resulted in a political homogenization that was made possible, in part, by a lack of political parties in the region and the fact that it was composed almost entirely of indigenous peoples—unlike municipal structures of authority in many other places in Chiapas. The ARIC-UU connected and integrated four paths of change: "the Catholic faith, Guevarist and Maoist socialist ideologies, and an ethnic consciousness opposed to Latinos" (persons of non-indigenous descent) (Leyva Solano 2003, 164). By the end of the 1980s, there were more than eight thousand catechists in Chiapas. In the Lacandon region, they were integrated into the governance structure of communities along with the ARIC-UU as elected deacons. Elected deacons had become permanent parts of local governance structures in many highland communities as well. Throughout the highlands and in other areas of Chiapas, other forms of indigenous organization also prospered in the 1980s, including a wide range of cultural production such as indigenous writers' cooperatives, radio shows, theatre groups, and history projects (Benjamin 2000).

The year 1989 was devastating for coffee producers. World prices fell by fifty percent when the International Coffee Organization failed to agree on production quotas. For the thousands of indigenous small coffee producers in Chiapas, the drop in prices was devastating. The inability of some of the regional peasant organizations to resolve the problem convinced some to begin to listen to an alternative peasant organization, ANCIEZ (described below), that was serving as a cover for the growing ranks of the clandestine Zapatista Army of National Liberation (EZLN).

While the origins of the EZLN are still being debated, self-histories of Zapatismos and other documentation suggest that it developed from two earlier guerrilla forces: the Mexican Insurgent Army (EIM), secretly organized in the 1960s and disbanded after action in Chiapas in 1968 and 1969, and the Forces of National Liberation (FLN), organized in Monterrey in 1969. In 1974, the federal police and army captured a guerrilla training camp of the FLN in Chiapas, killing five people. A few FLN members survived and regrouped in Mexico City, where they published their plans to form the Zapatista Army of National Liberation. By 1982, several cadres of the FLN were apparently secretly working on social programs in the highland municipality of San Andrés Larraínzar. Some of the initial recruits of the FLN were Tzotziles, who in 1983 joined the now-famous Subcomandante Marcos to organize in the Lacandon region. Throughout the 1980s, small cadres of FLN members organized the

Zapatista Army of Liberation in both the highlands and in the Lacandon.

In late 1991, the Mexican government announced a forthcoming amendment to Article 27 of the Constitution calling for the end of land redistribution and promoting but not requiring the titling and privatization of all communally held land. With over 25 percent of Mexico's unresolved land disputes set in Chiapas, the forthcoming reform was not welcome news. Shortly thereafter, a new peasant organization called the Independent Peasant Alliance "Emiliano Zapata" emerged in the Lacandon region, the highlands, and the northern region of Chiapas. It quickly began to pull people away from long-established regional peasant organizations and attracted interest from some catechists as well. In 1992, the Emiliano Zapata Independent Peasant Alliance (ACIEZ), founded in Puebla in 1991, became ANCIEZ (Independent National Peasant Alliance "Emiliano Zapata"), adding the word "national" to its title. ANCIEZ held several large-scale public demonstrations in 1992 protesting the reforms to Article 27 and the forthcoming North American Free Trade Agreement (NAFTA). In a foreshadowing event protesting the Columbian (1492) quincentary, more than 10,000 indigenous Chiapans marched through San Cristóbal; almost half of them were ANCIEZ members armed with bows and arrows and with signs denouncing NAFTA, 500 years of robbery and murder, and more. They pulled down the statue of the founder of the city, Mazariegos, broke it into pieces, and sold the pieces (see Stephen 2002, 138–140; Benjamin 2000, 12). After October 1992, ANCIEZ went underground and reemerged on January 1, 1994, as the Zapatista Army of National Liberation (EZLN). According to the EZLN, in the intervening two years, communities working with the social organizations of the EZLN voted to go to war and prepared to do so.

On January 1, 1994, Mexico awakened to news of the Zapatista Rebellion—a rebellion that in many ways had already taken place in Chiapas and now drew the attention of the rest of Mexico. Armed and unarmed EZLN troops of Tzeltal, Tzotzil, Tojolabal, Ch'ol, and Mam Indians from the central highlands of Chiapas and the Lacandon jungle had taken over five county seats in Chiapas. The group's name, method, and message invoked the spirit of the Mexican Revolution as it put forward a platform of work, land, housing, food, health, education, independence, liberty, democracy, justice, and peace. Twelve days into an armed confrontation between the very poorly equipped EZLN and the Mexican army, the government came to the negotiating table.

The Zapatistas released an important document in January of 1994 known as "The Revolutionary Law of Women," which called for women's right to participate in revolutionary struggles, to work and receive a just wage, to decide on the number of children they wanted to have, to hold leadership positions and participate in community affairs, to be educated, to choose their romantic partners instead of being forced to marry, and to not be sexually or physically abused. The law also called for severe punishments for rape. The issues highlighted in the "Revolutionary Law of Women" came out of sustained organizing in which women slowly articulated the need for attention to their life experiences. The law was inspirational to indigenous and other women all over Mexico (Stephen 2002, 176–198; Eber and Kovich 2003). As has been well documented, women make up about 30 percent of the armed forces and leadership of the military wing of the EZLN and have also been extremely active in base communities (Speed, Hernández-Castillo, and Stephen, forthcoming).

IMPACTS

The Zapatista movement has had three major impacts in Mexico. First, it has provided a political opening and international support for a national indigenous rights movement in Mexico that is still unfolding. Second, it has been part of a broader process of political maturity and democratization in Mexico that has resulted not only in the defeat of the PRI party in the 2000 presidential elections for the first time in seven decades, but has also solidified a broad range of civil-society movements as a critical part of how "politics" are understood. Third, the Zapatista movement has transformed the daily life of significant numbers of indigenous communities and regions in Chiapas and elsewhere who are living in self-declared autonomy and providing living role models for how local and regional participatory grassroots democracy can work. Here I focus primarily on the impact the Zapatista Rebellion has had for Mexico's indigenous peoples, estimated to be about 23.5 million, or about 22 percent of the population in 2004.

Since 1994, there have been several attempts to reach long-term agreements that would bring peace to Chiapas, but the process has been shattered repeatedly by ongoing military occupation of Chiapas communities by up to 70,000 federal army soldiers, the promotion of private paramilitary groups recruiting unemployed indigenous men to intimidate Zapatista communities and supporters, and the inability of both government negotiators and even the latest Mexican president (Vicente Fox) to deliver on negotiated peace settlements such as the San Andrés Accords on Indigenous Rights and Culture. In August of 1994, the Zapatistas organized the National Democratic Convention in La Realidad, allowing the EZLN to consult with more than 6,000 delegates and observers on issues, including a transition to democracy in the Mexican political system, a constitutional congress,

and new constitution. Many of the discussions initiated there continued and were influential in the organization of national movements, including the National Indigenous Congress (CNI), formed in 1996, and the National Coordinator of Indigenous Women of Mexico (CNMI), formed in 1997. In preparation for a second set of peace accords negotiated in 1995 and 1996, the Zapatistas convened several forums that pulled together representatives from different sectors of civil society to reflect on how to build a new relationship between the state and indigenous peoples, political reform, and indigenous rights and culture.

The San Andrés Accords on Indigenous Rights and Culture were signed by the Zapatista Army of National Liberation and the Mexican federal government in February of 1996, under President Ernesto Zedillo. The accords lay the groundwork for significant changes in the areas of indigenous rights, political participation, and cultural autonomy. Most importantly, they recognize the existence of political subjects called *pueblos indios* (indigenous peoples/towns/communities) and give conceptual validation to the terms "self-determination" and "autonomy" by using them in the signed accords. The accords emphasize that the government takes responsibility for not only reinforcing the political representation of indigenous peoples and their participation in legislatures, but also for guaranteeing the validity of internal forms of indigenous government. They further note that the government promises to create national legislation guaranteeing indigenous communities the right to (1) freely associate themselves with municipalities that are primarily indigenous in population, (2) to form associations between communities, and (3) to coordinate their actions as indigenous peoples.

In addition, the accords state that it is up to the legislatures of individual states to determine what the best criteria are for self-determination and autonomy. These criteria should accurately represent the diverse aspirations and distinctions of indigenous peoples. It is important to note that the accords do not deal with the key issues of land redistribution and agrarian policy, notably the revision of Article 27 of the Mexican Constitution in 1992 that ended land reform and encouraged privatization of communally held land.

Following the formation of the follow-up commission, a proposal for legislation elaborated by the National Commission of Concord and Pacification (COCOPA) and endorsed by the EZLN was rejected by the Mexican president, Ernesto Zedillo, in December of 1996. He stated that the COCOPA legislative proposal for the San Andrés Accords could result in the creation of a system of reservations and the balkanization of the country. In addition, he noted that Mexico's Indians should not be granted "special rights" but should be given the same rights as all Mexicans.

Zapatista military leader Marcos (center) and a security detail walk around the grounds of the meeting site between the Zapatista command and the CONAI, the mediation group involved in peace talks, September 1995. (AP/Wide World Photos)

The government's refusal to implement the accords it signed in 1996 was accompanied by increased paramilitary violence and army pressure in Chiapas. In December 1997, the low-intensity war burst into open flames. On December 22, forty-six Tzotzil indigenous women, children, and men, who were praying for peace in their chapel in the hamlet of Acteal, were massacred by a paramilitary group called Mascara Roja (the Red Mask). The shooting was carried out by approximately sixty men with AK-47s and lasted six hours. After the Acteal massacre, thousands of refugees fled to the mountains, and many eventually came to settle in some of the autonomous Zapatista communities in the region.

In July of 2000, federal elections that swept the PRI from power brought hope. President-elect Vicente Fox Quesada promised to send the approved San Andrés Accords for constitutional reforms to the senate. In Chiapas, gubernatorial elections held in August 2000 were won by Pablo Salazar Mendiguchía, who had become a critic of the PRI government and promised many reforms. In February of 2001, the Zapatistas organized a historic march in conjunction with the National Indigenous Congress (CNI), following the path Emiliano Zapata took to Mexico City during the Mexican Revolution. Thousands of people gathered along the way with the Zapatistas and other indigenous representatives to hear speeches about indigenous rights in seventeen cities.

In April of 2001, the Mexican senate passed legislation on indigenous rights and culture—a watered-down version of the San Andrés Accords signed in 1996 by the EZLN and the Mexican government. The legislation excluded key parts of the original accords, including recognition of indigenous territories, the use and collective enjoyment of natural resources in those territories, and the possibility of the federation of indigenous communities and municipalities. This governmental response was not a surprise to indigenous communities in Chiapas, who began to assert themselves as autonomous regional governments as early as 1995. Pluriethnic Autonomous Regions (RAP) organized by various groups from within civil society, including some affiliated with CIOAC, began to establish local and regional councils and a Chiapas-wide parliament in 1994 and 1995. Zapatista Autonomous Regions (RAZ) were established in the mid 1990s as well. By 2003, there were approximately thirty-one RAZ and seven to eight RAP (Burguete Cal y Mayor 2003, 192). Regional autonomy involves the demarcation of territory, demarcation of jurisdictional authority, the construction and acceptance of a normative framework regulating members of the region, election and establishment of authorities and government organs, the creation of governmental organizations, and infrastructure (Burguete Cal y Mayor 2003, 195). In the case of the RAZ, it also involved rejection of official government authorities, resources, and institutions, and the creation of real alternatives for people. Elsewhere in Mexico other indigenous communities and organizations are experimenting with ways to carry out the spirit of the 1996 San Andrés Accords.

In August of 2003, the Zapatistas announced the creation of five *caracoles* (literally, "shells") that are the seats for five Juntas (councils) of Good Government. Each of the five juntas includes one to two delegates from each of the already-existing Autonomous Councils in each zone. Currently there are thirty to thirty-one Zapatista Autonomous Municipalities in Rebellion that feed into the five juntas. Among other things, the functions of the juntas include monitoring projects and community works in Zapatista Autonomous Municipalities in Rebellion, monitoring the implementation of laws that function within the jurisdiction of the Zapatista Autonomous Municipalities in Rebellion, and care for Zapatista territory in rebellion that it manages. The juntas oversee education and health programs as a part of their work as well. Eleven years after their rebellion became public, the Zapatistas are continuing on their own path: in doing so, they have created a model that is being watched from many parts of the world. Internet and press coverage of the Zapatista Rebellion from its first days in January 1994 have made it a globally documented process that has enjoyed solidarity and support from around the world (Cleaver 1998).

PEOPLE AND ORGANIZATIONS

Ejido

Ejidos (communally owned parcels of land) were created after the Mexican Revolution to satisfy the demands of landless peasants who had seen their communal village lands eaten up by large agricultural estates and/or who had served as laborers on those estates. The formation of *ejidos* since the Mexican Revolution (until 1992) has involved the transference of over 70 million hectares from large estates to slightly more

than 3 million peasant beneficiaries. No new *ejidos* have been formed since 1992, when the Mexican government implemented a reform to Article 27 of the Mexican Constitution that eliminated the government's obligation to redistribute land.

Fox Quesada, Vicente (Born 1942)

President of Mexico from 2000 to 2006, he was the first opposition candidate to be elected (or allowed to be elected) in seven decades. A former Coca-Cola executive and candidate of the PAN, Fox promised wide-ranging reforms in Mexico and a resolution to the conflicts in Chiapas involving the EZLN, but had little success because of a stagnant congress and lack of leadership on key issues.

Institutional Revolutionary Party (Partido Revolucionario Institutional—PRI)

Founded in 1929 as the Revolutionary National Party (PRN) and consolidated under the administration of Lázaro Cárdenas as the Mexican Revolutionary Party (PRM), the PRI took its current name in 1946. Known as a corporatist political party, the precursor to the PRI created its own professional organizations, incorporating most sectors of Mexican society into these groups in 1946. Until the 1980s, the PRI had a lock on almost all political offices in Mexico. In the 1980s a series of political reforms began slowly permitting opposition parties to win elections. In 2000, the party lost the presidential election for the first time in seven decades.

National Action Party (Partido Acción National—PAN)

Founded in 1939, the PAN was established in reaction to the nationalization of industry and land redistribution carried out in the 1930s under President Lázaro Cárdenas. Socially conservative since its founding, the PAN's economic proposals have been consistently similar to those of the PRI. In 2000, the PAN won Mexico's presidential election.

North American Free Trade Agreement (NAFTA)

Implemented in 1994 to liberalize trade and capital flows between the United States and Mexico, NAFTA privatized Mexican national industries (airlines, telephones, mines, railroads, banks) and lowered trade barriers, allowing U.S. companies into all Mexican economic sectors. To allow U.S. products to compete in the Mexican market, Mexico eliminated price supports and subsidies on basic food items. This resulted in a decrease in the value of real wages. NAFTA led to the acceleration of corporate-led economic integration between Mexico and the United States.

Party of the Democratic Revolution (Partido de la Revolucion Democratica — PRD)

Established in 1989, from the earlier Democratic National Front (FDN), which ran Cuauhtémoc Cárdenas as a 1988 presidential candidate against Carlos Salinas de Gortari. After Cárdenas' defeat in what is widely viewed as a fraudulent election, the PRD was established. The PRD has favored a social welfare approach to governance and has opposed many of the neo-liberal reforms implemented by Salinas de Gortari and other recent PRI presidents.

Salinas de Gortari, Carlos (Born 1948)

President of Mexico from 1988 through 1994 as a member of the PRI party, Salinas was widely believed not to have won the 1988 presidential elections, but to have claimed power through electoral fraud. As a Harvard-trained economist he was one of the architects of NAFTA and a believer in neo-liberal economics. He was president when the Zapatista Rebellion erupted in January of 1994.

San Andrés Accords on Indigenous Rights and Culture

Document signed by the EZLN and the Mexican government in 1996 that would have given indigenous peoples far-reaching control over their forms of government, justice, education, and economic development.

Zapata, Emiliano (1879–1919)

Zapata fought during the Mexican Revolution alongside the peasants of Morelos trying to gain control over the land they worked. The original Zapatistas fashioned a land redistribution plan that was partially incorporated into the Mexican Constitution of 1917. Assassinated by government emissaries in 1919, Emiliano Zapata continues to serve as a symbol of peasant militancy.

Zapatista Army of National Liberation (Ejercito Zapatista de Liberacion Nacional — EZLN)

Taking its name from revolutionary hero Emiliano Zapata,

the EZLN was first contemplated as the military wing of the Forces of National Liberation in 1980 when the group published its program. The FLN was organized in Monterrey in 1971 and sent a few members to Chiapas, where they trained as the Emiliano Zapata Guerrilla Nucleus until most were captured or killed in 1974 by federal police and the Mexican army. The survivors regrouped in Mexico City and then returned to Chiapas in 1982. Subcomandante Marcos (non-indigenous spokesperson for the EZLN) and other FLN organizers came to the Lacandon region in 1983. There they worked slowly with local indigenous activists involved with a variety of organizations to build what would publicly emerge as the EZLN in 1994.

Zedillo Ponce de Leon, Ernesto (Born 1951)

President of Mexico from 1994 to 2000, Zedillo presided over the implementation of NAFTA and a major loss in the value of the peso in 1995. He refused to implement the San Andrés Accords on Indigenous Rights and Culture that his own government signed with the EZLN in 1996.

Lynn Stephen

See Also Documentaries of Revolution; Ethnic and Racial Conflict: From Bargaining to Violence; Guerrilla Warfare and Revolution; Inequality, Class, and Revolution; Mexican Revolution; Women and Revolution

References and Further Readings
Benjamin, Thomas, 1996, *A Rich Land, A Poor People: Politics and Society in Modern Chiapas.* Albuquerque: University of New Mexico Press.
———. 2000. "A Time of Reconquest: History, the Maya Revival, and the Zapatista Rebellion in Chiapas," *The American Historical Review* (105) 2: 417–451.
Burguete Cal y Mayor, Araceli. 2003. "The De Facto Autonomous Process: New Jurisdictions and Parallel Governments in Rebellion." Pp. 191–218 in *Mayan Lives, Mayan Utopias: The Indigenous Peoples of Chiapas and the Zapatista Rebellion,* edited by Jan Rus, Rosalva Aída Hernández Castillo, and Shannan Mattiace. Lanham, MD: Rowman and Littlefield Publishers
Cleaver, Harry. 1998. "The Zapatistas and the Electronic Fabric of Struggle." Pp. 81–103 in *Zapatista! Reinventing Revolution in Mexico,* edited by John Holloway and Eloina Peláez. Sterling, VA: Pluto Press.
Collier, George A., with Elizabeth Quaratiello. 1999. *Basta! Land and the Zapatista Rebellion in Chiapas.* Revised edition [original 1994]. Oakland, CA: Food First Books.
Eber, Christine, and Christine Kovich. 2003. *Women of Chiapas: Making History in Times of Struggle and Hope.* New York and London: Routledge.
Estrada-Belli, Fransisco, et al. 2003. "Preclassic Maya Monuments and Temples at Cival, Petén, Guatemala," *Antiquity* 77: 296. http://antiquity.ac.uk/ProjGall/belli/belli.html accessed May 31, 2005.

Gosner, Kevin. 1992. *Soldiers of the Virgin: The Moral Economy of a Colonial Maya Rebellion.* Tucson: University of Arizona Press.

Harvey, Neil. 1998. *The Chiapas Rebellion: The Struggle for Land and Democracy.* Durham, NC: Duke University Press.

Leyva Solano, Xóchitl. 2003. "Regional, Communal, and Organizational Transformations in Las Cañadas." Pp. 161–184 in *Mayan Lives, Mayan Utopias: The Indigenous Peoples of Chiapas and the Zapatista Rebellion,* edited by Jan Rus, Rosalva Aída Hernández Castillo, and Shannan Mattiace. Lanham, MD: Rowman and Littlefield Publishers.

Mattiace, Shannan. 2003a. *To See with Two Eyes: Peasant Activism and Indian Autonomy in Chiapas, Mexico.* Albuquerque: University of New Mexico Press.

———. 2003b. "Regional Renegotiation of Space: Tojolabal Ethnic Identity in Las Margaritas, Chiapas." Pp. 109–134 in *Mayan Lives, Mayan Utopias: The Indigenous Peoples of Chiapas and the Zapatista Rebellion,* edited by Jan Rus, Rosalva Aída Hernández Castillo, and Shannan Mattiace. Lanham, MD: Rowman and Littlefield Publishers.

Nash, June. 2001. *Mayan Visions: The Quest for Autonomy in an Age of Globalization.* New York: Routledge.

Rus, Jan. 1983. "Whose Caste War? Indians, Ladinos, and the 'Caste War' of 1869." Pp. 127–168 in *Spaniards and Indians in Southeastern Mesoamerica: Essays on the History of Ethnic Relations,* edited by Murdo J. Macleod and Robert Wasserstrom. Lincoln: University of Nebraska Press.

———. 1994 "The 'Comunidad Revolucionario Institutional': The Subversion of Native Government in Highland Chiapas, 1946–1968." Pp. 265–300 in *Everyday Forms of State Formation: Revolution and the Negotiation of Rule in Modern Mexico,* edited by Gilbert M. Joseph and Daniel Nugent. Durham, NC: Duke University Press.

Rus, Jan, and George Collier. 2003. "A Generation of Crisis in the Central Highlands of Chiapas: The Cases of Chamula and Zinacantán, 1974–2000." Pp. 33–62 in *Mayan Lives, Mayan Utopias: The Indigenous Peoples of Chiapas and the Zapatista Rebellion,* edited by Jan Rus, Rosalva Aída Hernández Castillo, and Shannan Mattiace. Lanham, MD: Rowman and Littlefield Publishers.

Speed, Shannon, Aída Hernández Castillo, and Lynn Stephen. Forthcoming. *Dissident Women: Gender and Cultural Politics in Chiapas.* Austin: University of Texas Press.

Stephen, Lynn. 2002. *Zapata Lives! Histories and Cultural Politics in Southern Mexico.* Berkeley: University of California Press.

Womack, John. 1999. *Rebellion in Chiapas: An Historical Reader.* New York: New Press.

Zimbabwean Revolution

CHRONOLOGY

1835–1836	Ndebele migrate north from south Africa, establish hegemony over southwestern Zimbabwe.
1888	Lobengula signs Rudd Concession.
1889	Lobengula renounces Rudd Concession. Cecil Rhodes acquires a British royal charter and forms the British South Africa Company (BSAC).
1890	BSAC's Pioneer Column enters Zimbabwe.
1892	Pass law requiring African men to carry identification documents enacted for Salisbury.
1893	War begins as Ndebele chiefs attempt to repulse BSAC control of Matabeleland. Lobengula attempts to negotiate peace but is ignored. After BSAC military successes, Lobengula abandons Bulawayo and is later reported dead. BSAC declares victory and the end of the Ndebele kingdom.
1894	BSAC commission demarcates reserves in Matabeleland, creating small areas deemed adequate for Ndebele subsistence; remaining areas are made available for sale to Europeans. By 1913 nearly one hundred various-sized reserves for indigenous Africans exist countrywide, establishing the land policy for the BSAC administration and later white settler governments.
1895	BSAC territories named "Rhodesia." The southern region renamed "Southern Rhodesia" in 1897, distinguishing it from "Northern Rhodesia."
1896–1897	Revolts against BSAC begin in Matabeleland, followed in Mashonaland. Rhodes meets Ndebele rebel chiefs and negotiates a peace. All Ndebele leaders eventually accept. The revolt in Mashonaland, resulting from land alienations in central Mashonaland, is supported by one-third of the population. Shona rebels prove more formidable than expected and are only suppressed after several campaigns against Shona strongholds that include dynamiting rebels hiding in caves. By October 1897 most rebels have surrendered.
1922	Europeans vote for self-governing status.
1923	BSAC rule ends and Southern Rhodesia becomes a European-settler-governed colony.

1930	Land Apportionment Act officially implements racial segregation of land use and ownership throughout Southern Rhodesia.
1934	African National Congress (ANC) [of Zimbabwe] is founded.
1951	Native Land Husbandry Act gives authority to assign African lands to government officials and calls for the mandatory destocking of African-owned cattle herds.
1953	Federation of Rhodesia and Nyasaland is launched by the British after approval in a Europeans-only referendum. Nyasaland (Malawi), Northern and Southern Rhodesia are amalgamated under a federal system. Southern Rhodesian Europeans support it for economic reasons, believing they can control the resources and labor supplies of the other members. African protests in the northern territories, coupled with the emerging support for majority rule in all of British Africa, eventually lead to Southern Rhodesian whites becoming disillusioned with the Federation. The Federation is dissolved on December 31, 1963.
1955–1957	The Youth League is founded in August 1955. A year later it leads a successful bus boycott against segregated public transportation in Salisbury. In 1957 it merges with the ANC, taking that organization's name but creating a more activist movement.
1959	The ANC leads demonstrations against European hegemony and is banned after the government declares a state of emergency.
1960	The National Democratic Party (NDP) is formed in January. In July, NDP leaders are arrested in a massive crackdown on African political protests. The government enacts the Law and Order (Maintenance) Act.
1961	The NDP is banned, and the Zimbabwe African National Union (ZAPU) is formed.
1962	The Rhodesian Front (RF) is formed in March. ZAPU is banned in September, and the RF wins December general elections and begins to govern the country.
1963	At a Dar es Salaam, Tanzania, meeting ZAPU leaders argue over tactics in confronting the RF policy of whites-only rule. Several leaders break away and form the Zimbabwe African National Union (ZANU).
1964	Ian Smith is named RF leader and becomes prime minister, pledging to gain independence under white rule. He immediately orders the arrest of ZAPU and ZANU leaders. ZANU is banned in mid year, and in November the white electorate approves a referendum calling for independence. ZANU creates a military wing of the party, the Zimbabwe African National Liberation Army (ZANLA).
1965	Following a visit by British prime minister Harold Wilson, Smith rejects calls for African participation in governing the country. On November 11, the government declares its Unilateral Declaration of Independence (UDI). The British impose economic sanctions in an effort to force Smith to reverse UDI, but Smith holds fast and sanctions remain in place for the next fifteen years. ZAPU forms a military command, the Zimbabwe People's Revolutionary Army (ZIPRA).
1966	In April, seven ZANLA combatants engage government security forces in the battle of Chinhoyi, the first military action by Africans against government forces since 1897.
1969	Land Tenure Act equalizes lands assigned to Africans and Europeans. However, the majority of African areas are marginally productive. Implementation results in overcrowding of African areas and heightens Africans' resentments against the government.
1972	ZANLA fighters attack Altena Farm a year after their commanders adopt guerrilla tactics. The thirty-minute attack marks a new phase of the revolution.
1975	Mozambique gains independence.
1976	ZAPU and ZANU form the Patriotic Front (PF). ZANLA and ZIPRA commands remain separate.

1977   Government amends the Land Tenure Act to increase support among rural Africans. The Organization of African States (OAU), along with many international groups and foreign governments, recognizes the PF as the legitimate representative of the Zimbabwean people.

1978   Smith signs an Internal Settlement with three African leaders. ZAPU and ZANU, as well as the vast majority of the international community, reject the settlement as not legitimate and call for talks between Smith and the PF.

1979   Following Internal Settlement guidelines, the country's first all-race elections are held. Abel Muzorewa wins the African vote and forms a government for "Zimbabwe Rhodesia." The OAU, Britain, the United States, and others refuse to recognize "Zimbabwe Rhodesia" and call for negotiations between the government and the PF. The Lancaster House Conference is convened, and the PF, Muzorewa, and Smith agree to a constitution and peace accord.

1980   In February 27–29 general elections, 94 percent of the African electorate participates. ZANU wins 63 percent of the vote, and Mugabe is asked to form a government for an independent Zimbabwe. On April 18, the Republic of Zimbabwe is declared.

1982   ZAPU rejects overtures to join ZANU. Nkomo is accused of planning a coup against Mugabe, and troops are sent into Matabeleland to suppress armed dissidents. Ndebele civilians report brutal treatment at the hands of government troops.

1987   Mugabe and Nkomo agree to merge ZAPU into ZANU. The Lancaster House Constitution is amended, replacing the office of prime minister with an executive president. In December, parliament elects Mugabe president.

1992   Land Acquisition Act is approved, giving the government authority to nationalize European-owned lands at prices set by government.

2000   African war veterans occupy European-owned farms.

2005   Zimbabwe government launches the controversial Operation Murambatsvina ("Clean Out the Garbage"), with the publicly proclaimed goal of clearing urban areas of criminal activities and illegal businesses and structures. The campaign reportedly uproots several hundred thousand people from their homes.

INTRODUCTION

Chimurenga, a Shona word meaning "resistance," is the term most commonly used to refer to the Zimbabwean Revolution of 1965 to 1980. However, it is also used to refer to the years 1896 and 1897, when the Shona and their Ndebele neighbors fought against land alienations throughout, and the imposition of colonial rule over, the area that is present-day Zimbabwe. The *Chimurenga* that ended with the independence of the country in 1980 can be seen as the culmination of ninety years of struggles by the African peoples of Zimbabwe to regain land and re-establish political authority. It can also be seen, at least initially, as a forward-looking process aimed at ending minority rule and replacing it with a multiracial, modern state with democratic institutions, laws applied to all Zimbabweans equally, and a land policy freed from principles of racial segregation. Unfortunately, *Chimurenga* has also come to mean a period of high ideals that, at the beginning of the twenty-first century, has been replaced by a period of fear, economic want, and an increasingly undemocratic government.

BACKGROUND: CULTURE AND HISTORY

Zimbabwe is in the southern tropics between 15°S and 23°S latitude, although much of the country has a temperate climate due to its relatively high altitude and inland location. Agriculturally, cattle ranching utilizes the southern and western areas of the country, while the eastern and northern regions have been involved in intensive maize, tobacco, cotton, tea, and other commercial crop cultivation. The country also has mineral deposits of gold, iron, copper, coal, chrome, asbestos, lithium, and mica.

The Iron Age came to the area around 200 B.C., brought by ancestors of modern Shona peoples. By 900 to 1000, the Shona had occupied most of the northeastern half of the territory and had begun to develop a hierarchical kingdom in south-central Zimbabwe. At the center of this kingdom (its name is unknown), the Shona built in stone at a site that is today known as Great Zimbabwe. The Shona word *zimbabwe* means a "venerated house" or "chiefly residence," and it has been applied by archaeologists to several sites in the southern and eastern regions of the country. Great Zimbabwe is merely the largest of those sites, in regard to acreage and building sizes; it is also the site from which the modern nation takes its name. That ancient kingdom was at its height in the early fifteenth century. By the end of that century, however, it had been replaced by two smaller states, Changamire and Togwa, with the latter apparently subsumed by Changamire in the late sixteenth century. From that time until the early nineteenth century, Changamire rulers claimed hegemony over much of the southern half of the area that became Zimbabwe. The foundation of the traditional Shona economy was a mixture of millet, maize, and sorghum cultivation and cattle herding. Cattle served as a form of wealth and a safeguard against drought and low crop yields. Rulers of the ancient kingdoms also traded gold and ivory to the East African coast for cloth and luxury items.

In the 1830s, elements of the Ndebele migrated north from south Africa and took control over the southwestern third of the territory. Mzilikazi had earlier created the Ndebele kingdom in ca. 1821 in the area being consolidated into the Zulu kingdom by the great south African ruler Shaka. Throughout the 1820s Mzilikazi led his people in a highly transient existence, often fleeing Zulu attacks. By the mid 1830s the Ndebele were relatively free from Zulu attacks but were being increasingly pressured by the presence of white settlers from the south. In 1836 or 1837, Mzilikazi decided for security reasons to move his kingdom north of the Limpopo River (the modern border between South Africa and Zimbabwe). Mzilikazi died thirty years later, after establishing control over the territory and its Shona inhabitants. His son, Lobengula, succeeded him as king in 1870. The Ndebele of the nineteenth century grew all the Shona crops as well as yams, pumpkins, beans, and other crops. The Ndebele also owned very large herds of cattle, but these were more emblematic of social standing than economic wealth.

The first Europeans to enter the territory were the Portuguese in the sixteenth century looking for the source of gold traded to the east coast of Africa. They were driven out of the region in the late seventeenth century by Changamire armies. The first group of Europeans to ultimately establish permanent contact was Christian missionaries, starting in 1859 with the founding of a London Missionary Society station in Inyati, in the southwest. By the 1860s missionaries were joined by Europeans hoping to exploit the supposed mineral wealth of the country. The most famous of these was Charles Rudd, who negotiated a concession with Lobengula in 1888. Lobengula believed that Rudd was assigned limited rights to look for minerals in a restricted area of his kingdom. What he didn't know at the time was that Rudd worked for Cecil Rhodes, a diamond baron and financier in south Africa. Rhodes wanted a concession with Lobengula that he could take to England and use to secure a royal charter granting Rhodes's company, the British South African Company (BSAC), the exclusive right to administer and economically exploit territories north of the Limpopo River. In 1889 Rhodes secured the charter, and in 1890 the BSAC's Pioneer Column entered Zimbabwe, marking the beginning of the colonial period of the country.

In the first decade of its administration, the BSAC fought two wars against the African inhabitants. In 1893, in the Ndebele War, the company provoked a conflict with Lobengula, one that eventually led to Lobengula's death, the confiscation of the majority of Ndebele cattle, the alienation (expropriation) of large tracts of Ndebele lands, and the assigning of the Ndebele to reserves. In March 1896, several Ndebele chiefs rose in rebellion against BSAC land encroachments, cattle seizures, and the company's refusal to allow Lobengula's successor to become king. In June, about one-third of the Shona population also revolted against BSAC rule. It is clear that several important Shona religious leaders who argued against Europeans' material culture and land alienations encouraged the rebels. The Ndebele revolt ended in August 1896, when Rhodes negotiated a peace with rebellious chiefs. The Shona revolt, however, continued until late the next year, when rebels were finally defeated through the use of extreme military actions, including dynamiting rebels' strongholds.

Once the country was under its undisputed control, the BSAC began exploiting its economic resources. Initially, it had been thought that gold mining would bring riches to the company. By 1908, however, the company announced that that was not the case and turned to the one commodity the company had in abundance, the land it had taken from the Shona and Ndebele. The company created a "white agricultural policy" through which it would sell land, to be used as farms and ranches, to European settlers. The BSAC government, called the Administration, instituted wide-ranging policies to support European settlers, giving them advantages over local African farmers and effectively cutting large numbers of Africans out of the commercial economy. For instance, a Land Bank provided low-interest loans for Europeans only to purchase and develop farms; government-run crop experiment stations were established to determine which crops grew best in European farming districts; and the government established a labor bureau to direct African labor to European farmers. The Administration also enacted pass laws, beginning in 1892, to control the movement of

African men, both indigenous and foreign. These laws had several goals: to keep unemployed Africans out of predominantly European towns, to regulate African labor, and to assist in the collection of taxes that had been levied on Africans as another means of forcing them to work for Europeans.

In 1923 the administration of the country was turned over to a settler government that continued to support white settlement schemes and assistance to European settlers. In 1930 the government enacted the Land Apportionment Act, which officially introduced the principle of racial segregation in land policy. Large areas of the country's most agriculturally productive lands were demarcated for European ownership only. Less arable lands were assigned to the much larger African populations. Within a decade the act had resulted in the overcrowding of African lands, with large numbers of African men being forced into wage employment to support their families. By the late 1940s, overcrowding was so bad that the government created the Native Land Husbandry Act to force African farmers to establish conservation schemes and sell off their cattle. Most importantly, the government wanted to turn the communally owned lands into privately owned plots, thereby creating a landowning peasantry. Africans responded to the Land Husbandry Act by ignoring it, flouting it as the latest attempt to control their lives. Ultimately more important for the Zimbabwe Revolution, for the first time chiefs and Western-educated Africans united in opposition to a government act.

CONTEXT AND PROCESS OF REVOLUTION

It was in the period of opposition to the Land Husbandry Act that the roots of the revolution of the 1960s and 1970s developed. Starting with that opposition, the African peoples of colonial Zimbabwe increasingly called for participation in the institutions of government that created the laws that governed their lives.

The country's first African political party was the Bantu Congress, formed in 1934. Although it quickly changed its name to the African National Congress (ANC), apparently inspired by the ANC organization in South Africa, it did not become a national movement. During the period before the Land Husbandry Act, it had a very small membership and focused on obtaining an exemption from discriminatory laws for educated Africans. By the early 1950s it only had one active branch in Bulawayo, the country's second-largest city. In 1955, the first of several truly African nationalist organizations was founded in Harare. The Youth League led a boycott against the local segregated public transport system in 1956. A year later it joined a reformed ANC and immediately began

to directly confront the government over issues of Africans' political and civil rights. In 1959, the government responded by banning the ANC and declaring a state of emergency, stating that the ANC program was a threat to public safety.

Over the next five years African nationalists created a series of successive political parties calling for African political rights, but in nearly every case they met increased government suppression. The National Democratic Party (NDP) was created in 1960 and was met by the arrest of its leaders and the enactment of the Law and Order (Maintenance) Act, which declared meetings of three or more people illegal. The party was then banned. In 1961 the Zimbabwe African People's Union (ZAPU) was formed, with Joshua Nkomo as president. Nkomo called for the creation of a government in exile, among other activities. Some ZAPU members who, in 1963, broke away and formed the Zimbabwe African National Union (ZANU), which favored a program of direct political action inside the country, denounced this strategy. ZANU's more aggressive stance was met with the imprisonment of its leaders and its banning in 1964. But this time, ZANU had anticipated the banning by sending one of its leaders, Herbert Chitepo, to Zambia to organize an armed wing of the party, the Zimbabwe African National Liberation Army (ZANLA). African nationalists had finally concluded that if all their aspirations were to be met by increased repression, then the only means of obtaining political and civil rights for Africans was through the use of force.

The beginning of the armed revolution against white rule is marked by the April 28, 1966, battle of Chinhoyi, northwest of Harare, where, in a three-hour battle, all seven ZANLA combatants were killed by government security forces (GSF). Several additional battles between ZANLA and GSF occurred over the next two years, each time resulting in the death of nearly all ZANLA combatants. In the late 1960s ZANLA commanders decided to shift tactics from direct assaults on GSF to guerrilla warfare. Adopting practices from liberation forces in Mozambique, and gaining financial support from China, by 1970 ZANLA had begun infiltrating political officers into the rural areas in the northeastern districts of the country. The function of these officers was to educate local African populations about the goals of the revolution. In *pungwes* (meetings often lasting all night) ZANLA political officers focused primarily on the land issue, promising that their victory would mean return of lands taken during the colonial period. They also discussed government taxes, the lack of health care and educational opportunities for Africans, and cattle dipping regulations. Liberation songs were sung and there were many instances when combatants punished or killed locals accused of being government collaborators. Combatants also often required donations of food and always stressed that they expected local inhabitants to inform them about GSF activities.

Members of the black nationalist guerrillas of the Zimbabwe African National Liberation Army (ZANLA), led by Robert Mugabe, stage a rally February 6, 1980, somewhere in Zimbabwe. (AFP/Getty Images)

By 1972, ZANLA believed the necessary groundwork had been laid and that it was time to introduce a new phase of the revolution—guerrilla attacks on European-owned farms and other isolated European sites in the rural areas. In accord with that decision, Altena Farm, 240 kilometers northeast of Harare, was attacked on December 21, 1972. Over the next seven years ZANLA insinuated more and more combatants into the country, primarily in the eastern provinces bordering Mozambique. With the independence of Mozambique from Portugal in 1975, ZANLA was able to move its forward bases from Zambia and increase its level of activity. Although rotation of ZANLA forces in and out of the country made it hard to know exactly, it is generally believed that by 1976 there were about 3,000 armed ZANLA men and women operating inside the country at any given time, with that number reaching 10,000 by 1979.

Upon gaining financial backing from the Soviet Union, ZAPU formed its armed force, the Zimbabwe People's Liberation Army (ZIPRA) in the mid 1960s. However, due to ZAPU's continued commitment to negotiations, ZIPRA did not become an operational fighting force until the mid 1970s.

Even then, ZIPRA operated as a conventional military force rather than as a guerrilla command. As a result, although they operated throughout the western part of the country, ZIPRA combatants did not enjoy the close local support that marked ZANLA operations. Still, it was ZIPRA that conducted two of the most notorious actions of the armed revolution, the shooting down of two civilian passenger airplanes in the late 1970s.

In 1976, ZAPU and ZANU announced the formation of a Patriotic Front, a political alliance that was established to present a united front on the international stage, thereby increasing international diplomatic support for their recognition. By 1978 they had received widespread international recognition. And, since Europeans were only about 4 percent of the population, the Patriotic Front had also forced the government to call on virtually every European male under sixty years of age to perform some form of military duty in response to the increased military actions by ZANLA and, to a lesser extent, by ZIPRA. In addition, an increasing proportion of the national budget was going to security. Into this milieu were added greater international pressures—from the

United States, the United Nations, and even South Africa, which, in part, feared that a PF victory in the field might inspire armed uprisings inside South Africa—to end the war. The white government's last attempt to do this without having to negotiate with ZAPU and ZANU occurred in early 1979, when Prime Minister Ian Smith agreed to an Internal Settlement with conservative African leaders Abel Muzorewa, Ndabaningi Sithole, and Jeremiah Chirau. In April general elections, the first in which Africans could vote, Muzorewa was elected prime minister of "Zimbabwe Rhodesia." Although many government ministerial posts were assigned to Africans, and Muzorewa claimed popular support, his government never gained international recognition.

Meanwhile, in August 1979 the recently elected British prime minister, Margaret Thatcher, agreed to a Commonwealth proposal calling for talks between representatives of the British government, ZAPU, ZANU, and Zimbabwe Rhodesia. She then announced a conference to be held at Lancaster House in London. All parties were invited, and despite reservations by many and political posturing by all, the conference was convened on September 10, with Nkomo and Mugabe representing the Patriotic Front, Muzorewa and Smith leading the government contingent (Smith really representing the country's Europeans), and the British foreign minister chairing the talks. By December, after extremely tense negotiations at times, the participants agreed on an end to the war. They negotiated a draft constitution granting majority rule but protecting certain rights of the white minority for ten years, including the right to maintain ownership of their lands and twenty guaranteed seats, out of a total of 100, in the new parliament; rules and procedures for a transition period, including disarming ZANLA and ZIPRA forces inside the country; and a peace accord officially ending the armed phase of the revolution. That accord took effect on December 28.

In January 1980, Nkomo and Mugabe returned to the country as heroes. Mugabe surprised Nkomo and international observers by announcing that ZANU would contest the upcoming elections as an independent entity, separate from the Patriotic Front. In February elections, ZANU won 63 percent of the African vote and Mugabe was asked by the interim British governor to form a government. At 12:01 a.m., April 18, at ceremonies in Harare, the Republic of Zimbabwe was born.

IMPACTS

Independence meant changes for all Zimbabweans. For Africans the impacts were substantial. Economically, opportunities that did not exist under white rule were opened. Support in the form of fertilizers, seeds, etc., and development loans became available to African farmers for the first time. They responded with increased crop production. For instance, in 1980 they produced a small percentage of the national maize and cotton crops; by 1987, they produced 50 percent of each. In the cities, the wages of industrial workers increased greatly. The government also increased support of African social programs. In education, by 1984 1,700 new primary and 900 secondary schools had been built, and 47,000 new teachers had been trained. Medical services also improved dramatically. The government instituted an innovative rural family planning program and began to provide free health care to the poorest rural people, with low fees for the rest. The government also built over 1,000 rural health clinics during the early 1980s (Chikuhwa 1998, 183,188).

As for Europeans, Mugabe surprised most by proposing reconciliation with those who chose to stay (about one-half of the pre-revolution white population left during the war or immediately after independence). European tobacco farmers in particular were encouraged to resume production and quickly regained their pre-revolution position as the country's top foreign exchange earners. Mugabe said that the country needed their financial skills and resources, and if they accepted that they no longer had political authority, they were welcome and necessary for Zimbabwe's future.

However, there were also indications of harder times ahead. For instance, the government extended the state of emergency declared during the revolution and refused to repeal the Law and Order (Maintenance) Act. By 1982 opposition-elected officials began to claim that the government was suppressing their efforts to campaign for policies opposed by the government. For example, after criticizing government policies in 1982, Nkomo and other ZAPU officials were dismissed from government posts and accused of planning a coup. The government claimed that former ZIPRA combatants were rearming. Citing Law and Order (Maintenance) Act regulations, the government sent military forces into Matabeleland in campaigns against so-called "dissidents." Reports of brutality and government atrocities against rural Ndebele began to emerge, but the government denied these and used its control of the media to try to suppress knowledge about its forces' actions.

By the beginning of the twenty-first century, many of the initial positive impacts of the 1965–1980 *Chimurenga* had been seriously eroded. In 2000, the government supported "land invasions" of European-owned farms by ZANU supporters, some of whom had been ZANLA fighters. Mugabe argued that these actions were a continuation of the revolution and were merely returning the land to its historically rightful owners. Both internally and internationally, however, the government was accused of using the constitutionally illegal land seizures as a means to undermine the country's hard-won democratic institutions and keeping the increasingly unpopular government in power. In addition, the land seizures virtually destroyed the agricultural export market and the economy rapidly deteriorated.

PEOPLE AND ORGANIZATIONS

African National Congress (ANC)

Founded in 1934 as the Bantu Congress, the ANC was the nation's first modern African political movement. It had a small membership through the 1950s, when it focused on attaining civil liberties for educated Africans. As a result of that limited goal, the ANC did not develop into a popularly supported movement before 1957. In that year it was energized when the Youth League took command of the organization. Using peaceful, constitutional means, the new leaders led mass protests against discriminatory laws. By 1959 the ANC claimed 30,000 members, alarming government officials. In an attempt to end African protests, the government in February 1959 banned the ANC.

British South Africa Company (BSAC)

The British South Africa Company, a private commercial organization, colonized Zimbabwe in 1890 and administered it until 1923. Citing the Rudd Concession, Cecil Rhodes obtained a royal charter from the British government in 1889 and formed the BSAC. The company was given authority over the regions of present-day Zimbabwe and Zambia, which were administratively separated in 1898. Company employees governed the country, alienated African lands, initiated discriminatory laws, and promoted European settlement. Settlers gained some political rights in 1898 when they formed a Legislative Council, although the company continued policies favorable to its own business concerns. In 1922 it surrendered administrative control of Zambia to the British government and in the following year relinquished control of Zimbabwe to a settler government.

Land Apportionment Act

Passed in 1930, the Land Apportionment Act officially introduced the principle of racial segregation into land policy. The act designated 50.8 percent of the country for European use only. These lands were the most productive farming and ranching areas. Reserves made up 22.4 percent of the land; Africans would live here in traditional communal societies. In addition, 7.7 percent of the country was assigned as African Purchase Areas, where Africans could own or lease private plots of land. The remaining lands were "unassigned lands" (Rubert and Rasmussen 2001, 146–147).

Land Tenure Act

Enacted in 1969, the act superseded the Land Apportionment Act. Although the act equalized European and African land holdings, each group being assigned 46.6%, the vast majority of the most productive areas were all within European-designated areas. The government's intention was to increase the segregation of European and African areas. (Rubert and Rasmussen 2001, 147–148).

Mugabe, Robert (Born 1924)

Robert Mugabe, first prime minister of an independent Zimbabwe, became executive president in 1987.

From 1941 to 1954 Mugabe taught in mission schools, with a one-year hiatus in 1951 to earn a B.A. in South Africa. He then taught outside the country, in present-day Zambia and Ghana. In 1960 he returned to the country and entered politics as the NDP's publicity secretary. When that party was banned, he acted as deputy to Joshua Nkomo in ZAPU. In 1963 he joined other disaffected ZAPU members to found ZANU. As secretary general of ZANU he was arrested several times before the party was banned in 1964 and he began a period of ten years in prison. In early 1974, Mugabe became party leader, although that was not well known at the time. Released from prison in late 1974, Mugabe went to Mozambique, where he played a crucial, though contested, role in reorganizing ZANU and ZANLA. As a result of growing support by ZANLA commanders, Mugabe was recognized as the uncontested leader of ZANU in late 1975. He joined with Nkomo to form the Patriotic Front in October 1976, and then traveled constantly, becoming one of the revolution's most recognized spokesmen. Following the Lancaster House Conference, he returned to Zimbabwe on January 27, 1980, and led ZANU to victory in February elections. During that campaign Mugabe called for reconciliation with the country's Europeans. On March 4, Mugabe was asked to form a government for an independent Republic of Zimbabwe. Once in office, he surprised many by continuing calls for reconciliation with the country's European farmers. He also began talks with Nkomo that aimed at unifying ZANU and ZAPU. Those talks eventually resulted in the Unity Pact of 1987. As of 2005, he remained the country's president, although he had ceased his calls for reconciliation with Europeans, his relations with former ZAPU supporters had deteriorated completely, and he was seen by many to be an authoritarian ruler.

Muzorewa, Abel (Born 1925)

Abel Muzorewa was ordained by the United Methodist Church in 1953 and named bishop in 1968. He gained notice in 1971, when he was arrested for entering reserves in defiance of government orders. In late 1971, supported by ZAPU and ZANU, he led African opposition to British and RF negotiations that excluded African political leaders. Because the use of violence was anathema to him, government officials initiated talks with him about constitutional reforms in the early 1970s. By 1978 he was disenchanted with PF policies and again entered into negotiations with the RF, this time with two other conservative African leaders. Those talks resulted in the Internal Settlement, which called for renaming the country "Zimbabwe Rhodesia" and for the first all-race elections. In April 1979, Muzorewa was elected the country's first African prime minister. He also served as defense minister and pursued the war against ZANLA and ZIPRA. Facing international calls to end the war, and escalating attacks by ZANLA and ZIPRA, Muzorewa agreed to attend the Lancaster House Conference. His reign as prime minister ended on December 12, 1979.

National Democratic Party (NDP)

Founded January 1, 1960, the National Democratic Party succeeded the ANC as the country's principal African political party. In response to massive demonstrations for political rights mounted by the NDP, the government enacted the Law and Order (Maintenance) Act. The NDP was banned on December 9, 1961. Although having many of the same members, the NDP differed from the ANC by directly confronting the constitutional basis for European rule and by demanding majority rule.

Ndebele

The second-largest African ethnic group in the country, about one-seventh of Zimbabwe's population, the Ndebele originated in southeastern south Africa in the early nineteenth century. Formed into a kingdom at that time, they eventually migrated to the southwestern region of Zimbabwe in the 1830s, where they established hegemony over local Shona-speaking peoples.

Nkomo, Joshua (1917–1999)

Joshua Nkomo was Zimbabwe's first African social worker. He entered politics in 1952 and became president of the Bulawayo chapter of the ANC in 1953. When the ANC was banned, he helped form the NDP. After it was banned, Nkomo founded ZAPU. He traveled extensively, calling the world's attention to the country's segregationist policies. His calls for creating a government in exile alienated many ZAPU members, eventually leading to several of them breaking away and establishing ZANU in 1963. He was arrested in 1964 and spent most of the next decade in prison. From 1974 to 1976, Nkomo was viewed as a moderate and participated in a series of talks with Ian Smith. In late 1976, however, he surprised many by announcing he was entering the PF. He stayed outside the country and used his considerable authority and international reputation to expand ZIPRA. After the Lancaster House Conference, he led ZAPU in the February 1980 elections. ZAPU placed second, ending Nkomo's dream to lead his country. Mugabe appointed him to a cabinet post but later dismissed him, claiming that Nkomo was plotting to overthrow the government. In December 1987, after several years of bitter political skirmishes, Nkomo agreed to merge ZAPU with ZANU. Mugabe named him second vice president in 1988, a largely ceremonial office he held until his death.

Patriotic Front (PF)

Formed in October 1976 as a political alliance between ZAPU and ZANU.

Reserves

Known as "Tribal Trust Lands" from 1970 to 1980, and as "Communal Lands" after independence, reserves were lands set aside for Africans. Initiated following the Ndebele War, this form of land segregation was applied to the entire country by 1930. In that year, the Land Apportionment Act officially instituted the racial segregation of land use and ownership. In general, reserves were inferior agricultural and rangelands, and were overpopulated by the 1940s.

Rhodes, Cecil (1853–1902)

Cecil Rhodes was a British-born south African financier and politician, and the force behind the BSAC. After forming that company in 1888, Rhodes used it to push British authority into south-central Africa.

Rhodesian Front (RF)

Formed in March 1962, the Rhodesian Front campaigned for the country's independence under European rule. The

RF won the whites-only general election that year and began to govern. Ian Smith became the party's leader, and prime minister in April 1964. The RF was extremely popular among the European community, especially after Smith declared the Unilateral Declaration of Independence (UDI) in late 1965. It retained control of the government until 1979.

Shona

Original black African inhabitants of Zimbabwe, four-fifths of the country's population.

Smith, Ian (Born 1919)

Ian Smith, the country's eighth prime minister, helped found the Rhodesian Front in 1962, becoming its leader and prime minister in 1964. He was uncompromising on the issue of continuing European rule, and for the first twelve years in office refused to concede even the possibility that Africans would ever rule the country. In 1976, clearly responding to ZANLA and ZIPRA attacks and growing international pressure, Smith announced he was willing to discuss African political participation in governing the country. Still, he attempted to control that possibility by negotiating only with conservative African leaders inside the country. Finally recognizing the failure of that tactic, Smith represented the country's Europeans at the Lancaster House Conference. After independence he continued to be a member of parliament and a vocal critic of the Mugabe government. Smith retired from active politics in 1987. He continued to live in Zimbabwe and to occasionally condemn government policies.

Youth League

Founded in Harare in 1955, the Youth League was the first African political organization to challenge the government's claim to exclusively govern the country, as well as the first to operate as a mass movement in both rural and urban areas.

Zimbabwe African National Liberation Army (ZANLA)

Armed wing of ZANU organized in 1964. Manned primarily by Shona men and women, ZANLA operated primarily in the eastern half of the country.

Zimbabwe African National Union (ZANU)

Founded in August 1963 by disgruntled members of ZAPU. Their primary concern was the extended absence of ZAPU's president, Joshua Nkomo, from the country. A more fundamental issue was a disagreement on tactics for confronting the government's intransigence on granting Africans political and civil rights. Nkomo called for the creation of a government in exile, while the founders of ZANU supported a policy of political action inside the country. In 1976 ZANU joined ZAPU in a political alliance to pressure the government to negotiate an end to the revolution. In early 1980, ZANU's president, Mugabe, announced that the party would participate in the coming elections separately from ZAPU, and ZANU won 63 percent of the votes. Under Mugabe, ZANU has controlled the government since those elections. Although a nationwide organization, its principal support is in the Shona-speaking regions of the country.

Zimbabwe African People's Union (ZAPU)

Established in December 1961, it succeeded the banned NDP, taking on virtually all of that organization's membership and programs. During the early 1970s, Joshua Nkomo, claiming to represent ZAPU, held a number of meetings with Ian Smith and moderate African leaders inside the country in attempts to negotiate a peaceful transition to African rule. Then in 1976 Nkomo announced that ZAPU was joining ZANU in the Patriotic Front. In February 1980 elections, ZAPU candidates won 24 percent of the votes and became the primary opposition party. After several years of bitter political fights with the ZANU-dominated government, in late 1987 Nkomo announced that ZAPU would be amalgamated into ZANU as part of a unity agreement between the two groups. Although it claimed national stature, ZAPU's support was generally restricted to the Ndebele-speaking region of Zimbabwe.

Zimbabwe People's Revolutionary Army (ZIPRA)

Armed wing of ZAPU organized in 1965. It recruited and operated almost exclusively in Matabeleland.

Steven C. Rubert

See Also Cinema of Revolution; Colonialism, Anti-Colonialism, and Neo-Colonialism; Documentaries of Revolution; Elites, Intellectuals, and Revolutionary Leadership; Ethnic and Racial Conflict: From Bargaining to Violence; Guerrilla Warfare and Revolution; Mozambique Revolution; South African Revolution; Student and Youth Movements, Activism and Revolution

References and Further Readings

Alexander, Jocelyn, Joanne McGregor, and T. O. Ranger. 2000. *Violence and Memory: One Hundred Years in the "Dark Forests" of Matabeleland.* London: Heinemann.

Barber, James. 1967. *Rhodesia: The Road to Rebellion.* London: OUP.

Bhebe, Ngwabii, and T. O. Ranger. 1996a. *Society in Zimbabwe's Liberation War.* London: James Currey.

———. 1996b. *Soldiers in Zimbabwe's Liberation War.* London: James Currey.

Chikuhwa, Jacob W. 1998. *Zimbabwe: The Rise to Nationhood.* London: Minerva.

Goodman, Peter. 1996. *Mukiwa.* New York: Atlantic Monthly Press.

Kriger, Norma. 1992. *Zimbabwe's Guerrilla War: Peasant Voices.* Cambridge: Cambridge University Press.

Lan, David. *Guns and Rain: Guerillas and Spirit Mediums in Zimbabwe.* London: James Currey.

Lyons, Tanya. 2004. *Guns and Guerrilla Girls: Women in the Zimbabwean Liberation Struggle.* New York: Africa World Press.

Martin, David, and Phyllis Johnson, eds. 1985. *The Struggle for Zimbabwe: The Chimurenga War.* Harare: Zimbabwe Publishing House.

Meredith, Martin. 2002. *Our Votes, Our Guns: Robert Mugabe and the Tragedy of Zimbabwe.* New York: Public Affairs.

Mugabe, Robert. 1983. *Our War of Liberation.* Gweru, Zimbabwe: Mambo Press.

Nkomo. Joshua. 1984. *Nkomo: The Story of My Life.* London: Methuen.

Phimister, Ian. 1988. *An Economic and Social History of Zimbabwe: Capitalist Accumulation and Class Struggles, 1890–1948.* New York: Longman.

Ranger, Terence O. 1985. *Peasant Consciousnesses and Guerrilla War in Zimbabwe.* London: James Currey.

Rubert, Steven C., and R. Kent Rasmussen. 2001. *Historical Dictionary of Zimbabwe*, 3rd edition. Lanham, MD: Scarecrow Press.

Zionist Revolution and the State of Israel

CHRONOLOGY

1843   Rabbi Yehuda Alkalai (1798–1878) publishes *Minchat Yehuda* ("Yehuda's Offering"), in which he makes the plea for human activities—settling the Holy Land—that would hasten the coming of Redemption. This book, along with the teachings of Rabbi Zvi Hirsch Kalisher (1795–1874), who in his 1862 book *Drishat Zion* ("Seeking Zion or Seeking a Homeland for the Jewish People") calls for the establishment of agricultural set-tlements in the Land of Israel in order to bring about the arrival of the messianic age, represents a break with the traditional Orthodox Jewish view, which stipulates that Jews should rebuild the Land of Israel only after the arrival of the Messiah.

1855   Moses Montefiore (1784–1885), the Anglo-Jewish financier and philanthropist, begins purchasing land for agricultural purposes outside the old cities of Jerusalem, Jaffa, Safed, and Tiberius.

1862   Moses Hess (1812–1875), the well-known German-Jewish socialist thinker, publishes *Rome and Jerusalem,* which calls for the Jewish nation to follow the model of Italian nationalism and to re-create Jewish national life in the Land of Israel. Hess is one of the first non-Orthodox Jews to articulate an argument in support of the resettlement of the ancient Jewish homeland.

1870   Mikve Israel, an agricultural school, is established outside the city of Jaffa by the French-Jewish organization Alliance Israelite Universelle. Traditionally Jews in the Land of Israel have relied on charity from Jewish communities in Europe and North America; the establishment of the school is part of an effort to make the Jewish community in the Land of Israel more self-reliant.

1878   Petah Tikavah ("Gate of Hope"), the first modern Jewish agricultural settlement, is founded by three Orthodox Jews from Jerusalem: Yehoshua Stampfer, David Meir Guttmann, and Rabbi Yoel Moshe Solomon.

1881   Pogroms in Russia devastate Jewish communities there. While millions of Jews migrate to North America and western Europe, a growing number of eastern European Jews come to see Jewish nationalism as a solution for their predicament; many Jewish nationalists become active in groups known as Hovevei Zion ("Lovers of Zion") that emerge in Russia as well as in Romania, where Jews experienced anti-Semitic outbursts similar to those experienced by their Russian counterparts.

1882–1903   The period of the First Aliya (the first wave of Zionist immigration), when Zionist pioneers, mainly from Russia and Romania, come to Turkish-ruled Palestine and settle in agricultural communities. Many of the Zionist immigrants are Hovevei Zion or members of Bilu, a student organization whose name is made of the initials of the words in Isaiah 2:5, "House of Jacob, come, let us go up."

1882   Leon Pinsker (1821–1891) publishes "Auto-Emancipation," a pamphlet claiming that anti-Jewish sentiments in Europe are largely the result of the fact that the Jews exist, unnaturally, as a people without a state of their own. His remedy is to call on the Jews to emancipate themselves outside Europe by establishing their own homeland.

1884   The first conference of Hovevei Zion (headed by Pinsker) convenes in Kattowicz. The thirty-four delegates agree that only in the Land of Israel can the Jewish nation be revived.

1894   The Dreyfus affair begins in Paris. The Jewish captain Alfred Dreyfus is falsely accused of treason; the trial leads to a growing wave of anti-Semitism in France. Theodor Herzl (1860–1904), a Jewish writer and journalist, covers the trial for the Austrian paper *Neue Freie Presse*. Herzl is, at this time, becoming increasingly interested in the condition of Jews in Europe, and the Dreyfus affair, which reveals the depths of anti-Semitism in France, one of the more enlightened European societies, leads him to become wholly committed to finding a solution to what he comes to regard as the "Jewish problem."

1896   Herzl publishes "The Jewish State," a pamphlet calling for an immediate political solution to the "Jewish problem": the creation of a Jewish State.

1897   The first Zionist Congress convenes in Basel, Switzerland (August 29–31), and adopts a program calling for the creation of a Jewish home in Palestine.

1901   The fifth Zionist Congress creates the Jewish National Fund. The fund's main function is to purchase land in Palestine for Jewish settlement.

1903   The Kishinev pogrom, which occurs in the Romanian town of Kishinev, then under czarist Russian control, sends shock waves across the Jewish and non-Jewish world and provides further motivation for Zionist activists.

1904–1914   The period of the Second Aliya. As opposed to the first major wave of Zionist migration to Palestine, which consisted mainly of middle-class Jews, this group of more than 40,000 includes large numbers of younger pioneers, many of whom come from Socialist circles.

1909   The city of Tel Aviv, the first "modern Hebrew" city, is founded north of Jaffa; it fast becomes the cultural and economic center of the Jewish community in Palestine. Ha-Shomer ("the Guard"), the first Jewish defense force, is created to protect Jewish settlements. Also in this year Degania, the first kibbutz, is established. The kibbutz is a Socialist-inspired commune, and it becomes one of the more popular forms of agricultural settlement for the Jewish pioneers in Palestine.

1916   The Sykes-Picot agreement divides the Near East into areas of British and French control, giving Britain control over Ottoman Palestine.

1917   In November the British foreign secretary, Lord Balfour, issues a statement in support of the establishment of a Jewish national home in Palestine. In December, under the command of General Allenby, the British army conquers Palestine and enters Jerusalem.

1919–1923   The period of the Third Aliya. This wave of immigration brings 35,000 Jews to Palestine, mainly from Russia and Poland. Many of the immigrants, like their Second Aliya predecessors, are Socialist pioneers.

1920   The British are awarded a mandate over Palestine by the League of Nations (it is officially confirmed two years later). The

Haganah, an underground military organization, is founded to provide defense to the Jewish community in light of growing numbers of attacks by Arabs against Jews in Palestine.

In March, the small Jewish settlement of Tel Hai is attacked. Among the casualities is Yoseph Trumpeldor, who was an officer in the Russian army in 1904–1905 during the Russo-Japanese War and played an important role in the establishment of the Zion Mule Corps that fought under British command in the Battle of Gallipoli. Trumpeldor becomes a symbol of the Zionist spirit of sacrifice, and the fall of Tel Hai becomes one of the first dates commemorated on the Zionist calendar.

1924–1928   The period of the Fourth Aliya. This wave of immigration brings over 65,000 Jews to Palestine, nearly half of them from Poland. Unlike the Second and Third Aliyot, this group of immigrants includes mainly middle-class Jews who settle primarily in urban centers.

1929–1939   The period of the Fifth Aliya brings nearly a quarter of a million Jews to Palestine. Most arrive in the years 1933–1936, following Hitler's rise to power. About a quarter of the Fifth Aliya immigrants come to Palestine illegally.

1929   Arab riots against Jews break out, mainly in Jerusalem and later in Hebron, where sixty-seven Jews are massacred. Following the riots, the British send the Shaw Commission to Palestine to look into the causes of the violence between Arabs and Jews. This leads, in the following year, to the Hope-Simpson report, which recommends imposing restrictions on Jewish immigration and land purchase in Palestine. These recommendations become the official public policy of the British in Palestine under the 1930 Passfield White Paper.

1934   The *Ha'apla*—"organized" illegal Jewish immigration to Palestine—begins. In response to the restrictions on the number of Jews allowed to enter Palestine imposed following the 1930 White Paper, the Jewish underground movement in Palestine begins to organize clandestine immigration. Many of the illegal immigrants are refugees fleeing Nazi Germany.

1936   The major Arab revolt and general strike in Palestine begin. The revolt, which lasts close to three years, leads to the creation of the Peel Commission, which is sent to investigate the turmoil in Palestine. In a report published in July 1937, the commission calls for the partition of Palestine into two states: a Jewish state that would include parts of the coastal plain and most of Galilee, and an Arab state that would include most of the remaining territories, including Transjordan. Growing Arab opposition to the plan leads to the formation of the Woodhead Commission in 1938, which concludes that the partition plan is not, for the time being, a practical solution.

1939   World War II breaks out in Europe. The British issue a new White Paper that imposes new limits on Jewish immigration to Palestine (75,000 immigrants over a period of five years).

1942   The Biltmore Conference, a Zionist conference held in New York City—during the war, Zionist congresses cannot convene in Europe—calls for the immediate lifting of restrictions on Jewish immigration to Palestine and the creation of a Jewish state in Palestine.

1944   A Jewish Brigade is created as part of the British army; it includes mainly Jews from Palestine. The brigade of nearly 5,000 soldiers participates in battles in Italy. (It is disbanded in 1946.) Under the leadership of Menachem Begin, the Irgun, the underground movement affiliated with the right-wing Revisionist movement, declares a revolt against the British in Palestine.

1946   The Zionist struggle against the British intensifies. The Irgun blows up the King David Hotel in Jerusalem; retaliating against the death sentences of Irgun members, they hang two British sergeants.

1947   On November 29 the United Nations votes in favor of a plan to partition Palestine and create two states, Arab and Jewish. The Zionist leadership accepts the resolution, whereas the Arab states and Arab leaders in Palestine reject it. Immediately following the UN vote, fighting breaks out between the Jews and Arabs in Palestine.

In December the British declare that they will end their mandate in Palestine on May 15, 1948.

1948   On May 14, David Ben Gurion declares the creation of the State of Israel. The IDF (Israel Defense Forces) is created. Five Arab states—Syria, Egypt, Lebanon, Jordan, and Iraq—join the Palestinian Arabs in the war against the Jewish state.

1949   On March 10, Israel signs an armistice agreement with Syria, Lebanon, Jordan, and Egypt, bringing Israel's war of independence to an end.

INTRODUCTION

Zionism, the Jewish national revival movement, emerged in Europe at the end of the nineteenth century in reaction to anti-Semitism as well as to modern nationalist trends in European societies that increased the threat of assimilation and the erosion of Jewish culture. Zionism sought to solve the "Jewish problem" by calling on the Jews to leave Europe and create an independent state in the ancient homeland. In less than seventy years, the Zionists succeeded in creating a viable Jewish community in Palestine and an international movement, manifested in the Zionist Organization and the Jewish National Fund, that paved the way for the creation of an independent Jewish state in 1948.

BACKGROUND: CULTURE AND HISTORY

In the year 70 A.D. the Romans, who then ruled the Middle East, including the Land of Israel, the historic home of the Jewish people, destroyed the Temple in Jerusalem in the midst of a Jewish revolt. But the Romans were not the first foreign rulers to conquer the Land of Israel. The Babylonians destroyed the Temple in the year 586 B.C. and exiled the lead-

ers of Judea; but several decades later the Temple was rebuilt and Jerusalem's centrality for the Jewish people was restored. However, the destruction of the Temple by the Romans marked the end of Jewish independence in the Land of Israel. After the destruction of the Temple (and the short-lived Bar-Kochva rebellion against the Romans, 132–135 A.D.), the Jewish community in the Land of Israel steadily decreased in numbers and influence, while Jewish communities in the Diaspora (first in the Near East and later also in Europe) became the centers of Jewish life.

In the Diaspora, Jews lived as members of dispersed religious communities. First in the Roman empire and then under Islam and in Christian Europe, Jews were a minority that lived separately from the rest of society, facing a host of restrictions, special taxes, and often persecutions fueled by religious hatred. There were periods in which different Jewish communities flourished, most notably perhaps in Moorish Spain—a period referred to in Jewish history as a Golden Age, when Jewish cultural life blossomed and Jewish individuals attained important political positions. But by and large, in the Diaspora, Jews were outsiders in the various countries and societies in which they lived, separated from the rest of society by legal, political, and cultural barriers. (This was not only the result of the attitudes of non-Jewish populations toward the Jewish communities; the Jews' own communal authorities sought to remain separate from the non-Jewish society to protect the Jewish traditional way of life.)

Although early on the Jewish communities in the Middle East and the Muslim world were dominant (they contributed the most important religious texts and religious authorities), in the modern period, with the general rise of Europe and the West, the Jewish communities in Europe became the more vital forces in Jewish life and the places where some of the most dramatic changes in Jewish life were to take place. The history of the Jews in Europe in the Middle Ages and in the early modern period is commonly associated with the image of the ghetto. (The term *ghetto* came into being in sixteenth-century Venice, but it came to symbolize the Jewish experience in Europe before and after that period.) The Jews were not a part of the general European society; they were prevented from owning land and had no political or social rights in the lands where they resided. They lived in special neighborhoods or areas, restricted from interacting with the general population and required, in some cases, to wear distinguishing marks. The Jews had their own educational and legal systems, with little interference from the political authorities.

Generally, Jews were invited by local rulers to settle in their lands to provide certain social and economic functions. In the Middle Ages, when the church forbade Christians to lend money with interest, Jews fulfilled this critical economic function. Later Jews held important banking and trading positions—and they were allowed to remain in a given territory only as long as they were needed and had a charter that gave them legal protection. In Christian Europe, Jews were regarded as the killers of Christ. They lived in an atmosphere of hate that often turned violent. The threat of expulsion was looming.

With the rise of absolute monarchies, the Enlightenment, and later national revolutions, the old corporate social system in Europe collapsed, paving the way to modern societies no longer based on different autonomous groups. This meant that first in western Europe (by the late eighteenth century) and later in the East (in the nineteenth century), the entire population of a country were now citizens of a state, sharing universal rights and obligations. This also meant that Jews were no longer living in an autonomous, separate sphere—they were gradually becoming citizens of the states in which they lived. These changes in the civic status of the Jews were accompanied by important cultural and social changes. The nineteenth century saw the emergence of the *Haskalah* (Jewish Enlightenment), which called on Jews to reform their educational system, to learn European languages and general subjects, and to enter the mainstream of European society. The nineteenth century also saw the rise of Reform Judaism, which challenged traditional Jewish practices and modernized the Jewish service and Jewish communal life. By the middle of the nineteenth century, Jews in the West were increasingly becoming part of the greater population.

These changes in civil status offered Jews great new opportunities, but at the same time they created new barriers and new forms of hatred that in some important ways were more dangerous than anything Jews had experienced before. In 1492, when the Jews were expelled from Spain, they had the option to convert to Christianity and avoid expulsion; by the nineteenth century, religion was no longer the only barrier preventing Jews from becoming full members of society. In the Middle Ages and the early modern period, hatred of the Jews was motivated almost exclusively by religion, but by the nineteenth century anti-Judaism was accompanied by a new form of hatred and discrimination: anti-Semitism—the hatred of the Jews as members of a distinct ethnic or racial group. As societies began to define themselves along ethnic, national, and, as in the case of Nazi Germany, racial lines, Jews were once again considered as outsiders.

The rise of modern anti-Semitism in the nineteenth century led to a renewed wave of anti-Jewish campaigns accompanied by pseudo-scientific ideologies; these became an integral part of the European political landscape. The situation was especially dire in the East. In the Russian empire, Jews enjoyed only a few of the political, social, and cultural benefits enjoyed by their brethren in the West. Under Russian rule, Jews were called upon to give up some of their old autonomous privileges (maintaining their own educational system, for example) and fulfill their obligations as subjects of the Russian empire (including lengthy military service). At the same time, many restrictions (on places of residence, on enrollment in schools and universities) were kept in place, and anti-Semitism—often encouraged by the authorities—was rampant.

The search for a solution for their plight led eastern European Jews on different paths. Many of them chose to emigrate to the West. Others embraced Socialism and radical politics. And a small number of Jews began to argue that if the society around them begins to define itself according to national parameters, perhaps the answer to the Jewish question lies in defining the Jewish people as a nation and finding a national solution to the plight of the Jews.

By the second half of the nineteenth century, more and more Jewish intellectuals came to the realization that only as an autonomous society, living in its own territory, could the Jews enjoy a normal existence. These intellectuals began to argue that the centuries of life in the Diaspora have turned the Jews into a people removed from the general course of history. They called for the development of a new Jewish mentality, one that does not call on Jews to live passively and accept the dictates of foreign authorities but demands that Jews take control of their own historical destiny. Increasingly these thinkers came to the realization that only in the Land of Israel, in the historical homeland of the Jewish people, could the Jewish nation emerge as a vital historical force.

Interestingly two of the first Jewish leaders who called for a return to the Land of Israel where Orthodox rabbis—Yehuda Alkalai (1798–1878) and Zvi Hirsch Kalisher (1795–1874). They argued that Jews had to take their historical destiny into their own hands and return to the Land of Israel to work the land as a source of vitality. (The traditional Jewish view was that only the Messiah could lead the Jews back to their land and reconstitute the Kingdom of Israel—any attempts by humans to do that would delay the arrival of the messianic age.) Soon, though, more secular Jews took the lead in articulating a vision of a Jewish national home. Moses Hess (1812–1875), the German-Jewish Socialist, in his book *Rome and Jerusalem*, which was inspired by Italian nationalism, declared the need for the development of Jewish national life in Israel. And Leon Pinsker (1821–1891), in his "Auto-Emancipation," argued that the plight of Jews in Europe was largely the result of the fact that the Jews were a people without a state of their own. He called on the Jews to liberate themselves outside Europe by establishing a new homeland for the Jewish people.

By the second half of the nineteenth century the idea of an independent Jewish state was gaining acceptance as a viable solution to the "Jewish problem" in Europe. All that was needed were individuals and groups who would turn this idea into a political movement. This process began in the last two decades of the nineteenth century and would ultimately lead to the creation of the modern State of Israel in the aftermath of World War II.

CONTEXT AND PROCESS OF REVOLUTION

The Zionist Revolution, which set off to create a Jewish state in the Land of Israel, started in the last two decades of the nineteenth century and realized its historical mission in 1948, when David Ben Gurion declared the establishment of the State of Israel.

By the 1880s the notion that only the creation of an independent state would solve the "Jewish problem" in Europe was gaining wider acceptance in Jewish circles. But in order to carry out this vision, Zionism had to move from the realm of intellectual and literary formulations into the world of concrete political actions. The Zionist movement operated on two parallel tracks in its effort to create a Jewish national home. One was creating a political body that operated in the international arena, trying to gather international support for the idea of a Jewish state. The second was carried out by pioneers who left Europe for the Land of Israel to lay the foundations for a new Jewish society that would lead the way for national independence.

While for nearly two millennia the centers of Jewish life were in Diaspora, Jews, in varying numbers, continued to live in the Land of Israel. In fact, since the end of the eighteenth century, the size of the Jewish community in the Land of Israel grew substantially. But the Jews who lived in the Land of Israel until the emergence of the Zionist movement did not seek to have political control over the country. In fact, their lives in Palestine were not all that different from those of their co-religionists outside the country. The members of the old Yishuv (Jewish community) were part of a religious community living under foreign rule. Many of the Jews who came to Israel did so in order to study and be buried in the Holy Land. They lived mainly in the old cities of Palestine—in Jerusalem, Hebron, Tiberius, and Safed—in harsh conditions, relying heavily on outside support. And even the attempts to better the circumstances of Jewish residents of Palestine by outside benefactors, most notably by the Anglo-Jewish philanthropist Moses Montefiore (1784–1885), who bought lands for agricultural purposes and helped create the first Jewish neighborhoods outside the walls of the Old City of Jerusalem, provided little if any improvement to life in this traditional community.

The Zionist pioneers who began arriving in Palestine in the 1880s had relatively little in common with the old Yishuv.

For them the goal of settling in the Land of Israel was not to join a religious community. Theirs was a revolutionary vision: to transform and modernize Jewish life by returning to the land and using it as the source of a new and vibrant society. The First Aliya (the first major wave of Jewish immigration to the Land of Israel) began in 1882 and was fueled to a large degree by pogroms that devastated Jewish communities in Russia. Over the next twenty years, nearly 25,000 Jews came to Palestine, among them the new Zionist pioneers. These pioneers were active in such groups as Hovevei Zion ("Lovers of Zion") and Bilu (a student organization whose name is made of the initials of the words in Isaiah 2:5, "House of Jacob, come, let us go up"). These groups had sprung up throughout Russia and Romania and included young Jews committed to the Zionist vision articulated by Rabbis Alkalai, Kalisher, and other Jewish leaders. In Turkish-ruled Palestine these pioneers formed the first Zionist agricultural settlements. Though highly motivated and committed to their vision, these mainly middle-class Jews had very little agricultural training, and the Israeli terrain proved to be overwhelming for them. Many of their initial efforts at working the land failed, and ultimately they had to rely on help from wealthy Jews abroad as members of the old Yishuv had done. (The wealthy Rothschild family, prominent in international banking and finance, played a critical role in saving these settlements and supporting the Zionist pioneers.)

While the Zionist pioneers were making initial steps, however modest, in the process of reclaiming the ancient homeland, in Europe Zionism was beginning to evolve as a political movement. The driving engine behind this development was Theodor Herzl (1860–1904). Herzl came from an assimilated Jewish-Hungarian family. Early on, as a writer and journalist, he showed little interest in Jewish affairs. By the early 1890s, however, he grew more aware of the challenges facing European Jewry. In 1894, working for the Viennese paper *Neue Freie Presse,* he covered the trial of Alfred Dreyfus, a Jewish officer in the French army wrongly charged with and convicted of spying against France. The Dreyfus affair brought about a wave of anti-Semitism in France; for Herzl, this was a sign that even in the most enlightened of European societies, where Jews had been equal citizens for over a century, the anti-Semitic demon could not be contained. The sole solution, Herzl believed, was the creation of a Jewish state.

In 1896 Herzl published "The Jewish State," a pamphlet in which he laid out his Zionist vision. In 1897 he organized the first Zionist Congress in Basel. Over 200 delegates from seventeen countries attended the congress, which would become a sort of parliament of the Zionist movement. Although he represented only a small segment of world Jewry, Herzl acted on the international scene as the representative of the entire Jewish world. He met with world leaders in Berlin and

Theodor Herzl was the founder of the modern Zionist Movement, whose core belief is that the Jewish people are entitled to a homeland and a state of their own. (Library of Congress)

Istanbul and tried to enlist their support for the movement. When he died in 1904, the Zionist movement was still in its infancy, but he left it with a vision and with the commitment to turn it into a player on the international scene.

In 1904, in Palestine the Second Aliya began and lasted until the start of World War I. Unlike the pioneers of the earlier wave, this group included a large number of young Socialist pioneers who wanted to combine their national vision with the ideals of social equality. These pioneers, who were better prepared for their mission, expanded the agricultural settlement of the country and created Tel Aviv, the first Hebrew city, which would become the cultural and social center of the Zionist community in Palestine. In their efforts, the Zionist settlers were aided by the Jewish National Fund, which was created to facilitate the purchase of lands in Palestine for Zionist settlement. One of the more popular forms of settlement that the pioneers of the Second Aliya developed was the kibbutz—an agricultural commune that was based on a utopian Socialist model.

The First World War led to the dismantling of the Ottoman empire, and by 1917, the area that included Palestine would fall under British control. During the war, Zionists under the leadership of Chaim Weizmann (1874–1952), a Russian-born

Jew who lived in Britain (a chemist, his work in the field of fermentation—on acetone—aided the British military) were able to reach the higher echelons of the British government and to win support for the Zionist cause. In November 1917, following sustained lobbying by Weizmann and other Zionist leaders, Lord Balfour, the British foreign minister, issued a declaration in support of the establishment of a Jewish national home in Palestine. After the war, the League of Nations granted Britain a mandate over Palestine with the intent of ultimately establishing a Jewish state. The Zionists welcomed the British mandate enthusiastically, and in its early years the British authorities indeed supported the Zionist cause. With time, however, as tensions between Jews and Arabs in Palestine escalated, the British changed their policies, withdrawing from the early parameters of the mandate.

In the Zionist imagination, the Land of Israel was an empty country that was waiting for the Jews to return back home. Of course, when they arrived there they realized that in fact the country was inhabited by local Palestinian Arabs. Initially there were few clashes between Jews and Arabs, but with the establishment of the mandate (that was supposed to prepare the conditions for a Jewish state) and the growing number of Jewish immigrants (in 1919–1923, the period of the Third Aliya, some 35,000 Jews came to Palestine; in the following four years, during the Fourth Aliya, over 65,000 Jews arrived in Palestine), tensions grew high.

The first wave of violent clashes between Jews and Arabs broke out in 1920. It was followed by a much more violent outbreak in 1929. These riots broke out in Jerusalem and Hebron (initially they were fueled by Arab fears that Jews were going to take over the holy sites in Jerusalem). The massacre in Hebron was especially vicious. Some of the Jewish families in Hebron had resided in the city for over four centuries and had warm, peaceful relations with their non-Jewish neighbors; sixty-seven Jews were massacred in that old city.

In the aftermath of the 1929 riots, the British became concerned with the growing tensions and sought to pacify the country. An investigation the following year produced the Hope-Simpson report, which viewed the rapid growth of the Jewish community as the cause of Arab anger. This conclusion would guide the British policy from 1930, which imposed restrictions on Jewish immigration and the ability of Jews to purchase land in Palestine. In 1936 the Arab leadership in Palestine declared a general strike, and a massive Arab revolt ensued. The revolt, which lasted in varying intensity for three years, would be crushed violently by the British. But it made it clear to the British that a radical new program must be instituted to solve the Palestinian question. One solution was that proposed by the Peel Commission, which had investigated the Arab revolt and called for a partition plan: the creation of an Arab state and a Jewish state in Palestine. However, this recommendation remained off the table for a decade. Instead, the British continued to impose more restrictions on Jewish immigration. In 1939, as war was breaking out in Europe and creating thousands of new Jewish refugees seeking a safe haven, the British constituted a new policy that limited Jewish immigration to 75,000 over a five year period.

During the early stages of the World War II, the Jewish community in Palestine faced the possibility of German occupation. But once this threat was removed, some Jews from Palestine joined the Jewish Brigade that fought in the British army. After the war, as the British were losing their colonial holdings around the globe, the Zionist leadership no longer spoke of a Jewish state and the need to create a new society in future terms. The focus was the immediate creation of a state. The Jews in Palestine, through their paramilitary organizations, concentrated their efforts on battling the British authorities, while the Zionist leadership began a concentrated international effort to compel the British to grant the Jews independence. On November 29, 1947, the United Nations passed a resolution (in the spirit of the partition plan) that called for the creation of two states in Palestine. Arab leadership rejected the plan, but Jews in the streets of Palestine celebrated the decision. Following the passage of the resolution a war broke out between the Jewish and Arab communities in Palestine. And in December of that year, the British announced that they would leave Palestine in May of 1948. On the eve of the termination of the mandate, May 14, 1948, David Ben Gurion declared the creation of the State of Israel.

IMPACTS

When David Ben Gurion declared the creation of the State of Israel, the country was in the midst of a bloody struggle between Arabs and Jews. On the day following Israeli independence, five Arab countries—Egypt, Syria, Lebanon, Jordan, and Iraq—declared war on the new state. What Israelis call the War of Independence lasted until 1949, when Israel signed armistice agreements with Syria, Lebanon, Jordan, and Egypt. These agreements created what became Israel's international borders, although West Jerusalem, which under the UN 1947 resolution was to become an international entity, was not recognized by the international community as Israel's capital. The 1948 War had a devastating effect on both sides in the conflict: Israel lost 6,000 people, about 1 percent of its Jewish population; on the Arab side, nearly three quarters of a million people lost their homes and became refugees.

One of the main reasons for the creation of Israel was to provide a refuge for Jews worldwide. One of the first laws that the Israeli Knesset (parliament) passed was the Law of Re-

turn, which guaranteed any Jew the right of Israeli citizenship. And indeed, throughout its history the State of Israel has absorbed millions of Jewish immigrants, mostly from areas where Jews faced hostile conditions. Initially it was Holocaust survivors who came to Israel; then in the 1950s and early 1960s, Jews from Arab and Muslim countries immigrated to Israel in large numbers; over the past thirty years, Jews from Russia and Ethiopia have found in Israel a home.

Although Jews flocked to Israel from troubled areas to find safety, Israel has found itself in a state of conflict with most of its neighboring countries since its inception. The armistice agreements of 1949 ended the 1948 War but did not bring peace between Israel and the Arab world. By the mid 1950s, facing a total Arab boycott and the emergence of a pan-Arab ideology (championed chiefly by Egypt's president, Gamal Abdel Nasser) that viewed Israel as a hindrance to Arab control over the region, the fear of another all-out war dominated Israeli policy. In November 1956, Israel joined Britain and France in their war against Nasser for control over the Suez Canal, and for a short while Israel controlled parts of the Sinai Peninsula, before returning it to Egypt.

The mid 1960s were the height of the "Arab Cold War" against Israel, which included a boycott and international pressure, along with redeployment of army units along Israel's borders and a blockade of strategic straits in the Red Sea. By the spring of 1967, Israelis felt that they were living in a state of siege. In June of that year, Israel launched a military strike against Syria, Jordan, and Egypt. In six days, Israel conquered the Golan Heights, the Sinai Peninsula, the Gaza Strip, and the West Bank, including East Jerusalem.

In 1973, on Yom Kippur, the holiest day on the Jewish calendar, Egypt and Syria launched a surprise attack against Israel. After initial advances by the Egyptian and Syrian armies, the Israeli army was able to reclaim territories and hold off the advancing armies. At the end of the war, with American diplomatic involvement, Israel and Egypt began negotiations that would lead to the first peace agreement between Israel and an Arab country. In the 1979 peace accord, Israel agreed to return the Sinai Peninsula to the Egyptians in return for the establishment of normal diplomatic relations between the two countries.

Until the mid 1960s, the Palestinians supported pan-Arabism and allowed other Arab states to represent them; in 1964, however, the Palestine Liberation Organization (PLO) was created, representing directly the interests of Palestinians. Already by the 1950s groups of Palestinians had infiltrated Israel and launched attacks against Israeli targets. But with the creation of the PLO, and especially after 1968, when control of the PLO shifted to authentic Palestinian leaders, their efforts became more organized. In its early years, Jordan, with a large Palestinian population, was the base of the PLO. But in September 1970, fearing instability, King

Hussein of Jordan expelled the Palestinian organizations from his kingdom, and they relocated mostly to Lebanon. From 1975 a civil war weakened the Lebanese central government and allowed the Palestinians in southern Lebanon to seize control of the area bordering Israel and launch attacks against civilian Israeli targets from there. In 1982 Israel invaded Lebanon in order the remove the immediate threat from Israel's northern border; however, Israel had grander plans—to lend support to a Christian faction that would make peace with Israel—a plan that proved to be a failure. (Initially Israel conquered nearly half of Lebanon, and then for another fifteen years it controlled a small security zone in southern Lebanon. Finally in 1999 Israel withdrew completely to the UN-recognized international border.)

In the 1967 War, Israel conquered the West Bank and Gaza, including the Palestinians who resided there. These areas remained under Israeli military rule, and while the population there did not become Israeli citizens, they became dependent on Israel economically (Arabs who lived in Israel at the end of the 1948 War became Israeli citizens). In 1987, the Palestinians in the territories launched the *Intifada*, an organized resistance against Israel that included general strikes and violent confrontations with the Israeli military. In 1992, in the aftermath of the first Gulf War, the American-organized Madrid Peace Conference brought Israelis and Palestinians to the negotiating table for the first time. A year later the Oslo Accords, which were signed by Israel and the PLO, led to the creation of the Palestinian Authority and put in motion a process that was to end the historic conflict between Arabs and Jews in the Middle East (Israel and Jordan signed a peace agreement following the Oslo Accords; Israel and Syria conducted peace negotiations throughout the 1990s but never reached a viable compromise). However, the implementation of the Oslo Accords proved to be fraught with obstacles, and by 2000 a second *Intifada* broke out, bringing the peace process between Israelis and Palestinians to a halt. Since its creation, then, Israel has provided a home for Jews around the world. Yet at the same time, its impact on the region has been a continued state of war between the Jewish State of Israel and most of the Arab world.

PEOPLE AND ORGANIZATIONS

Ben Gurion, David (1886–1973)

David Ben Gurion (born David Gruen) was born in Plonsk, Poland, in a Zionist home. At eighteen he joined the Zionist-Socialist movement Poalei Zion (workers of Zion). He came to Israel in 1906, during the Second Aliya, and was involved in the development of an agricultural commune. In the First World War he joined the Jewish Legion that was part of the British army and participated in the last battles against the Ottomans in Palestine. He was a founder of the Histadrut (a confederation of labor unions) and represented the Histadrut in the Zionist Organization. He was elected chairman of the Zionist Organization and the Jewish Agency in 1935. Ben Gurion coordinated and commanded the struggle for Israeli independence in the final years of British rule in Palestine, and after the creation of the state he became Israel's first prime minister. In 1953 he left politics and moved to a kibbutz in the Negev desert in southern Israel. He returned to public life in 1955 as defense minister and later assumed again the position of prime minister. He resigned from the post in 1963.

Gordon, A. D. (1856–1922)

Aharon David Gordon was born in Russia in a traditional Jewish home and worked in the family business until the age of forty-seven. Though he was involved with Hovevei Zion, it was only in 1903 that he decided to move to Israel and become a farmer. He worked in Israel in different communities, finally settling in Degania, the first kibbutz. Gordon believed that the return to manual labor would be the only way to transform the Jewish people into an independent and viable society. He enjoyed the position of prophet-like sage in Socialist Zionist circles, preaching the virtues of labor and the land in quasi-religious terms.

Haganah

The Haganah ("The Guard") was an underground military organization of the Jewish community in Palestine from 1920 to 1948. In its early years the Haganah lacked a central organization, but after the 1929 riots it became more centrally organized and grew in numbers. In addition to defending Jewish communities, the Haganah played an important role in the illegal immigration of Jews to Palestine. When in 1947 a war between Jews and Arabs broke out in Palestine, the Haganah served as the de facto army of the Jewish community. After the creation of Israel on May 14, 1948, it became the basis of the IDF (Israel Defense Forces).

Herzl, Theodor (1860–1904)

Herzl, the father of political Zionism, was born in Budapest and moved with his family to Vienna when he was eighteen. Educated in the spirit of the German Enlightenment, he showed little interest in Jewish affairs early in his career as a writer and journalist. But in the early 1890s he became more concerned with anti-Semitism and the prospects for Jews in

Europe. In 1894 Herzl covered the Dreyfus trial for the Viennese paper *Neue Freie Presse.* The Dreyfus affair flared anti-Semitic sentiments in France, and it served as a sign for Herzl that even in the country where Jews had been living as equal citizens for over a century, the specter of anti-Semitism loomed large. His solution, which he laid out in "The Jewish State" in 1896, was that the "Jewish problem" could only be solved by creating an internationally recognized Jewish state. In 1897 Herzl organized the first Zionist Congress in Basel, Switzerland. Nearly 200 delegates from seventeen countries participated in the congress and adopted the Basel Program, which called for the establishment of a home for the Jewish people in Palestine. In 1902 Herzl published *Altneuland* (Old New Land), a utopian novel depicting a future Jewish society that relies on science and technology in the Land of Israel.

Irgun

In 1931 a small group of Haganah members affiliated with the right-wing Revisionist faction created the Haganah B. During the Arab Revolt that began in 1936, the leaders of Haganah B returned to the Haganah, while the remaining Haganah B members created the Irgun Zvai Leumi ("National Military Organization"), a small underground military movement inspired by Jabotinsky's militaristic teachings, which carried out attacks against British and Arab targets. At the start of the Second World War, both the Haganah and Irgun agreed to halt any anti-British acts. Some members of the Irgun, however, refused to accept this decision and formed Lehi (also known as the Stern Gang), which continued to battle the British authorities throughout this period. In 1944 Menachem Begin, the Irgun commander, declared a revolt against the British in Palestine. This signaled a period in which both the Irgun and Lehi launched a series of daring attacks against the British in Palestine, including the bombing of the King David Hotel in Jerusalem in 1946.

Jabotinsky, Ze'ev (Vladimir) (1880–1940)

Jabotinsky, a writer, translator, and journalist from Odessa, became active in Zionist affairs in the aftermath of the Kishinev pogroms of 1903. Throughout his Zionist career, Jabotinsky was an advocate of Jewish militarism. During World War I he was one of the principal forces behind the creation of the Jewish Legion. In 1925 he founded the Revisionist faction within the Zionist movement. The Revisionists rejected the Zionist Socialist approach, which held that before national independence could be attained, a new society based on the values of labor and self-sufficiency must be created; instead, the Revisionists called for the immediate

creation of a Jewish state on both sides of the Jordan River with the aid of a strong Jewish military. The Revisionists were an opposition party within the Zionist movement, and in 1935 Jabotinsky decided to leave the Zionist Organization and created the New Zionist Organization.

Jewish National Fund (JNF)

This organization was created by the fourth Zionist Congress in 1901 for the purpose of purchasing land for Jewish settlement in Palestine. One of the more popular means by which the JNF raised money was the small blue collection box—nearly a million such boxes were distributed to Jewish homes around the world in the inter-war period. In addition to purchasing land, the JNF supported scientific research and development to aid the settlement of Jews in Israel, it helped in the development of towns and neighborhoods, and it took a leading role in forestation programs across Israel.

Kibbutz

An agricultural commune based on Socialist ideals that is a uniquely Zionist phenomenon. The name kibbutz comes from the Hebrew word *kevuzah* ("group"). The first kibbutz (Degania) was founded on the southern shore of the Lake of Galilee in 1910. The kibbutz became one of the more common forms of agricultural settlement in Israel. Over the years, kibbutzim turned to industry in addition to their agricultural basis. Recently, most kibbutzim have abandoned their strict Socialist principles and evolved into more free-market enterprises.

Weizmann, Chaim (1874–1952)

Weizmann was born near Pinsk in Russia and grew up in a traditional Jewish environment. He moved to Berlin to attend university and became involved in Zionist affairs. In 1904 he came to Manchester to teach and do research in chemistry. At the same time, he continued to be active in the Zionist movement and joined the Zionist Organization's executive. Weizmann quickly rose to a position of leadership in the Zionist movement and also cultivated relationships with British leaders. Weizmann's credentials as a chemist also helped his Zionist politics. He developed a formula for the production of acetone that aided the British military effort in World War I. Weizmann used his considerable influence to persuade the British government to produce what became known as the Balfour Declaration, in which the British foreign minister expressed his government's commitment to the creation of a Jewish national home in Palestine. In 1920 Weizmann became president of the Zionist Organization. During World War II, Weizmann played an important role in creating the Jewish Brigade. After the creation of the State of Israel, he became its first president—a mostly ceremonial position without executive powers.

Zionist Organization

The Zionist Organization was founded by Herzl in the first Zionist Congress in Basel. Members had to accept the Basel Program, which called for the creation of a Jewish home in Palestine, and to pay the Zionist *Shekel* ("dues"). The main organ of the Zionist Organization was the Zionist Congress, which acted as the elected assembly of the Zionist movement. In between congresses, the Zionist executive carried out the organization's policies. In 1929 an expanded institution, the Jewish Agency, was founded. It included members from the Zionist Organization and from non-Zionist Jewish groups. The Jewish agency became a de facto government of the Jewish community in pre-state Palestine involved in immigration, labor, and settlement.

Eran Kaplan

See Also Cinema of Revolution; Documentaries of Revolution; Elites, Intellectuals, and Revolutionary Leadership; Ethnic and Racial Conflict: From Bargaining to Violence; Nationalism and Revolution; Nazi Revolution: Politics and Racial Hierarchy; Palestinian Movement; Terrorism; War and Revolution

References and Further Readings

Avineri, Shlomo. 1981. *The Making of Modern Zionism: Intellectual Origins of the Jewish State.* New York: Basic Books.
Ben Israel, Hedva. 2003. "Zionism and European Nationalisms: Comparative Aspects," *Israel Studies* 8 (1) (Spring): 91–104.
Dieckhoff, Alain. 2003. *The Invention of a Nation: Zionist Thought and the Making of Modern Israel.* New York: Columbia University Press.
Halpern, Ben, and Jehuda Reinharz. 1998. *Zionism and the Creation of a New Society.* New York: Oxford University Press.
Kaplan, Eran. 2004. *The Jewish Radical Right: Revisionist Zionism and Its Ideological Legacy.* Madison: University of Wisconsin Press.
Kolatt, Israel. 1998. "Religion, Society, and State during the Period of the National Home." Pp. 273–301 in *Zionism and Religion,* edited by Shmuel Almog, Jehuda Reinharz, and Anita Shapira. Hanover, NH, and London: Brandeis University Press.
Kornberg, Jacques. 1993. *Theodor Herzl: From Assimilation to Zionism.* Bloomington: Indiana University Press.
Morris, Benny. 1999. *Righteous Victims: A History of the Zionist-Arab Conflict, 1881–1999.* New York: Knopf.
Penslar, Derek. 1991. *Zionism and Technocracy: The Engineering of Jewish Settlement in Palestine, 1870–1918.* Bloomington: Indiana University Press.
Ravitzky, Aviezer. 1996. *Messianism, Zionism, and Jewish Religious Radicalism.* Chicago: University of Chicago Press.
Roshwald, Aviel. 2004. "Jewish Identity and the Paradox of Nationalism." Pp. 11–24 in *Nationalism, Zionism and Ethnic Mobilization of the Jews in 1900 and Beyond,* edited by Michael Berkowitz. Leiden and Boston: Brill.
Shafir, Gershon. 1989. *Land, Labor and the Origins of Israeli-Palestinian Conflict, 1882–1914.* New York: Cambridge University Press.
Shapira, Anita. 1992. *Land and Power: The Zionist Resort to Force, 1881–1948.* New York: Oxford University Press.
Shimoni, Gideon. 1995. *The Zionist Ideology.* Hanover, NH, and London: Brandeis University Press.
Sofer, Sasson. 1998. *Zionism and the Foundations of Israeli Diplomacy.* New York: Cambridge University Press.
Stanislawski, Michael. 2001. *Zionism and the Fin de Siècle: Cosmopolitanism and Nationalism from Nordau to Jabotinsky.* Berkeley: University of California Press.
Stein, Leslie. 2003. *The Hope Fulfilled : The Rise of Modern Israel.* Westport, CT: Praeger.
Teveth, Shabtai. 1987. *Ben-Gurion: The Burning Ground, 1886–1948.* Boston: Houghton Mifflin.

Index

Editor Biography

James V. DeFronzo of the Sociology Department at the University of Connecticut has taught over 7,000 students in his revolutions course and over 9,000 students in his criminology course and is preparing the third edition of his textbook on revolutions, *Revolutions and Revolutionary Movements.* He has written dozens of research articles published in various academic journals dealing with topics such as criminology, social policy related to crime, demography, gender issues, teaching, and social stratification. Born in New Britain, Connecticut, he received a B.A. in Sociology from Fairfield University, Connecticut, and attended graduate school at Indiana University on a federal quantitative methodology fellowship and later on a research assistantship. He taught for three years in the Sociology Department at Indiana Univer-

sity-Purdue University at Fort Wayne, Indiana, and also taught as an adjunct instructor at Indiana University in Bloomington. He completed his Ph. D. the year after he began teaching at the University of Connecticut at Storrs. His teaching experience at Indiana University or the University of Connecticut includes Introductory Sociology, Social Problems, Social Psychology, Social Conflict, Criminology, Methods of Social Research, Social Stratification, and Revolutionary Movements Around the World. He is a member of the American Sociological Association and the American Society of Criminology. His writing and research interests include social movements, criminology, general sociology, social problems and political and historical sociology and developing textbooks for several of these areas.